The Collected Poems of
Muriel Rukeyser

Edited by Janet E. Kaufman
& Anne F. Herzog

with Jan Heller Levi

University of Pittsburgh Press

Published by the University of Pittsburgh Press, Pittsburgh, PA 15260

Manufactured in the United States of America

Printed on acid-free paper

10 9 8 7 6 5 4 3 2 1

LIBRARY OF CONGRESS CATALOGING-IN-PUBLICATION DATA

Rukeyser, Muriel, 1913-

    [Poems]

The collected poems of Muriel Rukeyser / edited by Janet E. Kaufman
and Anne F. Herzog with Jan Heller Levi.

       p. cm.

Includes bibliographical references (p.) and indexes.

ISBN 0-8229-4247-X (hardcover : alk. paper)

   I. Kaufman, Janet E., 1964-   II. Herzog, Anne F., 1959-   III. Levi,
Jan Heller.   IV. Title.

      PS3535.U4A17 2005

      811'.52--dc22

                      2005001790

Permissions information appears in the acknowledgments section.

For Jacob, Gabriel, Casey, and Rebecca Rukeyser

❧ Contents

Editors' Notes   xxiii
Acknowledgments   xxix
Introduction   xxxiii

Theory of Flight (1935)

1 Poem Out of Childhood
  Poem Out of Childhood   3
  Song for Dead Children   5
  In a Dark House   6
  Effort at Speech between Two People   9
  Notes for a Poem   11
  Place-Rituals   12
        Tradition of This Acre   *12*
        Ritual of Blessing   *12*
  Wooden Spring   13
  Sonnet   13
  Letter, Unposted   14
  Sand-Quarry with Moving Figures   15
  Wedding Presents   15
  Three Sides of a Coin   16
  Breathing Landscape   19
  Four in a Family   19
  This House, This Country   20

2 Theory of Flight
  Preamble   21
  The Gyroscope   24
  The Lynchings of Jesus   25
        1 Passage to Godhead   *25*
        2 The Committee-Room   *26*
        3 The Trial   *29*
  The Tunnel   31
  The Structure of the Plane   38
        1 The Structure of the Plane   *38*
        2 The Strike   *41*
        3 The Lover   *42*
  Night Flight : New York   44
  Theory of Flight   47

3 The Blood Is Justified

    For Memory   48
        Life and Works   48
        Holy Dying   49
        Ritual for Death   50
    City of Monuments   51
    Study in a Late Subway   53
    Child and Mother   53
    Eccentric Motion   55
    Sundays, They Sleep Late   56
    Thousands of Days   57
    The Surrounded   58
    Burlesque   59
    Movie   60
    Metaphor to Action   61
    Citation for Horace Gregory   62
    Cats and a Cock   63
    The Blood Is Justified   68

U.S. 1 (1938)

1 The Book of the Dead

    The Road   73
    West Virginia   74
    Statement: Phillippa Allen   75
    Gauley Bridge   77
    The Face of the Dam: Vivian Jones   78
    Praise of the Committee   79
    Mearl Blankenship   82
    Absalom   83
    The Disease   86
    George Robinson: Blues   87
    Juanita Tinsley   88
    The Doctors   89
    The Cornfield   92
    Arthur Peyton   94
    Alloy   95
    Power   96
    The Dam   99
    The Disease: After-Effects   102
    The Bill   104
    The Book of the Dead   106

2 Night-Music
     A Flashing Cliff   111
     Girl at the Play   111
     Burning Bush   112
     Eel   113
     Homage to Literature   115
     The Handclap   115
     Trophies   116
     Panacea   117
     In Hades, Orpheus   118
     The Drowning Young Man   119
     Boy with His Hair Cut Short   119
     Course   120
     More of a Corpse than a Woman   121
     Three Black Women   122
     Formosa   122
     Night-Music   123
          Time Exposures   *123*
          The Child Asleep   *124*
          Adventures, Midnight   *126*
          Night-Music   *127*
     Driveway   128
     Lover as Fox   129
     Gift-Poem   130
     Woman and Emblems   131
          Woman and Bird   *131*
          The Birthday   *131*
          Woman and Music   *132*
     Outpost   132

3 Two Voyages
     The Cruise   133
     Mediterranean   144

A Turning Wind (1939)

1 Moment of Proof
     Reading Time : 1 Minute 26 Seconds   155
     Song, the Brain-Coral   155
     Target Practice   156
     Otherworld   157
          Landing at Liverpool   *157*
          The Island   *158*

Otherworld   159
Nuns in the Wind   161
For Fun   162
Correspondences   164
   Democritus Laughed   164
   Tree of Days   164
   1/26/39   165
   Correspondences   166
Noguchi   168
Seventh Avenue   169
The Shortest Way Home   170
Palos Verdes Cliffs   171
Paper Anniversary   172
From the Duck-Pond to the Carousel   174
Asylum Song   174
The Victims, a Play for the Home   175
M–Day's Child   177
Speech for the Assistant, from *Houdini*   178
Judith   179

2 Lives
"The risen image shines, its force escapes, we are all named"   181
Gibbs   182
Ryder   185
Chapman   188
Ann Burlak   191
Ives   195

Wake Island (1942)   199

Beast in View (1944)
One Soldier   207

1 Beast in View
Ajanta   207
   1 The Journey   207
   2 The Cave   208
   3 Les Tendresses Bestiales   209
   4 Black Blood   210
   5 The Broken World   210
Mortal Girl   211
Child in the Great Wood   212

The Meeting   213
The Key   214
Darkness Music   215
Song   215
Shooting Gallery   216
Suicide Blues   216
Wreath of Women   217
Madboy's Song   221
Drunken Girl   222
Love and Its Doors and Windows   222
The Minotaur   223
Gift-Poem   224
Holy Family   228
Who in One Lifetime   228
from "To the Unborn Child"   229
Leg in a Plaster Cast   230
Bubble of Air   231
Sea Mercy   232
Long Past Moncada   232
Chapultepec Park—1   233
Chapultepec Park—2   234
A Game of Ball   235
Gold Leaf   236
All Souls   236
Evening Plaza, San Miguel   237
Beast in View   238

2

Letter to the Front   239

    1   *"Women and poets see the truth arrive"*   239

    2   *"Even during war, moments of delicate peace"*   239

    3   *"They called us to a change of heart"*   240

    4   *Sestina*   241

    5   *"Much later, I lie in a white seaport night"*   242

    6   *"Home thoughts from home; we read you every day"*   242

    7   *"To be a Jew in the twentieth century"*   243

    8   *"Evening, bringing me out of the government building"*   243

    9   *"Among all the waste there are the intense stories"*   244

    10   *"Surely it is time for the true grace of women"*   246

3

The Soul and Body of John Brown   247

The Green Wave (1948)
  "Let poems and bodies love and be given to air"   252
  Water Night   253
  Eyes of Night-Time   253
  This Place in the Ways   254
  Song, from "Mr. Amazeen on the River"   255
  Cloud, Airs, Carried Me Away   255
  Salamander   256
  His Head Is Full of Faces   257
  Mrs. Walpurga   257
  A Certain Music   259
  The Motive of All of It   259
  Green Limits   260
  The Children's Orchard   261
  Christmas Eve   261
  Crayon House   262
  A Charm for Cantinflas   263
  Traditional Tune   264
  Foghorn in Horror   265
  Summer, the Sacramento   265
  Speech of the Mother, from *The Middle of the Air*   266
  Then I Saw What the Calling Was   267

Translations: Six Poems by Octavio Paz
  The Bird   268
  Poet's Epitaph   268
  Spark   269
  Two Bodies   269
  The Street   269
  Lovers   270

Rari from the Marquesas
  Rari for Tahia and Piu   271
  Rari for O'Otua   272
  A True Confession   272
  Careful of the Day   273
  Rari for Hepuheku   273
  Rari   274
  Rari to Encourage Youth   274
  Rari, to Be Bothered by Mosquitoes   274
  Not Before I Fall Asleep   275

Easter Eve 1945

   Easter Eve 1945   276
   Private Life of the Sphinx   277
   Nine Poems for the unborn child   280

Orpheus (1949)   287

Elegies (1949)

   First Elegy. Rotten Lake   299
   Second Elegy. Age of Magicians   302
   Third Elegy. The Fear of Form   304
   Fourth Elegy. The Refugees   307
   Fifth Elegy. A Turning Wind   310
   Sixth Elegy. River Elegy   314
   Seventh Elegy. Dream-Singing Elegy   318
   Eighth Elegy. Children's Elegy   321
   Ninth Elegy. The Antagonists   325
   Tenth Elegy. Elegy in Joy   328

Body of Waking (1958)

I

   Haying Before Storm   333
   Phaneron   333
   The Young Girl of the Mississippi Valley   334
   A Birth   334
   King's Mountain   335
   Mother Garden's Round   336
   Rite   337
   Ringling   338
   After Their Quarrel   338
   Tree   339
   Night Feeding   340
   The Return   341
   Unborn Song   342
   The Two Illuminations   342
   F. O. M.   343
   Exile of Music   344
   On the Death of Her Mother   344
   "Make and be eaten, the poet says"   345
   Hero Speech   346
   The Watchers   347

A Ballad Theme   348

Asleep and Awake   349

Of Money. And the Past.   350

"Long enough. Long enough"   351

The Loan   352

Pouring Milk Away   353

Children, the Sandbar, that Summer   353

Born in December   354

The Sixth Night: Waking   354

Nevertheless the Moon   354

Speed, We Say   355

The Birth of Venus   356

The Place at Alert Bay   357

Voices of Waking   357

Divining Water   358

2 Translations: Octavio Paz

"The hand of day opens"   359

"At daybreak go looking for your newborn name"   360

Fable   360

Day   361

Proverbs   362

"In her splendor islanded"   362

"Like ivy the creeper with a thousand hands"   363

Life of the Poet   363

The Prisoner   364

from Sun Stone   366

3

Suite for Lord Timothy Dexter   367

    1 *"They face us in sea-noon sun, just
        as he saw them waiting"   367*

    2 *How to Impress Massachusetts   367*

    3 *Three Nights I Dreamed   369*

    4 *Kings and Contemporaries   370*

    5 *The Pickle, the Temple   372*

    6 *The Kind of Woman   376*

    7 *Guessing Time   377*

4

Are You Born?—I   379

"Murmurs from the earth of this land, from the caves and craters"   380

"The tree of rivers seen and forgotten"   380

"The power of war leads to a plan of lives"   381

"A tree of rivers flowing through our lives"   382
"The sea has opened, the limit of his dream"   382
Powerplant   383
"In the last hour of night, a zebra racing dawn"   384
Fields Where We Slept   384
Portrait of a Man, with a Background of Holdings   385
"A red bridge fastening this city to the forest"   386
"Power never dominion"   387
"The sky is as black as it was when you lay down"   388
"On your journey you will come to a time of waking"   389
"This is the net of begetting and belief"   389
Body of Waking   390
"Sounds of night in the country of the opposites"   395
Willkie in *The Gulliver*   396
"Then full awake you will recognize the voice"   396
"In your time, there have been those who spoke clearly"   397
He Had a Quality of Growth   398
Are You Born?—2   399

Waterlily Fire (1962)

The Speaking Tree   403
To Enter That Rhythm Where the Self Is Lost   403
For a Mexican Painter   404
A Song of Another Tribe   404
Song   405
Waterlily Fire   405
  1 The Burning   405
  2 The Island   406
  3 Journey Changes   408
  4 Fragile   409
  5 The Long Body   409

The Speed of Darkness (1968)

1 Clues
The Poem as Mask   413
  Orpheus   413
What Do I Give You?   413
The Transgress   414
The Conjugation of the Paramecium   414
Junk-Heap at Murano   415
Clues   416
In Our Time   417

Double Dialogue: 417
    Homage to Robert Frost 417
The Six Canons 418
Forerunners 418
Orgy 419
The Overthrow of One O'Clock at Night 420
Among Roses 420
What I See 421
Believing in Those Inexorable Laws 421
Song : Love in Whose Rich Honor 422
Niobe Now 422
Song : The Star in the Nets of Heaven 423
Air 423
Gift 424
Cries from Chiapas 424
The War Comes into My Room 425
Delta Poems 426
Spirals and Fugues 427
Anemone 428
Fighting for Roses 428
For My Son 429
Poem 430
The Power of Suicide 430
The Seeming 431
Song from *Puck Fair* 432
Not Yet 432
Landscape with Wave Approaching 433
Segre Song 434
Bunk Johnson Blowing 434
Cannibal Bratuscha 435
What Have You Brought Home from the Wars? 437
One Month 438
Silence of Volcanoes 439
What They Said 439
A Little Stone in the Middle of the Road, in Florida 440
The Blue Flower 440
Woman as Market 441
    Forgetting and Remembering 441
Word of Mouth 442
    1 *The Return* 442
    2 *Word of Mouth* 443
Endless 445

2 Games

    The Backside of the Academy   445

    Mountain : One from Bryant   447

    The Flying Red Horse   447

3

    The Outer Banks   448

4 Lives

    Akiba   454

        The Way Out   454

        for *the Song of Songs*   455

        The Bonds   457

        Akiba Martyr   458

        The Witness   459

    Käthe Kollwitz   460

        1 *"Held between wars"*   460

        2 *"Woman as gates, saying"*   461

        3 *"Held among wars, watching"*   462

        4 *Song : The Calling-Up*   463

        5 *Self-Portrait*   463

5

    The Speed of Darkness   465

Breaking Open (1973)

1 Searching / Not Searching

    Waking This Morning   471

    Despisals   471

    What Do We See?   472

    Looking at Each Other   473

    Desdichada   474

    Voices   475

    Fire   475

    Waiting for Icarus   476

    from City of Paradise   477

    The Question   477

    In Her Burning   478

    Rondel   479

    More Clues   479

    Myth   480

    Searching / Not Searching   480

        1 *"What kind of woman goes searching*
          and searching?"   480

2 *Miriam : The Red Sea* 481

3 *For Dolci* 481

4 *Concrete* 482

5 *Brecht's* Galileo 482

6 *Reading the* Kieu 482

7 *The Floor of Ocean* 483

8 *H. F. D.* 483

9 *The Artist as Social Critic* 484

10 *The President and the Laser Bomb* 484

11 *Not Searching* 485

12 *The Question* 485

13 *"Searching/not searching. To make closeness"* 486

14 *"What did I see? What did I not see?"* 486

A Simple Experiment 487

Along History 488

Boys of These Men Full Speed 488

All the Little Animals 489

Next 490

Two Years 490

Iris 490

2 Orange and Grape

Ballad of Orange and Grape 492

Rock Flow, River Mix 493

Martin Luther King, Malcolm X 494

Looking 494

Don Baty, the Draft Resister 495

Te Hanh : Long-Ago Garden 496

Welcome from War 496

Facing Sentencing 497

Secrets of American Civilization 497

Wherever 498

Bringing 498

A Louis Sonnet 499

After Melville 500

The Writer 502

Gradus Ad Parnassum 502

From a Play : Publisher's Song 503

In the Night the Sound Woke Us 503

In the Underworld 503

Afterwards 507

Flying to Hanoi 508

It Is There 508

The Running of the Grunion 509

Sacred Lake 511

3 Northern Poems

Songs of the Barren Grounds 512

    1 The Old Days 512

    2 Inland, Away 512

    3 I'm Here Again 513

    4 Not Much Good 514

    5 My Breath 514

I Recognize This Song 515

The Black Ones, the Great Ones 516

Trout Fishing 517

How Lovely It Is 517

The Word-Fisher 518

Stroking Songs 518

    A Girl for a Boy—Stroking Song 518

    The Baby on the Mountain—Stroking Song 519

    The Wiping Moss from the Ruins 519

Stroking Songs, Childhood Songs 520

    Being Born 520

    Shooting Star 520

4

Breaking Open 521

    Columbus 523

    Burning the Dreams 526

    Death and the Dancer 526

    Rational Man 526

    The Hostages 528

The Gates (1976)

I

St. Roach 533

Dream-Drumming 534

Double Ode 534

Painters 537

Rune 537

How We Did It 538

Islands 538

Blue Spruce 539

Artifact 540

Ms. Lot 540

Boys in the Branches   541
Song : Lying in Daylight   542
Hypnogogic Figure   542
The Lost Romans   543
Canal   544
For Kay Boyle   545
Resurrection of the Right Side   545
The Wards   546
The Sun-Artist   547
Poem   White Page   White Page   Poem   549
Fable   549
Neruda, the Wine   550
Before Danger   551
Song : Remembering Movies   551
Work, for the Day Is Coming   551
Recovering   552
Parallel Invention   553
Poem   554
Not to Be Printed, Not to Be Said, Not to Be Thought   554
Back Tooth   555
Destruction of Grief   555
Trinity Churchyard   556
Burnishing, Oakland   557
The Iris-Eaters   558
Slow Death of the Dragon   558
Mendings   560
Then   561

2

The Gates   561
    1   "Waiting to leave all day I hear the words"   561
    2   "Walking the world to find the poet of these cries"   562
    3   New Friends   562
    4   "The Cabinet minister speaks of liberation   563
    5   "Among the days"   563
    6   The Church of Galilee   564
    7   The Dream of Galilee   564
    8   Mother as Pitchfork   565
    9   "You grief woman   you gave me a scarlet coverlet"   565
    10   "Air fills with fear and the kinds of fear"   565
    11   "Long ago, soon after my son's birth"   567
    12   "For that I cannot name the names"   567

13 "Crucified child—is he crucified?
    he is tortured" *567*

14 "So I became very dark very large" *568*

15 "All day the rain" *568*

Juvenilia

Antigone *573*

Cities of the Morning *573*

Autumn in the Garden *574*

The Ballad of the Missing Lines *575*

November Sketches *576*

To a Lady Turning Middle-Aged *578*

Place-Poems: New York *579*

O City *579*

Fourteenth Street *579*

The New School for Social Research *580*

Sheridan Square Conversation *580*

The New Bridge *581*

Park Avenue *581*

College Special *582*

Empire State Tower *582*

"Dear place, sweet home" *583*

For an Aesthete *583*

Pastorale No. 2 *584*

A New Poem

An Unborn Poet *591*

Abbreviations *595*

Annotations *597*

Textual Notes *637*

Bibliography *651*

Index of Titles *655*

Index of First Lines *663*

✑ Editors' Notes

Rukeyser begins her preface to her 1978 *Collected Poems:* "'All the poems is a very curious idea." Indeed, that collection, which Rukeyser edited herself—to the best of her abilities, toward the end of her life and after she was debilitated by a series of illnesses and strokes—includes almost all the poems that Rukeyser published in her numerous volumes during her lifetime. As the coeditors of this newly envisioned *Collected Poems,* we have been acutely aware of the necessity of this new volume since we first began doctoral dissertations on Rukeyser in the early 1990s. It was frustrating at that time to realize that such a monumental figure of twentieth-century American poetry was no longer in print. Only readers who had access to libraries with extensive holdings or were motivated to pursue Rukeyser's work through used bookstores could piece together her poetry and prose works. Since that time, however, there has been a steady increase in new releases of portions of Rukeyser's writing: Kate Daniels's edition, *Out of Silence: Selected Poems of Muriel Rukeyser* (1992); Jan Heller Levi's poetry and prose collection, *A Muriel Rukeyser Reader* (1994); Jan Freeman and Paris Press's reissuing of *The Life of Poetry* (1996); *The Orgy* (1997); and *Houdini: A Musical* (2002); and most recently, Adrienne Rich's *Muriel Rukeyser: Selected Poems* (Library of America, 2004). The publication of our critical collection, *"How Shall We Tell Each Other of the Poet?": The Life and Writing of Muriel Rukeyser* (1999), along with the dozens of recent scholarly essays probing Rukeyser's work, all speak to the need for this newly edited and annotated *Collected Poems.* It is time that Rukeyser's oeuvre is more accessible, and we hope that this volume will continue to clarify the significance of Rukeyser as an American poet.

Rukeyser's preface to her 1978 *Collected Poems* indicates her intent to make that book comprehensive. She opened by meditating on the notion of "All the poems" and elaborated: "all the poems are included; only the translations have been removed" (v). In fact, though she acknowledged a desire to make "cuts," to rewrite and to leave out, she concluded: ". . . this is the truth of how the poems stand and how things formed for me" (v–vi). Throughout our work, we have striven to adhere to the spirit of openness and inclusivity Rukeyser professed when envisioning the 1978 *Collected Poems.* We have attempted to gather "all the poems," even while realizing the impossibility of following this mandate. Among Rukeyser's papers, primarily in the Library of Congress archives and the Henry W. and Albert A. Berg Collection of the New York Public Library, are drafts of poems written on scraps of paper, corners of envelopes, and backs of playbills. Some of these appear to be nearly completed. Other poems are handwritten on notebook paper with scribbled revisions penciled in. There are typed poems that were never published, but appear ready or near ready for publication, and drafts of tables of contents that include titles of poems we have not located. Additionally, there is a handful of poems that were published in journals and never appeared in Rukeyser's books. Ultimately, we determined that the transcription, analysis, and study of these previously unpublished, uncollected poems for the purpose of publication must wait for another project.

From the beginning, it has been our intent to produce an edition that once again makes available Rukeyser's collected poetry as she envisioned it. Throughout her life, when she articulated what was most important to her about poetry, she asserted the significance of the writer/poem/reader triad: poems are created and exist because of a relationship between the poet and her audience. In *The Life of Poetry*, Rukeyser told the story of asking a student in her writing workshop to tear up a poem he had written, ostensibly destroying the visible copy, and then asked her students if the poem still existed. For Rukeyser, the poem still existed as a work of art because it had been brought alive within the relationship of poet and witnesses, not by the materiality of ink on paper. She wrote, "I cannot say what poetry is; I know that our sufferings and our concentrated joy, our states of plunging far and dark and turning to come back to the world . . . all are here. . . . and there is an exchange here in which our lives are met, and created" (172). In presenting this collection with annotations, we hope to perpetuate and strengthen the exchange, the relation of poet, poem, and reader.

We have chosen not to construct this book as a variorum that would track the multiple appearances in text of Rukeyser poems, but rather to emphasize the essential triad of poet, poem, and audience. While Rukeyser published many of her poems from first drafts, others went through multiple drafts and were sometimes revised from one printing to the next. In the majority of these cases, such revisions were small: a word change or a shift in punctuation or spacing. In a handful of poems, she made substantial revisions from a typescript or early journal printing to the publication in one of her books. In instances where we have identified substantial changes, we refer the reader to the source of the earlier printing within our textual notes. We leave questions of the analysis of Rukeyser's revision process to future scholars, and hope that this edition will inspire enough interest to make possible further publications of her work.

Researching for this collection, we have made numerous discoveries and accompanying editorial decisions that result in an enriched *Collected Poems*, one that includes more poems than the 1978 edition. We have reproduced each of the twelve original volumes of poetry published in the 1978 *Collected Poems* in chronological order. To these, we have added translations, *Wake Island*, juvenilia, and a final poem of Rukeyser's that appeared in print just before her death. Additionally, we have included extensive annotations.

Rukeyser's translations of Octavio Paz were published in *The Green Wave*

(1948) and *Breaking Open* (1973), and a selection of translated Northern/Eskimo poems and rari poems was also published in *The Green Wave*. In other volumes, she published translations of individual poems of several other poets: Vicente Aleixandre, Charles Morice, Te Hanh, Hans Carossa, and Gunnar Ekelöf. In a typescript of the table of contents for the 1978 *Collected Poems,* Rukeyser included these translations, though they were ultimately omitted. After the *Collected Poems* was published, Rukeyser referred to "that big book that holds back a big door," and we suspect that publishing pressures to limit page length may have contributed to the decision to exclude the translations. Rukeyser gives us some clue to her ideas about translation in a few different places. In her endnote for the Northern Poems, she refers to her translation work as a type of "adaptation." Poet-critic Kate Daniels notes in her introduction to a double-issue of *Poetry East* focused on Rukeyser that translation is a kind of metaphor for the way Rukeyser envisioned her own eclectic, disciplinary, and boundary crossing aesthetic. Explaining Rukeyser's interest in joining scientific thinking and poetry, Daniels wrote: "she was 'translating' the phase rule in physics into poetic rhythms" (6). In a 1970 talk entitled "The Music of Translation," Rukeyser remarked that it takes a "mythological effort to bring a music over into another life" (*The World of Translation* 188). In typical Rukeyser fashion—her mind was constantly moving, refusing to remain wedded to any given position—she concludes at the end of her 1978 preface, "Only the translations have been taken out; and it now seems to me . . . might it not be that poetry and indeed all speech are a translation?" One can almost hear her questioning the rightness of leaving behind these translations. Or so we have heard her.

Our research in the archives of the Library of Congress yielded other translations by Rukeyser, completed but never published, such as those of the German poet Christian Morgenstern and an entry in a table of contents draft for a translation of the *Conference of the Birds* by the Sufi mystic Attar. It was tempting to publish these poems because we took such pleasure in reading them; it was an additional delight to see the drawings that Rukeyser created to accompany the Morgenstern translations. One wishes to share such pleasure. However, because space remains an interminable problem with Rukeyser's life's writing, we included only translations that she had already published in her books. Looking at both the translations she published and those she did not, we apprehended once again Rukeyser's vast reach, her vital curiosity and imagination, the boldness with which she explored poetry from so many languages, cultures, and times. These translations speak to Rukeyser's determination to live as a poet and citizen of the world.

The long poem *Wake Island* was published in its own slim edition in 1942, an omission from the 1978 *Collected Poems* for which no acknowledgement or explanation was given. When this poem was first published, Rukeyser was viciously attacked in various reviews, on *ad hominem* as well as literary and political grounds, for what was seen as her poem's naive rhetoric in response to the U.S. military conflict in the Pacific Ocean during World War II. Though we found no comment on this matter in her personal papers, it seems likely that the resistance to *Wake Island* when it was first published contributed to Rukeyser's perception that it remained particularly vulnerable to adverse criticism and therefore could be left out of the *Collected Poems*. It is also possible, given Rukeyser's declining health preceding the book's publication, that the exclusion of *Wake Island* was no more than an oversight. In preparing this new edition we chose to include *Wake Island,* first because Rukeyser did indeed publish it as a book, and second, because it represents an important moment in her consideration of what it means to be an American poet. As both Jim Brock and Louise Kertesz have argued, while the poem does not represent the zenith of Rukeyser's poetic talent, it is consistent with her lifelong vision that poetry should respond to questions of social justice and freedom, as well as to the historical moment, not only within her own country but globally. Perhaps now when the moment is less charged, readers will be interested in reconsidering this poem in the trajectory of Rukeyser's writing and as part of the writing to emerge from World War II.

Throughout her life, in poetry, prose, drama, biography, and fiction, Rukeyser experimented with genre and the boundaries of genre. In 1957, she published *One Life,* a book inspired by the life of the politician Wendell Willkie, which integrated prose, poems, prose poems, and sections of dialogue in verse. As Rukeyser wrote in her foreword to this work, she did not quite think of it as a biography, but rather, "a story, and a song" (xiii). When her first *Collected Poems* came out, Rukeyser included both poems and poem-like excerpts from *One Life.* The result was a large selection, comprising about one-sixth of the 1978 *Collected Poems.* Yet this selection is virtually inscrutable taken out of the context of *One Life.* Rukeyser herself, in a typescript titled "Note for One Life" that she left in her papers now housed in the Library of Congress, describes her ambivalence about including this selection. She writes: "The poems in this section [of the *Collected Poems*] are the poems in a book that is made of poems and documents, as well as these poems. But to tear the poems out, as has been done here, is to destroy the texture of the book and the arrangement which is edited as a film is edited, in those rhythms and sequences. I am glad to have the poems used here but both the sequence and the further meaning are destroyed. The arrangement is the life." After great deliberation, we have decided to publish a smaller selection of the *One Life* poems: we have included the eighteen poems that Rukeyser herself selected from this volume to be reprinted in *Body of Waking* (1958), the year after *One Life* was published. We hope that the smaller selection is sufficient to give current readers a taste of the poetic ambition of *One Life* while creating a more balanced book, not overly weighted by poems that are "torn," to use Rukeyser's term, from the larger work. The selection that

Rukeyser included in the 1978 *Collected Poems* deserves to be explored in *One Life* itself, where the reader has the opportunity to grasp the intensity of Rukeyser's genre experimentation and her effort to make a place for poetry in an ostensibly prose text, just as she worked with prose and documentary materials in ostensibly poetic works throughout her life (see, for example, "The Book of the Dead"). We look forward to the republication of *One Life* in its entirety.

The musical *Houdini,* written and revised by Rukeyser over the course of nearly forty years, represents a similar case. In 2002, Paris Press published what it considered to be the "completed" text, making Rukeyser's work on the song lyrics of this play available once again to readers. Interested readers may also wish to consider an alternate version published by Richard Jones and Kate Daniels. While we deeply admire the historical and imaginative work of the *Houdini* lyrics, we determined, as we did with the *One Life* poems, that excerpting from the work would diminish it.

One of the most significant additions to the present volume is a section of juvenilia. These poems were written in Rukeyser's early and late adolescence, during her years at the Ethical Culture and Fieldston schools, and at Vassar, where she matriculated at the age of sixteen. In some, Rukeyser can be seen straddling the border between adolescence and adulthood, just prior to the publication of *Theory of Flight,* her first book, selected when she was twenty-one for the Yale Younger Poets prize. In each of the poems we chose to include, it is remarkable to note the distinctness of voice, the breadth of vision, and the early feminist and political perspective; each one is completely consistent with what one may appreciate in Rukeyser's later published books.

The single substantive reordering we have done of the poems in this edition involves Rukeyser's elegies, a series of ten poems that she began publishing in clusters, first in *A Turning Wind* (1939), then in *Beast in View* (1944) and finally in *The Green Wave* (1948). In 1949, however, Rukeyser published *Elegies*—all ten poems together and by themselves for the first time—in a beautiful edition that highlights their continuity and progression. In her 1951 *Selected Poems,* Rukeyser again reprinted these elegies, again in their own separate grouping. Yet in the 1978 *Collected Poems,* the elegies were reprinted according to their original placement in three separate volumes. In considering the various groupings of these poems in print, we concluded that they are most powerful when presented together. Our conclusion is confirmed by Rukeyser's shaping of *Waterlily Fire: Poems 1935–1962,* a selection of favorite poems from earlier volumes. While she could easily have positioned the individual elegies within the sections of *Waterlily Fire* dedicated to the volumes in which they first appeared, Rukeyser chose, rather, to create a separate section for her elegies, printing them together. Thus, we have followed Rukeyser's example from 1949 and 1951, taking care to indicate in the annotations where individual elegies first appeared within

Rukeyser's books. The copy text for these poems is *Waterlily Fire,* as it most dependably reflects the printing of these poems separately in *A Turning Wind, Beast in View*, and *Green Wave*. However, the wide spaces in *Waterlily Fire* are bigger than in almost all other printings and thus we have worked between *Waterlily Fire* and the other versions to determine spacing.

As a general rule, we have relied on Rukeyser's original volumes for copy texts. Although the 1978 *Collected Poems* was her last published book, we found it was not entirely reliable because of numerous errors and differences from the original volumes. Rukeyser was suffering from the effects of strokes and illness at the time she was preparing her *Collected Poems;* she did not always have the energy to edit this book with the same meticulousness that her son, William L. Rukeyser, reports she devoted to her earlier publications. Additionally, the editor with whom she was working on the *Collected Poems* left mid-project. Thus, after studying Rukeyser's individual volumes, we chose them as the copy texts. In some cases, we found spelling, punctuation, and word changes in the 1978 *Collected Poems* that appear to be corrections to previous printings; where we had evidence for these changes or found them to be clear corrections, we incorporated and documented them in our section for textual notes at the end of the book. Additionally, if an alteration in the *Collected Poems* seemed as if it could not have been a typographical or printing error, we retained it. In another handful of cases, we found variations of word or punctuation choice in the 1978 *Collected Poems* that were plausible but for which we have no evidence of Rukeyser's intention or confidence that they were intentional revisions. In these situations, and for reasons of consistency, we have printed the version from Rukeyser's original volumes in the body of the text and offer the *Collected Poems'* version in the textual notes section.

～ Acknowledgments

This book has been a collaborative effort and numerous individuals have helped bring it to completion. First, it has been an added privilege of our work on Muriel Rukeyser's writing to know William L. Rukeyser, her son. From the earliest conception of this book, Bill has supported our efforts and has been an active participant in the project. All along, he has offered us guidance and insight into Rukeyser's writing and editing process. He has generously shared personal history and assisted with our understanding of the poet's life, has read and helped to develop annotations, and has trusted us with his mother's work. We have been honored to work with Bill and are grateful for his partnership.

Jan Heller Levi has been a consultant to us. She has contributed to the annotations and, as Rukeyser's biographer and a careful reader of her poetry, she has provided us with historical and personal details that would not have been accessible to us otherwise, helping us to make important connections between the details of Muriel Rukeyser's life and her poems. She has encouraged us to think about the scope and identity of this book, and her suggestions and challenges have strengthened the book.

Many colleagues, mentors, and friends have guided us along the way, questioned with us, offered multiple ways to think about a given concern, suggested readings, looked over archival materials with us, read our writing, and affirmed the work of this project. Thus we thank Charles Berger, Dan Fink, Karen Fitts, Ed Folsom, Ed Ochester, Kate Northrop, Alicia Ostriker, Michael Peich, Michael Rudick, Nancy Rumfield, Maeera Shreiber, Tom Stillinger, Carla Verderame, Cheryl Wanko, Barry Weller, Rebecca Wilks, Eleanor Wilner, and Hyoejin Yoon. We also thank an anonymous reviewer for offering generous and important suggestions toward our final drafting.

A number of research assistants have contributed to the formidable challenge of typing and formatting the poems, including Terri Borchers, Jason Pickavance, Rory Goughan, and Mark Hoefeletz. We are especially indebted to Eric Burger and Jocelyn Romano, whose eyes, commitment, and caring in the extensive preparation and review of the manuscript have made the completion of this project possible.

Jeslyn Medoff worked with the Houghton Library's Rukeyser manuscript materials, proving to be a valuable traveling scholar whose work was essential to the editorial project. Jes's work enhanced our sense of Rukeyser's drafting process, and contributed to the accuracy of this collection.

Alice Birney at the Library of Congress archives has guided us through Rukeyser's papers for many years, answered our questions, and made us feel welcome in the Library. It has been a pleasure and privilege to work with her. We thank the University Research Committee of the University of Utah, West Chester University's Graduate English Program, and West Chester University's CASSDA Grant for funding research assistance and for enabling our research trips to both the Library of Congress and the New York Public Library's Berg Collection.

We thank Isaac Gewirtz, curator of the Henry W. and Albert A. Berg Collection of English and American Literature at the New York Public Library, and especially Diana Burnham and Philip Milito, both of whom have kindly assisted us in accessing Rukeyser's papers at the Berg Reading Room. We thank the University of Utah and West Chester University librarians and, in particular, Dick Swain, Amanda Cain, Kimberly Klaus, Mary Sweeney, and Chris McCawley whose research expertise has provided us with access to materials that we could not locate on our own. We also appreciate the assistance of Ron Patkus and Dean Rogers, Vassar College Special Collections librarians, and Kathy Kienholz, the archivist at the Academy of Arts and Letters, who helped us with bits of research and offered levity.

Our sincere thanks goes to Deborah Meade, senior editor at the University of Pittsburgh Press. Her knowledgeable and careful responses to the final editing and production details for this book have been invaluable.

From Janet: For Lynn, Andrew, and Karen Kaufman, whose love, passion, and commitment to living life with all its contradictions sustains me and has helped me read this poetry. And for Rachel, whose joy and questions keep me celebrating and searching.

From Anne: My deepest gratitude to Emily, Lucas, and Hollis Graham, special ones, who have reminded me to laugh through the most intensive periods of completing this project. I also thank the extended Graham and Herzog families for their years of support and love. My work is dedicated to honoring and remembering the life of my father, Robert E. Herzog.

The editors acknowledge the following people and institutions for permission to reprint the named materials.

The following poems are reprinted by permission of New Directions Publishing Corporation:

"The Street," by Octavio Paz, translated by Muriel Rukeyser, from *Early Poems 1935–1955*, copyright © 1963, 1973 by Octavio Paz and Muriel Rukeyser.

"Lovers," "Spark," and "The Bird" by Octavio Paz, translated by Muriel Rukeyser, from *Early Poems 1935–1955*, copyright © 1973 by Octavio Paz and Muriel Rukeyser.

"Poet's Epitaph" and "Two Bodies" by Octavio Paz, translated by Muriel Rukeyser, from *Selected Poems*, copyright © 1973 by Octavio Paz and Muriel Rukeyser.

Quotations from the following materials, including notes explicating the poems, appear courtesy of the Henry W. and Albert A. Berg Collection of English and American Literature, The New York Public Library, Astor, Lenox, and Tilden Foundations:

"Antigone" (typescript, folder 6)

"Autumn in the Garden" (typescript, folder 6)

"The Ballad of the Missing Lines" (typescript, folder 9)

"Cities of the Morning" (typescript, folder 17, juvenilia)

"The Gates" (*The Gates*, folder 3)

Samuel Silens interview with Muriel Rukeyser (transcript, *U.S. 1* folder)

Quotations from poems and other materials held by the Library of Congress appear courtesy of the Muriel Rukeyser Papers, Manuscript Division, Library of Congress, Washington DC.

The excerpt of Muriel Rukeyser's translation of "To the Unborn Child" by Hans Carossa appears with the permission of Eva Kampmann-Carossa.

The translation of Leif Sjöberg and Muriel Rukeyser's translation of "Hypnogogic Figure" by Gunnar Ekelöf appears with the permission of Kaj Sjöberg.

❧ Introduction

When you hold this book in your hand you hold a living thing.
William Rose Benet

Throughout her life, Muriel Rukeyser maintained that poetry proved an essential means of communicating and acting in the world, a way "to meet the moment with our lives" and invite "a total response" (*Life of Poetry* 8–11). Rukeyser was a prolific and important writer during her publishing years, 1935–1980. In addition to the fifteen volumes of poetry she left at her death, she published biographies of the scientist Willard Gibbs and the explorer Thomas Hariot, a book that she called "a story and a song" about the politician Wendell Willkie, the musical *Houdini,* and *The Life of Poetry,* a series of essays explaining her poetics that challenged what she viewed as a cultural "fear of poetry" and asserted the potential power and importance of poetry in our lives. Rukeyser also published translations, six children's books, two novels, and uncollected articles, essays, criticism, plays, and filmscripts. At the age of twenty-one, her first book, *Theory of Flight,* was published as the winner of the Yale Younger Poets Award. This marked the beginning of a lifetime of recognition: the Harriet Monroe Poetry Award (1941), a Guggenheim Fellowship (1943), the Levinson Prize (1947), election to the National Institute of Arts and Letters (1967), the American Academy of Poets' Copernicus Prize (1977), the Shelley Prize (1977), and grants from the American Academy of Arts and Letters and the National Institute of Arts and Letters.

For Rukeyser, work on the poem was work on the self. This book challenges us to use poetry as Rukeyser imagined when she wrote of the experience of art, "It will apply to your life; and it is more than likely to lead you to thought or action, that is, you are likely to want to go further into the world, further into yourself, toward further experience" (*Life of Poetry* 26). This book invites us into relationship with the poems, with Rukeyser, and with ourselves.

While Rukeyser was much lauded during her lifetime, her place in modern American poetry has not been secure. Rukeyser was defined early as a Left-identified, political poet—ultimately a vexed identity for any American poet writing throughout the twentieth century. For while the 1930s—the decade her first volume of poetry was published—was a period in which poetry seeking to address public and political issues was taken seriously, in many ways it was also the peak decade of such openness within the literary history of the twentieth-century United States. As Michael Thurston explains in *Making Something Happen,* the unfolding of that period brought a "decoupling of poetry and politics" resulting from a variety of factors: "national politics, especially the anti-Communist inquisition . . . and literary politics, where new formalist methodologies wrought deep changes in the institutions that publish, recirculate, evaluate, and preserve literary works" (7).

We need look no further than the FBI file of more than one hundred pages focused on Rukeyser, the agency's labeling of her as a 'concealed Communist' (Dayton 12), or the House Un-American Activities Committee's censure of Sarah Lawrence College in November 1958 for employing her (Folsom 11) to appreciate the international reputation she earned as a powerful voice against the violence of war, poverty, racism, gender discrimination, and numerous other causes of the American Left. Yet even in terms of her political allegiances, Rukeyser never fit easily into prescriptive categories. She never functioned as a spokesperson for any partisan organization and never was a "card-carrying member" of the Communist Party as she was thought to be. Indeed, one of the most publicly humiliating events she experienced as a poet came at the hands of the *Partisan Review* editors in 1942, who mocked what they viewed as her overly patriotic stance in her book-length poem, *Wake Island*. Rukeyser wrote in response to her own vision, not the party line of the *Partisan Review* or any other editorial board. This vision was expansive, eclectic, and boundary crossing. Kenneth Rexroth wrote: "Her poems were the opposite of agitation and propaganda. They were expressions of responsibility, of abiding moral concern. As such they were part of a wider and more coherent life philosophy" (124). After Rukeyser's death, Denise Levertov wrote, "more than any other poet I know of (including Pablo Neruda) [Rukeyser] consistently fused lyricism and overt social and political concern" (189). Finally, in her introduction to the 1996 republication of *The Life of Poetry*, friend and fellow poet Jane Cooper asserted: "Reader, rarely will you encounter a mind or imagination of greater scope" (xxvi).

The opening line of Rukeyser's great poem "Käthe Kollwitz" tells us that Rukeyser viewed her lifetime as being "held between wars," and indeed, she was born on December 15, 1913, on the eve of World War I, and died on February 12, 1980, having lived through the Spanish Civil War, World War II, the Korean War, and the Vietnam War. She lived, as she wrote elsewhere, "in the first century of world wars" ("Poem"). Rukeyser benefited from a solid education in traditional literature and classics at the Ethical Culture School in Manhattan and the Fieldston School in the Bronx. Her mother worked as a bookkeeper and her father was a cofounder of Colonial Sand and Stone, which was at one time the biggest construction supply firm in the United States. Her family became quite wealthy during the formative years of her childhood. From a young age, Rukeyser was troubled by the discrepancy between her comfortable, sheltered childhood and what she learned from playing with members of street gangs, seeing prostitutes on the street, or hearing about the chauffeur's private life; she had a secret life apart from her parents, and it included "the wild, noisy, other world" of New York City (*Life of Poetry* 195). She developed an acute sense of the privileges and confinements of her social class. Reflecting on this period in her childhood, she writes, "It was clear to a growing child that the terrible, murderous differences between the way people lived were being upheld all over the city, that if you moved one block in any direction you would find an entirely different order of life" ("Education of a Poet" 221). Rukeyser's political consciousness was forged by her fascination for the difference that socioeconomic class made in people's lives and resulted in a lifelong concern for social justice.

Rukeyser matriculated at Vassar College when she was seventeen; she never graduated, due largely to her father's financial difficulties. At nineteen, she left college and traveled to Alabama to witness the Scottsboro trial of nine African American youths who were unjustly convicted of raping two white women. That venture marked the beginning of many such journeys. She went to Gauley Bridge, West Virginia, to report as a journalist on the vast industrial tragedy of the Hawk's Nest Tunnel construction project in which approximately two thousand migrant workers, mostly of African American descent, died of silicosis as a direct result of unhealthy working conditions. She traveled to Spain in 1936 to report on the People's Olympiad, an alternative, antifascist Olympics, and instead witnessed and wrote about the outbreak of the Spanish Civil War. In 1975 she went to South Korea to protest the imprisonment and death sentence of the poet Kim Chi-Ha, traveling in her official capacity as president of the P.E.N. American Center, an organization of writers promoting literature and reading and defending free expression.

Ultimately, Rukeyser viewed poetry as carrying tremendous power for witnessing on the part of both poet and audience. For the poet this meant testifying to one's perceptions of the world; for the reader this meant becoming accountable, responding with the writer through observations and personal experience, and by "the act of giving evidence" (*Life of Poetry* 175). We see Rukeyser's commitment to this conception of witnessing from the early years of her writing until the very end. She introduced *The Life of Poetry* with a story she frequently returned to at later points of her life: While evacuating Spain by boat at the outset of the Spanish Civil War, she was asked, "And poetry—among all this—where is there a place for poetry?" Rukeyser wrote: "Then I began to say what I believe" (3). In the concluding and title poem of *Speed of Darkness,* she issues a collective call for witnessing, "Who will speak these days, / if not I, / if not you?" And in her much quoted poetic question and answer in her biographical poem "Käthe Kollwitz," Rukeyser asks: "What would happen if one woman told the truth about her life? / The world would split open." In each of these lines, Rukeyser makes clear her intention to claim poetry's place off the page, outside the book, and within the larger world.

Even as she earned her impressive reputation as a political poet (e.g., "Poem Out of Childhood," "The Book of the Dead," "St. Roach," "The Backside of the Academy," "The Gates," and so many others), Rukeyser maintained a very fluid sense of the "political." Filmed in a 1978 documentary on three women artists, *They Are Their Own Gifts,* she stated, "I don't know what political is . . . it seems to me it's the thick of life . . . and it's the references and associations of life . . . I think it means the network of our lives, the ways in which we depend on each other and love and hate each other." Rukeyser simply did not accept conventional understandings of the political as a category separate from and defined in opposition to the personal. Perhaps she had an early appreciation of the feminist maxim brought to prominence in the 1960s: "The personal is political." Her *Collected Poems*, page by page, challenges the fracturing of political poetry from what some may view as private poetry and posits instead a world of poetic and political, personal and public, merging.

On more than one occasion, Rukeyser spoke of the origins of her first poems as a response to "the silence at home" ("Craft Interview" 153), and many of her poems speak to personal silences she felt and her yearning for language to fill them (e.g., "Effort at Speech Between Two People," "Four in a Family," "Asleep and Awake," "The Poem as Mask," "In Our Time," "The Speed of Darkness," "Double Ode," "The Gates"). Rukeyser's parents were both born in the United States, of German-Jewish and Romanian-Jewish descent. In regard to religion, she wrote: "There was not a trace of Jewish culture that I could feel—no stories, no songs, no special food—but then there was not *any* culture background that could make itself felt." She viewed her parents as part of what Margaret Mead called "second generation" culture — "split with the parent culture, leaning over backward to be 'American' at its most acceptable" ("Under Forty" 4–5). Yet we also know that Rukeyser cherished her mother's story that her family was descended from the great second-century scholar and martyr, Rabbi Akiba (see "Akiba"). Indeed, Rukeyser claims that she first fell in love with the poetry of the Bible when she turned to it during the Reform services her mother began taking her to at Temple Emanuel in New York City—the Bible, with "its clash and poetry and nakedness. . . .[was] closer to the city than anything that was going on or could possibly go on in the Temple" ("Under Forty" 7). Jo-Ann Mort links Rukeyser's political aesthetic to her Judaism, tracing Rukeyser's passion for social justice to the Deuteronomic call "intrinsic to Judaism": "'Justice, justice shalt thou follow, that thou mayst live, and inherit the land which the Lord thy God gaveth thee'" (20). Similarly, Robert Shulman frames Rukeyser's Jewish identity as "inseparable from her political radicalism . . . integral to her imagination" (34). In 1944, when she was only thirty and at the very beginning of her writing career, Rukeyser wrote: "To live as poet, woman, American, and Jew—this chalks in my position. If the four come together in one person, each strengthens the others" ("Under Forty" 8).

Still, Rukeyser resisted any turn toward religion for reassurance and comfort and sought a religious identity that would require an engaged struggle with both herself and the world. Thus she wrote that the value of her Jewish heritage was its value as a guarantee: "not only against fascism, but against many kinds of temptation to close the spirit" ("Under Forty" 9). Here again, we see her asserting a relationship between a term of political, institutional oppression—"fascism"—with the word "spirit," a term often relegated to personal, spiritual experience. Not so for Rukeyser. In a 1972 interview, Rukeyser commented on her essentially relational perspective, "It isn't that one brings life together—it's that one will not allow it to be torn apart" ("Craft Interview" 171).

Two other related facets of Rukeyser's work have complicated the critical assessment of her as a twentieth-century poet. First, she rejected some of the central developments of New Criticism, which rose in influence in the 1940s. Second, she maintained throughout her life an essentially visionary belief in the human capacity to create social change through language. The New Critical formalist emphasis, with its framing of the poem as a discrete art object separate from its historical-cultural context, was never consonant with Rukeyser's poetics, in particular because she emphasized the motion within language and the film-like elements of form. She stated that we, readers, should approach language and poetry "as we use it—as a process in which motion and relationship are always present . . ." She also recommended unequivocally that "we dismiss every static pronouncement and every verdict which treats poetry as static" (*Life of Poetry* 166–67). For Rukeyser, who resisted the fixedness essential to the New Critical idea of the poem-as-object, and who wrote poetry particular to its place, time, and political context, a critical approach seeking to detach a poem from its larger context would be mismatched. Rukeyser's later books do show a certain shift from the denser and more sprawling poems of her earlier volumes, perhaps a response to New Criticism's influence, yet she never completely turned away from the Whitmanesque lines of her youth. She insisted on writing poetry that emerged from—and was part and parcel of—distinct cultural, political, and historical moments.

Rukeyser's belief that poetry could enact change in the larger world shares no affinity for the ironic stance and world weariness of many high modernists. From her earliest poems, like "Theory of Flight," where she wrote, "Say yes, people. / Say yes. / YES," to her last book, where, in the poem "The Gates," addressing the political situation of imprisoned poet Kim Chi-Ha, she wrote, "How shall we free him? / How shall we speak to the infant beginning to run? / All those beginning to run?" Rukeyser writes from a position of hope, community, optimism, and faith in humanity. She concluded *The Life of Poetry* with the following assertion, "As we live our truths, we will communicate across all barriers, speaking for the sources of peace. Peace that is not lack of war, but fierce and positive" (214). From a position of cynicism, these lines would be trivialized and dismissed as naive. However, for readers who can entertain Rukeyser's sensibility, such lines throughout her writing are consistent with her courage and perseverance in trying to *use* poetry—the one kind of knowledge, she wrote in *The Life of Poetry*, that we are taught early not to use.

The resistance Rukeyser's poetry sometimes faced suggests that it touched deep nerves about what poetry and poets should be. For those who saw themselves as the guardians of the culture of poetry, the keepers of the gate, Rukeyser challenged notions of poetic propriety. In keeping with her integrated political-poetic aesthetic, Rukeyser's poems were accepted for publication in a wide array of journals, from left-wing publications such as *New Masses, Partisan Review,* and *The Nation,* to the more mainstream *Poetry* and *Harper's.* With fellow students Elizabeth Bishop, Mary McCarthy, and Eleanor Clark, Rukeyser founded an alternative literary magazine at Vassar, *Con Spirito;* at roughly the same period, she also began writing for the *Student Review,* a publication "sponsored by the National Student League, 'the militant vanguard of student revolt against war and reaction'" (Shulman 34). She published frequently in *Twice-a-Year: a Journal of Literature, the Arts, and Civil Liberties* and was for a time associate editor of *Decision,* a journal dedicated to exploring a "new humanism." She was regularly reviewed in an equally broad array of publications, from *Anvil* and *Common Sense* to the *New Yorker,* the *New York Times, American Poetry Review,* and the *Yale Review.* Her work was taken seriously but not always praised. As Louise Kertesz points out, Rukeyser was accused early on of having "romantic, bourgeois" concerns and, at the same time, "was hailed as an asset to the Communists" (58). She was, at times, accused of being obscure, erratic, complicated, too political, and for not reaching the heights of female lyricism. But as Kate Daniels has persuasively argued: "Rukeyser's politics and poetic imagination, . . . were far more complicated—and stubbornly individualistic—than any of her early critics realized. Her disinclination to conform to the dictates of any aesthetic or political program was not, as a number of later critics were to suggest, a carelessness or lack of intellectual rigor on her part. Throughout her life, she found herself astonished at the inability of most literary critics to consider work that departed from the conventions of a particular school or norm, and in her own critical writings she demonstrated her ability to transcend the contemporary and topical contexts of a work in favor of what she considered its more enduring artistic qualities" ("Muriel Rukeyser and Her Literary Critics" 250). Similarly, Richard Flynn states, "Rukeyser is far too risky and unusual a poet to fit neatly into our various master narratives of literary history; neither the conservative (and now largely discredited) New Critical version of modernism, nor a 'revisionist mythmaking' too narrowly based on identity politics has treated her work with any seriousness when they have treated it at all" (265).

On the other side of resistance, enormous admiration endures from critics, fellow poets, and students. Rukeyser has been called "an American genius," and "our twentieth-century Whitman." Kenneth Rexroth, leading poet of the San Francisco Renaissance, called her "the best poet of her exact generation" and Anne Sexton dubbed her "the mother of us all." Her words in "The Poem as Mask"—"No more masks! No more mythologies!—inspired the titles for two of the first anthologies of women's poetry in the 1970s—Florence Howe and Ellen Bass's *No More Masks!* and Louise Bernikow's *The World Split Open.* However, until recently, Rukeyser was virtually unacknowledged as a primary influence on writers who emerged during the last thirty years of the twentieth century in response to the women's movement. Grace Paley once recounted her excitement, while still a young girl, at finding Rukeyser's picture in a 1943 poetry anthology. She thought, "Well, there it is, a girl and a poet, it's a possibility at least—" (McEwen 1). Paley was born in 1922, a near contemporary of Rukeyser's; her remark reflects the anomaly of Rukeyser as an accomplished woman poet in what was then, unlike today, a tremendously male-dominated field. In her preface to the 1978 *Collected Poems* (reprinted in the annotations to this volume), reflecting on her love for reading other writers' collected poems, Rukeyser commented, "There were two differences then from today's books: the poets were all dead, and all were men." In some ways, it is difficult for readers today to appreciate the singularity of Rukeyser's accomplishments as a woman poet precisely because poetry now is enriched with great diversity, gendered and otherwise. It is important to remember that Rukeyser was born before women could vote in this country, and she was almost seventy years old when she died in 1980. Yet she broke silence in her poems about sex, lesbian erotics, motherhood, daughterhood, breastfeeding, menstruation, depression, and other experiences common among women that had rarely, if ever, been treated as suitable content for an American poet (see, among many others, "Effort at Speech," "Four in a Family," "Night Feeding," "Orgy," "Nine Poems," "More of a Corpse than a Woman," "The Question," "The Power of Suicide," "Looking at Each Other," and "For My Son").

Rukeyser lived her life, always writing and making her own, often unconventional, choices along the way. At sixteen, fascinated by the science and technology of aviation and wishing she could learn to fly, she enrolled in the Roosevelt School of Air to learn about flight mechanics. The title of *Theory of Flight* reflects this, and metaphors from flight to describe the human capacity to expand and connect, to find a "meeting-place" as the airplane does between air and earth, are prominent in her poems. In 1947 she became pregnant by a man who was never after involved in her or her child's life. When told that she could not both write and raise a child, that she had to choose between, she insisted on doing both (see "Nine Poems"). Not supported by her parents, she raised her son alone. She taught at the California Labor School in the early 1940s; in the 1950s and 1960s she taught at Sarah Lawrence College, where she invited the custodians to study along with the students. In that period she also worked and wrote closely with the well-known Jungian analyst Frances Wickes. She taught children in Harlem and adults in an array of schools, YWHA night programs, and community workshops. She wrote filmscripts and plays and designed exhibit plans for the San Francisco Exploratorium. She read widely among her contemporaries, irrespective of their national origins. Thus, she was well prepared to work closely with Octavio Paz on the first English translations of his poetry, and also to translate French, Vietnamese, Swedish, Spanish, Arabic, and German poets. In 1972, accompanied by Denise Levertov and Jane Hart, she traveled to downtown Hanoi, Vietnam, to protest the U.S. bombing. She was arrested for protesting on behalf of Civil Rights and against the Vietnam War. In 1978, only two years before her death, she planned to address a special session of the Modern Language Association on the topic "Lesbians and Literature," an address that would have made public her relationship with Monica McCall, her agent, but ultimately she could not attend due to illness.

She crossed boundaries at the life-sustaining intersections of all the various fields of human endeavor—science, history, modern dance, jazz, psychoanalysis, theater—and the connections among them enter her poetry. She searched everywhere for sources to feed her poetry and her own spirit. But truly remarkable—and indeed, postmodern before there was any such critical emphasis—is the way she dug deeply for the "buried voices" of this country's diverse history: Native American chants, mining songs, strike songs, Eskimo songs, African American spirituals, the songs of Chinese workmen building the American railway, the calypsos and ballads that made their way to jukeboxes and the roots of the American southern blues tradition. She wrote, "The continent in its voices is full of song; it is not to be heard easily, it must be listened for; among its shapes and weathers, the country is singing, among the lives of its people, its industries, its wild flamboyant venture, its waste, its buried search" (*Life of Poetry* 90). The relationship between poetry and the academy as it has evolved today would have been disconcerting to Rukeyser because of what is inevitably unheard and undiscovered in the process. A reading of her poem "The Backside of the Academy" makes clear her preference for the color and uncontained street life outside of the American Academy of Arts and Letters "Five brick panels, three small windows, six lions' heads with rings in their mouths, five pairs of closed bronze doors—."

The epigraph opening this introduction quotes from William Rose Benet's review of Rukeyser's first book, *Theory of Flight*: "When you hold this book in your hand you hold a living thing." If it was true of Rukeyser's first book, it most certainly can be said of these *Collected Poems*. Moving through the decades of Rukeyser's poems, we find the details of her life set in relation to individuals, cities, nations, cultures, wars—a vast list including John Brown, Sacco and Vanzetti, the Allies Advance, Tom Mooney, Ann Burlak, Gauley Bridge, Bunk Johnson, Chiapas, Hallie Flanagan, Willard Gibbs, Martin Luther King, Malcolm

X, the Vietnam War, and the Outer Banks. It is clear that Rukeyser viewed her poems as *living,* and she wanted them to go on living. She stated as much and more than once, echoing Walt Whitman's desire for his voice to reach beyond his lifetime: "If you want me again look for me under your boot-soles . . . I stop somewhere waiting for you" ("Song of Myself," section 52). In "Then," from her final volume *The Gates* (1976), Rukeyser writes: "When I am dead, even then / I am still listening to you. / I will still be making poems for you." And from 1964, handwritten on a piece of paper in Rukeyser's archives, is a piece she labeled "Dedication," written after the first of a series of strokes she suffered:

> My songs are for you
> And my silences.
> We are one life.
> We are many songs.
>
> My songs are for you.
> Lovers, the unborn—
> For you, stranger
> Now sing your songs.

Here, in two brief stanzas, we see Rukeyser's vision: her constant faith in the "we" of her readership, her awareness of the simultaneous singularity and multiplicity of human experience, and her hope for the future—strangers, lovers, and children alike. Rukeyser never faltered in her effort to speak directly to her readers, to make contact across silence and through speech, and to trust in poetry. The poems are here. She is waiting.

Theory of Flight

1935

❧ 1 Poem Out of Childhood

POEM OUT OF CHILDHOOD

1

Breathe-in experience, breathe-out poetry   :
Not Angles, angels   :   and the magnificent past
shot deep illuminations into high-school.
I opened the door into the concert-hall
and a rush of triumphant violins answered me
while the syphilitic woman turned her mouldered face
intruding upon Brahms.   Suddenly, in an accident
the girl's brother was killed, but her father had just died   :
she stood against the wall, leaning her cheek,
dumbly her arms fell, "What will become of me?" and
I went into the corridor for a drink of water.
These bandages of image wrap my head
when I put my hand up I hardly feel the wounds.
We sat on the steps of the unrented house
raining blood down on Loeb and Leopold,
creating again how they removed his glasses
and philosophically slit his throat.

> They who manipulated and misused our youth,
> smearing those centuries upon our hands,
> trapping us in a welter of dead names,
> snuffing and shaking heads at patent truth. . . .

We were ready to go the long descent with Virgil
the bough's gold shade advancing forever with us,
entering the populated cold of drawing-rooms;
Sappho, with her drowned hair trailing along Greek waters,
weed binding it, a fillet of kelp enclosing
the temples' ardent fruit   :

                            Not Sappho, Sacco.
Rebellion pioneered among our lives,
viewing from far-off many-branching deltas,
innumerable seas.

2

In adolescence I knew travellers
speakers digressing from the ink-pocked rooms,
bearing the unequivocal sunny word.

    Prinzip's year bore us :   see us turning at breast
    quietly while the air throbs over Sarajevo
    after the mechanic laugh of that bullet.
    How could they know what sinister knowledge finds
    its way among our brains' wet palpitance,
    what words would nudge and giggle at our spine,
    what murders dance?
    These horrors have approached the growing child;
    now that the factory is sealed-up brick
    the kids throw stones, smashing the windows,
    membranes of uselessness in desolation.

We grew older quickly, watching the father shave
and the splatter of lather hardening on the glass,
playing in sandboxes to escape paralysis,
being victimized by fataller sly things.
"Oh, and you," he said, scraping his jaw, "what will you be?"
"Maybe : something : like : Joan : of : Arc. . . ."
Allies Advance, we see,
Six Miles South to Soissons.   And we beat the drums.
Watchsprings snap in the mind, uncoil, relax,
the leafy years all somber with foreign war.
How could we know what exposed guts resembled?

A wave, shocked to motion, babbles margins
from Asia to Far Rockaway spiralling
among clocks in its four-dimensional circles.
Disturbed by war we pedalled bicycles
breakneck down the decline, until the treads
conquered our speed and pulled our feet behind them,
and pulled our heads.
We never knew the war, standing so small
looking at eye-level toward the puttees, searching
the picture-books for sceptres, pennants for truth;
see Galahad unaided by puberty.

Ratat a drum upon the armistice,
Kodak As You Go :   photo :   they danced late,
and we were a generation of grim children
leaning over the bedroom sills, watching
the music and the shoulders and how the war was over,
laughing until the blow on the mouth broke night
wide out from cover.
The child's curls blow in a forgotten wind,
immortal ivy trembles on the wall:
the sun has crystallized these scenes, and tall
shadows remember time cannot rescind.

    3

Organize the full results of that rich past
open the windows   :   potent catalyst,
harsh theory of knowledge, running down the aisles
crying out in the classrooms, March ravening on the plain,
inexorable sun and wind and natural thought.
Dialectically our youth unfolds   :
the pale child walking to the river, passional
in ignorance   in loneliness   demanding
its habitation for the leaping dream, kissing
quick air, the vibrations of transient light,
not knowing substance or reserve, walking
in valvular air, each person in the street
conceived surrounded by his life and pain,
fixed against time, subtly by these impaled   :
death and that shapeless war.   Listening at dead doors,
our youth assumes a thousand differing flesh
summoning fact from abandoned machines of trade,
knocking on the wall of the nailed-up power-plant,
telephoning hello, the deserted factory, ready
for the affirmative clap of truth
ricochetting from thought to thought among
the childhood, the gestures, the rigid travellers.

SONG FOR DEAD CHILDREN

We set great wreaths of brightness on the graves of the passionate
who required tribute of hot July flowers   :

for you, O brittle-hearted, we bring offering
remembering how your wrists were thin and your delicate bones
              not yet braced for conquering.

The sharp cries of ghost-boys are keen above the meadows,
the little girls continue graceful and wondering;
flickering evening on the lakes recalls those young
heirs whose developing years have sunk to earth
            their strength not tested, their praise unsung.

Weave grasses for their childhood   :   who will never see
love or disaster or take sides against decay
balancing the choices of maturity;
silent and coffin'd in silence while we pass
          loud in defiance of death, the helpless lie.

IN A DARK HOUSE

Two on the stairs in a house where they had loved   :
mounting, and the steps a long ascent before them
brown: a single step creaking high in the flight; the turn   :
the quiet house and the cheese-yellow walls shadowed by night,
dark; and the unlit lamps along the wall.
Dusk piles in old house-corners rapidly.   Shade grows
where corners round to flights of stairs again.   Evening
accumulates under the treads of mounting stairs.
They rise: he tightly-knit, clenched in anxiety, she calm,
massive in female beauty, precise line of brow
curving to generous cheek and mouth and throat,
and his face bright and strained with eagerness.

But the nights are restless with these dreams of ours
in which we cry, fling our arms abroad, and there is no one;
walls close in to a shaft and blur of brown:
out of the chaos and eclipse of mind rise stairs.
(Here, metrically and monotonously walks
each several person unprotectedly.)
Alone, the nightmare broadens in the rising,
dull step sinking behind dull step, now, here, here,
nothing in the world but the slow spiral rise, expectancy, and fear.

He turns his face to her, walk unbroken.   Her face
questioning turns: there is no help for each
in the other.   There are no eyes on them.   The shaft
is empty of voices, all but the creaking step, regularly
in the flights recurring, preknown, dreaded that sound.
There is no face that he can see but hers.
She knows his look, and has known it for a long time.
The creak of the one step is a punctuating rhyme.

But the nights are restless with receding faces
in massed battalions through the solemn air,
vivid with brightness, clangorous with sounds:
struck copper, chiming cylinders of silver, horns   :
presences in the outer air.   But here
only the empty shaft and the painful stairs.

He remembers the men and women he has loved:
fine-curved and brittle skulls housing strange ardency,
the male hard bravery of argument   :
lips of women, love-writhen, and their hands,
pale fruit of comfort, pliant, governing, white consolation
against small fear and human bodily pain,
never against the terror of the stairs.

Remembrances of words, human counsel in sounds, and pictures,
books, and the bleak rush of shining towers,
tunes crop through the tired brain: Ravel's "Bolero,"
an old blues going "Love, Oh Love, Oh Loveless Love,"
humping through air powerfully with its sound.

She remembers the men and women she has loved:
the full soft cheeks of girls, their secrecies,
grave words that fell with sweet continuance in her youth   :
men's eyes, dumb with meaning unspeakable and low-sounding
among the intricate memories deep in her recessed mind,
the length of their arms, the firm triangled backs, stalwart,
turning beautifully in their planes on the narrow hips,
dark ease beneath their arms and eyes, strength in their voices,
but ebbing away in the silence of the stairs.

Remembrances of wind shaking November evenings,
arpeggioed skyscrapers, clean-heavy-falling waters   :

"There's No Today, There's No Tomorrow"
debates against a symphony of Brahms',
and foot follows foot heavily in the row.

He had gone to play apart, by the hollows of the sand
cupped (a pale arm about the ocean's blue)   :
picked pebbles and the soft-voluted shells,
laver and dulse, dark flowers of the sea.
He had been a child in a fantastic wood
where the dim statues stood, posturing gothically,
and "Mother, mother, mother!" cried   :   but they
remained with closed lips ceremonially.
The ocean and his mother and his childhood let him be
until he had grown and finished his lessons and his prayers,
and then   :   these stairs.

Night is treacherous with dreams betraying us,
leaving us vulnerable to inherited shame,
crying out against our secret, naming an occult name.

And she had enjoyed narrow fields, shaven lawns,
tiny stones freckled brown and white and red,
green water troubled by waves of a twig's making,
grown out of these to wider thoughts that bred
high spaces and new knowledges, and cared for some
with mind and body, some with love only of eyes and head.
She had believed in the quick response to pain,
in union of crowds living in one belief,
a social order kept by a coöperative strain
steadily toward one thing, but aware of all   :
she had reached out her hand with the gesture of one who dares,
and found   :   these stairs.

The stairs still rise.   The halls remain, and dull
and somber stand to be trodden by the quiet two rising
laboriously along the fateful road.   They should be high now.
(If the dun walls should slide into the night,
faces might be disclosed, bitter, impotent, angered
above slant shoulders swinging toolless arms, great hands
jointed around no implements, and the silent mouths
opened to cry for law.   Some faces black, the rope
knotted beneath an ear, some black with the strong blood

of Negroes, some yellow and concentrate, all fixed
on the tower of stairs, should the walls sink, perhaps
all waiting, perhaps nothing but unanswering dark.)
They must be high.   There are no voices.   The shaft is very still.

Night is sick with our dreams.   Night is florid
with our by-reason-uncontested imagings.   We in our time
(not we : you : in your time : no credit ours)
have built brave stone on stone, and called their blazonry
Beauty Old Yet Ever New   :   Eternal Voice
And Inward Word   :   (a blur of fond noises signifying
a long thing) and raised signs, saying:
But Of All Things Truth Beareth Away
The Victory   :   (the pock-bitten pass to spit
gelatinously and obscenely on the bird-marked stones,
and shallow-carven letters fade).   The evil night
of our schooled minds is morbid with our dreams.

Whir.   Whirl of brown stairs.   Cool brow.   Athenian lips.
The creaking stairs.   Stupid   stupid   stupidly   stupidly
we go a long voyage on the stairs of a house
builded on stairs.   One stair creaks forever amen in the Name.
Treads rock under the feet.   The two go   :   he tight and harsh
(but limp with warm exhaustion), she plods   :   one, two, foot   :   on
up   mounting   up O lovely stairs, hideous and cruel
we propitiate you with incensuous words   stairs   lovely   loved
rise, idol of our walking days and nights,
travelled-forever road of the lordly mind   :   with shaking bannisters
and no sound crawling through the wall-hole-lips   :
love-writhen women's lips   :   the crackled lips of the mass
that must be there waiting for law at the wall's decay.
Large female   :   male   :   come tiredness and sleep
come peace   come generous power over no other, come Order here.
Steps mount.   The brown treads rise.   Stairs.   Rise up.   Stairs.

EFFORT AT SPEECH BETWEEN TWO PEOPLE

:   Speak to me.   Take my hand.   What are you now?
    I will tell you all.   I will conceal nothing.

When I was three, a little child read a story about a rabbit
who died, in the story, and I crawled under a chair   :
a pink rabbit   :   it was my birthday, and a candle
burnt a sore spot on my finger, and I was told to be happy.

:   Oh, grow to know me.   I am not happy.   I will be open:
Now I am thinking of white sails against a sky like music,
like glad horns blowing, and birds tilting, and an arm about me.
There was one I loved, who wanted to live, sailing.

:   Speak to me.   Take my hand.   What are you now?
When I was nine, I was fruitily sentimental,
fluid   :   and my widowed aunt played Chopin,
and I bent my head on the painted woodwork, and wept.
I want now to be close to you.   I would
link the minutes of my days close, somehow, to your days.

:   I am not happy.   I will be open.
I have liked lamps in evening corners, and quiet poems.
There has been fear in my life.   Sometimes I speculate
On what a tragedy his life was, really.

:   Take my hand.   Fist my mind in your hand.   What are you now?
When I was fourteen, I had dreams of suicide,
and I stood at a steep window, at sunset, hoping toward death   :
if the light had not melted clouds and plains to beauty,
if light had not transformed that day, I would have leapt.
I am unhappy.   I am lonely.   Speak to me.

:   I will be open.   I think he never loved me:
he loved the bright beaches, the little lips of foam
that ride small waves, he loved the veer of gulls:
he said with a gay mouth: I love you.   Grow to know me.

:   What are you now?   If we could touch one another,
if these our separate entities could come to grips,
clenched like a Chinese puzzle . . . yesterday
I stood in a crowded street that was live with people,
and no one spoke a word, and the morning shone.
Everyone silent, moving . . . . Take my hand.   Speak to me.

NOTES FOR A POEM

Here are the long fields inviolate of thought,
here are the planted fields raking the sky,
signs in the earth   :
water-cast shuttles of light flickering the underside of rock.
These have been shown before; but the fields know new hands,
the son's fingers grasp warmly at the father's hoe   ;
there will be new ways of seeing these ancestral lands.

 "In town, the munitions plant has been poor since the war,
 And nothing but a war will make it rich again."
 Holy, holy, holy, sings the church next door.

Time-ridden, a man strides the current of a stream's flowing,
stands, flexing the wand curvingly over his head,
tracking the water's prism with the flung line.
Summer becomes productive and mature.
Farmers watch tools like spikes of doom against the sure
condemning sky descending upon the hollow lands.

 The water is ridged in muscles on the rock,
  force for the State is planted in the stream-bed.
  Water springs from the stone   —   the State is fed.

Morning comes, brisk with light,
a broom of color over the threshold.
Long flights of shadows escape to the white sky   :
a spoon is straightened.   Day grows.   The sky is blued.

 The water rushes over the shelves of stone
 to anti-climax on the mills below the drop.
 The planted fields are bright and rake the sky.
 Power is common.   Earth is grown
 and overgrown in unrelated strength, the moral
 rehearsed already, often.
 (There must be the gearing of these facts
 into coördination, in a poem or numbers,
 rows of statistics, or the cool iambs.)
 The locked relationships which will be found
 are a design to build these factual timbers —
 a plough of thought to break this stubborn ground.

PLACE-RITUALS

TRADITION OF THIS ACRE
This is the word our lips caress, our teeth bite
on the pale spongy fruit of this, the name   :
mouthing the story, cowlike in dignity, and spitting it
in the tarnished cuspidor of present days.
And if there were radium in Plymouth Rock, they would not strike it
(bruising the fair stone), nor gawk at Semiramis on Main Street
nor measure the gentle Christ in terms of horse-power.
Cracked bells are severally struck at noon.
The furrow of their ways will cradle us all.
Amen, amen, to the ritual of our habit, fall
before the repetitions in the lips of doom.

RITUAL OF BLESSING
The proud colors and brittle cloths, the supple smoke rising,
the metal symbols precious to our dreams
loftily borne.   *Thy Kingdom come.*
                              We have blessed the fields with speech.
There are alp-passes in the travelled mind
(they have stood in the quiet air, making signs on the sky
to bless the cities of the shining plain).
The climate of the mind is the warmth of a shrine
and the air torn with incense.   *World without end.*
How can we bless this place   :   by the sweet horns,
the vaulted words, the pastoral lovers in the waist-deep grass,
remembrances linking back, hands raised like strict flames pointing,
the feet of priests tracking the smooth earth,
many hands binding corn   :   ?   *Thy Kingdom come.*
There are pale steeples erect among the green,
blood falling before the eyes of love   the lids fire-bright,
hands together in the fields, the born and unborn children,
and the wish for new blessing and the given blessing blend,
a glory clear in the man-tracks, in the blind
seeking for warmth in the climates of the mind.
                                        World without end.
                                                Amen.

WOODEN SPRING

How horrible late spring is, with the full death of the frozen tight bulbs
brownly rotting in earth; and each chord of light
rayed into slivers, a bunch of grapes plucked grape by grape apart,
a warm chord broken into the chilled single notes.

(Let us rely on cerebral titillation
for the red stimulus of sensuous supply;)
here is no heat, no fierce color: spring is no bacchante this year
eager to celebrate her carnal dedication.

The ghosts swim, lipless, eyeless, upward   :
the crazy hands point in five directions down   :
to the sea, the high ridge, the bush, the blade, the weak white root   :
thumping at life in an agony of birth, abortive fruit.

Spring is very mad for greenness now
(: suppose it would be beautiful, if we let ourselves be :),
but we must strip nascent earth bare of green mystery.
Trees do not grow high as skyscrapers in my town,

and flowers not so lovely as the pale bewildered youth,
hands pointing in five directions upward and out;
and spring in the fields and cities spreads to the north and south,
and is comforted in desire for the sun's mouth.

Earth does not seem wooden to the comforted spring   :
(spring could not seem so dull, I comforted   :
but there must be abstraction, where fields need not sprout, waves pound,
there must be silence where no rushing grasses sound,
life in this lack of death, comfort on this wide ground).

SONNET

My thoughts through yours refracted into speech
transmute this room musically tonight,
the notes of contact flowing, rhythmic, bright
with an informal art beyond my single reach.

Outside, dark birds fly in a greening time   :
wings of our sistered wishes beat these walls   :
and words afflict our minds in near footfalls
approaching with a latening hour's chime.

And if an essential thing has flown between us,
rare intellectual bird of communication,
let us seize it quickly   :   let our preference
choose it instead of softer things to screen us
each from the other's self   :   muteness or hesitation,
nor petrify live miracle by our indifference.

LETTER, UNPOSTED

*"My love, my love, my love,
why have you left me alone?"
    James Joyce*

If I could write   :   Summer waits your coming,
the flowers are colored, but half-alive and weak,
earth sickens, as I sicken, with waiting,
and the clouds print on the dull moon a dark and blotting streak.
If I could write   :   no energy is kinetic,
storm breaks nor foot falls until you arrive,
the trees thrive, but no fruit is born to hang
heavily   :   and the stale wind continues to drive
all pausing summer before it into the distance
from which you, shining, will come . . . . But summer lives,
and minds grow, and nerves are sensitized to power
and no winds wait, and no tree stands but gives
richly to the store of the burning harvest   :
the door stands open for you, and other figures pass,
and I receive them joyfully and live   :   but wait for you
(and sometimes secretly watch for wrinkles, in my glass).

SAND-QUARRY WITH MOVING FIGURES

Father and I drove to the sand-quarry across the ruined marshlands,
miles of black grass, burned for next summer's green.
I reached my hand to his beneath the lap-robe,
we looked at the stripe of fire, the blasted scene.

"It's all right," he said, "they can control the flames,
on one side men are standing, and on the other the sea;"
but I was terrified of stubble and waste of black
and his ugly villages he built and was showing me.

The countryside turned right and left about the car,
straight through October we drove to the pit's heart;
sand, and its yellow canyon and standing pools
and the wealth of the split country set us farther apart.
"Look," he said, "this quarry means rows of little houses,
stucco and a new bracelet for you are buried there;"
but I remembered the ruined patches, and I saw the land ruined,
exploded, burned away, and the fiery marshes bare.

"We'll own the countryside, you'll see how soon I will,
you'll have acres to play in"   :   I saw the written name
painted on stone in the face of the steep hill:
"That's your name, Father!"   "And yours!" he shouted, laughing.
"No, Father, no!"   He caught my hand as I cried,
and smiling, entered the pit, ran laughing down its side.

WEDDING PRESENTS

    1

                          Griefs
marking indelibly our later loves.

Fantastic juxtapose that sets the wish
opposite the insubordinate flesh
interring the fact of the inconstant rain
in the fixed lightly-palpitant brain,

the anthropoid hunger laid against the will
making small music in the ventricle
until evolved man hears with each breath-intake
the sweetly mathematical sound of Bach.

2

Be bold, friend   ;   all your nymphs have disappeared
dwindled upon those green and classic banks,
the goddesses are gone, and the chivalric ranks.
Where'er you walk, cool gales will fan the glade
breathing themselves to death, sighing against the towers
upon the firm and beautiful machines   ;
trees, where you sit, will crowd into a shade
eclipsing Handel, shining electric powers
of energy on polytechnic scenes.
Believe Eurydice unregained at last,
see that those idyll afternoons are past.
Accept the gathering skies that tell our morning,
open your hands   open your thighs   for strength
inviolate in beauty, ill-defined
ready for the Columbus of the mind.

Trembling, the mouth relaxes in the kiss.
The lemon body and purple blood beneath
award themselves in love, most perfect wreath.

THREE SIDES OF A COIN

1

Am I in your light?
                    No, go on reading
        (the hackneyed light of evening quarrelling with the bulbs;
            the book's bent rectangle solid on your knees)
only my fingers in your hair, only, my eyes
splitting the skull to tickle your brain with love
in a slow caress blurring the mind,
                            kissing your mouth awake
opening the body's mouth and stopping the words.
This light is thick with birds, and
evening warns us beautifully of death.

Slowly I bend over you, slowly your breath
runs rhythms through my blood
as if I said

                    I love you
and you should raise your head
listening, speaking into the covert night
    : Did someone say something?
                            Love, am I in your light?
Am I?

Refrain   See how love alters the living face
                go spin the immortal coin through time
                watch the thing flip through space
                        tick   tick

            2
We all had a good time

                            the throne was there and all
and there she was with that primitive unforgivable mouth
saying sophistications about nothing at all
as the young men cavorted up the room Darling
it's a swell party and those Martinis with
the olives so delicately soaked in alcohol
        and William Flesh, the inventor, being cute
about the revolution and the Negro Question
until Dick said "Lynch the Jews!" (his name was Fleischman
but the war brought about a number of changes)
and the Objectivist poet fresh from Butte
with his prePosterous suggestion. . . .
        After a while, of course, we left,
the room was getting so jammed with editors.
And William and Maurice and Del and I
went back and we took turns using the couch with them.
        We all had a good time
and Del had hysterics at about 3 A.M.
        we dashed water into her face
        I held her temples and Maurice said
        what could we hope to look for next:
        it's one thing to be faithful to the dead
        (he said) but for her to stick to an oversexed
old fool   :   but she only laughed and cried and beat the floor
until the neighbors rattled at the door.

Refrain   Runnels of wine ran down his chin and laughter
          softened his words until quite suddenly
          the walls fell and the night stood blank and after
                    tick   tick

          3

He turned the lights on and walked to the window   :
Son of a bitch   :   he said   :   if it isn't the reds again
parading through the streets with those lousy posters.
The Village was never like this in the old days,
throw a brick down the street and you'd hit a female poet
and life went on like a string of roller coasters.

                    Workers of the world   :
we've worked the world for all the damn thing's worth
                    tick   tick
I was little and they promised me the hills of glory
a great life and a sounding name on the earth   :
                    tick   tick
          this is a different story.
Here's a list I've been making   :   reasons for living
on the right, reasons for my sudden death on the left.
Right now they balance so I could flip a coin
determine the imperative tonight
                    tick   tick
flip that amazing coin through time and space this night
and the Village   :   and the army with banners
                              and the hot girls
and the rotgut all gone
                              like a blown fuse   :
I'd get a paragraph or two of news
obituary as a shutting door
meaning no more
leaving the world to the sun and the workers
the straight beautiful children   the coins   the clocks
                    tick   tick

BREATHING LANDSCAPE

Lying in the sun
and lying here so still
an egg might slowly hatch in this still hand.

The people pass
abruptly they nod   :   they smile
trailed in the air, silence follows their faces.

I know, lying
how the hills are fixed
and the day-moon runs at the head of the fixed hills.

Nothing crossed the field
all day but a bird
skirting the tall grass in briefest transit.

Their stern ideas
are a long work to each
and even armored we hardly touch each other.

The wind leans,
the air placed formally
about these faces and thoughts in formal dance.

Silence hangs in the air.
Nothing speaks but the sound
of certain rivers continuing underground.

FOUR IN A FAMILY

The father and mother sat, and the sister beside her.
I faced the two women across the table's width,
speaking, and all the time he looked at me,
sorrowing, saying nothing, with his hard tired breath.

Their faces said   :   This is your home; and I   :
I never come home, I never go away.
And they all answered   :   Stay.

All day the city turned about this room,
and silence had remained between our faces,
divisions outside to concentrate a world
tally here only to dead profits and losses.

We follow barrier voices, and we go fast,
unknown to each other, they race, I turn away.
No voice is strong enough to cry me Stay.

    My sister, I wished upon you those delights
    time never buries,
    more precious than heroes.

    Strange father, strange mother, who are you, who are you?
    Where have I come,
    how shall I prosper home?

THIS HOUSE, THIS COUNTRY

Always I travelled farther
dreading a barrier
starting at shadows scattered on the ground
fearful of the invisible night-sound,

till in that straight career
I crossed frontier
the questions asked   the proofs shown   the name
signed smiling   I reached knowledge of my home.

I praised their matings
and corner-meetings
their streets the brightest I had yet walked down   :
my family swore I did not leave my town

thought that I lied
and had not signed
those passports, tickets, contracts, bills of sale
but still rested among them and wished them well.

Over my shoulder
I see they grow older
their vision fails   :   observe I travel light
fear distance   hope I shall only spend the night.

But night in this country
is deep promise of day,
is busy with preparations and awake for fighting
and there is no time for leavetaking and regretting.

I know their tired house
full of remorse
I know in my body the door, the entrance-hall
a wall and my space and another wall.

I have left forever
house and maternal river
given up sitting in that private tomb
quitted that land   that house   that velvet room.

Frontiers admitted me
to a growing country
I carry the proofs of my birth and my mind's reasons
but reckon with their struggle and their seasons.

✧ 2 Theory of Flight

PREAMBLE

Earth, bind us close, and time   ;   nor, sky, deride
how violate we experiment again.
In many Januaries, many lips
have fastened on us while we deified
the waning flesh   :   now, fountain, spout for us,
mother, bear children   :   lover, yet once more   :
in final effort toward your mastery.

Many Decembers suffered their eclipse
death, and forgetfulness, and the year bore round   ;
now years, be summed in one access of power.
Fortresses, strengths, beauties, realities,
gather together, discover to us our wings
new special product of mortality.

Fortuitously have we gained loneliness,
fallen in waste places liberated,
relieved ourselves from weakness' loveliness   :
remain unpitied now, never descend
to that soft howling of the prostrate mind.
Cut with your certain wings;   engrave space now
to your ambition   :   stake off sky's dimensions.
We have plunged on nightmares to destruction
too long; and learned aggression divides wind,
pale early Venus is signature of night
and wish gnawed clean by plans precurses flight.
Distinguish the metaphor most chromium clear
for distant calendars to identify   :
Frail mouthings will fall diminished on old ears
in dusty whispers, light from extinctest stars
will let us sleep, nor may we replica
ourselves in hieroglyphs and broken things
but there is reproduction for this act
linking the flight's escape with strict contact.

Look!   Be   :   leap   ;
paint trees in flame
bushes burning
roar in the broad sky
know your color   :   be   :
produce that the widenesses
be full and burst their wombs
riot in redness, delirious with light,
swim bluely through the mind
shout green as the day breaks
put up your face to the wind
FLY

chant as the tomtom hubbubs crash
elephants in the flesh's jungle
reek with vigor   sweat   pour your life
in a libation to itself
drink from the ripe ground
make children over the world
lust in a heat of tropic orange
stamp and writhe   ;   stamp on a wet floor
know earth   know water   know lovers
know mastery
FLY

            Walks down the street
            Kaleidoscope   a man
            where patterns meet
            his mind colored
            with mirage
            Leonardo's tomb
            not in Italian earth
            but in a fuselage
            designed
            in the historic mind
            time's instrument
            blue-print of birth.

We know sky overhead, earth to be stepped
black under the toes, rubble between our fingers,
horizons are familiar   ;   we have been taught colors.
Rehearse these   ;   sky, earth, and their meeting-place,
confound them in a blur of distance, swallow
the blueness of guessed-at places, merge them now.
Sky being meeting of sky and no-sky
including our sources   the earth   water   air
fire to weld them   :   unity in knowing
all space in one unpunctuated flowing.
Flight, thus, is meeting of flight and no-flight.
We bear the seeds of our return forever,
the flowers of our leaving, fruit of flight,
perfect for present, fertile for its roots
in past   in future   in motility.

THE GYROSCOPE

But this is our desire, and of its worth. . . .
Power electric-clean, gravitating outward at all points,
moving in savage fire, fusing all durable stuff
but never itself being fused with any force
homing in no hand nor breast nor sex
for buried in these lips we rise again,
bent over these plans, our faces raise to see.
Direct spears are shot outward from the conscience
fulfilling what far circuits?   Orbit of thought
what axis do you lean on, what strictnesses evade
impelled to the long curves of the will's ambition?
Centrifugal power, expanding universe
within expanding universe, what stillnesses
lie at your center resting among motion?
Study communications, looking inward, find what traffic
you may have with your silences   :   looking outward, survey
what you have seen of places   :

                      many times this week I seemed
     to hear you speak my name
                    how you turn the flatnesses
   of your cheek and will not hear my words
                  then reaching the given latitude
  and longitude, we searched for the ship and found nothing
               and, gentlemen, shall we define desire
   including every impulse toward psychic progress?
Roads are cut into the earth leading away from our place
at the inevitable hub.   All directions are *out,*
all desire turns outward   :   we, introspective,
continuing to find in ourselves the microcosm
imaging continents, powers, relations, reflecting
all history in a bifurcated Engine.
Here is the gyroscope whirling out pulsing in tides illimitably
              widening, live force contained
in a sphere of rigid boundary   ;   concentrate
at the locus of all forces, spinning with black speed
revolving outward perpetually, turning with its torque
all the developments of the secret will.
Flaming origins were our fathers in the heat of the earth,
pushing to the crust, water and sea-flesh,
undulant tentacles ingrown on the ocean's floor,

frondy anemones and scales' armor gave us birth.
Bring us to air, ancestors! and we breathed
the young flesh wincing against naked December.
Masters of fire, fire gave us riches, gave us life.
Masters of water, water gave us riches, gave us life,
masters of earth, earth gave us riches, gave us life.
Air mocks, and desire whirls outward in strict frenzy, leaping,
elastic circles widening from the mind,
turning constricted to the mind again.
The dynamics of desire are explained
in terms of action outward and reaction to a core
obscured and undefined, except, perhaps, as "God in Heaven," "God in Man,"
Elohim intermittent with the soul, recurrent
as Father and Holy Ghost, Word and responsive Word,
merging with contact in continual sunbursts,
the promise, the response, the hands laid on,
the hammer swung to the anvil, mouth fallen on mouth,
the plane nose up into an open sky.
Roads are cut, purchase is gained on our wish,
the turbines gather momentum, tools are given   :
whirl in desire, hurry to ambition, return,
maintaining the soul's polarity   ;   be   :   fly.

THE LYNCHINGS OF JESUS

1 PASSAGE TO GODHEAD

Passage to godhead, fitfully glared upon
by bloody shinings over Calvary
this latest effort to revolution stabbed
against a bitter crucificial tree,
mild thighs split by the spearwound, opening
in fierce gestation of immortality.

Icarus' phoenix-flight fulfils itself,
desire's symbol swings full circle here,
eternal defeat by power, eternal death
of the soul and body in murder or despair
to be followed by eternal return, until
the thoughtful rebel may triumph everywhere.

Many murdered in war, crucified, starved,
loving their lives they are massacred and burned,
hating their lives as they have found them, but
killed while they look to enjoy what they have earned,
dismissed with peremptory words and hasty graves,
little calm tributes of the unconcerned.

Bruno, Copernicus, Shelley, Karl Marx   :   you
makers of victory for us   :   how long?
We love our lives, and the crucifixions come,
benevolent bugles smother rebellion's song,
blowing protection for the acquiescent,
and we need many strengths to continue strong.

Tendons bind us to earth, Antaeus-ridden
by desperate weakness disallied from ground,
bone of our bone; and the sky's plains above us
seduce us into powers still unfound,
and freedom's eagles scream above our faces,
misleading, sly, perverse, and unprofound.

Passage to godhead, shine illuminated
by other colors than blood and fire and pride.
Given wings, we looked downward on earth, seen
uniform from distance; and descended, tied
to the much-loved near places, moved to find
what numbers of lynched Jesuses have not been deified.

2 THE COMMITTEE-ROOM

Let us be introduced to our superiors, the voting men.
They are tired   ;   they are hungry   ;   from deciding all day
around the committee-table.
            Is it foggy outside?   It must be very foggy
            The room is white with it.
The years slope into a series of nights, rocking sea-like,
shouting a black rush, enveloping time and kingdom
and the flab faces
            Those people engendered my blood swarming
            over the altar to clasp the scrolls and Menorah
            the black lips, bruised cheeks, eye-reproaches   :
            as the floor burns, singing Shema
Our little writers go about, hurrying the towns along,

running from mine to luncheon, they can't afford
to let one note escape their holy jottings:
today the mother died, festering   :   he shot himself   :   the bullet entered
the roof of the mouth, piercing the brain-pan
    How the spears went down in a flurry of blood;
    how they died howling
          how the triumph marched
    all day and all night past the beleaguered town
    blowing trumpets at the fallen towers;
    how they pulled their shoulders over the hill, crying
    for the whole regiment to hear   The Sea   The Sea
Our young men opening the eyes and mouths together,
facing the new world with their open mouths
          gibbering war
          gibbering conquest

Ha. Will you lead us to discovery?

What did you do in school today, my darling?
    Tamburlaine rode over Genghis had a sword
    holding riot over Henry V Emperor of and
    the city of Elizabeth the tall sails
    crowding England into the world and Charles
    his head falling many times onto a dais
    how they have been monarchs and
    Calvin Coolidge who wouldn't say
         however, America

All day we have been seated around a table
        all these many days
One day we voted on whether he was Hamlet
or whether he was himself and yesterday
I cast the deciding vote to renounce our mouths.
Today we sentinel the avenue solemnly warning
the passers (who look the other way, and cough) that we
speak with the mouths of demons, perhaps the people's,
but not our own.
     Tomorrow
the vote's to be cast on the eyes, and sex, and brain.
Perhaps we will vote to disavow all three.
We are powerful now   :   we vote
      death to Sacco a man's name
      and Vanzetti a blood-brother; death

to Tom Mooney, or a wall, no matter;
poverty to Piers Plowman, shrieking anger
to Shelley, a cough and Fanny to Keats;
thus to Blake in a garden; thus to Whitman;
thus to D. H. Lawrence.

                        And to all you women,
dead and unspoken-for, what sentences,
to you dead children, little in the ground
all you sweet generous rebels, what sentences

This is the case of one Hilliard, a native of Texas,
in the year of our Lord 1897, a freeman.
Report . . . Hilliard's power of endurance seems to be
the most wonderful thing on record.   His lower limbs
burned off a while before he became unconscious;
and his body looked to be burned to the hollow.
Was it decreed (oh coyly coyly) by an avenging God
as well as an avenging people that he suffer so?

                                 We have

16 large views under magnifying glass.
8 views of the trial and the burning.
For place of exhibit watch the street bills.
                    Don't fail to see this.

Lie down dear, the day was long, the evening is smooth.
The day was long, and you were voting all day
              hammering down these heads
              tamping the mould about these diamond eyes
              filling the mouths with wax
                                lie down my dear
the bed is soft lie down to kindest dreams

              all night they carried leaves
              bore songs and garlands up the gradual hill
              the noise of singing kept the child awake
                but they were dead
                all Shakespeare's heroes   the saints   the Jews   the rebels
              but the noise stirred their graves' grass
              and the feet all falling in those places
              going up the hill with sheaves and tools
              and all the weapons of ascent together.

3 THE TRIAL

The South is green with coming spring ;   revival
flourishes in the fields of Alabama.   Spongy with rain,
plantations breathe April   :   carwheels suck mud in the roads,
the town expands warm in the afternoons.   At night the black boy
teeters no-handed on a bicycle, whistling The St. Louis Blues,
blood beating, and hot South.   A red brick courthouse
is vicious with men inviting death.   Array your judges; call your
                                                    jurors; come,
here is your justice, come out of the crazy jail.
Grass is green now in Alabama; Birmingham dusks are quiet
relaxed and soft in the park, stern at the yards:
a hundred boxcars shunted off to sidings, and the hoboes
gathering grains of sleep in forbidden corners.
In all the yards   :   Atlanta, Chattanooga,
Memphis, and New Orleans, the cars, and no jobs.

Every night the mail-planes burrow the sky,
carrying postcards to laughing girls in Texas,
passionate letters to the Charleston virgins,
words through the South   :   and no reprieve,
no pardon, no release.

A blinded statue attends before the courthouse,
bronze and black men lie on the grass, waiting,
the khaki dapper National Guard leans on its bayonets.
But the air is populous beyond our vision:
all the people's anger finds its vortex here
as the mythic lips of justice open, and speak.

Hammers and sickles are carried in a wave of strength, fire-tipped,
swinging passionately ninefold to a shore.
Answer the back-thrown Negro face of the lynched, the flat
    forehead knotted,
the eyes showing a wild iris, the mouth a welter of blood,
answer the broken shoulders and these twisted arms.
John Brown, Nat Turner, Toussaint stand in this courtroom,
Dred Scott wrestles for freedom there in the dark corner,
all our celebrated shambles are repeated here   :   now again
Sacco and Vanzetti walk to a chair, to the straps and rivets
and the switch spitting death and Massachusetts' will.
Wreaths are brought out of history

here are the well-nourished flowers of France, grown strong on blood,
Caesar twisting his thin throat toward conquest, turning
north from the Roman laurels,
the Istrian galleys slide again to sea.
How they waded through bloody Godfrey's Jerusalem   !
How the fires broke through Europe, and the rich
and the tall jails battened on revolution   !
The fastidious Louis', cousins to the sun, stamping
those ribboned heels on Calas, on the people;
the lynched five thousand of America.
Tom Mooney from San Quentin, Herndon   :   here
is an army for audience
                              all resolved
to a gobbet of tobacco, spat, and the empanelled hundred,
a jury of vengeance, the cheap pressed lips, the narrow eyes like
                      hardware;
the judge, his eye-sockets and cheeks dark and immutably secret,
the twisting mouth of the prosecuting attorney.
Nine dark boys spread their breasts against Alabama,
schooled in the cells, fathered by want.
    Mother   :   one writes   :   they treat us bad.   If they send us
    back to Kilby jail, I think I shall kill myself.
    I think I must hang myself by my overalls.

Alabama and the South are soft with spring;
in the North, the seasons change, sweet April, December and the air
loaded with snow.   There is time for meetings
during the years, they remaining in prison.
                          In the Square
a crowd listens, carrying banners.
Overhead, boring through the speaker's voice, a plane
circles with a snoring of motors revolving in the sky,
drowning the single voice.   It does not touch
the crowd's silence.   It circles.   The name stands   :
Scottsboro

       ⤜⤛

Earth, include sky   ;   air, be stable to our
feet, which have need of stone and iron stance;
all opposites, affirm your contradictions,
lead, all you prophets, our mechanic dance.

Arches over the earth, conform, be still,
calm Roman in the evening cool of grace,
dramatic Gothic, be finally rounded now
pared equal to the clean savannahs of space,

grind levels to one plane, unfold the stones
that shaped you pointed, return to ground, return,
bird be no more a brand upon the sky
no more a torch to which earth's bodies burn

fire attracting fire in magnetism
too subtle for dissection and proponence,
torturing fire, crucifying posture
with which dead Jesus quenches his opponents.

Shall we then straddle Jesus in a plane
the rigid crucified revived at last
the pale lips flattened in a wind a rain
of merging conquered blast and counterblast.
Shout to us   :   See   !
the wind   !
Shout to us   :
FLY

THE TUNNEL

1

NO WORK is master of the mine today
tyrant that walks with the feet of murder here
under his cracked shoes a grass-blade dusted
dingy with coal's smear.

The father's hand is rubbed with dust, his body
is witness to coal, black glosses all his skin.
Around the pithead they stand and do not talk
looking at the obvious sign.

Behind his shoulder stands the black mountain
of unbought coal, green-topped with grass growing

rank in the shag, as if coal were native earth
and the top a green snowing

down on the countryside.   In the whole valley
eleven mines, and five of them are closed,
two are on strike, but in the others, workers
scramble down the shafts, disposed

to grub all day and all night, lording it
in the town because of their jobs and their bosses
at work with all the other mines' graveyards.
These are the valley's losses

which even the company fails to itemize
in stubborn black and red in the company stores   :
the empty breasts like rinds, the father's hands,
the sign, the infected whores,

a puppy roasted for pregnant Mary's dinner . . .
On the cold evenings the jobless miners meet
wandering dully attracted to the poolroom,
walking down the grey street.

"Well," says the father, "nothing comes of this,
the strippings run to weeds, the roads all mucked.
A dead mine makes dead miners.   God, but I
was a fool not to have chucked

the whole damned ruin when I was a kid."
"And how'd you have a chance to throw it over?"
"Well," he said, "if I hadn't married   :   though then
the place had more in its favor.

Babies came quickly after summertimes.
You could work, and quit, and get a better job.
God knows if it'll ever be the same,
or if ever they'll think not to rob,

not to cut wages, not to weigh us short."
"All right," the other says, "maybe God does.
We'll be a long time dead, come that time, buried
under coal where our life was;

we were children and did not know our childhood,
we got infants, and never knew our wives,
year in and out, seeing no color but coal,
we were the living who could not have their lives."

2

Emerge, city, from your evening   :   allay me, sleep   :
but the city withdraws to night, sleep passes whitely
inanely over my eyelids mockcomforting pale dawn's
developing silver and I unloved.

Shall we no more, my love, pass down the lanes of grace
slowly together and in each other's safekeeping, no more
shall I watch evening touch hands to your face
and feel myself glisten in answer?

Day shines a last gloom quickening the street, and deep
grave-deep the subway files down space to a moment
over me a plane exterminates distance   ;   you
are unalterably removed   :   day touches you

nor night though tiger it may rage abroad   ;   you are
beyond its claws, if my love will not reach you.
O love, how am I surpassed how mocked   how
defiled and corroded untouched by your kiss.

I came to you riding on love with love in my hands, advancing
seaworn, hearing far bells   :   you have been a prow
carving a tragic sea to meet my love, you have been lamps
burning all night over tired waters.

You have been stone set upon fine-grained woods, buildings
of granite standing in a street of stone, roads
full of fallen flowers wet under the foot, ships
pointing an index to voyage among islands,

blue archipelagoes   :   your body being an island
set about with magnetic flowers and flesh and fruit   :
the sons I might bear you, the sons, the fragrant daughters.
Intrudes on this the bleak authentic voice   :

wherefore does the mouth stiffen, the cheeks freeze austere
as stone, affording special grief among the days
and cold days catalogued of comfort murdered,
the iron passage, estranged eyes, and the death

of all my logic   :   pale with the weakness of one
dead and not yet arisen, a hollow bath of flame
with my fire low along the oils of grace
how many deaths, body so torn from spirit.

Body, return   :   I love you   :   soul, come home!
I am gone down to death in a great bleeding.
All day the bleeding washes down my sides   ;   at night
darkly and helplessly my face is wet.

Open me a refuge where I may be renewed.   Speak to me
world hissing over cables, shining among steel strands,
plucking speech out on a wire, linking voices,
reach me now in my fierceness, or I am drowned

buried among my flesh, dead of a dead desire.
All night I went to the places of my love,
opened to one wished meeting, all unarmed.
And there was nothing but machine-loud streets.

All night I returned to the places of my love.
My love escaped me.   May not the blood's frail drums
ever pulse healing in wrists and lips made known
whispering convalescence through a mist of sleep?

Let me approach infinity in love and sorrow, waiting
with the doubled strength of my own will and love,
burning with copper-spun electric fire, unconsumed,
a bush upon a barren darkening plain.

My blood must be fed on foreign substance, lacking
the knowledge of those gestures, roots of words, unfeeling
the wet intestinal movings of another body, starving
not knowing the muscles' flexing.

Shall we losing our ego gain it, saddening
after no response and a turning away?   Sheer

the skyscrapers stand, pure without meaning, single
in desire rising to touch the sky   :

the diver waits, arms thrust in white dihedral
to air and next moment's water   :   the flash of shock
travels through diver   lover   tower   plane   reaching
sky, a contact in desire, leaving

bondage in flight.   Sever the cords binding our bones,
loosen us to each other, approach, night, return me love   :
unblind me, give me back myself, touch me now   :
slide, night, into the climates of the mind.

3

The cattle-trains edge along the river, bringing morning on a white vibration
breaking the darkness split with beast-cries   :   a milk-wagon proceeds
down the street leaving the cold bottles   :   the Mack truck pushes
around the corner, tires hissing on the washed asphalt.   A clear sky
growing candid and later bright.
                              Ceiling unlimited.   Visibility unlimited.

They stir on the pillows, her leg moving, her face swung windowward
vacant with sleep still, modeled with light's coming   ;   his dark head
among the softness of her arm and breast, nuzzled in dreams,
mumbling the old words, hardly roused.   They return to silence.
                              At the airport, the floodlights are snapped off.

Turning, he says, "Tell me how's the sky this morning?" "Fair," she answers,
"no clouds from where I lie; bluer and bluer."   "And later and later—
god, for some sleep into some noon, instead of all these mornings
with my mouth going stiff behind the cowling and wind brushing
away from me and my teeth freezing against the wind."
                              Light gales from the northwest   :   tomorrow, rain.

The street is long, with a sprinkling of ashcans   ;   panhandlers
begin to forage among banana-peels and cardboard boxes.
She moves to the window, tall and dark before a brightening sky,
full with her six-months' pregnancy molded in ripeness.
                              Stands, watching the sky's blankness.

Very soon   :   "How I love to see you when I wake," he says,
"How the child's meaning in you is my life's growing."

She faces him, hands brought to her belly's level, offering,
wordless, looking upon him.   She carries his desire well.
                        Sun rises   :   6:38 a.m.   Sun sets . . . .

"Flying is what makes you strange to me, dark as Asia,
almost removed from my world even in your closenesses   :
that you should be familiar with those intricacies
and a hero in mysteries which all the world has wanted."
                        Wind velocity changing from 19 to 30.

"No, that's wrong," and he laughs, "no personal hero's left
to make a legend.   Those centuries have gone.   If I fly,
why, I know that countries are not map-colored, that seas
belong to no one, that war's a pock-marking on Europe   :   "
                        The Weather Bureau's forecast, effective until noon.

"Your friends sleep with strange women desperately,
drink liquor and sleep heavily to forget those skies.
You fly all day and come home truly returning
to me who know only land.   And we will have this child."
                        New York to Boston   :   Scattered to broken clouds.

"The child will have a hard time to be an American,"
he says slowly, "fathered by a man whose country is air,
who believes there are no heroes to withstand
wind, or a loose bolt, or a tank empty of gas."
                        To Washington   :   Broken clouds becoming overcast.

"It will be a brave child," she answers, smiling.
"We will show planes to it, and the bums in the street.
You will teach it to fly, and I will love it
very much."   He thinks of his job, dressing.
                        Strong west northwest winds above 1000 feet.

He thinks how many men have wanted flight.
He ties his tie, looking into his face.
Finishes breakfast, hurrying to be gone,
crossing the river to the airport and his place.
                        To Cleveland   :   Broken clouds to overcast.

She does not imagine how the propeller turns
in a blinding speed, swinging the plane through space;

she never sees the cowling rattle and slip
forward and forward against the grim blades' grinding.
Cruising speed 1700 R.P.M.

Slipping, a failing desire   ;   slipping like death
insidious against the propeller, until the blades shake,
bitten by steel, jagged against steel, broken,
and his face angry and raked by death, staring.
Strong west northwest or west winds above 2000 feet.

She watches the clock as his return time hurries,
the schedule ticking off, eating the short minutes.
She watches evening advance   ;   she knows the child's stirring.
She knows night.   She knows he will not come.
Ceiling unlimited.   Visibility unlimited.

The rough skin dusty with coal on the slack hands   ;
lover trailing regret through the evening streets
uncomforted, walking toward destruction   :
the mouth of the young pilot stiffening
(I love to see you when I wake at morning)
hurtling, spiralling that plucks the breath from the throat
in a long chute to gauged mechanic death.

Greyly our vigor seeps away, the fingers
weak and the lips unspeaking, somberly
devoid of wholeness are we drowned again
mumbling death as our cheeks stiffen
as we go down these maelstroms   :   dissolution.
　　Harsh blue screams summer from behind the plane
　　the sea stiffens under it sculpturally.
　　Split space, monotonous and even-winged,
　　continue toward despair methodically.
Destruction and a burning fill these lives
unloved incompetent they compromise
with death and the bases of emotion fearing
the natural calm inclusiveness of time.
　　Tigers follow in a splendor of motion
　　sleek death treads unperturbed among these things,
　　time rages like a tiger and the
　　savage defeat swallows the fallen wings
plunging

O Icarus accurate white into the sea
the wax support too trusted   ;   the white pride
in sovereignty collapsed   ;   go down to harbor,
go down, plane, to the water's eagerness
engulfed, plunging

❧

We have prayed torrents of humility, open
in anguish to be hurt, in terror to be fooled.
We are beyond demand, waiting a minute
unconscious in attendance   :   here is strength to be used
delicately, most subtly on the controls and levers.
They begged that time be condensed.   Extend space for us,
let us include this memory in ourselves,
time and our dividend of history.

THE STRUCTURE OF THE PLANE

1 THE STRUCTURE OF THE PLANE

Kitty Hawk is a Caesar among monuments   ;
        the stiff bland soldiers predestined to their death
        the bombs piled neatly like children's marbles piled
        sperm to breed corpses eugenically by youth
        out of seductive death.
                        The hill outdoes our towers
        we might treasure a thistle grown from a cannon-mouth
        they have not permitted rust and scum and blossoms
        to dirty the steel,
                        however we have the plane
the hill, flower among monuments.

"To work intelligently" (Orville and Wilbur Wright)
"one needs to know the effects of variations
incorporated in the surfaces. . . . The pressures on squares
are different from those on rectangles, circles, triangles, or ellipses . . .
The shape of the edge also makes a difference."

The plane is wheeled out of the hangar.   The sleeves shake
fixing the wind, the four o'clock blue sky
blinks in the goggles swinging over his wrist.

The plane rests, the mechanic in cream-colored overalls
encourages the engine into idling speed.
The instructor looks at his class
and begins the demonstration.

"We finally became discouraged, and returned to kite-flying.
But as we grew older we had to give up this sport,
it was unbecoming to boys of our ages."

On the first stroke of the piston the intake valve opens,
the piston moves slowly from the head of the cylinder,
drawing in its mixture of gas and air.   On the second stroke
the piston returns, the valve closes.   The mixture is compressed.
A spark occurs, igniting America, opening India,
finding the Northwest Passage, Cipango spice,
causing the mixture to burn, expanding the gases
which push the piston away on the power stroke.
The final exhaust stroke serves to release the gases,
allowing the piston to scavenge the cylinder.
              We burn space, we sever galaxies,
              solar systems whirl about Shelley's head,
              we give ourselves ease, gentlemen, art and these explosions
              and Peter Ronsard finger-deep in roses   ;
gentlemen, remember these incandescent points,
remember to check, remember to drain the oil,
remember Plato O remember me
              the college pathways rise
              the president's voice intoning sonnets
              the impress of hoofmarks on the bridle path
              the shining girls the lost virginities
              the plane over a skeletal water-tower
              our youth dissolving O remember
              romantically dissolving remember me.

Blue smoke from the exhaust signifies too much oil.
Save yourselves from excesses, dirt, and tailspins.
These are the axioms   :   stability, control,
and equilibrium   :   in a yaw, in a roll, or pitch.
Here, gentlemen, are the wings, of fabric doped and painted
here is the rudder
here the propeller spins

: BE   hammers in the brain
   FLY and the footbeat of that drum
   may not be contradicted
   must be mine
   must be made ours, say the brothers Wright together
          although the general public had been invited
          few dared a cold December
          in order to see another plane not fly.

The helmet is strapped tight, orders are shouted
the elbows of steel move in oil
air is forced under the ship, the pilot's hand
is safe on the stick, the young student sits
with the wind mottling his eyelashes, rigidly.
Centuries fall behind his brain, the motor
pushes in a four-beat rhythm, his blood moves,
he dares look at the levels mounting in clouds
the dropping fields of the sky the diminishment of earth   ;
          now he thinks I am the child crying Mother
          this rim is the threshold into the hall's night
          or the windowsill livened with narcissus.
          The white edge of the bath a moment before
          slipping into watery ease, the windowsill
          eager for the jump into the street
          the hard stone under my back, the earth
          with its eyes and hands its eyes and hands
          its eyes
                    fixed eyes on the diminishing
          take me back the bath had fronds of steam
          escaping the hands held my head
          my eyes slipped in oil looking along your beauty
          earth is painful the distance hurts
          mother the night, the distance, dear
he is standing with one look of hate upon him
screams at the pilot you bastard, you bastard, jumps
trailing a long scream above him, the plane yaws down,
the motor pulls heavily, the ground is dark November,
his parachute opens a bright plume surrendering downward,
the plane heads up again, no good in following,
continues unfascinated by night or land or death.

2 THE STRIKE

"Well," he said, "George, I never thought you were with us.
You walked out of the shaft as if you'd spent years of your life
planning some day to walk out once without blinking
and not stop for a smoke but walk over to our side."

"No," he said, "I never expected to.   It was only the last cut:
before that, I'd have worked no matter who starved first."
The snow was stamped down with black nailprints
the stamping was a drum to warm them, stiff veins, crusted hands.

"Carrying guns, boys!" said the director.   "Now, boys;
I'll speak to the others and see what I can do."
The heavy-set miner spat on the peel of snow.
The fingers weighed on the triggers.   December bit
into the bone, into the tight skulls, creaking one word.

Tell how the men watched the table, a plate of light,
the rigid faces lit around it, the mouths
opening and clamping, the little warmth
watched against the shafts of the breakers.
Tell how the men watched.
Tell how the child chewed its shoe to strips.

That day broke equal grey, the lockers empty,
the cages hanging in a depth of silence.
Shall we say   :   there were two lines at last   :
death played like a current between them, playing,
the little flames of death ran along those eyes   :   ?

Death faced the men with a desperate seduction,
lifted a hand with the skill of a hypnotist.
They were so ready in khaki with bayonets.
      "George!" he heard.   That had once been his name.
      Very carefully he had stepped from his place,
      walked over his ground, over the last line.
      It seemed impossible he should not die.
            When a gun faces you, look down the bore,
            that is the well of death   :   when it confronts you
            it is not satisfied, it draws you steadily
            more loving than love, eagerer than hunger,
            resolving all unbalance.   He went to it.

However, the line held.   The plump men raised themselves
up from the chairs in a dreary passion of wrath,
hoisted themselves to the doorway.   Spoke.
There was his body, purpled, death casing him
in ice and velvet and sleep.   Indeed, they spoke,
this was unwarranted.   No, they conceded.   No.
Perhaps the strike might equal victory,
a company funeral, and the trucks of coal
                    ladled up from the earth,
                    heaped on this grave.

3 THE LOVER

Answer with me these certainties
of glands swelling with sentiment
the loves embittered the salts and waters mixing
a chemic threatening destruction.

Answer the men walking toward death
leaping to death meeting death in a kiss
able to find of equilibrium none
except that last of hard stone kissing stone.

Answer the lover's questioning in the streets
the evenings domed with purple, the bones
easing, the flesh slipping perfume upon the air   :
all surfaces of flight are pared to planes

equal, equilibrated, solid in fulfilment.   No way
is wanted to escape, no explosions craved,
only this desire must be met, this motion
be balanced with passion   ;

                    in the wreaths of time given to us what love
                    may reach us in the streets   the books   the years
                    what wreaths of love may touch our dreams,
                    what skeins of fine response may clothe our flesh,
                    robe us in valor brave as our dear wish

                    lover haunting the ghosts of rivers, letting time
                    slide a fluid runner into darkness
                    give over the sad eyes the marble face of pain

do not mourn   :   remember   :   do not forget
but never let this treason play you mate,

take to yourself the branches of green trees
watch the clean sky signed by the flight of planes
know rivers of love   be flooded thoroughly
by love and the years and the past and know
the green tree perishes and green trees grow.

Knock at the doors   ;   go to the windows   ;   run,
you will not find her soon who, lost in love,
relinquished last month to that silver music
repeating in her throat forsaken tunes.

Rigid and poised for the latest of these lovers
she stretches acute in waiting on the bed
most avaricious for the length of arms
the subtle thighs and heavy confident head.

Taut with a steel strut's singing tautness she
clinches her softness anguished at postponement
hardening all her thought she swears to be
unpacified by minutes of atonement.

The ticking of an ormolu clock taxes
her body with time's weight.   The opened door
adjusts such things   ;   responsive, she relaxes
ringing in answer to a word before

all tensity is changed to eagerness.
Translated and resolved, the anguish through,
sensitive altogether to the present   :
"Now?"   "Yes," she says, "yes," she says, "do."

⁓

Answer motion with motion, be birds flying
be the enormous movements of the snows,
be rain, be love, remain equilibrated
unseeking death,

                if you must have pilgrimages
go travelling to balance need with answer
suiting the explosion to the ensuing shock

the foil to the airstream running over it
food to the mouth, tools to the body, mind
to the bright mind that leaps in necessity
go answering   answering   FLY

NIGHT FLIGHT : NEW YORK

Lucid at dusk the city lies revealed
authentic purpose under masonry
emerging into emphasis.   Tenuous
the bodies grim at noon lie scattered, limp
on the beach of evening, and the long sea
of night softly encroaches on reality.

Pale the primitive blue of afternoon,
morning's bravado made ambiguous,
and all the bulwarks we relied upon
relapsed to fluid concept.   Now the night
opens a shady empire odorous
prodigal in sweetness, sweetly promiscuous.

Foliate evening opens in a blur
of even color on the risen stone   :
in unified unbroken shoulderings
of tower past planned tower, twilight-softened;
insanest noise resolves to monotone.
The theory of the city's fact made known

in a revelatory evening stillness.
Traffic and work and riot, triad of waking
are garbled into a full chord, drowning
identity in conquering vibration
impinging on the air, loud, rising, making
the city conscious of propellers shaking

hard frames of aircraft   ;   night cloven by twin wings,
incisive angles ripping evening where
blueness was closing deepest to the north
beyond the Bridge, beyond the island, planes   :

a burr of dissonance, a swoop of bare
fatal battalions black against the air.

Time is metric now with the regular advance   :   descend the skytrack
signal-red on the wingtips, defined by a glitter of bulbs   ;
we lean at the windows or roofrails, attentive
under inverted amphitheatre of sky.
The river is keen under blackness, weapon-malevolent,
crossed jagged marks mirrored against its steel.
Suddenly from a trance of speed are let fall bubbles slowly
blooming in pale light, but hardening to crystal
glows, into calcium brilliance, white bombs floating imperturbable
along the planes of the air, in chains of burning, destruction in the wake
of the beautiful transition.   City, shimmer in amusement,
spectators at the mocking of your bombardment.
City, cry out   :   the space is full of planes, you will be heard,
        the thin shark-bodies are concentrated to listen,
without a sound but the clean strength of the engines, dripping death-globes
        drifting down the wind
lifted by parachutes in a metaphor of death,
the symbol not the substance, merest detail of fact, going down
the wincing illuminated river, fading over the city.
Planes weave   :   the children laugh at the fireworks   :   "Oh, pretty stars!
                                Oh, see the white!"

Planes move in a calculated dance of war
each throwing, climax to superbest flight.

No whisper rises from the city   :   New York is quiet
as a doped man walking to the electric chair, fixed in memory,
suspended in an image of peace.   Skeins of light
are woven above the city, gathering-in evening in a harvest of peace,
from loveliest vessels falling, the buds of annihilation.
Turn and re-turn in precise advance, engines of power
subtle terrific potency, rays of destruction emitted from black suns
shining the faces of burial, loosing magnificence
in bombs, in a sardonic joke play games of death,
cancel the city to an achievement   :   zero.

Pregnant zero breeding annihilation. . . .
Futility stands clear on these horizons
marked in the zeros of a thousand clouds
pregnant above a harvested land, whose fruit

was peace infected with the germs of war.
In tragic streaks the planes' formations fly
across the black pavilions of the sky.

❧

Failure encompassed in success, the warplanes
dropping flares, as a historic sum of knowledge,
tallying Icarus loving the sun, and plunging,
Leonardo engraved on the Florentine pale evening
scheming toward wings, as toward an alchemy
transferring life to golden circumstance.
Following him, the warplanes travelling home,
flying over the cities, over the minds
of cities rising against imminent doom.
Icarus' passion, Da Vinci's skill, corrupt,
all rotted into war   :

Between murmur and murmur, birth and death,
is the earth's turning which follows the earth's turning,
a swift whisper of life, an ambiguous word spoken   ;
morning travelling quiet on mutinous fields,
muscles swollen tight in giant effort   ;   rain   ;   some stars   ;
a propeller's glimpsing silver whirl, intensely upward,
intensely forward, bearing the plane   :   flying.

❧

Believe that we bloom upon this stalk of time   ;
and in this expansion, time too grows for us
richer and richer towards infinity.
They promised us the gold and harps and seraphs.
Our rising and going to sleep is better than future pinions.
We surrender that hope, drawing our own days in,
covering space and time draped in tornadoes,
lightning invention, speed crushing the stars upon us,
stretching the accordion of our lives, sounding the same chord
longer and savoring it until the echo fails.
Believe that your presences are strong,
O be convinced without formula or rhyme
or any dogma   ;   use yourselves   :   be   :   fly.
Believe that we bloom upon this stalk of time.

THEORY OF FLIGHT

You dynamiting the structure of our loves
embrace your lovers solving antithesis,
open your flesh, people, to opposites
conclude the bold configuration, finish
the counterpoint   :   sky, include earth now.
Flying, a long vole of descent
renders us land again.
Flight is intolerable contradiction.
We bear the bursting seeds of our return
we will not retreat   ;   never be moved.
Stretch us onward   include in us the past
sow in us history, make us remember triumph.

    O golden fructifying, O the sonorous calls
    to arms and embattled mottoes in one war
    brain versus brain for absolutes, ring harsh!
    Miners rest from blackness   :   reapers, lay by the sheaves
    forgive us our tears   we go to victory
    in a commune of regenerated lives.
    The birds of flight return, crucified shapes
    old deaths restoring vigor through the sky
    mergent with earth, no more horizons now
    no more unvisioned capes, no death   ;   we fly.

Answer together the birds' flying
reconcile rest to rest
motion to motion's poise,
        the guns are dying the past is born again
        into these future minds the incarnate past
        gleaming upon the present

                    fliers, grave men,
    lovers   :   do not stop to remember these,
    think of them as you travel, the tall kind prophets,
    the flamboyant leapers toward death,
    the little painful children

                  how the veins were slit
    into the Roman basins to fill Europe with blood
    how our world has run over bloody with love and blood
    and the misuses of love and blood and veins.
    Now we arrive to meet ourselves at last,

we cry beginnings
the criers in the midnight streets call dawn   ;
respond   respond
you workers   poets   men of science and love.

Now we can look at our subtle jointures, study our hands,
the tools are assembled, the maps unrolled, propellers spun,
do we say *all is in readiness*   :
the times approach, here is the signal shock   :   ?

Master in the plane shouts "Contact"   :
master on the ground   :   "Contact!"
he looks up   :   "Now?" whispering   :   "Now."
"Yes," she says.   "Do."
Say yes, people.
Say yes.
YES

❧ 3 The Blood Is Justified

FOR MEMORY
for Ruth Lehman
obit February 10, 1934

LIFE AND WORKS

Open with care the journal of those years
firm years precipitating days to death
This was my friend walking in color and flame
walking through a texture of sense

no breath
deranges her fine hair   no voice changes her face.

It is hardly possible she will not come again
returned for a short while out of distances
to be re-given to distance and her loves.
It is hardly truth to say that soon
a letter will not come, postmarked Detroit,
New Orleans, Chicago, ultimate Mexico.
I think she must come, and go, and come again.

Throatfuls of life, arms crammed with brilliant days,
the colored years beat strength upon her youth,
pain-bombs exploded her body, joy rocketed in her,
the stranger forests, the books, the bitter times,
preluded college in a sheltered town.

               Remembering the pale suede jacket and russet coat
               swinging down avenues of trees together,
               the nights of talk   light cast from copper bowls,
               the fugitive journey to the coal-hills   :   names,
               Del Thomas, Tony Mancuso, Mrs. Silva
               the black river curdling under a midnight wind.
               Remembering how the pale wrists flickered love,
               the dark eye-sockets impelled her to the poor,
                    ring changes
                    tell of the loves in her life
                    tell how she loved.
This was my friend of whom I knew the face
the steel-straight intellect, broidered fantastic dreams
the quarrel by the lake
and knew the hopes

               She died.   And must be dead.
And is not dead where memory prevails.

Cut the stone, deepen her name.
Her mother did not know her.
Her friends were not enough, we missed essentials.
Love was enough and its blossoms.   Behind her life
stands a tall flower-tree, around her life
are worked her valid words into her testament
of love and writing and a ring of love.

HOLY DYING

Across the country, iron hands push up chimneys
black fingers stuck up from the blackened ground.
The rivers bend seaward urgent in blue reaches;
her pain turned seaward.   Her life extended past
the sea, the cities, the individual poor,
passionate and companioned, following life.

Through the bright years reckless and proud
dimming into that last impossible pain.
We cannot think she will not come again.
The words lean on the written line, the page
is a signal fire   all the letters shine.
Into this life is lowered now death's sign,
the younger days flicker up, the poems burn,
we cannot say Return.

Slowly her death is propelled into our lives
the yellow message   the clipped convenient style
the cancelled stamps   the telephone wires ring
confirming fear "You were right"   :   in a week's short while.
Her love was never handcuffed, her hates spoke up,
her life was a job of freedom.

                         Now the news comes, the *Times* prints a name
                         the telephone rings short music over her.
Drink your coffee, open your throat for words.
Loving, she died in passion and holiness.
They share remorse who had required less.

   RITUAL FOR DEATH
  Last night she died
  Turn down the lamps tonight
  shade the walls
                 let the proud voices rise
out of the midnight street,   the whistle flying
up and along and flying in the street
the harsh struck stone,   a brake squealing the pause
and the brave silence after a lapse of sound.

  Turn out the lights
  Her body does not move
is striding over no hill in all the world
there is no avenue in Illinois shall know
the eager mouth,   the fine voluptuous hands
touch no more Mexicos in dream again.
There was a shadow deep along her cheek,
her eyes and hair were intricate with sun.
Now lights are out.
: Stand to me in the dark
  Set your mouth on me for friends we did not know

Be strong in love
give strength to all we meet
the loving   the kind   the proletarian strong
convey our love to her in the grey fields
less grey for her, send her our breathing lives.
This was my friend
                    forget the "my," speak out
This was my friend who   eager   rash   and brave
has found one answer in an early grave.
This is my body   :   in its youth I find
strength given from the startle of her mind.
If we have strength in this evening, force life between her lips
        seal it   convey it   post it   the sheet discolored
        the ink already fading
                            the dead words fading
                            the dead all dead.

Out of the South are vivid flowers sent,
African daisies, red anemone   :
here are the riches of a continent,
and intellectual gifts   breaking you free,
poetry sounding in the narrow skull
sealing the sutures with music,   smoothing the cheek
with vocable comfort   the long hands of sorrow.
The full-blown flowers are given   :   our hands are full
of flowers and gestures   :   across New England dunes
where the stiff grasses rise against the sea,
across the city   the dark-red roofs, the stone,
across the Alleghanies,   down the Valley
the air speaks plenty   the words have all been spoken.

            Upon what skies are these ambitions written?
            across what field lies scattered the young wish,
            beneath what seas toll all those fallen dreams—?

CITY OF MONUMENTS

Washington 1934

Be proud   you people   of these graves
        these chiseled words   this precedent
From these blind ruins shines our monument.

Dead navies of the brain will sail
       stone celebrate its final choice
       when the air shakes, a single voice
a strong voice able to prevail   :

Entrust no hope to stone although the stone
shelter the root   :   see too-great burdens placed
with nothing certain but the risk
set on the infirm column of
the high memorial obelisk

erect in accusation sprung against
a barren sky taut over Anacostia   :
give over, Gettysburg   !   a word will shake your glory   :
blood of the starved fell thin upon this plain,
this battle is not buried with its slain.

       Gravestone and battlefield retire
       the whole green South is shadowed dark,
       the slick white domes are cast in night.
       But uneclipsed above the park

       the veteran of the Civil War
       sees havoc in the tended graves
       the midnight bugles blown to free
       still unemancipated slaves.

Blinded by chromium or transfiguration
we watch, as through a microscope, decay   :
    down the broad streets the limousines
advance in passions of display.

Air glints with diamonds, and these clavicles
emerge through orchids by whose trailing spoor
the sensitive cannot mistake
the implicit anguish of the poor.

The throats incline, the marble men rejoice
careless of torrents of despair.

Split by a tendril of revolt
stone cedes to blossom everywhere.

STUDY IN A LATE SUBWAY

The moon revolves outside; possibly, black air
turns so around them facing night's concave,
momentum the slogan of their hurling brains
swung into speed, crying for stillness   high
        suspended and rising on time's wave.

Did these tracks have a wilder life in the ground?
beaten from streams of metal in secret earth   :
energy travels along the veins of steel,
their faces rush forward, missiles of discontent
        thrown vaguely to the south and north.

That head is jointed loosely on his neck,
his glossy eyes turn on the walls and floor   :
her face is a blank breast with sorrow
spouting at the mouth's nipple.   All eyes move
        heavily to the opening door,

regarding in dullness how we also enter.
An angle of track charges up to us, swings
out and past in a firework of signals.
Sleepily others dangle by one hand
        tense and semi-crucified things.

Speed welcomes us in explosions of night   :   here
is wrath and fortitude and motion's burning   :
the world buries the directionless, until
the heads are sprung in awareness or drowned in peace.
        Sleep will happen.   We must give them morning.

CHILD AND MOTHER

for Vega Hustana

Revolution shall be a toy of peace to you,
children during our effort.   Storm covers all our days
the tracts of sunlight overcome with thunder
black on this ocean and our youth going.

Slowly our world is shaped to a new country
for living minute fingers, the duplicated flesh   :
The old will surrender, forced under; they endure
though dead adults walk stiffly in the street
cramming the dead poor in their mouths for meat.

        Seashores of centuries
        all cosmic whisperings
        ripple upon this beach,
        listen until she sings
        lullaby to all sudden
           all grievous things.

        Rome fashioned you blankets
        Asia, a coverlet,
        we live for your smiling   :
        sleep, we shall not forget   :
        these worlds are straining
           to make your Soviet.

Beaches of darkness! the transparent foam-lips hurrying, pouring
spent on the margin trailing sea-currents
mid-ocean streams   :   at the sand, ankle-deep
mother with child braced in the hip's firm socket
fronting the torrents.

Nakedly to the extreme of the world come bathers
advancing, the pale skin pathetic against the sea,
untried and bare   :   the flesh, the bones' thin tubes
facing dim oceans, raving hurricane, windspill,
leviathan-tyranny.

        Child, you shall grow to follow,
        survive, and find
        wet hollow, submarine terror
        not so unkind
        as to blast strength, your eyes
        unsealed, and an armed mind.

Child leans the dark head against protective side
turning its look softly to the horizon
moving its hand along the rapid wind.

The mother knows this ocean and will tell
clews to the young eyes' candor, fertile thoughts
will be asserted.
                           Rage, ocean   :   foam, oppressions,
We stand, and these children follow, and all will yet be well.

Chaos is split   :   the first slow definite strides
are taken against the open waters   ;   be
fresh growth, be confident for braveries
   we and our children meet these tides
prows of revolt launched among barbarous seas.

ECCENTRIC MOTION

Dashing in glass we race,
New York to Washington   :
encased with bubbles lie
in emerald spa   :
upholstered promenades
convey us far.
Have we reached the last limits?
What have we not done?

Shut into velvet we
survey the scene,
the locked-up building,
the frozen pier   :
before and before the events,
we loved our minds in fear   :
they wriggle into worms.
We watch.   We turn.   Surrounded,
we are at last closed in.

Coated in learning, do we
cause its crown to fall?
the plane, the bath, the car
extend our protection   :
(But have we seen it all?
Shall we continue
in this direction?   :   )

This is not the way
to save the day.
Get up and dress and go
nobly to and fro   :
Dashing in glass we race,
New York to Mexico. . . .

SUNDAYS, THEY SLEEP LATE

The days are incestuous, each with its yesterday,
and they, walking heavily in the streets, atone for the moment's
sin   :   their memories laboring under the weight of today
in its perverse alliance with the past.   Laments

are heard, droning from the city on all other mornings
but Sundays, they sleep late, and need not cry to wake,
sniffling in the pillow, realizing the day's churnings
of minute resolving to minute, and the whole day slack,

the wind bled of vigor, the talk in the parlor
of people pasturing on each other's minds, and sunset
evolving in the air, a quiet change against the duller
signs in pandemonium of day's gradual transit:

The klaxon voices through the roads, the picnickers joking
(returning from the fields), who wept before they dressed.
On Sundays their dreams are longer, and their waking
is a long exhalation of their weeks, decompressed.

There are these things to be remembered: the nine boys waiting,
battle-fronts of the rising army with holes bitten by death,
the man in the prison overland, and history beating
out the recurrent facts of power, suppression, wrath.

The days are incestuous.   They witness the daily binding
of minutes linking backwards.   Their remembering atones
in no part for the things they remember.   They sink in blinding
sleep too long, they dissolve in sleep their remembering bones.

THOUSANDS OF DAYS

Morning cried by the bed   :
at Seven I understood—
by Eight, I was very God,
happiness in my head.

At Nine, I went to work,
and all the machines spoke   :
Quiet there!   Don't talk,
make, break and make   !

At Ten, I opened my book
and all that hour I read
'The tallest men are dead,
their graveyard's in your look. . . .'

I rose, angered, through sky
in a plane of glass,
dreaming speed, I pass
very bright, very high.

As it went up toward Noon

I heard the sun scream   :
fly, suck your yellow dream,
we'll end it soon.

I fell all through One,
howling and threatening,
until at Two I sing
of a far reunion   :

On Three the masses spread,
a fist opening bare,
a great hand in the square
to vindicate the dead.

By Four the men had gone,
the land was wet with rain
and a fountain stood up plain
on every lawn.

The clock picked at Five,
those jets turned silver then
with the lovely words of men
who wrote and remained alive,

prophesying the night
of Six, and the dawn behind   ;
but, creeping down the wind,
Seven snatched all the light.

Now am I left alone
waiting for day   :
sometimes I turn away,
sometimes I sleep like stone.

Midnight is on my heels,
death bites about my legs.
While all my courage sags
the endless night wheels,

danger yells, and with
this blackness comes
back confidence, and blooms
in song and act and myth.

Call off your black dog, death,

it cannot bark me down   :
I'll travel past these wounds
and speak another breath   !

THE SURROUNDED

They escape before, but their shadows walk behind,
filling the city with formidable dark,
spilling black over the sun's run gold, speeding a rumor
of warfare and the sciences of death, and work
of treason and exposure, following
me for an easy mark.

The sky is travelled by brightness, clouds ignite,
flame is incised upon the martyred air　;
the city dissolves in foaming craters, stars
falling in multitudes dazzle the sky with fire,
and I pursue them, I am pursued, and
they are everywhere.

Now there is no more brightness, and no shadow
but the shadow of a thought, and I'm in jail enough
to know conviction with prisoner certainty,
haunted by protest, lacking completion's proof
surrounded by shadows
more plausible than love.

BURLESQUE

Up in the second balcony
the dark man's hand moves at his thigh,
he turns congested eyes to floor.
The crowd still stamps and brays for more　:

Magenta flares strip grace away
peeling attraction down to this　:
thighs' alternation, shrugging breasts,
silk tapping the mons veneris　;

The adequate trough inclines and dips
rising venereally to view　:
stained by the shifting light to blue,
the pearl scarf simmers at her hips.

With each contraction of desire
the appealing flesh is whipped entire,
ambushed in spasms.
　　　　　　　　　In the street,
　the raw light serves as index to
　upturning avid faces who
　shine all the signals of defeat.

An army of horns moves up the hall,
drums hurry to their crisis where
awkward in fear, the audience
at last confronts a dancer bare   :
these naked multitudes exposed to her   :
    bright shoulders, glossy length of leg,
    the lapsing beat persists, to beg
salving of lives of these thighs' stir.

We are drenched in confusion, drowning among lights
that flare across stormed waters   showing here
the faces pitiable with hesitation,
eyes groaning past the corpse's sneer,
the twisted words of all the unlucky, spent
on brightened flesh of these impossible dear   :

The blemished faces and impeccable thighs
are those we paint with lights to make us wise,
consigning our total beauty now to this   :
the clutching loins and intolerable kiss.

MOVIE

Spotlight her face   her face has no light in it
touch the cheek with light   inform the eyes
press meanings on those lips.
                            See cities from the air,
fix a cloud in the sky, one bird in the bright air,
one perfect mechanical flower in her hair.

Make your young men ride over the mesquite plains   ;
produce our country on film   :   here are the flaming shrubs,
the Negroes put up their hands in Hallelujahs,
the young men balance at the penthouse door.
We focus on the screen   :   look   they tell us
you are a nation of similar whores   remember the Maine
remember you have a democracy of champagne   —

And slowly the female face kisses the young man,
over his face the twelve-foot female head

the yard-long mouth enlarges and yawns

The End

Here is a city   here the village grows
here are the rich men standing rows on rows,
but the crowd seeps behind the cowboy the lover the king,
past the constructed sets America rises
the bevelled classic doorways   the alleys of trees are witness
America rises in a wave a mass
pushing away the rot.

The Director cries Cut!
hoarsely CUT   and the people send pistons of force
crashing against the CUT! CUT! of the straw men.

Light is superfluous upon these eyes,
across our minds push new portents of strength
destroying the sets, the flat faces, the mock skies.

METAPHOR TO ACTION

Whether it is a speaker, taut on a platform,
who battles a crowd with the hammers of his words,
whether it is the crash of lips on lips
after absence and wanting   :   we must close
the circuits of ideas, now generate,
that leap in the body's action or the mind's repose.

Over us is a striking on the walls of the sky,
here are the dynamos, steel-black, harboring flame,
here is the man night-walking who derives
tomorrow's manifestoes from this midnight's meeting   ;
here we require the proof in solidarity,
iron on iron, body on body, and the large single beating.

And behind us in time are the men who second us
as we continue.   And near us is our love   :
no forced contempt, no refusal in dogma, the close
of the circuit in a fierce dazzle of purity.
And over us is night a field of pansies unfolding,
charging with heat its softness in a symbol
to weld and prepare for action our minds' intensity.

CITATION FOR HORACE GREGORY

These are our brave, these with their hands in on the work,
hammering out beauty upon the painful stone
turning their grave heads passionately finding
truth and alone and each day subtly slain
and each day born.
                    Revolves
a measured system, world upon world, stemmed fires
and regulated galaxies behind the flattened head,
behind the immortal skull, ticking eternity
in blood and the symbols of living.

The brass voice speaks in the street
                              STRIKE   STRIKE
        the nervous fingers continue elaborately
        drawing consciousness, examining, doing.
Rise to a billboard world of Chesterfields,
Mae West hip-wriggles, Tarzan prowess, the little
nibbling and despicable minds.
                                Here, gentlemen,
here is our gallery of poets   :
                                Jeffers,
a long and tragic drum-roll beating anger,
sick of a catapulting nightmare world,
Eliot, who led us to the precipice
subtly and perfectly   ;   there striking an attitude
rigid and ageing on the penultimate step,
the thoughtful man MacLeish who bent his head
feeling the weight of the living; bent, and turned
the grave important face round to the dead.

And on your left, ladies and gentlemen   :   poets.

Young poets and makers, solve your anguish, see
the brave unmedalled, who dares to shape his mind,
printed with dignity, to the machines of change.
A procession of poets adds one footbeat to the
implacable metric line   :   the great and unbetrayed
        after the sunlight and the failing yellow,
        after the lips bitten with passion and

gentle, after the deaths, below
    dance-floors of celebration   we turn   we turn
these braveries are permanent.   These gifts
flare on our lives, clarifying, revealed.

We are too young to see our funerals
in pantomime nightly before uneasy beds,
too near beginnings for this hesitation
obliterated in death or carnival.
Deep into time extend the impersonal stairs,
    established barricades will stand,
before they die the brave have set their hand
on rich particular beauty for their heirs.

CATS AND A COCK

for Eleanor Clark

What hill can ever hold us?
        Standing high
we saw December packed, snow upon snow,
empty until the cars, leaping in beams below,
opened the shadow of the trees in fans
enormous on the plain, fragile and magnified.
Print of the delicate branch sweeping our feet
in hundred hugeness, passing to white again.

Up the dark hill a pack of cats   :
bursting from hollows, streaming to the crest,
streaming all night toward dawn
when green invaded east.
We stood to hear the rigid cock cry Five
a black cock crowing over cold water,
when all those cats found their sole proud objective
and whirled away to slaughter.

      ❧

        We walk the streets
        of the dark city,
        placards at back
        light in our heads,

Moon rides over us
town streams below   :
Strike and support us
the strike-songs go.

Ceilings of stars
disturb our faces,
tantrums of light
summon our eyes;

The daystar stands
hungry for day   :
we file, regarding
this twin morning.

Shall that bind us,
parade and planet,
mobile and point?
No, not yet,

there is a labor
before reunion.
Poets, pickets,
prepare for dawn!

∞

Come chop the days
lop off the moving hours,
we had not known there were disparate things.

Forget these syntheses and fade
peerless and distant into a distant grave
still hoping unity indeed be made?

I wish you to be saved . . . you wish . . . he wishes . . . she . . .
in conjugation of a destiny.
We were figures rubbed by wind passing upon a frieze,
galloping figures at a column's base
hungrily running from death and marble space.

I give you cats   :   I give you a cock on a hill   :
these stream in beauty   :   that stands blocked in pride

I pledge you death until
they fight and acquiesce, or one has died.

Earnestly and slowly I continue   :
no one could guess how the impact of a word
heard plain and plainly understood
can have attacked us so and so deferred.

Fight them down, deliver yourself, friend!
see, we all fight it down   :   poetry, picket-line,
to master pride and muscle fluid with sun,
conflicting graces moving to one end.

                       ⌒

Witness the unfailing war, season with season,
license and principle, sex with tortured sex,
class versus class, and help us to survey
this city for faces, this hill for tracks.

Sickness will bind itself upon our tissue
clipping off with restriction blood and heat and milk,
becoming real against all disbelief
a sly ghost coughing to advertise its bulk.

Climax to Egypt, our milestone pyramid
forces out history and we remember
conflict of thousands of April processions,
rival winds ripping at the heart's deep chamber.

No natural poison   :   a vicious, banker's thrust
nudges toward dissolution during war,
this peak of open battle points disgust
of decay, counterattacks backing us to our door.

This is when death thrives in the rot
and formal nightmare, zebra of sleep,
presents us madness, diffusion to remember,
to cherish, loss if we lose; and dust to keep.

Resent the nightmare, assume a waking stance,
this clock revolt, held in the hand and striking,
clapping, the violent wings of a struck bird,
speaks your top hour, marks your fatal chance.

"Still elegiac!   :   between two battles, when one is happy to be
   alive   !" — Rosa Luxemburg

Here was a battle forced by the brain's fortitude,
mapping machines of peace before crisis had come;
and by this planning we create a world
new-hearted, secure from common delirium.

If the strike was won, the prisoners freed at last,
the cataract tapped for power, parade-songs sung   :
Prepare for continuance, open your brilliant love,
your life,—front April, give it tongue   !

∽

   Below the flowering hedge
   rest in the light, forget
   grief's awful violet
   and indecision's wedge
   driven into your pride,
   and how the past has died.

   Here is transition   :
   pain, but no surgeon's knife
  :   anaesthetize your life?
   you lose the vision
   of how you simply walk
   toward a younger folk,

   simply, a flaming wire
   advancing on the night,
   reducing midnight
   to clear noon-fire   ;
   moving upon the future
   and large, clean stature
   nearer to all your nature.

∽

The latchpieces of consciousness unfasten.
We are stroked out of dream and night and myth,
and turning slowly to awareness, listen
to the soft bronchial whisperings of death.

Never forget in legendary darkness
the ways of the hands' turning and the mouth's ways,
wander in the fields of change and not remember
a voice and many voices and the evening's burning.

Turn and remember, this is the world made plain
by chart and signal, instrument and name   :

to some we say Master, others call Sister,
to some we offer nothing but love   :

flier in advance, the cloud over his mouth   ;
the inventor who produces the moment of proof   ;
a sun and moon and other several stars   ;
and those who know each other over wars.

Cats stream upon a hill,
the poet-cock breaks his throat now to say   :
Moment of Proof, May dawn transposing night,
partisan dawn's on the side of day!

$\sim\!\!\!\sim$

What hill can ever hold us?
                              Deeply night
found you intent upon this city river,
asleep at heart (turn light to her at last,
it shall be to her
as wellwater)   :
going all day along the gilded air
you saw at midnight
(going, down to the river, haunted by fog-horns) :
steam escaping over the spouting manhole,
a rout of white cats racing through the street.
Wet street, and the fight was ended there,
cats and that cock, fearful antagonists
resolved in fog, a quick pack running uphill
to a cock rigid with joy; running, but not to kill.

$\sim\!\!\!\sim$

"Forehead to forehead I meet thee, this third time, Moby Dick!" —
                              Herman Melville

Moment of proof, when the body holds its vision,
masses recognize masses, knowledge without all end   ;
face fathoms other face, all the hills open sunrise,
mouth sets on mouth   ;   Spring, and the tulips
                    totter in the wind.

Forfeit in love, forfeit in conflict, here
met and at last marked clear in principle,
desire meets desire, the chase expands, and now
forever we course, knowing the marks of growth,
                    seeing the signals.

Now we remember winter-tormented cities,
the August farm's overgrown hollow, thick with goldenrod,
the impetus of strain, and places where
love set its terminals, the vivid hunger
                    and satisfying food.

Mayday is moment of proof, when recognition
binds us in protest, binds us under a sun
of love and subtle thought and the ductile wish.
Tomorrow's Mayday. — How many are we?
                    We'll be everyone.

No hill can ever hold us, peak enlists peak,
climax forces out climax, proud cock, cats streaming,
poets and pickets contriving a valid country,
:   Mayday moment, forever provoking new
                    belief and blooming.

THE BLOOD IS JUSTIFIED

Beat out continuance in the choking veins
before emotion betrays us, and we find
staring behind our faces, accomplices of death.
Not to die, but slowly to validate our lives   :
simply to move, lightly burdened, alone,
carrying in this brain survival, carrying
within these ribs, history,
the past deep in the bone.

Unthread time till its empty needle prick your flesh
sewing your scars with air, treating the wounds
only by laceration   and the blood is fresh
blood on our skin on our lips over our eyes.

Living they move on a canvas of centuries
restored from death in artful poses, found
once more by us, descendants, foraging,
ravelling time back over American ground.
How did they wish, grandparents of these wars,
what cataracts of ambition fell across their brains?   :

The heavy boots kicked stones down Wisconsin roads,
Augusta Coller danced her début at Oshkosh   :
they spoke these names   :   Milwaukee, Waukesha,
the crackle and drawl of Indian strange words.

>   Jungle-savage the south
>   raw green and shining branches, the crying
>   of parakeets, the pointed stone,
>   the altars stained with oil   :
>   Mexico   :   and Canada wheaten and polar with
>   snow halfway up the sky   :
>   all these unknown.

: What treason to their race has fathered us?
  They walked in the towns, the men selling clothing etc.
  the women tatting and boiling down grape jelly.
: If they were asked this, surely they did not answer.

Over the country, Wisconsin, Chicago, Yonkers,
I was begotten, American branch no less because
I call on the great names of other countries.
I do not say   :   Forgive, to my kindred dead,
only   :   Understand my treason, See I betray you kissing,
I overthrow your milestones weeping among your tombs.

From out your knowing eyes I sprang, child of your distant wombs,
of your full lips.   Speaking allegiance, I turn,
steadfastly to destroy your hope.   Your cargo in me
swings to ports hostile to your old intent.

In us recurrences.   :   My generation feeds
the wise assault on your anticipation,
repeating historic sunderings, betraying our fathers,
all parricidal in our destinies.

How much are we American?   Not knowing
those other lands, being
blood wrung from your bone, our pioneers,
we call kindred to you, we claim links, speaking
your tongue, although we pass, shaking
your dream with revolution since we must.
By these roads shall we come upon our country.
Pillowed upon this birthright, we may wake
strong for such treason, brave with your fallen dust.

O, we are afflicted with these present evils,
they press between the mirror and our eyes,
obscuring your loaned mouths and borrowed hair.
We focus on our times, destroying you, fathers
in the long ground   :   you have given strange birth
to us who turn against you in our blood
needing to move in our integrity, accomplices
of life in revolution, though the past
be sweet with your tall shadows, and although
we turn from treasons, we shall accomplish these.

U.S. 1

1938

❧ 1 The Book of the Dead

THE ROAD

These are roads to take when you think of your country
and interested bring down the maps again,
phoning the statistician, asking the dear friend,

reading the papers with morning inquiry.
Or when you sit at the wheel and your small light
chooses gas gauge and clock; and the headlights

indicate future of road, your wish pursuing
past the junction, the fork, the suburban station,
well-travelled six-lane highway planned for safety.

Past your tall central city's influence,
outside its body: traffic, penumbral crowds,
are centers removed and strong, fighting for good reason.

These roads will take you into your own country.
Select the mountains, follow rivers back,
travel the passes. Touch West Virginia where

the Midland Trail leaves the Virginia furnace,
iron Clifton Forge, Covington iron, goes down
into the wealthy valley, resorts, the chalk hotel.

Pillars and fairway; spa; White Sulphur Springs.
Airport. Gay blank rich faces wishing to add
history to ballrooms, tradition to the first tee.

The simple mountains, sheer, dark-graded with pine
in the sudden weather, wet outbreak of spring,
crosscut by snow, wind at the hill's shoulder.

The land is fierce here, steep, braced against snow,
rivers and spring. KING COAL HOTEL, Lookout,
and swinging the vicious bend, New River Gorge.

Now the photographer unpacks camera and case,
surveying the deep country, follows discovery
viewing on groundglass an inverted image.

John Marshall named the rock (steep pines, a drop
he reckoned in 1812, called) Marshall's Pillar,
but later, Hawk's Nest. Here is your road, tying

you to its meanings: gorge, boulder, precipice.
Telescoped down, the hard and stone-green river
cutting fast and direct into the town.

WEST VIRGINIA

They saw rivers flow west and hoped again.
Virginia speeding to another sea!
1671—Thomes Batts, Robert Fallam,
Thomas Wood, the Indian Perecute,
and an unnamed indentured English servant
followed the forest past blazed trees, pillars of God,
were the first whites emergent from the east.
They left a record to our heritage,
breaking of records. Hoped now for the sea,
For all mountaines have their descents about them,
waters, descending naturally, doe alwaies resort
unto the seas invironing those lands . . .
Yea, at home amongst the mountaines in England.

Coming where this road comes,
flat stones spilled water which the still pools fed.
Kanawha Falls, the rapids of the mind,
fast waters spilling west.

Found Indian fields, standing low cornstalks left,
learned three Mohetons planted them; found-land
farmland, the planted home, discovered!

War-born:
The battle at Point Pleasant, Cornstalk's tribes,
last stand, Fort Henry, a revolution won;

the granite SITE OF THE precursor EXECUTION
sabres, apostles OF JOHN BROWN LEADER OF THE
War's brilliant cloudy RAID AT HARPERS FERRY.
Floods, heavy wind this spring, the beaten land
blown high by wind, fought wars, forming a state,
a surf, frontier defines two fighting halves,
two hundred battles in the four years: troops
here in Gauley Bridge, Union headquarters, lines
bring in the military telegraph.
Wires over the gash of gorge and height of pine.

But it was always the water
the power flying deep
green rivers cut the rock
rapids boiled down,
a scene of power.

Done by the dead.
Discovery learned it.
And the living?

Live country filling west,
knotted the glassy rivers;
like valleys, opening mines,
coming to life.

STATEMENT: PHILIPPA ALLEN

—You like the State of West Virginia very much, do you not?
—I do very much, in the summertime.
—How much time have you spent in West Virginia?
—During the summer of 1934, when I was doing social work
      down there, I first heard of what we were pleased to call the
      Gauley tunnel tragedy, which involved about 2,000 men.
—What was their salary?
—It started at 40¢ and dropped to 25¢ an hour.
—You have met these people personally?
—I have talked to people; yes.
   According to estimates of contractors
   2,000 men were

employed there
period, about 2 years
drilling, 3.75 miles of tunnel.
To divert water (from New River)
to a hydroelectric plant (at Gauley Junction).
The rock through which they were boring was of a high
silica content.
In tunnel No. 1 it ran 97–99% pure silica.
The contractors
knowing pure silica
30 years' experience
must have known danger for every man
neglected to provide the workmen with any safety device . . . .
—As a matter of fact, they originally intended to dig that
tunnel a certain size?
—Yes.
—And then enlarged the size of the tunnel, due to the fact
that they discovered silica and wanted to get it out?
—That is true for tunnel No. 1.
The tunnel is part of a huge water-power project
begun, latter part of 1929
direction: New Kanawha Power Co.
subsidiary of Union Carbide & Carbon Co.
That company—licensed:
to develop power for public sale.
Ostensibly it was to do that; but
(in reality) it was formed to sell all the power to
the Electro-Metallurgical Co.
subsidiary of Union Carbide & Carbon Co.
which by an act of the State legislature
was allowed to buy up
New Kanawha Power Co. in 1933.
—They were developing the power. What I am trying to get at,
Miss Allen, is, did they use this silica from the tunnel; did
they afterward sell it and use it in commerce?
—They used it in the electro-processing of steel.
SiO_2 SiO_2
The richest deposit.
Shipped on the C & O down to Alloy.
It was so pure that
$$SiO_2$$
they used it without refining.

—Where did you stay?
—I stayed at Cedar Grove. Some days I would have to hitch
    into Charleston, other days to Gauley Bridge.
—You found the people of West Virginia very happy to pick
    you up on the highway, did you not?
—Yes; they are delightfully obliging.
    (All were bewildered. Again at Vanetta they are asking,
        "What can be done about this?")
    I feel that this investigation may help in some manner.
    I do hope it may.
    I am now making a very general statement as a beginning.
        There are many points that I should like to develop later,
        but I shall try to give you a general history of this
        condition first . . . .

GAULEY BRIDGE

Camera at the crossing sees the city
a street of wooden walls and empty windows,
the doors shut handless in the empty street,
and the deserted Negro standing on the corner.

The little boy runs with his dog
up the street to the bridge over the river where
nine men are mending road for the government.
He blurs the camera-glass fixed on the street.

Railway tracks here and many panes of glass
tin under light, the grey shine of towns and forests:
in the commercial hotel (Switzerland of America)
the owner is keeping his books behind the public glass.

Post office window, a hive of private boxes,
the hand of the man who withdraws, the woman who reaches
        her hand
and the tall coughing man stamping an envelope.

The bus station and the great pale buses stopping for food;
April-glass-tinted, the yellow-aproned waitress;
coast-to-coast schedule on the plateglass window.

The man on the street and the camera eye:
he leaves the doctor's office, slammed door, doom,
any town looks like this one-street town.

Glass, wood, and naked eye : the movie-house
closed for the afternoon frames posters streaked with rain,
advertise "Racing Luck" and "Hitch-Hike Lady."

Whistling, the train comes from a long way away,
slow, and the Negro watches it grow in the grey air,
the hotel man makes a note behind his potted palm.

Eyes of the tourist house, red-and-white filling station,
the eyes of the Negro, looking down the track,
hotel-man and hotel, cafeteria, camera.

And in the beerplace on the other sidewalk
always one's harsh night eyes over the beerglass
follow the waitress and the yellow apron.

The road flows over the bridge,
Gamoca pointer at the underpass,
opposite, Alloy, after a block of town.

What do you want—a cliff over a city?
A foreland, sloped to sea and overgrown with roses?
These people live here.

THE FACE OF THE DAM:
VIVIAN JONES

On the hour he shuts the door and walks out of town;
he knows the place up the gorge where he can see
his locomotive rusted on the siding,
he sits and sees the river at his knee.

There, where the men crawl, landscaping the grounds
at the power-plant, he saw the blasts explode
the mouth of the tunnel that opened wider
when precious in the rock the white glass showed.

The old plantation-house (burned to the mud)
is a hill-acre of ground. The Negro woman throws
gay arches of water out from the front door.
It runs down, wild as grass, falls and flows.

On the quarter he remembers how they enlarged
the tunnel and the crews, finding the silica,
how the men came riding freights, got jobs here
and went into the tunnel-mouth to stay.

Never to be used, he thinks, never to spread its power,
jinx on the rock, curse on the power-plant,
hundreds breathed value, filled their lungs full of glass
(O the gay wind the clouds the many men).

On the half-hour he's at Hawk's Nest over the dam,
snow springs up as he reaches the great wall-face,
immense and pouring power, the mist of snow,
the fallen mist, the slope of water, glass.

O the gay snow the white dropped water, down,
all day the water rushes down its river,
unused, has done its death-work in the country,
proud gorge and festive water.

On the last quarter he pulls his heavy collar up,
feels in his pocket the picture of his girl,
touches for luck—he used to as he drove
after he left his engine; stamps in the deep snow.

And the snow clears and the dam stands in the gay weather,
O proud O white O water rolling down,
he turns and stamps this off his mind again
and on the hour walks again through town.

PRAISE OF THE COMMITTEE

These are the lines on which a committee is formed.
  Almost as soon as work was begun in the tunnel
  men began to die among dry drills. No masks.

Most of them were not from this valley.
The freights brought many every day from States
all up and down the Atlantic seaboard
and as far inland as Kentucky, Ohio.
After the work the camps were closed or burned.
The ambulance was going day and night,
White's undertaking business thriving and
his mother's cornfield put to a new use.
"Many of the shareholders at this meeting
were nervous about the division of the profits;
How much has the Company spent on lawsuits?
The man said $150,000. Special counsel:
I am familiar with the case. Not : one : cent.
'Terms of the contract. Master liable.'
No reply. Great corporation disowning men who made . . . ."
After the lawsuits had been instituted . . . .
The Committee is a true reflection of the will of the people.
Every man is ill. The women are not affected,
This is not a contagious disease. A medical commission,
Dr. Hughes, Dr. Hayhurst examined the chest
of Raymond Johnson, and Dr. Harless, a former
company doctor. But he saw too many die,
he has written his letter to Washington.
The Committee meets regularly, wherever it can.
Here are Mrs. Jones, three lost sons, husband sick,
Mrs. Leek, cook for the bus cafeteria,
the men : George Robinson, leader and voice,
four other Negroes (three drills, one camp-boy)
Blankenship, the thin friendly man, Peyton the engineer,
Juanita absent, the one outsider member.
Here in the noise, loud belts of the shoe-repair shop,
meeting around the stove beneath the one bulb hanging.
They come late in the day. Many come with them
who pack the hall, wait in the thorough dark.
This is a defense committee. Unfinished business:
Two rounds of lawsuits, 200 cases
Now as to the crooked lawyers
If the men had worn masks, their use would have involved
time every hour to wash the sponge at mouth.
Tunnel, 3⅛ miles long. Much larger than
the Holland Tunnel or Pittsburgh's Liberty Tubes.
Total cost, say, $16,000,000.

This is the procedure of such a committee:
　　To consider the bill before the Senate.
　　To discuss relief.
　　　　Active members may be cut off relief,
　　　　　　16-mile walk to Fayetteville for cheque—
　　　　　　WEST VIRGINIA RELIEF ADMINISTRATION, #22991,
　　　　　　TO JOE HENIGAN, GAULEY BRIDGE, ONE AND 50/100,
　　　　　　WINONA NATIONAL BANK. PAID FROM STATE FUNDS.
　　Unless the Defense Committee acts;
　　the *People's Press*, supporting this fight,
　　signed editorials, sent in funds.
　　Clothing for tunnel-workers.
　　　　Rumored, that in the post office
　　　　parcels are intercepted.
　　　　Suspected : Conley. Sheriff, hotelman,
　　　　head of the town ring—
　　　　Company whispers. Spies,
　　　　The Racket.
　　Resolved, resolved.
　　George Robinson holds all their strength together:
　　To fight the companies　　to make somehow a future.

"At any rate, it is inadvisable to keep a community of dying
persons intact."
"Senator Holt. Yes. This is the most barbarous example of
industrial construction that ever happened in the world."
Please proceed.
"In a very general way Hippocrates' *Epidemics* speaks
　of the metal digger who breathes with difficulty,
　having a pain and wan complexion.
　Pliny, the elder . . . ."
"Present work of the Bureau of Mines . . . ."

The dam's pure crystal slants upon the river.
　A dark and noisy room, frozen two feet from stove.
　The cough of habit. The sound of men in the hall
　waiting for word.

　　These men breathe hard
　　but the committee has a voice of steel.
　　One climbs the hill on canes.
　　They have broken the hills and cracked the riches wide.

In this man's face
family leans out from two worlds of graves—
here is a room of eyes,
a single force looks out, reading our life.

Who stands over the river?
Whose feet go running in these rigid hills?
Who comes, warning the night,
shouting and young to waken our eyes?

Who runs through electric wires?
Who speaks down every road?
Their hands touched mastery; now they
demand an answer.

MEARL BLANKENSHIP

He stood against the stove
facing the fire—
Little warmth, no words,
loud machines.

Voted relief,
wished money mailed,
quietly under the crashing:

"I wake up choking, and my wife
rolls me over on my left side;
then I'm asleep in the dream I always see:
the tunnel choked
the dark wall coughing dust.

I have written a letter.
Send it to the city,
maybe to a paper
if it's all right."

Dear Sir, my name is Mearl Blankenship.
I have Worked for the rhinehart & Dennis Co

Many days & many nights
& it was so dusty you couldn't hardly see the lights.
I helped nip steel for the drills
& helped lay the track in the tunnel
& done lots of drilling near the mouth of the tunnell
& when the shots went off the boss said
If you are going to work Venture back
& the boss was Mr. Andrews
& now he is dead and gone
But I am still here
a lingering along

He stood against the rock
facing the river
grey river grey face
the rock mottled behind him
like X-ray plate enlarged
diffuse and stony
his face against the stone.

J C Dunbar said that I was the very picture of health
when I went to Work at that tunnel.
I have lost eighteen lbs on that Rheinhart ground
and expecting to loose my life
& no settlement yet & I have sued the Co. twice
But when the lawyers got a settlement
they didn't want to talk to me
But I didn't know whether they were sleepy or not.
I am a Married Man and have a family.   God
knows if they can do anything for me
it will be appreciated
if you can do anything for me
let me know soon

ABSALOM

I first discovered what was killing these men.
I had three sons who worked with their father in the tunnel:
Cecil, aged 23, Owen, aged 21, Shirley, aged 17.
They used to work in a coal mine, not steady work

for the mines were not going much of the time.
A power Co. foreman learned that we made home brew,
he formed a habit of dropping in evenings to drink,
persuading the boys and my husband—
give up their jobs and take this other work.
It would pay them better.
Shirley was my youngest son; the boy.
He went into the tunnel.

> *My heart   my mother   my heart   my mother*
> *My heart   my coming into being.*

My husband is not able to work.
He has it, according to the doctor.
We have been having a very hard time making a living since
        this trouble came to us.
I saw the dust in the bottom of the tub.
The boy worked there about eighteen months,
came home one evening with a shortness of breath.
He said, "Mother, I cannot get my breath."
Shirley was sick about three months.
I would carry him from his bed to the table,
from his bed to the porch, in my arms.

> *My heart is mine in the place of hearts,*
> *They gave me back my heart, it lies in me.*

When they took sick, right at the start, I saw a doctor.
I tried to get Dr. Harless to X-ray the boys.
He was the only man I had any confidence in,
the company doctor in the Kopper's mine,
but he would not see Shirley.
He did not know where his money was coming from.
I promised him half if he'd work to get compensation,
but even then he would not do anything.
I went on the road and begged the X-ray money,
the Charleston hospital made the lung pictures,
he took the case after the pictures were made.
And two or three doctors said the same thing.
The youngest boy did not get to go down there with me,
he lay and said, "Mother, when I die,
I want you to have them open me up and

see if that dust killed me.
Try to get compensation,
you will not have any way of making your living
when we are gone,
and the rest are going too."

> *I have gained mastery over my heart*
> *I have gained mastery over my two hands*
> *I have gained mastery over the waters*
> *I have gained mastery over the river.*

The case of my son was the first of the line of lawsuits.
They sent the lawyers down and the doctors down;
they closed the electric sockets in the camps.
There was Shirley, and Cecil, Jeffrey and Oren,
Raymond Johnson, Clev and Oscar Anders,
Frank Lynch, Henry Palf, Mr. Pitch, a foreman;
a slim fellow who carried steel with my boys,
his name was Darnell, I believe. There were many others,
the towns of Glen Ferris, Alloy, where the white rock lies,
six miles away; Vanetta, Gauley Bridge,
Gamoca, Lockwood, the gullies,
the whole valley is witness.
I hitchhike eighteen miles, they make checks out.
They asked me how I keep the cow on $2.
I said one week, feed for the cow, one week, the children's
        flour.
The oldest son was twenty-three.
The next son was twenty-one.
The youngest son was eighteen.
They called it pneumonia at first.
They would pronounce it fever.
Shirley asked that we try to find out.
That's how they learned what the trouble was.

> *I open out a way, they have covered my sky with crystal*
> *I come forth by day, I am born a second time,*
> *I force a way through, and I know the gate*
> *I shall journey over the earth among the living.*

He shall not be diminished, never;
I shall give a mouth to my son.

THE DISEASE

This is a lung disease. Silicate dust makes it.
The dust causing the growth of

This is the X-ray picture taken last April.
I would point out to you : these are the ribs;
this is the region of the breastbone;
this is the heart (a wide white shadow filled with blood).
In here of course is the swallowing tube, esophagus.
The windpipe. Spaces between the lungs.

Between the ribs?

Between the ribs. These are the collar bones.
Now, this lung's mottled, beginning, in these areas.
You'd say a snowstorm had struck the fellow's lungs.
About alike, that side and this side, top and bottom.
The first stage in this period in this case.

Let us have the second.

Come to the window again. Here is the heart.
More numerous nodules, thicker, see, in the upper lobes.
You will notice the increase : here, streaked fibrous tissue—

Indicating?

That indicates the progress in ten months' time.
And now, this year—short breathing, solid scars
even over the ribs, thick on both sides.
Blood vessels shut. Model conglomeration.

What stage?

Third stage. Each time I place my pencil point:
There and there and there, there, there.

   "It is growing worse every day. At night
   I get up to catch my breath. If I remained
   flat on my back I believe I would die."

It gradually chokes off the air cells in the lungs?
I am trying to say it the best I can.
That is what happens, isn't it?
A choking-off in the air cells?

Yes.
There is difficulty in breathing.
Yes.
And a painful cough?
Yes.

Does silicosis cause death?

Yes, sir.

GEORGE ROBINSON: BLUES

Gauley Bridge is a good town for Negroes, they let us stand
  around, they let us stand
around on the sidewalks if we're black or brown.
Vanetta's over the trestle, and that's our town.

The hill makes breathing slow, slow breathing after you
  row the river,
and the graveyard's on the hill, cold in the springtime blow,
the graveyard's up on high, and the town is down below.

Did you ever bury thirty-five men in a place in back of your
  house,
thirty-five tunnel workers the doctors didn't attend,
died in the tunnel camps, under rocks, everywhere, world
  without end.

When a man said I feel poorly, for any reason, any weakness
  or such,
letting up when he couldn't keep going barely,
the Cap and company come and run him off the job surely.

I've put them
DOWN from the tunnel camps

to the graveyard on the hill,
tin-cans all about—it fixed them!—

TUNNELITIS
hold themselves up
at the side of a tree,
I can go right now
to that cemetery.

When the blast went off the boss would call out, Come, let's
        go back,
when that heavy loaded blast went white, Come, let's go back,
telling us hurry, hurry, into the falling rocks and muck.

The water they would bring had dust in it, our drinking
        water,
the camps and their groves were colored with the dust,
we cleaned our clothes in the groves, but we always had
        the dust.

Looked like somebody sprinkled flour all over the parks
        and groves,
it stayed and the rain couldn't wash it away and it twinkled
that white dust really looked pretty down around our ankles.

As dark as I am, when I came out at morning after the
        tunnel at night,
with a white man, nobody could have told which man was
        white.
The dust had covered us both, and the dust was white.

JUANITA TINSLEY

Even after the letters, there is work,
sweaters, the food, the shoes
and afternoon's quick dark

draws on the windowpane
my face, the shadowed hair,
the scattered papers fade.

Slow letters! I shall be
always—the stranger said
"To live stronger and free."

I know in America there are songs,
forgetful ballads to be sung,
but at home I see this wrong.

When I see my family house,
the gay gorge, the picture-books,
they raise the face of General Wise

aged by enemies, like faces
the stranger showed me in the town.
I saw that plain, and saw my place.

The scene of hope's ahead; look, April,
and next month with a softer wind,
maybe they'll rest upon their land,
and then maybe the happy song, and love,
a tall boy who was never in a tunnel.

THE DOCTORS

    —Tell the jury your name.
    —Emory R. Hayhurst.
    —State your education, Doctor, if you will.
       Don't be modest about it; just tell about it.

    High school Chicago 1899
    Univ. of Illinois 1903
    M.A. 1905, thesis on respiration
    P & S Chicago 1908
    2 years' hospital training;
    at Rush on occupational disease
    director of clinic 2½ years.
    Ph.D. Chicago 1916
    Ohio Dept. of Health, 20 years as
    consultant in occupational diseases.
    Hygienist, U.S. Public Health Service

and Bureau of Mines
and Bureau of Standards

Danger begins at 25%
here was pure danger
Dept. of Mines
came in, was kept away.

Miner's phthisis, fibroid phthisis,
grinder's rot, potter's rot,
whatever it used to be called,
these men did not need to die.

—Is silicosis an occupational disease?
—It is.
—Did anyone show you the lungs of Cecil Jones?
—Yes, sir.
—Who was that?
—It was Dr. Harless.

"We talked to Dr. L. R. Harless, who had handled many of the cases, more than any other doctor there. At first Dr. Harless did not like to talk about the matter. He said he had been subjected to so much publicity. It appeared that the doctor thought he had been involved in too many of the court cases; but finally he opened up and told us about the matter."

—Did he impress you as one who thought this was a very serious thing in that section of the country?

"Yes, he did. I would say that Dr. Harless has probably become very self-conscious about this matter. I cannot say that he has retracted what he told me, but possibly he had been thrust into the limelight so much that he is more conservative now than when the matter was simply something of local interest."

Dear Sir: Due to illness of my wife and urgent professional duties, I am unable to appear as per your telegram.

Situation exaggerated. Here are facts:
We examined. 13 dead. 139 had some lung damage.
2 have died since, making 15 deaths.
Press says 476 dead, 2,000 affected and doomed.
I am at a loss to know where those figures were obtained.
At this time, only a few cases here,

and these only moderately affected.

Last death occurred November, 1934.

It has been said that none of the men knew of the hazard connected with the work. This is not correct. Shortly after the work began many of these workers came to me complaining of chest conditions and I warned many of them of the dust hazard and advised them that continued work under these conditions would result in serious lung disease. Disregarding this warning many of the men continued at this work and later brought suit against their employer for damages.

While I am sure that many of these suits were based on meritorious grounds, I am also convinced that many others took advantage of this situation and made out of it nothing less than a racket.

In this letter I have endeavored to give you the facts which came under my observation . . . .

If I can supply further information . . . .

Mr. Marcantonio. A man may be examined a year after he has worked in a tunnel and not show a sign of silicosis, and yet the silicosis may develop later; is not that true?

—Yes, it may develop as many as ten years after.

Mr. Marcantonio. Even basing the statement on the figures, the doctor's claim that this is a racket is not justified?

—No; it would not seem to be justified.

Mr. Marcantonio. I should like to point out that Dr. Harless contradicts his "exaggeration" when he volunteers the following: "I warned many . . . ."

(Mr. Peyton. I do not know. Nobody knew the danger around there.)

Dr. Goldwater. First are the factors involving the individual.
      Under the heading B, external causes.
      Some of the factors which I have in mind—
      those are the facts upon the blackboard,
      the influencing and controlling factors.

Mr. Marcantonio. Those factors would bring about acute silicosis?

Dr. Goldwater. I hope you are not provoked when I say "might."
      Medicine has no hundred percent.
      We speak of possibilities, have opinions.

Mr. Griswold. Doctors testify answering "yes" and "no."
      Don't they?

Dr. Goldwater. Not by the choice of the doctor.

Mr. Griswold. But that is usual, isn't it?

Dr. Goldwater. They do not like to do that.
      A man with a scientific point of view—

unfortunately there are doctors without that—
I do not mean to say all doctors are angels—
but most doctors avoid dogmatic statements.
avoid assiduously "always," "never."
Mr. Griswold. Best doctor I ever knew said "no" and "yes."
Dr. Goldwater. There are different opinions on that, too.
We were talking about acute silicosis.

The man in the white coat is the man on the hill,
the man with the clean hands is the man with the drill,
the man who answers "yes" lies still.

—Did you make an examination of those sets of lungs?
—I did.
—I wish you would tell the jury whether or not those lungs
were silicotic.
—We object.
—Objection overruled.
—They were.

THE CORNFIELD

Error, disease, snow, sudden weather.
For those given to contemplation : this house,
wading in snow, its cracks are sealed with clay,
walls papered with print, newsprint repeating,
in-focus grey across the room, and squared
ads for a book : HEAVEN'S MY DESTINATION,
HEAVEN'S MY . . . HEAVEN . . . . THORNTON WILDER.
The long-faced man rises long-handed jams the door
tight against snow, long-boned, he shivers.
Contemplate.

Swear by the corn,
the found-land corn, those who like ritual. *He*
rides in a good car. They say blind corpses rode
with him in front, knees broken into angles,
head clamped ahead. Overalls. Affidavits.
He signs all papers. His office : where he sits.
feet on the stove, loaded trestles through door,

satin-lined, silk-lined, unlined, cheap,
The papers in the drawer. On the desk, photograph
H. C. White, Funeral Services (new car and eldest son);
tells about Negroes who got wet at work,
shot craps, drank and took cold, pneumonia, died.
Shows the sworn papers. Swear by the corn.
Pneumonia, pneumonia, pleurisy, t.b.

For those given to voyages : these roads
discover gullies, invade, Where does it go now?
Now turn upstream twenty-five yards. Now road again.
Ask the man on the road. Saying, That cornfield?
Over the second hill, through the gate,
watch for the dogs. Buried, five at a time,
pine boxes, Rinehart & Dennis paid him $55
a head for burying these men in plain pine boxes.
His mother is suing him : misuse of land.
George Robinson : I knew a man
who died at four in the morning at the camp.
At seven his wife took clothes to dress her dead
husband, and at the undertaker's
they told her the husband was already buried.
—Tell me this, the men with whom you are acquainted,
the men who have this disease
have been told that sooner or later they are going to die?
—Yes, sir.
—How does that seem to affect the majority of the people?
—It don't work on anything but their wind.
—Do they seem to be living in fear
or do they wish to die?
—They are getting to breathe a little faster.

For those given to keeping their own garden:
Here is the cornfield, white and wired by thorns,
old cornstalks, snow, the planted home.
Stands bare against a line of farther field,
unmarked except for wood stakes, charred at tip,
few scratched and named (pencil or nail).
Washed-off. Under the mounds,
all the anonymous.
Abel America, calling from under the corn,
Earth, uncover my blood!

Did the undertaker know the man was married?
Uncover.
Do they seem to fear death?
Contemplate.
Does Mellon's ghost walk, povertied at last,
walking in furrows of corn, still sowing,
do apparitions come?
Voyage.
Think of your gardens. But here is corn to keep.
Marked pointed sticks to name the crop beneath.
Sowing is over, harvest is coming ripe.

—No, sir; they want to go on.
They want to live as long as they can.

ARTHUR PEYTON

Consumed. Eaten away. And love across the street.
I had a letter in the mail this morning
Dear Sir, . . . pleasure . . . enclosing herewith our check . . .
payable to you, for $21.59
            being one-half of the residue which
                we were able to collect in your behalf
                in regard to the above case.
In winding up the various suits,
            after collecting all we could,
                we find this balance due you.
With regards, we are
            Very truly,

After collecting
                    the dust   the failure   the engineering corps
O love   consumed   eaten away   the foreman laughed
they wet the drills when the inspectors came
the moon blows glassy over our native river.

O love tell the committee that I know:
never repeat you mean to marry me.
In mines, the fans are large (2,000 men unmasked)
before his verdict the doctor asked me   How long

I said, Dr. Harless, tell me how long?
—Only never again tell me you'll marry me.
I watch how at the tables you all day
follow a line of clouds   the dance of drills,

and, love, the sky birds who crown the trees
the white white hills standing upon Alloy
—I charge negligence, all companies concerned—
two years O love two years he said he gave.

The swirl of river at the tidy house
the marble bank-face of the liquor store
I saw the Negroes driven with pick handles
on these other jobs I was not in tunnel work.

Between us, love
                    the buses at the door
the long glass street   two years, my death to yours
my death upon your lips
my face becoming glass
strong challenged time making me win immortal
the love a mirror of our valley
our street   our river   a deadly glass to hold.
Now they are feeding me into a steel mill furnace
O love the stream of glass a stream of living fire.

ALLOY

This is the most audacious landscape. The gangster's
stance with his gun smoking and out is not so
vicious as this commercial field, its hill of glass.

Sloping as gracefully as thighs, the foothills
narrow to this, clouds over every town
finally indicate the stored destruction.

Crystalline hill: a blinded field of white
murdering snow, seamed by convergent tracks;
the travelling cranes reach for the silica.

And down the track, the overhead conveyor
slides on its cable to the feet of chimneys.
Smoke rises, not white enough, not so barbaric.

Here the severe flame speaks from the brick throat,
electric furnaces produce this precious, this clean,
annealing the crystals, fusing at last alloys.

Hottest for silicon, blast furnaces raise flames,
spill fire, spill steel, quench the new shape to freeze,
tempering it to perfected metal.

Forced through this crucible, a million men.
Above this pasture, the highway passes those
who curse the air, breathing their fear again.

The roaring flowers of the chimney-stacks
less poison, at their lips in fire, than this
dust that is blown from off the field of glass;

blows and will blow, rising over the mills,
crystallized and beyond the fierce corrosion
disintegrated angel on these hills.

POWER

The quick sun brings, exciting mountains warm,
gay on the landscapers and green designs,
miracle, yielding the sex up under all the skin,
until the entire body watches the scene with love,
sees perfect cliffs ranging until the river
cuts sheer, mapped far below in delicate track,
surprise of grace, the water running in the sun,
magnificent flower on the mouth, surprise
as lovers who look too long on the desired face
startle to find the remote flesh so warm.
A day of heat shed on the gorge, a brilliant
day when love sees the sun behind its man
and the disguised marvel under familiar skin.

Steel-bright, light-pointed, the narrow-waisted towers
lift their protective network, the straight, the accurate
flex of distinction, economy of gift,
gymnast, they poise their freight; god's generosity! give
their voltage low enough for towns to handle.
The power-house stands skin-white at the transmitters' side
over the rapids   the brilliance   the blind foam.

This is the midway between water and flame,
this is the road to take when you think of your country,
between the dam and the furnace, terminal.
The clean park, fan of wires, landscapers,
the stone approach. And seen beyond the door,
the man with the flashlight in his metal hall.
Here, the effective green, grey-toned and shining,
tall immense chamber of cylinders. Green,
the rich paint catches light from three-story windows,
arches of light vibrate erratic panels on
sides of curved steel. Man pockets flashlight,
useless, the brilliant floor casts tiled reflection up,
bland walls return it, circles pass it round.
Wheels, control panels, dials, the vassal instruments.
This is the engineer Jones, the blueprint man,
loving the place he designed, visiting it alone.
Another blood, no cousin to the town;
rings his heels on stone, pride follows his eyes,
"This is the place."

Four generators, smooth green, and squares of black,
floored-over space for a fifth.

                              The stairs. Descend.
"They said I built the floor like the tiles of a bank,
I wanted the men who work here to be happy."
Light laughing on steel, the gay, the tall sun
given away; mottled; snow comes in clouds;
the iron steps go down as roads go down.

This is the second circle, world of inner shade,
hidden bulk of generators, governor shaft,
round gap of turbine pit. Flashlight, tool-panels,
heels beating on iron, cold of underground,

stairs, wire flooring, the voice's hollow cry.
This is the scroll, the volute case of night,
quick shadow and the empty galleries.

Go down; here are the outlets, butterfly valves
open from here, the tail-race, vault of steel,
the spiral staircase ending, last light in shaft.
"Gone," says the thin straight man.
"'Hail, holy light, offspring of Heav'n first-born,
'Or of th' Eternal Coeternal beam
'May I express thee unblamed?'"

                             And still go down.

Now ladder-mouth; and the precipitous fear,
uncertain rungs down into after-night.
"This is the place. Away from this my life
I am indeed Adam unparadiz'd.
Some fools call this the Black Hole of Calcutta,
I don't know how they ever get to Congress."

Gulfs, spirals, that the drunken ladder swings,
its rungs give, pliant, beneath the leaping heart.
Leaps twice at midnight. But a naked bulb
makes glare, turns paler, burns to dark again.
Brilliance begins, stutters. And comes upon
after the tall abstract, the ill, the unmasked men,
the independent figure of the welder
masked for his work; acts with unbearable flame.
His face is a cage of steel, the hands are covered,
points dazzle hot, fly from his writing torch,
brighten the face and hands marrying steel.
Says little, works : only : "A little down,
five men were killed in the widening of the tunnel."

Shell of bent metal; walking along an arc
the tube rounds up about your shoulders, black
circle, great circle, down infinite mountains rides,
echoes words, footsteps, testimonies.
"One said the air was thin, Fifth-Avenue clean."
The iron pillars mark a valve division,
four tunnels merging.   Iron on iron resounds,

echoes along created gorges. "Sing,
test echoes, sing : Pilgrim," he cries,
singing *Once More, Dear Home,*
as all the light burns out.
Down the reverberate channels of the hills
the suns declare midnight, go down, cannot ascend,
no ladder back; see this, your eyes can ride through steel,
this is the river Death, diversion of power,
the root of the tower and the tunnel's core,
this is the end.

THE DAM

All power is saved, having no end.   Rises
in the green season, in the sudden season
the white the budded

                        and the lost.
Water celebrates, yielding continually
sheeted and fast in its overfall
slips down the rock, evades the pillars
building its colonnades, repairs
in stream and standing wave
retains its seaward green
broken by obstacle rock; falling, the water sheet
spouts, and the mind dances, excess of white.
White brilliant function of the land's disease.

Many-spanned, lighted, the crest leans under
concrete arches and the channelled hills,
turns in the gorge toward its release;
kinetic and controlled, the sluice
urging the hollow, the thunder,
the major climax

                        energy
total and open watercourse
praising the spillway, fiery glaze,
crackle of light, cleanest velocity
flooding, the moulded force.

I open out a way over the water
I form a path between the Combatants:
Grant that I sail down like a living bird,
power over the fields and Pool of Fire.
Phoenix, I sail over the phoenix world.

Diverted water, the fern and fuming white
ascend in mist of continuous diffusion.
Rivers are turning inside their mountains,
streams line the stone, rest at the overflow
lake and in lanes of pliant color lie.
Blessing of this innumerable silver,
printed in silver, images of stone
walk on a screen of falling water
in film-silver in continual change
recurring colored, plunging with the wave.

Constellations of light, abundance of many rivers.
The sheeted island-cities, the white surf filling west,
the hope, fast water spilled where still pools fed.
Great power flying deep: between the rock and the sunset,
the caretaker's house and the steep abutment,
hypnotic water fallen and the tunnels under
the moist and fragile galleries of stone,
mile-long, under the wave. Whether snow fall,
the quick light fall, years of white cities fall,
flood that this valley built falls slipping down
the green turn in the river's green.
Steep gorge, the wedge of crystal in the sky.

How many feet of whirlpools?
What is a year in terms of falling water?
Cylinders; kilowatts; capacities.
Continuity: $\Sigma\, Q = 0$
Equations for falling water. The streaming motion.
The balance-sheet of energy that flows
passing along its infinite barrier.

It breaks the hills, cracking the riches wide,
runs through electric wires;
it comes, warning the night,

running among these rigid hills,
a single force to waken our eyes.

They poured the concrete and the columns stood,
laid bare the bedrock, set the cells of steel,
a dam for monument was what they hammered home.
Blasted, and stocks went up;
insured the base,
and limousines
wrote their own graphs upon
roadbed and lifeline.

Their hands touched mastery:
wait for defense, solid across the world.
Mr. Griswold. "A corporation is a body without a soul."
Mr. Dunn. When they were caught at it they resorted to the
    methods employed by gunmen, ordinary machine-gun
    racketeers. They cowardly tried to buy out the people who had
    the information on them.
Mr. Marcantonio. I agree that a racket has been practised, but the
    most damnable racketeering that I have ever known is the
    paying of a fee to the very attorney who represented these
    victims. That is the most outrageous racket that has ever come
    within my knowledge.
Miss Allen. Mr. Jesse J. Ricks, the president of the Union Carbide
    & Carbon Corporation, suggested that the stock-holder had better
    take this question up in a private conference.
The dam is safe. A scene of power.
The dam is the father of the tunnel.
This is the valley's work, the white, the shining.

High	Low	Stock and Dividend in Dollars	Open	High	Low	Last	Net Chge.	Closing		
								Bid	Ask	Sales
111	61¼	Union Carbide (3.20)...	67¼	69½	67¼	69½	+3	69¼	69½	3,400

The dam is used when the tunnel is used.
The men and the water are never idle,
have definitions.
This is a perfect fluid, having no age nor hours,
surviving scarless, unaltered, loving rest,
willing to run forever to find its peace

in equal seas in currents of still glass.
Effects of friction : to fight and pass again,
learning its power, conquering boundaries,
able to rise blind in revolts of tide,
broken and sacrificed to flow resumed.
Collecting eternally power. Spender of power,
torn, never can be killed, speeded in filaments,
million, its power can rest and rise forever,
wait and be flexible. Be born again.
Nothing is lost, even among the wars,
imperfect flow, confusion of force.
It will rise. These are the phases of its face.
It knows its seasons, the waiting, the sudden.
It changes. It does not die.

THE DISEASE: AFTER-EFFECTS

This is the life of a Congressman.
Now he is standing on the floor of the House,
the galleries full; raises his voice; presents the bill.
Legislative, the fanfare, greeting its heroes with
ringing of telephone bells preceding entrances,
snapshots (Grenz rays, recording structure) newsreels.
This is silent, and he proposes:

                            embargo on munitions
to Germany and Italy
as states at war with Spain.
He proposes
                Congress memorialize
the governor of California : free Tom Mooney.
A bill for a TVA at Fort Peck Dam.
A bill to prevent industrial silicosis.

This is the gentleman from Montana.
—I'm a child, I'm leaning from a bedroom window,
clipping the rose that climbs upon the wall,
the tea roses, and the red roses,
one for a wound, another for disease,
remembrance for strikers. I was five, going on six,

my father on strike at the Anaconda mine;
they broke the Socialist mayor we had in Butte,
the sheriff (friendly), found their judge. Strike-broke.
Shot father. He died : wounds and his disease.
My father had silicosis.

Copper contains it, we find it in limestone,
sand quarries, sandstone, potteries, foundries,
granite, abrasives, blasting; many kinds of grinding,
plate, mining, and glass.

Widespread in trade, widespread in space!
Butte, Montana; Joplin, Missouri; the New York tunnels,
the Catskill Aqueduct. In over thirty States.
A disease worse than consumption.

Only eleven States have laws.
There are today one million potential victims.
500,000 Americans have silicosis now.
These are the proportions of a war.

       Pictures rise, foreign parades, the living faces,
       Asturian miners with my father's face,
       wounded and fighting, the men at Gauley Bridge,
       my father's face enlarged; since now our house

       and all our meaning lies in this
       signature: power on a hill
       centered in its committee and its armies
       sources of anger, the mine of emphasis.

       No plane can ever lift us high enough
       to see forgetful countries underneath,
       but always now the map and X-ray seem
       resemblent pictures of one living breath
       one country marked by error
       and one air.

It sets up a gradual scar formation;
this increases, blocking all drainage from the lung,
eventually scars, blocking the blood supply,
and then they block the air passageways.

Shortness of breath,
pains around the chest,
he notices lack of vigor.

Bill blocked; investigation blocked.

These galleries produce their generations.
The Congressmen are restless, stare at the triple tier,
the flags, the ranks, the walnut foliage wall;
a row of empty seats, mask over a dead voice.
But over the country, a million look from work,
five hundred thousand stand.

THE BILL

The subcommittee submits:
Your committee held hearings, heard many witnesses; finds:

THAT the Hawk's Nest tunnel was constructed
        Dennis and Rinehart, Charlottesville, Va., for
        New Kanawha Power Co., subsidiary of
        Union Carbide & Carbon Co.

THAT a tunnel was drilled
        app. dist. 3.75 mis.
        to divert water (from New River)
        to hydroelectric plant (Gauley Junction).

THAT in most of the tunnel, drilled rock contained
        90—even 99 percent pure silica.

This is a fact that was known.

THAT silica is dangerous to lungs of human beings.
        When submitted to contact. Silicosis.

THAT the effects are well known.
        Disease incurable.
        Physical incapacity, cases fatal.

THAT the Bureau of Mines has warned for twenty years.

THAT prevention is: wet drilling, ventilation,
                         respirators, vacuum drills.
       Disregard : utter. Dust : collected. Visibility : low.
       Workmen left work, white with dust.
       Air system : inadequate.
       It was quite cloudy in there.
       When the drills were going, in all the smoke and dust,
         it seemed like a gang of airplanes going through
             that tunnel.
       Respirators, not furnished.
       I have seen men with masks, but simply on their breasts.
       I have seen two wear them.
       Drills : dry drilling, for speed, for saving.
       A fellow could drill three holes dry for one hole wet.
       They went so fast they didn't square at the top.
       Locomotives : gasoline. Suffering from monoxide gas.
       There have been men that fell in the tunnel. They had
         to be carried out.

The driving of the tunnel.
       It was begun, continued, completed, with gravest disregard.
       And the employees? Their health, lives, future?
Results and infection.
       Many died. Many are not yet dead.
       Of negligence. Wilful or inexcusable.
Further findings:
       Prevalence : many States, mine, tunnel operations.
       A greatest menace.
We suggest hearings be read.
       This is the dark. Lights strung up all the way.
       Depression; and, driven deeper in,
       by hunger, pistols, and despair,
       they took the tunnel.
Of the contracting firm
               P. H. Faulconer, Pres.
               E. J. Perkins, Vice-Pres.
       have declined to appear.
       They have no knowledge of deaths from silicosis.
       However, their firm paid claims.

I want to point out that under the statute $500 or
$1000, but no more, may be recovered.

We recommend.
        Bring them. Their books and records.
        Investigate. Require.
Can do no more.
        These citizens from many States
        paying the price for electric power,
        To Be Vindicated.

"If by their suffering and death they will have made a future life safer for
work beneath the earth, if they will have been able to establish a new
and greater regard for human life in industry, their suffering may not
have been in vain."
                    Respectfully,
                        Glenn Griswold
                Chairman, Subcommittee
                    Vito Marcantonio
                    W. P. Lambertson
                    Matthew A. Dunn

The subcommittee subcommits.

Words on a monument.
Capitoline thunder. It cannot be enough.
The origin of storms is not in clouds,
our lightning strikes when the earth rises,
spillways free authentic power:
dead John Brown's body walking from a tunnel
to break the armored and concluded mind.

THE BOOK OF THE DEAD

These roads will take you into your own country.
Seasons and maps coming where this road comes
into a landscape mirrored in these men.

Past all your influences, your home river,
constellations of cities, mottoes of childhood,
parents and easy cures, war, all evasion's wishes.

What one word must never be said?
Dead, and these men fight off our dying,
cough in the theatres of the war.

What two things shall never be seen?
They : what we did.   Enemy : what we mean.
This is a nation's scene and halfway house.

What three things can never be done?
Forget. Keep silent. Stand alone.
The hills of glass, the fatal brilliant plain.

The facts of war forced into actual grace.
Seasons and modern glory. Told in the histories,
          how first ships came

seeing on the Atlantic thirteen clouds
lining the west horizon with their white
          shining halations;

they conquered, throwing off impossible Europe—
could not be used to transform; created coast—
          breathed-in America.

See how they took the land, made after-life
fresh out of exile, planted the pioneer
          base and blockade,

pushed forests down in an implacable walk
west where new clouds lay at the desirable
          body of sunset;

taking the seaboard.   Replaced the isolation,
dropped cities where they stood, drew a tidewater
          frontier of Europe,

a moment, and another frontier held,
this land was planted home-land that we know.
          Ridge of discovery,

until we walk to windows, seeing America
lie in a photograph of power, widened
          before our forehead,

and still behind us falls another glory,
London unshaken, the long French road to Spain,
        the old Mediterranean

flashing new signals from the hero hills
near Barcelona, monuments and powers,
        parent defenses.

Before our face the broad and concrete west,
green ripened field, frontier pushed back like river
        controlled and dammed;

the flashing wheatfields, cities, lunar plains
grey in Nevada, the sane fantastic country
        sharp in the south,

liveoak, the hanging moss, a world of desert,
the dead, the lava, and the extreme arisen
        fountains of life,

the flourished land, peopled with watercourses
to California and the colored sea;
        sums of frontiers

and unmade boundaries of acts and poems,
the brilliant scene between the seas, and standing,
        this fact and this disease.

                    ✌

Half-memories absorb us, and our ritual world
carries its history in familiar eyes,
planted in flesh it signifies its music

in minds which turn to sleep and memory,
in music knowing all the shimmering names,
the spear, the castle, and the rose.

But planted in our flesh these valleys stand,
everywhere we begin to know the illness,
are forced up, and our times confirm us all.

In the museum life, centuries of ambition
yielded at last a fertilizing image:
the Carthaginian stone meaning a tall woman

carries in her two hands the book and cradled dove,
on her two thighs, wings folded from the waist
cross to her feet, a pointed human crown.

This valley is given to us like a glory.
To friends in the old world, and their lifting hands
that call for intercession.   Blow falling full in face.

All those whose childhood made learn skill to meet,
and art to see after the change of heart;
all the belligerents who know the world.

You standing over gorges, surveyors and planners,
you workers and hope of countries, first among powers;
you who give peace and bodily repose,

opening landscapes by grace, giving the marvel lowlands
physical peace, flooding old battlefields
with general brilliance, who best love your lives;

and you young, you who finishing the poem
wish new perfection and begin to make;
you men of fact, measure our times again.

      ✧

These are our strength, who strike against history.
These whose corrupt cells owe their new styles of weakness
        to our diseases;

these carrying light for safety on their foreheads
descended deeper for richer faults of ore,
        drilling their death.

These touching radium and the luminous poison,
carried their death on their lips and with their warning
        glow in their graves.

These weave and their eyes water and rust away,
these stand at wheels until their brains corrode,
these farm and starve,

all these men cry their doom across the world,
meeting avoidable death, fight against madness,
find every war.

Are known as strikers, soldiers, pioneers,
fight on all new frontiers, are set in solid
lines of defense.

Defense is sight; widen the lens and see
standing over the land myths of identity,
new signals, processes:

Alloys begin : certain dominant metals.
Deliberate combines add new qualities,
sums of new uses.

Over the country, from islands of Maine fading,
Cape Sable fading south into the orange
detail of sunset,

new processes, new signals, new possession.
A name for all the conquests, prediction of victory
deep in these powers.

Carry abroad the urgent need, the scene,
to photograph and to extend the voice,
to speak this meaning.

Voices to speak to us directly.   As we move.
As we enrich, growing in larger motion,
this word, this power.

Down coasts of taken countries, mastery,
discovery at one hand, and at the other
frontiers and forests,

fanatic cruel legend at our back and
speeding ahead the red and open west,
and this our region,

desire, field, beginning.   Name and road,
communication to these many men,
as epilogue, seeds of unending love.

2 Night-Music

A FLASHING CLIFF

Spinning on his heel, the traveller
sees across snow a flashing cliff.
Past the plain's freeze, past savage branches
immune in ice, a frozen waterfall,
clamped in December, glistens alive.

Love, will you recognize yourself displayed?
Or is the age defective, cold with storm
to lock fast water in iron artifice,
whitening cataracts?—contempt and loss,
and nothing, in the great world, can lie calm,

travel alive, but is frozen solid,
and will not face its mirror nor speak its pain.
Will you fight winter to break in immense speed
resisting and sensitive, a waterfall-flash
sparkling full across the vicious plain?

Fight down our age, the mad vindictive time?
No victory's here. Now, any passion suffers
against proud ice, flashing, angry, and jailed.
You, maniac, catalept!
And, love. You are all rivers.

GIRL AT THE PLAY

Long after you beat down the powerful hand
and leave the scene, prison's still there to break.

Brutalized by escape, you travel out to sit
in empty theatres, your stunned breast, hardened neck
waiting for warmth to venture back.

Gilded above the stage, staring archaic shapes
hang, like those men you learn submission from
whose majesty sits yellow on the night,
young indolent girls, long-handed, one's vague mouth
and cruel nose and jaw and throat.

Waiting's paralysis strikes, king-cobra hooded head's
infected fangs petrify body and face.
Emblems fade everyway, dissolving even
the bitter infantile boys who call for sleep's
winy breasts whose nipples are long grapes.

Seats fill. The curtain's up where strong lights act,
cut theatre to its theme; the quick fit's past.
Here's answer in masses moving; by light elect,
they turn the stage before into the street behind;
and nothing's so forgotten as your blind
female paralysis that takes the mind,
and nothing's so forgotten as your dead
fever, now that it's past and the swift play's ahead.

BURNING BUSH

Faced with furnace demands during its education,
the strictest spirit must take them all; it needs
to break down shame; but gasping into a pillow
later to nobody anywhere, claims I Love You.
It plays long tricks
upon itself—the stealthy girl locks doors,
the woman listens in single high rooms for music,
hears climbing elevators as the picket walks
in a dead street before tallest skyscrapers
far on the sidewalks;
all horrors enter all beds to purify
the critical spirit in a city of change,
twisted in flames, blazing among the secrets,

breaking the taut life with their harsh I Have You.
   It burns and never speaks
only is educated, when it assumes bright horror,
nourished against the time it hears its name—
until it is called will stand, witness to fire,
training a flame upward along its vine.

EEL

We started to walk but it was wading-slow.
Ran to the corner and boarded at the carstop,
impatient through the city, hating the noise of iron.
Shut it out of the head
until the city, quiet, goes submarine
and we are winding through, defended, winding, with
weird deepseas, the famous world, swimming, facing our youth.

Their faces royal in pain, useless children advance
down avenues shining a stormy cobalt sky.
The lights go green. They stare. Stop riding, cross the street,
here are rich avenues, a city's alibi,
here's your prophetic love and object lesson:
Shops will instruct you what to want.
Strangers will serve you, floorwalkers.
Condition : don't notice their disease.
be easy-going, and so, susceptible.
These to cultivate, perhaps have:
flippant defeat, good sportsmanship,
the miracle figure of the football-player:
a perfect husband, a promised income.

We were too earnest. We had to lose.
We wound past armies of strangers, waving love's
thin awkward plant among a crowd of salesmen.
"Sold the salesmen? Been loved, loving? You, too young?"
We stared at policemen, hypnotized by force,
holding the ball during games, forgetting to throw,
as they padlocked the bar, clapped boards across the door,
padlocked the union hall. Deported. Shut.

Winding through avenues, stone blocked our eyes,
we dreamed raw yellow hills of mustard-flower.
Mind's tropic scenery was farmed : Come back to stay,
return to the broken man across the subway,
read crinkled Atlantics, tabloid skies—your feet
slap stone; this is you, advancing down a street,
your ancestors being dead, your parents busy somewhere.
You have a class. You have your object lessons.

Radio City, largest of riches, leaning
against the flaming cobalt, fatal as Belgium,
flowers in neon on the winter air,
        All its theatres open padded lobbies
        all its windows run light
And adolescent breasts, alert for terror,
fingers ophelian white and quick with fear
flower aware, and the staring workman
walks down expensive streets. And all the adolescents,
winding, and submarine, waking, with sleep shaken
go weaving among the crowds; growing remember

Alexander, peacock of Macedon, Euclid building his circles
        on the flat Greek sand,
the violent empresses, Boone breaking through green country—
in the papers, Ann Burlak makes women pound kettles
for drums, for a loud band!

Miss Swan, the Latin teacher, hand laid on moulding,
speaks Cicero admirably, for massy syllables, hearing the
pompous Senate heave; we fidget until the hour—
we compare lipsticks, smudging our palms with red.
Know Rome is elsewhere and the street's outside.
And fast thoughts run like fire as the roads divide.

The adolescents, walking, at school, going through streets,
stop wavering, heal their minds snapped during mutiny.
Believing at first in easy cures, the floundering blood to
        be healed by love,
not yet knowing that thousands walk straightforward, wish
        the same,
young, and winding through cities, young, seeing time's disease.

Parading upon a stage lit with immense firm flame.
To change it. To mature. To find. To be these.

HOMAGE TO LITERATURE

When you imagine trumpet-faced musicians
blowing again inimitable jazz
no art can accuse nor cannonadings hurt,

or coming out of your dreams of dirigibles
again see the unreasonable cripple
throwing his crutch headlong as the headlights

streak down the torn street, as the three hammerers
go One, Two, Three on the stake, triphammer poundings
and not a sign of new worlds to still the heart;

then stare into the lake of sunset as it runs
boiling, over the west past all control
rolling and swamps the heartbeat and repeats
sea beyond sea after unbearable suns;
think : poems fixed this landscape : Blake, Donne, Keats.

THE HANDCLAP

The body cannot lie, but its betrayals,
narrower actions, cross even frontiers of night,
and your most delicate treason falls in a quick stroke,
                    undercuts sleep.

Now, if I bodily sometime betrayed myself,
the foolish play's curtain drops on your active exposure,
grotesque as a peepshow, definite as the axe
                    in instant effect.

The toppling high tree lets fall its heavy side
green on the air, goes anyway down to ground
after a clap of weight resting—but we descend to
                    imperfect peace.

Here's war!—body betrayed, but all nerves still exerted
to rise up whole, grasp the perpetual sun.
Echo the shock, handclaps of fact composing
              a blackest pattern,

a tyrant pace to dance, clatter of anger
spanking the fury up to publish treason,
ranting and clapping madness; while the dim
              blood groans forever love.

TROPHIES

The choice proposed : ascends, the nervy conductor
facing the strings as the stage shakes, as the plane
looms in the loud air, motor cut out,
and the musicians' black alters to violin-brown.
They lift their instruments. The choice.
Mr. Sceptre, the elegant instructor,
looks about the classroom sighing Keats,
emotion in torrents on adolescent cheeks
as teargas tranquilly saturates the college.
Choose: the workers will rise, or your heroes, tall as stone,
must face the fascist cruelties of pain.

Trapped in the valley—historian eloquence
reminds us of recurrent Civil War:
"To prevent repetition of this attack of the enemy
I directed Captain Gaw, chief topographer,
to reach the commanding officer of the other wing."
"Obtained abundance of corn, molasses, and sweet potatoes."
"The advance was then gallantly resumed, the enemy
driven from their guns, the heights handsomely carried."
But the choice *is* proposed: the active alternative,
people's Party in the streets, last year's heroes at home.

Who will take choice, demands the scientist
(the smiling friend sitting beside his mind),
now that the key is grincing in the lock?
Now that the sea has bitten on the ship
and bent it to the rock?

Here are insignia of reversed cities,
victorious slogans and the acts of war.
And we shall never know their poise again,
though we remember what we were,
now that our officers are no longer
in full golden summer regalia,
and we no longer well-dressed watchers
at the march-past and the fly-by—
or even attentive before the fire
haunted by certain safe compelling shoulders,
a trick of the head, lust of incautious eye;
fortified by the braver faces
of picket-line and commemorative parade,
the anniversary demonstration—
we cast about for love, lost between wars,
alone in the room and every street-light out.
Who's to rise to it, now that ruin's made,
now that we're petrified in the pale looking-glass,
our glossy scars, our books, our loss,
caught in the narrowest final pass?
And all our heroes are afraid.

PANACEA

Make me well, I said.—And the delighted touch.
You put dead sweet hand on my dead brain.
The window cleared and the night-street stood black.
As soon as I left your house others besieged me
forcing my motion, saying, Make me well.

Took sickness into the immense street,
but nothing was thriving   I saw blank light   the crazy
blink of torture   the lack   and there is no
personal sickness strong to intrude there.
Returned. Stood at the window. Make me well.

Cannot? The white sea, which is inviolable,
is no greater, the disallied world's unable,
daylight horizons of lakes cannot caress me well.

The hypocrite leper in the parable,
did he believe would be kissed whole by kisses?

I'll try beyond you now. I'll try all flame.
Some force must be whole, some eye inviolable—
look, here I am returned! No help. Gone high again;
legend's no precedent. This perseveres.
The sun, I say, sincere, the sun, the sun.

IN HADES, ORPHEUS

"Look!" he said, "all green!" but she,
leaning against him at her hospital door,
received it on her eyes as fireline blinding bright
and would not see.

"Come into the park!" he offered her,
but she was feverstruck still, brimful of white
monotonous weakness, and could not face the grass
and the bright water.

A boy skating upstreet
shouted; the gardener climbed at the doorway, pruning,
and the gay branches dropped where she stood, fearful
of her quick heartbeat

released, fearing the kiss
of vivid blood. The husband straightened in the sun,
risking their staggered histories against the violent
avenue's emphasis;

"A long pain, long fever!"
He faced her full for the first time, speaking,
turned with his hand her face to meet his mouth,
"but that death's over."

Lights out; noon falls
steeply away, blazing in green; he sees the sharp fear pass
verdict upon her, pitching and frothing toward the
mechanical white walls.

THE DROWNING YOUNG MAN

The drowning young man lifted his face from the river
to me, exhausted from calling for help and weeping;
"My love!" I said; but he kissed me once for ever
and returned to his privacy and secret keeping.

His close face dripped with the attractive water,
I stared in his eyes and saw there penalty,
for the city moved in its struggle, loud about us,
and the salt air blew down; but he would face the sea.

"Afraid, afraid, my love?" But he will never speak,
looking demands for rest, watching the wave come up,
too timid to turn, too loving to cry out,
lying face down in tide, biting his nervous lip.

Take him by shoulder and jaw, break his look back on us,
O hard to save, be saved, before we all shall drown!
But he has set his look, plunged his life deep for peace,
his face in the boiling river, and is surrendered down.

BOY WITH HIS HAIR CUT SHORT

Sunday shuts down on a twentieth-century evening.
The El passes. Twilight and bulb define
the brown room, the overstuffed plum sofa,
the boy, and the girl's thin hands above his head.
A neighbor radio sings stocks, news, serenade.

He sits at the table, head down, the young clear neck exposed,
watching the drugstore sign from the tail of his eye;
tattoo, neon, until the eye blears, while his
solicitous tall sister, simple in blue, bending
behind him, cuts his hair with her cheap shears.

The arrow's electric red always reaches its mark,
successful neon! He coughs, impressed by that precision.
His child's forehead, forever protected by his cap,

is bleached against the lamplight as he turns head
and steadies to let the snippets drop.

Erasing the failure of weeks with level fingers,
she sleeks the fine hair, combing: "You'll look fine tomorrow!
You'll surely find something, they can't keep turning you down;
the finest gentleman's not so trim as you!" Smiling, he raises
the adolescent forehead wrinkling ironic now.

He sees his decent suit laid out, new-pressed,
his carfare on the shelf. He lets his head fall, meeting
her earnest hopeless look, seeing the sharp blades splitting,
the darkened room, the impersonal sign, her motion,
the blue vein, bright on her temple, pitifully beating.

COURSE

for Betty Marshall

Years before action when the wish alone
has ammunition to threaten weakness down,
when thriving on discovery we speak
and wish a world
that wishing may not make.

Stretching our powers, we touch a broader street
crowded with hostile weapons and the weight
of death suggesting we see peace at last
and quiet cities,
rip out the eyes, and have our rest.

But we are set enough to clear a space
ample for action in this eccentric house.
An army of wishers in a dramatic grip
and crazy with
America has heat to keep its purpose up.

Determined to a world that Mr. Fist
and all his gang can't master or digest,
strengthened against the world that cannot hush

words singing down
the fever voice of death working against the wish.

MORE OF A CORPSE THAN A WOMAN

Give them my regards when you go to the school reunion;
and at the marriage-supper, say that I'm thinking about them.
They'll remember my name; I went to the movies with that one,
feeling the weight of their death where she sat at my elbow;
              she never said a word,
              but all of them were heard.

All of them alike, expensive girls, the leaden friends:
one used to play the piano, one of them once wrote a sonnet,
one even seemed awakened enough to photograph wheatfields—
the dull girls with the educated minds and technical passions—
              pure love was their employment,
              they tried it for enjoyment.

Meet them at the boat : they've brought the souvenirs of boredom,
a seashell from the faltering monarchy;
the nose of a marble saint; and from the battlefield,
an empty shell divulged from a flower-bed.
              The lady's wealthy breath
              perfumes the air with death.

The leaden lady faces the fine, voluptuous woman,
faces a rising world bearing its gifts in its hands.
Kisses her casual dreams upon the lips she kisses,
risen, she moves away; takes others; moves away.
              Inadequate to love,
              supposes she's enough.

Give my regards to the well-protected woman,
I knew the ice-cream girl, we went to school together.
There's something to bury, people, when you begin to bury.
When your women are ready and rich in their wish for the world,
              destroy the leaden heart,
              we've a new race to start.

THREE BLACK WOMEN

Invading nightmare, spinning up through sleep,
three loving Negresses ascend the night;
one sinks with Chinese eyes a despised man
shivering white in fear; mocking says "Take him,
I made him vastly unhappy;" dances, lifting
the purple belly pencilled delicate black.
The grandmother rises on the pointed shoulder
of the little black boy in the pink wool sweater,
bitterly asking about the deputies.
Burning, as dead skies over enemy cities
tip backward sliding, a third gleams on the South;
battlefields flicker, the scenery of doubt
dissolves in decoration on the night of
fire, black women, nightmare, dances, sleep.

FORMOSA

The sand's still blue with receding water, sky topples
                      its last brightness
down, day diminishing; two fishermen
walk over the sandbar, their thin indicative shadows
pointing tomorrow's sunrise on the whiteline horizon.
Tomorrow is only an interval, night's passing interval
cruises on open water here, anchored, while peace comes in.

Speedboat, run again before your smoking white
wake, while the light's collected on the hull,
until the evening turns, engaged with night.

The little dog races over the sandflats, the thin bathers
turn back to foamline, half-light discourages their daring
sea-dream. End it! omens are laughter, gay all morning,
gay before ogre midnight, spurless midnight—
midnight's an interval, darkness is promise, night's nothing,
nightmare is nothing, nothing but interval.

Eliminate all dreams : here, real : love come, high tide,
the risen, freehold moon, the fortunate island,
resting, blue-flooded, rests, delicately, the sea.

NIGHT-MUSIC

for Marya Zaturenska

TIME EXPOSURES

When the exposed spirit, busy in daytime,
searches out night, only renewer.
That time plants turn to. The world's table.
When any single thing's condemned again.
The changeable spirit finds itself out,
will not employ Saint Death, detective,
does its own hunting, runs at last to night.
Renewer, echo of judgment, morning-source, music.

Dark streets that light invents, one black tree standing,
struck by the street-light to raw electric green,
allow one man at a time to walk past, plain.
Cities lose size. The earth is field
and ranging these countries in sunset, we make quiet,
living in springtime, wish for nothing, see
glass bough, invented green, flower-sharp day
crackle into orange and be subdued to night.

The mind, propelled by work, reaches its evening:
slick streets, dog-tired, point the way to sleep,
walls rise in color, now summer shapes the Square
(and pastel five o'clock chalked on the sky).

We drive out to the suburbs, bizarre lawns
flicker a moment beside the speeding cars.
Speed haunts our ground, throws counties at us under
night, a black basin always spilling stars.

Waters trouble our quiet, vanishing down
reaches of hills whose image legend saves:
the foggy Venus hung above the flood

rising, rising, from the sea, with her arms full of waves
as ours are full of flowers.

Down polished airways a purple dove descending
sharp on the bodies of those so lately busy apart,
wingtip on breasttip, the deep body of feathers
in the breastgroove along the comforted heart.

The head inclined offers with love clear miles
of days simple in sun and action, bright
air poised about a face in ballet strictness
and pure pacific night.

But in our ears brute knocking at all doors,
factories bellow mutilation, and we live needy still
while strength and hours run
checkless downhill.

❧

Flattered by grief, the changeable spirit
puts on importance. Goes into the street,
adventures everywhere but places fear
is absent. Everywhere the face's look
is absent, the heart is flat,
the avenues haunted by a head whose eye
runs tears incessantly, the other eye
narrow in smiling. Everywhere, words fail,
men sunk to dust, houses condemned, walls ruined,
and dust is never an anachronism.
Everywhere the eye runs tears. And here
the hand, propelled somehow, marches the room
pulling dark windowshades down around the gaze.

And now, stately, jotting on lipstick, she
prepares to sexualize her thistle thought.
Loosens her earrings, smiling. Drives
herself far into night. Smiles, fornicating. Drives
herself deep into sleep. Sees children sleep.

THE CHILD ASLEEP

What's over England? A cloud. What's over France? A flame.
And over New York? The night.
Night is nameless, night has no name.

The crane leans down to drink the pit.
Look from the blackboard out the window.
Walk down the streets that lead to school.
Study, h'p! Pause, h'p! Recess, h'p!
I want to grow up.

Can you be direct as snow, straight to the face?
When the ball arrives, catch it! Who loves you?
What's around you and under you,
who bends above you?

> *Immortal* is miles away, and age.
> And Europe. But not so the sea.
> The sea is near, mother and father near.
> Not with the dirty children, dear.
> Not to look at the sea.

Quiet, music is playing! Never move your face.
Wear a mask if your face moves with your
love or anger moving. God first, then us.
Friday candles. Never discuss.

> See the full street—the war is over!
> The birdcage swung open to the storm.
> Do not love so much. Keep cool.
> Keep collected. Keep warm.

"And the harsh friend, pushing away the music."
The sand-pit high with money. The limousine.
The chauffeur filling the frost with suicide
smelling sick in garage. First strikers seen.

Death first, the stiff knees pointing up, gone breath.
"And the harsh lover: suddenly magic, making
me forget mother, sob through shut teeth, seeing
the kiss full on the palm erase the touch of death."

What's over us? The fancy snowfall. War.
What's at our hand for truth? The curious windlass
going into the well. Quaint. Why do those men parade?
What's after sitting at the window, reading?

Lying hot in the bath, weeping at night?
Going to bed at night and at last sleeping?

ADVENTURES, MIDNIGHT

1

Give a dime to a beggar for I have seen a sight
    children grown tall and tragic reason slight
    charity dealt the poor again
    I drove with my last love last night
    through Clinton Street where sick, sick, sick
    the pushcarts screened with oranges
    staggering avenues of brick
    and wealth and love were long away
    and this man wished the old love quick.

Give more and get your dollars back all dimes
    small change of love: so lied, and kissed him tight.
    I saw his tired body gone to crust
    and chuckling pigeons take him in their throats.
    —Now see us older, foolish, refugee,
    the child awake with an advertising look
    gathering speed in motors, love in dimes—
    what's after driving at night, answering joylessly?
    The wasted pity. Thieving charity.

2

With those two I went driving in the dark,
out from our town in a borrowed car whose light
ate forests as we drove deeper into the park.

Beloved, spoke the sweet equivocal night—
those two stood clapped, each breast warmly on breast,
I stood apart to remove them from my sight:

The creased brook ran in continual unrest,
rising to seastorm in the rioting mind.
Here night and they and I—and who was merriest?

He turned his face away refusing, and so signed
for her to stop who too was comfortless
and equally needy, as tender and as blind.

On the road to the city stood the hedge whose darkness
had covered me months ago with that tall stranger
as foreign to me as this loneliness,

as enemy to me as tonight's anger
of grief in the country, shut with those two in the park:
this crying, frantic at removal, the dark, the sorrowful
     danger.

3

Watching, on piers, exuberant travellers
enter the ocean where the beggar sits
desperate at exclusive waterfronts,
see how the feasted boat leaves port
covered with singing birds.

Cruising to cellophane islands, shaking off
this city's rock providing lonely tours,
grim single passports, persevering winter,
the ship slides down midnight's imperious harbor
The gilt-tiered galleries awake and dance.

What is it rippling across the deck?
What rising? What memory of ocean?
What is it ripples and rises?
The drowned heart, lifted a moment
answers clearly   Here it comes.

And get your feet wet in a drowning world?
Stand on a rotten dock, obsessed with tide?
The boat's condemned, the pier sinks. The long port
offers an only country to you, traveller,
a chance of upper air to hopeful, smothering heart.

NIGHT-MUSIC

When those who can never again forgive themselves
finish their dinner, rear up from the chair,
turning to movies are caught in demonstrations
sweeping the avenues—Meet them there.

Watch how their faces change like traffic-light
bold blood gone green as horses pound the street,

as plates of sweated muscle push
them squarely back into retreat.

Notice their tremulous late overthrow
caught irresponsible : as the first rank presses
up at the brown animal breast of law
defying government by horses.

And after the quick night-flurry, the few jailed,
the march stampeded, the meeting stopped, go down
night-streets to unique rooms where horror ends,
strike-songs are sung and the old songs remain.

Vaguely Ilonka draws her violin
along to Bach, greatest of trees, whereunder
earth is again familiar, grandmother,
and very god-music branches overhead.

Changeable spirit! build a newer music
rich enough to feed starvation on.
Course down the night, past scenes of horror, among
children awake, lands ruined, begging men.

Rebel against torment,
boats gone, night-battles, the sleepers up and shaking,
fear in the streets
cruelty on awaking.

Make music out of night will change the night.

DRIVEWAY

Speeding from city, feeling day
grimmer and more opaque,
a thousand times more Death than night
here on the pebbled roads, bled of all light and kind,
hastening darkness to the impatient mind,

we shook off nights our fever watched the street,
besieged by laughter from the outer room,

heard the pang, pang of bells bury our hope
for private warmth or time or bed or house
free from the failure public in that place.

Here was to be moment of proof, if any
conspiracy of night and speed and river
could lift us whole from danger, and make real
the veiny tree, the gleaming parallel
of railroad tracks and water, using our trespass well

to heal all breaches, prove our hope's disease
curable by annealing, bandage night,
blank out the city's bricked-up doors, the glare
of the night-watchman's ray, No Trespassing,
Don't Walk Here, Stay At Your Window, Keep On Looking.

Reaching the full-grown field, danger slowed down,
darkness enlarged around the blind, parked car.
No need to look; the brilliant fatal skim
of light swung over the acre, striking the night-proof dead,
the Caretaker's flashlight sending his shadow up ahead.

LOVER AS FOX

Driven, at midnight, to growth, the city's wistful turnings
lead you living on islands to some dark single house
where vacant windows mark increased pursuit,
chasing the runner outward beyond bounds
around the wildest circle of the night.

Circling returns! the city wreathed in rivers,
streaked skies surrounding islands of blank stone—
into this mythic track travelling breakneck,
a streaming furnace of escape, you, fox,
pursued, brick-red and vicious, circling bricks,

are followed as nimbly all mottled cloudy night;
fastened upon your path, the Floating Man
face down above the city, as shadow, changing shape,

as shadow of clouds, flying, and swiftly as
indifference running mad around the world.

Speed now! see city, houses across the water,
mosaic and bright over the riverfall
remote from the bursting eye, the open nostril,
flared lip (an image of angels singing speed),
caught in a nightlong visionary chase.

See the entire scene bright as you fly
round lots pauper all year, shacks lame with weather,
this sour fertile time teeming and ramshackle
before you, loving, clean sight in spyglass air.
And around town again. River, river.
Why do people live on islands?

GIFT-POEM

December steel done, flowers open color,
unshadowed brilliance enters the air again,
lets fear dissolve,

and convalescent brightness brush the face
until the subtlest rivers of sleep descend
over all eyelids,

and air lies gracious, lavishing general gold,
warming the lips, touching the salt away,
unlocking wishes,

until the lifelong travellers find their rest
in prodigal evening, marvel day, moonblaze,
superb ambassadors

whose power discloses sensual ease again
to these who come bringing flowers, standing still
past wandering arrived at open spring.

WOMAN AND EMBLEMS

WOMAN AND BIRD

A bird flew out of a cloud
(with a beak, flying),
broke its beak on my bone,
cried bird-cries over crying.

Sky, stranger, wilderness
(flying starry through flesh),
make an end; be me, bird.
It reverses my one wish.

Bird screams slavery among bones.
(I watch with a bird's eyes.)
Quarrel, wings; if I travel,
bird stays—stand, bird flies.

Bird sets feathers where flesh was
(my claws slide away on space).
Bird, here—now, bird, we fly!
Mourns, mourns, it turns a captive face.

THE BIRTHDAY

A sound lying on the fantastic air
opens the night and the child is born;
as the wind moves, the solemn crying
pioneers in the air, changes

to flame crusading among the grasses
fire-whitened, aroused before it,
rippled crops—and blazing races
into a central arena

where it stands as a fighting-cock
conqueror head, aggressive spur,
and the gilt feather, the bronze, the greenish,
flicker and threaten.

The feathers of the fighting-cock
become a tree, and casting seed,

raise potent forests at its side—
birth among burning.

The great magnetic branches sign
meaning on the record sky—
now rise, moon, stiffen, bird, and flames,
kill and engender.

Reversal, chameleon,
pursuing images—
recurrent birth offering other names,
a spool of brightness.

WOMAN AND MUSIC

This is a tall woman walking through a square
thinking what is a woman at midnight in a park
under bells, in the trivial and lovely hours
with images, violins, dancers approaching?

This is a woman sitting at a mirror
her back to the glass and all the dancers advancing,
or in a chair laughing at a bone
sitting upright in a chair
talking of ballet, flesh's impermanence.

This is a woman looking at a stage—
dancer receiving the floral blue and white,
balanced against a tallest blue decor,
dancing—and all the parks, walks, hours
descend in brilliant water past the eyes
pursuing and forgotten and subdued
to blinding music, the deliberate strings.

OUTPOST

After the last cold mountain
turns loaded with rock, the green iceberg
wheels at the ship
and gulls pass screaming:
sail out on trembling decks that cut
deepdigging into the ring of sea:

End of America! not so far out
as the home-storm of sickness,
furious seas, not like the arranged waves here
foreign in green, austere,
but, bright as household scene,
all the equipment of dismay,
teaching grave civilized man
nothing, feeding his sickest
dread of strong icy seas,
disgust with sunlight.

After the mountains turn, the Floating Man
raises his head (his shoulders are cold rock),
his face takes on the home-look : suffering,
sinking beneath the last iceberg horizon,
reminding us, risen to find us this last time.
He carries in his eyes street-images,
on forehead, protest, on sinking face, goodbye,
the sombre, bright, the unpredictable wind
laying a flag across his lips.

End of America! the ocean opening,
lighthouse and iceberg, vestige of vegetable green,
the sad face everywhere sinking backward last:
not rock, not ice, but here most civilized man,
outpost survivor,
the last and floating trace, streaming down every river
into the sea whose foreign colors waver,
hold to the end the images of violence
on rising overwave and underwave,
slave and slavedriver.

⊸ 3 Two Voyages

THE CRUISE

"Goodbye!" called the stockholders as the ship pulled out
    from the dock,

"Good trip, good luck!" as the captain saluted;
and the crew stared down from the top rungs, the passengers
     stormed confetti
from all the rails of the luxury liner, crowding
in imitation of a travel poster.
But the last words issued from the pier loudspeaker,
the admiral-president, shouting, guardian and serious,
"Orders: above all, not to put in at any port
doubtful or dangerous."
Already, sea
rose livid, boiling over the white expensive hull,
imperious completely, undeniable.

Beginning of a voyage, quiet and gay; dancing and games,
deck lectures, visits to polo ponies in the hold,
bulletins, engines, radio operator's important earphones,
poet, barmaid polishing bottles, union man, news,
deck-conversations, visits to the bridge,
the sailor wit, music and promenade,
scrolls watched in the water, the glaze, the celadon,
high sunrise lustre on the fretted waves.
Persons emerge:
gossip the captain walking with the blond,
emigrants, pleasure party, financier.

The exotic flowers were wilting in the staterooms.
Log's entry: "Quiet short voyage, last night unpleasant
     weather;
passengers sturdy, no sea-sickness, but the barmaid
fainted before lunch; waiting for diagnosis." Captain
writing, found confirmation in his heirloom mirror
freckled with tarnish, wishing him well, swaying. "Tomorrow, land."
About the bows, flyingfish, and island in the sea,
dove and appeared, and the chain of foam
followed the boat;
a spume of cirrus vanished with the sun,
safe water entertained a cloudless night.

Fourth day: first sight of rocks, a street of islands,
hazy and permanent, live green, the blues of mist,
bargaining cry of gulls. At the rail, radio operator
scouted for signs of houses. The blond stood alone. The captain

hardly looked at the land, a doubtful country.
"Very welcome," said passengers, watching swimming sea-grasses,
felt trigger joy the ocean should be past,
and foreign cities, doorless countries come.
No landing-place;
only the rock, moss, mist, a chiffon pageant,
suggesting harbors, a shore-image.

Deep cobalt morning sky, spring's melting ice in the sky,
softness in air, the port's nearness.
                                        But, the flavor of smoke
drifting across the bow like the last loudspeaker words;
but, the hypnotic thunder: cannon in that direction,
but, turning the promontory, the explosive city.
Flares, bombardments! Diamond hallucinations,
depth-bombs, ocean of waterspouts, fountains with strenuous
        trunks;
city of safety. The planted captain, straddled on his deck
thinks, Doubtful, thinks
grinning, Dangerous; must head for the next port:
radio asking advice, amuse all passengers.

        Chimes, clocks, rehearsals the radio invents.
        Stay away from here, there are planes falling,
        airliner crashes over Appalachians,
        two big amphibians lost above the Bay,
        no passengers recovered. Rumor: war,
        passages cancelled, no transatlantic sailings.
        One minute. Flash. One minute. Flash.
                                        Explosion!
        Death of children, none over thirteen injured,
        total unverified. Flash. Statement, song.
        Strange clouds visible over the prairies,
        blight on the wheat, dust in the middle air,
        unprecedented weather. To all planes:
        fly low, no flying blind, there will be flares on the ground.
        To all ships: make for port.

The deckrail hangs on the unaltered sea. Leaning, the poet
mentions danger. The pregnant barmaid half-hears his begging voice.
"Over the pointed hills, over the spit of sand,
harbor, we hurry down. Do you know the familiar

cat of superstition, feline terror?"
Sailors' mottoes. The barmaid dreads to make the land again,
losing her work; she watches. Clear sea, definite wave,
the picture of the last port taken fighting
deep on the brain;
"Talk to the union man," she volunteers,
"his cure is for your trouble."

The lighthouse seen at the spur, coastal clew, token.
But, over the new city, black, thunder of smoke,
the chilly shoal warm at the ship, the charred log rolling,
extensive flame, cries, broken walls. Laughter of falling glass.
Fiery capital, and the sea running hot, surf filmed with oil,
burning, the warehouses burning blue, sugar-blue,
and shadowless orange fire creeping seaward quickly.
Cliffs by the town metallic; menace of gold reflection,
and on their faces
pale of retreat, flattered by fire. The captain
orders backwater. The child says, "I want to stand on the ground."

But a boat can run down the coast, the shore is long,
(they said), one city stands by itself, unfortunate islands
breathe other air. We are equipped. We have
machines, being extensions of the hand and eye,
directile and very proud, discovering safety.
With foreign ports at war, foreign prime cities
burned to the ground, still we are navigators.
Stars come, a rose of stars, perfumed, circle of winds,
black Galileo
has taught us mastery. Choose southern voyage,
sun provides gentler beaches, the languid warless lands.

Easy to go south into the warm daybreak, faith in the course restored,
prepare to land, a captain to insure a safe end;
they filled the bar, stuck labels on their baggage,
planned weekends over roadmaps, walked the deck,
nodded, handled field-glasses, spied on the pasture water,
and the ship's new position was advanced in ink,
admired for accuracy, predicted by science,
the map consulted in nervous argument.
Only, the weakness;

only, the night sent rocking into
the floating ocean and the storm's renown.

When the light changed at last, the wake ran concentrated silver
and the blue northern sea dissolved to green, brightened,
the union man questioned the captain, urged a landing,
spoke to small groups. (Official entry, "First signs of
passengers' unrest. Insults, high temperatures.")
"They must be fighting for something we know," he said,
"I saw men advancing down those inspired hills,
guns and grenades are timed now against tyrants,
a wish to keep
us all alive! under its strictest grip
logical strength challenges conscience up."

"We must arrive at land," the union man kept saying,
"there's work." "You!" said the poet, "a wandering motive!
The captain knows here's a hot country coming
among rich water, I see it! the city at ease,
the islands braceletted with cloud, sky blue of mania."
"So long as we land." "We'll land in a port fit to receive us,
fleshly and bright, set in a frivolous growth,
giraffe plants, monster flowers."
Far off, the beach
lay white at the white water's edge, proclaiming
the hostile beauty of that savage coast.

Hot city, terraced by color, tropical among green,
vermilion blossom; and the mulatto cinnamon.
"This," said the poet, "my terror, my superstition,
here's a perfect city that we will dare not enter,
point me perfection, I'll show you warning and Captain's Orders,
or dangerous action; or tenderness, prelude to violence,
any promise painted in terms of acid Picasso
is signed Beware." And a small boat put smoothly out from harbor
and the man called
from it, below the ship, his least words taking on
significance, being in a foreign language.

The radio operator, translating; "I am here for Quarantine.
No quarantine man. Dead. Plague in the town—epidemic,

the ships bring it in, says the mayor. The doctors do not know.
Most of the town is dead. They have voted. Are laying mines
all through the harbor. Around you now. I'm instructed:
Torpedo all craft attempting to come in.
Our rich have donated handsomely for explosives."
Sand, green water, litter of wavy sunlight.
"No landing place,"
the captain, "you guessed," to the poet. He shivers, laughing,
"let them come after and make me cliché."

"But you're original now," said the captain; "we're sailing
        to Nothing
doubtful or dangerous, predict a landing-place." "I'll make
        my own landfall,"
answered the poet. "Not alone," said the union man.
        Individual harbor,
and you'll discover yours—man, most successful animal,
can disembark according to his need; you!" he accused the women,
"I must have love," insisted the blond; "What do you want,"
        asked the captain,
"another botched affair?" "My child," said the barmaid.
        "And you'll leave the ship!"
"Let them alone, they're right," said the union man. And
        the crew sang from the
lower deck—
*'Wade . . . in the water, chillen, wade . . . in the water, chillen, wade
        . . . in the water, chillen,*
Gods's a-gone to trouble the water.'

"Where is the cruise the travel posters promised? The dancing
        partners, quick landing?"
the blond demanded. "The epidemic harbor's faded, is the
        radio dead?"
"It answers only War." "Put in to port, if war is everywhere,"
the union man, "accept obtainable things." "I have my
        orders," answered the captain.
"Arbitrary commands!" "Do not be cynic at the captain's religion,"
the financier. "Commands are dead, he's a dead priest, the
        other's living,
this is a new voyage that you have not known."
"I've thought it out through orders," said the captain.

The sailor cried,
"We have our orders from you; but I saw a book,
and I saw a book, and I'll attempt before I die."

The poet called to the sailor, "What do you make of that city?
Of this rich water? Of captain's rules?" "I'll wait," shouted the sailor.
"If we are named," said the poet, "it is guilty generation."
"I'll wait a bit; and claim not guilt but anger,
and I see land!" The city on the cape
stood straight ahead, assuming the quality of dream,
silent, receptive, under the summer air.
The passengers sighted these last-chance piers, the towers
and over them,
over the color of street, roof, public pier,
and house : the vision, the puzzle in mid-air.

Is it the cloud? What's falling out of the sky? Is it
a storm falling? for a flame shot down, trailing
a falling plane, dropping behind the turning wings,
        clear flame in air,
and over it the dark cloud, spinning, noisy, resolving
to a cloud of planes, gunning. Among them, a white core,
the single parachute. As the flier descended
the planes circled him. Vertigo of machine-guns. And his
        dead body
swung, receiving bullets, sinking hooded by white
into the city.
Into the arson of the burning plane
fallen faster than flier in cage.

"That's our illness," concluded the poet, "the war our age
        must win,"
as the ship continued into pale sea, bright sea,
        hurrying south,
"I know its breath on my face, have noted all its symptoms,
have heard cats shouting, seen the worn eye stare
up from the doormat, the flowerbed, under the wave,
learned all the disease of this progressive time."
"Can it be cured?" asked the sailor. "At its root," said the
        union man,
"by reaching it." As the ship persevered out from land.

"Reach it,"
repeated the blond, "what must we take to our breast,
what must we kiss away?"

When the coast fell at last, the passengers' wish was apparent,
they dreamed of some simple convenient city, peaceful, wired
        for light.
Organization of lectures and modest entertainment.
But the audience struggled out after the second solo.
Log's entry: "Engines and instruments in good condition,
barmaid in labor, supply of fresh meat running low.
Insubordination common among the men. Fruit holding out.
Feeling against ship's orders is met with discipline."
But at night
confusion over the course, anger, lack of sleep,
ominous quarrels over strange constellations.

Distress of tourists; they dream of housedogs, house-animals,
the 6 a.m. cry of lapdogs as the child is delivered,
crying but not hungry, refusing food, mumbling.
Dreams of distress: ape-murder, invective, the autumnal escape,
stumbling dead in the dry leaves, hunting someone, not
        mentioning whom.
Dying. The barmaid's little baby's dying words
were the words with which its weekend life began:
Mother it said, enunciating distinctly,
refusing food.
They slid the two-foot coffin overboard,
a small white circle drowning in green water.

Identical sickness; but the barmaid did not speak, the crew
worked or looked up from work, waiting for shore,
worked with a mutinous hope. The poet spoke to the blond
mentioning love. She smiled when he said, "I praise the
marvel physical flowers upon your trellis skeleton, I welcome
from you, the discipline of every part." He thought, Elaborate,
I wait for the release, the explosive distorting act
with the same fever that they wait for land;
it fills the mind
it is my port, lighthouse, coastal clew, token,
suggesting harbors, a shore-image.

The close-up in the mind, the head enlarging to fill
the sky with its immense unique idea;
Homer wrote Helen blind, the unfree are praising freedom,
I know the exquisite taste of the sight of land.
If we saw grass, it would speak, it would say 'green,'
I dream of a boat riding on towery waves
overriding blond pebbles, grating on stone,
I have a superstition about land:
it is our wisdom,
contact and cause, without which only grows
abstinence, pestilence, unbalance.

But if a sound can travel to restore
the tight prophetic brain, but if a ringing
can travel out over electric seas:

Bells cannot ring from water, land must wait
where bells invite, strong, with their Latin chiming.
The crew looks up to the passenger rail; the poet
stands with his face into the vocal night:
Funera plango, fulgura frango, Sabbata pango,
excito lentos, dissipo ventos, paco cruentos.
"What do they ring?" shouted the sailor.
"Calling of funerals, breaking the lightning,
        pealing the Sabbath,
waking the lazy, dissolving wind, peace to the evil."
"They have power," shouted the sailor,
"read what they mean."
But the boat lost their *plango*
and on the wind *frango* night *pango,*
failing sifted over the water
until one bell repeated singular music,
only and loud.
Vox ego, ringing august,
vox ego sum vitae; voco vos.
"That hails us," shouted the sailor,
"who is that?"
"The voice of life," he interpreted, "calling you."
The cheer came.
"They can hear us!" shouted the sailor.

"Lucky you know the language," said the blond
as the hurrah went down. "What are the signals,
what do they mean?"

"God," he said, "revelation! closing over the world,
breaking on the air, the wasted sounds among
shouts and the violent bullet in the mouth,
our age broken like stone, all grace run out of grasp,
perfected music I could never reach.
Listen!" he shouted, "triumph of bells, swinging! And for me,
bells alive also under the sea," walking
the length of the deck, rising up tall, diving,
the arc, the avalanche.
"Insane!" the critic captain, "doesn't he
know that the sea is full of teeth?"

"Send boats out!" "You'll not reclaim that man," said the blond,
but the crew were dropping their small boats overside.
The body was gone. The sailor whistled. The rest of the crew
dropped down their lifeboats. "Who'll make the land, they
        hear us!" the sailor shouted,
"who's with us?" "Criminal fools!" threatened the captain,
and his pistol twitched the sea around them, "mutinous fools,
you'll hang or drown!" "Off your law-haunted ship! Trying
        for land!"
The union man, barmaid, radio operator, child who wanted
the ground jumped—
but the blond stood crying at the rail
not daring to be saved.

"Attempt land!" shouted the sailor, "fight for something we
        know!"
pulling on oars toward the origin of bells,
but the great ship was continuing, night advanced, the
        captain:
"Fanatic clowns, with their contamination,
laughter and mutiny!" and into severe morning,
the crazy alcohol blue, the bloodshot afternoon.
"I wanted to go," the blond. "Loved that suicide?" asked
        the captain,
"you'll love me too, you'll have your love, only believe
        their song was mad,

'*Free grace and dyin love, Free grace and dyin love*
Free grace and dyin love, to ring dem charmin bells.'"

Pool money. Slaughter the polo ponies for meat. Tamper
     with radio.
No sound from the world, and the water giving out.
A continent of sea: they wished formal December, blue snow,
suffering cold, but earth. And the sun came down
bare as the condor, elegant on the sea.
Mist rose, a threat of mist, ranging horizons,
the captain laughed, "Remember the landslide on Chartreuse,
and does the sea slide down on our monastics?
By God," he
swore, "they were correct, they knew, when they mutinied!"
"Oh no," said the blond, "oh no," as the mist arose.

Organization of simple banking system for passengers,
but the closed bar, the empty shops, the lack of cigarettes.
Dreams of distress : land passed in the night, with no one looking,
the rising mist, the subterfuge, disaster.
Log's entry: "Engines faltering, charts useless, meat maggotty,
passengers grown flabby with lack of confidence,
great trust in me while I believed in my orders.
But lately, doubts batter me. I do not confess.
The sea is
full of teeth, full of music, and there is war at home."
His mirror said, Order's tarnished, you drift insane.

Drift through continual waste of waters, under high heated clouds,
closing to storm-threat, guarding the ship, closing to fog,
and the passengers stared through shadow imagining
twirling cool springs, low-banked familiar flowers.
"Now," wrote the captain, "boats of madness ferry across
     the brain,
the blizzard sky's covered by fog and lost,
we'll sail by dead reckoning while the sun is covered;
saviors may rise which only can be seen
standing in mirrors."
He looked at the tarnished heirloom giving him back his face,
no word, no savior; raw forehead, open book.

On deck they lay obscured, bodily blanketed,
the faceless travellers, streaming fog bannering
between them let them forget the dangling lifeboat hooks,
the prison days, the reach of sea, the death
around them, mutinies, wars, suicides, angers,
the ineffective rancid idle engines.
The captain saw the fog taint brightening to ochre,
"Sulphur!" he cried, "that's hell, that's yellow, the color of
        madness,
we'll travel back to blue . . ."
tearing at his mirror, smashing it, smashing the radio,
        smashing the fog
until his arms were tied.

And deep into the galleries of fog, riding in silence, ship
drifted dead. The cloud came wave on wave,
the blond woman sang to the sleeping passengers, captain
shrieked from his straitjacket : Make her go, her hair is
        yellow fog.
Land, land, she sang, let them all attempt land.
Land, she sang, doubtful or dangerous. Barriers came
across her, filling up over her face.
Disaster of music in the yellow fog,
and she sang land
Drifting. Disaster. Drifted the world away
saner than angels, promise of safety, harbor.

MEDITERRANEAN

On the evening of July 25, 1936, five days after the outbreak of the Spanish
Civil War, Americans with the Anti-Fascist Olympic Games were evacuated
from Barcelona at the order of the Catalonian Government. In a small
Spanish boat, the *Ciudad di Ibiza,* which the Belgians had chartered, they and
a group of five hundred, including the Hungarian and Belgian teams as well
as the American, sailed overnight to Sète, the first port in France. The only
men who remained were those who had volunteered in the Loyalist forces :
the core of the future International Column.

1

At the end of July, exile. We watched the gangplank go
cutting the boat away, indicating : sea.
Barcelona, the sun, the fire-bright harbor, war.

Five days.
                    Here at the rail, foreign and refugee,
we saw the city, remembered that zero of attack,
alarm in the groves, snares through the olive hills,
rebel defeat : leaders, two regiments,
broadcasts of victory, tango, surrender.
The truckride to the city, barricades,
bricks pried at corners, rifle-shot in street,
car-burning, bombs, blank warnings, fists up, guns
busy sniping, the town walls, towers of smoke.
And order making, committees taking charge, foreigners
commanded out by boat.

I saw the city, sunwhite flew on glass,
trucewhite from window, the personal lighting found
eyes on the dock, sunset-lit faces of singers,
eyes, goodbye into exile. Saw where Columbus rides
black-pillared : discovery, turn back, explore
a new found Spain, coast-province, city-harbor.
Saw our parades ended, the last marchers on board
listed by nation.

I saw first of the faces going home into war
the brave man Otto Boch, the German exile, knowing
he quieted tourists during machine gun battle,
he kept his life straight as a single issue—
left at that dock we left, his gazing Breughel face,
square forehead and eyes, strong square breast fading,
the narrow runner's hips diminishing dark.
I see this man, dock, war, a latent image.

The boat *Ciudad di Ibiza,* built for 200,
loaded with 500, manned by loyal sailors,
chartered by Belgians when consulates were helpless,
through a garden of gunboats, margin of the port,
entered : Mediterranean.

        2

Frontier of Europe, the tideless sea, a field of power
touching desirable coasts, rocking in time conquests,
fertile, the moving water maintains its boundaries
layer on layer, Troy—seven civilized worlds:

Egypt, Greece, Rome, jewel Jerusalem,
giant feudal Spain, giant England, this last war.

The boat pulled into evening, underglaze blue
flared instant fire, blackened towards Africa.
Over the city alternate lights occurred;

                                  and pale

in the pale sky emerging stars.
No city now, a besieged line of lights
masking the darkness where the country lay.
But we knew guns
bright through mimosa
singe of powder
and reconnoitering plane
flying anonymous
scanning the Pyrenees
black now above the Catalonian Sea.
Boat of escape, dark on the water, hastening, safe,
holding non-combatants, the athlete, the child,
the printer, the boy from Antwerp, the black boxer,
lawyer and communist.

                     The Games had not been held.
       A week of Games, theatre and festival;
       world anti-fascist week. Pistol starts race.
       Machine gun marks the war. Answered unarmed,
       charged the Embarcadero, met those guns.
       And charging through the province, joined that army.
       Boys from the hills, the unmatched guns,
       the clumsy armored cars.
       Drilled in the bullring. Radio cries:
       To Saragossa! And this boat.

Escape, dark on the water, an overloaded ship.
Crowded the deck. Spoke little. Down to dinner.
Quiet on the sea: no guns.
The printer said, In Paris there is time,
but where's its place now; where is poetry?

       This is the sea of war; the first frontier
       blank on the maps, blank sea; Minoan boats
       maybe achieved this shore;
       mountains whose slope divides

one race, old insurrections, Narbo, now
moves at the colored beach
destroyer wardog. "Do not burn the church,
compañeros, it is beautiful. Besides,
it brings tourists." They smashed only the image
madness and persecution.
Exterminating wish; they forced the door,
lifted the rifle, broke the garden window,
removed only the drawings : cross and wrath.
Whenever we think of these, the poem is,
that week, the beginning, exile
remembered in continual poetry.

Voyage and exile, a midnight cold return,
dark to our left mountains begin the sky.
There, pointed the Belgian, I heard a pulse of war,
sharp guns while I ate grapes in the Pyrenees.
Alone, walking to Spain, the five o'clock of war.
In those cliffs run the sashed and sandalled men,
capture the car, arrest the priest, kill captain,
fight our war.
The poem is the fact, memory fails
under and seething lifts and will not pass.

Here is home-country, who fights our war.
Street-meeting speaker to us:

". . . came for Games,
you stay for victory; foreign? your job is:
go tell your countries what you saw in Spain."
The dark unguarded army left all night.
M. de Paîche said, "We can learn from Spain."
The face on the dock that turned to find the war.

3

Seething, and falling back, a sea of stars,
Black marked with virile silver. Peace all night,
over that land, planes
death-lists   a frantic bandage
the rubber tires burning   monuments
sandbag, overturned wagon, barricade
girl's hand with gun   food failing, water failing
the epidemic threat

the date in a diary   a blank page opposite
no entry—
however, met
the visible enemy heroes: madness, infatuation
the cache in the crypt, the breadline shelled,
the yachtclub arsenal, the foreign cheque.
History racing from an assumed name, peace,
a time used to perfect weapons.

If we had not seen fighting,
if we had not looked there
        the plane flew low
        the plaster ripped by shots
        the peasant's house
if we had stayed in our world
between the table and the desk
between the town and the suburb
slowly disintegration
male and female

If we had lived in our city
sixty years might not prove
        the power this week
        the overthrown past
        tourist and refugee
Emeric in the bow speaking his life
and the night on this ship
the night over Spain
quick recognition
male and female

And the war in peace, the war in war, the peace,
the faces on the dock
the faces in those hills.

        4

Near the end now, morning. Sleepers cover the decks,
cabins full, corridors full of sleep. But the light
vitreous, crosses water; analyzed darkness,
crosshatched in silver, passes up the shore,
touching limestone massif, deserted tableland,
bends with the down-warp of the coastal plain.

The colored sun stands on the route to Spain,
builds on the waves a series of mirrors
and on the scorched land rises hot.
Coasts change their names as the boat goes to
France, Costa Brava softens to Côte Vermeil,
Spain's a horizon ghost behind the shapeless sea.

Blue praising black, a wind above the waves
moves pursuing a jewel, this hieroglyph
boat passing under the sun to lose it on the
attractive sea, habitable and kind.
A barber sun, razing three races, met
from the north with a neurotic eagerness.

They rush to solar attraction; local daybreak finds
them on the red earth of the colored cliffs; the little islands
tempt worshippers, gulf-purple, pointed bay.
We crowd the deck,
welcome the islands with a sense of loss.

5

The wheel in the water, green, behind my head.
Turns with its light-spokes. Deep. And the drowning eyes
find under the water figures near
in their true picture, moving true,
the picture of that war enlarging clarified
as the boat perseveres away, always enlarging,
becoming clear.

Boat of escape, your water-photograph.
I see this man, dock, war, a latent image.
And at my back speaking the black boxer,
telling his education : porter, fighter, no school,
no travel but this, trade-union sent a team.
I saw Europe break apart
and artifice or martyr's will
cannot anneal this war, nor make
the loud triumphant future start
shouting from its tragic heart.

Deep in the water Spanish shadows turn,
assume their brightness past a cruel lens,
quick vision of loss. The pastoral lighting takes

the boat, deck, passengers, the pumice cliffs,
the winedark sweatshirt at my shoulder.
Cover away the fighting cities
but still your death-afflicted eyes
must hold the print of flowering guns,
bombs whose insanity craves size,
the lethal breath, the iron prize.

The clouds upon the water-barrier pass,
the boat may turn to land; the shapes endure,
rise up into our eyes, to bind
us back; an accident of time
set it upon us, exile burns it in.
Once the fanatic image shown,
enemy to enemy,
past and historic peace wear thin;
we see Europe break like stone,
hypocrite sovereignties go down
before this war the age must win.

6

The sea produced that town : Sète, which the boat turns to,
at peace. Its breakwater, casino, vermouth factory, beach.
They searched us for weapons. No currency went out.
The sign of war had been search for cameras,
pesetas and photographs go back to Spain,
the money for the army. Otto is fighting now, the lawyer said.
No highlight hero. Love's not a trick of light.

But. The town lay outside, peace, France.
And in the harbor the Russian boat *Schachter;*
sharp paint-smell, the bruise-colored shadow swung,
sailors with fists up, greeting us, asking news,
making the harbor real.
                              Barcelona.
Slow-motion splash. Anchor. Small from the beach
the boy paddles to meet us, legs hidden in canoe,
curve of his blade that drips.
Now gangplank falls to deck.
                              Barcelona
everywhere, Spain everywhere, the cry of Planes for Spain.

The picture at our eyes, past memory, poem,
to carry and spread and daily justify.
The single issue, the live man standing tall,
on the hill, the dock, the city, all the war.
Exile and refugee, we land, we take
nothing negotiable out of the new world;
we believe, we remember, we saw.
Mediterranean gave
image and peace, tideless for memory.

For that beginning
make of us each
a continent and inner sea
Atlantis buried outside
to be won.

A Turning Wind

1939

. . .for the forms of nature are awakened, and are as a turning wheel, and so they carry their spirit the wind.

Boehme

1 Moment of Proof

READING TIME :
1 MINUTE 26 SECONDS

The fear of poetry is the
fear : mystery and fury of a midnight street
of windows whose low voluptuous voice
issues, and after that there is no peace.

That round waiting moment in the
theatre : curtain rises, dies into the ceiling
and here is played the scene with the mother
bandaging a revealed son's head. The bandage is torn off.
Curtain goes down. And here is the moment of proof.

That climax when the brain acknowledges the world,
all values extended into the blood awake.
Moment of proof. And as they say Brancusi did,
building his bird to extend through soaring air,
as Kafka planned stories that draw to eternity
through time extended. And the climax strikes.

Love touches so, that months after the look of
blue stare of love, the footbeat on the heart
is translated into the pure cry of birds
following air-cries, or poems, the new scene.
Moment of proof. That strikes long after act.

They fear it. They turn away, hand up palm out
fending off moment of proof, the straight look, poem.
The prolonged wound-consciousness after the bullet's shot.
The prolonged love after the look is dead,
the yellow joy after the song of the sun.

SONG, THE BRAIN-CORAL

Lie still, be still, love, be thou not shaken,
it is for me to be shaken,
to bring tokens.

Among the yellow light in the hot gardens,
the thinned green light in the evening gardens,
I speak of gladness.

Let the great night, wearing its moods and shadows
find us so, stilled within its varied shadows
falling like feathers.

We change in images, color, visions, and change;
I bring you, speak you now a changeless stone,
the strange brain-coral,

thrown white on beaches beside the peacock Stream.
Lie still, love, while the many physical worlds stream
passionate by,

in dreams of the exterior intricate rainbow world,
dreaming the still white intricate stone of the world,
—bring you brain-coral,
a world's white seeming.

TARGET PRACTICE

Near Mexico, near April, in the morning.
Desert where the sun casts his circles of power
on acquiescent sand shifting beneath them. Car
speeding among white landscapes; suddenly
the permanent scene at the dead-center.

Photo, in circles of speed, how at raw barnside
father and son stand, man with his rifle up
levelled at heartpoint of a nailed-up bird
spread, wings against the wood. The boy's arm thrown
up over his eyes, flinching from coming shot.

Bullseye, you bullet! pinning down the scene.
And speed you car over the waste of noon
into the boundaries of distance where
the first ring lessens into memory.
Until, a little lower than the sun,

centered in that last circle, hangs a free
fierce bird down-staring on the target of land,
circle on circle of power spread, and speeding
eyes passing from zone to zone, from war to where
their bullets will never bring him down.

OTHERWORLD

LANDING AT LIVERPOOL

This is the dream-journey, knowing the earth slips under,
not knowing how the sea offers to ships
another sliding line. This is the otherworld
slipping among innumerable nets.

Color and love of land, the water-barrier spills
sleep on the gulls' waves, a sketch of ocean
like children's crayon-drawings, the long North
Sea fanged by icebergs, green and clanging hills.

This was the journey. Out of adolescence.
Past Anticosti, Labrador, past Belle Isle,
end of America. And islands come;
after the ocean, the seabird's complex eye.

Ship's wake at stern, the after-life.
And pass the Hebrides asleep.
Islands identified. Lighthouse and channel-blue
all day, pure Irish fields, a female sea.

Always ahead, new air. Falling behind
wide Firth, the lights of Greenock bank the Clyde.
Ayr, Arran, Ailsa Craig the single rock;
the Isle of Man points water-level Wales.

Coming among the living where we rise,
coming among the dead in whom we wade
kneedeep and undermined; through seas to the great island,
promising continents, the riding shores arrive.

That was the wanted voyage of a child with maps,
an adolescent at books and hearsay of lovers
telling desires dead with the end in sight.
I think now of that port, England ahead,
my clumsy porthole stare at landing-light.
I blessed my luck my landing could be loved.

Blessing my end-luck in this room again
steadily, for the first time steady. Watch
light, lying still, too awkward deep in joy.
All sliding globe-lines on the sea forgotten
and taken into shore where ships lose skill
after fierce water come to blessed end.

THE ISLAND

Land; and only to stand on the ground, stand on the brick of the dark-
      red city, stand on the car-crowded dock
with the city beating up at the face, and the harbor-land beating up at
      the feet, beating
its stony flatness after sea, with its strange tongues, strange turns of the
      head, strange
biddings, strange bracing, strange binding! but the car enters the tiled
      tunnel into the
turnings through summer country, among hills stippled with gardens,
      the shade-park forests
freaked with sunlight, the Shropshire hedges, the trenchings of lanes,
      the grassy
fallen shore-smooth places where this floor of island is a mowed fish-
      pond, the deep
grass, the stamping grass and parsley, marigold leaves and daisies,
the car run through a narrow bridge of speed winding the curving
      the standing shadows,
along the trellised stream, along the earth-wet-smelling cloisters
stopped by cascades from a loosely practised piano in Chester
shaking its scales loose over the city crowded with speech, the window
      where Herbert
and martyred Charles and Lancelot Andrewes are gone in their trance,
      in their triptych
of color to Chester's heaven, less vivid burning than blue-burning
      glass—
and the fields, and gooseberry lawns, and the ribbons of music broad-
      cast identical

over the roads, threading the shadows, thinned by the quick and
       ranging
eye of the sun who takes this fief with all lands captive daily, gathering
       the ripple of
speed and our knees before us and the car's leaning and the enamelled
       tree
whose flame is grassland and the tree a fire, sun-shadow, blocking
out black-caked industries, chimneys of blackened cities, hills, hollow
       streets
weighing down this driftless, this island, its scarps, its talismanic hills,
its wet-grass-wading counties, ocean-eye out, its moist color, its
       leaping
thought lifted to down-dipping suns, standing shadows of the barrow-
       buried race,
tombstones set out to pasture in fat grass—and the fashion
whose pulses match ours, an atrophied prince, a flier's career,
the pathic gunman, the gangster mayor, the voice of a mouse—and
       the profile of cities,
the cities, the old road through Roman cities, approaching the central
       city, the nave of horrible empire,
the proud, the evening-bold—over the last rolled cloudbanks, in a
       spume of light, we speed to,
curve to past distal cities. Starfall begins with the miracle over the hill.

                 ❧

And flat on this land the march, farm-foot, barn-foot, field-foot,
silent march on the London streets, come far : with slogans : and slowly,
the tithe-march moves, the farmers lift their flags : their faces break
the crust of nations once more, and farm-foot, barn-foot, field-foot,
pace London : their banners Invictus say We Will Not Be Druv: shoutless
move past the eyes of the stones, the guards, the horses, the houses
where the colonel with the undershot jaw sees the actress with the bulletproof face
see the cabman see the diplomat see the salesman see the colonial
rheumatic sub-secretary see cathedrals see the tourists
see the street see the marchers see the silence see the island
see the island see the island see the faces of the sky.

    OTHERWORLD
Coming among the living
              at railway stations   at the porter's smile
train for the south alone in the brisk winds
a rumor of nothing at all among the forest

coming among the dead
                    at Dover, a pebbled ridge of the known world
or water or the buffeting sight of that chalk forehead
a cloud over that head
tall over land
                    and feeling earth slip under
                    standing among innumerable nets
or Calais the rapid speech the warm hearth-colored brick
silver of trees the wheels in silver laid
Paris the fluent city running by like film
in landmarks of travelogues, the straddled tower,
the arch framing a gas-mask poster, travel on maps
south as the light decays vaulting the hills of a world
melted silver and speed, the water-silver trees
                    until night spends new air, the after-life sleep
                    wakes among the spurs and roots of mountains
the heat escaping, the cypress-licking sky
a country of cave-drawn mutilated hands
of water painted with the color of light
                    where the world ends as the wheels stop turning
                    people begin to live by their belief

Rites of initiation, if the whirlpool eye
see fire see buildings deformed and flowing to the ground
in a derangement of explosion falling
see the distorted face run through an olive grove
the rattle of hens scream of a cliff-face and the pylons filing
in an icing of sweat enter these tropics : war,
where initiation is a rite of passage,
simulation of death or real death, new name,
enjoying for a while the life of the spirits, may
travel, assume disguises, indeed absorb fear
see in this end of voyage love like that fabulous bird's
lit breast, the light of the black-crowned night heron
whose static soaring over the central world
identifies armies, takes the initiate
                    into a room where all the chairs fall down
                    and all the walls decay and all the world stands bare
                    until the world is a field of the Spanish War

ships with their tall stacks dipping crowd the air
seas of the sky cruised by anonymous planes

subjective myth becomes a province, a city
whose wish goes to the front with its final desire
monomanias come   their diaries   their days
                    the burning capitals
                    when the bricks of the last street are
                    up in a tall wave breaking
                    when cartwheels are targets are words are eyes
                    the bullring wheels in flame
                    the circles fire at the bleeding trees
the world slips under the footbeat of the living
everybody knows who lost the war

NUNS IN THE WIND

As I came out of the New York Public Library
you said your influence on my style would be noticed
and from now on there would be happy poems.
                    It was at that moment
the street was assaulted by a covey of nuns
going directly toward the physics textbooks.
Tragic fiascos shadowed that whole spring.
The children sang streetfuls, and I thought:
O to be the King in the carol
kissed and at peace; but recalling Costa Brava
the little blossoms in the mimosa tree
and later, the orange cliff, after they sent me out,
I knew there was no peace.
                    You smiled, saying : Take it easy.

That was the year of the five-day fall of cities.
                First day, no writers. Second, no telephones. Third
                no venereal diseases. Fourth, no income tax. And on
                the fifth, at noon.
The nuns blocked the intersections, reading.
I used to go walking in the triangle of park,
seeing that locked face, the coarse enemy skin,
the eyes with all the virtues of a good child,
but no child was there, even when I thought, Child!
The 4 a.m. cop could never understand.

You said, not smiling, You are the future for me,
but you were the present and immediate moment
and I am empty-armed without, until to me is given
two lights to carry : my life and the light of my death.

If the wind would rise, those black throbbing umbrellas
fly downstreet, the flapping robes unfolding,
my dream would be over, poisons cannot linger
when the wind rises . . .

All that year, the classical declaration of war was lacking.
There was a lot of lechery and disorder.
And I am queen on that island.

Well, I said suddenly in the tall and abstract room,
time to wake up.
Now make believe you can help yourself alone.
And there it was, the busy crosstown noontime
crossing, peopled with nuns.
                    Now, bragging now,
that flatfoot slambang victory,
                    thanks to a trick of wind
will you see faces blow, and though their bodies
by God's grace will never blow,
cities shake in the wind, the year's over,
calendars tear, and their clothes blow. O yes!

FOR FUN

It was long before the national performance,
preparing for heroes,
carnival-time, time of
political decorations and the tearing of treaties.
Long before the prophecies came true.
For cities also play their brilliant lives.
They have their nightmares. They have their nights of peace.
Senility, wisecracks, tomb, tomb.

Bunting, plaster of Paris whores, electrified unicorns.
Pyramids of mirrors and the winking sphinx,

flower mosaics on the floors of stores,
ballets of massacres. Cut-glass sewers,
red velvet hangings stained the walls of jails,
white lacquer chairs in the abortionists',
boxers, mummies for policemen, wigs
on the meat at the butchers', murderers
eating their last meal under the Arch of Peace.

The unemployed brought all the orange trees,
cypress trees, tubbed rubber-plants, and limes,
conifers, loblolly and the tamaracks,
incongruous flowers to a grove wherein
they sat, making oranges. For in that cold season
fruit was golden could not be guaranteed.

It was long before the riderless horse came streaming
hot to the Square. I walked at noon and saw
that face run screaming through the crowd saying Help
but its mouth would not open and they could not hear.

It was long before the troops entered the city
that I looked up and saw the Floating Man.
Explain yourself I cried at the last. I am
the angel waste, your need which is your guilt,
answered, affliction and a fascist death.

It was long before the city was bombed I saw
fireworks, mirrors, gilt, consumed in flame,
we show this you said the flames, speak it speak it
but I was employed then making straw oranges.
Everything spoke : flames, city, glass, but I
had heavy mystery thrown against the heart.

It was long before the fall of the city.
Ten days before the appearance of the skull.
Five days until the skull showed clean,
and now the entry is prepared.
Carnival's ready.
Let's dance a little before we go home to hell.

CORRESPONDENCES

*. . . the primary purpose here being simply to indicate that,
whatever "free play" there may be in esthetic enterprise, it is held
down by the gravitational pull of historical necessities . . .*

Kenneth Burke, *in* Attitudes toward History

DEMOCRITUS LAUGHED

Democritus laughed when he
saw his whole universe
combined of atoms, and
the gods destroyed—
He killed the ghostly
vengeance deep at the source,
holding bright philosophical sand
up for a threat—
laughing his soldier laughter
with ages of troops after
who grin with reason in
the trenches of
metaphysics, astronomy, disease,
philosophy, the state, and poetry,
the black-and-white war on sin,
the dead wars, the impossible dark wars,
the war on starve, the war on kill, the war on love,
the war on peace.

TREE OF DAYS

I was born in winter when
Europe heard the early guns,
when I was five, the drums
welcomed home the men.

The spring after my birth
a tree came out of the lake,
I laughed, for I could not speak;
the world was there to learn.

The richest season in
the headlines fell as I was ten,
but the crazies were forgotten,
the fine men, the bravest men.

When I had reached fifteen,
that pliant tree was dark,
breadlines haunted the parks—
the books tricked-in that scene.

No work in any town
when I was twenty, cured
the thin and desperate poor
from being forced alone.

Clear to half a brain
in a blind man's head,
war must follow that tide
of running milk and grain.

Now China's long begun,
that tree is dense and strong,
spreading, continuing—
and Austria; and Spain.

If some long unborn friend
looks at photos in pity,
we say, sure we were happy,
but it was not in the wind.

Half my twenties are gone
as the crazies take to the planes,
the fine men, the bravest men,
and the war goes on.

1/26/39

When Barcelona fell, the darkened glass
turned on the world an immense ruinous gaze,
mirror of prophecy in a series of mirrors.
I meet it in all the faces that I see.

Decisions of history the radios reverse;
storm over continents, black rays around the chief,
finished in lightning, the little chaos raves.
I meet it in all the faces that I see.

Inverted year with one prophetic day,
high wind, forgetful cities, and the war,

the terrible time when everyone writes "hope."
I meet it in all the faces that I see.

When Barcelona fell, the cry on the roads
assembled horizons, and the circle of eyes
looked with a lifetime look upon that image,
defeat among us, and war, and prophecy,
I meet it in all the faces that I see.

CORRESPONDENCES

Wars between wars, laughter behind the lines.
Fighting behind the lines. Not children laughing,
but the trench-laughter of the wounded, of radios,
of animal cartoons, the lonely broadcast
on the taxi dashboard, behind the wrecking crew
lit by a naked bulb—to the forgetful bars
prisms and amber shaken with laughter, to the ships at sea.
To the maleficent walls of cities, and an old actress
trying against the trying wind under the skyscrapers,
blind ageing face up, still the look of the lioness,
walking close to the buildings, along the wall,
she licks her lips in panic of loneliness.
She understands the laughter that rides around the streets,
blowing the news to the stone-lands, the swamp-lands, the dust-land,
where omens of war, restless in clouds of dust,
mean dust is never an anachronism
and ruin's news.

The actress knows. Laughter takes up the slack,
changes the fact, narrowing it to nothing,
hardly a thing but silence on a stage.
Crack of laughter. Walls go white, and the plain open note
talks in a houseful of noise. Reply : Now hide!

Over the air, the blindfold answer, the news of force,
the male and hairless hand of fear
in a shiny leather sleeve
armed.

The radiations of harm : black grooves in photographs,
blackness in spokes playing from Hitler's head.
A head with one nightmare.
Expect failure of plans, the floodgates closing,

failure of traffic-control, loss of voice, fog.
Wires dead, defection of your central power-plant.
A code : Laughter. What alphabet are they using?

Many wished for little.
Many asked unity.

We had our characters as we had our cities,
or as a lyric poet has his voices, audible
as separate lives, maturing in poise, and symbols
coming to their "great period," too big to kill,
able to batter at the jetties of hell.

Rites of initiation of our lives:
by filth in childhood,
by wealth in the middle,
by death at the end.
We knew the dear, the enemy, we saw the spy
whisper at ear, the agency suggest,
and where no secrecy and treason were
we saw the novelist, pimp of character,
develop the age so it be understood
to read like his book, a city of the dead.

But the century had its rites, its politics,
machineries whose characters were wars.
Ceremonies of further separation. And now, our backs to brick,
war closes in, calling us to the guns
to make accounting how our time was spent.
And the planes fall. Soon the whole incident is
over, all but the consequences.

Laughter, and childhood; and laughter; and age; or death.
Call to the male puppet, Croak,
and to the female puppet, Shriek,
and turn on me your gun for luck.

Take us our sacrifices, a wish for the living,
this foil of thought, this soil from which we sprang,
fugal music of peace, the promises well-kept,
the big and little diaries of the dead.
The song of occupations and the ghosts,

the historian, pimp of centuries, the general, pimp of wars,
the Floating Man, gentle above the cities,
afraid to touch, a cloud before his head,
laughing the laugh of a man about to be drafted,
the flier, mock–protagonist of his time,
refugees who reserve a final condemnation
and see a richer horror in the sky.

Humor, saliva of terror, will not save the day
or even one moment when the cities are
high in a boneyard where clowns ride up and down
and a night crew works quickly before morning;
while news arrives of the death of others,
laughter of brothers and the brother wars,
works of an age among such characters.

Violent electric night! and the age spiralling past
and the sky turning over, and the wind turning the stars.

NOGUCHI

Since very soon it is required of you.
Even here, on this bed, your face turned up and away,
a strong statue's face turning up and away,
the spangled eye staring live and away.
And the call comes : Open and now obey.

Now it is coming from a roomful of cats,
the dead man on the cot, desert outside,
mesa and goldmine around a tombstone town.
The cat flies shouting from the dead man's mouth.
News of the world : Open and now obey.

Now it is coming during the major climax,
when the brain is suprised and singing only medley.
Or in the meeting. Or at lunch around the rink
with the stranger and the stories of Libyan maneuvers,
horror's imperative the heart obeys.

When they ask you What were you doing at that hour,
When the headlines predicted it What street did you walk down?
When they insist Prove yourself alive that afternoon
It was coming then And everybody saw it
Your life pointed to that That was your world.

I think of effort. Brought us to birth in force.
Noguchi's mother with her scalded child
wedged her awake with splinters in the eyes.
If you are falling fallen failing, force
will suffice, must fix yourself alert.

Sleeping, I saw awake a widened world.
I saw a well full of men's eyes that weep,
wrong ghosts sailing the cities praised our night,
but effort of light comes, overflow morning
waking no weeping, the series of twelve doors
strike shut like clock, but my light will not go;
woke. Love, we'll stay awake until it's healed,
until the time is brought to a fair hour,
obey the heart that calls to prove alive
a love, an age, all soldiers home again,
the growing time a child up and alive,
until the world is done.

SEVENTH AVENUE

This is the cripples' hour on Seventh Avenue
when they emerge, the two o'clock night-walkers,
the cane, the crutch, and the black suit.

Oblique early mirages send the eyes:
light dramatized in puddles, the animal glare
that makes indignity, makes the brute.

Not enough effort in the sky for morning.
No color, pantomime of blackness, landscape
where the third layer back is always phantom.

Here come the fat man, the attractive dog-chested
legless—and the wounded infirm king
with nobody to use him as a saint.

Now they parade in the dark, the cripples' hour
to the drugstore, the bar, the newspaper-stand,
past kissing shadows on a window-shade to

colors of alcohol, reflectors, light.
Wishing for trial to prove their innocence
with one straight simple look:

the look to set this avenue in its colors—
two o'clock on a black street instead of
wounds, mysteries, fables, kings
in a kingdom of cripples.

THE SHORTEST WAY HOME

There was no place on that plain for a city,
no city can break through the blank of the Black Prairie,
its stiff grass tufted grey and aluminum birds;
a province whose design holds fertile seasons,
black earth, basis for growth; travellers whose approach
bends daylight through ghosts, the reasonable dread,
frontier familiar form, through color without water.

There was no place on that prairie for relief,
until the Blue Marl Lands, relics of ancestors
passed us, belted by rocks, the tribal poles;
tourist, we hunt the past as the farmer hunts rain,
as the manic depressive in tired hunt for equilibrium
hunts sleep, swarm up the totems for a view,
see older beds outcropping, dipping seaward and blue.

There was no room on that road for a shadow.
Far off the sand-hills blew, domes over rock salt blowing
echo slant fields in the colors of winter still,
we pass white obelisks of pioneers, the square hero women
and also settlers who control the language,

riding the continent tilting seaward, seeing
the coastal plain stand faithful as a wall.

Down-lying, the drowned valleys, the captured streams, the fall
of barrier beach and hills embayed, the red, the orange,
the chocolate, the sulphur, the cuesta yellow.
Profile of waves, a jaw of sand, surface of breakers,
and there the end of the trip, and the five swimmers
finding, dive like spread hand into the lit water
seaming the ocean with silver. Tantrum of light on water.
The ladies watch whose jewels sparkle as they breathe,
the stander in wet boat, his net flinching with fish,
the city at the lagoon, surfboat and speedcar
see the whole country : Snow Mountain, under which leaps the rose,
the tops of ranges where no lazy are,
through Black, Marl, Salt, to coast-land, vein to vein.

Down-lying, prophetic, the long veins of this land
passing into the sea without a change of slope.
Vein of this land feeding on rest again
eats central freshness, the white implacable root.
Each birth was earned with convulsions, each traveller's birth
spoke its word every time the tilt was changed.
But the ruined mills, but the ghost-towns, but the gaunt adolescent
short-sleeved, torn-trouser, before the final beach!
Pathologies of lightnings turn to prose,
broken and jarring forms to peace.
A fugue of landscapes resolved, the hunt
levelled on equilibrium, that totemic head seeing
a natural sleep, a place for people and peace.

PALOS VERDES CLIFFS

And if the cliffs themselves produced the major illusion.
Cannot without the sun, the flaming instroke
direct and personal, the haystack on the peak.

And if the flashing hay could produce the illusion.
Cannot without the sea beneath and blue

on accurate margin the surfboard boy returned
tiny from the Pacific to a fabulous shore.

And if the seascape could produce the illusion.
Cannot without whole scene : city and oilfield
in metal forests to the hills' mirage,
Hollywood and the high bare brilliant mountains.
Illusion of calm over a minute plain
in steepness opened, an overheated landscape
familiar in movies and recurrent dreams.

O prism of summer and produced illusion:
absolute calm. Past newsreel, print, and view,
vicarious true images, do you see, over the
high-flying plane below you, over the harbor,
over the city, over this precipice,
do you see hot grass, mile-off counties, fire-surfaced sea,
obsessions of sight cliff-hung, as movie, as peace?

PAPER ANNIVERSARY

The concert-hall was crowded the night of the crash
but the wives were away; many mothers gone sick to their beds
or waiting at home for late extras and latest telephone calls
had sent their sons and daughters to hear music instead.

I came late with my father; and as the car flowed stop
I heard the Mozart developing through the door
where the latecomers listened; water-leap, season of coolness,
talisman of relief; but they worried, they did not hear.

Into the hall of formal rows and the straight-sitting seats
(they took out pencils, they muttered at the program's margins)
began the double concerto, Brahms' season of fruit
but they could not meet it with love; they were lost with their fortunes.

In that hall was no love where love was often felt
reaching for music, or for the listener beside:
orchids and violins—precision dances of pencils
rode down the paper as the music rode.

Intermission with its spill of lights found heavy
breathing and failure pushing up the aisles,
or the daughters of failure greeting each other under
the eyes of an old man who has gone mad and fails.

And this to end the cars, the trips abroad, the summer
countries of palmtrees, toy moneys, curt affairs,
ending all music for the evening-dress audience.
Fainting in telephone booth, the broker swears.

"I was cleaned out at Forty—" "No golf tomorrow" "Father!"
but fathers there were none, only a rout of men
stampeded in a flaming circle; and they return
from the telephones and run down the velvet lane

as the lights go down and the Stravinsky explodes
spasms of rockets to levels near delight,
and the lawyer thinks of his ostrich-feather wife
lying alone, and knows it is getting late.

He journeys up the aisle, and as Debussy begins,
drowning the concert-hall, many swim up and out,
distortions of water carry their bodies through
the deformed image of a crippled heart.

The age of the sleepless and the sealed arrives.
The music spent. Hard-breathing, they descend,
wait at the door or at the telephone.
While from the river streams a flaw of wind,

washing our sight; while all the fathers lie
heavy upon their graves, the line of cars progresses
toward the blue park, and the lobby darkens, and we
go home again to the insane governess.

The night is joy, and the music was joy alive,
alive is joy, but it will never be
upon this scene upon these fathers these cars
for the windows already hold photography

of the drowned faces the fat the unemployed—
pressed faces lie upon the million glass

and the sons and daughters turn their startled faces
and see that startled face.

FROM THE DUCK-POND TO
THE CAROUSEL

Playing a phonograph record of a windy morning
you gay   you imitation summer
                let's see you slice up the Park
in green from the lake drawn bright in silver salt
while the little girl playing   (in iodine and pink)
tosses her crumbs and they all rise to catch
lifting up their white and saying Quack.

O you pastoral lighting what are you getting away with?
Wound-up lovers   fidgeting balloons   and a popsicle man
running up the road on the first day of spring.
And the baby carriages whose nurses with flat heels
(for sufferance is the badge of all their tribe)
mark turning sunlight on far avenues
etch beacons on the grass. You strenuous baby
rushing up to the wooden horses
with their stiff necks, their eyes,
and all their music!

Fountains!   sheepfolds!   merry-go-round!
The seal that barking slips Pacifics dark-
diving into his well until up! with a fish!
The tiglon resembling his Siberian sire,
ice-cream and terraces and twelve o'clock.
O mister with the attractive moustache,
        How does it happen to be you?
Mademoiselle   in   cinnamon   zoo,
        Hello,   hello.

ASYLUM SONG

As I went down the road to the water, the river to the sea,
the valley narrowed to a cat's-eye jewel,

one middle streak of highlight straightening;
and nothing was plain in the river-light,
not even what I was hurrying for
as I walked and thought
At the waterfront they are free.

As I went down past the low barren orchards hanging in the dark
(They are free at the waterfront),
I heard the night-bird answer : "The trees suffered too much,
"now they are sterile; but in your city
"the ghosts of houses struggle to put down roots,
"and in the rooms, they have nightmares of freedom,
"they are jealous of any fruit."

As I crossed over Gravelly Run, I looked into the water
(They are free at the waterfront),
not one cloud whitening the brown black water,
but there I saw my face so bare
not blemished but unlit,
I thought, if I am not almost free
there's an end of wit.

As I came toward the sea, I saw the marks of night
walk on and over the sky and night went over
without a sound on the wide water
but the sea's sound and the windspin
talking to ships slave under the sea
and on the sea obsessed with tide
as the long tides came in.

THE VICTIMS, A PLAY FOR THE HOME

And if the curtain lifts, it is a window-shade,
and if there is a stage, it is the room at home.
Furnished as we remember it. Not too well lit.
The wooden chair   the bed quite neatly made.
The face is discovered in shadow, but someone is there.
If we look without fear, we will all know who it is.
This is a theatre and many masks have played
the part; female or male : it will not matter here.

The role is traditional. It does what others did,
if anything is said, it is what others said.

The exits are a window and a door, both shut.
We in the audience know what is in that head,
see only the fixtures of that room, but hear the loud
and ringing world; doorbell, radio, phones, and voices in the hall;
the words in the parents' bedroom; the shot in the street.
The play could be anywhere; the stage could expand. It does not.
Its acts are single actions in the player's head;
watch Act One. Player crosses—hero and bride and clown—
and flings the window up letting the dark shine down,
the black in whom no coward is afraid.

Stares from the window into the audience,
a mirror of the world that stays and stares
and sees the player staring think, dismayed,
of an immense vaudeville of a century
when anyone may sit in a row of chairs
dummy of a ventriloquist who made
a head lying in his hand speak with a candid voice.
The play the player sees is at the margin of the mind.
The player thinks : Who speaks for me? What road
takes me away from here? The door's or window's? Act Two.

The player crosses the room to the desk; looks down.
Letters from friends are clews, the child at the shore,
the oversize girl, and the adolescent swayed
by every attraction. The letters are appeals : We Need.
Come out and help us. We did not remain.
The little boy runs into his green wave,
movies are teaching the slickhaired shortstop love,
the fat girl is seen entering cafeterias
pretending she's pregnant so people will be kind.
They show the player no exit of rescue. Act Three.

Stands at the door, flattened against the wood,
hearing the parents' quarrel, thinking of father
who was the mother's favorite child, the mother
who was the father's favorite daughter, drawing
comfort from the bodies of her children, lowered

resistance in them, told them to love one person
which was impossible : they needed first two parents,
they were lost : there came upon them confusion of sex
and the maternal was male, and the great breast was drawn
forever in remembrance over the stammering mouth.

The player runs to the bed, slaps tired body down.
Act Four. Radio playing Sweet Mystery of Life.
The hands are hidden and the sobbing's hard.
The loyal, the little; and the father is absent,
his feet are on a desk, trucks roll over his heart,
and the mother's hysterics menace the whole house,
resolving nothing. They change; cancers invade them.
The player gets up in hatred, goes to the window, leans
out over the audience, speculates, Should you jump?
Walk down that roomlong road? It will not take you home.
As each step falls, a birth arrives. It is not you.

The sky of the Fifth Act is slant and tall,
sails on its kelson cloud. A champion angel stands,
possibly, on an arch in a spill of gold.
But if it does, it is a statue. The end's prepared.
This victim must come to death as the shade goes down.
The player turns in the middle of the room, and speaks.
"Bargain," shouts to the audience, "bargain, but answer!
"I will tell you what I am if you tell me where you are.
"Not everything that happens happens in the street!
"You are souls riding me, and I'm to be your ghost—
"I have more in me than that! Ticket-taker, their money back!
"I know a way to start!" Laughs, and slams out the door.

M-DAY'S CHILD

M-Day's child is fair of face,
Drill-day's child is full of grace,
Gun-day's child is breastless and blind,
Shell-day's child is out of its mind,
Bomb-day's child will always be dumb,
Cannon-day's child can never quite come,

but the child that's born on the Battle-day
is blithe and bonny and rotted away.

SPEECH FOR THE ASSISTANT, FROM *HOUDINI*
for Marya Zaturenska

And for the man with one nightmare, the student of clouds, the bitter
hero whose silly laurels, kept on his head, confess he knows his Brutus,
the tall political speaker, alone on his platform, the wooden echoes, the batter
words, who wishes he could sail in the middle of the ocean, and never move at all,
for all those who freeze alone in the middle of madness, of sleep, of the better
madness of speed, hands frozen to the frozen steering-wheel, a circuit of cold coming
around through their lives, their current of loneliness, I tell of the single face;
a windowpane, two stains where eyes should stammer;
the head in the barber-chair, nothing behind it but hands;
ghosts, boat-burial, a headless coat on the dancing clothesline.
A shouting single dream of alone,
or the islanded paranoiac insisting
my dear dear dear dear dear dear dear
my dear my dear dear.

The one dream spoken, or the bird more alone,
rising to spill that lake, his music, over
repeated cities whose ragmen crowd the docks
staring at scraps, whose brutes, whose chinless villains
under the flag speak to their crowds
alone, howling; alone, falling; alone and alone among
all the anonymous who work and meet and scatter
and write the criminal words, "Burn this," under the letter.
And the pillars of the cities with their poor against them,
the men in the sky, riding the cylinder hung on hero chains,
the men in the airlock, waiting; in the subway, sitting
at puzzles and headlines, waiting.
And always these figures with the averted face.
Winter advancing, the white, the witless season,
and the spirit waiting.

The cold comes fast, an appetite of air—
earth-eating serpent, my Faust, swallowing

the alone and the falling and the howls of day.
The core is in the head, five-fingered wrong
throws a switch in the head; loneliness, fear,
the deaf indifferent suicide seeking the water,
abnormal batters who will not hit the ball,
magicians imagining rack and oubliette;
the athlete owning his gun; the priest his persecution,
the speaker his curse; the uniform its muscle.
But I remember I am hands and whole,
head, breasts, and white, and to be used.
Only those passed through madness have any sense for us,
whose eyes say I have seen, whose mouths read I have been there.
Alone and waiting cold so long.
Race up, race up, you fiery man.
He does not try; he dares not; or caring, cannot cure.
When song is insecure, again
the solo lark goes mad for song.

JUDITH

This is a dark woman at a telephone
thinking 'brown blood, brown blood' and calling
numbers, saying to her friend, "I will be gone
"a month or two," breaking a weekend saying
"I will be back in a week," in an undertone
to her doctor, "I will take care of the child,
"I may be back within the year," thinking alone
'brown blood' and staring hard at the furniture
remembering the nightmares of a room
she leaves, forever clamped at her breastbone.

This is a woman recalling waters of Babylon,
seeing all charted life as a homicide map
flooded up to the X which marks her life's
threatened last waterline. Safety now for her husband,
no taint—brown blood for him, the naked blond,
the tall and safe. For her, the bottomless ship
inviting to voyage—the sly advertisement,
as the enemy in war invites to luxury:

"Our side has its meat, wine, and cigarettes."
Prediction of no safety for the bone.

This is a woman putting away close pain,
child of a stolid mother whose family runs wild,
abandons fear, abandons legend; while the insane
French peasant is caught, stalking and barking Heil,
fire, anemia, famine, the long smoky madness
a broken century cannot reconcile.
Agons of blood, brown blood, and a dark woman
leaves the blond country with a backward look,
adventures into the royal furious dark
already spread from Kishinev to York.

At the green sources of the Amazon
a bird develops, who repeats his race
whole in a lifetime; hatched with primitive claws
he grows and can absorb them and is grown
to a green prime of feathers. This is known.
A woman sitting at a telephone
repeats her race, hopes for the trap's defence.
Defenders rumored nothing but skeleton.
Applause of news. Suicides reaching for
ritual certainty in their last impatience.

These dragon-surrounded young cannot obtain,
and the white children who become unreal,
live responsive as smoke and travel alone,
wish revocation of fugitives and banned,
know sun-roar, fatal telephones, the hand
palm placing out, the fact wanting its rant.
Cry to the newborn, the youngest in the world
for a new twisting wind to be all winds
to cancel this, rejuvenating rain
to wash it away, forces to fight it down.

A dark-faced woman at a telephone
answered by silence and cruelest dragon-silence;
she knows the weakness of the dim and alone,
compunctive bitter essence of the wound,
the world-spike that is driven through all our hearts.
She will go like a woman sweated from a stone

out from these boundaries, while a running cloud
in that bruised night no bigger than a brain
joins in a cloud-race over the flat of sky
in persecution of the whitened moon.

❧ 2 Lives

[UNTITLED]

The risen image shines, its force escapes, we are all named.
Now that the threads are held; now that the footcuts hold
where these intent finders of tumult climbed
in music or mathematical intensity,
and paint, or fire, or order, found and held,
their achieved spirits gleam. In the dark perfect sky
a hand is risen firm under its crackling globe of flame.
Against the stare it floats, over our agony of street,
repeated eyes, disclosures and closures of walls,
glimpses of centuries until the shining fails.

The faces are normal; the superhuman light saves, kills, and saves;
is mixed, and they fall fighting; and wake to climb the streets
in the vigor of their blood grown changed and abstract,
whose faces begotten of faces crack in their bitterness
light through all faces with the familiar strain
of features that have earned a general grace;
in a fountain of energy shining among the graves
earned human meaning and fantastic flame—
hold pitiless under street-flares colors of night, react,
remain in a passion of daybreak effort when the day arrives.

They are real whereof the ancestors were dreams,
hallucination and loneliness and the creative yoke.
And they may break the eyes to water or ease like starlight in
tormented cities whose shops and savage parks
are the star-chamber of a furious race,
whose warehouses, tenements, equations, song

have risen in complexity among
old portraits, flayed men, skeletons of slaves, and women
with brilliant carriage and averted face
proving a paranoiac rule tricking to death its children.

But there are more in the scheme : the many-born
charging our latest moment with their wave,
a shaking sphere whose center names us all as core,
risen among the timid and the torn
toward the sun-cities which the brain has known
whose moment of proof races through time to live.
These faces have risen, destroyed, found and still find
antagonisms of life, the dreamed and half-known world,
awakened forms among the profuse creative
promises of the mind.

GIBBS

It was much later in his life he rose
in the professors' room, the frail bones rising
among that fume of mathematical meaning,
symbols, the language of symbols, literature . . . threw
air, simple life, in the dead lungs of their meeting,
said, "Mathematics *is* a language."

Withdrew. Into a silent world beyond New Haven,
the street-fights gone, the long youth of undergraduate
riots down Church Street, initiation violence,
secret societies gone : a broken-glass isolation,
bottles smashed flat, windows out, street-fronts broken :

                                    to quiet,
the little portico, wrought-iron and shutters' house.
A usable town, a usable tradition.
                                    In war or politics.
Not science.
                    Withdrew.
                                    Civil War generates, but

Not here. Tutors Latin after his doctorate
when all of Yale is disappearing south.

There is no disorganization, for there is no passion.
Condense, he is thinking.   Concentrate, restrict.
This is the state permits the whole to stand,
the whole which is simpler than any of its parts.
And the mortars fired, the tent-lines, lines of trains,
earthworks, breastworks of war, field-hospitals,
Whitman forever saying, "Identify."
Gibbs saying
                    "I wish to know systems."

To be in this work. Prepare an apocryphal
cool life in which nothing is not discovery
and all is given, levelly, after clearest
most disciplined research.
                              The German years
of voyage, calmer than Kant in Koenigsberg, to states
where laws are passed and truth's a daylight gift.

Return to a house inheriting Julia's keys,
sister receiving all the gifts of the world,
white papers on your desk.
                              Spiritual gift
she never took.
                    Books of discovery,
haunted by steam, ghost of the disembodied engine,
industrialists in their imperious designs
made flower an age to be driven far by this
serene impartial acumen.
                              Years of driving
his sister's coach in the city, knowing the
rose of direction loosing its petals down
atoms and galaxies.   Diffusion's absolute.
Phases of matter!   The shouldering horses pass
turnings (snow, water, steam) echoing plotted curves,
statues of diagrams, the forms of schemes
to stand white on a table, real as phase,
or as the mountainous summer curves when he
under New Hampshire lay while shouldering night
came down upon him then with all its stars.

Gearing that power-spire to the wide air.
Exacting symbols of rediscovered worlds.

Through evening New Haven drove. The yellow window
of Sloane Lab all night shone.

Shining an image whole, as a streak of brightness
bland on the quartz, light-blade on Iceland spar
doubled! and the refraction carrying fresh clews.
Withdrew.
          It will be an age of experiment,
or mysticism, anyway vastest assumption.
He makes no experiments.   Impregnable retires.
Anyone having these desires will make these researches.
Laws are the gifts of their systems, and the man
in constant tension of experience drives
moments of coexistence into light.
It is the constitution of matter I must touch.

Deduction from deduction : entropy,
heat flowing down a gradient of nature,
perpetual glacier driving down the side
of the known world in an equilibrium tending
to uniformity, the single dream.
               He binds
himself to know the public life of systems.
Look through the wounds of law
at the composite face of the world.

        If Scott had known,
he would not die at the Pole, he would have been
saved, and again saved—here, gifts from overseas,
and grapes in January past Faustus' grasp.
Austerity, continence, veracity, the full truth flowing
not out from the beginning and the base,
but from accords of components whose end is truth.
Thought resting on these laws enough becomes
an image of the world, restraint among
breaks manacles, breaks the known life before
Gibbs' pale and steady eyes.

He knew the composite
many-dimensioned spirit, the phases of its face,
found the tremendous level of the world,
Energy : Constant, but entropy, the spending,
tends toward a maximum—a "mixed-up-ness,"
and in this end of levels to which we drive
in isolation, to which all systems tend,
Withdraw, he said clearly.

The soul says to the self : I will withdraw,
the self saying to the soul : I will withdraw,
and soon they are asleep together
spiralling through one dream.

                              Withdrew, but in
his eager imperfect timidities, rose and dared
sever waterspouts, bring the great changing world
time makes more random, into its unity.

RYDER

Call himself unbegun, for the sea made him;   assemblages of waters
                    gave him his color.
But not the sea; coast-line, coast-water, rising sfumato from smoke-
                    holes of the sea,
pitching onto the black rock of the ocean-edge.   But not the coast-
                    line;
the Atlantic coast, flinging him headlong from its rigors into his art.
Great salt-swept boldface captain, big-boned New Englander
                    drowning deep
among the mysteries of the painful western adventure, circling
in unappeased circles into America.

Tempests, phantasmagoria!   Impervious, first of all
to paint the tragic landscape that breeds us here,
the deep life, the terrible foreboding whose soil
is in our mind, the imagination of this geography.
Whose whaling port acknowledges the fearful
content of evil and the swift-lit blessed light,
Melville's 'latent horror of life' in the whale water

that Ryder, whose racecourse with its big horse Death
runs round the brain, knew.
                              In his room
wreckage of boxes, propped-leg, easel, couch, ashes, coal-keg, shells,
bronzed tarnished coffee-pot, books, paints, piled broken furniture,
varnish drippings, matches, cans, newspapers stacked up,
plaster falling with a scurrying like mice, paper bannering from the
                walls,
the stains, the path cleared to the stuffed chair crammed with poems,
money, checks, poems, the bathtub filled with clothes—
the unseen room, after a moment there.
He stood
              laying the paint on
                              stacking color on,
more pigment, dark and stormy, thickness, depth, more black, stove-
                ashes maybe,
and at the last slashed poker through the cloth, a knife of lightning,
                white as space, leaping white! out of darkness!
Out black night leaping, rider to flame.

He walks through the rainy streets, the great grey sweater;
fog walking through rain, wool worn on his giant head,
his giant beard stowed in the collar.   Walks black pavement.
Is seen on corners beaten by storms of night.
He gives a painting to the tubercular seamstress
"to look at while she lives," talks poetry
and philosophy to the woman at the newsstand.
He believes with his eye, he lives in the foreboding
empty tempests of the mind, thunder revolving
among his blackest noons; remembers voyages
to fabulous harbors whose event was sea.

He looks through the plateglass window at his formal dinner,
turns down the street, "I have been there," looks through glass
at formal painting, inch by inch, reaching the corner
stands back, "That's a fine place." And moves away
to mystic reconciliations, feeling the world enlarge
and never complete itself, a bone riding a horse
around a track, dead angels from the sea resurrected
to lend a metaphor of waves, to sound the abstract
Jonah who rolls under a pitch of ocean,

knows God with his arms up among the teeth of waves,
the moon stark in the sky as a center of whirlpool.
All these invoke the image, a sea-belief in the sea
whose waters open swallow the army whole and save the tribe.

He is your irresponsible pioneer. He is deprived. Fearful of sex.
        Desire, God's blossoming rod
points to assemblages of waters, heroes Macbeth kneedeep,
the foggy Dutchman riding, salt eyelids see
the fall of waters, the distinction and power, the shock,
the helplessness immanent in things.
Ghosts of oxen, stiff-grappled claws of a dead bird,
romantic wish that mourns from an Opera seat
over the spotlit love, wishes housekeeper love,
Elaine of wish, bends over an empty big suit of armor,
over the giant fallen bones of the dead horse.

Historic disherison : Ryder, emblematist,
divorced from the arts, believing in art alone,
master of meaning and never mastering means,
wasteful and slow, without tradition.   He shortens
the life of his paintings in their friable colors
by ignorance, by storms.   Refusing the dead life
like a nest of tables whose next is always smaller
refined and congruent, slashes American sky
by derelict lightning, turning all landscape into
sublunar ocean.   He is chained under water,
chained under rain, under paint, no hold on daylight,
his fixed moon stares into a tragic coast
whose people are little figures pasted on.
"Not you," he cries, "the human document."
These are not paintings for comfort hung on walls.
Paint over it, paint.   It is a monument
cracking and supernatural, an obelisk at the sea,
three sides shadowed with names, the sea-slab empty.
A big-boned charging figure under rain
seen by the visionary moon and dark,
unbegun among assemblages of waves.
His head that was moon the center of the storm.
His boulders that were eyes washed by the drift of ocean.

CHAPMAN

Returns to punishment as we all return, in agonized initiation proving America,
a country returning to moments of conversion, in agony supporting its changes,
    receiving
the past, the clews of instinct, and the rich return:
conviction in our people's face, all in pain.
He dances in Boston, the young and turning side
turned to a room of marvellous skirts whose rustle
like burning paper alters, rustling black to flame.
He looks across all rooms to a sibyl-minded woman
the dark   the clew to life   whose afternoons
he shares through Dante's climbing Paradise
to break his youth, the handsome turning side
dancing and turning again to her dark head
in rings of darkness whose God is ringed in light
which coils and revolves around him—
in the smoky garden
after the word was spoken
the blow to the rival's smoky head echoing in the hand
ringed round with darkness;
dark passages through streets unknown; and now, at home,
he sees his braced arm, ringing with the shock,
given before him to the ringing fire.
Blaze of hard-coal.   Disapparition of flesh.
He draws his hand out of flame; charred to the bone,
white knuckles and finger-bones exposed.
His soul rises screaming in the shape of an eagle.
He says, quietly and exactly, "This will never do."

"The one time in my life I lived was twenty days of pain."
And later, after the healing, after the marriage,
alone among red desert, the wild bushes' grey-green,
the red buttes cancelling half the sky, he writes
"It was not waste land in Colorado.   Not waste time, for
you are here and many lives packed into one life,
the green shoot out of the heart of the plant, springing up blossoms in the night;
many old things have put on immortality,
and lost things have come back knocking within
from before the time I was conceived in the womb,
there were you also.
And of the pain! it was false,

and the rending, unnecessary.
The breaking down of dams that ought never be up,
but being up it was the sweeping away
that the waters might flow together."

The life all burning on the public hill,
the men living tramort, travelling through their deaths,
arrive with marks by which they know one another
at the center of systems.   By a breach of childhood
symptoms of health declare all the signs leading through,
until the crisis comes,
air seethes, and all the bushes flicker up,
memories parasite in the life underground
irrupt with convulsions and the speech of fire.

At the focus, the cool life is insufficient.
He knows his conversion.   He speaks of Whitman as tramp:
"By an act as simple as death, he puts off effort and lives in peace."
Knowing by what redemption he claims his house,
he stands on the balcony of a burning building.

The ghosts come near the blood.   Sits at the bedside reading
to the dropped quiet head, Dante and fire and coexistent death
at his wife's bedside.
Fire, rage, splendor;   and terror
who judges the judgment of men.
He is broken, his face is broken back,
his spirit's legs are broken, crutches hold him,
a second wife holds him while he becomes
incredible to himself, fulgurite fused by lightning,
health shaking its flag of death in his frenetic head.
Death of his son, and he heals, he is born again,
fed on his agonies, wanting again
his gritty taste of truth.

There are those who are many-born.   There is the man
who will plunge his hand in the fire this evening, who goes out every day
seeing Prometheus in mirrors, finding
comets, men of the people, conscious, who take their place
in national revulsion producing a nation's poems,
belong to the present, are not sterilized
by breaks from the past.

He fights for the acute senses, terror, passion, and need.
"I make it a policy to say nothing I will not regret."
Speaks from a cart-end, manhandles his hecklers,
knows the struggles of treason making it easy for death
to arrive when the living have passed the perfection of youth.

The century bursts upward in shocks of flame,
fireworks' starfish of imperial spirit,
ordeals by fire : he fights the finished wars,
looks back to slavery.   They burn the shingles down,
the lynched face broken back, mouth filled with fire,
firebrand full in face.   The ashes rise.
Chapman arrives to face his empty hall,
courtly, one-handed, turning his handsome side
upon the hall to face his audience,
one Negro woman come to hear. Undoings
walking in all forms, treacheries of the deep
spirit caught in the net.   Our need is of new life.
There are these tendencies in America:
they planned John Brown;   they do what will be done.

Birth after birth, in the spanned democratic
passage of birth, the incubation motive,
desire's experience, tense for finality.
He is reborn too often;   the shock cannot take.
He loosens;   fights for war;   fights Harvard's plans:
a stone for both sides—he rants, upholstered deep
in Harvard Club armchairs—a monument to Zero.
He is charred out, is calling vengeance on Jews,
he is old and charred.   He has been many-born.
Blinks in the fire-world, sees started birds
blinked red and black, the wing a dark log burning
against the sun;   flashes of cypress and swamps,
a watery forest of red birds.
Goes down
his altering ash smothers the shock of peace,
he carried flame
but selling-out is not a dramatic moment,
it is the chain of memories parasite,
the thin flame of existence travelling down
until the yellow and alizarin red
flares out.   The whole of any life, he said,

is always unmistakably one thing.
And a dream-voice said Freiheit
a crackling globe flew down
fire and punishment, returning grace;
vortex of parable through modes of life
simple and imperceptible transitions
in countries of transition giving other lives
the long remorseless logic of their love.

ANN BURLAK

Let her be seen, a voice on a platform, heard
as a city is heard in its prophetic sleep when
one shadow hangs over one side of a total wall
of houses, factories, stacks, and on the faces
around her tallies, shadow from one form.

An open square shields the voice, reflecting it
to faces who receive its reflections of light as
change on their features. She stands alone, sending
her voice out to the edges, seeing approach people
to make the ring ragged, to fill in blacker
answers.
    This is an open square of the lit world
whose dark sky over hills rimmed white with evening
squares lofts where sunset lies in dirty patterns
and rivers of mill-towns beating their broken bridges
as under another country full of air.
Dark offices evening reaches where letters take the light
even from palest faces over script.
Many abandon machines, shut off the looms,
hurry on glooming cobbles to the square. And many
are absent, as in the sky about her face, the birds
retreat from charcoal rivers and fly far.

The words cluster about the superstition mountains.
The sky breaks back over the torn and timid
her early city whose stacks along the river
flourished darkness over all, whose mottled sky

shielded the faces of those asleep in doorways
spread dark on narrow fields through which the father
comes home without meat, the forest in the ground
whose trees are coal, the lurching roads of autumn
where the flesh of the eager hangs, heavier by
its thirty bullets, barbed on wire. Truckdrivers
swing ungrazed trailers past, the woman in the fog
can never speak her poems of unemployment,
the brakeman slows the last freight round the curve.
And riveters in their hardshell fling short fiery
steel, and the servant groans in his narrow room,
and the girl limps away from the door of the shady doctor.
Or the child new-born into a company town
whose life can be seen at birth as child, woman, widow.
The neighbor called in to nurse the baby of a spy,
the schoolboy washing off the painted word
"scab" on the front stoop, his mother watering flowers
pouring the milk-bottle of water from the ledge,
who stops in horror, seeing. The grandmother going
down to her cellar with a full clothes-basket,
turns at the shot, sees men running past brick,
smoke-spurt and fallen face.

       She speaks of these:
the chase down through the canal, the filling-station,
stones through the windshield. The woman in the bank
who topples, the premature birth brought on by tear-gas,
the charge leaving its gun slow-motion, finding those
who sit at windows knowing what they see;
who look up at the door, the brutalized face appraising
strangers with holsters; little blackened boys
with their animal grins, quick hands salvaging coal
among the slag of patriotic hills.

She knows the field of faces at her feet,
remembrances of childhood, likenesses of parents,
a system of looms in constellation whirled,
disasters dancing.
      And behind her head
the world of the unpossessed, steel mills in snow flaming,
nine o'clock towns whose deputies' overnight power
hurls waste into killed eyes, whose guns predict

mirages of order, an empty coat before the blind.
Doorways within which nobody is at home.
The spies who wait for the spy at the deserted crossing,
a little dead since they are going to kill.
Those women who stitch their lives to their machines
and daughters at the symmetry of looms.

She speaks to the ten greatest American women:
The anonymous farmer's wife, the anonymous clubbed picket,
the anonymous Negro woman who held off the guns,
the anonymous prisoner, anonymous cotton-picker
trailing her robe of sack in a proud train,
anonymous writer of these and mill-hand, anonymous city walker,
anonymous organizer, anonymous binder of the illegally wounded,
anonymous feeder and speaker to anonymous squares.

She knows their faces, their impatient songs
of passionate grief risen, the desperate music
poverty makes, she knows women cut down
by poverty, by stupid obscure days,
their moments over the dishes, speaks them now,
wrecks with the whole necessity of the past
behind the debris, behind the ordinary
smell of coffee, the ravelling clean wash,
the turning to bed, undone among savage night
planning and unplanning seasons of happiness
broken in dreams or in the jaundiced morning
over a tub or over a loom or over
the tired face of death.
                              She knows
the songs : *Hope to die, Mo I try, I comes out,*
Owin boss mo, I comes out, Lawd, Owin boss mo
food, money and life.
                    Praise breakers,
praise the unpraised who cannot speak their name.
Their asking what they need as unbelieved
as a statue talking to a skeleton.
They are the animals who devour their mother
from need, and they know in their bodies other places,
their minds are cities whose avenues are named
each after a foreign city. They fall when cities fall.

They have the cruelty and sympathy of those
whose texture is the stress of existence woven
into revenge, the crime we all must claim.
They hold the old world in their new world's arms.
And they are the victims, all the splinters of war
run through their eyes, their black escaping face
and runaway eyes are the Negro in the subway
whose shadowy detective brings his stick
down on the naked head as the express pulls in,
swinging in locomotive roars on skull.
They are the question to the ambassador
long-jawed and grim, they stand on marble, waiting
to ask how the terms of the strike have affected him.
Answer : "I've never seen snow before. It's marvellous."
They stand with Ann Burlak in the rotunda, knowing
her insistent promise of life, remembering
the letter of the tear-gas salesman :"I hope
"this strike develops and a damn bad one too.
"We need the money."
                              This is the boundary
behind a speaker : Main Street and railroad tracks,
post office, furniture store. The soft moment before storm.
Since there are many years.
And the first years were the years of need,
the bleeding, the dragged foot, the wilderness,
and the second years were the years of bread
fat cow, square house, favorite work,
and the third years are the years of death.
The glittering eye all golden. Full of tears.
Years when the enemy is in our street,
and liberty, safe in the people's hands,
is never safe and peace is never safe.

Insults of attack arrive, insults
of mutilation. She knows the prophetic past,
many have marched behind her, and she knows
Rosa whose face drifts in the black canal,
the superstitions of a tragic winter
when children, their heads together, put on tears.
The tears fall at their throats, their chains are made
of tears, and as bullets melted and as bombs let down
upon the ominous cities where she stands

fluid and conscious. Suddenly perceives
the world will never daily prove her words,
but her words live, they issue from this life.
She scatters clews. She speaks from all these faces
and from the center of a system of lives
who speak the desire of worlds moving unmade
saying, "Who owns the world?" and waiting for the cry.

IVES

Knowing the voices of the country, gathering
voices of other harvests, farm-hands who gather in
sources of music on the blueberry hills,
the village band, lines at the schoolhouse singing—
lit cheeks and lips over the blown-glass lamps
in the broad houses, along the pebble beach,
or up the baldface mountain's granite sky
above New England, voices of wilderness,
scorch of the sun where ranges all run west,
snow-glare on seaward slopes, sea-breeze and tea,
the voices of stinted music in the towns.
There are strange herbs in the pasture, and the stiff
death angels on the red assyrian stones.
Daguerreotypes and family quiet, wells,
woodwork and panelling, the cloaks of the forest,
all the blinds drawn on the imagination's
immediate mystery of the passer-by.
Intense as instruments to split these sounds
into component memory, and reduce
memory to uncompromising sound.

To whom do I speak today?   I've heard their oarlocks turning
at dawn on the river, in the warm bankside light
heard cut trees fall, hickory pull the head
toward violent foreground laughter of torn wood,
watched steeples diminishing in low day before sunset,
and found the evening train riding the bend.
That train will never speak again of tracks
routed to outland counties, but the firm

sumac and corn, broadleaf tobacco farms,
a churchyard murmur for the air of truth,
acres where birds I did not know till now
fly sharp-reflected in water, a field of sky;
over the human lake, the gods make the swallows fly.

To whom do I speak today?   Call off your wit and write
for silent implicated men, a crabbed line
of intercepted music with the world between.
Networks of songs, white seagull in white air,
cliff edge and stripe of sand's immovable gulls
hung over women's morning festivals.
Affection of villages whose boy guitarist,
blond, with his rolled sleeve and the girl behind
sings into fire-darkness goodbye after pleasure
and the streets, our liberty, the village store,
songs of the sorrow and mystery of pavilions'
slow carousel-music, bulbs and mirrors in sunlight,
processions of godly animals revolving;
or big October mornings, cider and perry noon
when the child comes open-mouth round the corner singing;
that music of the imagination here
which is the only sound lives after war.

Acoustics of sideshows! and the organist
playing the mirror of the mind again.
Concord whose choice between repose and truth
colors our memory, whose outer islands of thought
are fugal movements in one dignity.
Rebellion of outposts whose deepest results arrive
when the rebellion, not from worst to greatest,
but great to greater goes. The sequent movements
of that developing know supernatural
Hawthorne as dripping wet with guilt, a ghost
personal at first, and national at twilight,
and tries to be universal suddenly at midnight;
know in their pace the supernatural future
and the future of human coarseness, and Emerson's
future, eternity, whose forecast is the past,
and Alcott's suffering, whipping his innocent
boy next to the guilty, since guilt need not suffer;
and Thoreau who did not die of his consumption

but lived with it.
                    Raise us an instrument
limitless, without the scarecrow keyboard
can give repose and fame to successful painists
playing to camouflage dullness.   A scale for truth,
obscurities of a village organist
who satisfies his life on Sunday.

                              Songs.
Young men singing on stoops, the sickle pears of Concord,
the wheels scraping the curb, lockets of childhood
faith, barn dances, ballads; or those revealing men
I gave a mask, and they to me the secrets
of sensual thought, music and thunderbolt.
The concentrated man bent over drums,
a skeleton over drums, a fritter of triangles
played without aim, spasms of arabesques
in decoration of nothing.   I speak a flute over frost,
hypnotisms of trumpets, the plain and open voice
of the walk toward the future, commonplace transcendent
chores and melodeons, band-concert morning
or the ultimate Negro over his white piano
meaning O Saint!   O Blues!

                    This is Charles Ives.
Gold-lettered insurance windows frame his day.
He is eclectic, he sorts tunes like potatoes
for better next-year crops, catching the variable
wildest improvisations, his clusters of meaning;
railing against the fake sonorities, "sadness
"of a bathtub when the water is being let out,"
knowing the local hope knocking in any blood.
"Today we do not choose To die or to dance,
"but to live and walk."
                    Inventor, beginner of strong
coherent substance of music, knowing all
apple-reflecting streams, loons across echoing lake,
cities and men, as liners aloof in voyage,
and their dead eyes, so much blue in the ground
as water, as running song he loves and pours
as water into water, music in music.
                              Walks

at starfall or under the yellow dragons of sunset
among the ritual answers and the secular wish,
among spruce, and maroon of fallen needles, walks
the pauper light of dawn imagining truth,
turning from recommended madness, from Europe
who must be forced to eat what she kills, from cities
where all the throats are playing the same tune
mechanically.

He was young.   He did not climb
four flights on hands and knees to the piano. Heard
the band in the square, Jerusalem the Golden
from all the rooftops, blare of foreground horns,
violins past the common;   in the street
the oral dissonance, the drum's array.
Far breaking music indistinct with wheels'
irregular talk, the moving world, the real
personal disagreement of many voices;
clusters of meaning break in fantastic flame,
silver of instruments rising behind the eye.

He gathers the known world total into music,
passion of sense, perspective's mask of light
into suggestion's inarticulate
gesture, invention.   Knowing the voices, knowing
these faces and music and this breeding landscape
balanced between the crisis and the cold
which bears the many-born, he parcels silence
into a music which submerges prayer,
rising as rivers of faces overhead,
naming the instruments we all must hold.

Wake Island

1942

1

PROOF OF AMERICA! A fire on the sea,
a tower of flame rising, flame falling out of the sky,
a wave of flame like a great sea-wave breaking
over this fighting island in its rain of wounds—
fighting until the flames grew tall, fighting while waves
broke and the enemy landed on each wave;
fighting as if they were the fist of the world
and they had a world to save.

⚬

Their backs to the immense cloud-melting sea
empty of help, and the enemy eyes were close,
and deadly close; they saw those fatal eyes
and a flag striped on the night in fire and stars.
The radio spoke its word: "The issue is in doubt,"
that word went flying out.

⚬

We built this island flashing in the sea,
younger than the children of these men.
In the cloud country, among the breathless calm
Wake was built for a link.
            Eyes of the plane look down,
find a green footprint in the unmarked sea.

⚬

Eyes of the plane sight the lagoon at Wake.
There was another look on Christmas Week
when every fighting man looked in his neighbor's eyes
and found more will to fight.

⚬

There are two looks in the world: the plane's gaze down
on a scene of unrolled sea and open land
as it becomes a single map of space.
There is the close look of a fighting face
when the earth screams and fire falls from the air
and those fighting together look at each other's lives
and wish, in that moment of proof, more life for the world
and stand their ground.

2

These are the brave of our time, who in
        a new-found world
stand where the morning lights them and the war,
throw bravery into the sky while their planes hold,
read challenge on the sea, the word Surrender
shining on smoking water, and fire at the word
as long as their guns load.

           ❧

Fight on the beaches in the bloody fighting
as long as their bodies last. And then they send their word
into the war that closes on the world.
They fought at this island for the air we breathe;
one war, one enemy seething at the beach.

           ❧

Without their hills underfoot, not holding the fields
        of home,
not fighting for land or their streets or the voice
        of American evening
filling through treetops and into the lighted doorway,
not for the trumpets and the recruiting kiss
or the most loved caress, did they look down
        at their flesh,
see in surprise the sudden wound opening.

           ❧

Not flesh, not roses, not our Indian summer,
the sea-surf at our shores, the flashing cities,
the multiple Mississippi, the little secret lakes—
prairie in green winds of spring, smell of
        our mountain snow,
the radio word of promise in our sky.

3

This battle is not finished. They shouted and went down
in the sky, in the flaming water, on the unknown sand.
They did not hear our millions as they fell

who follow the proof of the brave, that the world
       is one world,
who set our lives and bodies at the sea
between the future and the enemy.

      ❧

The world's the only island, and our men
and women fight one war; it will be won again.
They were never cut off from us. We were cut off
       from them.
This is our age's discovery; sailing fathers
knew an impossible continent of promise
existed past danger and named in America.
We know the world is one; we name it Freedom.

      ❧

O many-memoried America!
This island may be set among your stars;
planted in freedom, deep in a war for life,
that war will never rest among the dead,
the war belongs to the living of the world.
Shadows of our loss darken the land,
under their night new armies form and stand.

      ❧

Impossible courage that finds impossible chance,
America planted in a sea of war,
free as our hope is free over all mountains
flying, and looking down; and our eyes looking
directly into the eyes of all the brave
under a night striped with our fire and stars
until the war's first weapon is liberty,
and there is no slaveholder and no slave,
not even in the mind; but only the free.

      ❧

Proof of America in a fighting age—
we see the face of the world, and its eyes are brave,
the men and women we stand with fight to save
our hope, our discovery, our unappeasable rage
against the enemy cutting us apart.

      ❧

The future rises from the fighting heart
to fly over the world, riding where cities fall,

where the brave stand again, where voices call
to us to take their proof, proof of a world to win,
proof of America to lift the soul—
fighting to prove us whole.

Beast in View

1944

All, all of a piece throughout;
Thy chase had a beast in view;
Thy wars brought nothing about;
Thy lovers were all untrue.
'Tis well an old age is out,
And time to begin a new.

   John Dryden

ONE SOLDIER

When I think of him, midnight
Opens about me, and I am more alone;
But then the poems flower from the bone.—

You came to me bearing the truth in your two hands;
I sit and look down at my hand like an astonished
Fortune-teller, seeing the mortal flesh.

Your wish was strong the first day of the war
For it had been strong before, and then we knew
All that I had to be, you had to do.

Once when you stood before me, kisses rose
About my lips; poems at my lips rise,
Your live belief fills midnight and my eyes.

❧ I Beast in View

AJANTA

1 THE JOURNEY

Came in my full youth to the midnight cave
Nerves ringing; and this thing I did alone.
Wanting my fulness and not a field of war,
For the world considered annihilation, a star
Called Wormwood rose and flickered, shattering
Bent light over the dead boiling up in the ground,
The biting yellow of their corrupted lives
Streaming to war, denying all our words.
Nothing was left among the tainted weather
But world-walking and shadowless Ajanta.
Hallucination and the metal laugh
In clouds, and the mountain-spectre riding storm.
Nothing was certain but a moment of peace,
A hollow behind the unbreakable waterfall.

All the way to the cave, the teeming forms of death,
And death, the price of the body, cheap as air.
I blessed my heart on the expiation journey
For it had never been unable to suffer:
When I met the man whose face looked like the future,
When I met the whore with the dying red hair,
The child myself who is my murderer.
So came I between heaven and my grave
Past the serene smile of the *voyeur,* to
This cave where the myth enters the heart again.

2 THE CAVE

Space to the mind, the painted cave of dream.
This is not a womb, nothing but good emerges:
This is a stage, neither unreal nor real,
Where the walls are the world, the rocks and palaces
Stand on a borderland of blossoming ground.
If you stretch your hand, you touch the slope of the world
Reaching in interlaced gods, animals, and men.
There is no background.   The figures hold their peace
In a web of movement.   There is no frustration,
Every gesture is taken, everything yields connections.
The heavy sensual shoulders, the thighs, the blood-born flesh
And earth turning into color, rocks into their crystals,
Water to sound, fire to form; life flickers
Uncounted into the supple arms of love.
The space of these walls is the body's living space;
Tear open your ribs and breathe the color of time
Where nothing leads away, the world comes forward
In flaming sequences.   Pillars and prisms.   Riders
And horses and the figures of consciousness,
Red cow grows long, goes running through the world.
Flung into movement in carnal purity,
These bodies are sealed—warm lip and crystal hand
In a jungle of light.   Color-sheeted, seductive
Foreboding eyelid lowered on the long eye,
Fluid and vulnerable.   The spaces of the body
Are suddenly limitless, and riding flesh
Shapes constellations over the golden breast,
Confusion of scents and illuminated touch—
Monster touch, the throat printed with brightness,
Wide outlined gesture where the bodies ride.

Bells, and the spirit flashing.   The religious bells,
Bronze under the sunlight like breasts ringing,
Bronze in the closed air, the memory of walls,
Great sensual shoulders in the web of time.

3 LES TENDRESSES BESTIALES

A procession of caresses alters the ancient sky
Until new constellations are the body shining:
There's the Hand to steer by, there the horizon Breast,
And the Great Stars kindling the fluid hill.
All the rooms open into magical boxes,
Nothing is tilted, everything flickers
Sexual and exquisite.
The panther with its throat along my arm
Turns black and flows away.
Deep in all streets passes a faceless whore
And the checkered men are whispering one word.
The face I know becomes the night-black rose.
The sharp face is now an electric fan
And says one word to me.
The dice and the alcohol and the destruction
Have drunk themselves and cast.
Broken bottle of loss, and the glass
Turned bloody into the face.
Now the scene comes forward, very clear.
Dream-singing, airborne, surrenders the recalled,
The gesture arrives riding over the breast,
Singing, singing, tender atrocity,
The silver derelict wearing fur and claws.
O love, I stood under the apple branch,
I saw the whipped bay and the small dark islands,
And night sailing the river and the foghorn's word.
My life said to you: I want to love you well.
The wheel goes back and I shall live again,
But the wave turns, my birth arrives and spills
Over my breast the world bearing my grave,
And your eyes open in earth.   You touched my life.
My life reaches the skin, moves under your smile,
And your throat and your shoulders and your face and your thighs
Flash.
              I am haunted by interrupted acts,
Introspective as a leper, enchanted

By a repulsive clew,
A gross and fugitive movement of the limbs.
Is this the love that shook the lights to flame?
Sheeted avenues thrash in the wind,
Torn streets, the savage parks.
I am plunged deep.   Must find the midnight cave.

4 BLACK BLOOD

A habit leading to murder, smoky laughter
Hated at first, but necessary later.
Alteration of motives.   To stamp in terror
Around the deserted harbor, down the hill
Until the woman laced into a harp
Screams and screams and the great clock strikes,
Swinging its giant figures past the face.
The Floating Man rides on the ragged sunset
Asking and asking.   Do not say, Which loved?
Which was beloved? Only, Who most enjoyed?
Armored ghost of rage, screaming and powerless.
Only find me and touch my blood again.
Find me.   A girl runs down the street
Singing Take me, yelling Take me Take
Hang me from the clapper of a bell
And you as hangman ring it sweet tonight,
For nothing clean in me is more than cloud
Unless you call it.   —As I ran I heard
A black voice beating among all that blood:
"Try to live as if there were a God."

5 THE BROKEN WORLD

Came to Ajanta cave, the painted space of the breast,
The real world where everything is complete,
There are no shadows, the forms of incompleteness.
The great cloak blows in the light, rider and horse arrive,
The shoulders turn and every gift is made.
No shadows fall.   There is no source of distortion.
In our world, a tree casts the shadow of a woman,
A man the shadow of a phallus, a hand raised
The shadow of the whip.
Here everything is itself,
Here all may stand
On summer earth.

Brightness has overtaken every light,
And every myth netted itself in flesh.
New origins, and peace given entire
And the spirit alive.
In the shadowless cave
The naked arm is raised.

Animals arrive,
Interlaced, and gods
Interlaced, and men
Flame-woven.
I stand and am complete.
Crawls from the door,
Black at my two feet
The shadow of the world.

World, not yet one,
Enters the heart again.
The naked world, and the old noise of tears,
The fear, the expiation and the love,
A world of the shadowed and alone.

The journey, and the struggles of the moon.

MORTAL GIRL

The girl being chosen stood in her naked room
Singing at last alone naked and proud
Now that the god had departed and his doom
Guarded her door forever and the sky
Would flame in trophies all night and every day.

Sang: When your white sun stood still, I put away
My garments and my crafts and you came down.
When you took me as a flame, I turned to flame;
In whiteness I lay on the mist-flower river-bank
When you as a swan arrived, and cloudy in my tower
For you as a shower of gold, the lily bright in my hand
Once, you as unthinkable light.

                              Make me more human,
Give me the consciousness
Of every natural shape, to lie here ready
For love as every power.
I wait in all my hopes,
Poet beast and woman,
Wait for the superhuman,
The god who invaded the gold lady,
The god who spoke to the naked princess,
The storm over the fiery wanderer.

Within me your city burning, and your desperate tree.
All that the song and the apparition gave
To seal my mouth with fire, make me mad
With song and pain and waiting, leave me free
In all my own shapes, deep in the spirit's cave
To sing again the entrance of the god.

CHILD IN THE GREAT WOOD

It is all much worse than I dreamed.
The trees are all here,
Trunk, limb, and leaf,
Nothing beyond belief
In danger's atmosphere
And the underbrush is cursed.
But the animals,
Some are as I have dreamed,
Appear and do their worst
Until more animals
With recognizable faces
Arrive and take their places
And do their worst.

It is all a little like dreaming,
But this forest is silent,
This acts out anxiety
In a midnight stillness.
My blood that sparkles in me

Cannot endure this voiceless
Forest, this is not sleep
Not peace but a lack of words.
And the mechanical birds
Wing, claw, and sharpened eye.
I cannot see their sky.

Even this war is not unlike the dream,
But in the dream-war there were armies,
Armies and armor and death's etiquette,
Here there are no troops and no protection,
Only this wrestling of the heart
and a demon-song that goes
For sensual friction
Is largely fiction
And partly fact
And so is tact
And so is love,
And so is love.

The thin leaves chatter. There is a sound at last
Begun at last by the demon-song.
Behind the wildest trees I see the men together
Confessing their lives and the women together.
But really I cannot hear the words.   I cannot hear the song.
This may still be my dream
But the night seems very long.

THE MEETING

One o'clock in the letter-box
Very black and I will go home early.
Now I have put off my dancing-dress
And over a sheet of distance write my love.
I walk in the city with my pride of theme
While the lean girls at their betrayal smiling
Dance, do their sea-green dance, and laugh in dancing.
And all the stars fade out of my sky.

Early in the morning on a windy ocean.
My sleep opens upon your face to kiss and find

And take diversion of the meeting waters,
The flameless sky of peace, blue-sided white air.
I leave you as the trivial birds careen
In separation, a dream of easy parting.
I see you through a door. The door sails away,
And all the ships move into the real sea.

Let that far day arrive, that evening stain!
Down the alleys of the night I trail a cloak;
Field-dusk and mountain-dusk and final darkness—
Each absence brings me nearer to that night
When I stone-still in desire standing
Shall see the masked body of love enter the garden
To reach the night-burning, the perpetual fountain.
And all the birds fly out of my scene.

THE KEY

I hold a key in my hand
And it is cold, cold;
The sign of a lost house
That framed a symbolic face.
Its windows now are black,
Its walls are blank remorse,
Here is a brass key
Freezing to the touch.

Of that house I say here
Goodness came through its door,
There every name was known,
And of all its faces
Unaligned beauty gives
Me one forever
That made itself most dear
By killing the cruelest bond:
Father murder and mother fear.

What perception in that face
Nothing but loneliness

Can ever again retrace—
Conflict and isolation,
A man among copper rocks,
Human among inhuman
Formal immune and cold,
Or a wonderful young woman
In the world of the old.

I walk the world with these:
A wish for quick speech
Of heathen storm-beaten poems
In pure-lined English sound,
A key in my hand that freezes
Like memories of faces
Whose intellectual color
Relieves their cruelty,
Until the wishes be found
And the symbols of worship speak,
And all may in peace, in peace,
Guiltless turn to that mouth.

DARKNESS MUSIC

The days grow and the stars cross over
    And my wild bed turns slowly among the stars.

SONG

The world is full of loss; bring, wind, my love,
    My home is where we make our meeting-place,
    And love whatever I shall touch and read
    Within that face.

Lift, wind, my exile from my eyes;
    Peace to look, life to listen and confess,
    Freedom to find to find to find
    That nakedness.

SHOOTING GALLERY

For Donald B. Elder

These images will parade until the morning
When every symptom is a sign of health.
Man in repose is armed to kill, his sign
The bomber diving down the iron funnel—
Until he is free and the screaming of the boy
Becomes no more than a knitting of the brows.

But now they parade in the city and the cloud.
Or, Don, your gallery, where all images
Pass as a line of targets and the bells
Ring for perfection and the birds go down,
With one dark figure always aiming where
Any right-minded fool sees only air.

If anyone call it supernatural,
Say that all shapes seduce: this space is real,
Say that his trigger-finger can contrive
The Middle West be Spain, the hostile child
At last be reconciled; until this death
Through skill dissolve in the body with all myth.

Monsters of understanding will deny
The body holds all images, but myth
Is in this shape, shape of a target space
That can be filled by the flicker of a face
Until the parade dissolve to peace, the eye
Of the sacred hunter assume his own identity.

SUICIDE BLUES

I want to speak in my voice!
I want to speak in my real voice!

This street leads into the white wind
I am not yet ready to go there.
Not in my real voice.

The river.   Do you know where the river springs?
The river issues from a tall man,
From his real voice.

Do you know where the river is flowing?
The river flows into a singing woman,
In her real voice.

Are you able to imagine truth?
Evil has conspired a world of death,
An unreal voice.

The death-world killed me when the flowers shine,
In spring, in front of the little children,
It threw me burning out of the window
And all my enemies phoned my friends,
But my legs went running around that building
Dancing to the suicide blues.

They flung me into the sea
The sunlight ran all over my face,
The water was blue the water was dark brown
And my severed head swam around that ship
Three times around and it wouldn't go down.

Too much life, my darling, embraces and strong veins,
Every sense speaking in my real voice,
Too many flowers, a too-knowing sun,
Too much life to kill.

WREATH OF WOMEN

Raging from every quarter
The winds attack this house
With its great gardens
Whose rose-established order
Gives it its graciousness,
Its legendary fountains

The darkness of whose forest
Gives it its long repose.

Among these fountains walks
Walpurga, goddess of springs,
And of her summer stalks
A gift has been given—
Old sorrows, old beginnings,
Matured a summer wreath.
I offer it to you.
There is no storm can tear
Miracles made of grief,
Horror, and deepest love.
Under enchantment
I lived a frightful summer
Before I understood.
It had its roots in God
And it bred good love
And hatred and the rare
Revelation of fear.

Women who in my time
Move toward a wider giving
Than warm kitchen offering
And warm steady living
Know million ignorance
Or petty village shame,
And come to acknowledge the world
As a world of common blame.
Beyond the men of letters,
Of business and of death,
They draw a rarer breath,
Have no career but choice.
Choice is their image; they
Choose the myth they obey.

The world of man's selection
May widen more and more.
Women in drudgery knew
They must be one of four:
Whores, artists, saints, and wives.
There are composite lives

That women always live
Whose greatness is to give
Weakness its reasons
And strength its reassurance;
To kiss away the waste
Places and start them well.

From three such women I
Accepted gifts of life
Grown in these gardens
And nourished in a season
That forced our choices on us
Taking away our pardons,
Showing us in a mirror
Interminable girlhood
Or the free pain and terror
To accept and choose
Before we could be free.

Toward such a victory
Crusades have moved, and peace,
And holy stillnesses.
These women moved alone,
Clothed in their suffering—
The fiery pain of children,
The horror of the grown,
And the pure, the intense
Moments of music and light
That let us live in the night
Of the soul and the world's pain.
O flayed Vesalian man
Bent over your shovel,
You will find agony
And all the fears that rave:
Dig in anyone's shadow,
You find a turning grave.

But there are victories
That finally are given:
A child's awareness
Listening at a wall
To Mozart's heaven of music

In a forgetful town.
The flowering wild call
From a dark balcony
Through fever, war and madness
To the world's lover.

The suffering that discovers
Gambler and saint, and brings
A possibility
Wherein we breathe and live.
These three are emblems of need:
Now they struggle together
In a dark forest
Bound as a painful wreath;
Are in that war defiled,
Obsessive to be freed.

Let the last meanings arrive!
These three will be reconciled,
Young and immortal and lovely:
The tall and truthful child,
The challenger's intricacies,
Her struggles and her tenderness;
And the pursued, who cries
"Renunciation!" in a scarlet dress—
Three naked women saying Yes
Among the calling lakes, the silver trees,
The bird-calling and the fallen grass,
The wood-shadow and the water-shadow.

I know your gifts, you women offering.
Whatever attacks your lives, your images,
And in what net of time you are trapped, or freed,
I tell you that all of you make gifts that we
Need in their opposition and will need
While earth contains ambivalence.
I praise you in the dark and intense forest,
I will always remember you,
Fair head, pale head, shining head;
Your rich eyes and generous hands
And the links underneath

Your lives.
                    Now, led
By this unbreakable wreath
Mrs. Walpurga moves
Among her fountains.

MADBOY'S SONG

Fly down, Death: Call me:
I have become a lost name.

One I loved, she put me away,
                    Fly down, Death;
Myself renounced myself that day,
                    Fly down, Death.

My eyes in whom she looked so deep
                    Long ago flowed away,
My hands which slept on her asleep
                    Withered away,
My living voice I meant to keep,
                    Faded and gray.

Fly down, Death: Call me:
I have become a lost name.

Evening closes in whispers,
          Dark words buried in flame—
My love, my mother, my sister,
          I know there is no blame,
But you have your living voice,
          Speak my forgotten name.

Fly down, Death: Call me:
I have become a lost name.

Don't come for me in a car
To drive me through the town;
Don't rise up out of the water,
Once is enough to drown;

Only drop out of the sky,
For I am fallen down.

Fly down Death.

DRUNKEN GIRL

Do you know the name of the average animal?
Not the dog,
    Nor the green-beaded frog,
Nor the white ocean monster lying flat—
    Lower than that.
The curling one who comes out in the storm—
The middle one's the worm.

Lift up your face, my love, lift up your mouth,
Kiss me and come to bed
    And do not bow your head
Longer on what is bad or what is good—
    The dead are terribly misunderstood,
And sin and godhead are in the worm's blind eye,
We'll come to averages by and by.

LOVE AND ITS DOORS
AND WINDOWS

History melts my houses,
But they were all one house
Where in the dark beginning
A tall and maniac nurse
Hid tortures behind the door
And afterwards kissed me
Promising all as before.

The second house was music;
The childish hands of fear
Lying on a piano
That was blackness and light,
Opened my life with sound—

Extorting promises
Loud in the ringing air.

After that, broken houses,
The wealthy halls of cloud
Haunted by living parents
And the possessive face.
Power and outrage looking
At the great river
Marvellous filthy and gold.

When love lay in my arms
I all night kissed that mouth,
And the incredible body
Slept warm at my side;
But the walls fell apart
Among my lifetime dream—
O, a voice said crying,
My mother's broken heart.

Nothing was true in the sense
I wanted it to be true.
Victory came late,
Excitement returned too soon.
If my love were for the dead,
Desire would restore
Me to my life again.

My love is for the living;
They point me down to death,
And death I will not take.
My promises have grown,
My kiss was never false,
The faint clear-colored walls
Are not forever down.

THE MINOTAUR

Trapped, blinded, led; and in the end betrayed
Daily by new betrayals as he stays

Deep in his labyrinth, shaking and going mad.
Betrayed.   Betrayed.   Raving, the beaten head
Heavy with madness, he stands, half-dead and proud.
No one again will ever see his pride.
No one will find him by walking to him straight
But must be led circuitously about,
Calling to him and close and, losing the subtle thread,
Lose him again; while he waits, brutalized
By loneliness.   Later, afraid
Of his own suffering.   At last, savage and made
Ravenous, ready to prey upon the race
If it so much as learn the clews of blood
Into his pride his fear his glistening heart.
Now is the patient deserted in his fright
And love carrying salvage round the world
Lost in a crooked city; roundabout,
By the sea, the precipice, all the fantastic ways
Betrayal weaves its trap; loneliness knows the thread,
And the heart is lost, lost, trapped, blinded and led,
Deserted at the middle of the maze.

GIFT-POEM

The year in its cold beginning
Promises more than cold;
The old contrary rhyming
Will never again hold—
The great moon in its timing
Making the empty sky
A continent of light
Creates fine bombing weather,
Assures a safer flight
For fliers, and many will die
Who in their backwardness
Cannot leave the ground.
Weather is not what it was:
The losers are not winning,
The lost will never be found.
The year in its cold beginning
Finds us a good deal farther

From our good weather
Than we had ever dreamed.

Darling, dead words sublimed
May be read out loud at last:
The legendary past
Cannot scare us again.
This is what I have known
After a New Year's Eve
Of a desperate time.
There will be great sorrow,
Great pain, and detailed joy,
The gladness of flowering
Minutes, green living leaf.
You recommend me grief:
There will be no more grief;
Terrible battle that tears the world apart,
Terrible health that takes the world to bed,
Sickness that, broken, jets across the room
Into the future time;
Not the mild ways of grief,
Mourning that feels at home.

I see your gardens from here,
I see on your terraces
The shadowy awful regiment;
The weak man, the impossible man,
The curly-headed impotent
Whose failure did not reach his face,
And then the struggle for grace, and then
The school'd attenuated men.

I know you are moved by these:
The vice of self-desire
That does not lead to crime,
Leads to no action, is rather
Liquid seductive fire
Before the final blame
When there is no forgiveness.

And many lovers fail to love,
Lose the ability to move

Before the supernatural fear
Calls to the natural need
Come to the feast and feed
On a supernatural meal:
The taproot and the sacrifice.
Nothing can arrive to heal
The dead wish, the living face
That sees its disgrace and loss,
But the loss of its dear wish:
The word spoken across
Distance and loneliness—
Communication to the flesh.

There will be small joy:
There will be great rage,
Do not tell me the feeble
Grief of the very weak;
Only turn, only speak.
I see all the possible ends.
But the impossible;
I know it in its weakness,
Unborn and unprized,
It still commands my faith.
And then I remember the page
Of other words for death.
Then I remember the voices,
The voice not recognized
Or overheard too soon;
Rejected offerings,
Letter and telephone,
And I think of the bombing weather
Fine in the full of the moon.

I think of the big moon
Plain on the gardens,
And the clews of the year.
The haunted gardens wear it,
Knowledge like furniture;
The white frame of the spirit
Whose painting is naked fear.

The girl whose father raped her first
Should have used a little knife;
Failing that, her touch is cursed
By the omissive sin for life;
This bitter year's event and change
Turned to personal revenge.
Paint out the tortured painting,
The scene is too well done
But this processional
Must find some other saint,
Must find some other colors,
Some better expiation
Even more strange.

Murder is not the link;
Meaning must set it right.
Never recommend me grief
Nor deny my horror's straightness,
Early and late I see
The fire in the leaf
The minute's appetite.
If horror fire and change
Bring us our success
The word is indeed lost—
If the frosty world
Start its newest year
In fear and loss and belief,
Something may yet be safe.

Joy may touch the eyes again,
Night restore the walls of sleep,
Ease the will's incessant strain
And the forehead and the breast
And the lung where death lies sleeping.
Darling, if there should be tears,
They'll be no easy movie weeping,
Never the soft tears of grief
That go as simply as they start;
The rage and horror of the heart
In conflict with its love.

January 1941

HOLY FAMILY

A long road and a village.
A bloody road and a village.
A road away from war.
Born, born, we know how it goes.

A man and woman riding.
Riding, the new-born child.
White sky, clever and wild.
Born, born, we know how it goes.

The wheel goes back.
How is it with the child?
How is it with the world?
Born, born, we know how it goes.

Never look at the child.
Give it to bloody ground.
By this dream we are bound.
Born, born, we know how it goes.

Riding between these hills,
Woman and man alone
Enter the battle-line.
Born, born, we know how it goes.

They childless disappear
Among the fighting men.
Two thousand years until they come again.
Born, born, we know how it goes.

WHO IN ONE LIFETIME

Who in one lifetime sees all causes lost,
Herself dismayed and helpless, cities down,
Love made monotonous fear and the sad-faced
Inexorable armies and the falling plane,
Has sickness, sickness.   Introspective and whole,
She knows how several madnesses are born,

Seeing the integrated never fighting well,
The flesh too vulnerable, the eyes tear-torn.

She finds a pre-surrender on all sides:
Treaty before the war, ritual impatience turn
The camps of ambush to chambers of imagery.
She holds belief in the world, she stays and hides
Life in her own defeat, stands, though her whole world burn,
A childless goddess of fertility.

June 1941

FROM "TO THE UNBORN CHILD"

A translation, from Hans Carossa

To keep and conceal may be, in times of crisis,
a godly service.   No one's too weak for this.
I have heard often about our ancestress,
who was a stupid child, learning her lessons
slowly.   In time the village turned
the cattle over to her, and she loved her labor.
Until, in a darkened spring, the war-ghost came.
The arrogant strange leader rushed with his army
across our country and over the frontier.
One evening they heard distant insistent drums.
The farmers ran and stared at each other in the road.
The girl was silent; but her still spirit planned
the act which reaches our village now as legend.
She stole by night from farm to farm unchaining
in every stable the finest and most perfect beasts
and led them from that village, chained in dreams.
Not a dog barked; animals knew the girl.
She drove the herd through towns and off the highway
past fragrant reaches to the mountain pastures'
deep meadows; and she talked to her animals;
they were quieted by the voice of the wise child.
A bellow would have betrayed their hiding-place;
they were never betrayed to the terrible enemy
ransacking their village.   And for a long time
she lived in this way, on milk and bitter berries.

At home they listed her among the missing,
lost in the meadows of the underworld.

One day the last of the soldiers left the land,
the soft land lay, green in the light of peace.
And then she gathered her leaves and flowers, and singing
led the wreathed marvellous herd down from the forests;
and the new-born calves leapt along in the field.
The girl had grown tall and lovely in that time.
She walked behind them, tall and garlanded.
She sang; she sang.   And the young and old ran out.
And all the cattle streamed back to their farms.
The shouts of the children.   The weeping of the old.

To whom do I speak today?   Who shall tell us
that you are alive again?   Who shall tell us today
that you will eat the bread of the earthly fields?
Ah, this star we live on is burning full in danger.
All we know is this: across existence
and across its lapse passes something unknown.
We name it love.   And, love, we pray to you.
— It takes only a second to walk around a man.
Whoever wishes to circle the soul of a lover
needs longer than his pilgrimage of years.

LEG IN A PLASTER CAST

When at last he was well enough to take the sun
He leaned on the nearest railing and summed up his sins,
Criminal weaknesses, deeds done and undone.
He felt he was healing.   He guessed he was sane.

The convalescent gleam upon his skin,
With his supported leg and an unknown
Recovery approaching let him black out pain.
The world promised recovery from his veins.

People said "Sin"; in the park everyone
Mentioned one miracle: "We must all be reborn."

Across an accidental past the horns
Blasted through stone and barriers of sense

And the sound of a plaster cast knocking on stone.
He recognized the sound of fearful airmen
Returning, forerunners, and he could not run.
He saw they were not flying home alone.

He stood in a down-torn town of men and women
Whose wasted days poured on their heads as rain,
As sin, as fire—too lame, too late to turn,
For there, the air, everywhere full of planes.

BUBBLE OF AIR

The bubbles in the blood sprang free,
crying from roots, from Darwin's beard.
The angel of the century
stood on the night and would be heard;
turned to my dream of tears and sang:
Woman, American, and Jew,
three guardians watch over you,
three lions of heritage
resist the evil of your age:
life, freedom, and memory.
And all the dreams cried from the camps
and all the steel of torture rang.
The angel of the century
stood on the night and cried the great
notes Give Create and Fight—
while war
runs through your veins, while life
a bubble of air stands in your throat,
answer the silence of the weak:
Speak!

SEA MERCY

The sea dances its morning
On my enlightened bones,
Stones of the lip-warm land
Clap my awakening.
The land is partly lost,
The sea is all water,
Half horror and half blue
Shaking its appetites
Among my senses.
History has commanded
All the rivers—
A ship entered the bay
And the sky sailed in.
The twentieth century
Stares from the high air—
The skin of the land
Is shallow and very green
But the sea   the sea
Is still, the deep scene
Contains the unbroken
Tides of man.
Horror is appetite,
Hell is lonely,
War's a breath.
Wake us   you black
You white   you water.
The scream of the gull:
Land's too shallow
Life's a breath
Sea mercy.
Worms be my carnival
Who cries there is no death?

LONG PAST MONCADA

Nothing was less than it seemed, my darling:
The danger was greater, the love was greater, the suffering
                    Grows daily great—

And the fear we saw gathering into that Spanish valley
Is rank in all countries, a garden of growing death;
Your death, my darling, the threat to our lifetime
          And to all we love.

Whether you fell at Huesca during the lack of guns,
Or later, at Barcelona, as the city fell,
          You reach my days;
Among the heckling of clocks, the incessant failures,
I know how you recognized our war, and ran
To it as a runner to his eager wedding
          Or our immediate love.

If I indeed killed you, my darling, if my cable killed
Arriving the afternoon the city fell,
          No further guilt
Could more irrevocably drive my days
Through the disordered battles and the cities down
In a clash of metal on murder, a stampede of
          Hunger and death.

Other loves, other children, other gifts, as you said,
"Of the revolution," arrive—but, darling, where
          You entered, life
Entered my hours, whether you lie fallen
Among those sunlight fields, or by miracle somewhere stand,
Your words of war and love, death and another promise
          Survive as a lifetime sound.

CHAPULTEPEC PARK—1

The calling and the melody all night long
And then in the first stillness, morning
Leaning over the dark, over the night-park
Combing her blue hair.
After the guitars, after the tide of bells,
Surge, calls, and furious song,
Very softly the trees emerge,
A tree of light beside a tree of darkness.
And in the silent park

A girl opens her eyes and combs her hair.
Freshness of blue wavers among the lakes;
Two people wake, look at the calm forest,
Turn an iron wheelbarrow on its back
And, fanning a little fire under it,
Cook their tortillas.
Morning leans down; morning lifts out of the stone
The angry archaic statue of a god
Watching from live rock.
The Palace whitens, and all the standing fountains.
Snow is shining on the far volcanoes,
We walk smiling down the Philosopher's Footpath.
A young horse runs into the sunlight.

CHAPULTEPEC PARK—2

The city of the heart
Is like this city.   Its names commemorate
Beliefs and lovers, books and the body's forms.
I walk among these avenues whose great
Names speak of places and saints, revolts and flowers.

I walk through the night city; walking hear a cry
Calling, "Slaves demand promises, we need no promises,
We are free; we promise ourselves a living world."
Shadows after the lamps, bruise-color and bronze
On the pure walls of midnight.   Dark, my brothers,
Where your dark faces watch against a stubborn sky.

Mystical passion, fury, the taste of the world.
The calling of the world, and everything man fears:
Poetry, poetry, bravery, poverty, war.
And if we weep, it is ourselves we weep,
Not our belief.   But in these streets we see
The cheapest tourists, the twisted cross parade.

The city of the heart knows creeping fire
That beats its towers into storms of flame.
Cynics of power come with their shout of blame.
We wake among the dreams; grace has its ways:

Fire and gleam of blood on stone will fade
Into the moment of proof, blood of our days.

Dawn comes to the city and the spirit's city,
Laughs in the heart like a child, and midday flies
Over the dogs with their sharp and primitive faces
Coursing gay and masterless to the zoo.
The live heart laughs and courses and is free,
For the city contains poverty, bravery, war,
But most, a deepened hope, sunlight and memory.

A GAME OF BALL

On a ground beaten gold by running and
Over the Aztec crest of the sky and
Past the white religious faces of the
Bulls and far beyond, the ball goes flying.

Sun and moon and all the stars of the moon
Are dancing across our eyes like the flight of armies
And the loser dies.   Dark player and bright
Play for the twinned stiff god of life and death.
They die and become the law by which they fight.

Walls grow out of this light, branches out of the stone,
And fire running from the farthest winds
Pours broken flame on these fantastic sands
Where, sunlit, stands the goddess of earth and death,
A frightful peasant with work-hardened hands.

But over the field flash all the colors of summer,
The battle flickers in play, a game like sacrifice.
The sun rides over, the moon and all her stars.
Whatever is ready to eat us, we have found
This place where the gods play out the game of the sky
And bandy life and death across a summer ground.

GOLD LEAF

A shadowy arch calling the clouds of the sun
To enter, enter.   Enter.   But they run.

Their seeking whiteness refuses the false, the thief.
This shadow is rich twilight of gold leaf.

A mask of gold beaten upon the stone
Is a live cheek painted on martyr bone.

If you go through the gold you find a hand
Delicate as foam and at the wrist

Foam and the scarlet cloth of a sick priest.
Until he coughs you will not understand.

You must go deeper to find the pure dark way,
The many crying "Sangre!" "Sangre!" "Sangre!"

Deeper than death the faithful blood will flow
Singing "Mexico!" "Mexico!" "Mexico!"

A serpent in the passionate garden says
"This," looking at men and saying "this, this."

Pain and the desperate music of the poor.
The true darkness.   A naked human door.

Out of this darkness music of the crowd,
Bells raise their circles of truth and find the cloud.

ALL SOULS

The day of life and death offers its flowers:
Branches of flame toward a midnight lake of stars,
And the harsh sunny smell of weeds at noon.
In the clear season, we sit upon the graves
(Northern red leaf, frost-witches and toy ghost):
Here are the crystal skull and flowering bone.

The cloak of blood down the shoulder of the bull.

Whirl of mirrors and light about the blade
And the bullring turning groaning to the sun.—
We are all sitting on graves, drinking together,
Each grave a family gay on the hot grass,
Its bottle, its loaf of bread in a basket,
And a few peaches too perfect ever to wither.

And the river of light down the shoulder of the hill.

The drink of flowers and fire in the sun,
The child in pink holding her sugar skull—
This appetite raving on death's high holiday:
Love of the dead, fierce love of the alive.
We eat the feast of our mortality,
Drink fiery joy, and death sinks down with day.

O in the burning day of life and death
The strong drink running down the shoulder of the grave!

EVENING PLAZA, SAN MIGUEL

No one will ever understand that evening
Who has not lain the night with a changeable lover,
Changeable as that last evening.

No one who has not ever seen that color
Change and travel the hills, the irrelevant bells
Ringing the changes,

And seen the green enter the evening sky,
Reluctant yellow come and the cathedral
Unfold in rose—

And stood under that rose of stone, remembering rose
Spattered in feasts of rockets, interrupted
By the black downdrawn line

Of the down-turning wheel of carnival—will ever know
The evening color filtered through cinnamon
And how the birds came down

Through the bars of yellow and the bars of green
Into the brandy dusk and the leaves of night,
A touch, a shadow of touch, when breasts

Lift their little branches, and showers and flares of fire
Rise in the blood, in spite of the word of war,
In spite of evening coming down like a lover,

Like the birds falling among the trees, like music
As the trees close, and the cathedral closes.
No one will know who in a stranger land

Has never stood while night came down
In shadows of roses, a cloud of tree-drawn birds,
And said, "I must go home."

BEAST IN VIEW

Configurations of time and singing
    Bring me to a dark harbor where
    The chase is drawn to a beginning.
    And all the myths are gathered there.

I know the trees as fountains and the stars'
    Far fires fountains and your love
    A vivid fountain, and the bars
    Broken about me let me move

Among the fountains.   At last seeing
    I came here by obscure preparing,
    In vigils and encounters being
    Both running hunter and fierce prey waring.

I hunted and became the followed,
    Through many lives fleeing the last me,
    And changing fought down a far road
    Through time to myself as I will be.

Chaos prepared me, and I find the track,
　　Through life and darkness seek my myth—
　　Move toward it, hunting grow more like,
　　Draw near, and know it through our path.
　　Know only that we run one path.

❧ 2

LETTER TO THE FRONT

1

Women and poets see the truth arrive.
Then it is acted out,
The lives are lost, and all the newsboys shout.

Horror of cities follows, and the maze
Of compromise and grief.
The feeble cry Defeat be my belief.

All the strong agonized men
Wear the hard clothes of war,
Try to remember what they are fighting for.

But in dark weeping helpless moments of peace
Women and poets believe and resist forever:
The blind inventor finds the underground river.

2

Even during war, moments of delicate peace
Arrive; ceaseless the water ripples, love
Speaks through the river in its human voices.
Through every power to affirm and heal
The unknown world suggests the air and golden
Familiar flowers, and the brief glitter of waves,
And dreams, and leads me always to the real.
Even among these calendars of fire.

Sings: There is much to fear, but not our power.
The stars turn over us; let us not fear the many.
All mortal intricacies tremble upon this flower.
Let us not fear the hidden.   Or each other.
We are alive in an hour whose burning face
Looks into our death, death of our dear wish.
And time that will be eating away our flesh
Gives us this moment when blue settles on rose
And evening suddenly seems limitless silver.
The cold wind streaming over the cold hill-grasses
Remembers and remembers.   Mountains lift into night.
And I am remembering the face of peace.

I have seen a ship lying upon the water
Rise like a great bird, like a lifted promise.

3

They called us to a change of heart
But it was not enough.
Not half enough, not half enough
For all their bargaining and their art.

After the change of heart there comes
The savage waste of battlefield;
The flame of that wild battlefield
Rushes in fire through our rooms.

The heart that comes to know its war
When gambling powers try for place
Must live to wrestle for a place
For every burning human care:

To know a war begins the day
Ideas of peace are bargained for.
Surrender and death are bargained for—
Peace and belief must fight their way.

Begin the day we change and so
Open the spirit to the world.
Wars of the spirit in the world
Make us continually know
We fight continually to grow.

4 SESTINA

Coming to Spain on the first day of the fighting,
Flame in the mountains, and the exotic soldiers,
I gave up ideas of strangeness, but now, keeping
All I profoundly hoped for, I saw fearing
Travelers and the unprepared and the fast-changing
Foothills.   The train stopped in a silver country.

Coast-water lit the valleys of this country—
All mysteries stood human in the fighting.
We came from far.   We wondered, Were they changing,
Our mild companions, turning into soldiers?
But the cowards were persistent in their fearing,
Each of us narrowed to one wish he was keeping.

There was no change of heart here; we were keeping
Our deepest wish, meeting with hope this country.
The enemies among us went on fearing
The frontier was too far behind.   This fighting
Was clear to us all at last.   The belted soldiers
Vanished into white hills that dark was changing.

The train stood naked in flowery midnight changing
All complex marvellous hope to war, and keeping
Among us only the main wish, and the soldiers.
We loved each other, believed in the war; this country
Meant to us the arrival of the fighting
At home; we began to know what we were fearing.

As continents broke apart, we saw our fearing
Reflect our nations' fears; we acted as changing
Cities at home would act, with one wish, fighting
This threat or falling under it; we were keeping
The knowledge of fiery promises; this country
Struck at our lives, struck deeper than its soldiers.

Those who among us were sure became our soldiers.
The dreams of peace resolved our subtle fearing.
This was the first day of war in a strange country.
Free Catalonia offered that day our changing
Age's hope and resistance, held in its keeping
The war this age must win in love and fighting.

This first day of fighting showed us all men as soldiers.
It offered one wish for keeping.   Hope.   Deep fearing.
Our changing spirits awake in the soul's country.

5

Much later, I lie in a white seaport night
Of gongs and mystery and bewildered mist
Giving me a strange harbor in these white
Scenes, white rivers, my white dreams of peace.
And a ship lifted up on a sign of freedom.
Peace sharp and immediate as our winter stars.
A blue sailor with a cargo of guitars.

I saw a white ship rise as peace was made
In Spain, the first peace the world would not keep.
The ship pulled away from the harbor where Columbus
Standing on his black pillar sees new worlds;
And suddenly all the people at all the rails
Lifted their hands in a gesture of belief
That climbs among my dreams like a bird flying.
Until the world is lifted by one bird flying
An instant drawing to itself the world.

6

Home thoughts from home; we read you every day,
Soldiers of distances.   You wish most to be here.
In the strange lands of war, I woke and thought of home.
Remembering how war came, I wake and think of you,
In the city of water and stone where I was born,
My home of complex light.   What we were fighting for,
In the beginning, in Spain, was not to be defined.
More human than abstract, more direction than end.
Terror arrived intact, lit with the tragic fire
Of hope before its time, tore us from lover and friend.
We came to the violent act with all that we had learned.

But now we are that home you dream across a war.
You fight; and we must go in poetry and hope
Moving into the future that no one can escape.
Peace will in time arrive, but war defined our years.
We are like that young saint at the spring who bent
Her face over dry earth the vision told her flowed,

Miring herself.   She knew it was water.   But for
Herself, it was filth.   Later, for all to come
Following her faith, miraculous crystal ran.

O saint, O poet, O wounded of these wars
To find life flowing from the heart of man.
We hold belief.   You fight and are maimed and mad.
We believe, though all you want be bed with one
Whose mouth is bread and wine, whose flesh is home.

        7

To be a Jew in the twentieth century
Is to be offered a gift.   If you refuse,
Wishing to be invisible, you choose
Death of the spirit, the stone insanity.
Accepting, take full life.   Full agonies:
Your evening deep in labyrinthine blood
Of those who resist, fail, and resist; and God
Reduced to a hostage among hostages.

The gift is torment.   Not alone the still
Torture, isolation; or torture of the flesh.
That may come also.   But the accepting wish,
The whole and fertile spirit as guarantee
For every human freedom, suffering to be free,
Daring to live for the impossible.

        8

Evening, bringing me out of the government building,
Spills her blue air, her great Atlantic clouds
Over my hair, reminds me of my land.
My back to high stone and that man's golden bands
Who said of our time which has only its freedom,
"I will not ever say 'for a free world,'
'A better world' or whatever it is;
A man fights to win a war,
To hang on to what is his—"
Consider this man in the clothes of a commander.
Remember that his field is bottled fizz.

O the blue air and the nightsound of heartbeats—
Planes or poems or dreams direct as prayer.

The belief in the world, and we can stand with them,
Whoever clearly fights the order of despair.
In spite of the fascist, Malicioso King,
Contractor, business man and publisher,
Who will hire a man to hire another man
To hire someone to murder the man of strong belief.
Look at him at the Radio City bar;
Remember that he functions best as thief.

O the clouds and the towers are not enough to hide
The little sneer at freedom, the whisper that art died.
Here is the man who changed his name, the man who dyed his hair;
One praises only his own birth; one only his own whore.
Unable to create or fight or commit suicide,
Will make a job of weakness, be the impotent editor,
The sad and pathic bull always wishing he were
The bullfighter.   But we remember the changes that he made,
Screaming "Betrayed!" He forever betrays.   He alone is betrayed.

They are all here in this divided time:
Dies the inquisitor against the truth,
Wheeler, Nye, Pegler, Hearst, each with his crews,
McCormick, the Representatives whose crime
Is against history, the state, and love.
I hold their dead skulls in my hand; this death
Worked against labor, women, Jews,
Reds, Negroes.   But our freedom lives
To fight the war the world must win.
The fevers of confusion's touch
Leap to confusion in the land.
We shall grow and fight again.
The sickness of our divided state
Calls to the anger and the great
Imaginative gifts of man.
The enemy does his rigid work.
We live fighting in that dark.
Let all the living fight in proof
They start the world this war must win.

9

Among all the waste there are the intense stories
And tellers of stories.   One saw a peasant die.

One guarded a soldier through disease.   And one
Saw all the women look at each other in hope.
And came back, saying, "All things must be known."

They come home to the rat-faced investigator
Who sneers and asks, "Who is your favorite poet?"
Voices of scissors and grinders asking their questions:
"How did you ever happen to be against fascism?"
And they remember the general's white hair,
The food-administrator, alone and full of tears.

They come home to the powder-plant at twilight,
The girls emerging like discolored shadows.
But this is a land where there is time, and time;
This is the country where there is time for thinking.
"Is he a 'fellow-traveler'?—   No.   —Are you sure?   —No."
The fear.   Voices of clawhammers and spikes clinking.

If they bomb the cities, they must offer the choice.
Taking away the sons, they must create a reason.
The cities and women cry in a frightful voice,
"I care not who makes the laws, let me make the sons."
But look at their eyes, like drinking animals'
Full of assurance and flowing with reward.
The seeds of answering are in their voice.
The spirit lives, against the time's disease.
You little children, come down out of your mothers
And tell us about peace.

I hear the singing of the lives of women,
The clear mystery, the offering and pride.
But here also the orange lights of a bar, and an
Old biddy singing inside:

    Rain and tomorrow more
    They say there will be rain
    They lean together and tell
    The sorrow of the loin.

    Telling each other, saying
     "But can you understand?"

They recount separate sorrows.
Throat.   Forehead.   Hand.

On the bars and walls of buildings
They passed when they were young
They vomit out their pain,
The sorrow of the lung.

Who would suspect it of women?
They have not any rest.
Sad dreams of the belly, of the lip,
Of the deep warm breast.

All sorrows have their place in flesh,
All flesh will with its sorrow die—
All but the patch of sunlight over,
Over the sorrowful sunlit eye.

10

Surely it is time for the true grace of women
Emerging, in their lives' colors, from the rooms, from the harvests,
From the delicate prisons, to speak their promises.
The spirit's dreaming delight and the fluid senses'
Involvement in the world.   Surely the day's beginning
In midnight, in time of war, flickers upon the wind.

O on the wasted midnight of our pain
Remember the wasted ones, lost as surely as soldiers
Surrendered to the barbarians, gone down under centuries
Of the starved spirit, in desperate mortal midnight
With the pure throats and cries of blessing, the clearest
Fountains of mercy and continual love.

These years know separation.   O the future shining
In far countries or suddenly at home in a look, in a season,
In music freeing a new myth among the male
Steep landscapes, the familiar cliffs, trees, towers
That stand and assert the earth, saying: "Come here, come to me.
Here are your children."   Not as traditional man
But love's great insight—"your children and your song."

Coming close to the source of belief, these have created
Resistance, the flowering fire of memory,
Given the bread and the dance and the breathing midnight.
Nothing has been begun.   No peace, no word of marvellous
Possible hillsides, the warm lips of the living
Who fought for the spirit's grace among despair,
Beginning with signs of belief, offered in time of war,
As I now send you, for a beginning, praise.

 3

THE SOUL AND BODY OF JOHN BROWN

Multitudes, multitudes in the valley of decision!
Joel III : 14

His life is in the body of the living.
When they hanged him the first time, his image leaped
into the blackened air.   His grave was the floating faces
of the crowd, and he refusing them release
rose open-eyed in autumn, a fanatic
beacon of fierceness leaping to meet them there,
match the white prophets of the storm,
the streaming meteors of the war.

Dreaming Ezekiel, threaten me alive!

Voices:Why don't you rip up that guitar?
Or must we listen to those blistering strings?

The trial of heroes follows their execution.   The striding
wind of nations with new rain, new lightning,
destroyed in magnificent noon shining straight down
the fiery pines.   Brown wanted freedom.   Could not himself be free
until more grace reached a corroded world.   Our guilt his own.
Under the hooded century drops the trap—
There in October's fruition-fire three
tall images of him, Brown as he stood on the ground,
Brown as he stood on sudden air, Brown

standing to our fatal topmost hills
faded through dying altitudes, and low
through faces living under the dregs of the air,
deprived childhood and thwarted youth and change:
      fantastic sweetness gone to rags
      and incorruptible anger blurred by age.

Compel the steps of lovers, watch them lie silvery
attractive in naked embrace over the brilliant gorge,
and open them to love: enlarge their welcome
to sharp-faced countrysides, vicious familiar windows
whose lopped-off worlds say *I am promise,* holding
stopgap slogans of a thin season's offering,
false initials, blind address, dummy name—
enemies who reply in smiles; mild slavers; moderate whores.
There is another gorge to remember, where soldiers give
terrible answers of lechery after death.
Brown said at last, with a living look,
"I designed to have done the same thing
again on a larger scale." Brown sees his tree
grow in the land to leap these mountains.
Not mountains, but men and women sleeping.

      O my scene! My mother!
      America who offers many births.

Over the tier of barriers, compel the connected steps
past the attacks of sympathy, past black capitals,
to arrive with horizon sharpness, marching
in quick embrace toward people
faltering among hills among the symptoms of ice,
small lights of the shifting winter, the rapid snow-blue stars.
This must be done by armies.   Nothing is free.
Brown refuses to speak direct again,
      "If I tell them the truth,
      they will say I speak in symbols."

White landscapes emphasize his nakedness
reflected in counties of naked who shiver at fires,
their backs to the hands that unroll worlds around them.
They go down the valleys. They shamble in the streets,
Blind to the sun-storming image in their eyes.

They dread the surface of their victim life,
lying helpless and savage in shade parks,
  asking the towers only what beggars dare:
  food, fire, water, and air.

Spring: the great hieroglyph : the mighty, whose first hour
collects the winter invalids, whose cloudless
pastures train swarms of mutable apple-trees
to blond delusions of light, the touch of whiter
more memorable breasts each evening, the resistant
male shoulders riding under sold terrible eyes.
The soldier-face persists, the victorious head
asks, kissing those breasts, more miracles—
Untarnished hair! Set them free! "Without the snap of a gun—"
More failures—but the season is a garden after sickness;
  Then the song begins,
  "The clearing of the sky
  brings fulness to heroes—
  Call Death out of the city
  and ring the summer in."

Whether they sleep alone. Whether they understand darkness
of mine or tunnel or store. Whether they lay branches
with skill to entice their visions out of fire.
Whether she lie awake, whether he walk in guilt
down padded corridors, leaving no fingerprints.
Whether he weaken searching for power in papers,
or shut out every fantasy but the fragile eyelid to
  commemorate delight . . .
  They believe in their dreams.

They more and more, secretly, tell their dreams.
They listen oftener for certain words, look deeper
in faces for features of one remembered image.
They almost forget the face. They cannot miss the look.
It waits until faces have gathered darkness,
and country guitars a wide and subtle music.
It rouses love. It has mastered its origin:
  Death was its method. It will surpass its
  furious birth when it is known again.

  Dreaming Ezekiel, threaten me alive!

Greengrown with sun on it. All the living summer.
They tell their dreams on the cool hill reclining
after a twilight daytime painting machines on the sky,
the spite of tractors and the toothless cannon.
Slaves under factories deal out identical
gestures of reaching—cathedral-color-rose
resumes the bricks as the brick walls lean
away from the windows, blank in bellwavering air,
a slave's mechanical cat's-claw reaping sky.
The cities of horror are down. These are called born,
and Hungry Hill is a farm again.

> I know your face, deepdrowned
> prophet, and seablown eyes.

Darkflowing peoples. A tall tree, prophet, fallen,
your arms in their flesh laid on the mountains, all
your branches in the scattered valleys down.
Your boughs lie broken in channels of the land,
dim anniversaries written on many clouds.
There is no partial help. Lost in the face of a child,
lost in the factory repetitions, lost
on the steel plateaus, in a ghost distorted.
Calling More Life. In all the harm calling.
Pointing disaster of death and lifting up the bone,
heroic drug and the intoxication gone.

> I see your mouth calling
> before the words arrive.

Buzz of guitars repeat it in streamy
summernoon song, the whitelight of the meaning
changed to demand. More life, challenging
this hatred, this Hallelloo—risk it upon yourselves.
Free all the dangers of promise, clear the image
of freedom for the body of the world.
After the tree is fallen and has become the land,
when the hand in the earth declined rises and touches and
after the walls go down and all the faces turn,
the diamond shoals of eyes demanding life
deep in the prophet eyes, a wish to be again
threatened alive, in agonies of decision
part of our nation of our fanatic sun.

The Green Wave

1948

Let poems and bodies love and be given to air,
Earth having us real in her seasons, our fire and savor;
And, reader, love well, imagine forward, for
All of the testaments are in your favor.

WATER NIGHT

The sky behind the farthest shore
Is darker than I go to sleep.

Blackness of water, the crater at the core,
The many blacknesses begin to gleam.

Rivers of darkness bind me to this land
While overhead the moon goes far to shine,

And now nothing nobody is my own.
The motion of streams glitters before my eyes:

Sources and entrances, they lie no more,
Now darkly keep, now flow now bright

Until all wandering end, a hand
Shine, and the leadings homeward of delight

Seem to begin my deepest sleep
To make a lake of dream.

EYES OF NIGHT-TIME

On the roads at night I saw the glitter of eyes:
my dark around me let shine one ray;   that black
allowed their eyes   :   spangles in the cat's, air in the moth's
    eye shine,
mosaic of the fly, ruby-eyed beetle, the eyes that never weep,
the horned toad sitting and its tear of blood,
fighters and prisoners in the forest, people
aware in this almost total dark, with the difference,
the one broad fact of light.

Eyes on the road at night, sides of a road like rhyme;
the floor of the illumined shadow sea
and shallows with their assembling flash and show
of sight, root, holdfast, eyes of the brittle stars.

And your eyes in the shadowy red room,
scent of the forest entering, various time
calling and the light of wood along the ceiling
and over us birds calling and their circuit eyes.
And in our bodies the eyes of the dead and the living
giving us gifts at hand, the glitter of all their eyes.

THIS PLACE IN THE WAYS

Having come to this place
I set out once again
on the dark and marvelous way
from where I began:
belief in the love of the world,
woman, spirit, and man.

Having failed in all things
I enter a new age
seeing the old ways as toys,
the houses of a stage
painted and long forgot;
and I find love and rage.

Rage for the world as it is
but for what it may be
more love now than last year
and always less self-pity
since I know in a clearer light
the strength of the mystery.

And at this place in the ways
I wait for song.
My poem-hand still, on the paper,
all night long.
Poems in throat and hand, asleep,
and my storm beating strong!

SONG, FROM "MR. AMAZEEN ON THE RIVER"

Over the water, where I lie alive,
   Grass burns green where the buried are,
   Tall stone is standing   "And the sea
   Gave up its dead."   The wave, the living star,
   Evening and house at river-mouth shine.

The hour of voices on the water and oars
   Speaking of blue, speaking of time.
   His colors, colors of deepness will arrive,
   Island-sleep, keel-sleep, cloud-controlling evening.
   They say to me at last "I am your home."

CLOUDS, AIRS, CARRIED ME AWAY

Clouds, airs, carried me away,
but here we stand
and newborn we begin.
Having seen all the people of the play,
the lights, the map in the hand,
we know there will be wars
all acted out, and know not who may win.

Deep now in your great eyes, and in my gross
flesh—heavy as ever, woman of mud—
shine sunset, sunrise and the advancing stars.
But past all loss
and all forbidding a thing is understood.

Orpheus in hell remembered rivers
and a music rose
full of all human voices;
all words you wish are in that living sound.
And even torn to pieces
one piece sang
Come all ye torn and wounded here
together
and one sang to its brother
remembering.

One piece in tatters sang among its blood:
man is a weapon, woman's a trap;
and so is the hand with the map, my dear,
so is the hand with the colored map.
And I to myself the tightest trap.

Now all is young again:
in a wet night among the household music,
the new time,
by miracle my traps are sprung.
I wished you all your good again
and all your good is here with you,
smiling, various, and true,
your living friends, as live as we.

I believed because I saw not;
now I see,
with love become
so haunted by a living face
that all the dead rise up and stare;
and the dumb time, the year that was
passes away.   Memory is reborn,
form and forgiveness shine.
So in this brilliant dark, dark of the year,
shining is born.
We know what we do,
and turn, and act in hope.
Now the wounds of time
have healed and are grown.
They are not wounds, they are mine,
they are healed into mouths.
They speak past wrongs.   I am born;
you bring shining, and births.
Here are the stories they tell you,
here are their songs.

SALAMANDER

Red leaf.   And beside it, a red leaf alive
flickers, the eyes set wide in the leaf head,

small broad chest, a little taper of flame for tail
moving a little among the leaves like fear.

Flickering red in the wet week of rain
while a bird falls safely through his mile of air.

HIS HEAD IS FULL OF FACES

for Bernard Perlin

Now he has become one who upon that coast
landed by night and found the starving army.
Fed on their cheese and wine.   In those ravines
hidden by orphaned furious children lay
while cries and wounds and hour past hour of war
flamed past the broken pillars of that sky.

He saw the enemy.   His head is full of faces—
the living, the brave, a pure blazing alone
to fight a domination to the end.
And now he sees the rigid terrible friend
inert, peopled by armies, winning.   Now
he has become one given his life by those
fighting in Greece forever under a star
and now he knows how many wars there are.

MRS. WALPURGA

In wet green midspring, midnight and the wind
floodladen and ground-wet, and the immense dry moon.
Mrs. Walpurga under neon saw
the fluid airs stream over fluid evening,
ground, memory, give way and rivers run
into her sticky obsessive kiss of branches,
kiss of a real and visionary mouth,
the moon, the mountain, the round breast's sleepless eye.

Shapes of her fantasy in music from the bars,
swarming like juke-box lights the avenues;

no longer parked in the forest, from these cars,
these velvet rooms and wooden tourist camps,
sheetless under the naked white of the moon.
Wet gaze of eye, plum-color shadow and young
streams of these mouths, the streaming surface of earth
flowing alive with water, the egg and its becoming.

Coming in silence.   The shapes of every dread
seducing the isolated will.   They do not care.
They are not tortured, not tired, not alone.
They break to an arm, a leg, half of a mouth,
kissing disintegrate, flow whole, couple again;
she is changed along, she is a stream in a stream.

These are her endless years, woman and child, in dream
molded and wet, a bowl growing on a wheel,
not mud, not bowl, not clay, but this *becoming,*
winter and split of darkness, years of wish.
To want these couples, want these coupling pairs,
emblems of many parents, of the bed,
of love divided by dream, love with his dead wife,
love with her husband dead, love with his living love.

Mrs. Walpurga cries out : "It is not true!"
The light shifts, flowing away.   "It was never like—"
She stops, but nothing stops.   It moves.   It moves.
And not like anything.   And it is true.
The shapes disfigure.   Here is the feature man,
not whole, he is detail, he gleams and goes.
Here is the woman all cloth, black velvet face,
black, head to ground, close black fit to the skin,
slashed at the mouth and eyes, slashed at the breasts,
slashed at the triangle, showing rose everywhere.

Nights are disturbed, here is a crying river
running through years, here is the flight among
all the Objects of Love.   This wish, this gesture
irresisted, immortal seduction!   The young sea
streams over the land of dream, and there
the mountain like a mist-flower, the dark upright peak.
And over the sheet-flood Mrs. Walpurga
in whitened cycles of her changing moon.

The silence and the music change;   this song
rises and sharps, and never quite can scream—
but this is laughter harsher than nakedness
can take—in the shady shady grove the leaves
move over, the men and women move and part,
the river braids and unfolds in mingling song;
and here is the rain of summer from the moon,
relenting, wet, and giving life at last,
and Mrs. Walpurga and we may wake.

A CERTAIN MUSIC

Never to hear, I know in myself complete
that naked integrated music;   now
it has become me, now it is nerve, song, gut,
and my gross hand writes only through Mozart; see
even in withholding what you have brought to me.

Renewed, foolish, reconciled to myself, I walk
this winter-country, I fly over its still-flock'd clouds,
always in my isolated flesh I take
that theme's light certainty of absolute purpose
to make quick spirit when spirit most might break.

Naked you walked through my body and I turned
to you with this far music you now withhold.
O my destroyed hope!   Though I never again
hear developing heaven, the growing grave-bearing earth,
my poem, my promise, my love, my sleep after love;
my hours, listening, along that music move,
and have been saved and hardly know the cold.

THE MOTIVE OF ALL OF IT

The motive of all of it was loneliness,
All the panic encounters and despair
Were bred in fear of the lost night, apart,
Outlined by pain, alone.   Promiscuous

As mercy.   Fear-led and led again to fear
At evening toward the cave where part fire, part
Pity lived in that voluptuousness
To end one and begin another loneliness.

This is the most intolerable motive   :   this
Must be given back to life again,
Made superhuman, made human, out of pain
Turned to the personal, the pure release:
The rings of Plato and Homer's golden chain
Or Lenin with his cry of Dare We Win.

GREEN LIMITS

My limits crowd around me
like years, like those I loved
whose narrow hope could never
carry themselves.

My limits stand beside me
like those two widowed aunts
who from an empty beach
tore me into the wave.

Green over my low head
the surf threw itself down
tall as my aunts whose hands
locked me past help.

The sand was far behind
and rushing underfoot
water and fear and childhood,
surf of love.

Green limits walled me, water
stood higher than I saw—
glass walls, fall back!   let me
dive and be saved.

My limits stand inside me
forever like that wave
on which I ride at last
over and under me.

THE CHILDREN'S ORCHARD

In the full sun.   In the fruitfall season.
Against my knees the earth and the bucket, and the soft blue prunes
echoing red   echoing purple   echoing in the silver bucket
sun, and over the flames of earth the sun flies down.

Over my head the little trees tremble alive in their black branches
and bare-ribbed boys golden and shouting stoop here to gather the blue,
the wild-red, the dark.   Colors of ripeness in the fruitfall season.
I will remember the last light on the lowest branch.

Will see these trees as they were in spring, wild black rooted in light,
root-deep in noon, the piercing yellow noon of mustard-blossom.
Sun breathing on us the scent of heat, richness of air where my hands know
blue, full summer, strong sun.   I tell you harvest.

CHRISTMAS EVE

The secret child walks down the street
of the year's winter black and white,
while evening flames, blue-green and high—
the smooth face turns in the snow-smooth street
to lights, star-bubbles, the dark tree,
the giant star in the sacred sky.

Children behind their windows sing
a cradle, a birth, the pilgrim kings,
praising the still and wild.
They praise the face, the quickening,
the various joy, the wound!   They sing
a new prophetic child.

Out of the street, out of the spire,
a slow voice, radio or king,
begins above the mystery.
Tells pain and sweetness, pain and fire.
The bells begin to cast their rings
of celebration down the sky.

The secret child walks down the street
of needle-dark December smells.
She walks with wonder everywhere.
Who is that Child?   Where is that sweet
face of the songs and silver bells,
the broad red saint, the angelhair?

The voice tells ragged ships that sailed
to find that birth and piercèd hand,
a little child among the Jews.
"But I," she says, "I am a child
of Jews—"   Says, "This is Christianland
and things are otherwise.

"People, beasts, and a winter rose,
procession and thorn, the suffering
that had to be, the needed loss
led to this flame among the snows.
Three agents brought about this thing:
the Father, the Jews, the blessèd cross.

"And one of these is ours and overhead;
and one is God;   and one is still outside."
Sure of the birth then, the people all went to sleep.
But the child was awake, and grieved for the time ahead,
awake all night, watching the land and the sky.
Did the child weep?   No the child did not weep.

CRAYON HOUSE

Two or three lines across;   the black ones, down,
into the ground where grass sparkles and shines;

but the foundation is the green and the shine.
Windows are drawn in.   Overhead the sun
surrounded by his crown, continually given.
It is a real place, door, floor, and windows.

I float past it.   I look in at the little children.
I climb up the straight and planted path, alone.
In the city today grown, walking on stone,
a suddenness of doors, windows, bread and rolls.

Roads are in all I know   :   weapon and refugee,
color of thunder calling   Leave this room,
Get out of this house.   Even then, joy began,
went seeking through the green world, wild and no longer wild,
always beginning again.   Steady giving and green decision,
and the beginning was real.   The drawing of a child.

A CHARM FOR CANTINFLAS

After the lights and after the rumba and after the bourbon
                              and after the beer
and after the drums and after the samba and after the
                              ice cream and not long after
failure, loss, despair, and loss and despair
There was the laughter and there was Cantinflas at last
                              and his polka
doing the bumps with a hot guitar
turning unique.   Slow.   Slow.   Slow.   Deprecating
                              shoulder up.
                              Hand up.
                              All the fingers tall.
Panache and rags and triumph and smile—
beggar of light in ridiculous sunlight.

All things human clumsy and fair
as graceful as loving as stupid as true.

And on this floor
the dancers, in this square the little trees,
and on this stage always the clown of our living

gives us our sunlight and our incantation
as sun does, laughing, shining, reciting dawn, noon, and down,
making all delight and healing all ills
like faraway words on jars, the labels in Protopapas' window:
marshmallow, myrtle, peppermint, pumpkin, sesame, sesame, squills.

TRADITIONAL TUNE

After the revolution came the Fuehrer;
And after the resurrection, the Christian Era.
Not yet simple and not yet free.

Just after the Exodus, in the divided sea
The chariots drowned, and then the tempering
By forty sandy years of misery.

And after the King of the Jews came Godfrey King;
Kneedeep in blood the children wandering,
Holy Holy Holy hear the children sing.

Now mouthdeep nosedeep the fires reach our eye.
Teach us from torment to fly and not to fly.
Not yet safe, not ready to die.

Illumination and night cast on the eyes of those
Believing and fighting, playing the Worldly Fool,
Fool of Thy Word, who feel the century

Rule, under whose deep wave explosion waits;
We know the dead power of Thy Allied States.
Not yet simple and not yet free.

Sailing, remembering the rock and the child,
Sailing remember the sand, the city, the wild
Holy songs.   Deaths!   Pillar of cloud and sun,

Remember us and remember them and all
Not safe, not free sailing again upon
The sacred dangerous harbor, Jerusalem.

FOGHORN IN HORROR

I know that behind these walls is the city, over these rooftops is the sun.
But I see black clothes only and white clothes with the fog running in
and all their shadows.
Every minute the sound of the harbor
intruding on horror with a bellow of horror:
blu–a!   blu–aa!   Ao. . . .

I try to write to you, but here too I meet failure.
It has a face like mine.
Silence and in me and over the water
only the bellowing,
Niobe howling for her life and her children.
Did you think this sorrow of women was a graceful thing?
Horrible Niobe down on her knees:
Blu–a!   Blu–aa!   Ao. . . .

Thirty years, and my full strength, and all I touch has failed.
I sit and see
the black clothes on the line are beautiful, the sky drifting away.
The white clothes of the fog beyond me, beautiful, and the shadows.
Blu–aa!   Blu–aa!   AO.

SUMMER, THE SACRAMENTO

To this bridge the pale river and flickers away in images of blue.
And is gone.   While behind me the stone mountains
stand brown with blue lights;   at my right shoulder standing
Shasta, in summer standing, blue with her white lights
near a twilight summer moon, whiter than snow
where the light of evening changes among these legends.

Under me islands lie green, planted with green feathers,
green growing, shadowy grown, gathering streams of the green trees.
A hundred streams full of shadows and your upland source
pulled past sun-islands, green in this light as grace,
risen from your sun-mountains where your voices go
returning to water and music is your face.

Flows to the flower-haunted sea, naming and singing, under my eyes
coursing, the day of the world.   And the time of my spirit streams
before me, slow autumn colors, the cars of a long train;
earth-red, earth-orange, leaf, rust, twilight of earth
stream past the evening river and over into the dark of north,
stream slow like wishes continuing toward those snows.

SPEECH OF THE MOTHER, FROM
THE MIDDLE OF THE AIR

Act I, Sc. 4.   She is lit, standing high, with the lit line of Anne's
sleeping body at her knee.   Darkness around.
Her soliloquy will indicate the passage of a year.

A year passes behind me.   Shadows grow larger.   Time
dissolves to a moment.   I look to my children.   They
change. A smile, a brush of the lips against my heart;   things
brighten and vanish into a kind of joy, a kind of light.
Chaos began us, war in my own time, war in my children's time,
irrevocable accusation!   I have heard the music of the sounds of
        peace:
music of rivers, of street-corners, of our South,
blues, harvest-songs;   and in the faces of lovers
seen all our challenge shining as a sign
                to shape the future in love and birth.
Women standing in their houses set around with order—
the bread, the doorways and tables of everyday living
through all the walls have heard the shouts of fighting,
                planes in the air,
and a shrill cry of women tortured under time,
each one carrying loss like conception : a lover gone,
or a son, or her brothers disappeared. One saying, "Spain!   Spain!"
One desolate for her unborn children.   One standing alone
outside of lighted windows, or black against raving fires
                of this year and next year.
Chaos began us, a people skillful in war, young in love,
and in peace unbegun.   A people various as life
whose strength is in our many voices and our hope
of a future of many, each singing his own song.
For we know this struggle   :   more than forces in conflict,

we know it as always the rising changing shadow of a dream.
A woman moving in my own house among my daughters,
I remember their hands when they were little, and smoothing
their shining hair.   They change.   And one will have her child.
                    The year passes.   Around me chaos grows.
     And darkly
our time renews itself.   And equilibrium, the healer, the young one,
the beginning of new life, poises itself on war.   And life
moves in its sharpened color into another year.
As I grow old, I face the strange seasons, I rejoice in the young,
and I say, in suffering, in joy, among the marvelous changes,
                    among the accusations, all things glow.

THEN I SAW WHAT THE CALLING WAS

All the voices of the wood called "Muriel!"
but it was soon solved;   it was nothing, it was not for me.
The words were a little like Mortal and More and Endure
and a word like Real, a sound like Health or Hell.
Then I saw what the calling was   :   it was the road I traveled, the clear
time and these colors of orchards, gold behind gold and the full
shadow behind each tree and behind each slope.   Not to me
the calling, but to anyone, and at last I saw   :   where
the road lay through sunlight and many voices and the marvel
orchards, not for me, not for me, not for me.
I came into my clear being;   uncalled, alive, and sure.
Nothing was speaking to me, but I offered and all was well.

And then I arrived at the powerful green hill.

Translations: Six Poems by Octavio Paz

THE BIRD

Silence of the air, of the light, of sky.
In this transparent silence
day was resting:
the transparency of space
was silence's transparency.
Motionless light of the sky was slowing
the growth of the grass.
Small things of earth, among the stones,
under identical light, were stone.
Time was sated in a minute.
And in the absorbed stillness
Noonday consumed itself.

And a bird sang, slender arrow.
The wounded silver breast shivered the sky,
the leaves moved,
and grass awoke.
And I knew that death was an arrow
who cannot know the finger on the string
and in the flicker of an eye we die.

POET'S EPITAPH

He sang until his death
singing to close his eyes
to his true life, his real life of lies;
and to remember till he died
how it had lied, his unreal life of truth.

SPARK

Sparks of fishes
in the night of the sea
and birds, sparks
in the forest night.
Our bones are sparks
in the night of the flesh.
O world, night everywhere,
the spark being life.

TWO BODIES

Two bodies face to face
are at times two waves
and night is an ocean.

Two bodies face to face
are at times two stones
and night is a desert.

Two bodies face to face
are at times two knives
and night strikes sparks.

Two bodies face to face
are at times two roots
and night is the earth.

Two bodies face to face
are two stars falling down
in an empty sky.

THE STREET

Here is a long and silent street.
I walk in blackness and I stumble and fall

and rise, and I walk blind, my feet
trampling the silent stones and the dry leaves.
Someone behind me also tramples, stones, leaves:
if I slow down, he slows;
if I run, he runs.   I turn : nobody.
Everything dark and doorless,
only my steps aware of me,
I turning and turning among these corners
which lead forever to the street
where nobody waits for, nobody follows me,
where I pursue a man who stumbles
and rises and says when he sees me : nobody.

LOVERS

Lying in the grass
girl and boy.
Eating oranges, exchanging kisses
like waves exchanging whiteness.

Lying on the beach
girl and boy.
Eating apples, exchanging kisses
like clouds exchanging whiteness.

Lying underground
girl and boy.
Saying nothing, never kissing,
exchanging silence for silence.

❧ Rari from the Marquesas

RARI FOR TAHIA AND PIU

by Moa Tetua

The dream-image fades, with its red pandanu keys
Strung with leaves, wet in the small rain!
He is a handsome garland.
Tahia's mouth is brave, but her eyes tremble at the spring.
Desire aroused for the valley-side boy,
Bringing the gifts of a valiant husband,
A rare fan of speckled feathers
And the loin-cloth.

Come and find the fruit!
Hold your breath!
Pressed close to my lover in the mountain,
Hidden away like children, he and I
Until the shadows of the sun climb past the mountain-top.
The *kawa* leaves have risen high toward me!
Climb the high tree, break off, O piu,
The branch of the treasure.
Swing over the precipice we call Flowers-at-the-Peak.
My garland makes my lover happy.
Lightning flashes on the mountainflowers
Like my eyes calling you
To sleep in shame at the house of songs.
For the first time, you see the ripe and lovely fruit.
I also have seen you before, while you were tabu.

When I lay down with the chief, the sun was hot,
Handsome, you came along the stream,
My chief, my love, my soul, my palm-leaf.
My shining leaf. Farewell. The cloth is wet with tears,
    mucus and tears.
I am wet, swollen and wet and left alone.
You are away on the far, silent river.

RARI FOR O'OTUA

by Moa Tetua

The sun climbs, hot and burning overhead
And they return, deep in me, thoughts of love.
I sail a surf-board, landing on your shore,
And my soul walks toward you, stops.   I startle you.
In the night, it is good for man to be unwed,
We are locked together till dawn is on the sea.
The last day, when I have to go, we weep.
I cannot take my eyes from your tattooing.
My garlands, my potent fruit-plucking pole, go down to the shadows.
—You are the virile one, scented with oils, the lover.
Pick my flower, O'Otua.
Kiss the superb wide-awake flower,
It is love burning in my heart.
Cut it . . . hurry up the path!
My hand, haphazard, crushes the whiteness of love.
My opened clothes were torn like this, and the clasps.

A TRUE CONFESSION

by Moa Tetua

A true confession!
My love is gone in an earth-clinging rainbow!
She is gone!   My eyes are blind with tears, mist before mountains,
The sea grows smaller, feebler,
And rain pours down indeed.
My tears flow from the prison.
I dream of the after-life and of my love.
The sea of my sweetheart is at low tide,
Love in my heart.
Then dawn-clouds come, the clouds dear to the god,
Great clouds rise up, up to the source of love.
Two lovers parted, and my finished dream.
The surf rises, I am held fast, taken,
Held fast, flung away, cast out on coral reefs.
Into the depths, roar upon roar!

CAREFUL OF THE DAY

by Moa Tetua

Care for love tenderly, it is deep in me.
Be careful of the day when you are old,
And old, the garlands are gone and the love-making.
Can you forget
The day we wandered into the strange cave
When we were lost?
The moon was new;
When we were parted from each other
There was only hunger.   —
I turn my head,
My head is in the shadow of a high-standing flower.
I know my real food.

RARI FOR HEPUHEKU

by Puko'i

O my singing lover
Bringing strength and love.
O my singing lover
Bring me a child!
Uncover the Chinese cloth!

O my singing lover,
I gave you a hat and garland
Of vanilla flowers,
Half-opened laurel blossoms,
Half-opened laurel blossoms,
Half-opened laurel flowers!

Come, gardenia of Tahiti,
Strike with the rice-white weapon,
Into heaven twist and turn
The circumcised end—
Raise the blue flower!

RARI

by Taman

I wear a garland and take my beloved's hand,
Dewdrops are in my song, dewdrops.
A gift of a wreath, a gift of peace.

Strong fires disturb her, the girl is mad with love.
My thoughts are sad, in the cruel mists and mountains.
I weep as I make my clothes.   I sing.   Why has he gone?

I wear a garland of seven-petaled flowers.
The mountains are our love, the sky our clothing,
And wreaths our destruction.

RARI TO ENCOURAGE YOUTH

by Kahu'Einui

When a man's body is young
At night he gives up his sleep
And sings, and sings!

Lovesick, with the singing sickness,
With the dizzy sickness,
When even earth and clouds flame with desire!

Chorus.   Until the body is like an old woman,
             Like an eel in a hole in the sea,
             Pounding, pounding!

RARI, TO BE BOTHERED
BY MOSQUITOES

by Te'i'i Puei

Here's the story, my darling, of the dancing flower.
Song of nothing, song of nothing at all.
What about it?

Chorus.   How can I stay alone?
             How can I live alone?
             How can I love alone?
             How can I sing alone?

From Sombre-water came the love
I dreamed of in the night.
Until the cock crowed I had my joy,
And I sweated.

My lover is carried on currents of the sea!
And I stay to sleep alone,
Bothered by mosquitoes,
And sleeping all alone!

NOT BEFORE I FALL ASLEEP

The clouds are dark
Above the mountain-top —
The sweet-smelling skin
Of my love, and her gay garlands!
O not too soon, not too soon,
Not before I fall asleep. . . .

Chorus.   You desire me!   You love me!
             You make me fall with you in a comet.
             A song, a song.
             For your brow a wreath and a song.

Easter Eve 1945

EASTER EVE 1945

Wary of time O it seizes the soul tonight
I wait for the great morning of the west
confessing with every breath mortality.
Moon of this wild sky struggles to stay whole
and on the water silvers the ships of war.
I go alone in the black-yellow light
all night waiting for day, while everywhere the sure
death of light, the leaf's sure return to the root
is repeated in million, death of all man to share.
Whatever world I know shines ritual death,
wide under this moon they stand gathering fire,
fighting with flame, stand fighting in their graves.
All shining with life as the leaf, as the wing shines,
the stone deep in the mountain, the drop in the green wave.
Lit by their energies, secretly, all things shine.
Nothing can black that glow of life;   although
　　　.　　each part go crumbling down
　　　　itself shall rise up whole.

Now I say there are new meanings;   now I name
death our black honor and feast of possibility
to celebrate casting of life on life.   This earth-long day
between blood and resurrection where we wait
remembering sun, seed, fire;   remembering
that fierce Judaean Innocent who risked
every immortal meaning on one life.
Given to our year as sun and spirit are,
as seed we are blessed only in needing freedom.
Now I say that the peace the spirit needs is peace,
not lack of war, but fierce continual flame.
For all men　:　effort is freedom, effort's peace,
it fights.   And along these truths the soul goes home,
　　　flies in its blazing to a place
　　　more safe and round than Paradise.

Night of the soul, our dreams in the arms of dreams
dissolving into eyes that look upon us.
Dreams the sources of action, the meeting and the end,
a resting-place among the flight of things.
And love which contains all human spirit, all wish,
the eyes and hands, sex, mouth, hair, the whole woman—
fierce peace I say at last, and the sense of the world.
In the time of conviction of mortality
whatever survive, I remember what I am.—
The nets of this night are on fire with sun and moon
pouring both lights into the open tomb.
Whatever arise, it comes in the shape of peace,
fierce peace which is love, in which move all the stars,
and the breathing of universes, filling, falling away,
and death on earth cast into the human dream.
        What fire survive forever
        myself is for my time.

PRIVATE LIFE OF THE SPHINX

for Ella Winter

1

Simply because of a question, my life is implicated:
my flesh and answer fly between chaos and their need.
On the rock I asked the shaky king
one foolish question to make him look at himself—
He looked.   Beheld himself and kingdoms.   Took.
My claws and smile transferred into his myth.

Babble of demand, and answers building the brilliant cities
the standing battlefields and the fields of the fallen down.

Now in this city in the Lounge of Time,
I tell you it was a legend founded on fire,
founded on what we are.   Simply because I asked one question,
"What is this, What?"   so that the answer must be "Man."
Because of that they bring their riddles and rhyme
to my door if I houseless run throughout the world,
torse of a woman and quarters of a lion.

2

Open war with its images of love and death—
man, an explosion walking through the night in
rich and intolerable loneliness.
Cathedrals writhing gold against their clouds
and a child asking the fiery pure questions.
The monkey-dark, a month of smoky violets,
delicate repose of my reality among
dreams, and the angel of the resurrection,
a mouth overhead, the sky planted with stars.

My questions are my body.   And among this glowing, this sure,
this fact, this mooncolored breast, I make memorial.

3

My body is set against disorder.   Risen among enigmas,
time and the question carry a rose of form,
sing a life-song.   Strangler and bitch, they said,
but they mistook the meaning of my name:
I am the root who embraces and the source.
I sing.   I sing.

In these cities, all suffer from their weaknesses—
they lack some gut, they are ill, they have womb-envy,
run howling from the question and the act.
They bring me their need for answers in their hands and eyes.
To embody truth, the Irish old man said.

I remember in Calabria a peasant
broad, smiling, and sly, with a bird throbbing and small
behind his back, in his hands;   and he asked his question.
Is it alive? and he smiled at me.   Then I knew
if I said Yes, he would twist the sparrow's neck.
The fool of time!   I gave him my only answer,
that answer of time:
Fool, I said, you know it depends on you
whether it live or die.

4

I answer!   I fly reborn from deep escape!
Listen to their cries, the selfsame crying throats,
crying the selfsame need.

Here is my self.   I touch you, life reaches me.
You touch me, I am able to give my gifts.
All the acts flow together, a form being made.
I know a garden beyond questioning—
can almost see night-flowering white mallows,
can almost tell you below the sound of water,
white lilac like a voluptuous light
shining at full on our two faces—
It goes ahead of our hope.   It is the secret that moves
with the speed of life,
    secrets of night and   the street
secrets of milk and dinner and daylight,
enigmas of gardens, the kitchen and the bed,
the riddle and sacrament in the knot of wood,
in the wine, in the water and root the coil of life.

They ask for answers, they starving eat their shadows.
The beginning is always here.   Its green demand.

        5

They think I answer and strangle.   They are wrong.
I set my life among the questioning.
The peasant, the wars, the wounded powerful king.
The shining of questions which cannot be concealed
lies in that mirror.   The little child to the mother
of the father's unspoken death, said   :   "You have told me
    yourself."
Even alone, away from daily life, the fire
and monster crown of the legend over me
reaches their eyes—children, friendship of lions,
the sense of the world at last broken through to man
in all fury, all sacred open mystery,
is in my question.
                    The stranger, the foreign and strong,
the child and king, wide village eyes of the farm,
the demand loud, or choking in surf-foam,
density of flowers, the faces of all love,
the core of our hope;   stronger than kill,
stronger almost than question, almost than song.

NINE POEMS FOR THE UNBORN CHILD

1

The childless years alone without a home
Flashed daily with the world's glimpse, happiness.
Always behind was the dark screen of loss
Hardly moving, like heavy hardly-moving cloud.
"Give me myself," or "Take me," I said aloud;
There was little to give, and always less to take.
Except the promise, except the promise darkness
Makes, night and daylight, miracle to come.

Flying over, I suddenly saw the traces
Of man : where man is, you may read the wind
In shadow and smoke, know how the wind is gone
And know the way of man;   in the fall of the plane
Into its levels, encounter the ancient spaces:
The fall to life, the cliff and strait of bone.

2

They came to me and said, "There is a child."
Fountains of images broke through my land.
My swords, my fountains spouted past my eyes
And in my flesh at last I saw.   Returned
To when we drove in the high forest, and earth
Turned to glass in the sunset where the wild
Trees struck their roots as deep and visible
As their high branches, the double planted world.

"There is no father," they came and said to me.
—I have known fatherless children, the searching, walk
The world, look at all faces for their father's life.
Their choice is death or the world.   And they do choose.
Earn their brave set of bone, the seeking marvelous look
Of those who lose and use and know their lives.

3

There is a place.   There is a miracle.
I know the nightmare, the black and bone piano,
The statues in the kitchen, a house dissolving in air.
I know the lilac-turreted cathedral
Taking its roots from willows that changed before my eyes

When all became real, real as the sound of bells.
We earthly are aware of transformation;
Miraculously, life, from the old despair.

The wave of smooth water approaches on the sea-
Surface, a live wave individual
Linking, massing its color.   Moving, is struck by wind,
Ribbed, steepened, until the slope and ridge begin;
Comes nearer, brightens.   Now curls, its vanishing
Hollows darken and disappear;   now high above
Me, the scroll, froth, foam of the overfall.

4

Now the ideas all change to animals
Loping and gay, now all the images
Transform to leaves, now all these screens of leaves
Are flowing into rivers, I am in love
With rivers, these changing waters carry voices,
Carry all children;   carry all delight.
The water-soothed winds move warm above these waves.
The child changes and moves among these waves.

The waves are changing, they tremble from waves of waters
To other essentials—they become waves of light
And wander through my sleep and through my waking,
And through my hands and over my lips and over
Me;   brilliant and transformed and clear,
The pure light.   Now I am light and nothing more.

5

Eating sleep, eating sunlight, eating meat,
Lying in the sun to stare
At deliverance, the rapid cloud,
Gull-wing opposing sun-bright wind,
I see the born who dare
Walk on green, walk against blue,
Move in the nightlong flare
Of love on darkness, traveling
Among the rings of light to simple light,
From nowhere to nowhere.
And in my body feel the seasons grow.
Who is it in the dim room?   Who is there?

6

Death's threat!   Today I have known laughter
As if for the first time;   have seen into your eyes,
Death, past the still gaze, and found two I love.
One chose you gladly with a laugh advancing,
His hands full of guns, on the enemy in Spain.
The other living with the choice of life
Turning each day of living to the living day.
The strength, the grossness, spirit and gall of choice.

They came to me and said, "If you must choose,
Is it yourself or the child?"   Laughter I learned
In that moment, laughter and choice of life.
I saw an immense ship trembling on the water
Lift by a gesture of hands.   I saw a child.   I saw
A red room, the eyes, the hands, the hands and eyes.

7

You will enter the world where death by fear and explosion
Is waited;   longed for by many;   by all dreamed.
You will enter the world where various poverty
Makes thin the imagination and the bone.
You will enter the world where birth is walled about,
Where years are walled journeys, death a walled-in act.
You will enter the world which eats itself
Naming faith, reason, naming love, truth, fact.

You in your dark lake moving darkly now
Will leave a house that time makes, times to come
Enter the present, where all the deaths and all
The old betrayals have come home again.
World where again Judas, the little child,
May grow and choose.   You will enter the world.

8

Child who within me gives me dreams and sleep,
Your sleep, your dreams;   you hold me in your flesh
Including me where nothing has included
Until I said : I will include, will wish
And in my belly be a birth, will keep
All delicacy, all delight unclouded.

Dreams of an unborn child move through my dreams,
The sun is not alone in making fire and wave
Find meeting-place, for flesh and future meet,
The seal in the green wave like you in me,
Child.   My blood at night full of your dreams,
Sleep coming by day as strong as sun on me,
Coming with sun-dreams where leaves and rivers meet,
And I at last alive sunlight and wave.

9

Rider of dream, the body as an image
Alone in crisis.   I have seen the wind,
Its tall cloud standing on a pillar of air,
The toe of the whirlwind turning on the ground.
Have known in myself hollow bodiless shade,
The shadow falling from the tree to the ground,
Have lost and lost and now at last am found
For a moment of sleep and waking, striking root.

Praise that the homeless may in their bodies be
A house that time makes, where the future moves
In his dark lake.   Praise that the cities of men,
The fields of men, may at all moments choose.
Lose, use, and live.   And at this daylight, praise
To the grace of the world and time that I may hope
To live, to write, to see my human child.

Orpheus

1949

1

The mountaintop stands in silence a minute after the murder.
    The women are furies racing down the slope;   far down,
    copper and black of hair, the white heel running,
    escaped line of skirt and foot,
among the leaves and needles of these witness trees.
    Overhead, clouds, lions and towers of the sky.
Darkness masses among the treetops;   dense shapes bulk
    among treetrunks over the murdered ground,
    stain of light glancing on the jointed branches.
Light of water, blaze of the comet-tailed stars.
The scene is the mountain, just after the murder,
    with a dry concentrated moon
rocking back and forth between the crowns of trees,
    back and forth, until over this black crown,
attacking the sharp black and the secrecy, moon comes to rest.
    And the exhausted
women are streaming down the paths at the foot
    of the mountain, now fleeing,
now halted by the sleep that follows murder.
From this moment, the darkness fills the walls of rivers,
and the walls of houses and in the villages
the walls, the olive groves, remembrances and pillars
of dark.   Murder.   Scattered and done.
Down in his blood on a holy mountaintop.
All the voices are done; very deep, they rest, they are alone.
Only the breath around the earth moves, in a slow rested rhythm,
    as the moon
comes to rest over that treepoint swaying like the breast
of an escaping woman.   Down
from the moon one cloud falls and it passes, sails upon
this place in the forest where the god is slain.
These golden breasts have troubled heaven.
But they are breasts of tears;   their act is done;   and down,
here on wet ground, scattered, the flowing man.
Scattered, there lit, in black and golden blood :
his hand, a foot, a flat breast, phallus, a foot,
shoulder and sloping back and lyre and murdered head.

Hacked, stopped, he bleeds with the long dayblood's life.
Has bled until the moon cleared range and rose, female and male,
shining on treetops and water and on the pieces of a man.

Very quiet, the trees awake.   And find their voices.   But
the clouds are first, they have begun their song
over these air-cut, over these river-cut mountains—
Lost!   they build the sound of Lost!   the dark level clouds
voice under voice arranged in white arpeggios
on the high air, the statement of the sky
rides across, very high, very clear,
singing Lost;   lost man.
And the river falls among the plunging forests,
the heartshaped waterfall goes down like the fall of man

seeking, and crying one word, earth's water speaking of harvest.
But moon says No : in finished night the great moon overrides,
promising new moons only, saying I know no harvests—
My harvest, declares in whiteness, are the tides to come.
These words are called in a silence
over the scattered man.
The clouds move, the river moves,
the great moon slowly moves;   even more slowly now,
the first finger of the right hand.

The right hand stirred in the small grass and said
"Do more;   for this is how it is,"   and died again.

2

1

Scattered.   The fool of things.   For here is Orpheus,
without his origin   :   the body, mother of self,
the earliest self, the mother of permanence.
He is sensation and matter, all forms and no form.
He is the pieces of Orpheus and he is chaos.

All myths are within the body when it is most whole,
all positions being referred to flesh in unity—
slow changes of form, the child and growing man

as friends have seen him, altered by absences and years.
Scatterings cannot discern changes of quality:

This scattered on the mountain is no man
but body as circus.

Sideshow of parts, the freaks of Orpheus.

2

The wounds   :   Touch me!   Love me!   Speak to me!
The hand risen to reap, standing upon its wrist
and singing, "I will do," among its dreams.
The hunter eye in the forest, going mad.
The waste and shed of song that ritual made,
and the wandering, loss of forms, the darkened light,
as the eye said:

I looked at night, to rainbow-crested moon,
as to round-crested sun I looked at day.
Stare that fertilizes the threshold of square Hell,
stare pacing the forest, staring the death away.

Give everything.   Ask not beyond the daily light.
I shine, am reflected in all that is and will be,
names, surfaces, the void where light is born.
There was something I saw.   Something not to be seen.
But I cannot remember;   and I cannot see.

3

The wounds   :   Touch me!   Speak to me!   Love me!
In darklit death, the strong pyramid heart
knows something of the source, the maze of blood
the deeper fountains and dance of certain colors.
Something was founded at the base of the heart,
it cannot find it now, but the blood's pilgrimage
carries its relics and the sacred banners
far from this mountaintop to the beating valves of the sea.
It cannot clench.

There was song, and the tomb of song,
there was love, but it all escapes.   What love?   For whom?

4

The wounds   :   Speak to me!
The arm that living held the lyre
understands touch me, the thrill of string on hand
saying to fingers   Who am I?
Father of songs,
when all the doors are open,
beyond the clasp of power,
the mastery of undiscovered music,
what laying on of grace?
Healing of the valleys of sacrifice
and five rivers finally trembling down
to open sea.
I almost remember another body,
I almost, another face.

5

The wounds   :   Love me!
Something turned back, something looked Hellward round.
Not this hard heelbone, something that lived and ran.
The muscles of the thigh are the rapids of a stream,
the knee a monument stone among fast waters,
light flowing under the skin, the current hardnesses,
channels where, secret, the awareness streamed.

                                         No!

That was not how it was!

                          They will say I turned to a face.
That was forbidden. There was a moment of turning,
but not to a face. This leg did turn,
there was a turn, and then there was a journey,
and after many dances and wanderings
Yes;   but there was a face.

6

Who will speak to the wounds?   Who will have grace,
who will touch this broken, who will dare being whole
to offer healing?   Who broken enough to know
that the gift is the only real, who will heal these wounds?

Rolled like a stone in a riverbed
The stone exposed in the dry riverbed
This head of dreams, horizon of this murder,
rolled on the mountaintop.   The man who is all head,
this is, in the circus.   Arches of music, arches of the brain,
furrows and harvests plowed by song.   Whom song
could never capture.   This it was alive
led Jason past the sirens, this
in Egypt and in Hell had heard of Heaven
and reading Moses found the breath of life,
looked up and listening felt the breath of death
at the left ear, finding then every life
among the men of mud and the men of sunlight
the women turned to light in the eyes of this head.
The head;   the song;   and the way to transcend.
The song and chance.   The way beyond the wound.
Rolled, like the music of an old ballad,
a song of heroes, a stone, a hope, a star over head.

The head turns into a cloud and the cloud rises
unwounded, the cloud assumes the shape of plants,
a giant plant.   Rolls to the great anvil storm-cloud,
creates the storm.   This is the head of dream.

      7

Only there is a wound that cries all night.
We have not yet come through.   It cries Speak, it cries Turn.

Majesty, lifted omen.   The power to make.
The burning ship that sails to the burning sun
a sun half sky half water wholly flame,
the burning ship half wood half water all fire.
There is no riddle but all is mystery.
There is only life.   To live is to create.

Father of song, in the seed and vaults of the sea,
the wall of light and pillars of desire,
the dark.   The dark.   But I will know again,
I will know more and again,
woman and man.

8

And turn and arise and give these wounds their song.
They have no song and no music.   They are wounds.
And the air-tree, the air-heart
cannot propose old death-breath any song.
Fountain of air, I see you offering,
this air is a bird among the scenes of the body,
a golden plover, a blackheart plover.
Here is his body and the trees of life,
the red tree, the ivory, the tree of nerves,
powerless to bear another song.
Chopped like the chopped gold of fields harvested,
air falling through many seductive shapes,
cascades of air.
The shadow falling from the tree to the ground.

9

Let the wounds change.   Let them not cry aloud.

Blood-clothed structure, bone of body's being,
there is no sin here, all the giant emotions
were uncorrupted, but there is no sign.
The bones and the skein of flowing, the many-chaining
blood and the chain of dreams and chain of silver nerves
cannot remember.   They cannot imagine.   No space
is here, no chance nor geometry,
any more than this mountain has its space or chance.
The mountain looks down the road.   It sees the last of the women
escaped and alone, running away the road.
It sees one woman in a million shapes,
procession of women down the road of time.
They have changed into weapons;   now they need be whole.
And the pieces of the body cannot be.
They do not even know they need be whole.
Only the wounds in their endless crying.
Now they know.

10

Touch me!   Love me!   Speak to me!
One effort and one risk.
The hand is risen.   It braces itself, it flattens,
and the third finger touches the lyre.   Wounds of hand.

But it finds thick gold of frame, grasps the frame
with its old fingering of bone and gold.
Now there is blood, a train of blood on grass
as hand swings high and with a sowing gesture
throws the lyre upward.   The lyre is going up:
the old lyre of Orpheus, four strings of song
of the dawn of all things, daystar, daymoon, and man,
hurtles up, whistling through black air.
Tingles in moon-air.   Reaches the other stars.
And these four strings now sing:
Eurydice.

3

Standing in silence on the mountaintop, the trees incline
        before the breath of fire.
Very slowly, the sounds awake.   Breathing that is the
        consciousness, the lifting
and the resting of life, and surf-sounds of many flames.
Flame in its flowing streams about these pieces
and under the sides of clouds and chars the branches.
It does not touch the flesh.   Now the flesh moves,
the hacked foot and the hand and the head,
buttocks and heart, phallus and breast, compose.
Now the body is formed;   and the blood of Orpheus,
spilled, soaked, and deep under the wet ground,
rises in fountains playing into the wounds.
Now the body is whole;   but it is covered with murder.
A mist of blood and fire shines over the body,
shining upon the mountain, a rose of form.
And now the wounds losing self-pity change,
they are mouths, they are the many mouths of music.
And now they, disappear.   He is made whole.
The mist dissolves into the body of song.

A lake of fire lowers, tendrils level to source,
over the mountaintop many young streams.
Standing newborn and naked, Orpheus.
He has died the death of the god.

His gifts are to be made, in a newfound voice,
his body his voice.   His truth has turned into life.
—When I looked back in that night, I looked beyond love at hell.
           All the poets and powers will recognize.
           I thought the kings of Hell would recognize.
           I misjudged evil. —
                                    He has opened the door of pain.
It is a door and a window and a lens
opening on another land;   pain standing wide
and the world crystallized in broken rains.

Nightmares of scatterings are past, the disc of music and day
makes dawn and the streams make seed of towering fern.
The green night rising in flower,
helmet-flower, nebula-flower, lilacs in their turrets of air,
and stain of morningside bright on the low sky under
new constellations of anatomy.
Ripple of grape, trembling star in the vine of water,
the night-goer rises in color before a parade of clouds.
Now he remembers the real;   remembers love.
His life is simpler than the sum of its parts.
The arrangement is the life.   It is the song.

His death is the birth of the god.
He sings the coming things, he sings arrivals,
the blood reversing from the soaked ground, warmth
passing over the lands where now barren resists,
fertile and wet invite, all in their way receive.
And all the weapons meld into his song.
The weapons, the wounds, the women his murderers.
He sings the leaves of the trees, the music of immense forests,
the young arriving, the leaf of time and their selves
their crying for their needs and their successes,
developing through these to make their gifts.   In flower.
All who through crises of the body pass
to the human life and the music of the source.

Are there songs rising from the broken sources?
The mountain   the bright cloud   and the cities risen.
The faceless and the unborn in their transfigured song.
The god a god because there are birth and death
approaching each other in their blood and fragments,

the death and birth at last identified.
He has died the birth of the god.

The animal and song beneath the skin,
seeking an exit, baited with food and wounds;
no, not an exit.   What are they seeking?

Cyclic dependence   the god and the miracle
needing each other,   and all the wounds are mouths,
weapon to song transfigured.

Song of the air between us, of the voiceless alone,
the cloud diffusing over the island country
pulled down in the shape of a plant, shape of a brain,
collected into the ground and will of man.
Song of the dam destroyed   over the widening river
in a triumph of hope;   song of the flute in the kitchen,
a little bright water boiling on the stove.
Song.   The frozen man, his axe in the sequoia;
blueberries, toyon berries, black galleries of coal,
ferocious gestures of work and the bed of the poor.
The unmade music of the power to rise,
the young and unborn, the throat and hand of song.
The body risen past its other life.

Among the acts and the memories he remembers—
he brings together and he binds—
among the firewind and the cloud chamber,
he is aware, he knows the nature of power,
the nature of music and the nature of love.
Knowing the enemies, those who, deprived at the root,
flourish in thorny action, having lost the power
to act essentially, they fall into the sin
of all the powerless.   They commit their acts of evil
in order to repent, repent and forgive, murder and begin again.

To have gone through.
To live and begin again.
The body alive and offering,
whole, up and alive,
and to all men, man and woman,
and to all the unborn,

the mouth shall sing
music past wounding
and the song begin:

SONG

Voices and days, the exile of our music
and the dividing airs are gathered home.
The hour of light and birth at last appears
among the alone, in prisons of scattering.
Seeming of promise, the shining of new stars,
the stars of the real over the body of love.
The cloud, the mountain, and the cities risen.
Solving the wars of the dead, and offering dream
making and morning.   Days and voices, sing
creation not yet come.

Elegies

1949

FIRST ELEGY. ROTTEN LAKE

As I went down to Rotten Lake I remembered
the wrecked season, haunted by plans of salvage,
snow, the closed door, footsteps and resurrections,
      machinery of sorrow.

The warm grass gave to the feet and the stilltide water
was floor of evening and magnetic light and
reflection of wish, the black-haired beast with my eyes
      walking beside me.

The green and yellow lights, the street of water standing
point to the image of that house whose destruction
I weep when I weep you. My door (no), poems, rest,
      (don't say it!) untamable need.

When you have left the river you are a little way
nearer the lake; but I leave many times.
Parents parried my past; the present was poverty,
the future depended on my unfinished spirit.
There were no misgivings because there was no choice,
only regret for waste, and the wild knowledge:
growth and sorrow and discovery.

When you have left the river you proceed alone;
all love is likely to be illicit; and few
friends to command the soul; they are too feeble.
Rejecting the subtle and contemplative minds
as being too thin in the bone; and the gross thighs
and unevocative hands fail also. But the poet
and his wife, those who say Survive, remain;
and those two who were with me on the ship
leading me to the sum of the years, in Spain.

When you have left the river you will hear the war.
In the mountains, with tourists, in the insanest groves
the sound of kill, the precious face of peace.
And the sad frightened child, continual minor,
returns, nearer whole circle, O and nearer
all that was loved, the lake, the naked river,

what must be crossed and cut out of your heart,
what must be stood beside and straightly seen.

&

As I went down to Rotten Lake I remembered
how the one crime is need. The man lifting the loaf
with hunger as motive can offer no alibi, is
        always condemned.

These are the lines at the employment bureau
and the tense students at their examinations;
needing makes clumsy and robs them of their wish,
        in one fast gesture

plants on them failure of the imagination;
and lovers who lower their bodies into the chair
gently and sternly as if the flesh had been wounded,
        never can conquer.

Their need is too great, their vulnerable bodies
rigidly joined will snap, turn love away,
fear parts them, they lose their hands and voices, never
        get used to the world.

Walking at night, they are asked Are you your best friend's
best friend?   and must say No, not yet, they are
love's vulnerable, and they go down to Rotten Lake
        hoping for wonders.

Dare it arrive, the day when weakness ends?
When the insistence is strong, the wish converted?
I prophesy the meeting by the water
        of these desires.

I know what this is, I have known the waking
when every night ended in one cliff-dream
of faces drowned beneath the porous rock
        brushed by the sea;

suffered the change : deprived erotic dreams
to images of that small house where peace
walked room to room and always with one face
        telling her stories,

and needed that, past loss, past fever, and the
attractive enemy who in my bed
touches all night the body of my sleep,
      improves my summer

with madness, impossible loss, and the dead music
of altered promise, a room torn up by the roots,
the desert that crosses from the door to the wall,
      continual bleeding,

and all the time that will which cancels enmity,
seeks its own Easter, arrives at the water-barrier;
must face it now, biting the lakeside ground;
      looks for its double,

the twin that must be met again, changeling need,
blazing in color somewhere, flying yellow
into the forest with its lucid edict:
      take to the world,

this is the honor of your flesh, the offering
of strangers, the faces of cities, honor of all your wish.
Immortal undoing!   I say in my own voice.   These prophecies
      may all come true,

out of the beaten season.   I look in Rotten Lake
wait for the flame reflection, seeing only
the free beast flickering black along my side
      animal of my need,

and cry I want!   I want!   rising among the world
to gain my converted wish, the amazing desire
that keeps me alive, though the face be still, be still,
the slow dilated heart know nothing but lack,
now I begin again the private rising,
the ride to survival of that consuming bird
beating, up from dead lakes, ascents of fire.

SECOND ELEGY. AGE OF MAGICIANS

A baroque night advances in its clouds,
maps strain loose and are lost, the flash-flood breaks,
the lifting moonflare lights this field a moment,
while death as a skier curves along the snows,
death as an acrobat swings year to year,
turns down to us the big face of a nurse.
Roads open black, and the magicians come.

The aim of magicians is inward pleasure.
The prophet lives by faith and not by sight,
Being a visionary, he is divided,
or Cain, forever shaken by his crime.
Magnetic ecstasy, a trance of doom
mean the magician, worshipping a darkness
with gongs and lurid guns, the colors of force.
He is against the unity of light.

The Magician has his symbols, brings up his children by them:
the march-step, the staircase at night, the long cannon.
The children grow in authority and become
Molitor, Dr. Passavant, powerful Dr. Falcon,
bring their professors, and soon may govern
the zone, the zodiac, the king on his throne.
"Because the age holds its own dangers.
Because snow comes with lightnings, omens with all seasons."
(The Prophet covers his face against the wall,
weeps, fights to think again, to plan to start
the dragon, the ecliptic, and the heart.)

The Magician lifts himself higher than the world.
The Prophets were more casual. They endured,
and in the passive dread of solitude
heard calls, followed veiled, in midnight humility.
They claimed no preference;   they separated
unity from blindness
living from burning
tribute from tribute.

They have gone under, and do they come again?
The index of prophecy is light

and steeped therein
the world with all its signatures visible.

and steeped therein

Does this life permit its living to wear strength?
Who gives it, protects it.   It is food.
Who refuses it, it eats in time as food.
It is the world and it eats the world.
Who knows this, knows.   This has been said.

This is the vision in the age of magicians:
it stands at immense barriers, before mountains:
'I came to you in the form of a line of men,
and when you threw down the paper, and when you sat at the play,
and when you killed the spider, and when you saw the shadow
of the fast plane skim fast over your lover's face.
And when you saw the table of diplomats,
the newsreel of ministers, the paycut slip,
the crushed child's head, clean steel, factories,
the chessmen on the marble of the floor,
each flag a country, each chessman a live man,
one side advancing southward to the pit,
one side advancing northward to the lake,
and when you saw the tree, half bright half burning.
You never inquired into these meanings.
If you had done this, you would have been restored.'

The word is war.
And there is a prediction that you are the avenger.

They cut the people's hands, and their shoulders were left,
they cut their feet off, and their thighs were whole,
they cut them down to the torse, but the voice shouted,
they cut the head off, but the heart rang out.

And in the residential districts, where nothing ever happens,
armies of magicians filled the streets,
shouting
Need! Bread! Blood! Death!

And all this is because of you.
And all this is avenged by you.

Your index light, your voice the voice,
your tree half green and half burning,
half dead half bright,
your cairns, your beacons, your tree in green and flames,
unbending smoke in the sky, planes' noise, the darkness,
magic to fight.   Much to restore, now know.   Now be
Seer son of Sight, Hearer, of Ear, at last.

THIRD ELEGY. THE FEAR OF FORM

Tyranny of method!   the outrageous smile
seals the museums, pours a mob skidding
up to the formal staircase, stopped, mouths open.
And do they stare?   They do.
At what?   A sunset?

Blackness, obscurity, bravado were the three colors;
wit-play, movement, and wartime the three moments;
formal groups, fire, facility, the three hounds.

This was their art : a wall daubed like a face,
a penis or finger dipped in a red pigment.
The sentimental frown gave them their praise,
prized the wry color, the twisted definition,
and said, "You are right to copy."

But the car full of Communists put out hands and guns,
blew 1–2–3 on the horn before the
surrealist house, a spiral in Cataluña.

New combinations : set out materials now,
combine them again!   the existence is the test.
What do you want?   Lincoln blacking his lessons
in charcoal on an Indiana shovel?
or the dilettante, the impresario's beautiful skull
choosing the tulip crimson satin, the yellow satin
as the ballet dances its tenth time to the mirror?
Or the general's nephew, epaulets from birth,
run down the concourse, shouting Planes for Spain?

New methods, the staring circle given again
force, a phoenix of power, another Ancient
sits in his circle, while the plaster model
of an equation slowly rotates beneath him,
and all his golden compass leans.
Create an anti-sentimental : Sing!
"For children's art is not asylum art,
there are these formal plays in living, for
the equal triangle does not spell youth,
the cube nor age, the sphere nor ever soul.
Asylum art is never children's art.
They cut the bones down, but the line remained.
They cut the line for good, and reached the point
blazing at the bottom of its night."

&

A man is walking, wearing the world, swearing
saying You damn fools come out into the open.
Whose dislocated wish?   Whose terrors whine?
I'll fuse him straight.
The usable present starts my calendar.
Chorus of bootblacks, printers, collectors of shit.
Your witwork works, your artwork shatters, die.
Hammer up your abstractions.   Divide, O zoo.
—He's a queer bird, a hero, a kangaroo.
What is he going to do?

He calls Rise out of cities, you memorable ghosts
scraps of an age whose choice is seen
to lie between evils.   Dazzle-paint the rest,
it burns my eyes with its acetylene.
Look through the wounds, mystic and human fly,
you spiritual unicorn, you clew of eyes.

Ghosts to approach the blood in fifteen cities.
Did you walk through the walls of the Comtesse de Noailles?
Was there a horror in Chicago?
Or ocean?   Or ditches at the road.   Or France,
while bearing guarding shadowing painting in Paris,
Picasso like an ass Picasso like a dragon Picasso like a
romantic movement
and immediately after, stations of swastikas

Prague and a thousand boys swing circles clean
girls by the thousand curve their arms together
geometries of wire
the barbed, starred
Heil

Will you have capitals with their tarnished countesses
their varnished cemetery life
vanished Picassos
or clean acceptable Copenhagen
or by God a pure high monument
white yellow and red
up against Minnesota?

Does the sea permit its dead to wear jewels?

Flame, fusion, defiance are your three guards,
the sphere, the circle, the cluster your three guides,
the bare, the blond and the bland are your three goads.

Adam, Godfinger, only these contacts function:
light and the high accompanied design,
contact of points   the fusion say of sex
the atombuster too along these laws.
Put in a sphere, here, at the focal joint,
he said, put it in.   The moment is arrangement.
Currents washed through it, spun, blew white,
fused.   For!   the sphere!   proving!

This was the nightmare of a room alone,
the posture of grave figure, finger on other head,
he puts the finger of power on him,
optic of grandiose delusion.
All you adjacent and contagious points,
make room for fusion;   fall,
you monuments, snow on your heads,
your power, your pockets, your dead parts.

Standing at midnight corners under corner-lamps
we wear the coat and the shadow of the coat.
The mind sailing over a scene lets light arrive
conspicuous sunrise, the knotted smoke rising,

the world with all its signatures visible.
Play of materials in balance,
carrying the strain of a new process.
Of the white root, the nature of the base,
contacts, making an index.
And do they stare?   They do.
Our needs, our violences.
At what?   Contortion of body and spirit.
To fuse it straight.

FOURTH ELEGY. THE REFUGEES

And the child sitting alone planning her hope:
I want to write for my race.   But what race will you speak,
being American?   I want to write for the living.
But the young grow more around us every day.
They show new faces, they come from far, they live
occupied with escape, freeze in the passes, sail
early in the morning.   A few arrive to help.
        Mother, those were not angels, they were knights.

Many are cast out, become artists at rejection.
They saw the chute, the intelligible world
so wild become, it fell, a hairy apparent star
this time with not a public saint in sight
to record miracle. The age of the masked and the alone begins,
we look for sinister states, a loss shall learning suffer
before the circle of this sun be done,
the palace birds of the new tyrants rise
flying into the wounded sky, sky of catastrophe;
help may be near, but remedy is far,
rain, blood, milk, famine, iron, and epidemic
pour in the sky where a comet drags his tail.
The characters of the spectacles are dead,
nothing is left but ventriloquists and children,
and bodies without souls are not a sacrifice.

It is the children's voyage must be done
before the refugees come home again.

They run like lemmings out
building their suffocated bodies up
to let the full stream pass.
The predatory birds sail over them.
They dash themselves into lighthouses, where the great
        lights hold up,
they laugh at sympathy : "Have you nothing better to do
        in the trenches?"
And at that brink, that bending over doom,
become superior to themselves, in crisis.
There is an addition and fusion of qualities.

They are the children. They have their games.
They made a circle on a map of time,
skipping they entered it, laughing lifted the agate.
I will get you an orange cat, and a pig called Tangerine.
The gladness-bird beats wings against an opaque glass.
There is a white bird in the top of the tree.
They leave their games, and pass.

Cut. Frozen and cut. Off at the ankle. Off at the hip.
        Off at the knee. Cut off.
Crossing the mountains many died of cold.

We have spoken of guilt to you too long.
The blame grows on us who carry you the news.
And as the man bringing the story of suicide
lives with the fact, feels murder in himself,
as murderous regents with their gentle kings
know the seductions of crime long before death takes hold,
we bear their—
                a child crying shrill in a white street
"Aviación!" among the dust of geysers,
the curling rust of Spanish tile.
We bear their smile, we smile under the guilt,
in an access of sickness, "Let me alone, I'm healthy!"
cry. And in danger, the sexually witty
speak in short sentences, the unfulfilled.
While definition levels others out.
Wish : the unreality of fulfilled action.
Wish : the reality of fulfilled thought.
Images of luxury. Image of life.

A phoenix at play among the peonies.
The random torture predicts the random thought.
Over the thought and bird and flowers, the plane.

Coming to strange countries refugee children find
land burned over by winter, a white field and black star
falling like firework where no rockets are
into hell-cities with blank brick and church-bells
(I like this city. This is a peaceful city)
ringing the bees in the hot garden with their mixing sounds,
ringing the love that falters among these hills,
red-flowering maple and the laugh of peace.
It will take a bell-ringing god tremendous imagined descending
for the healing of hell.

A line of birds, a line of gods. Of bells.
And all the birds have settled on their shadows.
And down the shadowed street a line of children.
You can make out the child ahead of you.
It turns with a gesture that asks for a soft answer.
It sees the smaller child ahead of it.
The child ahead of it turns. Now, in the close-up
faces throw shadow off. It is yourself
walks down this street at five-year intervals,
seeing yourself diminishing ahead,
five years younger, and five years younger, and young,
until the farthest infant has a face
ready to grow into any child in the world.

They take to boats. The shipwreck of New York.
To trains whose sets of lines pass along boxes,
children's constructions.
Rush to rejection
foreknowing the steps,
        disfigurement of women, insults of disease,
        negations of power. They people the earth.
        They are the strong. They see the enemy.
        They dream the relaxed heart, coming again to power,
        the struggle, the Milk-Tree of Children's Paradise.

They are the real creation of a fictional character.
They fuse a dead world straight.

A line of shadowy children issues, surf issues it,
sickness boiled in their flesh, but they are whole,
insular strength surrounds them, hunger feeds them strong,
the ripened sun finds them, they are the first of the world,
free of the ferryman Nostalgia, who stares at the backward shore.
Growing free of the old in their slow growth of death,
they hold the flaming apples of the spring.
They are exposed to danger.
Ledges of water trick them,
they fall through the raw colors of excavations,
are crushed by monuments, high stone like whale-blow rising,
the backwash of machines can strike them down.
A hill on a map claims them, their procession reaches
a wavy topographical circle where
two gunners lie behind their steelwork margins,
spray shot across the line, do random death.
They fire in a world infected by trenches,
through epidemics of injuries, Madrid, Shanghai,
Vienna, Barcelona, all cities of contagion,
issue survivors from the surf of the age.
Free to be very hungry and very lonely.
And in the countries of the mind, Cut off at the knee.   Cut off at the
          armpit.   Cut off at the throat.
Free to reclaim the world and sow a legend,
to make the adjustments never made,
repair the promises broken and the promise kept.
They blame our lives, lie on our wishes with their eyes our own,
to say and to remember and avenge.   A lullaby for a believing child.

FIFTH ELEGY. A TURNING WIND

Knowing the shape of the country.   Knowing the midway travels of
migrant fanatics, living that life, up with the dawn and
moving as long as the light lasts, and when the sun is falling
          to wait, still standing;

and when the black has come, at last lie down, too tired to
turn to each other, feeling only the land's demand under them.
Shape that exists not as permanent quality, but varies with
          even the movement of bone.

Even in skeletons, it depends on the choices of action.
A definite plan is visible. We are either free-moving or
fixed to some ground. The shape has no meaning
   outside of the function.

Fixed to Europe, the distant, adjacent, we lived, with the land-
promise of life of our own. Course down the East—frontiers
meet you at every turn—the headlights find them, the plain's,
   and the solar cities'

recurrent centers. And at the middle of the great world the wind
answers the shape of the country, a turning traveller
follows the hinge-line of coast, the first indefinite
   axis of symmetry

torn off from sympathy with the past and planted,
a primitive streak prefiguring the west, an ideal
which had to be modified for stability,
   to make it work.

Architecture is fixed not only by present needs but
also by ancestors. The actual structure means a plan determined
by the nature of ancestors;   its details are determined by
   function and interference.

There are these major divisions : for those attached to the seafloor,
a fan at freedom, flexible, wavering, designed to catch food
from all directions.   For the sedentary, for those who crouch and look,
   radial symmetry,

spokes to all margins for support.   For those who want movement,
this is achieved through bilateral symmetry only,
a spine and straight attack, all muscles working,
   up and alive.

   ∽

And there are years of roads, and centuries of need,
of walking along the shadow of a wall, of visiting houses,
hearing the birds trapped in the wall, the framework trembling
   with struggles of birds,

years of nightwalking in stranger cities, relost and unnamed,
recurrent familiar rooms, furnished only with nightmare,

recurrent loves, the glass eye of unreal ambition,
        years of initiation,

of dishallucination on the diamond meadows,
seeing the distances of false capes ahead,
feeling the tide-following and turning wind,
        travelling farther

under abrasive weather, to the bronzy river,
the rust, the brown, the terrible dead swamps,
the hanging moss the color of all the hanged,
        cities whose heels

ring out their news of hell upon all streets,
churches where you betray yourself, pray ended desire,
white wooden houses of village squares. Always one gesture:
        rejecting of backdrops.

These are the ritual years, whose lore is names of shapes,
Grabtown, Cockade Alley, Skid Row where jobless live,
their emblem a hitch-hiker with lips basted together,
        and marvel rivers,

the flooded James, a double rainbow standing over Richmond,
the remnant sky above the Cape Fear River, blue stain on red water,
the Waccamaw with its bone-trees, Piscataqua's rich mouth,
        red Sound and flesh of sand.

—A nation of refugees that will not learn its name;
still shows these mothers enduring, their hidden faces,
the cry of the hurt child at a high night-window,
        hand-to-hand warfare,

the young sitting in libraries at their only rest
or making love in the hallway under an orange bulb,
the boy playing baseball at Hungry Mother State Park,
        bestiaries of cities

and this shape, this meaning that promises seasonal joy.
Whose form is unquietness and yet the seeker of rest,
whose travelling hunger has range enough, its root
        grips through the world.

The austere fire-world of night : Gary or Bethlehem,
in sacred stacks of flame—or stainless morning,
anti-sunlight of lakes' reflection, matchlight on face,
        the thorny light of fireworks

lighting a way for the shape, this country of celebrations
deep in a passage of rebirth. Adventures of countries,
adventures of travellers, visions, or Christ's adventures
        forever following him

lit by the night-light of history, persevering
into the incredible washed morning air.
The luisarne swamp is our guide and the glare ice,
        the glow of tracklights,

the lights winding themselves into a single beacon,
big whooping riders of night, a wind that whirls
all of our motives into a single stroke,
        shows us a country

of which the birds know mountains that we have not dreamed,
climbing these unsuspected slopes they fade. Butte and pavilion
vanish into a larger scape, morning vaults all those hills
        rising on ranges

that stand gigantic on the roots of the world,
where points expand in pleasure of raw sweeping
gestures of joy, whose winds sweep down like stairs,
        and the felled forests

on hurricane ridges show a second growth. The dances
of turkeys near storm, a pouring light, tornado
umbilical to earth, fountains of rain, a development
        controlled by centers,

until the organs of this anatomy are fleshed away at last
of gross, and determining self, develop a final structure
in isolation. Masterpieces of happiness arrive,
        alive again in another land,

remembering pain, faces of suffering, but they know growth,
go through the world, hunger and rest desiring life.

Mountains are spines to their conquest, these wrecked houses
      (vines spiral the pillars)

are leaning their splintered sides on tornadoes, lifted careening
in wheels, in whirlwind, in a spool of power
drawing a spiral on the sun, drawing a sign of
      strength on the mountains,

the fusing stars lighting initiated cities.
The thin poor whiteness raining on the ground
forgotten in fickle eclipses, thunderbirds of dream
      following omens,

following charts of the moving constellations.
Charts of the country of all visions, imperishable
stars of our old dream : process, which having neither
      sorrow nor joy

remains as promise, the embryo in the fire.
The tilted cities of America, fields of metal,
the seamless wheatfields, the current of cities running
      below our wings

promise that knowledge of systems which may bless.
May permit knowledge of self, a lover's wish of conversion
until the time when the dead lake rises in light,
the shape is organized in travelling space,
this hope of travel, to find the place again,
rest in the triumph of the reconceived,
lie down again together face to face.

SIXTH ELEGY. RIVER ELEGY

In burning summer I saw a season of betrayal,
the world fell away, and wasteful climbing green
covered the breaking of bodies, covered our hearts.
Unreal in the burning, many-motioned life
lay like a sea, but fevers found my grief.
I turned in that year to retrieve the stainless river,
the lost, the flowing line of escaped music.

Year of judgment!   Century of betrayal!
They built their cities on the banks of war
and all their cities are down, the Floating Man
swims in the smoke of their sky, the Double Woman
smiles up through the water with her distorted mouth.
I stand over reflection as the world darkens in
destruction of countries, all souls downward set,
life narrowing to one color of a choked river
and hell on both its banks.   My city, my city!
They never built cities.   Cities are for the living.
They built for the half-dead and the half-alive.
Their history is a half-history.   And we go down.
They built their villages whose lame towers fell
where error was overgrown until the long
tentacular ruin touches all fields.   My love!
Did I in that country build you villages?
Great joy my love, even there, until they fell
and green betrayal climbed over the wall.

Defeat and raging and a burning river.
Half-faced, half-sexed, the living dead arrive
passing, a lip, a breast, half of a hand.
Gaudy sadistic streets, dishonest avenues
where every face has bargained for its eyes.
And they come down to the river, driven down.
And all the faces fly out of my city.
The rich streets full of empty coats parading
and one adolescent protesting violin,
the slums full of their flayed and faceless bodies,
they shiver, they are working to buy their skin.
They are lost.   They come down to look for life in a river,
plunge, turn and plunge, they cannot change their life,
swimming, their head is in another world.

World without form.   Chaos beaten and beaten,
raging and suffering and hoping to take shape.
I saw your summer.   I saw your river flow.
I being wasted everywhere saw waste.
Hell's entropy at work and torment general,
friend against most-known friend, love fighting off love.
They asked for an end to emptiness; their sick throats filled
        with foam,

prayed to be solved, and rose to deal betrayal.
And I falling through hell passed many friends, and love,
and a haunted woman warned me as I fell.
Downward through currents, the horrors with little hands.

The chaos, the web of the heart, this bleeding knot;
raises me swimming now, one moment in the air
and light is on my face, the fans over the river
of wind, of goodness.   Lie gasping on this shore,
there is nothing in the world but an honest word
which the severed away may speak before we die.
Let me tell you what I have held to all along:
when I said that I loved you, when I crossed the frontier,
when I learned the obscurities of a frightened child,
when I shut the door, and felt the sprouting tears,
when I saw the river, when I learned resurrection,
the joy of your hands in a pain that called More Life.
Let me tell you what I have meant all along:
meaning of poetry and personal love,
a world of peace and freedom, man's need recognized,
and all the agonies that will begin that world.

Betrayed, we are betrayed.   The set of the great faces
mean it, the following eyes.   They are the flayed men,
their strength is at the center, love and the time's disease
lie at their skin.   The kiss in the flaring garden
when all the trees closed in.   The knotted terrible lips.
The black blood risen and the animal rage.
The last fierce accident, whose back-thrown drowning head
among the escaping sound of water hears
slow insane music groping for a theme.

My love, reach me again.   The smell of the sea,
wind-flower, sea-flower, the fallen gull-feather.
Clear water and order and an end to dreams:
ether-dreams, surrounded beasts, the aftertoll of fear,
the world reduced to a rising line of water,
the patient deserted by the analyst.
To keep the knowledge that holds my race alive:
spiritual grace of the material world.

I walked under the sky, and the high clouds
hollowed in ribs arched over their living heart:
the world, the corporeal world that will not die.
No, world's no heart—here is yourself walking
in a cage of clouds looking up wanting one face
over you and that look to fill the sky.
Carrying counter-agony into the world,
dream-singing, river-madness, the tragic fugal love
of a theme balancing another theme.

Disorder of suffering, a flight of details, a world
with no shadows at noontime and never at night a light.
Suddenly the flame-blue of a drunken sky
and it is the change, the reds and metals of autumn.
But I curse autumn, for I do not change,
I love, I love, and we are far from peace,
and the great river moves unbearably;
actual gestures of giving, and I may not give.
Water will hold my shadows, the kiss of darkness,
maternal death's tender and delicate promises
seethe at the lips, release and the full sleep.

Even now the bright corporeal hand
might come to redeem the long moment of dying.
Even now if I could rest my life,
my forehead on those knees and the arriving shadows
in rising quiet as the long night arrives.
Terror, war, terror, black blood and wasted love.
The most terrible country, in the heads of men.
This is the war imagination made;
it must be strong enough to make a peace.
My peace is strong enough if it will come
flowing, the color of eyes. When the world burns away
nothing is left can ever be betrayed.

All broken promises, adulterate release—
cast in the river Death, charred surface of waste,
a downward soulset, never the old heaven
held for a moment as breath held underwater;
but we must rise into a breathing world.
And this dark bellowing century, on its knees—?
If all this must go down, it must.

And all this brilliance go to dust?
Only the meanings can remain alive.
When the cemeteries are military objectives
and love's a downward drawing at the heart
and every letter bears the stamp of death.

There is no solution. There is no happiness.
Only the range must be taken, a way be found to use
the inmost frenzy and the outer doom.
They are here, they run their riot in the clouds,
fly in our blood and over all our mountains,
corrupt all waters, poison the pride of theme.

Years of judgment!   Century screaming for
the flowing, the life, the intellectual leap
of waters over a world grown old and wild,
a broken crying for seasonal change until
O God my love in time the waste become
the sure magnificent music of the defeated heart.

Summer 1940

SEVENTH ELEGY.
DREAM-SINGING ELEGY

Darkness, giving us dream's black unity.
Images in procession start to flow
among the river-currents down the years of judgment
and past the cities to another world.

There are flat places. After the waterfall
arched like the torso of love, after the voices
singing behind the waterfall, after the water
lying like a lover on the heart,
there is defeat.

And moving through our spirit in the night
memories of these places.
Not ritual, not nostalgia, but our cries,
the axe at the heart, continual rebirth,
the crying of our raw desire,
young. O many-memoried America!

In defeat there are no prophets and no magicians,
only the look in the loved and tortured eyes
when every fantasy restores, and day denies.
The act of war debased to the act of treason
in an age of treason. We were strong at the first.
We resisted. We did not plan enough. We killed.
But the enemy came like thunder in the wood,
a storm over the treetops like a horse's head
reared to a great galloping, and war
trampled us down. We lost our young men in the fighting,
we lost our homeland, our crops went under the frost,
our children under the hunger. Now we stand
around this fire, our black hills far behind,
black water far before us, a glitter of time on the sea,
glitter of fire on our faces, the still faces—
stillness waiting for dreams
and only the shadows moving,
shadows and revelations.

In the spring of the year, this new fighting broke out.
No, when the fields were blond. No, the leaves crimson.
When the old fighting was over, we knew what we were
seeing as if for a first time our dark hills masked with green,
our blond fields with the trees flame-shaped and black
in burning darkness on the unconsumed.
Seeing for a first time the body of our love,
our wish and our love for each other.
Then word came from a runner, a stranger:
"They are dancing to bring the dead back, in the mountains."
We danced at an autumn fire, we danced the old hate and change,
the coming again of our leaders. But they did not come.
Our singers lifted their arms, and a singer cried,
"You must sing like me and believe, or be turned to rock!"

The winter dawned, but the dead did not come back.
News came on the frost, "The dead are on the march!"
We danced in prison to a winter music,
many we loved began to dream of the dead.
They made no promises, we never dreamed a threat.
And the dreams spread.

But there were no armies, and the dead were dead,
there was only ourselves, the strong and symbol self
dreaming among defeat, our torture and our flesh.
We made the most private image and religion,
stripped to the last resistance of the wish,
remembering the fighting and the lava beds,
the ground that opened, the red wounds opening,
remembering the triumph in the night,
the big triumph and the little triumph—
wide singing and the battle-flash—
assassination and whisper.

In the summer, dreaming was common to all of us,
the drumbeat hope, the bursting heart of wish,
music to bind us as the visions streamed
and midnight brightened to belief.
In the morning we told our dreams.
They all were the same dream.

Dreamers wake in the night and sing their songs.
In the flame-brilliant midnight, promises
arrive, singing to each of us with tongues of flame:
"We are hopes, you should have hoped us,
We are dreams, you should have dreamed us."
Calling our name.

When we began to fight, we sang hatred and death.
The new songs say, "Soon all people on earth
will live together." We resist and bless
and we begin to travel from defeat.
Now, as you sing your dream, you ask the dancers,
in the night, in the still night, in the night,
"Do you believe what I say?"
And all the dancers answer "Yes."

⤙⤚

To the farthest west, the sea and the striped country
and deep in the camps among the wounded cities
half-world over, the waking dreams of night
outrange the horrors. Past fierce and tossing skies
the rare desires shine in constellation.
I hear your cries, you little voices of children

swaying wild, nightlost, in black fields calling.
I hear you as the seething dreams arrive
over the sea and past the flaming mountains.
Now the great human dream as great as birth or death,
only that we are not given to remember birth,
only that we are not given to hand down death,
this we hand down and remember.

Brothers in dream, naked-standing friend
rising over the night, crying aloud,
beaten and beaten and rising from defeat,
crying as we cry : We are the world together.
Here is the place in hope, on time's hillside,
where hope, in one's image, wavers for the last time
and moves out of one's body up the slope.
That place in love, where one's self, as the body of love,
moves out of the old lifetime towards the beloved.
Singing.

Who looks at the many colors of the world
knowing the peace of the spaces and the eyes of love,
who resists beyond suffering, travels beyond dream,
knowing the promise of the night-flowering worlds
sees in a clear day love and child and brother
living, resisting, and the world one world
dreaming together.

EIGHTH ELEGY. CHILDREN'S ELEGY

Yes, I have seen their eyes.   In peaceful gardens
the dark flowers now are always children's eyes,
full-colored, haunted as evening under fires
showered from the sky of a burning country.

Shallow-featured children under trees
look up among green shadows of the leaves.
The angel, flaming, gives—into his hands
all is given and he does not change.
The child changes and takes.

All is given.   He makes and changes.
The angel stands.

A flame over the tree.   Night calling in the cloud.
And shadow among winds.   Where does the darkness lie?
It comes out of the person, says the child.
A shadow tied and alive, trying to be.

In the tremendous child-world, everything is high,
active and fiery, sun-cats run through the walls,
the tree blows overhead like a green joy,
and cloudy leopards go hunting in the sky.

The shadow in us sings, "Stand out of the light!"
But I live, I live, I travel in the sun.

On burning voyages of war they go.
Like starving ghosts they stumble after nuns.
Children of heroes, Defeat the dark companion.
But if they are told they are happy, they will know.

Who kills the father burns up the children's tears.
Some suffering blazes beyond all human touch,
some sounds of suffering cry, far out of reach.
These children bring to us their mother's fears.

Singing, "O make us strong O let us go—"
The new world comes among the old one's harms,
old world carrying new world in her arms.
But if you say they are free, then they will know.

War means to me, sings a small skeleton,
only the separation,
mother no good and gone,
taken away in lines of fire and foam.
The end of war
will bring me, bring me home.

The children of the defeated, sparrow-poor and starved,
create, create, must make their world again.
Dead games and false salutes must be their grace.

One wish must move us, flicker from our lives
to the marred face.

My child, my victim, my wish this moment come!
But the martyr-face cries to us fiercely
"I search to learn the way out of childhood;
I need to fight.   I wish, I wish for home."

                    ⌒⌽⌒

This is what they say, who were broken off from love:
However long we were loved, it was not long enough.

We were afraid of the broad big policeman,
of lions and tigers, the dark hall and the moon.

After our father went, nothing was ever the same,
when mother did not come back, we made up a war game.

My cat was sitting in the doorway when the planes
went over, and my cat saw mother cry;
furry tears, fire fell, wall went down;
did my cat see mother die?

Mother is gone away, my cat sits here coughing.
I cough and sit.   I am nobody's nothing.

However long they loved us, it was not long enough.
For we have to be strong, to know what they did, and then
our people are saved in time, our houses built again.

You will not know, you have a sister and brother;
my doll is not my child, my doll is my mother.

However strong we are, it is not strong enough.
I want to grow up. To come back to love.

                    ⌒⌽⌒

I see it pass before me in parade,
my entire life as a procession of images.
The toy, the golden kernel, the glass lamp.
The present she gave me, the first page I read,
the little animal, the shadowless tall angel.
The angel stands. The child changes and takes.
He makes a world, stands up among the cousins,

cries to the family, "Ladies and gentlemen—
The world is falling *down!*" After the smooth hair
darkens, and summer lengthens the smooth cheek,
and the diffuse gestures are no longer weak,
he begins to be the new one, to have what happened,
to do what must be done.

O, when the clouds and the blue horse of childhood
melt away and the golden weapons,
and we remember the first public day's
drums and parades and the first angel
standing in the garden, his dark lips
and silver blood, how he stood,
giving, for all he was was given.

I begin to have what happened to me.

O, when the music of carousels and stars
is known, and the music of the scene
makes a clear meeting, greeting and claim of gods,
we see through the hanging curtain of the year
they change each other with one change of love!
see, in one breath, in a look!
See, in pure midnight a flare of broken color
clears to a constellation.
Peace is asleep, war's lost. It is love.
I wanted to die. The masked and the alone
seemed the whole world, and all the gods at war,
and all the people dead and depraved. Today
the constellation and the music! Love.

You who seeking yourself arrive at these lines,
look once, and you see the world,
look twice and you see your self.

And all the children moving in their change.

To have what has happened, the pattern and the shock;
and all of them walk out of their childhood,
give to you one blue look.

And all the children bowing in their game,
saying Farewell, Goodbye; Goodbye, Farewell.

NINTH ELEGY. THE ANTAGONISTS

Pieces of animals, pieces of all my friends
prepare assassinations while I sleep.
They shape my being, a gallery of lives
fighting within me, and all unreconciled.
Before them move my waking dreams, and ways
of the spirit, and simple action.   Among these
I can be well and holy.   Torn by them I am wild,
smile, and revenge myself upon my friends
and find myself among my enemies.
But all these forms of incompleteness pass
out of their broken power to a place
where dream and dream meet and resolve in grace.

The closing of this conflict is the end
of the initiation.   I have known the cliff
and known the cliff-dream of the faces drowned.
Stood in the high sun, a dark girl looking down,
seeing the colors of water swaying beneath me, dense
in the flood-summer, various as my love
and like my hope enchanted.   Drawn to blue
chance and horizons, and back as sea-grasses move
drawn landward slowly by incoming tides—
and then the final cancelling and choice,
not tilted as flowers under wind, but deep
blessing of root and heart, underwater swung,
wrenched, swayed, and given fully to the sea.
Heaven not of rest, but of intensity.

The forms of incompleteness in our land
pass from the eastern and western mountains where
the seas meet the dark islands, where the light
glitters white series on the snowlands, pours its wine
of lenient evening to the center.   Green
on shadows of Indiana, level yellow miles . . .
The prairie emblems and the slopes of the sky
and desert stars enlarging in the frost
redeem us like our love and will not die.
All origins are here, and in this range
the changing spirit can make itself again,
continually love, continually change.

Out of the myth the mother leaned;
From out the mother shines the child;
Man rises, in the mass contained;
And from this growth creation grows.
The fire through all the spiral flows:
Create the creative, many-born!
And use your love, unreconciled!

❧

In wheels, in whirlwind, in a storm of power
alive again and over every land
the thunderbird with lightnings at his wrists.
Eclipses uncloud and show us miracle,
gleaming, our ancestors, all antagonists:
Slave and Conquistador, dead hand-to-hand,
scented fastidious Tory with his whore,
distinguished rebel and woman at the plow.
The fiery embryo umbilical
always to failure, and form developing
American out of conflict.

Fierce dissenting ghosts,
the second Adams' fever and eagle voice
and Jackson's muscular democratic sense.
Sprung in one birth John Brown, a mad old man
whose blood in a single broken gesture freed
many beliefs;   and Lincoln's agony
condemning and confirming.   O, they cry,
the oppositions cry, O fight for me!
Fight, you are bound to freedom, and be free!
When Hawthorne saw the fabulous gift, he tore
flesh from his guilt, and found more guilt; the bells
rang barter of the self, but Melville drowned.
The doubled phantoms bring to our terrible
chaos the order of a meeting-place
where the exchange is made, the agonies
lie down at last together face to face.

In the black night of blood, the forms begin
to glitter alive, fathers of constellations,
the shining and the music moving on.
We are bound by the deepest feuds to unity.
To make the connections and be born again,
create the creative, that will love the world.

Not glistening Indies, not continents, but the world
opening now, and the greatness of our age
that makes its own antagonists of the wish.
We want to find and will spend our lives in finding:
the landfall of our broken voyages
is still our America of contradictions.
Ancestors of that dream lie coupled in our flesh,
pieces of animals, pieces of all our friends
meet in us and we live. We do not die.

Magical keen Magellan sought a rose
among the compass and legendary winds.
Green sequels rocked his eyes in water;   he
hung with the scorpion sun on noon's glass wall,
stared down, down into the future as he sailed.
Fanatic travels, recurrent mysteries.
Those who want the far shore spend their lives on the ocean.
The hand of God flowers in coasts for these.

Those who want only home spend their lives in the sky.
Flying over tonight, while thirteen searchlights join
high incandescent asters on black air.
The blinding center fastens on a plane
floating and white, glare–white; he wanting land
and intimate fertile hours, hangs there.   Sails
great scends of danger, or wades through crazy sand.

Those who most long for peace now pour their lives on war.
Our conflicts carry creation and its guilt,
these years' great arms are full of death and flowers.
A world is to be fought for, sung, and built:
Love must imagine the world.
                              The wish of love
moving upon the body of love describes
closing of conflict, repeats the sacred ways
in which the spirit dances and survives.

To that far meeting-place call home the enemies—
they keep their oppositions, for the strong
ironic joy of old intensities
still carries virile music.

                                    O, the young
will come up
                    after us
                                    and make the dream,
the real world of our myth.
                                        But now, the song
they will discover is a shadowy theme—

Today we are bound, for freedom binds us—we
live out the conflict of our time, until
Love, finding all the antagonists in the dance,
moved by its moods and given to its grace,
resolves the doom
                    and the deliverance.

TENTH ELEGY. ELEGY IN JOY

Now green, now burning, I make a way for peace.
After the green and long beyond my lake,
among those fields of people, on these illuminated
hills, gold, burnt gold, spilled gold and shadowed blue,
the light of enormous flame, the flowing light of the sea,
where all the lights and nights are reconciled.
The sea at last, where all the waters lead.
And all the wars to this peace.

For the sea does not lie like the death you imagine;
this sea is the real sea, here it is.
This is the living. This peace is the face of the world,
a fierce angel who in one lifetime lives
fighting a lifetime, dying as we all die,
becoming forever, the continual god.
Years of our time, this heart! The binding of the alone,
bells of all loneliness, binding our lands and our music,
branches full of motion each opening its own flower,
lands of all song, each speaking in his own voice.
Praise in every grace
among the old same war.

Years of betrayal, million death breeding its weaknesses
and hope, buried more deep more black than dream.

Every elegy is the present : freedom eating our hearts,
death and explosion, and the world unbegun.
Now burning and unbegun, I sing earth with its war,
and God the future, and the wish of man.

&

Though you die, your war lives : the years fought it,
fusing a dead world straight.

The living will be giving you your meanings,
widening to love because of the love of man.
All the wounds crying
I feare, and hope : I burne, and frese like yse . . .
saying to the beloved
For your sake I love cities,
on your love I love the many,
saying to the people,
for your sake I love the world.
The old wounds crying
I find no peace, and all my warres are done.

   Out of our life the living eyes
   See peace in our own image made,
   Able to give only what we can give:
   Bearing two days like midnight. "Live,"
   The moment offers;   the night requires
   Promise effort love and praise.

Now there are no maps and no magicians.
No prophets but the young prophet, the sense of the world.
The gift of our time, the world to be discovered.
All the continents giving off their several lights,
the one sea, and the air. And all things glow.

Move as this sea moves, as water, as force.
Peace shines from its life, its war can become
at any moment the fierce shining of peace,
and all the life-night long many voices are saying
The name of all things is Glowing.

A beginning, a moment of rest that imagines.
And again I go wandering far and alone,
I rise at night, I start up in the silence—

lovely and silver-black the night remembers.
In the cities of America I make my peace;
among the bombs and commands,
the sound that war makes
NO   NO
We see their weeping and their lifetime dreams.

All this, they say to us, because of you.
Much to begin.   Now be your green, your burning,
bear also our joy, come to our meeting-place
and in the triumph of the reconceived
lie down at last together face to face.

We tell beginnings : for the flesh and answer,
for the look, the lake in the eye that knows,
for the despair that flows down in widest rivers,
cloud of home;   and also the green tree of grace,
all in the leaf, in the love that gives us ourselves.
The word of nourishment passes through the women,
soldiers and orchards rooted in constellations,
white towers, eyes of children:
saying in time of war What shall we feed?
I cannot say the end.

Nourish beginnings, let us nourish beginnings.
Not all things are blest, but the
seeds of all things are blest.
The blessing is in the seed.

This moment, this seed, this wave of the sea, this look,
    this instant of love.
Years over wars and an imagining of peace.   Or the expiation
    journey
toward peace which is many wishes flaming together,
fierce pure life, the many-living home.
Love that gives us ourselves, in the world known to all
new techniques for the healing of a wound,
and the unknown world.   One life, or the faring stars.

Body of Waking

1958

HAYING BEFORE STORM

This sky is unmistakable. Not lurid, not low, not black.
Illuminated and bruise-color, limitless, to the noon
Full of its floods to come. Under it, field, wheels, and mountain,
The valley scattered with friends, gathering in
Live-colored harvest, filling their arms; not seeming to hope
Not seeming to dread, doing.
       I stand where I can see
Holding a small pitcher, coming in toward
The doers and the day.
      These images are all
Themselves emerging: they face their moment: love or go down,
A blade of the strong hay stands like light before me.
The sky is a torment on our eyes, the sky
Will not wait for this golden, it will not wait for form.
There is hardly a moment to stand before the storm.
There is hardly time to lay hand to the great earth.
Or time to tell again what power shines past storm.

PHANERON

Whatever roams the air is traveling
Over these griefs, these wars and this good.
Whatever cries and changes, lives and reaches
Across the threshold of sense; I know the piercing name;
Among my silence, in cold, the birth-cry came.
Salt of these tears whitens my eyelashes.

Whatever plows the body turns to food:
Before my face, flowers, color which is form.
Cries plow the sea and air and turn to birth
Upon the people-sown, people-flowering earth.
A year turns in its crisis. In its sleep.
Whatever plows our dreams is ours to keep.

Whatever plows our dreams is ours to give:
The threshold rises and changes.
I give, I perceive;
Here are the gifts of day risen at last;
Blood of desire, the riding of belief
Beyond our fury and our silences.

THE YOUNG GIRL OF THE MISSISSIPPI VALLEY

Stallions go leap, and rimfire knows,
Where there was sleep the ware eye goes,
Out of the rotten climbs the rose.
    I will remember how the music went
    When he sang down my fears.

A murder ballad blown by the moon away,
And all your dreaming could not make him stay.
He wants the blue counties, the way to Africa.
    Lean east lean west, the thousand ocean knows,
    How soon do you come to the center again?

Nightmary, zip me up, the avenue
Is black, I'll start in the dark of the moon—
Flat miles away my love who never knew
    Wakes and leans on the windowsill,
    Wanting the sea-breasts of an unborn girl.

Hills climb, songs climb, and I will find him out,
My child will leap like stallions from my mouth
Before the traveler moon can light my heart.
    There'll be a gun, and there'll be storms of roses,
    All Indiana crystal in my tears.

A BIRTH

Lately having escaped three-kinded death
Not by evasion but by coming through

I celebrate what may be true beginning.
But new begun am most without resource
Stupid and stopped. How do the newborn grow?
I am of them. Freshness has taken our hearts;
Pain strips us to the source, infants of further life
Waiting for childhood as we wait for form.

So came I into the world of all the living
The maimed triumphant middle of my way
Where there is giving needing no forgiving.
Saw now the present that is here to say:
Nothing I wrote is what I must see written,
Nothing I did is what I now need done.—
The smile of darkness on my song and my son.

Lately emerged I have seen unfounded houses,
Have seen spirits not opened, surrounded as by sun,
And have, among limitless consensual faces
Watched all things change, an unbuilt house inherit
Materials of desire, that stone and wood and air.
Lit by a birth, I defend dark beginnings,
Waste that is never waste, most-human giving,
Declared and clear as the mortal body of grace.

Beginnings of truth-in-life, the rooms of wilderness
Where truth feeds and the ramifying heart,
Even mine, praising even the past in its pieces,
My tearflesh beckoner who brought me to this place.

KING'S MOUNTAIN

In all the cities of this year
I have longed for the other city.

In all the rooms of this year
I have entered one red room.

In all the futures I have walked toward
I have seen a future I can hardly name.

But here the road we drive
Turns upon another country.

I have seen white beginnings,
A slow sea without glaze or speed,
Movement of land, a long lying-down dance.

This is fog-country. Milk. Country of time.

I see your tormented color, the steep front of your storm
Break dissipated among limitless profiles.

I see the shapes of waves in the cross-sea
Advance, a fog-surface over the fog-floor.
Seamounts, slow-flowing. Color. Plunge-point of air.

In all the meanings of this year
There will be the ferny meaning.

It rises leaning and green, streams through star-lattices;
After the last cliff, wave-eroded silver,
Forgets the limitations of our love,
These drifts and caves dissolve and pillars of these countries
Long-crested dissolve to the future, a new form.

MOTHER GARDEN'S ROUND

The year was river-throated, with the stare of legend,
Then truth the whirlwind and Mother Garden. Death.
And now these stars, antlers, the masks of speech,
And the one ghost a glove in the middle of the floor.
        Garden my green may grow.

If you were here tonight, my heart would rest,
Would rest on a support, happy thereon.
Something is dancing on leafdrift, dancing across the graves:
A child is watching while the world breaks open.
        Garden my green may grow.

Speed of a red fox running along this street.
Everyone could have seen it, no one is now awake.
Separations all year and the seeking of roots.
It was a lie, Mother Garden, they do not wish for death.
        Garden my green may grow.

They wish only to live again. No more the whirlwind.
One colored pebble now, one look, the singular
Opening of the lips; a leaf happens to speak.
I remember in love you walked to me straight across that room.
        Garden my green may grow.

The suffering of your absence flies around me now,
No house can keep out this flying of small birds.
Feathers, bird-feathers, settle upon my waking.
The agonies are open. Faces, dead within them; and on these faces
And filling the clefts and on my hands and eyes
The little fresh pain flutters. Whitening the grass,
Snowing through the windows. Drifting over the floor.
Touching my face when, almost, touch means kindness.
My dear dream, Mother Garden. We wish to be born again.
        Death death may my green grow.

RITE

My father groaned; my mother wept.
Among the mountains of the west
A deer lifted her golden throat.

They tore the pieces of the kill
While two dark sisters laughed and sang.—
The hidden lions blare until

The hunters charge and burn them all.
And in the black apartment halls
Of every city in the land

A father groans; a mother weeps;
A girl to puberty has come;
They shriek this, this is the crime

The gathering of the powers in.
At this first sign of her next life
America is stricken dumb.

The sharpening of your rocky knife!
The first blood of a woman shed!
The sacred word: Stand Up You Dead.

Mothers go weep; let fathers groan,
The flag of infinity is shown.
Now you will never be alone.

RINGLING

for Toni

Lattice of his back grows, the dolphin-arching, till
That ripple, that stress, dance on a board on a ball,
Bracing are planted among the unbalanced seas
Rooted in whirlwind, flanks of a man whose torse
Unknots becoming the face of all control
Trembling past his tornadoes, rouse of storm
Walking upon one point of make and build.
Black copper acrobat from Ecuador.

Is followed by the blonde and summer one
Fallen in whiteness upon her smooth trapeze,
Swung to no heavier and softer force
Than Monet's waterlilies in his light suspended
Or floating in our joy, or floating in circus air,
The calm eye at the core of the hurricane.

AFTER THEIR QUARREL

After the quarrel in the house I walked the grasses of the field
Until the hissing of breakers and the hissing on the sand
Lowered, and I could see the seed heads and the sky.

A pod of the milkweed burst; it was speaking to me:
Never mind, never mind. All splits open. There is new inside,
We witness. Downwind, the softened asters let me see

A lengthened sky in its mixed oranges of sunset
Gone east and west, glazing the first bare branches.
The branches said: We know you. I remembered a tiger

The winter I was five not leaping in my dream but fusing
All my wishes to run, with his endless glowing look telling:
I recognize you. Kill them if they deny; or wake them. Now wake!

Autumn announcing birds, the flights calling from sunset.
One bird crying: I see you down there, bird! The quick furry ground
Moves with me in small animals whispering:
You are like us, too. And the stars.—I my own evidence

That even the half-eaten and accursed can be a season.
Search yourself, said all the field, understand growth.
When lack consents to leave its seed, waste opens, you will see
Even there, the husband of the spring, who knows his time.

TREE

It seemed at the time like a slow road and late afternoon
When I walked past a summery turning and saw that tree in the sun.
That was my first sight of it. It stood blasted open,
Its trunk black with tar on its unsealed destruction.
You could see blue through that window, endless sky in the wound
Bright blue past the shining of black harm. And sound
Fresh wood supported branches like judge's arms,
Crutch under branch, crutch where the low hand leaned,
Strong new wood propping that apple-tree's crown.

And the crown? World-full, beneficent, round,
Many-branching; and red, apple-red, full of juices and color-ripe,
The great crown spread on the hollow bark and lived.
Lavish and fertile, stood on her death and thrived.

For three years remembering that apple-tree,
I saw in it the life of life in crisis,
Moving over its seasons, meeting death with fruition.
I have been recognizing all I loved.

Now, after crisis of day and crisis of dream,
That tree is burning and black before my years.
I know it for a tree. Rooted and red it bears.
Apple and branch and seed.
Real, and no need to prove, never a need
For images: of process, or death, or flame; of love, or seeming, or speed.

NIGHT FEEDING

Deeper than sleep but not so deep as death
I lay there dreaming and my magic head
remembered and forgot. On first cry I
remembered and forgot and did believe.
I knew love and I knew evil:
woke to the burning song and the tree burning blind,
despair of our days and the calm milk-giver who
knows sleep, knows growth, the sex of fire and grass,
renewal of all waters and the time of the stars
and the black snake with gold bones.

Black sleeps, gold burns; on second cry I woke
fully and gave to feed and fed on feeding.
Gold seed, green pain, my wizards in the earth
walked through the house, black in the morning dark.
Shadows grew in my veins, my bright belief,
my head of dreams deeper than night and sleep.
Voices of all black animals crying to drink,
cries of all birth arise, simple as we,
found in the leaves, in clouds and dark, in dream,
deep as this hour, ready again to sleep.

THE RETURN

An Idea ran about the world
screaming with the pain of the mind
until it met a child
who stopped it with a word.

The Idea leaned over those newborn eyes
and dreamed of the nature of things:
the nature of memory and the nature of love;
and forgave itself and all men.

Quieted in a sea of sleeping
the Idea began its long return—
renewed by the child's sea-colored eyes
remembered the flesh, smiled and said:

I see birds, spring and the birthplace
unknown by the stable stone.
I know light and I know motion
and I remember I am not alone.

The Idea voyaged nearer my breathing, saying
Come balance come
into the love of these faces and forces
find us our equilibrium.

And the child stirred, asking his questions.

The Idea grew more fleshly and spoke:
Beaten down I was
Down I knew very long
Newborn I begin.

And the child went on asking his questions.

The Idea journeying into my body
returned, and I knew the nature of One,
and could forget One, and turn to the child,
and whole could turn to the world again.

Until the pain turns into answers
And all the masters become askers
And all the victims again doers
And all the sources break in light.

The child goes alive, asking his questions.

UNBORN SONG

Rabbits breed, flies breed, said the virgin lady;
But I
Cannot find my fulness where they rise,
My many children, their burning mouths and eyes,
Their bodies that have other fathers made.

The wife gone sterile in her weeping said
Flies breed, rabbits breed;
Faith of our time falls hissing on the sand,
Hard sand, is the hand of man set against hope? My bed
Whispers to me all year my love my hope my land.

Rabbits breed, flies breed, cried the infinite hearts of all the unborn,
In shady leafy places, underseas and in dim rooms, in the prodigal
        dark, all things are made again, but here
Among the new dreams and new nightmares, who listens, who
        believes? They give their stone demand
To the born, to the seed and seeking. While change emerges like
        another power from power, no longer the old good and evil,
        but a blessing that fares in the world, among the cities torn down
Crying awake, among the clouds who move calling do.
The mouth saying nothing. The air saying live and die.
The womb saying welcome, the sun saying Dare.

THE TWO ILLUMINATIONS

Storm and disorder and the giant emotions,
The seven deadly sins, they scatter all my hope.
To gather them in change I summon up the image

Of all arrangement in equilibrium.
Moments of poise in the middle of madness;
Sharpened as a forest is sharpened by fire,
I mean destroyed.

O abstract jealousy, half angel and half bird,
The bird smashing itself on the lighthouse's flying eye.
Tonight able at last to imagine perfect love—
Out of all murders
                midnight in desire.

Now in a twilight moment I summon up twilight,
The two illuminations that can tell
Nothing in any second by themselves—
Only the body's knowledge, many fresh mornings,
Newborn experience says this flicker of air
Over the face, this time's quick light is dawn.

I think too of a longhanded mime of form,
A dancer carrying two great eggs, intricacies
Of music and equilibrium: the boy
A Javanese temple-dancer, thin-fingered, dancing
Turret-crowned, in his dark hands balancing
The eggs.

           Come back to me soon. You are my breath and wine.
Did we then wrestle as if we were our angels?
There is peace also,
              love changing like religion.
Around your image now my prodigal wishes
Gather in, like the eye's color in brightened rooms,
Contract like a cloud of birds about a tree.

F. O. M.

The Death of Matthiessen

It was much stronger than they said. Noisier.
Everything in it more colored. Wilder.
More at the center calm.

Everything was more violent than ever they said,
Who tried to guard us from suicide and life.
We in our wars were more than they had told us.
Now that descent figures stand about the horizon,
I have begun to see the living faces,
The storm, the morning, all more than they ever said.
Of the new dead, that friend who died today,
Angel of suicides, gather him in now.
Defend us from doing what he had to do
Who threw himself away.

EXILE OF MUSIC

for Naginski

In the last bus last night that dead musician
Rode, I saw him riding, all his orchestras
Lost past belief and under Egypt plowed
By rusty knives, the noise-machines of grief.

Thunder of the senses died,
Stabbed in their singing by a sleepwalker.
You were the man in whose voices the green leaf
Of form was singing, the bird riding the cloud.

Minotaur underwater in the cedar lake,
Naginski, you are your own exile of music.
There were three roads going through that whole land:
The bird's, the bed's, or suicide.

He meant to drown his self. He drowned his life.
Silence lay down fanatically straight.
I am your exile, he sang from his dead mouth,
From the water-maze reaching out his hand and one green leaf.

ON THE DEATH OF HER MOTHER

A seacoast late at night and a wheel of wind.
All those years, Mother, your arms were full of absence

And all the running of arrows could never not once find
Anything but your panic among all that substance,
Until your wide eyes opened forever. Until it all was true.
The fears were true. In that cold country, winter,
The wordless king, went isolate and cruel,
And he alone real. His armies all that entered.

But here is peacock daybreak; thought-yoked and warm, the light,
The cloud-companions and the greenest star.
Starflash on water; the embryo in the foam.
Dives through my body in the waking bright,
Watchmen of birth; I see. You are here, Mother, and you are
Dead, and here is your gift: my life which is my home.

[UNTITLED]

Make and be eaten, the poet says,
Lie in the arms of nightlong fire,
To celebrate the waking, wake.
Burn in the daylong light; and praise
Even the mother unappeased,
Even the fathers of desire.

Blind go the days, but joy will see
Agreements of music; they will wind
The shaking of your dance; no more
Will the ambiguous arm-waves spell
Confusion of the blessing given.

Only and finally declare
Among the purest shapes of grace
The waking of the face of fire,
The body of waking and the skill
To make your body such a shape
That all the eyes of hope shall stare.

That all the cries of fear shall know,
Staring in their bird-pierced song;
Lines of such penetration make
That shall bind our loves at last.

Then from the mountains of the lost,
All the fantasies shall wake,
Strong and real and speaking turn
Wherever flickers your unreal.

And my strong ghosts shall fade and pass
My love start fiery as grass
Wherever burn my fantasies,
Wherever burn my fantasies.

HERO SPEECH

from a play

When the hero of the threshold enters our lives and our houses
The wish that is most human in all of us deepens and feels saved;
    it rises
To another level of desire. Himself the man, himself the animal,
Himself the moment makes new the forms, makes our song
    and our prayer.
We look at our lives renewed, we have let go of the fear
That went through the old minutes. Our selves begin to speak:
"There was curse on his house. Or blessing. But there is choice."
Say of this flier, "A skill has taken possession of the man."
The young saying Dare, the old Praise air, but keep on land.

When we see the hero, his act seeming accomplished, we wish
    for him the leader's lifetime,
The drums being here, the loudspeakers, sharp trumpets,
    acclaim of sunlight;
The joy of time is the leap forward of a man or a people.
The moment of the leap is ready today.
We look again for the laws of history in the hero's face and his
    lifetime,
But it is not like that—he has his speech of thanks, his dazzled
    smile of sunlight.
Our acceptance is flowering and sheds on his air triumph.
Our delight is the herald of certain public voices
Arriving to tell us as they always tell us
Take the act and postpone the meanings.
In the world of listen and touch, shining and sounding,

Love and the hero,
God give us each his sin to awaken him.

When in our deep delight we take the gifts of the hero
We are glad, we become responsible. And in an age at war,
Dead power, the lying opposites, the great cities fighting in the air,
We think of flying, the flying of all dreams,
The ancient reaching for the chance to return changed.
In deepest power the changing and opening, the seed obeying
        its own law.
When we at last take the moment and meanings
There will be set in motion our most dear wish—
For the wish for escape is only a part of the wish,
The wish for death is not what they say it is.
It is a dancing tribal woman who stands among a room
And says, "Won't somebody come and kill me?" and somebody does;
This is in order that she dance the dance of rebirth. Tomorrow.
For the plane is not over power, and the weapons are all weapons,
But the seeds of all things are the ways of choice, of the forms
Declaring the energy we breathe and man,
Breaking. Changing. Forever broken and made.

Through our own need
We come again to our own deep,
We go and grow.
The peace of growth may follow; now we see war in loss,
When we imagine peace it is process, is seed.
It will be given its body when we give it.

But here the nearest: this moment, this hero.

THE WATCHERS

for Carson and Reeves

She said to me, He lay there sleeping
Upon my bed cast down
With all the bitterness dissolved at last,
An innocent peace within a sleeping head;
He could not find his infant war, nor turn
To that particular zoo, his family of the dead.

I saw her smile of power against his deep
Heart, his waking heart,
Her enmity, her sexual dread.

He said to me, She slept and dreaming
Brought round her face
Closer to me in silence than in fire,
But smiled, but smiled, entering her dark life
Whose hours I never knew, wherein she smiles.
Wherein she dim descending breathes upon
My daylight and the color of waking goes.
Deep in his face, the wanderer
Bringing the gifts of legend and the wars,
Conspiracy of opposing images.

In the long room of dream I saw them sleep,
Turned to each other, clear,
With an obliterated look—
Love, god of foreheads, touching then
Their bending foreheads while the voice of sleep
Wept and sang and sang again
In a chanting of fountains,
A chattering of watches,
Love, sang my sleep, the wavelight on the stone.
I weep to go beyond this stone and the waterlight,
To kiss their eyelids for the last time and pass
From the delicate confidence of their sly throats,
The conversation of their flesh of dreams.
And though I weep in my dream,
When I wake I will not weep.

A BALLAD THEME

She tells:

Sing I chant I
To music in new morning heard
My need has become a bird
And is flown and is free

My need grew stormy and wild
No love of mine had made a child
No song of mine had made my love
To plant my life

Need grew deep about my heart.
They came then with their steely knives
They said Your song has many lives
Now choose you

They split my life while I did sleep
The joy of chance was in my dream
Loving and remembering
The nature of memory

Of the nature of time was all my dream
The nature of love and of forgetting
I dreamed the series of eternity
While I lay bleeding

The joy of choice I sing
That out my wound did spring
My son and my song
Sing I chant I

Now the child is alive and young
And the child I among my veins
Sings and says with every breath
Sing I chant I

ASLEEP AND AWAKE

Asleep and awake, I wake.
Never having written
What I have to say.
No poem offers of me
My central meaning,
I have danced to my naming
And danced away.

Now I move past my dreams:
They yield processions of
Changing images.
I want to speak the clear
The intricate meeting-place
Of all things with all desires:
Cut down by risk to the root
Where everything is given.
The finding of the child,
The lost voices, songs of all
Who take their meanings.
They are beginning the songs.

Mortal, awake, I sing and say
All is immortal, all
Save personality.
Yes, your passion, yes, the time of a flower.
Move in all your meanings,
Go lit by many fires,
Deep in the secret fires
All speak to all.
The deep life lives and dies
Changes, sings, and sings.
Speak before I sleep,
Before the keepings are given,
I find my time, and speak,
Driven toward love and music,
Music of forms and desires.

OF MONEY. AND THE PAST.

These coins and calendars stood for the moon, strong boys,
And the resinous storerooms of a house in silence.
Too many losses among the possible.
But only when you hear their fearful music:
Nothing at all and then the front door slamming,
The cave of sound at the station after all hope has gone,
Fifteen wire hangers jangling in emptied closets.

When you discover the real, lying under, and still,
Among the silences green morning reopening.

Now your invisible path between the brambles opens
To the hill of oyster-shells under the hills of cloud
And the hard knuckles of a boy poverty-driven
And the moon rising in a smell of vanilla.

Voices of money, voices of your past,
The swinging music in these voices telling:
No, no, you must go. Now. Go from this bay to where
You can bridge backward and forward and move toward form.
For here there is nothing. Nothing for you here.
Somewhere you may find something. But not here.
Do not look here, not now. Not anywhere here.
Nowhere, nowhere, nothing anywhere here.

Beyond these coins and seasons, then look back.
When the black voices turn brilliant and call: Here!

[UNTITLED]

"Long enough. Long enough,"
I heard a woman say—
I am that woman who too long
Under the web lay.
Long enough in the empire
Of his darkened eyes
Bewildered in the greying silver
Light of his fantasies.

I have been lying here too long,
From shadow-begin to shadow-began
Where stretches over me the subtle
Rule of the Floating Man.
A young man and an old-young woman
May dive in the river between
And rise, the children of another country;
That riverbank, that green.

But too long, too long, too long
Is the journey through the ice
And too secret are the entrances
To my stretched hidingplace.

Walk out of the pudorweb
And into a lifetime
Said the woman; and I sleeper began to wake
And to say my own name.

THE LOAN

You told me resurrection in images of roots,
Taking upon your summer my defeats.
Now I take on myself your wound's meaning
Private self-given torment, on my mouth.

The open grave stood in your eyes
Past the colors of our meeting—
Stain-moon, accepted curse of a false sun
Your guardians rising at your head.
A mask sang out, swinging away,
The verdicts proven fallacies,
"Lay you sweetly down to bed!"—
But the mask cannot kiss this away, nor wake—
Only you can wake, making go on to make;
Even when all your hope
Is buried dreaming,
The meanings move. Though my words are a loan,
Though your body I love vanish
Evading through our century among
These nightmare judgments of innocence and guilt.

All that I know from you of resurrection
Be passed on as branches, as one leaf.
Even the root of need.
The wound reaches its opposite, shines on my face, a flower
Bright among violence, the passion that is peace.
We have promises to make:
We saw that in each other's eyes.
Not to accept the curse, but wake,
Never to act in formal innocence.
It was not the maze of the time
But possibility we felt
In full gaze as we began to wake.

Not the lock of these years of silence,
We knew lack, we knew withholding, but there was more,
    the body of love said so—
Deep it was buried, but it lay there, in all eyes, in the meaning
    of sex
Waiting for more life, for it was more, and lively,
More a child running in the fields for his joy of running,
A running like creation, beginning now to make
Day and idea, his acts, his dreams, his waking,
His live ideas of innocence.

POURING MILK AWAY

Here, again. A smell of dying in the milk-pale carton,
And nothing then but pour the milk away.
More of the small and killed, the child's, wasted,
Little white arch of the drink and taste of day.
Spoiled, gone and forgotten; thrown away.

Day after day I do what I condemned in countries.
Look, the horror, the waste of food and bone.
You will know why when you have lived alone.

CHILDREN, THE SANDBAR,
THAT SUMMER

Sunlight the tall women may never have seen.
Men, perhaps, going headfirst into the breakers,
But certainly the children at the sandbar.
Shallow glints in the wave suspended
We knew at the breaker line, running that shore
At low tide, when it was safe. The grasses whipped
And nothing was what they said: not safety, nor the sea.
And the sand was not what they said, but various,
Lion-grained, beard-grey. And blue. And green.
And each grain casting its shadow down before
Childhood in tide-pools where all things are food.
Behind us the shores emerged and fed on tide.

We fed on summer, the round flowers in our hands
From the snowball bush entered us, and prisoner wings,
And shells in spirals, all food.
                              All keys to unlock
Some world, glinting as strong as noon on the sandbar,
Where men and women give each other children.

BORN IN DECEMBER

for Nancy Marshall

You are like me born at the end of the year;
When in our city day closes blueness comes
We see a beginning in the ritual end.

Never mind: I know it is never what it seems,
That ending: for we are born, we are born there,
There is an entrance we may always find.

They reckon by the wheel of the year. Our birth's before.
From the dark birthday to the young year's first stay
We are the ones who wait and look for ways:

Ways of beginning, ways to be born, ways for
Solvings, turnings, wakings; we are always
A little younger than they think we are.

THE SIXTH NIGHT: WAKING

That first green night of their dreaming, asleep beneath the Tree,
God said, "Let meanings move," and there was poetry.

NEVERTHELESS THE MOON

Nevertheless the moon
Heightens the secret
Sleep long withheld

Dry for a rain of dreams—
Flies straight above me
White, hot-hearted,
Among the streaming
Firmament armies.
A monk of flames
Stands shaking in my heart
Where sleep might lie.

Where you all night have lain.
And now hang dreaming,
Faded acute, fade full,
Calling your cloudy fame,
A keen high nightlong cry.
Rises my silent, turning
Heart. Heart where my love
Might lie, try toward my love
Flying, let go all need,
Brighten and burn—
Rain down, raging for life
Light my love's dream tonight.

SPEED, WE SAY

Speed, we say of our time: racing my writing word
The jet now, the whole sky screaming his name, Speed.
But I know rapider, someone hauling horizons in
Beside whom the racing of the suns seems tame.

I know faster than the flashing of suddenly recognized love
Or yellow spring going glimpsing his green fame,
Love after long suffering like inward lightning,
Assumed and lived through where now lovers lie warm,

Wild and at peace among their colors. Speed. And now
One quick-color mouth saying, "Now, love, now;
I have my spirit now, newborn and given,
The live delight;

It now is immediately not only spirit, not only mine,
        but delight the forerunner
Of the depth of joy, most subtle, most rapid.
My two speeds, now, at last
Related, now at last in the same music—
Light running before light."

THE BIRTH OF VENUS

Risen in a
welter of waters.

Not as he saw her
standing upon a frayed and lovely surf
clean-riding the graceful leafy breezes
clean-poised and easy. Not yet.

But born in a
tidal wave of the father's overthrow,
the old rule killed and its mutilated sex.

The testicles of the father-god, father of fathers,
sickled off by his son, the next god Time.
Sickled off. Hurled into the ocean.
In all that blood and foam,
among raving and generation,
of semen and the sea born, the
great goddess rises.

                However, possibly,
on the long worldward voyage flowing,
horror gone down in birth, the curse, being changed,
being used, is translated far at the margin into
our rose and saving image, curling toward a shore
early and April, with certainly shells, certainly blossoms.

And the girl, the wellborn goddess, human love—
young-known, new-knowing, mouth flickering, sure eyes—
rides shoreward, from death to us as we are at this moment, on
the crisp delightful Botticellian wave.

THE PLACE AT ALERT BAY

Standing high on the shoulders of all things, all things.
Creation pole reaching over my teeming island
That plays me at last a fountain of images.
Away from the road, life rising from all of us,
The grove of animals and our souls built in towers.
A music to be resumed in God.

Our branched belief, the power-winged tree.
Tree of meanings where the first mothers pour
Their totems, their images, up among the sun.
We build our gifts: language of process offers
Life above life moving, a ladder of lives
Reaching to time that is resumed in God.

Did the thunderbird give you yourself? The man mourning?
The cedar forest between the cryings of ravens?
Everfound mother, streaming of dolphins, whale-white moon.
Father of salmon-clouded seas, your face.
Water. Weatherbeaten image of us all.
All forms to be resumed in God.

For here, all energy is form: the dead, the unborn,
All supported on the shoulders of us all,
And all forever reaching from the source of all things.
Pillars of process, the growing of the soul,
Form that is energy from these seas risen,
Identified. Resumed in God.

VOICES OF WAKING

for the eightieth birthday of Frances G. Wickes

Whenever you wake, you will find journeying—
Even in deep night, dreams surrounding your dreams—
The song of waking begun, prepared in silence,
Planted in silence as her life is planted
Among the constellations and the days.

Whenever you wake, you will hear entering
The song of meanings, a melody of green;
The image of a legendary woman
Dancing among her mercies, in essence emerging
Female to leap into the dragon-throning sea.

Voices of nourishing, lifting the newborn up,
Away,—they lift away, newborn to all,
To the nourisher, to self born, to new life.
Voices of waking that journey in our lives
As renaissance and rain of images.

All of the people of the play are here,
In a storm of light; birthday; at any moment.
Full in their powers, and the voice of waking
Sings for beginnings; she sings, wherever waking is.

Wherever the deep moon stands, the song arrives.
Nevertheless the moon goes voyages.

Nevertheless, the journeying is time:
Makes birthdays, makes this birthday a resonance
And the remote boundaries of imagining
Acknowledge the voices, her daily human voice,
Blessing this birthday moment her monument.

Deep in the waking, her life builds in light
The vision of the body of the soul.

DIVINING WATER

We stood around the raw new-planted garden
Parables green and yellow in the ground
The old man with his branch paced the diagonal

The rare Negro girl accepted a forked branch
And paced her line   The corners of an ancient
Dance-figure now we were as we stood watching

Everything was there in the moment there
Random and light in the dance on young grass flaming up
While the old man held his branch and walked toward water

Walked to that moment where the branch dives down
We stood in the moment random funny rare
Everything here and everything contained

In a strong diving a diving of the swan's strong neck
Diving of prayer leaping to find deep under
Reason and rock the cold sweet-driven springs

Everything being here in the moment here
Belief and disbelief the dry light on the grass
And the old man with lit eyes

Calculations of willow, predictions done in peach-branch
Dancing of the young dark over wellwater
The way we guess where lies the buried life

But not for days after the eyes and dance
Did the deep fountain show   Do they divine each other?
The man drove true   the moment was all water

And time the branch drove and the hand of man
It shines awake it glitters on the grass
Now waters divine man we all know what he was

❧ 2 Translations: Octavio Paz

[UNTITLED]

The hand of day opens
Three clouds
Becoming a few words

[UNTITLED]

At daybreak go looking for your newborn name
Over the thrones of sleep glittering the light
Gallops across all mountains to the sea
The sun with his spurs on is entering the waves
Stony attack breaking the clarities
The sea resists rearing to the horizon
Confusion of land approaching the state of sculpture
The naked forehead of the world is raised
Rock smoothed and polished to cut a poem on
Display of light that opens its fan of names
Here is the seed of a singing like a tree
Here are the wind and names beautiful in the wind

FABLE

The state of fire and the state of air
Prancing of water
From green to yellow
       Yellow to red
From dream to vigil
       From desire to act
You needed only a step and that taken without effort
The insects then were jewels who were alive
The heat lay down to rest at the edge of the pool
Rain was the light hair of a willow-tree
There was a tree growing within your hand
And as it grew it sang laughed prophesied
It cast the spells that cover space with wings
There were the simple miracles called birds
Everything belonged to everyone
       Everyone was everything
Only one word existed immense without opposite
A word like a sun
One day it exploded into tiny fragments
They were the words of the language that we speak
They are fragments which never will unite
They are the splintered mirrors where the world
       can see itself shattered

DAY

A day is lost
In a sky suddenly there
Light leaves no footprints in the snow
A day is lost
Opening and shutting all the doors
The seed of the sun splits open soundlessly
A day begins
The fog goes up in the foothills
A man goes down to the river
They meet and are together in your eyes
And you are lost in this day
Singing among the leaves of light
The bells making their music far away
Every call of theirs a wave
Every wave gone down for ever
One move one word light against cloud
You laugh and you do your hair distractedly
A day begins at your feet
Skin hand whiteness these are not names
For this skin this hand and this whiteness
The visible and palpable which is outside
That which is within and which is nameless
By acts of touch they go searching in us
Following the turns that language made
Crossing the bridge this image strung from them
As light pouring itself among the fingers
As you yourself between my hands
As your hand interlaced within my hands
A day begins in my words
Light which goes ripening until it becomes flesh
Until it becomes shadow of your flesh light of your shadow
Armor of warmth skin of your light
A day begins in your mouth
Day which is lost in our eyes
Day which begins in our night

PROVERBS

One cornstalk is all cornfields
A feather is a bird alive and singing
A man of flesh is a man of dream
Truth is indivisible
One clap of thunder proclaims the acts of the lightning
One dreaming woman gives us the form of love forever
The sleeping tree speaks all green oracles
Water talks ceaseless never repeating a word
There are eyelids whose poise is never disturbed by dream
And the poise of delirium which dream never disturbs
The mouth of a woman saying Yes to life
The bird of paradise opening his wings

[UNTITLED]

In her splendor islanded
This woman burning like a charm of jewels
An army terrifying and asleep
This woman lying within the night
Like clear water lying on closed eyes
In a tree's shadow
A waterfall halted halfway in its flight
A rapid narrow river suddenly frozen
At the foot of a great and seamless rock
At the foot of a mountain
She is lake-water in April as she lies
In her depths binding poplar and eucalyptus
Fishes or stars burning between her thighs
Shadow of birds scarcely hiding her sex
Her breasts two still villages under a peaceful sky
This woman lying here like a white stone
Like water on the moon in a dead crater
Not a sound in the night not moss nor sand
Only the slow budding of my words
At the ear of water at the ear of flesh
Unhurried running
And clear memorial

Here is the moment burning and returned
Drowning itself in itself and never consumed

[UNTITLED]

Like ivy the creeper with a thousand hands
Like fire and the avid plumes of fire
Like Spring arriving to assault the year
The fingers of music
The talons of music
The burning bush of music
Covering our bodies covering our souls
Tattooing our bodies with those burning sounds
Like the body of god in images constellated
Like the body of heaven tattooed by the raging stars
Souls blazing bodies blazing
Music arrives here to tear out our eyes
(We will see only if music gives us sight
We will not hear without the swords of light)
Music arrives here to tear out our tongues
Now its huge mouth is devouring the bodies
The world arrives
Burning its name the names that clothe the world
Nothing remains but an enormous sound
Tower of glass that shelters birds of glass
Invisible birds
Made of a substance identical with light

LIFE OF THE POET

Words? Yes, made of air,
and in the air dissolved.
Give me your gift, to lose my self in words,
let me become the air on living lips,
one breath that goes wandering without barriers,
scent of a moment in the air diffused.

Even so light in itself is lost.

THE PRISONER

Homage to D. A. F. de Sade

les traces de ma tombe disparaissent
de dessus la surface de la terre
comme je me flatte que ma memoire
s'effacent de l'esprit des homes . . .
        Testament of Sade

You have not disappeared.
The letters of your name are still a scar that will not heal,
the tattoo of disgrace on certain faces.

Comet whose body is substance, whose tail glitters in dialectics.
You rush through the nineteenth century holding a grain of truth,
exploding as you come to our own time.

A mask that smiles beneath a veil of pink
made of the eyelids of the executed,
truth broken into a thousand flames of fire.
What is the meaning of these giant fragments,
this herd of icebergs sailing from your pen and from the high seas
        heading toward the nameless coasts?
these delicate surgical instruments made for cutting away
        the chancre of God?
these howls interrupting your kingly elephant thoughts?
the frightful striking of out-of-order clocks?
all of this rusty armament of torture?

The learned man and the poet,
the scholar, the writer, the lover, the maniac,
and the man who has cancelled out our threat from reality, who
        goes along drugged in his dream,
they fight like dogs over the bones of your work.
You who stood against all of them,
you are today a name, a leader, a banner.

Bending over life like Saturn over his sons
you scan with your steady look of love and wonder
the white ridges left by semen, by love, by blood.
These bodies, face to face like blazing stars,
are made of the same substance as the suns.

We call this love or death; liberty, doom.
Is it catastrophe? Is it the grave of man?
Where is the borderline between spasm and earthquake,
eruption and coitus?

Prisoner in your castle of crystal of rock
you pass through dungeons, chambers and galleries,
enormous courts whose vines twist on ancestral pillars,
seductive graveyards where the still black poplars dance.
Walls, things, bodies, reflecting you.
All is mirror!
Your image follows you.

Man is inhabited by silence and by space.
How can this hunger be met and satisfied?
How can you still the silence? How can the void be filled?
How can my image ever be escaped?
Only in my resemblant can I transcend myself,
only his blood affirms another life.
Justine is alive only through Juliette,
the victims breed their executioners.
This body which today we sacrifice,
is it not the god, tomorrow's sacrifice?

Imagination is desire's spur,
whose territory is endless, it is infinite
like boredom's who is its opposite and twin.
Pleasure or death, vomit or flooding in,
autumn, resembling daybreak,
sex or volcano,
high wind, and spring that sets the fields on fire,
talons or galaxies,
the stony woman riding the horse called Dread,
red foam of desire, slaughter on the seas,
and the great azure hill, delirium,
forms, images, bubbles, and the rage for life,
eternities in flashes,
excesses: it is you who are the measure of man.
Now dare forward:
freedom is the willing choice of necessity.
You are the arrow, the bow, the chord and the cry.
Dream is explosive. It bursts. And becomes the sun.

And in your castle on fire with diamonds, your image destroying
    itself, remaking itself, unweakened, tirelessly.

FROM SUN STONE

. . . .

now the world stands visible through your body,
the world, transparent through your transparency.

I go a journey in galleries of sound,
I flow among the resonant presences,
going, a blind man passing transparencies
one mirror cancels me, I rise from another,
forest whose trees are the pillars of magic,
under the arches of light I go among
the corridors of a dissolving autumn,

I go among your body as among the world
your belly the sunlit center of the city
your breasts two churches where are celebrated
the great parallel mysteries of the blood,
the looks of my eyes cover you like ivy,
you are a city by the sea assaulted,
you are a rampart by the light divided
into two halves, distinct, color of peaches,
and you are a saltiness, you are rocks and birds
beneath the edict of concentrated noon,

and dressed in the coloring of my desire
as soon you will be stripped by my thought naked,
I go among your eyes as I swim water,
the tigers come to these eyes to drink their dreams,
the hummingbird is burning among these cries,
I go upon your forehead as on the moon,
like cloud I go among your imagining
journey your belly as I journey your dream

. . . .

SUITE FOR LORD TIMOTHY DEXTER

1

They face us in sea-noon sun, just as he saw them waiting,
Bolted down, fastened together by their nailhead proverbs.
The sun still pouring all male all female through their blood
And away through the salt marsh and the white salt sand
Sea-blaze over their shoulders, fantasy
A blue invisible mountain up whose side
Laughter and sharp clouds race as he saw them ride
In witness when he as a boy walked down
With morning for a sign.
Smelling of acid, like his trade.
Ready to throw their lifeday down their throats like wine,
Death-rotten proverbs and the jokes all made,
Himself the wine-bottle burning in the sun.

More here than power over proverbs. But that power pours here.
And the sure sun of story, on top the live gold mast.
What's strong, what's lost? What boy walked salty in the light?
A raging worshipping fantastic man,
Tasting money and words, live-breasted women,
The tanner's boy streaked with truth. In the young States
He saw young morning. Wild he was.
And most
A clap of mockery clean in the sea-brightness,
A legend of this coast.

2 HOW TO IMPRESS MASSACHUSETTS

A name's a name but
Nothing's the same,
Now King-No-More knows
Lady-No-More;
There may be shame but
He's Mr. Guilt, and
Hell is Mr. War.

The wooden golden eagle
Announces from the rooftree:
Miss Equal, Mr. E.,
Dr. and Mrs. Eden, and
I am Miss Liberty.
But we see Timothy,
No more the colonized,
Look around after labor.
Not a single neighbor
Gives him his due acclaim.
Timothy's surprised:
A harsh laugh, a short knife,
Started his prodigious life.
But he took hold of fate,
Invested in the State, with
Money not worth a damn.
"I," he said, "am what I am,
What's to be done will be done,
The capital will be Washington.
Mr. Hamilton keeps his word,
This country's bond's as sound as me,
Timothy.
What' dyou say?
'Sound as I'—?
Very well; me is I,
I the tree
Flourishing."
Mr. Hamilton truly meant
An almost infinite per cent
Would accrue
Quickly to
The trustful and the nourishing.
The newborn Federal bank has stirred.
Timothy is a sword.
A sword without blessing,
A sword without fame,
A sword bearing no signal name.
If Newburyport
Will be blind,
Will seem bored,
Never mind.

The tanner's boy,
after we become
the United States,
invests in our
currency, which
is generally
regarded as
worthless;

becomes rich,

New Hampshire's kind, and
Calls him "Lord."   and acquires
Apprentice then, on the road   his new
Next day wore his freedom suit,   first name.
Brided widow and won his house,
Ground their proverbs underfoot.
A poor boy made and found
And funding came to his own tune.
"Lord" is the center of that sound,
And all the songs proclaim
He is the bright blue morning rhyme,
A great name rides before his name.
Turn, burn, and overturn!
Among the squarest houses, he
Is more than Timothy,
And more than merry.
Can forever now retort
Very much Newbury-
Port:
The voice of the people and I can't help it,
But all's easy and no bones broken,
All is well, all in Love.
The first Lord of the age has spoken.
Now all the torment Massachusetts bore
Triumphs in a blaze of love.
Love, love, fantasy,
For
Out of shame and poverty,
From oppression, commerce, war,
Rose a new sovereignty:
The states are free and trade is free
And Dexter's Lord Timothy.

3 THREE NIGHTS I DREAMED

Sharp clouds and a sea-moon sang to me
Where were you born my young my dear
I said nowhere vary your singing   He makes his
Now where was your mother shaded, they sang,   fortune as
Nowhere I answered the ring the rung   a merchant:
Dark bells rang and I was young—

O on the water then, wine on the sea—
Nowhere they cried and they sang to me—
Nowhere my dear my darling,
My dearly darling beware.

Where and nowhere and then the singing changed
Past hills of prophecy the words went ranging,
The colors of the words to images
Went formed. And all I saw was warming-pans,   selling warming-
Three nights of warming-pans until I woke   pans in the
And a great ship's bare spars sailing my window,   West Indies,
Up to my tall room window a ship's spars,
And I remembered all the nights and wars,
Sang in my waking of poverty and dream:
My dearly darling beware.

The sun all male and female through me poured,
Awake I bought a cargo all of dream,   where they are
Warming-pans for the South, to all the roaring   snapped up for
Nothing, to those who mock at my song.   molasses-ladles;
I have entrusted south my folly cargo,
A full hold coming home now showers gold.
My warming-pans sailed gently to Jamaica—
The lids ripped off, made fine molasses-ladles,
Rum, rum, my darling beware.

Gold I am, lord of the cats of gold,   And then, to spite
Mittens and kittens and coals of gold,   their business
Malta, the Baltic, the Caribbee,   sayings, cats to
And Britain commend their money to me   Malta; mittens
As I go funding among the dreamers,   north; and,
Among their golden nightmares ringing   finally, coals
Among their proverbs a wine-gold bell,   to Newcastle.
Sounding a folly my dear my darling
My dearly darling dream well.

4 KINGS AND CONTEMPORARIES

How can I speak to them today? What can I know,
What can I show so that we see ourselves?
Voices of stinted singing in the towns,
Voices of wildness and fear of wilderness.

The rhythm, the root. Gathering in
Sources of music and the wild sea-rose.

Sea-music and the sea building its waters,
The weathervane beast. My song.

Whenever I say what I mean
They mock and call me mad.
They slip my meaning—
When I mock at them, I
always make money—
How can this go on?
Harum scarum, merchant marum,
My house is built, and my wall of pillars,
A noted house to the Isles of Shoals.
My kings, my presidents, stand round:
I speak in images so they may know
My gold spread-eagle on the cupalow.

⁓

Dr. Franklin, Mr. Hamilton, John Hancock, Rufus King,
John Jay, two grenadiers.
Four lions, and here the roof runs so,
That a lamb can lie down with one of the lions,
And an eagle on the cupalow.

He sets up, around his house, the figures of those he most admires.

One unicorn, one dog, one horse,
And in the Garden Adam and Eve—
I will if I please have Adam and Eve.
If no man murders me summer or snow
I'll carry this to its fair concluding
With an eagle on the cupalow.

Three of the apostles, viz.
St. Paul St. Peter and St. John.
Venus, Hiram, and Solomon—
The President's platform and columns grow—
I meant marble, but wood it is,
And an eagle on the cupalow.

The Royal Arch, with lifesize painted figures carved by Joseph Wilson, the figurehead sculptor.

George Third, L'Ouverture,
Lord Nelson Baron of the Nile.

Constantinople's Grand Signior,
All heroes, each one in his style—
The Chief Cornplanter with his bow,
His moccasins, arrows, and tomahawk,
And an eagle on the cupalow.

❧

Black rum and silver gin,
Drink for this company.
For the resident poet, Jonathan Plummer,
With a wheelbarrow full of broadsides and haddock—
Malaga wine for Madam Hooper,
Timothy Dexter's fortune-teller;
And for brandy-breasted Lucy, Lucy Lancaster,
Daughter of princes in Africa,
Feathers and majesty—what for her?
Black rum and silver gin
And a coach with cream-color horses.

Filisy, folosy, silver gin,
Stingalum, stangalum, wine for day,
Ram pan, muski dan,
And wine for night on the sound blind sea.
Stingalum, stangalum, buck.

Rum, whalerbone, whackerbone,
Waterfront, turnpike, Merrimack bridge,
Sea-berry, sea-gold, pine-forest edge;
Wire, briar, limber lock,
Timothy's a red red rock
Surrounded by waves of whisky and wine,
Loving waves called Jonathan,
Lucy Lancaster, Madam Hooper,
And a coach with cream-color horses.

5 THE PICKLE, THE TEMPLE

The Pickle
I will say what I mean here; in a book;
I wants to make
My Enemies grin
Like a cat over
A hot puddin.

If you can bear the truth
Then I will tell the truth:
Man's the best animal,
And the worst—
All men, I say, are more or
Less the Devil's.
Odds make the difference
And there's a sight of odds.
Some half, some quarters.
Odds make the difference.
I see in all places God, the God
Of nature in all things.
We live and move in God,
We live in God.

From *A Pickle For*
the Knowing Ones,
Timothy Dexter's book.

❧

When great powers ruled,
I was born.
In a snowstorm, the signs
In the seventh house.
Mars came forward
Holding the candle—
Jupiter stood by.
I was to be
One great man.
(I think I am a Quaker
But have so little sense
I can't deceive.)
The bubble is the soul . . .
Man is the giant toad . . .
I have thoughts about clocks
Nobody will believe.
Ask me and I will tell.

Of his birth
and becoming.

❧

Now turn the system of knowledge
Into light—
Parents and masters begin, begin schoolmasters
At Cadameys and Collegeys,
Begin ministers,
Leave off, scarecrows in courage,
Brave good apelets—
One thing masters must teach:

Have good manners
To parents and people in streets,
And don't be too nosey.
I recommend a school   A plan for
Of languages,   the young:
Scholars to go to
Far parts to trade—
Go supercargo
To learn navigation
And character.
There will in time take
Many brave men,
Advantage to merchants
And funding to country—
Wise men pos-pos on this.
Goodbye—Timothy Dexter.

I command peace and the
Gratest brotherly love
And Not fade, be linked
Together with that best of troue Love
So as to govern all nasions
On the fass of the gloub
Not to
Tiranize over them   A Congress of Nations;
But to
Put them to order . . .
A Congress of nasions
To be allways in france
All Despouts is
To be there settled
And this way be Dun
This will balless power
And then all was Dun
A Way—there-for I have the Lam
To Lay Dow with the Lion
Now this may be dun
If the powers would
A geray to Lay whats called
Devel to one side

I being a man without learning
Please to give me Light.   His appeal.

❧

The knowing ones complain
Of my book
The first edition
Had no stops
I put in a Nuf here
And they may peper
And solt it as they plese

,,
,,
....
,,
..............!!!!!!!!!!!..............
...............!!!!!!!..............
.................!!!...............
..................!...............
,,
.......???????????..............

The Temple

Then with a touch of the gout, and being
A little sober in the morning
I raised in the garden a Temple of Reason
For my own funeral,
Furnished with pipes and tobacco, a speaking trumpet
And fireworks in the tomb,
A Bible to read, and some good songs.
I sent out invitations.
Now it was time to begin.   He holds his
                                                         own funeral,

It was a fine clear day,
I had fine pallbearers
Lord East Lord West Lord North and Lord South
Lord Megul and Lord Shambow.
The minister made his prayer—
Doctor Strong, he was—
And the flimsy sextons were there
And very much crying.
About 3000 came,
Oh, half the town, I'd say.

375 ❧

The procession wound   and watches from
Under my window   an upper window
Across the garden to my
Temple of Reason.
My coffin was long ready,
Painted in my house.
White lead inside
And outside touched with green.
Noble trimmings, eight handles
And an uncommon lock.
Now it was put into the
Temple of Reason.
Out in the kitchen I was
Beating my wife;
The ghostly lady
Had hardly mourned at all.

Very few people
Should attend funerals.
Many catch cold, and we
Want to settle Ohio;
We can't spare these beauties
To die so soon.

6 THE KIND OF WOMAN
Ghostly in my house
A woman I married—
Ghostly up the stairs,
Like snow in the hall.
At midnight in her bed
The ghostly-breasted;
I cannot have her ghost
Walking my palace.   He is haunted by
They say she is alive.   his living wife.
I say she will ever be
Mrs. Dexter that was.
The attacks of the ghost
Will not let me sleep.—
Now to save my life.

I will sell the house,
Horses, the cream-color horses
And the coach.

If not I will let it.
Wait. I can sweep my house
And get all anew
And go out of hell.
I will advertise.

"I must have a
Companon four
good by all."

"A very colding wife
Is poison to me.
I wish to be still
And master of my cash;
And therefore I wish for
One very good housekeeper.
Them that know me know
The kind of woman.
Now I will say
What kind of a person,
From thirty to forty
And a good jade
That will trot pace and gallop—
Not to heave one off
But, rather of the two,
Heave on.—I mean right well.
Now stop, I got off the path;
Now I am honest: I wish for
A middling woman for size,
Sensible honest and comely,
Knowing when to speak
and when to be silent,
With a nose like mine."

7 GUESSING TIME

A feat of laughter and a coastwise dance
Among the ills of ocean, in pauper light
Imagining truth, at dawn turning from madness
Into the unknown world, up blue invisible
Mountains of fantasy climbing
To the sea.
Where he as a boy walked down, salty, in brightness
Raging and worshipping.
Their faces turn again the nailhead stare
Of proverbs glaring at the intuitive.
My old head has

Worn out three bodies.
Amen. Clean truth.
Pay the whole debt, it will make nations tremble.
Keep up to what we set out to be, honest republicans,
No king, but you won't go it long without being honest;
If dishonest, you must have a king.
Keep Judas out of your councils.
Watch day and night, for mankind is mankind.
Jockey-handed priests, deacons, grunters, whiners—
(And I will show you one more private torture:
Abraham Bishop my son-in-law from whom
I live in hell on earth; pity me, fellow mortals,
A.B. mad with learning, as poor as a snake,
As proud as Lucifer. A.B. is a beast,
A Connecticut bull, short neck, thick curly hair.
When I see my father, the great good man,
Father Thomas Jefferson, he'll shed great tears with grief.)

A sortment, a sortment is good in a shop.

How many nicknames three things have:
Sex and glory and the grave.

Now I suppose I may guess
As it is guessing time:
I guess the world is all one
Very large living creature;
Mankind is the master beast,
As in the sea the whale
Is head fish—master over the
Whole of beasts and fish,
But still we're all one creature.
Man is the masterly beast,
And also the worst of the whole,
Knowing the most and acting the worst
According to what we know.

I think when the candle goes out
Men and women are done at one blow,
We will lie then as dirt of rocks
Until the great gun go—
9,000,000,000 tons

Of the best good powder.
That will shake and bring all the
Bones together,
Then the world will be to an end.
All kinds of music then,
And funding laid aside,
The melody will be very great,—
Now why won't you believe me?

It is as true as apple-seed,
The sea and sea-music.
True as the voices that through me burn—
As true as we died and we are born,
Apple-seed and apple-thorn
Calling root and calling hand,
Saying Amen, mockery, Amen, fantasy,
Sea-music and the sea.

 4

ARE YOU BORN?—1

A man riding on the meaning of rivers
Sang to me from the cloud of the world:
Are you born? Are you born?
My name is gone into the burning heart
That knows the change deep in the form of things.
—I saw from the treeline all our cities shine.
A woman riding on the moon of ocean
Sang to me through the cloud of the world:
Are you born? Are you born?
The form of growing in leaf and crystal flows,
And in the eyes and rivers of the land.
—From the rock of our sky, I came to recognize.

A voice riding on the morning of air
Sang to me from the cloud of the world:

Are you born? Are you born?
Bring all the singing home;
There is a word of lightning in the grass.
—I stood alive in the young cloud.

[UNTITLED]

Murmurs from the earth of this land, from the caves and craters,
	from the bowl of darkness. Down watercourses of our
	dragon childhood, where we ran barefoot.
We stand as growing women and men. Murmurs come down
	where water has not run for sixty years.
Murmurs from the tulip tree and the catalpa, from the ax of
	the stars, from the house on fire, ringing of glass; from
	the abandoned iron-black mill.
Stars with voices crying like mountain lions over forgotten
	colors.
Blue directions and a horizon, milky around the cities where the
	murmurs are deep enough to penetrate deep rock,
Trapping the lightning-bird, trapping the red central roots.
You know the murmurs. They come from your own throat.
You are the bridges to the city and the blazing food-plant green;
The sun of plants speaks in your voice, and the infinite shells of
	accretion
A beach of dream before the smoking mirror.
You are close to that surf, and the leaves heated by noon, and
	the star-ax, the miner's glitter walls. The crests of the sea
Are the same strength you wake with, the darkness is the eyes
	of children forming for a blaze of sight and soon, soon,
Everywhere your own silence, who drink from the crater, the
	nebula, one another, the changes of the soul.

[UNTITLED]

The tree of rivers seen and forgotten,
With all its lightnings laid over it, the white law.
Strokes of the spirit on the flowing spirit
Seen, forgotten, and seen, until the source.

But the source, simple and various
As possibility, the nest of light,
Is open; what do you forget who have forgotten?
At home or hunting, forgetting takes your throat.

This dream of rivers responding, as many lives respond:
The cant of a dam and the running of fresh waters
Allow discovery deep in the city of your days
Starting up, before your faces born,
Born and reborn of your perceive,
Of your smile that you recognize
The meanings as they move.

[UNTITLED]

The power of war leads to a plan of lives
Involving rivers. The many-stated million
Human concerns. This touches, this gives life
To all its forms. Now clothe our force,
Make it as flexible as a man venturing
To fend for himself in his own enterprise.

Now in the unity of all vision, unity of the land, the forests
        and water,
See nature, the nation, as a web of lives
On the earth together, full of their potencies.
The total unity, reached past images,
Reaching past the naming of religions.
We reach to create. That is our central meaning,
Suggestion of art and altar in all our passwords,
For the meaning of "mirror of nature," the meaning of "image
        of God"
Is a simple fiery meaning : man is to create.
Making, singing, bring the potential to day.

[UNTITLED]

A tree of rivers flowing through our lives;
These lives moving through their starvation and greatness,
Masked away from each other, masked in lack.
Each woman seen as a river through whom lifetime
Gives, and feeds. Each man seen giving and feeding.
Under all the images, under all growth and form. The energy
       of each, which is relation,
A flare of linked fire which is the need to grow,
The human wish for meaning.
                        Roots of diversity
Each being witness to itself, entering to relate,
Bearing the flood, the food, the becoming of power,
Which is our eyes and our lives
Related, in bonds of flow.

[UNTITLED]

The sea has opened, the limit of his dream
Has split; now lights announce him to the day.
He is born; and asleep, awake, and soon the warm
Taste of the second world calls him to understand
Power drawn on the tides of sweetness in.
His strength allowing change, letting him choose and grow
Again, and the curve of the world is breast, the breathing land
With his own breathing tells of peace and form.

Not now, but much later, does the world fall away.
This is myself, says the child. My self, we all did say.
There is my mother, whose pleasure, whose deep need
It was to feed me singing, or recoil.
And then the fable, the terrible forgetting.
A cold distortion twisting past the leaves.
Was there a Garden? Was there a Tree of Sin?
What was my exile but from memory?
Refusal, flowering, was the only tree.
It grew until the truth was almost lost.
Cast, the obliterate spirit sang its loss.
Dream and the sea open.

All things find their change.
        The child remembers : the child is the tree;
The tides, the leaves, the city, the true relation.
The world was the mother, the world; it was always the world
Pure, fierce, all moving and all reconciled.

POWERPLANT

A structure is rising. It takes on shape, it takes on meaning
Where there was formless waste. Go down the valley,
Eye of creation, sings the voice of the girl
Through cloverfield. Green water is the spring of the year,
Jade green in summer; autumn bright blue, for winter water-black.
The wall's detail, discrimination of blue
Standing above the wall, where developing water
Coils, sheathes, transforms itself turning, into light.
Fusing of images and further change.
Fire and music, interchangeable.
Fusing of flow, dividing and further blue.

There is control here, for all things in relation
Find their offerings and give. A tendency toward life.
The man at peace with his life and its flashing,
A climax forest at peace with its fields.
When the storms come, there is something in us
That has always been ready to greet the storm.
An impulse running through a valley of process
Quickens the blossoming, whose orange on evening
The fiery action of men and women emerges.
And daughter-stars, daughter-forests of our range
Dance with the central prince the dance of reign.
We know the light incarnate, we have seen
At last that the flashing is our old light, and flesh.

Under stones, under leaves, under links of purpose,
Appetite up so tall, the power is given
Along the hillsides of risk, the spiral dances
Within its own symmetry. But women, but men, but women
And men in the dances and risks of birth
In which love and the spirit are reborn.

This also from lightning given and growing power.
Lightning which is the word. The gift and power. Love.

[UNTITLED]

In the last hour of night, a zebra racing dawn,
Black-and-white hour that feeds the night and the light,
Feeding the strong infants; when the well is open;
When all the birds of day begin to sing.
He turning in sleep finds through a journey of dream
One woman in whom all the rivers of his storm
Cluster and fill, as words, as woman. Finds
The running of stones in a riverbed
Troubling hillsides with their leaves
Over black branches. Swinging-to of mountains
No heavier than sails riding to rendezvous.
Dense in our blood, abstract as the idea of God.
As smoky misereres, as the birthcry.
The big few clusters, the body of a man.
The clusters of her body. Sleep of gardens,
Sleep of rain, always distant and present
As your own deprived childhood. No. Not deprived.
Yes. For it never saw it was deprived.
But there was the unknown, the great dream of the poor
And of all men; your childhood found that friend.
Was it the faceless, the man in the purple graveyard?
No. Hidden. And kind. In endless offering.
And now in early sleep, a ripple uncovering
The roots of the diverse, the city of love.

A note in music. His sleep going long and along.

FIELDS WHERE WE SLEPT

Fields where we slept
Lie underwater now
Clay meadows of nightmare
Beneath the shallow wave.

A tremor of speech
On all lips and all mirrors,
Pink sweater and tornado
Act out the spiral dawn.

South lies evocative
On one fine Negro mouth.
Play of silver in streams
Half lake under.

High on the unplowed red
And waterweeds respond
Where Sheriff Fever
Ordered me to trial,

Where once hatred and fear
Touched me the branch of death,
I may float waves of making
Hung above my lost field.

Remember they say and Incarnatus Est,
The fire-tailed waves, never forget the eyes
Of the distorted jailers or their kindness
Even while they were torturing Mr. Crystal.

Psalms awake and asleep, remember the manmade
Lake where those barren treecrowns rode.
Where air of curses hung, keel of my calm
Rides our created tide.

PORTRAIT OF A MAN, WITH A BACKGROUND OF HOLDINGS

Standing against the gorge, he sees the slides of light.
Where lightning lay, they are building. The surfaces are lit.
The dam that is almost finished stands in seamless night
Declaring its form with a clear speaking.
The man leans on his railing. He thinks : I will listen.
Bulbs of violent light swing on their own wires,

Lines of the downstream face flow down the slope of dream.
Spillway of loyalties shining, the gate of fire.

He forgets the police on a hot summer night long past
Later finding the wound between his shoulder blades;
He thinks of the women opened before him, flowers of summer,
The first cry of his son at which all waterfalls
Waited like streams of wine bitter in Spain.
Riches of breathing, fantastic poverty.
The running of stones in this riverbed.

Corngreen and fields of thirst, he thinks. I know a woman
The river of whose mouth, whose sea of flowers
I saw in the hot fields of the past, at night.
Over all images a lightning stroke of law
Has been laid across, white structure on the river
To stop my profit's streams, to make a tree
Celebrating the years of growth and form.

The pacemaker image. A pulse and pattern of light.
The mirror image of my waste, in the ferocious cities
Whose roaring and giant fibres find my exultation
Outward in the shout, while what I stare at is
The dam I tried to murder for years; or sail
In a boat the color of violins among
A school of condoms floating in the Sound.
Beyond naming, waste! The legs of the withered man.
My summons from the great web and the woman
In glimpses accepted, for long forgot. I think
I am wheat dormant in the seedman's hand.

[UNTITLED]

A red bridge fastening this city to the forest,
Telling relationship in a stroke of steel;
Cloud-hung among the mist it speaks the real,
In the morning of need asserts the purest
Of our connections : for the opposites
To call direct, to be the word that goes,

Glowing from fires of thought to thought's dense snows,
Growing among the treason and the threats.

Between the summer strung and the young city,
Linking the stonefall to the treefall slope,
Beyond the old namings of body and mind
A red bridge building a new-made identity:
Communion of love opened to cross and find
Self the enemy, this moment and our hope.

[UNTITLED]

Power never dominion.
Some other power.
Some force flaking in light, avalanches of lilies,
Days and the sun renewed in semen, pure
Among the uncorrupted fires, fire's ancestor,
Forgotten; worshipped secretly;
Where the vestigial Lucifer regales
Craters of memory; where leans
Some fleshly girl, the shaped stones of desire
Leaping in color at her human cunt.
They will translate this girl. She will appear
In textbooks as a sacrificed antelope
Guilt running shiny over the short fur.
Ideas of shame did split that throat.
But none of that is true tonight.
The girl was leaning over the crater, I dreamt it,
The shriveled flowers twisted in her hair,
And jewels budded at her throat.
The girl of choice, remembering the past fires,
Praising the word, the columns in the grove,
Arbor vitae uterinae
Locked by such branches, light in the dense forest,
Praising the world unknown and feeling beat
Among her branches
A human child.
Brambles of sense! and that responding power
Rocking the fullness of time.

Until it shall be, what never was:
River and born and dream.

Canals of music downward serenade
New satin gleams under her haunches;
And, running laterally,
And backwards across ripples,
Passing the lower stairs,
Even above the unforgettable murmur,
The sound of oars.

Body of the splendid, bear me now!
Completed by orbits of unhorsèd comets,
The bronze, paternal stars.

Cave of their messengers,
Thalamic cleft where the divorcèd myth
Begged to be nursed through hysteria that leap year,
Sank at the window—O the famous view!
This side or that side of the balcony
Falling, the graceless sanatorium swan,
Breaking nobody's kneecaps but her own.

Passes the pear orchard near the middle hill
At the wind's moment when all sails are lowered,
A small bird kiares, slope of his flight, the blue
Yielding flutes of his feathers, that small wing
Bounds us above—kiar! Inscribing our horizon.
A high note over our necessity.

[UNTITLED]

The sky is as black as it was when you lay down
But it is shining; the setting constellations
Are under now. You fell asleep listening.
Yes, you are off the road. But showers of fire
Are running through night, and now your daybreak eyes
Remember the forest and the invisible city,
You will always know what there is loose in the world,
God of your early morning childhood and your dreams,

Visible sparkling in these women and men.
That you can learn alone and by loving them
That act through all things seeming unstill or still
And turns your painful spirit to face the light.

[UNTITLED]

On your journey you will come to a time of waking.
The others may be asleep. Or you may be alone.

Immediacy of song moving the titled
Visions of children and the linking stars.

You will begin then to remember. You
Hear the voice relating after late listening.

You remember even falling asleep, or a dream of sleep.
For now the song is given and you remember.

At every clear waking you have known this song,
The cities of this music identified

By the white springs of singing, and their fountains
Reflected in windows, in all the human eyes.

The wishes, the need growing. The song growing.

[UNTITLED]

This is the net of begetting and belief :
The laws of relation, of seed, urging all things to form
Through growth which develops on the dreams of law

The waking of each day, the theatres of the night
Afford us responsibility, the king and queen
Of fire in its running through all things.
Our only rest is in going with our meanings
In life and holiness,

All the creative acts drawing from the deep source
Their air of wildness and peace,
Their blessing and energy,
Making forever the world.

BODY OF WAKING

Fire-thread in the valley. Bird-voice in darkness.
Before the opening of the world. In our own time.
Days we then heard the cities in their singing,
Armies standing in their graves imagining certain mornings,
Hours a naked man in the stream high on the mountain
Imagined this, too, among the cold water,
Looking up at the forming sky.

Century of absence in the valley of confusion.

When you wake, even startled awake, even in shadowless night, even
        alone, the song
Will be growing. The song begun will be growing in fiery night ; in
        blackness, voices
Pouring over the unseen cities, and the mountains wake,
Riverlands unseen, immediacy of song.

Silence prepares the sleepers. Silence prepares
Our night of the dark branches of the world.

Century of absence. It could be like a time
When the soul that has slept leaps from its priests,
Spring when the old idea is at last available to all children,
And God in the world is on the lips of love.
Hot out of the dried blood of the separate churches,
The nations, separate wards in the same hospital.
Revenge which spikes the cross and splits the star
Withers the crescent. The world circles among
The solitude of Spain, the solitude of Stalingrad,
Solitude in the hills of loess and the caves of Africa,
And now your solitude, New York, who raised yourself above.

Now the buried questions flicker on all faces.
Does the flat belly know its heart is broken?
Do you drag yourself through the wilderness saying
Never mind how we got here; that will come later?
Much later, after you speak of the weapon birds
And the spies in your milk and the little split children
Bleeding models of cars; you told their fortunes
According to a harvest of slot-machines;
According to the obscene pattern of bombers.
Much later, after you glare for eight days, silent,
After you howl for a century and a half,
You look at the clock and see it has not moved.
What do you do then? Weep for the generations?
You change your life. No. You begin again
Going on from the moment in which you stand today.
Will there be suffering? Perhaps not as much as now.
But there will be suffering, in the healing? Yes.
Only with a difference. You will know it then.
Walking down Basin Street, will be aware.
And that, my darling, my dear dear, is what Mother prays for,
Beside the cradle, lighting the candles of the days,
In retreat, in the kitchen, watching by living bodies
And waiting endlessly by the unmoving face
While the door is still not, not really, not yet, opened.
My darling, my baby, my people, my own self.

The words rising from the sleep of America:
I had all my children, and they locked themselves in,
My babies are sick to death, and the doctor is not well.
Ruddy we are, strong we are, and insane.
They built doors around themselves, and then they locked the doors.
Some believe they are doctors. Some believe they are patients,
Some think they are statisticians. Some are ambassadors.
We eat very well. We keep the pictures on.
Sometimes the clocks jump fifty minutes. Some days they do not
    Move.
Some play they are parents. Some always are the children.
We are careful to flush the toilet. Of course we take exercise.
Of course it's a toilet. Of course it's a swimming pool.

The force that split the spirit could found a city,
That held the split could shine the lights of science.
This rigid energy could still break and run dancing
Over the rockies and smokies of all lives.
How many moons circle our dreams? America,
Did you think only of wars and luxury?
Can you remember your early dreaming?

Who of us fully living
Among these inward murders,
Among the ritual
Of domination?

I remember the structure of towers
Torches over New York
I remember the structure of crystals
A single sheet of flow
I know an immortal journey
And we all walk hypnotized by a cliff
Speed and explosion.

Voices of process, river of human meanings.
Put your hand in, come into the dance,
Turn around fine, take out your hand,
Dance yourself once.
You know this music.
You were born among these songs.

No we tell, sing, and relate.
The buried life and the body of waking.

❧

Bird-voice in darkness. Tremor of night moving.
The rocks accept blackness. Now I remember trees.
Across the crystals of time forming I suddenly feel
The flow of a cold breeze following a bird-voice
The river remade, the invitation of water
Moving in praise of process.
In time the river turns, in time turn the wakers
Among their colored dreams,
In time our frightful processions
May turn toward morning and turn toward form.

Now the praise of the moving into light,
The melody of this walking, the broken breathing even of us
Who moved to discover the children in the forest,
The children of our own dreams who would save us.
Even among our broken failing years
And the acts to bind us, the look between two faces,
Ways and grace,
The melody of praise and the whisper of green
Before the opening of the world,
In our own time.
That was long before we knew what was required,
Before we began ever to hear the questions.

But the young, talking together of growth and form,
Arrived once more at the terms. In praise of process,
Our songs were, of the seed; we took the joy
Of the eye dancing unborn, its precise fore-lighting
Moving in unborn dark toward the achieved gaze,
Seeking continually developing light.
Seeking as we began to grow, and resting without distrust,
We moved toward a requirement still unknown.

We spoke of the heroes, the generous ones, who gave their meanings,
Knowing again meaning as music,
Meaning in all its moving, as process, as song,
As the enlightened seed transformed in dark and light.
Color transformed us. We knew the dance of selves,
Growing, meaning giving us our green.
And toward a future the music goes.

Flashing of meaning as the light we breathe,
And through the whole night moving, coming as music.
Music that grows in silence, along dark a single voice
On its long stair of sound going up darkness
Moving toward form, moving becoming meaning
That makes our sleeping.
                              Silent
Until the river under the voice discovers
Its own currents, a flowing in a stream.
While air follows its own music.

Throat of song. The air-achieving bird
Sings in the blackness.
Hours past midnight and a throat of music,
The dark night offering.
Fleet of voices in a single turning
Stair of calling and the flying pauses
Go as darkness and grow as constellations.
Voices of all music going toward its form
In human meanings and in silences.
Arriving again as the weather of our days
Over born water, on waking faces.
Growing to feed each other, lover, mother of gesture
To turn against fear and withholden reach,
The movement at the center of all things
Making a stillness never a refusal.
Dream and creation and sea,
Violent precise act,
Movement to match our lives,
Wish at the center of growth
We feel as peace.
Peace the love of the process of our lives
For the movement at the center of all things.

Voice diving deep.
Deep in the lights of silence.
When night no longer imagines sunlight,
And we going darker come to all music,
Deep in the clearoscure, where we alone
And all alone go through the texture of time
To the flowing present that becomes all things,
The energy of myth and star and bone.

Now the heroes of process
Not leaders but lives
Is even the lost girl walking the length of the forest
Even the child whose January wrists
Stuck out below his blowing sleeves. Weeping, he was,
Along the avenue. And the man who faced the spies
At the Segre River. Long ago. In Spain.

Another image of the born, the next woman,
Another image of the next power of man

Finds itself dreaming in the world of form.
Entering, long before we enter,
The new requirement, the world of morning.

⁓

Here's day beginning, the blessed, the unbegun, the song, the given.
For that the human wish to grow acts through his giving
The living will be giving you your doors and apples.
Self torn from its old lies, walking and eating,
Becoming music and bone,
All incomplete without the rest
And powerful over time
No longer cruel in partial truth,
Knowledge of giving and taking
Enters now and lets us live.
Lets us arrive at the present when the world
Has the choice of each of us, to make life or suicide,
To give or die.

⁓

They have eluded us. They are not here.
Statues turning to cloud among the music
Float overhead, promising rain and seasons
In the black, the day in midnight.
Dayray before the way.
Rides on a flickering breath, the changes of darkness,
Exchange of murders. Bodies exchanging life.
Where the belief flows somewhere
Uncorrupt, hidden, under violence,
Making its own and dawn-announcing act,
River of daybreak, where the waking is,
Still to be sung among the deaths and days.

These meanings become the light we breathe,
The breathing of a theme; in our own time.

[UNTITLED]

Sounds of night in the country of the opposites.
Music for the first time, on incredible instruments:
The rapids of a river, a woman's kitchen stove,

A village crossroads with its forgotten language;
Clank and chuckle of gambling; one line of a song;
The strings of lost limitless time. Music.
Voice of a cat you knew before you learned to speak.
Voices of waterfalls, steel whirls, many small flowers,
Voices of a dream of the animals of heaven
          Raised through the hungering
Of some one thin wavering unransomed boy
          In starved and golden air.
A sheer black music, rare-lit joining of waters.
Night-sound in the country of the opposites.

WILLKIE IN *THE GULLIVER*

When after the screens of the evening of defeat
You try the remote clean air, withdrawal, think of him.
He was like many of us. He had lost.
He flew to the many, making a crisis of choice
Lead toward the solving of barriers; learning, flying, crossed
Level after level of process, where we come
To ourselves, to the voiceless many who never in time
Choose against life. We find the direct voice.

Remembering limits, in the days of death,
All the faring that follows our first sight of the face
Of all things beginning again past deepest defeat.
Think now all of us of our loved and great,
Traveling new to make human the bonds of breath
After defeat; for all men; by God's grace.

[UNTITLED]

Then full awake you will recognize the voice,
You will know pouring through your journey
Bird-voice, voices of crystal, human voice
Whose body is your love
Opening the valleys of your love.

Dreaming we were awake, we saw the clusters
Moving, and the swarm of crystal forming, faces
Spiked down by stars who could not speak their bonds.
And forgot. And forget. Averted our souls. Forgot.

All I can promise if you go your journey
Is that you will come to a place of fire
And a place of night and then another place
Nobody now alive has ever predicted.
The gate of that place is water. It is called Process.

But on the way to the place, I saw a tower,
The children took me to it, and there the old men
Stood on the high rim. But the tower was hollow.
Within was a pit as deep as the tower was high.
Whatever arose, arose from the depth of the pit.
The name of the tower was The Place of Praise.

When you reach the place, will you live forever?
Surely not. You will leave again, often. You will forget,
In rigid afternoons, a power of flowing. But now
You will remember again, again return, and find
Again that changing fire, that changing
Water, that waking, and your self, and all men.

[UNTITLED]

In your time, there have been those who spoke clearly
For the moment of lightning.
Were we all brave, but at different times?
Even raped open and split, even anonymous,
They spoke. They are not forgotten.
But they are. In late summer; forgot; caught at cross–purposes,
Interrupted in an hour of purity,
Their lives careening along in the fierce cities,
Through atrocious poverties and magnificence,
The unforgotten, the early gone forgot.

Late daytime, and nothing left to hide but an eye endowed
With the charred, guilty, gouged by war, the raging splendor;

Despised like you, criminal in intent; sunburnt, in love and
      splendid;
This heart, naked and knocking, going in clouds,
Smoke and a cry of light.
In pain, the voice of pain. The shadow of your cry.
And never forget : you are magnificent beyond all colors.

HE HAD A QUALITY OF GROWTH

No one ever walking this our only earth, various, very clouded,
      in our forests, in all the valleys of our early dreams,
No one has ever for long seen any thing in full, not live
As any one river or man has run his changes, child
Of the swarms and sowings. Death nor the woman, seed
Of the born, all growing, going through the grass.
However deep you have looked into the well of the cradle
Or into any dream or open eyed the grave
While the soul, many-leaved and waiting,
Began to assume another exact flower.
Smoke and smell in the wind, a single life!
However true you tell, you never have told.
And even that is not altogether true. It changes, we say,
      changes, for yes,
Indeed we all know this, any, any of us, there are secrets known
      to all.
Was it indeed shown you in a flash of journey, the flicker along
      change?
In the fine shadow between the curve of lips, shadow of days
      lengthening,
In the flicker of meaning revealed by many windows;
In the form of the eye, the form of words, of the word; meaning that formed
These marvelous genitals, nameless as God;
Or in the informing light behind his dream, and he was dreaming of you.
Did his own self escape him, now to reach us, reaving the edge of cloud?

Has a gift then been given, each other giving our lives?

As air is given to the mouth of all?

ARE YOU BORN?—2

A child riding the stormy mane of noon
Sang to me past the cloud of the world:
Are you born? Are you born?
The form of this hope is the law of all things,
Our foaming sun is the toy of that force.
Touch us alive, developing light! Today,
Revealed over the mountains, every living eyes.

Child of the possible, who rides the hour
Of dream and process, lit by every fire.
Glittering blood of song, a man who changed
And hardly changed, only flickered, letting pass
A glint of time, showers of human meanings
Flashing upon us all : his story and his song.
The song of a child; the song of the cloud of the world,
Born, born, born. Cloud became real,

                                    and change,
The starry form of love.

Waterlily Fire

1962

THE SPEAKING TREE

for Robert Payne

Great Alexander sailing was from his true course turned
By a young wind from a cloud in Asia moving
Like a most recognizable most silvery woman;
Tall Alexander to the island came.
The small breeze blew behind his turning head.
He walked the foam of ripples into this scene.

The trunk of the speaking tree looks like a tree-trunk
Until you look again.   Then people and animals
Are ripening on the branches;   the broad leaves
Are leaves;   pale horses, sharp fine foxes
Blossom;   the red rabbit falls
Ready and running.   The trunk coils, turns,
Snakes, fishes.   Now the ripe people fall and run,
Three of them in their shore-dance, flames that stand
Where reeds are creatures and the foam is flame.

Stiff Alexander stands.   He cannot turn.
But he is free to turn : this is the speaking tree,
It calls your name.   It tells us what we mean.

TO ENTER THAT RHYTHM WHERE
THE SELF IS LOST

To enter that rhythm where the self is lost,
where breathing : heartbeat : and the subtle music
of their relation make our dance, and hasten
us to the moment when all things become
magic, another possibility.
That blind moment, midnight, when all sight
begins, and the dance itself is all our breath,
and we ourselves the moment of life and death.
Blinded;   but given now another saving,
the self as vision, at all times perceiving,
all arts all senses being languages,
delivered of will, being transformed in truth—
for life's sake surrendering moment and images,
writing the poem;   in love making;   bringing to birth.

FOR A MEXICAN PAINTER

Carlos, your art is embryos,
These eyes are shaping in the dark;
There is a fate map in this red
Line and that bright red line,
The earliest map of all.

These eyes are shaping in the dark
Toward the requirement of light
And all will grow as they have grown;
Even transplanted will perform
Selfwise, themselves, this one, that one.

Deep in the hieratic blood
Toward sleep toward dream the process goes,
Toward waking move the sex, the heart,
The self as woman man and rose.
Carlos, your art is embryos.

A SONG OF ANOTHER TRIBE

Guilt   said the bony man
Do you feel guilt
At your desires?
No   I said   my guilt comes when
My desires find no way.
Country of sand and claws;
I wait for my rescuer.
No one will venture there.

Out of long silences
Come I to wordless song
O let my singing bring me
To that place
Where live waters
Rise and go.
There may the living arrive,
Go and return.
Find me, and I find,

And go finding.
A beating sound, I hear
A sound of riding.
Speed after silence
And at last music,
Words of another tribe:

My riding is on swift mares,
My love is by the green water-springs;
For a short moment I will sit there,
I will look upon her wandering face,
I will put an end to the black delay.

SONG

A voice flew out of the river as morning flew
    out of the body of night, a voice sending
    out from the night of the sleeping
Morning : a voice in its own voice, naked, made
    of the whole body and the whole life
But without anything
Breath
Breath of the fire love
Smoke of the poems voices

WATERLILY FIRE

for Richard Griffith

1 THE BURNING

Girl grown woman   fire   mother of fire
I go to the stone street turning to fire.   Voices
Go screaming   Fire   to the green glass wall.
And there where my youth flies blazing into fire
The   dance   of sane and insane images, noon
Of seasons and days.   Noontime of my one hour.

Saw down the bright noon street the crooked faces
Among the tall daylight in the city of change.

The scene has walls   stone   glass   all my gone life
One wall a web through which the moment walks
And I am open, and the opened hour
The world as water-garden   lying behind it.
In a city of stone, necessity of fountains,
Forced water fallen on glass, men with their axes.

An arm of flame reaches from water-green glass,
Behind the wall I know waterlilies
Drinking their light, transforming light and our eyes
Skythrown under water, clouds under those flowers,
Walls standing on all things stand in a city noon
Who will not believe a waterlily fire.
Whatever can happen in a city of stone,
Whatever can come to a wall can come to this wall.

I walk in the river of crisis toward the real,
I pass guards, finding the center of my fear
And you, Dick, endlessly my friend during storm.

The arm of flame striking through the wall of form.

2 THE ISLAND

Born of this river and this rock island, I relate
The changes : I born when the whirling snow
Rained past the general's grave and the amiable child
White past the windows of the house of Gyp the Blood.
General, gangster, child.   I know in myself the island.

I was the island without bridges, the child down whose blazing
Eye the men of plumes and bone raced their canoes and fire
Among the building of my young childhood, houses;
I was those changes, the live darknesses
Of wood, the pale grain of a grove in the fields
Over the river fronting red cliffs across—
And always surrounding her the river, birdcries, the wild
Father building his sand, the mother in panic her parks—
Bridges were thrown across, the girl arose
From sleeping streams of change in the change city.
The violent forgetting, the naked sides of darkness.
Fountain of a city in growth, an island of light and water.
Snow striking up past the graves, the yellow cry of spring.

Whatever can come to a city can come to this city.
Under the tall compulsion
                              of the past
I see the city
                    change like a man changing
I love this man
                          with my lifelong body of love
I know you
                    among your changes
                                            wherever I go
Hearing the sounds of building
                                    the syllables of wrecking
A young girl watching
                          the man throwing red hot rivets
Coals in a bucket of change
How can you love a city that will not stay?
I love you
            like a man of life in change.

Leaves like yesterday shed, the yellow of green spring
Like today accepted and become one's self
I go, I am a city with bridges and tunnels,
Rock, cloud, ships, voices.   To the man where the river met
The tracks, now buried deep along the Drive
Where blossoms like sex pink, dense pink, rose, pink, red.

Towers falling.   A dream of towers.
Necessity of fountains.   And my poor,
Stirring among our dreams,
Poor of my own spirit, and tribes, hope of towers
And lives, looking out through my eyes.
The city the growing body of our hate and love,
The root of the soul, and war in its black doorways.
A male sustained cry interrupting nightmare.
Male flower heading upstream.

Among a city of light, the stone that grows.
Stigma of dead stone, inert water, the tattered
Monuments rivetted against flesh.
Blue noon where the wall made big agonized men
Stand like sailors pinned howling on their lines, and I

See stopped in time a crime behind green glass,
Lilies of all my life on fire.
Flash faith in a city building its fantasies.

I walk past the guards into my city of change.

3 JOURNEY CHANGES

Many of us   Each in his own life waiting
Waiting to move   Beginning to move   Walking
And early on the road of the hill of the world
Come to my landscapes emerging on the grass

The stages of the theatre of the journey

I see the time of willingness between plays
Waiting and walking and the play of the body
Silver body with its bosses and places
One by one touched awakened into into

Touched and turned one by one into   flame

The theatre of the advancing goddess   Blossoming
Smiles as she stands intensely being in stillness
Slowness in her blue dress advancing standing I go
And far across a field over the jewel grass

The play of the family stroke by stroke acted out

Gestures of deep acknowledging on the journey stages
Of the playings the play of the goddess and the god
A supple god of searching and reaching
Who weaves his strength   Who dances her more alive

The theatre of all animals, my snakes, my great horses

Always the journey   long   patient   many haltings
Many waitings for choice and again easy breathing
When the decision to go on is made
Along the long slopes of choice and again the world

The play of poetry approaching in its solving

Solvings of relations in poems and silences
For we were born to express   born for a journey
Caves, theatres, the companioned solitary way
And then I came to the place of mournful labor

A turn in the road and the long sight from the cliff

Over the scene of the land dug away to nothing and many
Seen to a stripped horizon carrying barrows of earth
A hod of earth taken and emptied and thrown away
Repeated farther than sight.   The voice saying slowly

But it is hell.   I heard my own voice in the words
Or it could be a foundation   And after the words
My chance came.   To enter.   The theatres of the world.

4 FRAGILE

I think of the image brought into my room
Of the sage and the thin young man who flickers and asks.
He is asking about the moment when the Buddha
Offers the lotus, a flower held out as declaration.
"Isn't that fragile?" he asks.   The sage answers:
"I speak to you.   You speak to me.   Is that fragile?"

5 THE LONG BODY

This journey is exploring us. Where the child stood
An island in a river of crisis, now
The bridges bind us in symbol, the sea
Is a bond, the sky reaches into our bodies.
We pray : we dive into each other's eyes.

Whatever can come to a woman can come to me.

This is the long body : into life from the beginning,
Big-headed infant unfolding into child, who stretches and finds
And then flowing the young one going tall, sunward,
And now full-grown, held, tense, setting feet to the ground,
Going as we go in the changes of the body,
As it is changes, in the long strip of our many
Shapes, as we range shifting through time.
The long body : a procession of images.

This moment in a city, in its dream of war.
                         We chose to be,
Becoming the only ones under the trees
                                    when the harsh sound
Of the machine sirens spoke. There were these two men,
And the bearded one, the boys, the Negro mother feeding
Her baby. And threats, the ambulances with open doors.
Now silence. Everyone else within the walls. We sang.
                    We are the living island,
We the flesh of this island, being lived,
Whoever knows us is part of us today.

Whatever can happen to anyone can happen to me.

Fire striking its word among us, waterlilies
Reaching from darkness upward to a sun
Of rebirth, the implacable.   And in our myth
The Changing Woman who is still and who offers.

Eyes drinking light, transforming light, this day
That struggles with itself, brings itself to birth.
In ways of being, through silence, sources of light
Arriving behind my eye, a dialogue of light.

And everything a witness of the buried life.
This moment flowing across the sun, this force
Of flowers and voices body in body through space.
The city of endless cycles of the sun.

I speak to you   You speak to me

The Speed of Darkness

1968

THE POEM AS MASK

ORPHEUS

When I wrote of the women in their dances and wildness,
    it was a mask,
on their mountain, god-hunting, singing, in orgy,
it was a mask; when I wrote of the god,
fragmented, exiled from himself, his life, the love gone
    down with song,
it was myself, split open, unable to speak, in exile from
    myself.

There is no mountain, there is no god, there is memory
of my torn life, myself split open in sleep, the rescued child
beside me among the doctors, and a word
of rescue from the great eyes.

No more masks! No more mythologies!

Now, for the first time, the god lifts his hand,
the fragments join in me with their own music.

WHAT DO I GIVE YOU?

What do I give you?   This memory
I cannot give you.   Force of a memory
I cannot give you : it rings my nerves among.
None of these songs
Are made in their images.
Seeds of all memory
Given me give I you
My own self.   Voice of my days.
Blessing;   the seed and pain,
Green of the praise of growth.
The sacred body of thirst.

THE TRANSGRESS

That summer midnight under her aurora
northern and still we passed the barrier.

Two make a curse, one giving, one accepting.
It takes two to break a curse

transformed at last in each other's eyes.

I sat on the naked bed of space,
all things becoming other than what they seem

in the night-waking, in the revelation
thundering on tabu after the broken

imperative, while the grotesque ancestors fade
with you breathing beside me through our dream:

bed of forbidden things finally known—
art from the symbol struck, living and made.

Branch lifted green from the dead shock of stone.

THE CONJUGATION OF THE
PARAMECIUM

This has nothing
to do with
propagating

The species
is continued
as so many are
(among the smaller creatures)
by fission

(and this species
is very small
next in order to
the amoeba, the beginning one)

The paramecium
achieves, then,
immortality
by dividing

But when
the paramecium
desires renewal
strength   another joy
this is what
the paramecium does:

The paramecium
lies down beside
another
paramecium

Slowly   inexplicably
the exchange
takes place
in which
some bits
of the nucleus of each
are exchanged

for some bits
of the nucleus
of the other

This is called
the conjugation of the paramecium.

JUNK-HEAP AT MURANO

for Joby West

You told me : they all went in and saw the glass,
The tourists, and I with them, a busload of them,
        a boatload
Out from Venice. We saw the glass making.

Until I, longing for air—longing for something—walked
       outside
And found my way along the building and around.
Suddenly there the dazzle, all the colors, fireworks and
       jewels in a mound
Flashing from the heap of glass thrown away. Not quite
       perfect. Perhaps a little flawed. Chipped, perhaps.
              Here is one.
And handed me the blue.

I looked into your eyes
Who walked around Murano
And I saw far behind, the face of the child I carried outdoors
       that night.
You were four. You looked up into the great tree netting
       all of night
And saw fire-points in the tree, and asked, "Do birds eat
       stars?"

Behind your eyes the seasons, the times,
assemble; dazzle; are here.

CLUES

How will you catch these clues at the moment of waking
take them, make them yours?   Wake, do you,
and light the lamp of sharpest whitest beam
and write them down in the room of night on white—
night opening and opening white
paper under white light, write what streamed
from you in darkness
into you by dark?

Indian Baptiste saying, We painted our dreams.
We painted our dreams on our faces and bodies.
We took them into us by painting them on ourselves.

    When we saw the water mystery of the lake
after the bad dream, we painted the lines and masks,
when the bear wounded me, I painted for healing.

When we were told in our dreams, in the colors of day
red for earth, black for the opposite, rare green, white.
Yellow. When I dreamed of weeping and dreamed of sorrow
I painted my face with tears, with joy.
Our ghost paintings and our dreams of war.
The whole brow, the streak, the hands and sex, the breast.
The spot of white, one hand black, one hand red.
The morning star appearing over the hill.
We took our dreams into our selves.
We took our dreams into our bodies.

IN OUR TIME

In our period, they say there is free speech.
They say there is no penalty for poets,
There is no penalty for writing poems.
They say this.   This is the penalty.

DOUBLE DIALOGUE:

HOMAGE TO ROBERT FROST

In agony saying : "The last night of his life,
My son and I in the kitchen : At half-past one
He said, 'I have failed as a husband. Now my wife
Is ill again and suffering.' At two
He said, 'I have failed as a farmer, for the sun
Is never there, the rain is never there.'
At three he said, 'I have failed as a poet who
Has never not once found my listener.
There is no sense to my life.' But then he heard me out.
I argued point by point. Seemed to win. Won.
He spoke to me once more when I was done:
'Even in argument, father, I have lost.'
He went and shot himself. Now tell me this one thing:
Should I have let him win then? Was I wrong?"

To answer for the land for love for song
Arguing life for life even at your life's cost.

THE SIX CANONS

after Binyon

Seize structure.
Correspond with the real.
Fuse spirit and matter.
Know your own secrets.
Announce your soul in discovery.
Go toward the essence, the impulse of creation,
    where power comes in music from the sex,
    where power comes in music from the spirit,
    where sex and spirit are one self
    passing among
    and acting on all things
    and their relationships,
    moving the constellations of all things.

FORERUNNERS

Forerunners of images.
In morning, on the river-mouth,
I came to my waking
seeing carried in air
seaward, a ship.
Standing on stillness
before the bowsprit
the man of spirit
—lookout aloft, steersman at wheel, silence on water—
and the young graceful man holding the lily iron.
I dream of all harpooning and the sea.

Out of Seville, after Holy Week I heard the
story of the black carriage and a lordly woman.
Her four daughters, their skirts of black foam,
lace seethed about them; drawn by four horses,
reined in, their black threads in the coachman's hands.
Far ahead on invisible wire
a circus horse making his shapes on the air.
Between us forever enlarges Spain and the war.

Far in New Jersey, among split-level houses,
behind the concrete filling-station I found
a yellow building and the flags of prayer.
Two Tibetans in their saffron bowed, priests
of their robes, their banners, their powers.
Little Tibetan children playing stickball
on the black road.
Day conscious and unconscious.
Words on the air.
Before the great
images arrive, riderless horses.
Words on an uproar silent hour.
In our own time.

ORGY

There were three of them that night.
They wanted it to happen in the first woman's room.
The man called her; the phone rang high.
Then she put fresh lipstick on.
Pretty soon he rang the bell.
She dreamed, she dreamed, she dreamed.
She scarcely looked him in the face
But gently took him to his place.
And after that the bell, the bell.
They looked each other in the eyes,
A hot July it was that night,
And he then slow took off his tie,
And she then slow took off her scarf,
The second one took off her scarf,
And he then slow his heavy shoe,
And she then slow took off her shoe,
The other one took off her shoe,
He then took off his other shoe,
The second one, her other shoe,
A hot July it was that night.
And he then slow took off his belt,
And she then slow took off her belt,
The second one took off her belt . . .

THE OVERTHROW OF ONE O'CLOCK
AT NIGHT

is my concern.   That's this moment,
when I lean on my elbows out the windowsill
and feel the city among its time-zones, among its seas,
among its late night news, the pouring in
of everything meeting, wars, dreams, winter night.
Light in snowdrifts causing the young girls
lying awake to fall in love tonight
alone in bed; or the little children
half world over tonight rained on by fire—that's us—
calling on somebody—that's us—to come
and help them.
                        Now I see at the boundary of darkness
extreme of moonlight.
                              Alone.   All my hopes
scattered in people quarter world away
half world away, out of all hearing.
                                        Tell myself:
Trust in experience.   And in the rhythms.
The deep rhythms of your experience.

AMONG ROSES

Lying here among grass, am I dead am I sleeping
amazed among silences   you touch me never
Here deep under, the small white moon
cries like a dime and do I hear?

The sun gone copper or I dissolve
no touch no touch   a tactless land
denies my death my fallen hand
silence runs down the riverbeds

One tall wind walks over my skin
                                    breeze, memory
bears to my body (as the world fades)
                                    going in

very late in the world's night to see roses opening
Remember, love, lying among roses.
Did we not lie among roses?

WHAT I SEE

Lie there, in sweat and dream, I do, and "there"
Is here, my bed, on which I dream
You, lying there, on yours, locked, pouring love,
While I tormented here see in my reins
You, perfectly at climax. And the lion strikes.
I want you with whatever obsessions come—
I wanted your obsession to be mine
But if it is that unknown half-suggested strange
Other figure locked in your climax, then
I here, I want you and the other, want your obsession, want
Whatever is locked into you now while I sweat and dream.

BELIEVING IN THOSE
INEXORABLE LAWS

Believing in those inexorable laws
After long rebellion and long discipline
I am cut down to the moment in all my flaws
Creeping to the feet of my master the sun
On the sea-beach, tides beaten by the moon woman,
And will not think of you, but lie at my full length
Among the great breakers. I find the clear outwater
Shine crash speaking of truth behind the law.

The many-following waves turn into you.
I see in vision that northern bay : pines, villages,
And the flat water suddenly rears up
The high wave races against all edicts, taller,
Finally powerful. Water becomes your mouth,
And all laws all polarities your truth.

SONG : LOVE IN WHOSE RICH HONOR

Love
in whose rich honor
I stand looking from my window
over the starved trees of a dry September
Love
deep and so far forbidden
is bringing me
a gift
to claw at my skin
to break open my eyes
the gift longed for so long
The power
to write
out of the desperate ecstasy at last
death and madness

NIOBE NOW

Niobe
    wild
        with unbelief
                as all
                    her ending
                        turns to stone
Not gentle
    weeping
        and souvenirs
            but hammering
                honking
                  agonies
Forty-nine tragic years
        are done
            and the twentieth century
                not begun:
All tears,
    all tears,
        all tears.

Water
        from her rock
                is sprung
                        and in this water
                                lives a seed
That must endure
                and grow
                        and shine
                                beasts, gardens
                                        at last rivers
A man
        to be born
                to start again
                        to tear
                                a woman
                                        from his side
And wake
        to start
                the world again.

SONG : THE STAR IN THE NETS
OF HEAVEN

The star in the nets of heaven blazed past your breastbone,
Willing to shine among the nets of your growth,
The nets of your love,
The bonds of your dreams.

AIR

Flowers of air
with lilac defining air;
buildings of air
with walls defining air;
this May, people of air
advance along the street;
framed in their bodies, air,
their eyes speaking to me,

air in their mouths made
into live meanings.

GIFT

the child, the poems, the child, the poems, the journeys
      back and forth across our long country
          of opposites,
and through myself, through you, away from you, toward
      you, the dreams of madness and of an
          impossible complete time—
gift be forgiven.

CRIES FROM CHIAPAS

Hunger
      of mountains
             spoke
                  from a tiger's throat.
Tiger-tooth peaks.
          The moon.
              A thousand mists
turning.
      Desires of mountains
             like the desires of women,
moon-drawn,
        distant,
          clear black among
             confusions of silver.
Women of Chiapas!
        Dream-borne
           voices of women.
Splinters of mountains,
        broken obsidian,
           silver.
White tigers
      haunting
        your forehead here
          sloped in shadow—

black hungers of women,

confusion

turning like tigers

And your voice—

I am

almost asleep

almost awake

in your arms.

THE WAR COMES INTO MY ROOM

Knowing again

that nothing

has been spoken

not now

not this night time

the broken singing

as we move

or of

the endless war

our lives

that above all

there is not said

nothing

of this moment

in the poems

our love

in all the songs

now I will

live out

this moment

saying

it

in my breath

to you

across the air

DELTA POEMS

Among leaf-green
this morning, they
walk near water-blue,
near water-green
of the river-mouths
this boy   this girl
they die with their heads near each other,
their young mouths

        ❧

A sharp glint out among the sea
These are lives coming out of their craft
Men who resemble. . . .
Sound is bursting the sun
Two dead bodies against the leaves
A young man and a girl
Their heads close together
No weapons, only grasses and waves
Lives, grasses

        ❧

Something is flying through the high air over the river-mouth country,
Something higher than the look can go,
Higher than herons fly,
Higher than planes is it?
It is nothing now
But now it is sound beyond bigness
Turns into the hugeness : death. A leaf shakes on the sky.

        ❧

Of the children in flames, of the grown man
his face burned to the bones, of the full woman
her body stopped from the nipples down, nursing
the live strong baby at her breast
I do not speak.

I am a woman
in a New York room
late in the twentieth century.

I am crying. I will write no more.—
Young man and girl walking along the sea,
among the leaves.

⁙

Fresh hot day among the river-mouths,
yellow-green leaves   green rivers running to sea.
A young man and a girl
go walking in the delta country
The war has lasted their entire lifetime.
They look at each other with their mouths.
They look at each other with their whole bodies.
A glint as of bright fire, metal over the sea-waters.

⁙

A girl has died upon green leaves,
a young man has died against the sky.
A girl is walking printed against green leaves,
A young man walks printed upon the sky.

⁙

I remember you. We walked near the harbor.
You a young man believing in the future of summer,
in yellow, in green, in touch, in entering,
in the night-sky, in the gifts of this effort.
He believes in January,
he believes in the pulses beating along his body,
he believes in her young year.

I walk near the rivers.

⁙

They are walking again at the edge of waters.
They are killed again near the lives, near the waves.
They are walking, their heads are close together,
their mouths are close as they die.
A girl and a young man walk near the water.

SPIRALS AND FUGUES

Spirals and fugues, the power most like music
Turneth all worlds to meaning

And meaning to matter, all continually,
And sweeps in the sacred motion,
Spirals and fugues its lifetime,
To move my life to yours,
   and all women and men and the children in their light,
The little stone in the middle of the road, its veins and
   patience,
Moving the constellations of all things.

ANEMONE

My eyes are closing, my eyes are opening.
You are looking into me with your waking look.

My mouth is closing, my mouth is opening.
You are waiting with your red promises.

My sex is closing, my sex is opening.
You are singing and offering : the way in.

My life is closing, my life is opening.
You are here.

FIGHTING FOR ROSES

After the last freeze, in easy air,
Once the danger is past, we cut them back severely;
Pruning the weakest hardest, pruning for size
Of flower, we deprived will not deprive the sturdy.
The new shoots are preserved, the future bush
Cut down to a couple of young dormant buds.

But the early sun of April does not burn our lives :
Light straight and fiery brings back the enemies.
Claw, jaw, and crawler, all those that devour.
We work with smoke against the robber blights,
With copper against rust; the season fights itself
In deep strong rich loam under swarm attacks.

Head hidden from the wind, the power of form
Rises among these brightnesses, thorned and blowing.
Where they glow on the earth, water-drops tremble on them.
Soon we must cut them back, against damage of storms.
But those days gave us flower budded on flower,
A moment of light achieved, deep in the air of roses.

FOR MY SON

You come from poets, kings, bankrupts, preachers,
        attempted bankrupts, builders of cities, salesmen,
the great rabbis, the kings of Ireland, failed drygoods
        storekeepers, beautiful women of the songs,
great horsemen, tyrannical fathers at the shore of ocean,
        the western mothers looking west beyond from their
            windows,
the families escaping over the sea hurriedly and by night—
the roundtowers of the Celtic violet sunset,
the diseased, the radiant, fliers, men thrown out of town,
        the man bribed by his cousins to stay out of town,
            teachers, the cantor on Friday evening, the lurid
                newspapers,
strong women gracefully holding relationship, the Jewish girl
        going to parochial school, the boys racing their iceboats
            on the Lakes,
the woman still before the diamond in the velvet window,
        saying "Wonder of nature."
Like all men,
you come from singers, the ghettoes, the famines, wars and
        refusal of wars, men who built villages
that grew to our solar cities, students, revolutionists, the
        pouring of buildings, the market newspapers,
a poor tailor in a darkening room,
a wilderness man, the hero of mines, the astronomer, a
        white-faced woman hour on hour teaching piano and
            her crippled wrist,
like all men,
you have not seen your father's face
but he is known to you forever in song, the coast of the skies,

in dream, wherever you find man playing his
      part as father, father among our light, among our
        darkness,
and in your self made whole, whole with yourself and
      whole with others,
the stars your ancestors.

POEM

I lived in the first century of world wars.
Most mornings I would be more or less insane,
The newspapers would arrive with their careless stories,
The news would pour out of various devices
Interrupted by attempts to sell products to the unseen.
I would call my friends on other devices;
They would be more or less mad for similar reasons.
Slowly I would get to pen and paper,
Make my poems for others unseen and unborn.
In the day I would be reminded of those men and women
Brave, setting up signals across vast distances,
Considering a nameless way of living, of almost unimagined values.
As the lights darkened, as the lights of night brightened,
We would try to imagine them, try to find each other.
To construct peace, to make love, to reconcile
Waking with sleeping, ourselves with each other,
Ourselves with ourselves. We would try by any means
To reach the limits of ourselves, to reach beyond ourselves,
To let go the means, to wake.

I lived in the first century of these wars.

THE POWER OF SUICIDE

The potflower on the windowsill says to me
In words that are green-edged red leaves :
Flower   flower   flower   flower
Today for the sake of all the dead   Burst into flower.

1963

THE SEEMING

for Helen Lynd

Between the illuminations of great mornings
there comes the dailiness of doing and being
and the hand as it makes as it brightens   burnishes
the surfaces   seemings   mirrors of the world

We do not know the springs of these colored and loving
acts   or what triggers birth   what sleep is
but name them as we name bird-wakened morning
having our verbs of the world
to which all action seems
to resolve, being

to go, to grow, to flow, to shine, to sound, to glow,
to give and to take, to bind and to separate,
to injure   and to defend

we do not even   not even know why we wake

but some of us showing the others
a kind of welcoming
bringing a form to morning
as a woman who recognizes
may offer us the moment and the names
turning all shame into a declaration
immediately to be followed by
an act of truth
until all seemings are
                                        illumination
we see in a man a theme
a dream taking over
or in this woman going today who has shown us
fear, and form, and storm turned into light
the dailiness of our being and doing
morning and every time the way to naming
and we see more now coming into being

see in her goings as in her arrivings
the opening of a door

SONG FROM *PUCK FAIR*

Torrent that rushes down
Knocknadober,
Make the channel deeper
Where I ferry home.

Winds go west over
Left-handed Reaper
Mountain that gathered me
Out of my old shame—

Your white beard streaming,
Puck of summertime,
At last gave me
My woman's name.

NOT YET

A time of destruction. Of the most rigid powers in ascendance.
Secret plots against them, open work against them in round buildings.
All fail. Any work for fluency, for freedom, fails.
Battles. The wiping out of cities full of people.
Long tracts of devastation.

In one city : a scene of refugees, each allowed to take
a suitcase of bedding, blankets, no more. An old man, a professor.
He has hidden a few books and two small statues in a blanket
and packed his case. He comes in his turn to the examining desk.
He struggles about the lie he needs to tell. He lies, he declares nothing.
Even after the lie, the suitcase is thrown over the cliff
where all the statues lie broken, the books, pictures, the records.

Long landscapes of devastation. Color modulated between
sparse rigid monuments. Long orange landscapes
shifting to yellow-orange to show a generation.
Long passage of time to yellow. Only these elite,
their army tread on yellow terrain. Their schools. Their children.

A tradition of rigor, hatred and doom is now
—generations after—the only sole tradition.
I am looking at the times and time as at a dream.
As at the recurrent dream of a locked room.
I think of the solution of the sealed room mystery
of the chicken and the egg, in which the chicken
feeds on his cell, grows strong on the sealed room
and finally
                    in strength
                                        eating his prison
pierces the shell.
                            How can this room change state?
I see its sky, its children. I cannot imagine.

I look at the young faces of the children
in this tradition, far down the colors of the years.
They are still repeating their shut slogans
with "war" substituted for freedom. But their faces glow.
The children are marvelous, singing among the wars.
They have needed the meanings, and their faces show
this : the solution.
                            The words have taken on
all their forbidden meanings. The words mean their opposites.
They must, they are needed.

Children's faces, lit, unlit,
the face of a child.

LANDSCAPE WITH WAVE
APPROACHING

1

All of the people of the play were there,
swam in the mile-long wave, among cliff-flowers
were pierced, hung and remembered a sunlit year.

2

By day white moths, the nightlong meteors
flying like snow among the flowery trees—
hissing like prophecy above those seas.

3

The city of the past. The past as a city
and all the people in it, your childhood faces,
their dances, their words developing, their hands.

4

The fertile season ending in a glitter;
blight of the forest, orange, burning the trees away,
the checkered light. Full length on naked sand.

5

All of the people of the play were there,
smiling, telling their truths, coming to crisis.
This water, this water, this water. These rocks, this piercing sea.

6

Flower of time, and a plague of white trilling in sunlight,
the season advancing on the people of the play,
the scars on the mountains and the body of fire.

Carmel, California

SEGRE SONG

Your song where you lie long dead on the shore of a Spanish river—
your song moves under the earth and through time, through air—
your song I sing to the sun as we move
and to the cities
sing to the mimosa
sing to the moon over my face

BUNK JOHNSON BLOWING

in memory of Leadbelly
and his house on 59th Street

They found him in the fields and called him back to music.
Can't, he said, my teeth are gone.   They bought him teeth.

Bunk Johnson's trumpet on a California
early May evening, calling me to

breath of . . .
up those stairs . . .
calling me to
look into
the face of that
trumpet
experience
and past it
his eyes

Jim and Rita beside me. We drank it. Jim had just come back
from Sacramento the houses made of piano boxes the bar without
a sign and the Mexicans drinking we drank the trumpet music
and drank that black park moonlit beneath the willow trees,

Bunk Johnson blowing all night out of that full moon.
Two-towered church. Rita listening to it, all night
music! said, I'm supposed to, despise them.
Tears streaming down her face. Said, don't tell my ancestors.

We three slid down that San Francisco hill.

CANNIBAL BRATUSCHA

Have you heard about Mr. Bratuscha?
He led an orderly life
With a splendid twelve-year-old daughter,
A young and passionate wife—
    Bratuscha, the one they call Cannibal.

Spring evening on Wednesday,
The sky is years ago;
The girl has been missing since Monday,
Why don't the birches blow?
    And where's their daughter?

Nine miles to the next village
Deep in the forested past—
Wheatland, marshland, daisies
And a gold slender ghost.
    It's very difficult to keep them safe.

She hasn't been seen and it's Thursday.
Down by the river, raped?
Under the birches, murdered?
Don't let the fiend escape,
　First, we'll track him down and catch him.

The river glittering in sunlight,
The woods almost black—and she
Was always a darling, the blonde young daughter,
Gone gone vanished away.
　They say Bratuscha is ready to talk.

O God he has told the whole story;
Everything; he has said
That he killed his golden daughter
He ate her, he said it!
　Eaten by the cannibal, Cannibal Bratuscha.

Down at the church her mother
In the confession booth—
She has supported his story,
She has told the priest the truth;
　Horror, and now the villagers gather.

They are ready to lynch Bratuscha,
Pounding at his door—
Over the outcries of the good people
Hear the cannibal roar—
　He will hold out, bar the doorway, fight to the death.

But who is this coming, whose shadow
Runs down the river road?
She is coming, she is running, she is
Alive and abroad—
　She is here, she is well, she was in the next village.

The roaring dreams of her father :
He believed all he confessed—
And the mother was threatened with hellfire
By the village priest
　If she didn't tell everything, back up what Bratuscha said.

This all took place some time ago
Before all villages joined—
When there were separate, uncivilized people,
Only the birds, only the river, only dreams and the wind.
　　She had just gone off for a few days, with a friend.

But O God the little Bratuscha girl
What will become of her?
Her mother is guilt suggestion panic
Her father of dreams, a murderer
　　And in waking and in fantasy and now and forever.

Who will help her and you and me and all those
Children of the assumption of guilt
And the roaring fantasy of nightmare
The bomb the loathing all dreams spilt
　　Upon this moment and the future and all unborn children.

We must go deep go deep in our lives and our dreams—
Remember Cannibal Bratuscha his wife and his young child
And preserve our own ideas of guilt
Of innocence and of the blessed wild
　　To live out our own lives to make our own freedom to make
　　　　the world.

WHAT HAVE YOU BROUGHT HOME FROM THE WARS?

What have you brought
home from the wars, father?
Scars.
We fought far overseas; we knew
the victory must
be at home.
But here I see
only a trial by time
of those
who know.
The public men all shout : Come bomb,

come burn
our hate.
I do not
want it shot;
I want it solved.
This is the word
the dead men said.
They said peace.
I saw in the hot light
of our century
each face killed.

ONE MONTH

for Dorothy Lear

All this time
you were dead and I did not know
I was learning to speak
and speaking to you
and you were not there
I was seeing you
tall, walking the corridor
of that tall shining building
I was learning to walk
and walking to you
and it was not true
you were still living still lying still
it was not true
that you were giving me a rose
telling me stories
pouring a wine-story, there were bubbles in it
all this time
I was remembering untrue
speaking untrue, seeing a lie.

It is true.

SILENCE OF VOLCANOES

1

The mountains and the shadows move away
Under their snows to show an immense scene:
A field of cathedrals. Green domes eye-green,
Domes the color of trumpets. Obliterated rose
And impure copper. Vaults are pale shoulders.
Grass-haired and deformed,
The dome-capped pyramid to the god of the air.
A white dome under these volcanoes.
This is the field that glittered in massacre,
Time is boiling with domes.

2

A woman has been begging for ninety-seven years.
The singing of her words against shadows of gold.
I see her lean her face against this scene.
The domes dissolve. All her unfallen tears.
I remember a room for sale in a picture
Torn as this landscape
Obsessed by a single thing.

3

A hall at the National Pawnshop crowded with unsold bureaus.
In sharp paint at the end of a blind aisle
Red-robed and listening, the saint looks at the Sign.
Books fold him in, strict black-and-white tile
Lead to a sleeping garden where his lion,
The guardian, lies in a silence of volcanoes.
Hung in that air, there pierces his leaning soul
The cheap tin trumpet that is the voice of God.

Mexico

WHAT THEY SAID

:   After I am dead, darling,
          my seventeen senses gone,

I shall love you as you wish,
      no sex, no mouth, but bone—
      in the way you long for now,
with my soul alone.

:   When we are neither woman nor man
         but bleached to skeleton—
when you have changed, my darling,
         and all your senses gone,
         it is not me that you will love:
you will love everyone.

A LITTLE STONE IN THE MIDDLE OF
THE ROAD, IN FLORIDA

My son as child saying
God
is anything, even a little stone in the middle of the road,
      in Florida.
Yesterday
Nancy, my friend, after long illness:
You know what can lift me up, take me right out of despair?
No, what?
Anything.

THE BLUE FLOWER

for Frances G. Wickes on her ninetieth birthday, August 28, 1965

Stroke by stroke, in the country of the fragile
stroke by stroke, each act a season
speaking the years of making
this flower
shining over the fears
over the cities
and the camps of death.
Shines from a field
of eighty-seven years,
the young child and the dream.

In my city of stone,
water and light
I saw the blue flower
held still, and flying—
never seen by me
but in your words given;
fragile, mortal
that endures.

By turns flying and still.
"AngkorVat, a gray stone city
but the flight of kingfishers
all day enlivened it"—
a blue flash given to us, past stone and time.

Blaze of mortality
piercing, tense
the structure of a dream
speaking and fragile,
momentary,
for now
and ever and all
your blue flower.

WOMAN AS MARKET

FORGETTING AND REMEMBERING

What was it? What was it?
Flashing beside me, lightning in daylight at the orange stand?
Along the ranks of eggs, beside the loaves of dark and light?
In a moment of morning, providing:
the moment of the eggplant?
                    the lemons? the fresh eggs?
with their bright curves and curves of shadow?
the reds, the yellows, all the calling boxes.
What did those forms say? What words have I forgotten?
what spoke to me from the day?
God in the cloud? my life in my forgetting?
I have forgotten what it was
that I have been trying to remember

WORD OF MOUTH

1 THE RETURN

Westward from Sète
      as I went long before
along my life
   as I went
       wave by wave—
the long words of the sea
        the orange rooftop tiles
back to the boundary
     where I had been before.

Spain.
    Sex of cactus and of cypresses,
Tile-orange, green; olive; black. The sea.
One man. Beethoven radio. War.
Threat of all life. Within my belief's body.
Within my morning, music. High colored mountain
along the seacoast
     where the swallows fly.

Prolonged
beyond your cries and your cities.

Along my life and death backward toward that morning
when all things fell open and I went into Spain.

One man. Sardana music. This frontier.
Where I now come again.
     I stop.
       I do not pass.

Wave under wave
     like the divisive South
afire in the country of my birth.

A moment of glass. All down the coast I face
as far as vision, blue, memory of blue.

Seen now. Why do I not go in? I stand.

I cannot pass.   History, destroyed music.

I need to go into.
                    In a dream I have seen
Spain, *sleeping children:*
                              before me:
                                              as I drive

as I go
            (I need to go into
                              this country
of love and)
                wave after wave
                                    they lie

in a deep forest.
                    As the driving light
touches them
                (I need this country
                                      of love and death)
they begin to rouse.
                    They wake.

2 WORD OF MOUTH

Speeding back from the border.
                                    A rock came spinning up
cast from the wheels of a car.
                                    Crackled the windshield glass.
Glitter before my eyes like a man made of snow
lying over the hood, blind white except for glints
an inch of sight where Languedoc shines through.

You on my one side, you on the other!
What I have is dazzle.   My son; my friend;
tell me this side and tell me that side,
news of the road near Agde.

Word from this side, word from the tree-side—
Spain at our back : agony : before me, glitter,
                                              today
blinding my eyes, blind diamonds, one clear wound.

Something is flying out of the sky behind me.

Turning, stirring of dream, something is speeding,
something is overtaking.

Stirrings in prisons, on beds, the mouths of the young,
resist, dance, love.   It drives through the back of my head,
through my eyes and breasts and mouth.
I know a harvest : mass in the wine country.
A lifetime after, and still alive.

Something out of Spain, into the general light!
I drive blind white, trusting news of this side,
news of that side, all the time the line of the poem:
Amor, pena, desig, somni, dolor.
The grapes have become wine by the hand of man.
Sea risen from the sea, a bearded king.

The seaward cemetery risen from the sea
like a woman rising.

                    Amor.

                              Phases of sun.
The wine declared god by the hand of man.
Pena.
               A rumor given me by this side and that side.
We drive in brilliant glitter, in jungle night, in distant war,
in all our cities, in a word, overtaking.

                              Desig.

A cry received, gone past me into all men,
speaking, into all women.
                         A man goes into the sea,
bearded fire and all things rise from this blaze of eyes,
living, it speaks, driving forth from Spain,

                                   somni, dolor,

These cliffs, these years.   Do we drive into light?
Driven, live, overtaken?

                         Amor, pena, desig.

ENDLESS

Under the tall black sky you look out of your body
lit by a white flare of the time between us
your body with its touch its weight   smelling of new wood
as on the day the news of battle reached us
falls beside the endless river
flowing to the endless sea
whose waves come to this shore a world away.

Your body of new wood your eyes alive barkbrown of treetrunks
the leaves and flowers of trees   stars all caught in crowns of trees
your life gone down, broken into endless earth
no longer a world away but under my feet and everywhere
I look down at the one earth under me,
through to you and all the fallen
the broken and their children born and unborn
of the endless war.

～ 2 Games

THE BACKSIDE OF THE ACADEMY

Five brick panels, three small windows, six lions' heads
        with rings in their mouths, five pairs of closed bronze doors—
the shut wall with the words carved across its head
ART REMAINS THE ONE WAY POSSIBLE OF
        SPEAKING TRUTH.—
On this May morning, light swimming in this street,
        the children running,
on the church beside the Academy the lines are flying
of little yellow-and-white plastic flags flapping in the light;
and on the great shut wall, the words are carved across:
WE ARE YOUNG AND WE ARE FRIENDS OF TIME.—
Below that, a light blue asterisk in chalk
and in white chalk, Hector, Joey, Lynn, Rudolfo.
A little up the street, a woman shakes a small dark boy,

she shouts What's wrong with you, ringing that bell!
In the street of rape and singing, poems, small robberies,
carved in an oblong panel of the stone:
CONSCIOUS UTTERANCE OF THOUGHT BY
    SPEECH OR ACTION
TO ANY END IS ART.—
On the lowest reach of the walls are chalked the words:
    Jack is a object,
Walter and Trina, Goo Goo, I love Trina,
and further along Viva Fidel now altered to Muera Fidel.
A deep blue marble is lodged against the curb.
A phone booth on one corner; on the other, the big mesh
    basket for trash.
Beyond them, the little park is always locked. For the two
    soldier brothers.
And past that goes on an eternal football game
which sometimes, as on this day in May, transforms to stickball
as, for one day in May,
five pairs of closed bronze doors will open
and the Academy of writers, sculptors, painters, composers,
    their guests and publishers will all roll in and
the wave of organ music come rolling out into
the street where light now blows and papers and little
        children and words, some breezes of Spanish blow
            and many colors of people.

A watch cap lies fallen against a cellophane which used
        to hold pistachio nuts
and here before me, on my street,
five brick panels, three small windows, six lions' heads with
        rings in their mouths, five pairs of closed bronze doors,
light flooding the street I live and write in; and across the
        river the one word FREE against the ferris wheel and
            the roller coaster,
and here, painted upon the stones, Chino, Bobby, Joey,
        Fatmoma, Willy, Holy of God
and also Margaret is a shit and also fuck and shit;
far up, invisible at the side of the building:
WITHOUT VISION THE PEO
and on the other side, the church side,
where shadows of trees and branches, this day in May, are
        printed balanced on the church wall,

in-focus trunks and softened-focus branches
below the roof where the two structures stand,
bell and cross, antenna and weathervane,
I can see past the church the words of an ending line:
IVE BY BREAD ALONE.

MOUNTAIN : ONE FROM BRYANT

Wildflowers withering with the same death.
Grave a slope, threw she long shadows,
Mountains o'erlooking earth, affect and places
High.   On God that time, the elder worshipper,
Deemed spirit, made here a tribe of offering,
Bear and wolf of skins shaggy, maze of ears
And garlands lay.   Mother, my dreams, night and
Mockings like friends, pastimes hate I
And business accursed upon me glares;
The life of the sick is sorrow, guilt, and love.
Eye her then, vain in might, simple as heart.
Heaven props earth with columns; mountains raise
Distances, blue in hills, upward swell fields.
Man has ages for soil, mining himself
To paradise.   The scene murmurs.   Struggle with winds,
Hear depth dizzy the ear, a thunderbolt of whiteness.
Centuries of growth, darkness of capitals,
Pinnacles and trees shaggy and wild.
North to the drowned!   and nations separate the world.
Shriek eagle in your torrent solitude.
Glens of secret, down into forest-tops,
Beneath a wide-spread earth; majesty and beauty
Fail.   Foot mountains.   Though rocky our ascent,
Face nature in harmony, lovely, and face it!   wild.

THE FLYING RED HORSE

On all the streetcorners the children are standing,
They ask What can it mean?
The grownups answer   A flying red horse
Signifies gasoline.

The man at the Planetarium,
Pointing beyond the sky,
Is not going to say that Pegasus
Means poetry.

Some of our people feel like death,
And some feel rather worse.
His energy, in this night of lies,
Flies right against the curse.

What's *red?*   What is the *flying horse?*
They swear they do not know,
But just the same, and every night,
All the streetcorners glow.

Even the Pentagon, even the senators,
Even the President sitting on his arse—
Never mind—over all cities
The flying red horse.

❦ 3

THE OUTER BANKS

1

Horizon of islands shifting
Sea-light flame on my voice
                              burn in me
                                        Light
flows from the water from sands   islands of this horizon
The sea comes toward me across the sea.   The sand
moves over the sand in waves
between the guardians of this landscape
the great commemorative statue on one hand
        —the first flight of man, outside of dream,
              seen as stone wing and stainless steel—
and at the other hand

        banded black-and-white, climbing
the spiral lighthouse.

        2

Flood over ocean,
avalanche on the flat beach. Pouring.
Indians holding branches up, to
placate the tempest,
the one-legged twisting god that is
a standing wind.
Rays are branching from all things:
great serpent, great plume, constellation:
sands from which colors and light pass,
the lives of plants.   Animals.   Men.
A man and a woman reach for each other.

        3

Wave of the sea.

        4

Sands have washed, sea has flown over us.
Between the two guardians, spiral, truncated wing,
history and these wild birds
Bird-voiced discoverers : Hariot,   Hart Crane,
the brothers who watched gulls.
"No bird soars in a calm,"   said Wilbur Wright.
Dragon of the winds forms over me.
Your dance, goddesses in your circle
sea-wreath, whirling of the event
behind me on land as deep in our own lives
we begin to know the movement to come.
Sunken, drowned spirals,
hurricane-dance.

        5

Shifting of islands on this horizon.
The cycle of changes in the Book of Changes.
Two islands making an open female line
That powerful long straight bar a male island.
The building of the surf
constructing immensities
between the pale flat Sound

and ocean ever
birds as before earthquake
winds fly from all origins
the length of this wave goes from the great wing
down coast, the barrier beach in all its miles
road of the sun and the moon to
a spiral lighthouse
to the depth turbulence
lifts up its wave like cities
the ocean in the air
spills down the world.

6

A man is walking toward me across the water.
From far out, the flat waters of the Sound,
he walks pulling his small boat

In the shoal water.

A man who is white and has been fishing.
Walks steadily upon the light of day
Coming closer to me where I stand
looking into the sun and the blaze inner water.
Clear factual surface over which he pulls
a boat over a closing quarter-mile.

7

Speak to it, says the light.
Speak to it music,
voices of the sea and human throats.
Origins of spirals,
the ballad and original sweet grape
dark on the vines near Hatteras,
tendrils of those vines, whose spiral tower
now rears its light, accompanying
all my voices.

8

He walks toward me.   A black man in the sun.
He now is a black man speaking to my heart
crisis of darkness in this century
of moments of this speech.

The boat is slowly nearer drawn, this man.

The zigzag power coming straight, in stones,
        in arcs, metal, crystal, the spiral
in sacred wet
                        schematic elements of
cities, music, arrangement
spin these stones of home
                                under the sea
return to the stations of the stars
and the sea, speaking across its lives.

        9

A man who is bones is close to me
drawing a boat of bones
the sun behind him
is another color of fire,
the sea behind me
rears its flame.

A man whose body flames and tapers in flame
twisted tines of remembrance that dissolve
a pitchfork of the land worn thin
flame up and dissolve again
                        draw   small   boat

Nets of the stars at sunset over us.
This draws me home to the home of the wild birds
long-throated birds of this passage.
This is the edge of experience, *grenzen der seele*
where those on the verge of human understanding
the borderline people stand on the shifting islands
among the drowned stars and the tempest.
"Everyman's mind, like the dumbest,
claws at his own furthest limits of knowing the world,"
a man in a locked room said.

Open to the sky
I stand before this boat that looks at me.
The man's flames are arms and legs.
Body, eyes, head, stars, sands look at me.

I walk out into the shoal water
and throw my leg over the wall of the boat.

10

At one shock, speechlessness.
I am in the bow, on the short thwart.
He is standing before me amidships, rowing forward
like my old northern sea–captain in his dory.
All things have spun.
The words gone,
I facing sternwards, looking at the gate
between the barrier islands.   As he rows.
Sand islands shifting and the last of land
a pale and open line   horizon
sea.

With whose face did he look at me?
What did I say?   or did I say?
in speechlessness
move to the change.
These strokes provide the music,
and the accused boy on land today saying
What did I say?   or did I say?
The dream on land last night built this the boat of death
but in the suffering of the light
moving across the sea
do we in our moving
move toward life or death

11

Hurricane, skullface, the sky's size
winds streaming through his teeth
doing the madman's twist

and not a beach not flooded

nevertheless, here
stability of light
my other silence
and at my left hand and at my right hand
no longer wing and lighthouse

no longer the guardians.
They are in me, in my speechless
life of barrier beach.
As it lies open
to the night, out there.

Now seeing my death before me
starting again, among the drowned men,
desperate men, unprotected discoverers,
and the man before me
here.
Stroke by stroke drawing us.
Out there? Father of rhythms,
deep wave, mother.
There is no *out there.*
All is open.
Open water. Open I.

    12

The wreck of the *Tiger,* the early pirate, the blood-clam's
        ark, the tern's acute eye, all buried mathematical
                instruments, castaways, pelicans, drowned five-
                        strand pearl necklaces, hopes of livelihood,
                                hopes of grace,
walls of houses, sepia sea-fences, the writhen octopus and
        those tall masts and sails,
marked hulls of ships and last month's plane, dipping his salute
        to the stone wing of dream,
turbulence, Diamond Shoals, the dark young living people:
"Sing one more song and you are under arrest."
"Sing another song."
Women, ships, lost voices.
Whatever has dissolved into our waves.
I a lost voice
moving, calling you
on the edge of the moment that is now the center.
From the open sea.

❧4 Lives

AKIBA

THE WAY OUT

The night is covered with signs. The body and face of man,
with signs, and his journeys.   Where the rock is split
and speaks to the water;   the flame speaks to the cloud;
the red splatter, abstraction, on the door
speaks to the angel and the constellations.
The grains of sand on the sea-floor speak at last to the noon.
And the loud hammering of the land behind
speaks ringing up the bones of our thighs, the hoofs,
we hear the hoofs over the seethe of the sea.

All night down the centuries, have heard, music of passage.

Music of one child carried into the desert;
firstborn forbidden by law of the pyramid.
Drawn through the water with the water-drawn people
led by the water-drawn man to the smoke mountain.
The voice of the world speaking, the world covered by signs,
the burning, the loving, the speaking, the opening.
Strong throat of sound from the smoking mountain.
Still flame, the spoken singing of a young child.
The meaning beginning to move, which is the song.

Music of those who have walked out of slavery.

Into that journey where all things speak to all things
refusing to accept the curse, and taking
for signs the signs of all things, the world, the body
which is part of the soul, and speaks to the world,
all creation being created in one image, creation.
This is not the past walking into the future,
the walk is painful, into the present, the dance
not visible as dance until much later.
These dancers are discoverers of God.

We knew we had all crossed over when we heard the song.

Out of a life of building lack on lack:
the slaves refusing slavery, escaping into faith:
an army who came to the ocean: the walkers
who walked through the opposites, from I to opened Thou,
city and cleave of the sea. Those at flaming Nauvoo,
the ice on the great river: the escaping Negroes,
swamp and wild city: the shivering children of Paris
and the glass black hearses; those on the Long March:
all those who together are the frontier, forehead of man.

Where the wilderness enters, the world, the song of the world.

Akiba rescued, secretly, in the clothes of death
by his disciples carried from Jerusalem
in blackness journeying to find his journey
to whatever he was loving with his life.
The wilderness journey through which we move
under the whirlwind truth into the new,
the only accurate. A cluster of lights at night:
faces before the pillar of fire. A child watching
while the sea breaks open. This night. The way in.

Barbarian music, a new song.

Acknowledging opened water, possibility:
open like a woman to this meaning.
In a time of building statues of the stars,
valuing certain partial ferocious skills
while past us the chill and immense wilderness
spreads its one-color wings until we know
rock, water, flame, cloud, or the floor of the sea,
the world is a sign, a way of speaking. To find.
What shall we find? Energies, rhythms, journey.

Ways to discover. The song of the way in.

FOR THE SONG OF SONGS

However the voices rise
They are the shepherd, the king,

The woman; dreams,
Holy desire.

Whether the voices
Be many the dance around
Or body led by one body
Whose bed is green,

I defend the desire
Lightning and poetry
Alone in the dark city
Or breast to breast.

Champion of light I am
The wounded holy light,
The woman in her dreams
And the man answering.

You who answer their dreams
Are the ruler of wine
Emperor of clouds
And the riches of men.

This song
Is the creation
The day of this song
The day of the birth of the world.

Whether a thousand years
Forget this woman, this king,
Whether two thousand years
Forget the shepherd of dreams.

If none remember
Who is lover, who the beloved,
Whether the poet be
Woman or man,

The desire will make
A way through the wilderness
The leopard mountains
And the lips of the sleepers.

Holy way of desire,
King, lion, the mouth of the poet,
The woman who dreams
And the answerer of dreams.

In these delights
Is eternity of seed,
The verge of life,
Body of dreaming.

THE BONDS

In the wine country, poverty, they drink no wine—
In the endless night of love he lies, apart from love—
In the landscape of the Word he stares, he has no word.

He hates and hungers for his immense need.

He is young. This is a shepherd who rages at learning,
Having no words. Looks past green grass and sees a woman.
She, Rachel, who is come to recognize.
In the huge wordless shepherd she finds Akiba.

To find the burning Word. To learn to speak.

The body of Rachel says, the marriage says,
The eyes of Rachel say, and water upon rock
Cutting its groove all year says All things learn.
He learns with his new son whose eyes are wine.

To sing continually, to find the word.

He comes to teaching, greater than the deed
Because it begets the deed, he comes to the stone
Of long ordeal, and suddenly knows the brook
Offering water, the citron fragrance, the light of candles.

All given, and always the giver loses nothing.

In giving, praising, we move beneath clouds of honor,
In giving, in praise, we take gifts that are given,
The spark from one to the other leaping, a bond
Of light, and we come to recognize the rock;

457 ❧

We are the rock acknowledging water, and water
Fire, and woman man, all brought through wilderness;
And Rachel finding in the wordless shepherd
Akiba who can now come to his power and speak:
The need to give having found the need to become:

More than the calf wants to suck, the cow wants to give such.

AKIBA MARTYR

When his death confronted him, it had the face of his friend
Rufus the Roman general with his claws of pain,
His executioner. This was an old man under iron rakes
Tearing through to the bone. He made no cry.

After the failure of all missions. At ninety, going
To Hadrian in Egypt, the silver-helmed,
Named for a sea. To intercede. Do not build in the rebuilt Temple.
Your statue, do not make it a shrine to you.
Antinous smiling. Interpreters. This is an old man, pleading.
Incense of fans. The emperor does not understand.

He accepts his harvest, failures. He accepts faithlessness,
Madness of friends, a failed life; and now the face of storm.

Does the old man during uprising speak for compromise?
In all but the last things. Not in the study itself.
For this religion is a system of knowledge;
Points may be one by one abandoned, but not the study.
Does he preach passion and non-violence?
Yes, and trees, crops, children honestly taught. He says:
Prepare yourselves for suffering.

Now the rule closes in, the last things are forbidden.
There is no real survival without these.
Now it is time for prison and the unknown.
The old man flowers into spiritual fire.

Streaking of agony across the sky.
Torn black. Red racing on blackness. Dawn.
Rufus looks at him over the rakes of death
Asking, "What is it?
Have you magic powers? Or do you feel no pain?"

The old man answers, "No. But there is a commandment
    saying
Thou shalt love the Lord thy God with all thy heart,
    with all thy soul and with all thy might.
I knew that I loved him with all my heart and might.
Now I know that I love him with all my life."

The look of delight of the martyr
Among the colors of pain, at last knowing his own response
Total and unified.
To love God with all the heart, all passion,
Every desire called evil, turned toward unity,
All the opposites, all in the dialogue.
All the dark and light of the heart, of life made whole.

Surpassing the known life, day and ideas.
My hope, my life, my burst of consciousness:
To confirm my life in the time of confrontation.

The old man saying Shema.
The death of Akiba.

THE WITNESS

Who is the witness? What voice moves across time,
Speaks for the life and death as witness voice?
Moving tonight on this city, this river, my winter street?

He saw it, the one witness. Tonight the life as legend
Goes building a meeting for me in the veins of night
Adding its scenes and its songs. Here is the man transformed,

The tall shepherd, the law, the false messiah, all;
You who come after me far from tonight finding
These lives that ask you always Who is the witness—

Take from us acts of encounter we at night
Wake to attempt, as signs, seeds of beginning,
Given from darkness and remembering darkness,

Take from our light given to you our meetings.
Time tells us men and women, tells us You
The witness, your moment covered with signs, your self.

Tells us this moment, saying You are the meeting.
You are made of signs, your eyes and your song.
Your dance the dance, the walk into the present.

All this we are and accept, being made of signs, speaking
To you, in time not yet born.
                                        The witness is myself.
                                                        And you,
The signs, the journeys of the night, survive.

KÄTHE KOLLWITZ

1

Held between wars
my lifetime
                among wars, the big hands of the world of death
my lifetime
listens to yours.

The faces of the sufferers
in the street, in dailiness,
their lives showing
through their bodies
a look as of music
the revolutionary look
that says   I am in the world
to change the world
my lifetime
is to love to endure to suffer the music
to set its portrait
up as a sheet of the world
the most moving the most alive
Easter and bone
and Faust walking among flowers of the world
and the child alive within the living woman, music of man,
and death holding my lifetime between great hands
the hands of enduring life
that suffers the gifts and madness of full life, on earth, in our time,
and through my life, through my eyes, through my arms and hands
may give the face of this music in portrait waiting for

the unknown person
held in the two hands, you.

2

Woman as gates, saying :
"The process is after all like music,
like the development of a piece of music.
The fugues come back and
again and again
interweave.
A theme may seem to have been put aside,
but it keeps returning—
the same thing modulated,
somewhat changed in form.
Usually richer.
And it is very good that this is so."

A woman pouring her opposites.
"After all there are happy things in life too.
Why do you show only the dark side?"
"I could not answer this. But I know—
in the beginning my impulse to know
the working life
had little to do with
pity or sympathy.
I simply felt
that the life of the workers was beautiful."

She said, "I am groping in the dark."

She said, "When the door opens, of sensuality,
then you will understand it too. The struggle begins.
Never again to be free of it,
often you will feel it to be your enemy.
Sometimes
you will almost suffocate,
such joy it brings."

Saying of her husband : "My wish
is to die after Karl.
I know no person who can love as he can,
with his whole soul.

Often this love has oppressed me;
I wanted to be free.
But often too it has made me
so terribly happy."

She said : "We rowed over to Carrara at dawn,
climbed up to the marble quarries
and rowed back at night. The drops of water
fell like glittering stars
from our oars."

She said : "As a matter of fact,
I believe
          that bisexuality
is almost   a necessary factor
in artistic production; at any rate,
the tinge of masculinity within me
helped me
          in my work."

She said : "The only technique I can still manage.
It's hardly a technique at all, lithography.
In it
          only the essentials count."

A tight-lipped man in a restaurant last night saying to me :
"Kollwitz?   She's too black-and-white."

      3
Held among wars, watching
  all of them
  all these people
  weavers,
  Carmagnole

Looking at
  all of them
  death, the children
  patients in waiting-rooms
  famine
  the street

the corpse with the baby
floating, on the dark river

A woman seeing
the violent, inexorable
movement of nakedness
and the confession of No
the confession of great weakness, war,
all streaming to one son killed, Peter;
even the son left living; repeated,
the father, the mother; the grandson
another Peter killed in another war; firestorm;
dark, light, as two hands,
this pole and that pole as the gates.

What would happen if one woman told the truth about her life?
The world would split open

4 SONG : THE CALLING-UP

Rumor, stir of ripeness
rising within this girl
sensual blossoming
of meaning, its light and form.

The birth-cry summoning
out of the male, the father
from the warm woman
a mother in response.

The word of death
calls up the fight with stone
wrestle with grief with time
from the material make
an art harder than bronze.

5 SELF-PORTRAIT

Mouth looking directly at you
eyes in their inwardness looking
directly at you
half light   half darkness
woman, strong, German, young artist
flows into

wide sensual mouth meditating
looking right at you
eyes shadowed with brave hand
looking deep at you
flows into
wounded brave mouth
grieving and hooded eyes
alive, German, in her first War
flows into
strength of the worn face
a skein of lines
broods, flows into
mothers among the war graves
bent over death
facing the father
stubborn upon the field
flows into
the marks of her knowing—
Nie Wieder Krieg
repeated in the eyes
flows into
"Seedcorn must not be ground"
and the grooved cheek
lips drawn fine
the down-drawn grief
face of our age
flows into
Pieta, mother and
between her knees
life as her son in death
pouring from the sky of
one more war
flows into
face almost obliterated
hand over the mouth forever
hand over one eye now
the other great eye
closed

THE SPEED OF DARKNESS

1

Whoever despises the clitoris despises the penis
Whoever despises the penis despises the cunt
Whoever despises the cunt despises the life of the child.

Resurrection music,   silence,   and surf.

2

No longer speaking
Listening with the whole body
And with every drop of blood
Overtaken by silence

But this same silence is become speech
With the speed of darkness.

3

Stillness during war, the lake.
The unmoving spruces.
Glints over the water.
Faces, voices.   You are far away.
A tree that trembles.

I am the tree that trembles and trembles.

4

After the lifting of the mist
after the lift of the heavy rains
the sky stands clear
and the cries of the city risen in day
I remember the buildings are space
walled, to let space be used for living
I mind this room is space

this drinking glass is space
whose boundary of glass
lets me give you drink and space to drink
your hand, my hand being space
containing skies and constellations
your face
carries the reaches of air
I know I am space
my words are air.

5

Between   between
the man : act   exact
woman : in curve   senses in their maze
frail orbits, green tries,   games of stars
shape of the body speaking its evidence

6

I look across at the real
vulnerable   involved   naked
devoted to the present of all I care for
the world of its history leading to this moment.

7

Life the announcer.
I assure you
there are many ways to have a child.
I bastard mother
promise you
there are many ways to be born.
They all come forth
in their own grace.

8

Ends of the earth join tonight
with blazing stars upon their meeting.

These sons,   these sons
fall burning into Asia.

9

Time comes into it.
Say it.   Say it.
The universe is made of stories,
not of atoms.

10

Lying
blazing beside me
you rear beautifully and up—
your thinking face—
erotic body reaching
in all its colors and lights—
your erotic face
colored and lit—
not colored body-and-face
but now entire,
colors   lights   the world thinking and reaching.

11

The river flows past the city.

Water goes down to tomorrow
making its children   I hear their unborn voices
I am working out the vocabulary of my silence.

12

Big-boned man young and of my dream
Struggles to get the live bird out of his throat.
I am he am I?   Dreaming?
I am the bird am I?   I am the throat?

A bird with a curved beak.
It could slit anything, the throat-bird.

Drawn up slowly.   The curved blades, not large.
Bird emerges   wet   being born
Begins to sing.

13

My night awake
staring at the broad rough jewel

the copper roof across the way
thinking of the poet
yet unborn in this dark
who will be the throat of these hours.
No.   Of those hours.
Who will speak these days,
if not I,
if not you?

Breaking Open

1973

WAKING THIS MORNING

Waking this morning,
a violent woman in the violent day
Laughing.
                    Past the line of memory
along the long body of your life
in which move childhood, youth, your lifetime of touch,
eyes, lips, chest, belly, sex, legs, to the waves of the sheet.
I look past the little plant
on the city windowsill
to the tall towers bookshaped, crushed together in greed,
the river flashing flowing corroded,
the intricate harbor and the sea, the wars, the moon, the
    planets, all who people space
in the sun visible invisible.
African violets in the light
breathing, in a breathing universe.   I want strong peace,
    and delight,
the wild good.
I want to make my touch poems:
to find my morning, to find you entire
alive moving among the anti-touch people.

                    I say across the waves of the air to you:
today once more
I will try to be non-violent
one more day
this morning, waking the world away
in the violent day.

DESPISALS

In the human cities, never again to
despise the backside of the city, the ghetto,

or build it again as we build the despised
backsides of houses.   Look at your own building.
You are the city.

Among our secrecies, not to despise our Jews
(that is, ourselves) or our darkness, our blacks,
or in our sexuality   wherever it takes us
and we now know we are productive
too productive, too reproductive
for our present invention—never to despise
the homosexual who goes building another

with touch   with touch   (not to despise any touch)
each like himself, like herself each.
You are this.
                              In the body's ghetto
never to go despising the asshole
nor the useful shit that is our clean clue
to what we need.   Never to despise
the clitoris in her least speech.

Never to despise in myself what I have been taught
to despise.   Not to despise the other.
Not to despise the *it*.   To make this relation
with the it : to know that I am it.

WHAT DO WE SEE?

When they're decent about women, they're frightful about children,
When they're decent about children, they're rotten about artists,
When they're decent about artists, they're vicious about whores,
          What do we see?   What do we not see?

When they're kind to whores, they're death on communists,
When they respect communists, they're foul to bastards,
When they're human to bastards, they mock at hysterectomy—
          What do we see?   What do we not see?

When they're decent about surgery, they bomb the Vietnamese,
When they're decent to Vietnamese, they're frightful to police,

When they're human to police, they rough up lesbians,
        What do we see?   What do we not see?

When they're decent to old women, they kick homosexuals,
When they're good to homosexuals, they can't stand drug people,
When they're calm about drug people, they hate all Germans,
        What do we see?   What do we not see?

Cadenza for the reader

When they're decent to Jews, they dread the blacks,
When they know blacks, there's always something : roaches
And the future and children and all potential.   Can't stand themselves
        Will we never see?   Will we ever know?

LOOKING AT EACH OTHER

Yes, we were looking at each other
Yes, we knew each other very well
Yes, we had made love with each other many times
Yes, we had heard music together
Yes, we had gone to the sea together
Yes, we had cooked and eaten together
Yes, we had laughed often day and night
Yes, we fought violence and knew violence
Yes, we hated the inner and outer oppression
Yes, that day we were looking at each other
Yes, we saw the sunlight pouring down
Yes, the corner of the table was between us
Yes, bread and flowers were on the table
Yes, our eyes saw each other's eyes
Yes, our mouths saw each other's mouth
Yes, our breasts saw each other's breasts
Yes, our bodies entire saw each other
Yes, it was beginning in each
Yes, it threw waves across our lives
Yes, the pulses were becoming very strong
Yes, the beating became very delicate
Yes, the calling   the arousal
Yes, the arriving   the coming

Yes, there it was for both entire
Yes, we were looking at each other

DESDICHADA

1

For that you never acknowledged me, I acknowledge
the spring's yellow detail, the every drop of rain,
the anonymous unacknowledged men and women.
The shine as it glitters in our child's wild eyes,
one o'clock at night.   This river, this city,
the years of the shadow on the delicate skin
of my hand, moving in time.
Disinherited, annulled, finally disacknowledged
and all of my own asking.   I keep that wild dimension
of life and making and the spasm
upon my mouth as I say this word of acknowledge
to you forever.   *Ewig.*   Two o'clock at night.

2

While this my day and my people are a country not yet born
it has become an earth I can
acknowledge.   I must.   I know what the
disacknowledgment does.   Then I do take you,
but far under consciousness, knowing
that under under flows a river wanting
the other : to go open-handed in Asia,
to cleanse the tributaries and the air, to make for making,
to stop selling death and its trash, pour plastic down
    men's throats,
to let this child find, to let men and women find,
knowing the seeds in us all.   They do say Find.
I cannot acknowledge it entire.   But I will.
A beginning, this moment, perhaps, and you.

3

Death flowing down past me, past me, death
marvelous, filthy, gold,
in my spine in my sex upon my broken mouth

and the whole beautiful mouth of the child;
shedding power over me
death
if I acknowledge him.
Leading me
in my own body
at last in the dance.

VOICES

Voices of all our voices, running past an imagined race.
Pouring out morning light, the pouring mists of Mil Cumbres.
Out of the poured cities of our world.
Out of the black voice of one child
Who sleeps in our poverty and is dreaming.

The child perceives and the cycles are fulfilled.

Cities being poured; and war-fire over the poor.
Mist over the peak.
One child in his voices, many voices.
The suffering runs past the end of the racing
Making us run the next race. The child sleeps.
Lovers, makers, this child, enter into our voices.
Speak to the child.   Now something else is waking:
The look of the lover, the rebel and learning look,
The look of the runner just beyond the tape, go into
The child's look at the world.   In all its voices.

FIRE
  after Vicente Aleixandre

The fire entire
                    withholds
passion.
          Light alone!
Look—
          it leaps up pure

to lick at heaven,
while all the wings
fly through.
                    It won't burn!
And man?
                Never.
                            This fire
is still
free of you, man.

Light, innocent light.

And you, human:
better never be born.

WAITING FOR ICARUS

He said he would be back and we'd drink wine together
He said that everything would be better than before
He said we were on the edge of a new relation
He said he would never again cringe before his father
He said that he was going to invent full-time
He said he loved me that going into me
He said was going into the world and the sky
He said all the buckles were very firm
He said the wax was the best wax
He said Wait for me here on the beach
He said Just don't cry

I remember the gulls and the waves
I remember the islands going dark on the sea
I remember the girls laughing
I remember they said he only wanted to get away from me
I remember mother saying : Inventors are like poets,
                                        a trashy lot
I remember she told me those who try out inventions are
    worse
I remember she added : Women who love such are the worst
    of all

I have been waiting all day, or perhaps longer.
I would have liked to try those wings myself.
It would have been better than this.

FROM CITY OF PARADISE

after Vicente Aleixandre
To my city of Malaga

There was I led by a maternal hand.
Accident of flowering grillwork, that sad guitar
singing a song abruptly held in time;
the night went quiet, more quieted the lover,
the moon forever, in interrupted light.

One breath of eternity could destroy you,
prodigious city, moment emerged from a god's mind.
According to a dream man lives and does not live,
eternally gleaming like a breath of heaven.

Garden, flowers. The sea breathing, someone's arm
stretched gasping to the city swinging from peak to gulf,
white in air, have you seen birds in the wind held by gusts
and not rising in flight?   O city not of earth!

By what maternal hand was I borne lightly
along your weightless streets. Barefoot by day.
Barefoot by night.   Big moon.   Pure sun.
The sky was you, city who lived in the sky.
You took flight in the sky with open wings.

THE QUESTION

Mother and listener she is, but she does not listen.
I look at her profile as I ask, the sweet blue-grey of eye
going obdurate to my youth as I ask the first grown sexual
question.   She cannot reply.
And from then on even past her death, I cannot fully
have language with my mother, not as daughter
and mother through all the maze and silences

of all the turnings.
Until my own child grows and asks, and until
I discover what appalled my mother long before, discover
who never delivered her, until their double weakness and
strength in myself
rouse and deliver me from that refusal.
I threw myself down on the pine-needle evening.
Although that old ancient poem never did come to me,
not from you, mother,
although in answer you did only panic, you did only grieve,
and I went silent alone, my cheek to the red pine-needle
earth, and although it has taken me all these years
and sunsets to come to you, past the dying, I know,
I come with my word alive.

IN HER BURNING

The randy old
woman said
Tickle me up
I'll be
dead very soon—
Nothing will
touch me then
but the clouds
of the sky
and the bone-
white light
off the moon
Touch me
before I go
down
among the bones
My dear one
alone
to the night—
I said
I know I know

But all I know
tonight
Is that the sun
and the moon
they burn
with the one
one light.

In her burning
signing
what does the
white moon say?
The moon says
The sun
is shining.

RONDEL

Now that I am fifty-six
Come and celebrate with me—

What happens to song and sex
Now that I am fifty-six?

They dance, but differently,
Death and distance in the mix;
Now that I'm fifty-six
Come and celebrate with me.

MORE CLUES

Mother, because you never spoke to me
I go my life, do I, searching in women's faces
the lost word, a word in the shape of a breast?

Father, because both of you never touched me
do I search for men building space on space?
There was no touch, both my hands bandaged close.

I come from that, but I come far, to touch to word.
Can they reach me now, or inside out in a universe
of touch, of speech is it? somewhere in me, clues?

MYTH

Long afterward, Oedipus, old and blinded, walked the
roads.   He smelled a familiar smell.   It was
the Sphinx.   Oedipus said, "I want to ask one question.
Why didn't I recognize my mother?"   "You gave the
wrong answer," said the Sphinx.   "But that was what
made everything possible," said Oedipus.   "No," she said.
"When I asked, What walks on four legs in the morning,
two at noon, and three in the evening, you answered,
Man.   You didn't say anything about woman."
"When you say Man," said Oedipus, "you include women
too. Everyone knows that."   She said, "That's what
you think."

SEARCHING / NOT SEARCHING

Responsibility is to use the power to respond.
                after Robert Duncan

1

What kind of woman goes searching and searching?
Among the furrows of dark April, along the sea-beach,
in the faces of children, in what they could not tell;
in the pages of centuries—
for what man? for what magic?

In corridors under the earth, in castles of the North,
among the blackened miners, among the old
I have gone searching.
The island-woman told me, against the glitter of sun
on the stalks and leaves of a London hospital.
I searched for that Elizabethan man,
the lost discoverer, the servant of time;
and that man forgotten for belief, in Spain,

and among the faces of students, at Coventry,
finding and finding in glimpses. And at home.
Among the dead I too have gone searching,
a blue light in the brain.
Suddenly I come to these living eyes,
I a live woman look up at you this day
I see all the colors in your look.

2   MIRIAM : THE RED SEA

High above shores and times,
I on the shore
forever and ever.
Moses my brother
has crossed over
to milk, honey,
that holy land.
Building Jerusalem.
I sing forever
on the seashore.
I do remember
horseman and horses,
waves of passage
poured into war,
all poured into journey.
My unseen brothers
have gone over;
chariots
deep seas under.
I alone stand here
ankle-deep
and I sing, I sing,
until the lands
sing to each other.

3   FOR DOLCI

Angel of declaring, you opened before us walls,
the lives of children, water as power.
To control the water is to control our days,
to build a dam is to face the enemy.

We will form a new person who will step forward,
he it is, she it is, assumes full life,

fully responsible. We will bring all the children,
they will decide together.

We will ask these children : what is before you?
They will say what they see.
They will say what they don't see.
Once again we breathe in discovery.

A man, a woman,
will discover
we are each other's sources.

4 CONCRETE

They are pouring the city:
they tear down the towers,
grind their lives,
laughing tainted, the river
flows down to tomorrow.

They are setting the forms,
pouring the new buildings.
Our days pour down.
I am pouring my poems.

5 BRECHT'S *GALILEO*

Brecht saying : Galileo talking astronomy
Stripped to the torso, the intellectual life
Pouring from this gross man in his nakedness.

Galileo, his physical contentment
Is having his back rubbed by his student; the boy mauls;
The man sighs and transforms it; intellectual product!

Galileo spins a toy of the earth around
The spinning sun; he looks at the student boy.
Learning is teaching, teaching is learning.
Galileo
Demonstrates how horrible is betrayal,
Particularly on the shore of a new era.

6 READING THE *KIEU*

There was always a murder within another murder.
Red leaves and rosy threads bind them together.

The hero of Vietnam's epic is a woman
and she has sold herself to save her father.

Odor of massacres spread on the sky.
Loneliness, the windy, dusty world.
The roads crowded with armor and betrayal.
Mirror of the sun and moon, this land,

in which being handed to soldiers is the journey.
Shame, disgrace, change of seas into burnt fields.
Banners, loudspeakers, violation of each day,
everything being unjust. But she does save him,
and we find everything in another way.

7 THE FLOOR OF OCEAN

Sistine Chapel

Climbing the air, prophet beyond prophet
leaning upon creation backward to the first
creation the great spark of night
breathing sun energy   a gap between finger-tips
across all of space or nothing, infinity.

But beyond this, with this, these
arms raising reaching wavering
as from the floor of ocean
wavering showing swaying like sea-plants
pointing straight up closing the gap between
continual creation and the daily touch.

8 H. F. D.

From you I learned the dark potential
theatres of the acts of man holding
on a rehearsal stage   people and lights.
You in your red hair ran down the darkened
aisle, making documents and poems
in their people form the play.

Hallie it was from you I learned this:
you told the company in dress-rehearsal
in that ultimate equipped building   what they lacked:
among the lighting, the sight-lines, the acoustics,
the perfect revolving stage, they lacked only one thing

the most important thing.   It would come tonight:
The audience   the response

Hallie I learned from you this summer, this
Hallie I saw you lying all gone to bone
the tremor of bone   I stroked the head all sculpture
I held the hands of birds   I spoke to the sealed eyes
the soft live red mouth of a red-headed woman.
I knew Hallie then I could move without answer,
like the veterans for peace, hurling back their medals
and not expecting an answer from the grass.
You taught me this in your dying, for poems and theatre
and love and peace-making that living and my love
are where response and no-response
meet at last, Hallie, in infinity.

9 THE ARTIST AS SOCIAL CRITIC

They have asked me to speak in public
and set me a subject.

I hate anything that begins : the artist as . . .
and as for "social critic"
at the last quarter of the twentieth century
I know what that is:

late at night, among radio music
the voice of my son speaking half-world away
coming clear on the radio into my room
out of blazing Belfast.

Long enough for me to walk around
in that strong voice.

10 THE PRESIDENT AND THE LASER BOMB

He speaks in a big voice through all the air
saying : we have made strength,
we have made a beginning,
we will have lasting peace.

Something shouts on the river.

All night long the acts speak:
the new laser bomb falls impeccably

along the beam of a strict light
finding inevitably a narrow footbridge
in Asia.

11 NOT SEARCHING

What did I miss as I went searching?
What did I not see?
I renounce all this regret.
Now I will make another try.

One step and I am free.

When it happens to us again and again,
sometimes we know it for we are prepared
but to discover, to live at the edge of things,
to fall out of routine into invention
and recognize at the other edge of ocean
a new kind of man   a new kind of woman
walking toward me into the little surf.
This is the next me   and the next child
daybreak in continual creation.
Dayray we see, we say,
we sing what we don't see.

Picasso saying : I don't search, I find!

And in us our need, the traces of the future,
the egg and its becoming.

I come to you searching and searching.

12 THE QUESTION

After this crisis,
nothing being conquered,
the theme is set:

to move with the forces,

how to go on
from the moment that
changed our life,

the moment of revelation,

proceeding from the crisis,
from the dream,
and not from the moment
of sleep before it?

        13

Searching/not searching.   To make closeness.
For if this communication was the truth,
then it was this communication itself
which was the value to be supported.

And for this communication to endure,
men and women must move freely.   And to make
this communication renew itself always
we must renew justice.
And to make this communication
lasting, we must live to eliminate
violence and the lie.

Yes, we set the communication
we have achieved
against the world of murder.

Searching/not searching.

                                    after Camus, 1946

        14

What did I see? What did I not see?
The river flowing past my window.
The night-lit city. My white pointed light.
Pieces of world away
within my room.

Unseen and seen, the bodies within my life.
Voices under the leaves of Asia,
and America, in sex, in possibility.
We are trying to make, to let our closeness be made,
not torn apart tonight by our dead skills.

The shadow of my hand.
The shadow of the pen.
Morning of the day we reach or do not reach.
In our bodies, we find each other.
On our mouths, inner greet,
in our eyes.

A SIMPLE EXPERIMENT

When a magnet is
struck by a hammer
the magnetism spills out of
the iron.

The molecules
are jarred,
they are a mob going
in all directions

The magnet is
shockéd back
it is no magnet but
simple iron.

There is no more
of its former
kind of accord
or force.

But if you take
another magnet
and stroke the iron
with this,

it can be
remagnetized
if you stroke it
and stroke it,

stroke it
stroke it,

the molecules
can be given
their tending grace

by a strong magnet
stroking stroking
always in the same direction,
of course.

ALONG HISTORY

Along history, forever ·
     some woman dancing,
     making shapes on the air;
     forever a man
     riding a good horse,
     sitting the dark horse well,
     his penis erect with
                fantasy

BOYS OF THESE MEN
FULL SPEED

for Jane Cooper

Boys of these men
     full speed across free,
     my father's boyhood eyes.
     Sail-skating with friends
     bright on Wisconsin ice
     those years away.

Sails strung across their backs
     boys racing toward
     fierce bitter middle-age
     in the great glitter of
     corrupted cities.
     Father, your dark mouth
     speaking its rancor.

Alive not yet, the girl
    I would become
    stares at that ice
    stippled with skaters,
    a story you tell.

Boys of those men
    call across winter
    where I stand and shake,
    woman of that girl.

ALL THE LITTLE ANIMALS

"You are not pregnant," said the man
with the probe and the white white coat;
"Yes she is," said all the little animals.
Then the great gynecologist examined. "You are not now,
   and I doubt that you ever have been," he said with
   authority.
"Test me again." He looked at his nurse and shrugged.
"Yes she is," said all the little animals, and laid down their
   lives for my son and me.

Twenty-one years later, my son a grown man and far away
   at the other ocean,
I hear them : "Yes you are," say all the little animals.
I see them, they move in great jumping procession through my waking hours,
those frogs and rabbits look at me with their round eyes,
   they kick powerfully with their strong hind legs,
they lay down their lives in silence,
all the rabbits saying Yes, all the frogs saying Yes,
in the face of all men and all institutions,
all the doctors, all the parents, all the worldly friends, all the
   psychiatrists, all the abortionists, all the lawyers.
The little animals whom I bless and praise and thank forever,
they are part of my living,
go leap through my waking and my sleep, go leap through
   my life and my birth-giving and my death,
go leap through my dreams,
and my son's life
and whatever streams from him.

NEXT

after Charles Morice

Come : you are the one chosen, by them, to serve them.
Now, in the evening of L'Amour and La Mort.
Come : you are the one chosen, by them, to love them.

. . . The child perceives and the cycles are fulfilled.
Man's dead.   Dead never to be reborn.
The Islands and Waters serve another lord,
New, better.   His eyes are the flowering of light.
He is beautiful.   The child smiles at him in his tears.

TWO YEARS

Two years of my sister's bitter illness;
the wind whips the river of her last spring.
I have burned the beans again.

IRIS

1

Middle of May, when the iris blows,
blue below blue, the bearded patriarch-
face on the green flute body of a boy
Poseidon   torso of Eros
blue
sky below sea
day over daybreak violet behind twilight
the May iris
midnight on midday

2

Something is over and under this deep blue.
Over and under this movement, *etwas*
before and after, *alguna cosa*
blue before blue

is it

      perhaps

            death?

That may be the wrong word.

The iris stands in the light.

   3

Death is here, death is guarded by swords.
No. By shapes of swords
flicker of green leaves
under all the speaking and crying
shadowing the words the eyes   here they all die
racing withering   blue evening
my sister death the iris
stands clear in light.

   4

In the water-cave
ferocious needles of teeth
the green morays
in blue water   rays
a maleficence   ribbon of green   the flat look of
eyes staring   fatal mouth staring
the rippling potent force
curving into any hole
death finding his way.

   5

Depth of petals, May iris
transparent   infinitely deep they are
petal-thin   with light behind them
and you, death,
and you
behind them
blue under blue.
What I cannot say
in adequate music
something being born
transparency   blue of
light standing on light

this stalk of
(among mortal petals-and-leaves)
light

✢ 2 Orange and Grape

BALLAD OF ORANGE AND GRAPE

After you finish your work
after you do your day
after you've read your reading
after you've written your say—
you go down the street to the hot dog stand,
one block down and across the way.
On a blistering afternoon in East Harlem in the twentieth century.

Most of the windows are boarded up,
the rats run out of a sack—
sticking out of the crummy garage
one shiny long Cadillac;
at the glass door of the drug-addiction center,
a man who'd like to break your back.
But here's a brown woman with a little girl dressed in rose and pink, too.

Frankfurters frankfurters sizzle on the steel
where the hot-dog-man leans—
nothing else on the counter
but the usual two machines,
the grape one, empty, and the orange one, empty,
I face him in between.
A black boy comes along, looks at the hot dogs, goes on walking.

I watch the man as he stands and pours
in the familiar shape
bright purple in the one marked ORANGE
orange in the one marked GRAPE,
the grape drink in the machine marked ORANGE

and orange drink in the GRAPE.
Just the one word large and clear, unmistakable, on each machine.

I ask him : How can we go on reading
and make sense out of what we read?—
How can they write and believe what they're writing,
the young ones across the street,
while you go on pouring grape into ORANGE
and orange into the one marked GRAPE—?
(How are we going to believe what we read and we write
    and we hear and we say and we do?)

He looks at the two machines and he smiles
and he shrugs and smiles and pours again.
It could be violence and nonviolence
it could be white and black   women and men
it could be war and peace or any
binary system, love and hate, enemy, friend.
Yes and no, be and not-be, what we do and what we don't do.

On a corner in East Harlem
garbage, reading, a deep smile, rape,
forgetfulness, a hot street of murder,
misery, withered hope,
a man keeps pouring grape into ORANGE
and orange into the one marked GRAPE,
pouring orange into GRAPE and grape into ORANGE forever.

ROCK FLOW, RIVER MIX

Flickering
in the buildings
they dance now
hip   face   and knee
dances I hunted for
when at nineteen
I stood at the river
here, the Hudson
hunting for Africa—
something rumored

caught, poured in shadow and light
face of ecstasy
on film
swivel neck, eternal smile
suffer the night
water flows down
to
today
black theatre, road dusted with light
streaking down over our heads
setting before us, around us
sound track
image track

MARTIN LUTHER KING, MALCOLM X

Bleeding of the mountains
the noon bleeding
he is shot through the voice
all things being broken

The moon returning in her blood
looks down   grows white
loses color
and blazes

. . . and the near star gone—

voices of cities
drumming in the moon

bleeding of my right hand
my black voice bleeding

LOOKING

Battles whose names I do not know
Weapons whose wish they dare not teach

Wars whose need they will not show
Tear us tear us each from each,
O my dear
Great sun and daily touch.
Fallen beside a river in Europe,
Burned to grey ash in Africa,
Lain down in the California jail,
O my dear,
Great sun and daily touch.

Flaming in Asia today.

I saw you stare out over Canada
As I stare over the Hudson River.

DON BATY, THE DRAFT RESISTER

I Muriel stood at the altar-table
The young man Don Baty stood with us
I Muriel fell away in me
in dread but in a welcoming
I am Don Baty then I said
before the blue-coated police
ever entered and took him.

I am Don Baty, say we all
we eat our bread, we drink our wine.
Our heritance has come, we know,
your arrest is mine. Yes.
Beethoven saying Amen Amen Amen Amen Amen
and all a singing, earth and eyes,
strong and weaponless.

There is a pounding at the door;
now we bring our lives entire.
I am Don Baty. My dear, my dear,
in a kind of welcoming,
here we meet, here we bring
ourselves. They pound on the wall of time.
The newborn are with us singing.

TE HANH : LONG-AGO GARDEN

The long-ago garden is green deepened on green
Day after day our mother's hair, whiter
We are all far away, each at our own work
When do we return to the long-ago garden?

We are a shining day following rain
Like the sun like the moon
The morning star, evening star, they never cross over
When will we go back to the long-ago garden?

We are summer lotus, autumn chrysanthemum,
Ripe tenth-month fig, and fifth-month dragon-eye
You followed the eighth-month migratory birds
Third month, I left with those who crossed over

You went back into the house one day in spring
I was out picking guava, Mother said
You looked up at the tree-top, where the wind blew through
The leaves touched; lips, speaking my name

When I returned one summer day,
You were at the well washing clothes, Mother said
I looked in the pure deep water past the well-rim
Saw only the surface and myself, alone

The long-ago garden is green deepened on green
Day after day our mother's hair, whiter
We are all far away, each at our work
When will we return to the long-ago garden?

WELCOME FROM WAR

The woman to the man :
What is that on your hands?
It is also on my hands.

What is that in your eyes?
You see it in my eyes, do you?

Is your sex intact? Is mine?
Can it be about life now?

You went out to war.
War came over our house.

Our bed is not the same.
We will set about beginnings.

I kiss your hands, I kiss your eyes,
I kiss your sex.

I will kiss, I will bless
all the beginnings.

FACING SENTENCING

Children remembering sadness grieve, they grieve.
But sadness is not so terrible.   Children
Grown old speak of fear saying, we are to
Fear only this fear itself.   But fear is not to be so feared.
Numbness is.   To stand before my judge
Not knowing what I mean : to walk up
To him, my judge, and back to nobody
For the courtroom is almost empty, the world
Is almost silent, and suppose we did not know
This power to fall into each other's eyes
And say We love; and say We know each other
And say among silence We will help stop this war.

SECRETS OF AMERICAN CIVILIZATION

for Staughton Lynd

Jefferson spoke of freedom but he held slaves.
Were ten of them his sons by black women?
Did he sell them? or was his land their graves?
Do we asking our questions become more human?

497 ⤳

Are our lives the parable which, living,
We all have, we all know, we all can move?
Then they said : The earth belongs to the living,
We refuse allegiance, we resign office, and we love.

They are writing at their desks, the thinking fathers,
They do not recognize their live sons' faces;
Slave and slaveholder they are chained together
And one is ancestor and one is child.
Escape the birthplace; walk into the world
Refusing to be either slave or slaveholder.

WHEREVER

Wherever
we walk
we will make

Wherever
we protest
we will go planting

Make poems
seed grass
feed a child growing
build a house
Whatever we stand against
We will stand feeding and seeding

Wherever
I walk
I will make

BRINGING

Bringing their life   these young
bringing their life   rise from their wakings
bringing their life   come to a place
where they make their gifts

The grapes of life of death   of transformation
round they hang at hand   desires   like peace
or seed of revolutions that make all things new
and must be lived out, washed in rivers, and themselves made new
and bringing their life   the young   they reach
in their griefs   their mistakes   their discovering
bringing their life   they touch   they take
bringing their life   they come to a place

It is raining fire   they are bringing their life
their sex speaks for them   their ideas all speak
their acts arrive   bringing their life entire
They resist a system of wars and rewards
They offer their open faces   they offer their bodies
They offer their hands   bringing their life entire
They offer their life   they are their own gifts
Make life   resist   resist   make life
Bringing their life entire   they come to this moment
Bringing their life entire   they come to this place

A LOUIS SONNET

for Louis Untermeyer, his 80th birthday

The jokes, the feuds, the puns, the punishments,
This traditional man being brave, going in grace,
Finding the structure of lives more than perfected line;
The forms of poetry are his time and space.
He's quirky, he rhymes like daily life; light wine
Is all his flavor, till fierce reverence
Turns delicatessen into delicatesse—
The man who anthologizes experience.

He is anthologized; like a wave of the sea
He is here, he is there, he changes;   impossibly,
He is blue surface, green suspended, the dark deep notes.
A stain of brilliance spreading upward floats
In luminous air; we are luminous, he makes us be
The jokes of Job and Heine's anecdotes.

AFTER MELVILLE

for Bett and Walter Bezanson

1

The sea-coast looks at the sea, and the cities pour.
The sea pours embassies of music : murder-sonata, birth-sonata,
the seashore celebrates the deep ocean.

Ocean dreaming all day all night of mountains
lifts a forehead to the wakes of stars;
one star dives into a still circle : birth, known to all.

A shore of the sea, one man as the shore of the sea;
one young man lying out over configurations of water
never two wave-patterns the same, never two same dreamings.

He writes these actualities, these dreamings,
transformed into themselves, his acts, his islands,
his animals ourselves within his full man's hand.

Bitter contempt and bitter poverty,
Judaean desert of our life, being locked
in white in black, a lock of essences.

Not graves not ocean but ourselves tonight
swing in his knowledge, his living and its wake,
travelling in the sea that goes pouring, dreaming
where we flash in our lifetime wave, these breathing shallows
of a shore that looks at the deep land, this island
that looks forever at the sea; deep sexual sea
that breathes one man at the shoreline of emergence.
He is the sea we carry to our star.

2

They come into our lives, Melville and Whitman who
ran contradictions of cities and the one-sparing sea
held in the long male arms—Identify.

They enter our evenings speaking—Melville and Crane
taking the wars of our parentage, silence and smoke,
tearing the live man open till we wake.

Emily Dickinson, Melville in our breathing,
isolate among powers, telling us the sea
and the slow dance of the absence of the sea.

Hawthorne whose forehead knew the revelation—
how can we receive the vision at noonday?
Move with the revelation?   Move away?

More violent than Melville   diving the sea deeper
no man has ever gone.   He swims our world
violence and dream safe only in full danger.

Revealing us, who are his afterlife.

   3

A woman looks at the sea.
   Woman in whose waiting is held ocean
   faces the other sea where his life drowns and is saved,
   recurrent singing, the reborn wave.

A man looking into the sea.
   He sails, he swims among the opposites,
   diving, making a life among many unknowns,
   he takes for his knowledge the future wake of stars.

The sea looking and not looking.
   Among the old enemies, a transparent lake.
   Wars of the sea and land, wars of air;   space;
   against the corroded wars and sources of wars, a lake of being born.

A man and a woman look into each other.
   One man giving us forever the grapes of the sea.
   Gives us marriage; gives us suicide and birth; he drowns
   for the sake of our look into each other's body and life.
   Allowing the great life : sex, time, the feeding powers.
   He is part of our look into each other's face.

THE WRITER

for Isaac Bashevis Singer

His tears fell from his veins
They spoke for six million
From his veins all their blood.
He told his stories.
But noone spoke this language
Noone knew this music.

His music went into all people
Not knowing this language.
It ran through their bodies
And they began to take his words
Everyone the tears
Everyone the veins
But everyone said
Noone spoke this language.

GRADUS AD PARNASSUM

Oh I know
If I'd practised the piano
I'd never be so low
As I now am

Where's Sylvia Beerman?
Married, rich and cool
In New Rochelle
She was nobody's fool,

She didn't write in verse
She hardly wrote at all
She rose she didn't fall
She never gave a damn

But got up early
To practise Gradus
Ad Parnassum—she
Feels fine. I know.

FROM A PLAY : PUBLISHER'S SONG

I lie in the bath and I contemplate the toilet-paper:
Scottissue, 1000 sheets—
    What a lot of pissin and shittin,
    What a lot of pissin and shittin,
Enough for the poems of Shelley and Keats—
All the poems of Shelley and Keats.

IN THE NIGHT THE SOUND WOKE US

In the night the sound woke us.
We went up to the deck.
Brightness of brightness in the black night.
The ship standing still, her hold wide open.
Light shining orange on the lumber
her cargo, fresh strong-smelling wood.
A tall elder sailor standing at the winches,
his arms still, down; not seeming to move,
his hands hidden behind
black leather balcony.
The silver-hair tall sailor, stern and serene his face
turning from side to side.
The winches fell and rose with the newborn wood.
Orange and blazing in the lights it rose.
Vancouver straits, a northern midnight.
Delivered from death I stood awake
seeing it brought to the cool shining air.
O death, skillful, at night, in the bright light
bringing to birth.

Over my head
I see it in the air.

IN THE UNDERWORLD

I go a road
among the upturned

faces in their colors
to the great arch
of a theatre stage

I the high queen
starting in the air
far above my head
royal of the crown
I the tower
go through the wide arch
proscenium queen

❧

The arch shuts down like December
very small all about me
the entrance to this country

❧

Many whispers in the quick dark
Fingers in swarms, breath is busy,
they have reached above my head
and taken off my crown
I go and I go
I have been searching
since the light of all mornings

I remember only a pale brightness
and no more.   What do I remember?
I no longer

They have reached to my jewels
green in this cave, that one, iceberg the blue,
whirled into diamond
in the deep dark taken.

I move into thicker dark,
moss, earth-smell, wet coal.
Their hands are on my stiff robe.
I walk out of my robe.

At my surfaces
they unfasten my dress of softness.
Naked the naked wind
of the underworld.

Rankness at my breasts,
over my flank
giggle and stink
They have taken little knives
my skin lifts off
I go in pain-colored black
trying to find

I walk into their asking
Where is he
they sing on one note
Your lord memory
He your delight
I cannot hear their music
it scrapes along my muscles
they make my flesh go
among the gusts and whispers
they take off my eyes
my lips no more
the delicate fierce places
of identity
everywhere
taken

I, despoiled and clacking
walk, a chain of bones
into the boneyard dark.
One by one.
Something
reaches for my bones.

Something walks here
a little breath in hell
without its ghost.
A breath after nothing.
Gone.
Nothing turns the place
where perceiving was
from side to side.
There is no place.   It has dissolved.
The lowest point, back there, has slid away.

—What are you working on?
—Istar in the underworld.
—Baby, you *are* in trouble.

What calls her?
The body of a woman alive
but at the point of death,
the very old body lying there riddled with life,
gone, gasping at pain,
fighting for words
fighting for breath.
One clear breast looks up out of this gone body
young, the white clear light of this breast
speaks across distance

Remember is
come back.
Remember is
Who is here?
I am here.

At the pit of the underworld
something flickers in her
without anything

Now I remember love
who has set my being on me,
who permits me move
into all being,
who puts on me perceiving
and my bones
in a live chain
and my flesh that perceives
and acts
and my acknowledging skin
my underdress, my dress
and my robe
the jewels of the world
I touch and find

—I know him and I know
the breast speaking
out of a gone woman
across distances

And my crown a tower.

A voice saying : She went in a queen,
she died and came out,
goddess.

All our faces in their colors
staring at the
arch of this world.

The breast smiles : Do not
think you are invulnerable!
The breast smiles : Do not
think you are immortal!

AFTERWARDS

We are the antlers of that white animal
That great white animal
Asleep under the sea
He forgets and dreams so deep he does not
Know his whiteness in the sea-black
Among the plants of night.
His antlers have legs and arms.   Our heads
together being joined
Journey tonight, dreamed in his ocean.

Where we lie afterwards, smoke of our dreams
Goes coiling up, a plant in the dark room.
You were a young boy, you sang in the Polish woods
Limping away away.   I in this city, held
In a dream of children.   Some mythic animal
Rises now, flies up, white from the sea-floor.
In all our death, the glow behind his eyes
Speaks under all knowing : our lives burn.

FLYING TO HANOI

I thought I was going to the poets, but I am
   going to the children.
I thought I was going to the children, but I am
   going to the women.
I thought I was going to the women, but I am going
   to the fighters.
I thought I was going to the fighters, but I am going
   to the men and women who are inventing peace.
I thought I was going to the inventors of peace,
   but I am going to the poets.
My life is flying to your life.

IT IS THERE

Yes, it is there, the city full of music,
Flute music, sounds of children, voices of poets,
The unknown bird in his long call.   The bells of peace.
Essential peace, it sounds across the water
In the long parks where the lovers are walking,
Along the lake with its island and pagoda,
And a boy learning to fish.   His father threads the line.
Essential peace, it sounds and it stills.   Cockcrow.
It is there, the human place.

On what does it depend, this music, the children's games?
A long tradition of rest? Meditation? What peace is so profound
That it can reach all habitants, all children,
The eyes at worship, the shattered in hospitals?
All voyagers?
               Meditation, yes; but within a tension
Of long resistance to all invasion, all seduction of hate.
Generations of holding to resistance; and within this resistance
Fluid change that can respond, that can show the children
A long future of finding, of responsibility; change within
Change and tension of sharing consciousness
Village to city, city to village, person to person entire
With unchanging cockcrow and unchanging endurance
Under the
           skies of war.

THE RUNNING OF
THE GRUNION

for Denise Levertov and Mitchell Goodman

1

Launching themselves
beating silver
on that precise
moment of tide & moon.

Exact in act
outer limit
stranded on high sand.
With an arched back he
digs their bed
she under him
releases he
fertilizes and
with back arched
covers (sand)
the gleam spawn.

On the lit beach
the hunt begins:
silver buckets.
People run down
for the huge catch.
Pulsing on sand
countless silver.
Highest wave
stretches
among the hunt.
A few of the fish
are washed to sea.

The spawn enclosed
in high sand

rhythms of hot & cool;
a full moon later
the wave foams over;

young grunion
wash to ocean.

Eleven later,
mature, silver,
they return.

People with pails.

2

Sand nailed down
by beating silver
nailed
by live nails

Sand is not crucified
only people
only animals

3

These creatures
cruciform.
To make life.

In the act of life
murder
people with pails

4

Silver
on silver
birth
and
murder

Not birth
conception

5

Seawave
moon
seasand

at the moment of life
They throw themselves
million silver
upon making

Whether or not
people with pails

SACRED LAKE

some flushed–earth–color pueblo
holding the long–light sunset
shadows go into this ground
the mountain lifting the lake
in an orante gesture
like the men
in their white shirt-sleeves
in the basement of the Planetarium
the mailman the policeman the highschool-teacher
these winter evenings   making their own telescopes
they hold them up to test them the only way
against a ray of light in a gesture of offering.

This long wide gorge and mesa make the gesture
holding each man up against sunset light
and holding Blue Lake up.

SONGS OF THE BARREN GROUNDS

Eskimo Songs translated by Paul Radin
and Muriel Rukeyser

1 THE OLD DAYS

Song-calling,
Breathing deep, my heart laboring,
Calling the song.
Hearing the news:
Faraway villages in their
Terrible fishing seasons,
Breathing deep and
Calling the song;
Come down, song.
Now I forget
The laboring breast,
I remember the old days:
My strength, butchering
Caribou bulls,
Calling the song—
I call the song.
Three bulls butchered
While the sun climbed morning—
I call the song
Breathing deep
—Aya ayee—
Calling the song.

2 INLAND, AWAY

Inland, away
Grieving I know I
Shall not leave again
This bench, this place.
Wanderwishing troubles me:
Going inland, going away.
My thoughts keep playing with a thing that seems

Animal flesh
And yet I know I
Shall not leave again
This bench, this place.
Feeling the old wish to go
Inland, away.
Here I am, I—
Never again to go out with the rest.
I was the one who shot them down, both:
The widespread antlers, old caribou,
And the young one too.
Once
When heaven-twilight
Lay over the land—

—Aya, yee, ya.—
All this, unforgotten,
All my fantasy,
That hunting, and my fortunes,
That caribou and calf,
While all the earth
Whitened with snow.
Inlandaway.
Inlandaway.

3 I'M HERE AGAIN

I'm here again—
What's the matter?   Want to say something?
Something I heard told around:
I'm here to tell,
I'm here to tell,
I'm here to tell
How you and your
Uncle's
Younger sister
Went to bed.
Just at the coming of the great springtime.
I'm here to tell,
I'm here to tell,
I'm here to tell,
You sure have been fucking, you two.
What do you say now?   How about it?

"Open your legs now, nice and wide!"
When you got there, hard,
How was she?
I'm here again.
Here I am.

4 NOT MUCH GOOD

I'm not much good at any of this.
Is the song too long, is the song too long?
He wanted his sister, he did he did—
That's what they said that people said.
Well you rascal, you rascal you.
Think I'd sing a pack of lies,
Lies about a fellow who never
Made a pass at his little sister?
Well you rascal, you rascal you—
Know what they said, they said you did?
Came sneaking in to your little sister,
Sneaked in to screw your little sister.
Know what she asked you?
"Well, what you doing?"
Pretty silly, you looked—
Sneaking in, to screw his sister!
. . . . To show him up
I'm singing this song.

5 MY BREATH

A song I sing, strong I sing.
Helpless as my own child, ever since last fall.

My house and my wife, I wish they were gone.
With me, she's with a worthless man;
Her man should be strong as winter ice.
I am bedridden and
I wish she were gone.

Do we know ourselves?

Beasts of the hunt!   Can I remember one?
Faintly remembering the polar bear,
White back high, head lowered, charging,

Sure he was the one male there,
Full speed at me.

Had me down again and again—
He didn't lie over me, he went away.
Hadn't expected another male there
At the edge of the ice-floe
He knew who he was, he rested.

I can never forget the fjord-seal
On the sea ice;   I killed it early
When my comrades, my land-sharers
Were just waking.
Reaching the breathing-hole,
I discovered it,
And then I was standing over the hole—
I hadn't scratched the ice, the firm ice,
And the bear hooked under—
It heard me, that good seal, that cunning seal.
And just tasting my disappointment if I lost it
I caught it with my harpoon head!

My house and wife are here.
I have no oil for her lamp and spring has come,
Dawn gives way to dawn;   when will I be well?
My house;   my wife, by neighbors
Clothed, by charity
Eating meat.
Not my providing; when will I be well?

Do we know ourselves?
Little you know of yourself,
Dawn giving way to dawn.

Orpingalik

I RECOGNIZE THIS SONG

I recognize this little song—
It's a fellow being.
Sure, I should be ashamed

Of the child I carried,
I've heard
The neighbors talking—
Sure, I should be ashamed
Because his mother
Wasn't as pure
As the pure blue sky;
I got what was coming;
Gossip will teach him
And finish his schooling.
Sure, I should be ashamed
The child I love won't ever take care of me.
When others go hunting
Out on the flat ice
And far behind, people
Stand looking at them
A person feels envy!
I've just remembered
Once in wintertime
At Cross-Eye Island, breaking camp,
The weather was—Down there
Footsteps creaked faintly in the snow,
Sinking.   I followed close, like a tame animal.
Oh, that's the way to be.
But when the message came
Of murder done by my son
I staggered.   I could not keep my foothold.

THE BLACK ONES, THE
GREAT ONES

After the black ones!
Racing the great ones!
Over the plain-flowers
With all my strength.
Running breakneck
Forever after
Horizon-animals.
Obsessed!   They're growing
Out of the ground!

The giants!   I shot them,
The great ones, the black ones,
Faraway
In the summer-hunting.

TROUT FISHING

Well, I'm back again
To this song—
Back again, standing over
My old fishing-place.
And I'm not one who's good at going back,
A hook waiting for trout.
Upstream and up the stream.
There aren't any trout around here
Unless you wait.
I keep saying There aren't many trout this year.
There are those I eat and those I don't wait for
Because I give up so soon.
Upstream and up the stream;
Well, and it's glorious
On snowy ice-surfaces
Walking and walking.
I can't even go errands—
I, a falling-down old man.
Everything else is fine. . . .
I cannot even make my difficult song,
For easy birdsong is not given to me,
Even though I turn to it again,
And I'm not one who's good at going back.

O difficult things!   And I want everything.
                                                    Ikinilik

HOW LOVELY IT IS

How lovely it is to
Put a little song together.

Many of mine fail, yes they do.
How lovely it all is,
But me, I seldom burn with luck,
Hunting across the ice, alas.
How lovely it all is
To wish and bring it through.
But again and again
My wishes slip away!
How very hard, how very hard it all is, yes, alas.

Ikinilik

THE WORD-FISHER

I know what I want in my words
But it will not turn into song
And it's not worth the listening!
To make my song
Really good listening,
That's pretty hard—
But listen : Some clumsy song . . .
Is in the making . . .
And is made!

STROKING SONGS

A GIRL FOR A BOY—
STROKING SONG

It's still my little big "big brother," isn't it?
The one I wanted to make new, isn't it?
The one I didn't do such a good job on, isn't it?

I'm going to have to prime my tool again,
There'll have to be work done in the bag.
I didn't do a good job, that's what the man says now.

THE BABY ON THE MOUNTAIN—
STROKING SONG

Up against the mountain-side
The little early-born—
No stopping-place, no hiding-place
Pushing it out, pushing it out.—

White skin, furless skin,
Great skin of harbor seal,
Great skin, hanging soft,
Great skin hanging free.

Roughened by the east wind
Pushing pushing,
I'm sorry, it's only
The southern winds.

This is the way we
This is the way we open it,
This is the way we
Make it hard.

This is the way we
Stroke the baby,
Stroking the baby's
Parts.

This is the way of the baby's groin,
This is the way the baby'll marry,
A real man with a fine one,
A real man with a darling one.

Stroking, stroking, stroke the baby.

THE WIPING MOSS FROM THE RUINS

Running to me—
My wiping moss—
Breakneck from the ruined house.

Well, a nipple full of milk
And a fine pot-stone, yes,

Welcome as the light of spring,
Welcome as a seal in spring!

Well, the milk of the nipple, listen,
Listen : hear them shout
Where is that milk?
All the way up from Ipsetaleq.

Then what, what, what's the matter?
Pinch you, pinch you, pinch your crotch.
Falling all over yourself, darling.

STROKING SONGS, CHILDHOOD SONGS

BEING BORN

She was unloaded and delivered to us, glory be!
Unloaded from her mother, the little one, delivered,
And we all say Glory Be!

SHOOTING STAR

You star up there,
Starer up there,
Your fingers up there
Not holding very tight,
Not catching—not tight—
And falling downwards,
Downwards and falling falling
Downward down the night.

BREAKING OPEN

I come into the room   The room stands waiting
river   books   flowers   you are far away
black river   a language just forgotten
traveling blaze of light   dreams of endurance
racing into this moment   outstretched faces
and you are far away

                            The stars cross over
fire-flood   extremes of singing
filth and corrupted promises   my river
A white triangle of need

                     my reflected face
laced with a black triangle   of need

Naked among the silent of my own time
and Zig Zag Zag that last letter
     of a secret or forgotten alphabet
     shaped like our own last letter but it means
Something in our experience you do not know
When will it open open opening
River-watching all night

                   will the river
swing open we are Asia and New York
Bombs, roaches, mutilation   River-watching

Looking out at the river
the city-flow seen as river
the flow seen as a flow of possibility
and I too to that sea.

Summer repetitive. The machine screaming
Beating outside, on the corrupted
Waterfront.
On my good days it appears digging
And building,

On others, its monstrous word
Says on one note Gone, killed, laid waste.

The whole thing—waterfront, war, city,
        sons, daughters, me—
Must be re-imagined.
Sun on the orange-red roof.

            ❧

Walking into the elevator at Westbeth
Yelling in the empty stainless-steel
Room like the room of this tormented year.
Like the year
The metal nor absorbs nor reflects
My yelling.
My pulled face looks at me
From the steel walls.

            ❧

And then we go to Washington as if it were
Jerusalem;
and then we present our petition, clearly,
rightfully;
and then some of us walk away;
and then do others of us stay;
and some of us lie gravely down
on that cool mosaic floor,
the Senate.
Washington! Your bombs rain down!
I mourn, I lie down, I grieve.

            ❧

Written on the plane:

The conviction that what is meant by the unconscious is the same
as what is meant by history. The collective unconscious is the living
history brought to the present in consciousness, waking or sleeping.
The personal "unconscious" is the personal history. This is an
identity.
We will now explore further ways of reaching our lives, the new
world. My own life, yours; this earth, this moon, this system, the
"space" we share, which is consciousness.

Turbulence of air now. A pause of nine minutes.

⌘

Written on the plane. After turbulence:

The movement of life : to live more fully in the present. This movement includes the work of bringing this history to "light" and understanding. The "unconscious" of the race, and its traces in art and in social structure and "inventions"—these are our inheritance. In facing history, we look at each other, and in facing our entire personal life, we look at each other.

I want to break open. On the plane, a white cloud seen through rainbow. The rainbow is, optically, on the glass of the window.

⌘

The jury said Guilty, Guilty, Guilty,
Guilty, Guilty.   Each closed face.
I see myself in the river-window.   River
Slow going to its sea.
An old, crushed, perverse, waiting,
In loss, in dread, dead tree.

⌘

COLUMBUS

Inner greet.   Greenberg said it,
Even the tallest man needs inner greet.
This is the great word
brought back, in swinging seas.   The new world.

⌘

End of summer.
Dark-red butterflies on the river
Dark-orange butterflies in the city.
The young men still going to war
Or away from war, to the prisons, to other countries.
To the high cold mountains, to the source of the river, I too go,
Deeper into this room.

⌘

A dream remembered only in other dreams.
The voice saying:
All you dreaded as a child
Came to pass in storms of light;
All you dreaded as a girl

Falls and falls in avalanche—
Dread and the dream of love will make
All that time and men may build,
All that women dance and make.
They become you.   Your own face
Dances through the night and day,
Leading your body into this
Body-led dance, its mysteries.
Answer me.   Dance my dance.

∽

River-watching from the big Westbeth windows:
Powerful miles of Hudson, an east-blowing wind
All the way to Asia.
No.   Lost in our breath,
Sobbing, lost, alone.   The river darkens.
Black flow, bronze lights, white lights.
Something must answer that light, that dark.
Love,
The door opens, you walk in.

∽

The old man said, "The introversion of war
Is the main task of our time."
Now it makes its poems, when the sky stops killing.
I try to turn my acts inward and deeper.
Almost a poem.   If it splash outside,
All right.
My teacher says, "Go deeper."
The day when the salmon-colored flowers
Open.
I will essay.   Go deeper.

Make my poem.

∽

Going to prison. The clang of the steel door.
It is my choice. But the steel door does clang.
The introversion of this act
Past its seeming, past all thought of effect,
Until it is something like
Writing a poem in my silent room.

∽

In prison, the thick air,
still, loaded, heat on heat.
Around your throat
for the doors are locks,
the windows are locked doors,
the hot smell locked around us,
the machine shouting at us,
trying to sell us meat and carpets.
In prison, the prisoners,
all of us, all the objects,
chairs, cots, mops, tables.
Only the young cat.
He does not know he is locked in.

&

In prison, the prisoners.
One black girl, 19 years.
She has killed her child
and she grieves, she grieves.
She crosses to my bed.
"What do *Free* mean?"
I look at her.
"You don't understand English."
"Yes, I understand English."
"What do *Free* mean?"

&

In prison a
brown paper bag
I put it beside my cot.
All my things.
Comb, notebook, underwear,
letterpaper, toothbrush, book.
I am rich—
they have given me another toothbrush.
The guard saying:
"You'll find people share here."

&

Photos, more precise than any face can be.
    The broken static moment, life never by
    any eye seen.

&

My contradictions set me tasks, errands.

This I know:
What I reap, that shall I sow.

How we live:
I look into my face in the square glass.
Under it, a bright flow of cold water.
At once, a strong arrangement of presences:
I am holding a small glass
under the little flow
at Fern Spring, among the western forest.
A cool flaw among the silence.
The taste of the waterfall.

Some rare battered she-poet, old girl in the Village
racketing home past low buildings some freezing night,
come face to face with that broad roiling river.
Nothing buried in her but is lit and transformed.

BURNING THE DREAMS

on a spring morning of young wood, green wood
it will not burn, but the dreams burn.
My hands have ashes on them.
They fear it
and so they destroy the nearest things.

DEATH AND THE DANCER

Running from death
throwing his teeth at the ghost
dipping into his belly, staving off death with a throw
tearing his brains out, throwing them at Death
death-baby is being born
scythe clock and banner come
trumpet of bone   and drum made of something—
the callous-handed goddess
her kiss is resurrection

RATIONAL MAN

The marker at Auschwitz
The scientists torturing male genitals
The learned scientists, they torture female genitals

The 3-year-old girl, what she did to her kitten
The collar made of leather for drowning a man in his chair
The scatter-bomb with the nails that drive into the brain
The thread through the young man's splendid penis
The babies in flames.   The thrust
Infected reptile dead in the live wombs of girls
We did not know we were insane.
We do not know we are insane.
We say to them : you are insane
Anything you can imagine
        on punishable drugs, or calm and young
        with a fever of 105, or on your knees,
        with the word of Hanoi bombed
        with the legless boy in Bach Mai
        with the sons of man torn by man
Rational man has done.

Mercy, Lord.   On every living life.

        ०৯৯

In tall whirlpools of mirrors
Unshapen body and face
middle of the depth
of a night that will not turn
the unshapen all night
trying for form

        ०৯৯

I do and I do.
Life and this under-war.
Deep under protest, make.
For we are makers more.

but touching teaching going
the young and the old
they reach they break they are moving
to make the world

        ०৯৯

something about desire
something about murder
something about my death
something about madness

something about light
something of breaking open
sing me to sleep and morning
my dreams are all a waking

❧

In the night
wandering room to room of this world
I move by touch
and then something says
let the city pour
the sleep of the beloved
Let the night pour down
all its meanings
Let the images pour
the light is dreaming

❧

THE HOSTAGES

When I stand with these three
My new brothers my new sister
These who bind themselves offering
Hostages to go at a word, hostages
to go deeper here among our own cities
When I look into your faces
Karl, Martin, Andrea.

When I look into your faces
Offered men and women, I can speak,
And I speak openly on the church steps,
At the peace center saying : We affirm
Our closeness forever with the eyes in Asia,
Those who resist the forces we resist.
One more hostage comes forward, his eyes: Joe,
With Karl, Martin, Andrea, me.

And now alone in the river-watching room,
Allen, your voice comes, the deep prophetic word.
And we are one more, Joe, Andrea, Karl, Martin,
Allen, me.   The hostages.   Reaching.   Beginning.

❧

That I looked at them with my living eyes.
That they looked at me with their living eyes.

That we embraced.
That we began to learn each other's language.

It is something like the breaking open of my youth
but unlike too, leading not only to consummation
of the bed and of the edge of the sea.
Although that, surely, also.

But this music is
itself
needing only other selving
It is defeated but a way is open:
transformation

&

Then came I entire to this moment
process and light
        to discover the country of our waking
breaking open

&

The Gates

1976

ST. ROACH

For that I never knew you, I only learned to dread you,
for that I never touched you, they told me you are filth,
they showed me by every action to despise your kind;
for that I saw my people making war on you,
I could not tell you apart, one from another,
for that in childhood I lived in places clear of you,
for that all the people I knew met you by
crushing you, stamping you to death, they poured boiling
    water on you, they flushed you down,
for that I could not tell one from another
only that you were dark, fast on your feet, and slender.
    Not like me.
For that I did not know your poems
And that I do not know any of your sayings
And that I cannot speak or read your language
And that I do not sing your songs
And that I do not teach our children
                to eat your food
                or know your poems
                or sing your songs
But that we say you are filthing our food
But that we know you not at all.

Yesterday I looked at one of you for the first time.
You were lighter than the others in color, that was
    neither good nor bad.
I was really looking for the first time.
You seemed troubled and witty.

Today I touched one of you for the first time.
You were startled, you ran, you fled away
Fast as a dancer, light, strange and lovely to the touch.
I reach, I touch, I begin to know you.

DREAM-DRUMMING

I braced the drum to my arm, a flat drum, and began to play.
He heard me and she heard me.   I had never seen this drum before.
As I played, weakness went through me; weakness left me.
   I held my arms high, the drum and the soft-headed long stick
I drummed past my tiredness vibrating weakness, past it into music,
As in ragas past exhaustion into the country of all music.

Held my arms high, became that vibration, drummed the sacrifice of my belly.
He heard me, she heard me,
I turned into the infinity figure, reaching down into
 the earth of music with my legs at last,
Reaching up from the two circles, my pelvic sea,
 mountains and air of breast, with my arms up into music
At last turned into music, drumming on that possessed
 vibration,
Drumming my dream.

DOUBLE ODE

 for Bill & Alison

  1

Wine and oil gleaming within their heads,
I poured it into the hollow of their bodies
but they did not speak.   The light glittered.
Lit from underneath they were.   Water
pouring over her face, it
made the lips move and the eyes move, she
spoke:
Break open.
He did not speak.
A still lake shining in his head,
until I knew that the sun and the moon
stood in me with one light.

  2

They began to breathe and glitter.   Morning
overflowed, gifts poured from their sex
upon my throat and my breast.

They knew. They laughed. In their tremendous games
night revolved and shook my bed. I
woke in a cold morning.
Your presences
allow me to begin to make myself
carried on your shoulders, swayed in your arms.
Something is flashing among the colors. I
move without being allowed. I
move with the blessing of the sky and the sea.

3

Tonight I will try again for the music of truth
since this one and that one of mine are met with death.
It is a blind lottery, a cheap military trumpet
with all these great roots black under the earth
while a muscle-legged man
stamps in his red and gold
rough wine, creatures in nets, swords through their spines
and all their cantillation in our thought.

Glitter and pedestal under my female powers
a woman singing horses, blind cities of concrete, moon
comes to moonrise as a dark daughter.
I am the poet of the night of women
and my two parents are the sun and the moon,
a strong father of that black double likeness,
a bell kicking out of the bell-tower,
and a mother who shines and shines his light.

Who is the double ghost whose head is smoke?
Her thighs hold the wild infant, a trampled country
and I will fly in, in all my fears.
Those two have terrified me, but I live,
their silvery line of music gave me girlhood
and fierce male prowess and a woman's grave
eternal double music male and female,
inevitable blue, repeated evening
of the two. Of the two.

4

But these two figures are not the statues east and west
at my long window on the river they are mother and father

but not my actual parents only their memory.
Not memory but something builded in my cells

Father with your feet cut off
mother cut down to death
cut down my sister in the selfsame way
and my abandoned husband a madman of the sun
and you dark outlaw the other one when do we speak
The song flies out of all of you the song
starts in my body, the song
it is in my mouth, the song
it is on my teeth, the song
it is pouring the song
wine and lightning
the rivers coming to confluence
in me entire.

     5

But that was years ago.   My child is grown.
His wife and he in exile, that is, home,
longing for home, and I home, that is exile, the much-loved country
like the country called parents, much-loved that was, and exile.
His wife and he turning toward the thought
of their own child, conceive we say, a child.
Now rise in me the old dealings : father, mother,
not years ago, but in my last-night dream,
waking this morning, the two Mexican figures
black stone with their stone hollows I fill with water,
fill with wine, with oil, poems and lightning.
Black in morning dark, the sky going blue,
the river going blue.

Moving toward new form I am—
carry again
all the old gifts and wars.

     6

Black parental mysteries
groan and mingle in the night.
Something will be born of this.

Pay attention to what they tell you to forget
pay attention to what they tell you to forget
pay attention to what they tell you to forget

Farewell the madness of the guardians
the river, the window, they are the guardians,
there is no guardian, it is all built into me.

Do I move toward form, do I use all my fears?

PAINTERS

In the cave with a long-ago flare
a woman stands, her arm up. Red twig, black twig, brown twig.
A wall of leaping darkness over her.
The men are out hunting in the early light
But here in this flicker, one or two men, painting
and a woman among them.
Great living animals grow on the stone walls,
their pelts, their eyes, their sex, their hearts,
and the cave-painters touch them with life, red, brown, black,
a woman among them, painting.

RUNE

The word in the bread feeds me,
The word in the moon leads me,
The word in the seed breeds me,
The word in the child needs me.

The word in the sand builds me,
The word in the fruit fills me,
The word in the body mills me,
The word in the war kills me.

The word in the man takes me,
The word in the storm shakes me,
The word in the work makes me,

The word in the woman rakes me,
The word in the word wakes me.

HOW WE DID IT

We all traveled into that big room,
some from very far away
we smiled at some we knew
we did not as we talked agree
our hearts went fast thinking of morning
when we would walk along the path.
We spoke. Late night. We disagreed.
We knew we would climb the Senate steps.
We knew we would present our claim
we would demand : be strong now : end the war.
How would we do it?   What would we ask?
"We will be warned," one said. "They will warn us and take us."
"We can speak and walk away."
"We can lie down as if in mourning."
"We can lie down as a way of speech,
speaking of all the dead in Asia."
Then Eqbal said, "We are not at this moment
a revolutionary group, we are
a group of dissenters.   Let some, then,
walk away, let some stand until they want to leave,
let some lie down and let some be arrested.   Some of us.
Let each do what he feels at that moment
tomorrow."   Eqbal's dark face.
The doctor spoke, of friendships made in jail.
We looked into each other's eyes
and went all to our rooms, to sleep,
waiting for morning.

ISLANDS

O for God's sake
they are connected
underneath

They look at each other
across the glittering sea
some keep a low profile

Some are cliffs
The bathers think
islands are separate like them

BLUE SPRUCE

Of all green trees, I love a nevergreen
blue among dark blue, these almost black
needles guarded the door there was, years
before the white guardians over Sète
. . . that's Sea France at the Sea Cemetery
near Spain where Valéry . . .
those short square Mediterranean
man and woman
couple at the black-cut shadow door
within the immense marine
glare of noon,
and on the beach
leaning from one strong hip
a bearded Poseidon
looking along the surface of the sea
father and husband there he stands
and an invisible woman him beside
blue-eyed   blue-haired   blue-shadowed
under the sun and the moon
they blaze upon us
and we   waiting   waiting
swim to the source
very blue   evening now deepening
needles of light   ever new
a tree of light   and a tree of darkness
blue spruce

ARTIFACT

When this hand is gone to earth,
this writing hand and the paper beneath it,
long gone, and the words on the paper forgotten,
and the breath that slowly curls around earth with
                              its old spoken words
gone into lives unborn and they too gone to earth—
and their memory, memory of any of these gone,
and all who remembered them absorbed in air and dirt,
words, earth, breeze over the oceans, all these now other,
there may as in the past be something left,
some artifact. This pen. Will it tell my? Will it tell our?
This thing made in bright metal by thousands unknown to me,
will it arrive with that unnameable wish to speak a music,
offering something out of all I moved among?
singing for others unknown a long-gone moment in old time sung?

                                  The pen—
will some broken pieces be assembled by women, by guessing men
(or future mutations, beings unnamed by us)—
can these dry pieces join? Again go bright? Speak to you then?

MS. LOT

Well, if he treats me like a young girl still,
That father of mine, and here's my sister
And we're still traveling into the hills—
But everyone on the road knows he offered us
To the Strangers when all they wanted was men,
And the cloud of smoke still over the twin cities
And mother a salt lick the animals come to—
Who's going to want me now?
Mother did not even know
She was not to turn around and look.
God spoke to Lot, my father.
She was hard of hearing. He knew that.
I don't believe he told her, anyway.
What kind of father is that, or husband?
He offered us to those men. They didn't want women.

Mother always used to say:
Some normal man will come along and need you.

BOYS IN THE BRANCHES

Blue in the green trees, what are they climbing?
And girls bringing water, what are they watering
With their buckets spilling the wet dark on dry ground?

And up the hill the concrete-mixers rolling
Owned by my father when I was the same youth
As these who are my students, boys in the branches,
Young women in the young trees.

The last few drops from the faucet, carried
To the tan crumbling earth.
The earth belongs to the authorities
Of this college, and the authorities
Have turned the water off, have they?

Ask the owners of colleges, who is in the trees?
Ask the owners of concrete-mixers, who is holding
This acre of city land against the concrete?
We know where the water is.

Blue green students in the branches
Defending the tree. The trees begin to shudder.
The concrete-mixers roll over exposed roots.

But isn't all this a romantic delusion?
You love the pouring of the city, don't you?
You need the buildings, don't you?
Sift the seeds. We need to sift the seeds.

We know where the water is.
They have turned the water off.
You don't want buildings not to be built, do you?
The blueprint lies on the flat-top desk.

The building now is two years built,
Most of the boys went off to war,
I don't teach there any more.

Here we go, swimming to civilization,
We who stand and water and sift the seeds,
My students saying their word, it flies behind what I hear in the air:
"Time is God's blood," Warren said.   Avra wrote:
"Forgive me, Mother.   I am alive."

SONG : LYING IN DAYLIGHT

Lying in daylight, in the strong
light of all our fantasies,
now touch speaking to touch, touch sees—
night and light, the darkness-stare,
your long look that pierces where
light never came till now—
moving is what we do,
moving we are, searching,
going high and underground,
rain behind rain pouring down,
river under river going
silence on silence
sound under sound.

HYPNOGOGIC FIGURE

A translation, from Gunnar Ekelöf

In woods you know stands the wonder-working madonna
You stub your foot on the plinth when you walk lost
    among trees
She looks like your small bronze bell, the one in the
    shape of
a little girl with a stand-up collar
But it is limitless and dark, of tarnished silver
When you crawl under her skirt, you will see the inside
but up there, the clapper is gone, nothing is hanging down;

bulging like Atreus' treasure-chamber, a great bell
Ask for her sons, there are many, X, Y and Z
You may find a door in the creases of underwear
and grope your way up along peculiar stairways
winding in precarious spirals like the climb up the tower at Pisa
You are dizzy already. The risers are irregular
Gravity works against the spiral and the balance
you thought built-in no longer functions, you stumble
Above the vault is her waist, you see it as her belt
from the inside, a shimmer of colors, yellow violet and blood-red
It is studded with square-cut stones rose-stones garnets
aquamarines and chrysolites and amethysts
Each stone is a chamber, a triangle pointing inward
along two sides are divans, the hypotenuse is the window
or a rectangle with three divans and a table in the middle
You can walk from room to room or take your ease
responding to color and your state of being. You can go all the way
You will still never get back. Your vision has changed.
I have been higher up—I could not see the heart
but saw the jewel on her breast like a rose-window shimmering
upon her breasts. Once I went higher up, once only:
in her Head. There was empty space. You floated in
                                        weightlessness.

THE LOST ROMANS

Where are they, not those young men, not those
                        young women
Who walked among the bullet-headed Romans with their
                        roads, their symmetry, their iron rule—
We know the dust and bones they are gone to, those
                        young Romans
Who stood against the bitter imperial, their young
                        green life with its poems—
Where are the poems made music against the purple
Setting their own purple up for a living sign,
Bright fire of some forgotten future against empire,
Their poems in the beautiful Roman tongue
Sex-songs, love-poems, freedom-songs?

Not only the young, but the old and in chains,
The slaves in their singing, the fierce northern
                                   gentle blond rhythms,
The Judean cantillations, lullabies of Carthage,
Gaul with her cries, all the young Roman rebels,
Where are their songs?   Who will unlock them,
Who will find them for us, in some undiscovered
                                   painted cave
For we need you, sisters, far brothers, poems
                                   of our lost Rome.

CANAL

Sea-shouldering Ithaca
staring past sunset
after the islands
darkening   closing
The narrow night. We
came in from Ithaca
into the inland
narrow water
trying to keep awake
while the ship went forward
but sleep came down
shouldering
down like Ithaca.
Night smites, light smites
and again light
in a narrow place
of old whiteness.
We are in
the narrowest place
moving in still
through an ash-white canal
a whitened plant
grappled to this wall
deep-cut, Judean slaves
cut the narrowest place
the ship fares into,
light smites again

the olive-plant in the crevice
captained through light.

FOR KAY BOYLE

What is the skill of this waking?   Heard the singing
of that man rambling up Frederick Street in music
and his repeated ecstasy, in a long shaken line.

After many and many a February storm, cyclamen
and many a curtain of rain, the tearing of all curtains
and, as you said, making love and facing the police

in one afternoon.   A few bright colors in permanent ink:
black sea, light like streetlight green, blue sees in you
the sun and the moon that stand as your guardians.

And the young bearded rebels and students tearing it all away,
all of it, down to the truth that barefaced naked act of
light, streamings of the courage of the sources,
the sun and the moon that stand at your ears.

RESURRECTION OF THE RIGHT SIDE

When the half-body dies its frightful death
forked pain, infection of snakes, lightning, pull down the
    voice. Waking
and I begin to climb the mountain on my mouth,
word by stammer, walk stammered, the lurching deck of earth.
Left-right with none of my own rhythms
the long-established sex and poetry.
                                        I go running in sleep,
but waking stumble down corridors of self, all rhythms gone.

The broken movement of love   sex out of rhythm
one halted name   in a shattered language
ruin of French-blue lights behind the eyes
slowly the left hand extends a hundred feet

and the right hand follows follows
but still the power of sight is very weak
but I go rolling this ball of life, it rolls
and I follow it whole up the slowly-brightening slope

A whisper attempts me, I whisper without stammer
I walk the long hall to the time of a metronome
set by a child's gun-target   left-right
the power of eyesight is very slowly arriving
                in this late impossible daybreak
                all the blue flowers open

THE WARDS

St. George's Hospital, Hyde Park Corner

Lying in the moment, she climbs white snows;
At the foot of the bed the chart relates.
Here a man burns in fever; he is here, he is there,
Five thousand years ago in the cave country.
In this bed, I go wandering in Macao,
I run all night the black alleys. Time runs
Over the edge and all exists in all. We hold
All human history, all geography,
I cannot remember the word for what I need.
Our explorations, all at the precipice,
The night-table, a landscape of zebras,
Transistor constellations. All this music,
I heard it forming before I was born. I come
In this way, to the place.
                          Our selves lit clear,
This moment giving me necessity
Gives us ourselves and we risk everything,
Walking into our life.

THE SUN-ARTIST

for Bob Miller

1

The opening of the doors.   Dark.
The opening of the large doors.
Out of the daylight and the scent of trees
and that lake where generations of swans
no longer move among children.   In a poisoned time.
But the bright-headed children move.
Dark, high, the beams of a huge building
exposed in the high dark air.
I see brightness with a shock of joy.

2

Past the darkness a lashing of color.
Not color, strands of light.
Not light but pure deep color beyond color,
like the pure fierce light I once knew, before
a minute of blindness.   These colors are deeper;
the entire range in its millions,
twisting and brilliant traveling.

3

I stand in the strong sun before a bank of prisms.
On the screen in front of me, tangled colors of light,
                              twined, intertwined.
A sensitive web of light changing, for the sun moves, the air moves.
The perceiver moves.
                    I dance my slow dance.

4

The deepest blue, green, not the streams of the sea,
the clear yellow of yellows, not California, more,
not Mediterranean, not the Judean steeps.   Red beyond
                              blood over flame,
more even than visionary America.   All light.
A man braced on the sun, where the sun enters
through the roof, where the sun-follower,
a man-made motor with a gentle motion
just counters the movement of the earth, holds this scene
in front of us on the man-made screen.
Light traveling, meets, leaps and becomes art.

5

Colors move on a screen. The doors open again.
They run in, the California children.
They run past the colors and the colors change.
The laughter of running. They cry out, bird-voices,
ninety-seven children, Wow! Wow! How come?

6

Another day. I stand before the screen,
Alone I move, selecting out my green,
choose out the red with my arm, I let the orange stand,
a web of yellow, the blue stays and shines.
I am part of the color, I am part of the sun.

7

You have made an art in which the sun is standing.
It changes, goes dark, goes grey. The sun appears.
You have led me through eleven states of being.
You have invited us all. Allow the sunlight,
dance your dance.

8

Another day. No sun. The fog is down,
Doing its slow dance into the city,
It enters the Gate and my waking.
There will be no colors but the range of white.
Before the screen, I wait.

9

Night. What do you know about the light?

10

Waiting. A good deal like real life.
Waiting before the sea for the fish to run
Waiting before the paper for the poem
Waiting for a man's life to be, to be.

11

Break of light! Sun in his colors,
streaming into our lives.
This artist dreams of the sun, the sun, the children of the sun.

12

Frail it is and can be intercepted.
Fragile, like ourselves.   Mirrors and prisms, they
                        can be broken.
Children shattered by anything.
Strong, pouring strong, wild as the power of the great sun.
Not art, but light.   In distance, in smiting winter,
the artist speaks : No art.
This is not art.
What is *an artist?*   I bear the song of the sun.

POEM   WHITE PAGE   WHITE PAGE   POEM

Poem   white page   white page   poem
something is streaming out of a body in waves
something is beginning from the fingertips
they are starting to declare for my whole life
all the despair and the making music
something like wave after wave
that breaks on a beach
something like bringing the entire life
to this moment
the small waves bringing themselves to white paper
something like light stands up and is alive

FABLE

   for Herbert Kohl

Yes it was the prince's kiss.
But the way was prepared for the prince.
It had to be.

When the attendants carrying the woman
—dead they thought her lying on the litter—
stumbled over the root of a tree
the bit of deathly apple in her throat
jolted free.

Not strangled, not poisoned!
She
can come alive.

It was an "accident" they hardly noticed.

The threshold here comes when they stumble.
The jolt. And better if we notice,
However, their noticing is not
Essential to the story.

A miracle has even deeper roots,
Something like error, some profound defeat.
Stumbled-over, the startle, the arousal,
Something never perceived till now, the taproot.

NERUDA, THE WINE

We are the seas through whom the great fish passed
And passes. He died in a moment of general dying.
Something was reborn. What was it, Pablo?
Something is being reborn : poems, death, ourselves,
The link deep in our peoples, the dead link in our dead regimes,
The last of our encounters transformed from the first
Long ago in Xavier's house, where you lay sick,
Speaking of poems, the sheet pushed away
Growth of beard pressing up, fierce grass, as you spoke.
And that last moment in the hall of students,
Speaking at last of Spain, that core of all our lives,
The long defeat that brings us what we know.
Meaning, poems, lifelong in loss and presence passing forever.
I spilled the wine at the table
And you, Pablo, dipped your finger in it and marked my forehead.
Words, blood, rivers, cities, days. I go, a woman signed by you—
The poems of the wine.

BEFORE DANGER

There were poems all over Broadway that morning.
Blowing across traffic. Against the legs.
Held for a moment on the backs of hands.
Drifts of poems in doorways.
The crowd was a river to the highest tower
all the way down that avenue.
Snow on that river, torn paper
of their faces.

Late at night, in a dark-blue sleep,
the paper stopped blowing.
Lightning struck at me from behind my eyes.

SONG : REMEMBERING MOVIES

remembering movies   love
remembering songs
remembering the scenes and flashes of your life
given to me as we lay dreaming
giving dreams
in the sharp flashes of light
raining from the scenes of your life
the faithless stories, adventures, discovery
sexuality opening range after range
and the sharp music driven forever into my life
I sing the movies of your life
the sequences cut in rhythms of collision
rhythms of linkage, love,
I sing the songs

WORK, FOR THE DAY IS COMING

It is the poem, yes
that it exist   that it grow in reach
that it grow into lives not yet born not yet speaking.
That its sounds move with the grace of meaning

the liquid sharing, the abrupt clash of lives.
That its suggestions climb to
    descend to   the fire of finding
        the last breath of the poem
          and further.
For that I move through states of being,
the struggle to wake, the frightful morning,
the flash of ecstasy among our mutilations,
the recognizing light   shining   and all night long
am invited led whipped dragged through states of being
toward the
        inviting you through states of being

                    poem.

RECOVERING

Dream of the world
speaking to me.

The dream of the dead
acted out in me.

The fathers shouting
across their blue gulf.

A storm in each word,
an incomplete universe.

Lightning in brain,
slow-time recovery.

In the light of October
things emerge clear.

The force of looking
returns to my eyes.

Darkness arrives
splitting the mind open.

Something again
is beginning to be born.

A dance is
dancing me.

I wake in the dark.

PARALLEL INVENTION

We in our season like progress and inventions.
The inventor is really the invention.
But who made the inventions?   To what uses
Were they put, by whom, and for what purposes?

You made an innovation and then
did you give it to me without writing it down?
Did you give it to her, too?
Did I develop it and give it to him,
or to her, or to them?

Did you quicken communication,
Did you central-control?   And war?   And the soul?

Let's not talk about communication
any more.

Did we deepen our integration ties
did we subsequently grow—
in strength?   in complexity?

Or did we think of doing the same things
at the same time and do them to each other?

And then out of our lovemaking
emergence of priests and kings,
out of our smiles and twists
full-time craft specialists,
out of our mouths and asses
division into social classes,

art and architecture and writing
from meditation and delighting
from our terrors and our pities
"of course," you say, "the growth of cities."

But parallels do not imply
identities—there is no iron law;
we are richly variable
levels of heaven and levels of hell;
ripples of change out from the center
of me, of you, of love the inventor.

POEM

Green going through the jungle of those years
I see the brilliant bodies of the invaders
And the birds cry in the high trees, the sky
Flashes above me in bright crevices; time is,
And I go on and the birds fly blurred
And I pass, my eyes seeing through corpses of dead cells
Glassy, a world hardening with my hardening eyes
My look is through the corpses of all the living
Men and women who stood with me and died before
But my young look still blazes from my changing
Eyes and the jungle asserts fiery green
Even though the trees are the trees of home
And we look out of eyes filled with dead cells
See through these hours, faces of what we are.

NOT TO BE PRINTED, NOT TO BE SAID, NOT TO BE THOUGHT

I'd rather be Muriel
than be dead and be Ariel.

BACK TOOTH

My large back tooth, without a mate for years,
at last has been given one. The dentist ground her down
a bit. She had been growing wild, nothing to meet her, keep her sane.
Now she fits the new one, they work together, sleep together,
she is a little diminished but functioning, all night all day.

DESTRUCTION OF GRIEF

Today I asked Aileen
at the Film Library to help me find
those girl twins of the long-gone summer.
Aileen, who were they?
I was seven, the lion circus
was pitched in the field of sand and swordgrass
near the ocean, behind the Tackapoosha Garage.
The ancient land of the Waramaug Indians.
Now there's a summer hotel.
The first day of that circus dazzles me forever.
I stayed. That evening
the police came looking for me.
Easy to find, behind
the bales of hay, with Caesar's tamer,
the clowns, and the girl twins.
My father and mother forgave me, for they loved
circuses, opera, carnivals, New York, popular songs.
All day that summer, all July and August,
I stayed behind the tents with the twin girls,
with Caesar the lion my friend,
with the lion-tamer.
Do you know their names, Aileen?
The girls went into the early movies.
Late August, Caesar mauled the man's right hand.
I want to remember the names of those twins.
You could see he would not ever keep his hand.
Smell of the ocean, straw,
lordly animal rankness, gunpowder.
"Yes, they destroyed Caesar," I was told that night.
Those twins became movie stars.

Those of us who were there that summer—
Joey killed himself, I saw Tommy
just before the war; is Henry around?
Helene is in real estate—and the twins—
can you tell me their names, Aileen?

TRINITY CHURCHYARD

for my mother & her ancestor, Akiba

Wherever I walked I went green among young growing
Along the same song, Mother, even along this grass
Where, Mother, tombstones stand each in its pail of shade
In Trinity yard where you at lunchtime came
As a young workingwoman, Mother, bunches of your days, grapes
Pressing your life into mine, Mother,
And I never cared for these tombs and graves
But they are your book-keeper hours.

You said to me summers later, deep in your shiniest car
As a different woman, Mother, and I your poem-making daughter—
"Each evening after I worked all day for the lock-people
"I wished under a green sky on the young evening star—
"What did I wish for?" What did you wish for, Mother?
"I wished for a man, of course, anywhere in my world,
"And there was Trinity graveyard and the tall New York steeples."

Wherever I go, Mother, I stay away from graves
But they turn everywhere in the turning world; now,
Mother Rachel's, on the road from Jerusalem.
And mine is somewhere turning unprepared
In the earth or among the whirling air.
My workingwoman mother is saying to me, Girl—
Years before her rich needy unreal years—
Whatever work you do, always make sure
You can go walking, not like me, shut in your hours.

Mother I walk, going even here in green Galilee
Where our ancestor, Akiba, resisted Rome,
Singing forever for the Song of Songs
Even in torture knowing. Mother, I walk, this blue,
The Sea, Mother, this hillside, to his great white stone.

And again here in New York later I come alone
To you, Mother, I walk, making our poems.

BURNISHING, OAKLAND

Near the waterfront
mouth of a wide shed   open
many-shining bronze flat
ship-propellors hanging in air
propellors lying blunt on ground
The vast sound and shine
screaming its word

One man masked
holding a heavy weight
on the end of a weighted boom
counterbalanced
I see him draw
his burnisher
along the bronze
high scream of burnishing
a path of brightness

Outside, the prowl cars
Oakland police
cruising past
behind them the trailing
Panther cars
to witness to
any encounter

Statement of light
I see as we drive past
act of light
among sleeping houses
in our need
the dark people

Behind my head
the shoulders of hills

and the dark houses.
Here the shine, the singing cry
near the extreme
of the range of knowing
one masked man
working alone
burnishing

THE IRIS-EATERS

for John Cage

It was like everything else, like everything—
nothing at all like what they say it is.
The petals of iris were slightly cinnamon,
a smooth beard in the mouth
transforming to strong drink,
light violet turning purple in the throat
and flashed and went deep red
burning and burning.
Well, no, more an extreme warmth,
but we thought of burning,
we thought of poisons,
we thought of the closing of the throat
forever, of dying, of the end of song.
We were doing it, you understand,
for the first time.
You were the only one of us who knew
and you saved us, John,
with music, with a
         complex
                smile.

SLOW DEATH OF THE DRAGON

The sickness poured through the roads,
The vineyards shook.
A clot formed on the wild river.
The streets and squares were full of crevices.

Poison ran on the church-towers.
The olive trees!
He shook for thirty years,
Held his buttocks tense while his varnished officers
Broke thighs, broke fingers.
A man dies.
The genitals of the South are broken.
Venom pours
Into his provinces of pain.

The surgeons come.
Are there children left alive
Among his bones?   The drugs of choice are used,
Sleep-poison, torture-dream-drink, elixir of silence,
Rousing of memory : the inquisition.
Purgation of the future. "Cut off this lobe," they said.
"The heart is rejecting the present."   On the roads
The dead of the resistance tried to stand
Again, they tried to stand again.
But they were dead.

The surgeons are cutting out his words.
Too late; all the children are silent.
On the central plateau, snow is falling.
Incisions split the open country. On the coast of pain,
All craft becalmed. The surgeons are singing.
No, of course the dragon is not dead.
A branch of a tree is dead.
A generation is dead.
Most of the living are silent.
Prepare the ink on the rollers;
This has been a long time coming.
The posters carry one word:
Today!

Send the word underground, where water flows,
Clear, pure, black.
Is it beyond taint?
No, it is not beyond taint.
Certain women and men look at us out of their eyes.
Do they begin to speak
They have been speaking all along.

We can tell by their eyes,
Although their mouths are broken.
Now they are healing their mouths;
They have been speaking during all this dead lifetime.
Has the dragon died?
Something is beginning to be born,
But the seeds of the dragon are also growing in the fresh
    wombs of girls.
O love. Make the song start.

Summer 1936–Winter 1975

MENDINGS

for Alfred Marshak

You made healing as you wanted us to make bread and poems.
In your abrasive life of gifts,
In the little ravine telling the life of the future
When your science would be given to all,
A broken smile.
In the sun, speaking of the joining of nerve-endings,
Make the wounds part of the well body.
Make a healed life.
You shouted, waving your hand with the last phalange
Of the little finger missing, you whole man,
"Make it well!   Make things accessible!"
He is a pollinating man.   We are his seedlings.
Marshak, I was your broken nerve-endings,
You made your man-made bridges over the broken nerves.
What did you do?   Inspect potatoes, wait for passports, do your research,
While the State Department lady was saying, "Let him swim,"
While the chief who had the power to allow your uses
To move, a proper use of plastic, a bridge across broken nerves
Stopped you there (and asked me to marry him).
Saying to you, Marshak, full of creation as the time
Went deeper into war, and you to death:
"The war will be over before your work is ready."

THEN

When I am dead, even then,
I will still love you, I will wait in these poems,
When I am dead, even then
I am still listening to you.
I will still be making poems for you
out of silence;
silence will be falling into that silence,
it is building music.

❧2

THE GATES

Scaffolding.   *A poet is in solitary; the expectation is that he will be tried and summarily executed on a certain day in autumn. He has been on this cycle before : condemned to death, the sentence changed to life imprisonment, and then a pardon from his President during a time of many arrests and exe-cutions, a time of terror. The poet has written his stinging work—like that of Burns or Brecht—and it has got under the skin of the highest officials. He is Kim Chi Ha.*

An American woman is sent to make an appeal for the poet's life. She speaks to Cabinet ministers, the Cardinal, university people, writers, the poet's family and his infant son. She stands in the mud and rain at the prison gates—also the gates of perception, the gates of the body. She is before the house of the poet. He is in solitary.

1

Waiting to leave all day I hear the words;
That poet in prison, that poet newly-died
whose words we wear, reading, all of us.   I and my son.

All day we read the words:
friends, lovers, daughters, grandson,
and all night the distant loves
and I who had never seen him am drawn to him

Through acts, through poems,
through our closenesses—
whatever links us in our variousness;
across worlds, love and poems and justices
wishing to be born.

2

Walking the world to find the poet of these cries.
But this walking is flying the streets of all the air.

Walking the world, through the people at airports,
this city of hills, this island ocean fire-blue and now this city.

Walking this world is driving the roads of houses
endless tiles   houses, fast streams, now this child's house.

Walking under the sharp mountains through the sharp city
circled in time by rulers, their grip; the marvelous
hard-gripped people silent among their rulers, looking at me.

3 NEW FRIENDS

The new friend comes into my hotel room
smiling.   He does a curious thing.
He walks around the room, touching
all the pictures hanging on the wall.
One picture does not move.

A new friend assures me : Foreigners are safe,
You speak for writers, you are safe, he says.
There will be no car
driving up behind you, there will be
no accident, he says.   I know these accidents.
Nothing will follow you, he says.
O the Mafia at home, I know, Black Hand
of childhood, the death of Tresca whom I mourn,
the building of New York.   Many I know.
This morning I go early to see the Cardinal.
When I return, the new friend is waiting.   His face
wax-candle-pool-color, he saying
"I thought you were kidnapped."

A missionary comes to visit me.
Looks into my eyes.   Says,
"Turn on the music so we can talk."

4

The Cabinet minister speaks of liberation.
"Do you know how the Communists use this word?"
We all use the word.   Liberation.

No, but look—these are his diaries,
says the Cabinet minister.
These were found in the house of the poet.
Look, Liberation, Liberation, he is speaking in praise.

He says, this poet, It is not wrong
to take from the rich and give to the poor.

Yes.   He says it in prose speech, he says it in his plays,
he says it in his poems that bind me to him,
that bind his people and mine in these new ways
for the first time past strangeness and despisal.

It also means that you broke into his house and stole his papers.

5

Among the days,
among the nights of the poet in solitary,
a strong infant is just beginning to run.
I go up the stepping-stones
to where the young wife of the poet
stands holding the infant in her arms.
She weeps, she weeps.
But the poet's son looks at me
and the wife's mother looks at me with a keen look
across her grief.   Lights in the house, books making every wall
a wall of speech.
                    The clasp of the woman's hand
around my wrist, a keen band
more steel than the words
Save his life.

I feel that clasp on my bones.

A strong infant is beginning to run.

6 THE CHURCH OF GALILEE

As we climb to the church of Galilee
Three harsh men on the corner.
As we go to the worship-meeting of the dismissed,
three state police on the street.
As we all join at the place of the dispossessed,
three dark men asking their rote questions.
As we go ahead to stand with our new friends
that will be our friends our lifetime.
Introduced as dismissed from this faculty, this college,
this faculty, this university.
'Dismissed' is now an honorary degree.
The harsh police are everywhere,
they have hunted this fellowship away before
and they are everywhere, at the street-corner,
listening to all hymns,
standing before all doors,
hearing over all wires.
We go up to Galilee.
Let them listen to the dispossessed
and to all women and men who stand firm and sing
wanting a shared and honest lifetime.
Let them listen to Galilee.

7 THE DREAM OF GALILEE

That night, a flute
across the dark, the sound
opening times to me, a time
when I stood on the green hillside
before the great white stone.
Grave of my ancestor
Akiba at rest over Kinneret.
The holy poem, he said to me,
the Song of Songs always;
and know what I know, to love
your belief with all your life,
and resist the Romans, as I did,
even to the torture and beyond.
Over Kinneret, with all of them,
Jesus, all the Judeans,
that other Galilee
in dream across war I see.

8 MOTHER AS PITCHFORK

Woman seen as a slender instrument,
woman at vigil in the prison-yard,
woman seen as the fine tines of a pitchfork
that works hard, that is worn down, rusted down
to a fine sculpture standing in a yard
where her son's body is confined.
Woman as fine tines blazing against sunset,
wavering lines against yellow brightness
where her fine body becomes transparent in bravery,
where she will live and die as the tines of a pitchfork
that stands to us as her son's voice does stand
across the world speaking

The rumor comes that if this son is killed
this mother will kill herself

But she is here, she lives,
the slender tines of this pitchfork standing in flames of light.

9

You grief woman   you gave me a scarlet coverlet
thick-sown with all the flowers
and all the while your poet sleeps in stone

Grief woman, the waves of this coverlet,
roses of Asia,
they flicker soft and bright over my sleep

all night while the poet waits in solitary

All you vigil women, I start up in the night,
fling back this cover of red;
in long despair we work   write   speak   pray   call to others
Free our night   free our lives   free our poet

10

Air fills with fear and the kinds of fear:

The fear of the child among the tyrannical
unanswerable men and women, they dominate day and night.

Fear of the young lover in the huge rejection
ambush of sex and of imagination;
fear that the world will not allow your work.

Fear of the overarching wars and poverties,
the terrible exiles,
all bound by corruption until at last!   we speak!

And those at home in jail who protest the frightful war
and the beginning : The woman-guard says to me, Spread your cheeks,
the search begins and I begin to know.

And also at home the nameless multitude
of fears : fear in childbirth for the living child,
fear for the child deformed and loved, fear
among the surgeries that can cure her, fear
for the child's father, and for oneself, fear.
Fear of the cunt and cock in their terrible powers
and here a world away fear of the jailers' tortures
for we invent our fear and act it out
in ripping, in burning, in blood, in the terrible scream
and in tearing away every mouth that screams.

Giant fears : massacres, the butchered that across the fields of the world
lie screaming, and their screams are heard as silence.
O love, knowing your love across a world of fear,
I lie in a strange country, in pale yellow, swamp-green, woods
and a night of music while a poet lies in solitary
somewhere in a concrete cell.   Glare-lit, I hear,
without books, without pen and paper.
Does he draw a pencil out of his throat,
out of his veins, out of his sex?
There are cells all around him, emptied.
He can signal on these walls till he runs mad.
He is signalling to me across the night.

He is signalling.   Many of us speak,
we do teach each other, we do act through our fears.

Where is the world that will touch life to this prison?

We run through the night.   We are given his gifts.

11

Long ago, soon after my son's birth
—this scene comes in arousal with the sight of a strong child
just beginning to run—
when all life seemed prisoned off, because the father's other son
born three weeks before my child
had opened the world
that other son and his father closed the world—
in my fierce loneliness and fine well-being
torn apart but with my amazing child
I celebrated and grieved.
And before that baby
had ever started to begin to run
then Mary said,
smiling and looking out of her Irish eyes,
"Never mind, Muriel.
Life will come will come again
knocking and coughing and farting at your door."

12

For that I cannot name the names,
my child's own father, the flashing, the horseman,
the son of the poet—
for that he never told me another child was started,
to come to birth three weeks before my own.
Tragic timing that sets the hands of time.
O wind from our own coast, turning
around the turning world.

Wind from the continents, this other child,
child of this moment and this moment's poet.
Again I am struck nameless, unable to name,
and the axe-blows fall heavy heavy and sharp
and the moon strikes his white light down over the continents
on this strong infant and the heroic friends
silent in this terrifying moment under all moonlight,
all sunlight turning in all our unfree lands.
Name them, name them all, light of our own time.

13

Crucified child—is he crucified?   he is tortured,
kept away from his father, spiked on time,

crucified we say, cut off from the man
they want to kill—
he runs toward me in Asia, crying.
Flash gives me my own son strong and those years ago
cut off from his own father and running toward me
holding a strong flower.

Child of this moment, you are your father's child
wherever your father is prisoned, by what tyrannies
or jailed as my child's father
by his own fantasies—
child of the age running among the world,
standing among us who carry our own time.

14

So I became very dark very large
a silent woman this time given to speech
a woman of the river   of that song
and on the beach of the world in storm given
in long lightning seeing the rhyming of those scenes
that make our lives.
Anne Sexton the poet saying
ten days ago to that receptive friend,
the friend of the hand-held camera:
"Muriel is serene."
Am I that in their sight?
Word comes today of Anne's
of Anne's long-approaching
of Anne's over-riding over-falling
suicide. Speak for   sing for   pray for
everyone in solitary
every living life.

15

All day the rain
all day waiting within the prison gate
before another prison gate
The house of the poet
He is in there somewhere
among the muscular wardens
I have arrived at the house of the poet
in the mud in the interior music of all poems

and the grey rain of the world
whose gates do not open.
I stand, and for this religion and that religion
do not eat but remember all the things I know
and a strong infant beginning to run.
Nothing is happening.   Mud, silence, rain.

Near the end of the day
with the rain and the knowledge pulling at my legs
a movement behind me makes me move aside.
A bus full of people turns in the mud, drives to the gate.
The gate that never opens
opens at last.   Beyond it, slender
Chinese-red posts of the inner gates.
The gate of the house of the poet.

The bus is crowded, a rush-hour bus that waits.
Nobody moves.

"Who are these people?" I say.
How can these gates open?

My new friend has run up beside me.
He has been standing guard in the far corner.
"They are prisoners," he says, "brought here from trial.
Don't you see?   They are all tied together."

Fool that I am!   I had not seen the ropes,
down at their wrists in the crowded rush-hour bus.

The gates are open.   The prisoners go in.
The house of the poet who stays in solitary,
not allowed reading   not allowed writing
not allowed   his woman   his friends   his unknown friends
and the strong infant beginning to run.

We go down the prison hill.   On our right, sheds
full of people all leaning forward, blown on some ferry.
"They are the families of the prisoners.   Some can visit.
They are waiting for their numbers to be called."

How shall we venture home?
How shall we tell each other of the poet?
How can we meet the judgment on the poet,
or his execution?   How shall we free him?
How shall we speak to the infant beginning to run?
All those beginning to run?

Juvenilia

ANTIGONE

Faithful ever to thy brother,
Risking everything, e'en life,
Careless of the scorn of others,
Quelling all internal strife.

While in the bare cave around you,
Stood the somber shades of night,
Did you pray that Jove would save you,
Did you wish again for light?

Antigone! Through song and story
Lives your name and ever will,
While the sages, gray and hoary,
See the rock-cave on the hill.

When you died for Polynices,
To save him from endless shame,
Did you tear your soul in pieces,
Just to save your brother's name?

Faithful ever to thy brother,
Yes, you gave your all, your life,
Did not heed the scorn of others,
And you quelled the inward strife.

CITIES OF THE MORNING

This is the music of the cities of the morning:
Pounding of steel girders, clank of broken chains,
Cries of wordy prophets, shouting out a warning
To the silent, smiling watchers in the busy crowd;
Shouting out a warning to the new generations,
Bidding them look up, shoulder to the morning,
Brush back the clouds from the foreheads of the nations,
Beat their drums of challenge in the Eastern countries,
Stack up golden grain in the larders of the city.
Exploit the farmers, use all their produce,
Harry their homes and their land without pity . . . .

In one of the houses a woman is singing,
Singing this refrain to an infant in a cradle:
"—All the sons of morning to your hands are bringing
    Gifts of gold, and gifts of jewels, and their flags unfurled—
The journey's just started, the joy is yet yours,
    Gather the blossoms of the wide, wide world."
This is the music of the cities of the morning:
Pounding of the girders, rattling of trains,
Paeans of church organs, sound of children singing,
And the soft, sweet stillness of the glad refrains:
"All the sons of morning to our hands are bringing
Gifts of gold, and gifts of silver, and their flags unfurled—
The journey's just started, the joy is yet ours,
We'll gather the blossoms of the wide, wide world."

AUTUMN IN THE GARDEN

More lovely this,
With the pale dying flowers that fall and hide
The pebbles of the path,
Than the profusion of the budding Spring.

More holy this,
With the dim gentleness of failing winds,
Than any hour blessed
By sacral book and ritual-mouthing priest.

More fragrant this,
The sweet grass in a russet, sheltered place,
Than soothest incense borne
Aslant through dusky aisles in some rich shrine.

Less bitter this
Grape, whose blue globe you crush in plucking it,
Than witching honey-dew
Drunk by enchanters on Midsummer Eve.

More mellow these
Fugitive colors of an Autumn day,
With deeper reds and golds
Than dyers use to tinge their finest stuffs.

More happy I
In falling flowers, gentle winds, smooth grapes,
Than ever mortal was
In the bright plenty of budding spring.

THE BALLAD OF THE MISSING LINES

Eve walked in the Garden of a Sunday morning,

Sunlight was her kirtle and her book a rose—
Where was she going, down the aisle of trees so primly?
                No one knows.

Helen in her bower looked into her dressing-glass,
(Although of course the mirror was not invented yet,)
What did she think as she preened herself for Paris?
                The songs forget.

Vivien was subtle by the age-old oak tree,
But that Merlin the enchanter was her dupe, I doubt,
What did she do when he loosed the magic bondage?
                There are lines left out.

Isolt didn't worry if she'd make a good impression—
She was lovely in the daytime, she was charming in the dark—
We wonder how she looked when she woke up in the morning—
                The answer rests with Mark.

Rapunzel in her tower was a witch—well, a beauty,
She made of her tow-head a long and golden snare;
But the fairy-tales forget what she said to her Prince Charming
                The first time he tugged her hair.

Oh, the ladies of the romances were certainly alluring,
—No understanding reader entertains a single doubt—
But there must be more than one who'd be glad to get a glimpse of
                Just a few of the lines they left out.

NOVEMBER SKETCHES

1

The brown, dead leaves
Are a flock of birds that hovers listlessly
Above the City—a flock of swallows
Wheeling and pirouetting
In an antique dance.
A brown, torn garment
On the grey, still city.

2

The thin, black fingers of the ash-tree
Are combing the wind in her bereavement.
The ash-tree is a dark, lone widow
Searching the winds
For her husband, the Springtime.
Searching the winds with tremulous fingers,
And mourning in loneliness.

3

Come back to us, little grey sister,
Grey ghost of the birch-tree.
Come back to us,
Your elderly relations.
We are prim old great-aunts,
We the pine-trees,
And bearded uncles,
We the old oak-trees.
Your little brothers, the maples,
Weep for you.
Come back to us, little grey sister,
Pale little ghost of the birch-tree.

4

There was frost on my window
This morning.—A delicate stencil
Of silvery patterns,
Of deep-drooping willows,
And heavy, fantastic, the ferns
That were scattered over the sill.

—An age-honored sign of the Winter,
An infallible omen of Winter.

5

The moon is not a crescent
As in September, (it shone above the rose-bush)
Nor a great globe of false sunlight
As in mid-July.
It is only a half-moon,
Half-moon of November,
High over the City,
Waiting for Winter.

6

The wind is an insolent braggart
That is hushed for an instant
In touching with arrogant lips the dead face
Of his mother, the Earth.
And whispering sadly the old, old promise
Of resurrection.—
He has just come from kissing
The white shoulders of mountains,
And laughing and vowing
With a smile on his lips
The same promise of Springtime.
It is strange mockery that he should enter
The dark death-chamber
After revelry such as his.

7

No pagan gods are dancing in these fields,
But the wraith of Autumn,
The breath of Winter
Have made a rendez-vous in the orchard.
The fields
Are barren, and the young acacia-tree
Is numbed and frozen by the laugh of Death.
No pagan gods are dancing in November

8

These things are the heart of Autumn:
The fading of day,—

The mourning of all Nature—
A lighted window in the dreary darkness—
And the shallow laughter of heedless children
In the grey stone streets,
   After the flowers have withered.

TO A LADY TURNING MIDDLE-AGED

Two years ago,
Four years ago,
Eight years ago,
Your hands were not iris-veined,
And red, and growing shrivelled,
Your voice was never like it is today
When, after tea, you say harmonious nothings
In a strange tone.
That has none of its old timbre.
Two years ago,
Four years ago,
When middle age was but an ugly dream
As now your youth is but a sweet brief dream
You were still lovely.
Now you sit
In the clustering twilight, and sip tea
And wonder about things you never thought of
In the old days.
Of course, you may say now,
Shrugging your shoulders,
(Once narrow as a countess',)
"I have but grown mature,
This is all stupid—I am quite young yet."
But—
Two years ago,
Four years ago,
I never knew you to sit at windows
And watch the people passing in the street.
The other day you spoke about
The people and their faces,
And yet, three summers past,
You watched the lilacs in the little roadway,

And laughed, and sang gay songs
You may enjoy sitting there
By a narrow window
Looking down into a narrow street,
But you never used to like to sit there in the evening.
Two years ago,
Four years ago,
Eight years ago.

PLACE-POEMS: NEW YORK

O CITY

City,
O my delight! Nourishment to the fat,
Sword of abstraction killing the criers at the gate,
Flower of the world on a stem of wicked stone,
Call in the misted night, poem in monotone.
There is no standing above this city, no weeping Jesus
Pedestalled on tall cliffs above a sleeping town.
And the high world is made of white and shine and brown
(The people's maskings cemented straitly on them).
Sow the bridges, watch with smiling eyes,
the lines of pale lights bloom in the blue evenings.
(A man walks over the new bridge, feeling his weakness
and drops a penny into the sheer of blue space below,
and thinks during the long whistle of its fall:
          "Their power, their power, their power."

FOURTEENTH STREET

Oranges smell of the south. Chestnuts are warm. The paint
Savors and shines on the toys. The five-and-ten
Boxes so much color away from the mute faces
Serried outside. The subway swallows many. A few stand
To hear a shout that rises from the curb:
"Here, the world changes.—This is new, that one
Should stop on the street to cry a kind revolt
On the things that they tell us in chalk
Words set on blackboards for rows of years, that have won
Wars against gray uniforms and our own swordless tribes.
Here, my people, know yourselves: you are a beast that has foaled

A fabulous thing, a unicorn of truth at last, the Day has lit
The sky with a strange light, and your light part of it."
No prophecies, no useless diatribes.
A soap-box is like a coffin, or an altar.
The crowd bears on in the runnels of its knowing,
And the brave words like a branch in a strong water's flowing.
But they will hear, they will falter,
They quicken and turn, and the mute faces speak.

THE NEW SCHOOL FOR SOCIAL RESEARCH

St. Thomas' House: "And now I will believe;
Help Thou my unbelief." Let us prod the wounds
Of the poor with a gentle finger, but let us prod the wounds
We must know if they bleed in truth,
We must know—we must have the truth.
Let us be decorously Liberal, O Lord,
Let us look around us gravely and quietly
Never forgetting that we have Faith and Traditions.
Yes, we recant our Bourgeois Superstitions,
But let us conduct our Research Quietly.
O Lord, help the poor people.—Lord, look at Mexico,
Dear Lord, watch over them on the Lower East Side
And intercede for us if we go to war with China.
Dear Lord, we really are interested in social experiment,
And Russia, we know, is Stimulating and Large—
Dear Lord, watch over us—we are such Very Nice People.

SHERIDAN SQUARE CONVERSATION

Mr. T. S. Eliot knows the potency of music,
Mr. T. S. Eliot knows the impact of bright words—
He has forgotten the caked hands, the muscle-banded shoulders,
In loving sounds swift birds.

This year's winter closes down upon the Square
In a cry of wind and a burden of batting-snow—
A bricklayer stands, and plunges into the subway;
Shall we use him as symbol? No,

Let us be done with symbols, we who talk
Over the healthy wood of the tables here,
Let us take him and point him out to the others,
Might forget his fears,

Not with a shallow Whitman-ish acceptation,
Not for what he is, but for what he gives his years,
Mr. T. S. Eliot (whom we consider) would forget the desert,
Might forget his fears.

Carrying a hod beside this man. We might do better
Than sit here mouthing opinions, by carrying a hod,
Raising a made thing high instead of a sentence,
Worshipping with this offering our literate god.

THE NEW BRIDGE

"Look," the city child said, "they have built over the river.
It is a lovely curve. But think what might be:
A circle on that arch would be really something to see:—"

The toll-taker heard, and grinned, and spat. "Lord, what a kid!
Like them all,—wants a good thing to go on and on forever.
Tell him he ought to be glad they made what they did."

Made what they did! . . . I saw the bridge built. One spring
A riveter stood high on the iron skeleton,
And the flakes of white fire fell and his hard face shone.

Men strung out cables. They were beautiful,
Cables and men, hard, polished, gleaming,—
The pride that the man-work should now prove fruitful!—

The states send automobiles over the Hudson River.
A man stands on the abyss, dropping a penny down,
Breathlessly watching the rush. Stand. The light of the town

Shine down the Drive, and the grim towers of empire
Are bright, burst, to kindle the evening; the torches shiver,
Flaming high, whirling the city into one strong wind of fire.

PARK AVENUE

Idols of luxury,
Gogs, Magogs,—
"The place where bad women
Walk good dogs."
The dogs strut down
Park Avenue,

Their growls cultured,
Their blankets new,
Proud that their harness
Is well-shined.
They look well-dinnered
And well-wined.
They parley gravely
About the weather,
And never bother
To test their tether.
The wolfhounds amble,
The spaniels waddle
Each city pampers
Its special twaddle.

COLLEGE SPECIAL

Plush lines the metal train, making the steel
Furry and warm. And Araminta's mind
Is furry, as she paces the stone hall.
The flowers lie along her shoulder, breathing.
The pale young man trots dutifully beside.
The Terminal is smooth and proud and wide,
And a neat, painted sky roofs it down from the wind.
The tastes of earth grow blander here and thinned
as Araminta clicks along the tiling,
as Araminta buys her single ticket
From a face at a window, as Araminta walks
patiently and serenely to her train.
The young pale gentleman farewelled, she sits.
The engineer is hot; he grinds the butt at his heel.
The locomotive feels the sharp rebuke of steel on steel.

EMPIRE STATE TOWER

The far lands melt to orange and to grey.
The city lies, quiet but for a rumor,
A single voice. People are guessed. We hazard
The world we know is there, below, unseen.
And in the street the many beautiful
Unstaring walk unwaiting the knives of doom
In sleep, or death, or love—the beautiful people
Setting up parapets against space and time,
like this one where small contact is forgotten.

Pitiable remove, that we should ask to go
Away from earth, from the nudge of other minds;
Clumsy abstraction, that human beings forego
For a short quiet the sight of their own kinds;
O strong unlove against our fellows here,
Never again set me so high, away
From action, pocketed in loneliness from fear,
And hurt, perhaps, but from the working-day.

[UNTITLED]

Dear place, sweet home.
I do not know the streets of London, the Parisian squares,
The Berlin parks, nor the far ways of Rome.
I do not know this city.
But I have seen
White mothers, and the bearded foreigners,
Workers with hands, and merchants of exchange,
Their places. My places: the broad avenues,
The rivers with their momentary changes,
Places housing the small and beautiful acts
That are accomplished, and the ugly facts. My people, these,
who may disown me even against my wish,
the people of my birth.
City   city   city
O my delight
New York.

FOR AN AESTHETE

You would have loveliness in a cup and spoon,
Fragile and brittle, perishable fine,
Given to you by useless, servile hands
In a politely appetizing manner.
You might, perhaps, pause in your languid way
To make some small remark about
Its smooth and tepid insipidity.
You will never feel the rush and surge of beauty
Upon your eyes and lips and throat, never rejoice
In the great loveliness that this earth holds,
In the white glory of a blinding patch of sunlight

Illuminating an unknown and hidden place,
Never exult in a triumph over land and sea and the angels,
Feeling the muscularity of all things,
Or hear the chorals of the wheeling stars.
You will only smile, and be bored, and cultivate
A way of walking and a dinner-pose,
And play with trifles of a flimsy wit,
Thinking its little candle-light to be
The flame that sears all things of earth away
And is the shadow of Eternity.
You will live, sipping tea, nibbling life,
Finding the sum of beauty in a cup
Given to you by the gracious, useless hands.

PASTORALE NO. 2

High wind, and spring restless in the ground.

> The earth is ribbed with water,
> vaulted with wind, peopled with motions
> of life rising in the times of the changing seasons.
> The sky blows blue and milky, March draws on
> multiplex in growth, and spring's green daughters,
> and strident with a high wind overriding rain.
> There will be new children to be born, new foison
> lifted from the creases of the ground.
> Spring lifts with a confused and shaking sound.
> Here is high wind, new spring consoling us,
> and an obscure deep restlessness in the ground.

1

The mountains rear, and are deathly terrifying,
    their names are trumpets in the lists of men—
    they rush up strenuously to the ghastly moon:
                      high,
and are unshaken by any sound of ours,
    resisting the nibbling picks that chip their ice,
    thunders, impregnable before the gales that race
                     (wind

tickling the cliffs of time), and the snow beats down
        in the season of snows, and the sun in another season,
        decay in autumn, and life bursting from prison
                and spring
when the cropped grass jostles around the stunted bush,
        and the rocks split with the sound of rippling husks,
        rivulets trickle cold down, trees green, life
                is restless
in new vigor, the brittle serpent renews itself, the fish
        makes curved sparkles leaping above the falls, death
        is given the lie once more, and life climbs
                in the ground.

2

Inverted torrents, fountains with strong trunks of water,
geysers that rush away from exhausted earth—
land straining away from matrix-land, gathering,
shouldering up, subsiding to our familiar hills.
Greenness rises from the soil, the shouts of waking
arrow straight to the sun, mountains assume new pride:
Everest, the Indian pinnacles, the Swiss magnificent Alps,
and the American clear heights rise and deride
conformity to earth's compulsion, the clay even bed,
flatness, quiescence—pulling, tugging up, straining to sky,
eager for the quick air, the moon's gleam, sun's red,
brave and presumptuous, captains of earth.   High.

3

A child is in the dark room where the dim lights swim,
reflected from the living street passing below, and alone.
And the grown people far, the few lights very dim,
nothing present in the room but the March wind's moan;
nothing by the bed but the rising screams of the wind,
piercing and bleak and cold—lowering to monotone.

In the corners of the world awaken the melted sleeping,
forged into a bar of hardness, stiffened against the cry
of the malevolent wind, bitterly creeping,
and there is no escape, no way to put it by—
music on the pipes of stone, a loud whine dripping
into the rooms of the sleeping from the black hell of sky.

And here, the child shudders against the blast,
and ribbons of sound tangle, and knot, and are thinned,
twine: and the hills shout, and the towers are cast
with a falling noise in unearthly seas; all life is pinned
against a bending pillar of sound, held fast,
transfixed to an embodied shrieking. Wind.

4

The light tumbles in cubes, boxes of light through my window,
there are sticks of pale light frozen on the floor—
outside, trees glisten with convalescent brightness,
the gleam in a healing sick man's face. (This winter tore
the woods with sleet, crumpled long branches, pricked the sky
with cold stars, slashed the clouds with a moon like a sickle,
in the almost artificial fury of a late season
hung every cornice with a fiercer icicle.)
March follows with a bubble of drenched ground,
washed hills, expanding earth—the massed stars sing,
we wait the blossom of the flowing fields
in tall grass mad with flowers. In new spring.

5

    Microscopically, the ground moves. Dark creases in the soil
    wrinkle a garden patch. The pale stems split.
    A bud bursts into locked small leaves in the sunlight.
    Evening quivers with strange light. The night is lit.
    Streams dive down the hillsides. Fat rivers hurtle
    through the mixed greens and duns of wilderness.
    Sap stirs in maples. Laden branches swing
    slowly with new motion. Moves new loveliness.
    Life crackles the husk of earth. And no more consciousless,
    the wet and growing soil quickens, sunned, restless.

6

Antaeus was once strong, when his feet, locked in earth,
made him firm and reliant. We wander and we fail,
Not for our wandering, but that we have denied.

The planter's hand in spring is red with clay.
Rubble avalanches deeply in quarried sand. Our land
is lined with the proud ores, and is fertile earth.

The younger beasts nuzzle gladly in grasses,
little snouted things root in the mud, are content,
and we have learned to straddle the winds, and leave earth.

O ground, O broken rock that makes us whole,
The unborn hills, the winds that flow in the fields,
black depths, and blinding heights, quiet and roll
of life in the moving soil, fall, winter, spring,
blithe summer—sudden stillness and brave sound,
cyclical growth, green life, eternal wave,
set our feet firmly on this mother-ground.

A New Poem

AN UNBORN POET

for Alice Walker

1

Early, before the reservoir,
driving up to a work day
you see the eleven trees
and put the poem aside
deep in the water. For the day.

But a word rings beside your cheek
all day long. A bone of the poem.

2

A young woman stands at the door of my small room,
a marvelous young woman, the daughter I never had,
no poems yet, only the digging questions
about the South, about love, about this moment.
The woman suffering the hurt of her parents.
The blood of her hurt eye forever rising
a river in flood on the life of the girl,
a girl in the North shudders, collecting blankets,
collecting heat from where she can.

3

We look through our lives at each other
after the woman's conference, at the airport.
He sang to me (noises of the planes):
"I'm not a woman. And I don't write poems.
And I just. Don't. Know."

4

Peddler, drowned pier, birdcage—images
caught in your lens forever, Berenice.
You said, "I need a light
great as the sun. No. Greater than the sun."
You said, "I must invent: clothes, architecture,
a camera that is a room, the child of
camera obscura."
I went journeying in Baptista della Porta.
I went marketing on Sixth Avenue

and so we found the fish-head, Berenice,
you turned his teeth to icicles,
and his great tongue—
I found the apple and the ear of corn.
Twelve huge lights went off blazing at my left eye.
Visionary lavender, flaming. Then lime-green burning. A vision of sight.
Then blindness. Blindness. Black, returning me to night.

 5

Working with these students. This
returns me to the poem, returns me
to other lives. The young woman
comes from the South, shivering, one perfect eye
one hurt eye, asking my friend her question:
"Can a black person love a white person?"
The beautiful man answers:
"In this world, it's very hard
for any one person to love any other person."

 6

I told myself coming after a long time to my poem,
to the songs of the bodies that I met, in sleep in waking
who are at last turning returning to this moment.
Zora, you looked at me
and asked me South on a journey I never went.
"If I go with you," I questioned in my white blackness
"Will I pass? How will I pass, Zora?"
"Honey," she said, "you travellin' with me,
don't worry, you passin'."

Alice, we're handed down.
Alice, there is a road of long descent.
Cold and shivering and something of ascent.

 7

Early, before the huge explosions,
Woman with her lens under the massive roadbed,
in the stillness speaks to me, "You feel it,
don't you? The entire city vibrating,
causing me to tremble,
causing my picture
and the world to tremble."

And now, Berenice,
I feel it and we feel it, huge,
My friends go to trial, Grace, Denise,
These energies speaking to us at last
for evil and for life.

8

To the poem. Alice, you left a sheet
of first working under the door of the small house.
Red leaves, Africa, the house itself, were here.
Pointing our eyes to poems,
never again to leave,
to hold to the poems,
hold to simplicities.
Alice, landscaper of grief, love, anger, bring me to birth,
bring back my poems. No. Bring me my next poem!
Here it is, to give to all of you.
To do what we mean, in poetry and sex,
to give each other what we really are.

End of a time of intercepted music.

✎ ABBREVIATIONS

The following abbreviations are used throughout the annotations and textual notes.

29P	*29 Poems*
B	Berg collection
BO	*Breaking Open*
BV	*Beast in View*
BW	*Body of Waking*
CP	*The Collected Poems* (1978)
E	*Elegies*
G	*The Gates*
GA	Galley
GW	*The Green Wave*
JB	*The Soul and Body of John Brown*
LCI	Library of Congress collection, part I
LCII	Library of Congress collection, part II
LP	*The Life of Poetry*
MS	Manuscript
NP	"Notes for a Preface"
O	*Orpheus*
OB	*The Outer Banks*
OL	*One Life*
P	"Preface to the Reader"
PP	Page Proof
S	*Selected Poems*
SD	*Speed of Darkness*
SP	*Selected Poems* typescript (TS) and page proofs (PP), identified by catalogue number
TF	*Theory of Flight*
TS	Typescript
TW	*A Turning Wind*

US1   *U.S. 1*
WF   *Waterlily Fire*
WI   *Wake Island*
WLR   William L. Rukeyser personal collection

ANNOTATIONS

Collected Poems. *New York: McGraw-Hill, 1978.*

Rukeyser's "Preface to the Reader," written for her 1978 *Collected Poems,* was signed "Muriel Rukeyser, New York":

"All the poems" is a very curious idea. Here you have a book that is like a film strip of a life in poetry: like that idea in Asia of the long body, the person seen as big-headed infant, then as reaching adolescent, then as fuller young woman, mature grown one, mother, desperate in other ways, hopeful in other ways, and so on into older life. The *Collected Poems* shows the movement of phases, too. Here are the early lyrics and two kinds of reaching in poetry, one based on the document, the evidence itself; the other kind informed by the unverifiable fact, as in sex, dream, the parts of life in which we dive deep and sometimes—with strength of expression and skill and luck—reach that place where things are shared and we all recognize the secrets.

Underneath all, the experience itself—a trust in the rhythms of experience.

When I began to read, I loved the collected poems I found—they invited me through the poems of all the years of a loved poet. There were two differences then from today's books: the poets were all dead, and all were men.

It never occurred to me that my poems would be collected until after my lifetime. The big books of my childhood were gathered from those published by one firm. My books have been issued by many publishers: I seem promiscuous, and this is chiefly because of the wanderings of my editors, as they moved from house to house. My present publisher, McGraw-Hill, is a small experimental press as far as poetry is concerned, but a great vast publishing house of science; and I care very much about that meeting-place, of science and poetry.

In this book, all the poems are included; only the translations have been removed. The text is left as it was. It seems to me that the perseverance of certain meanings and certain rhythms can be followed here, and also the changes of perception as a life and life-work go on, can be seen.

As I read the poems in preparation for you, I saw many cuts I wanted to make; many of the large castings-forth of childhood and youth I have wanted rewritten or left out, but this is the truth of how the poems stand and how things formed for me. I do not wish to lie; many references are here without names, so as not to hurt the living and not to intrude a kind of slang of fact into poems.

That slang is a trap of the documentary. For example, fliers do not call out "Contact!" now that planes have self-starters; but "Contact!" was the truth of that moment, and of the relation between flier and groundman. It is that toward which my poems are reaching; and I believe that poetry can extend the document. Today, too, I would change the title "Three Negresses" to "Three Black Women" in our usage and I would bring "fine black mouth" to the truer colors of nature.

I have rectified two or three titles to those titles I have used in reading the poems to audiences.

Only the translations have been taken out; and it now seems to me . . . might it not be that poetry and indeed all speech are a translation? This translation, this music, speaks to our silence. It in my childhood did, and ever since. I hope these may speak to yours, as my silence goes on speaking.

Theory of Flight. New Haven: Yale University Press, 1935.

Rukeyser's original dedication read: "I wish here to thank Horace and Marya Gregory, Nancy Naumburg, Stephen Vincent Benet, Elizabeth Ames, Henry Fuller, Flora Rosenmeyer, and my parents, Lawrence and Myra Rukeyser.

Rukeyser's original acknowledgments read:

Some of these poems have appeared in *Poetry, Dynamo, New Republic, New Masses, Herald-Tribune Books, The Magazine, Partisan Review, Housatonic, Trend, Vassar Review, Trial Balances, Student Outlook, Con Spirito, Kosmos, Alcestis, Student Review, Smoke,* and *Westminster Review.*

Stephen Vincent Benet wrote the following foreword to the 1935 Yale Series of Younger Poets edition of *Theory of Flight:*

Some people are born with their craft already in their hand, and, from her first book, Miss Rukeyser seems to be one of these. There is little of the uncertainty, the fumbling, the innocently direct imitation of admirations which one unconsciously associates with a first book of verse. It is, some of it, work in a method, but the method is handled maturely and the occasional uncertainties are rather from experimentation than any technical insufficiency. Moreover, there is a great deal of power—a remarkable power for twenty-one. I don't know quite what Miss Rukeyser will do with the future but she certainly will be a writer. It sticks out all over the book.

Politically, she is a Left Winger and a revolutionary. She speaks for her part of the generation born "in Prinzip's year" that found the world they grew up in too bitterly tainted by that year to accept.

> We focus on our times, destroying you, fathers
> in the long ground—you have given strange birth
> to us who turn against you in our blood,

she says in "The Blood Is Justified" and again

> I do not say : Forgive, to my kindred dead,
> only : Understand my treason, See I betray you kissing,
> I overthrow your milestones weeping among your tombs.

I do not intend to add, in this preface, to the dreary and unreal discussion about unconscious fascists, conscious proletarians, and other figures of straw which has afflicted recent criticism with head noises and small specks in front of the eyes. But I will remark that when Miss Rukeyser speaks her politics—and she speaks with sincerity and fire—she does so like a poet, not like a slightly worn phonograph record, and she does so in poetic terms. For evidence, I offer the section "The Lynchings of Jesus" in the long poem "Theory of Flight"; the short "shot" of the coal-mine in the elegy for Ruth Lehman and the poem "The Blood Is Justified," among others. They are worth reading, to see what a young and talented person thinks of certain contemporary things—and how a poet of talent can make poetry out of them.

I use the word "shot" advisedly—for the mind behind these poems is an urban and a modern one. It has fed on the quick jerk of the news-reel, the hard lights in the sky, the long deserted night-street, the take-off of the plane from the ground. It knows nature as well—the look of landscape, the quietness of hills. But its experience has been largely an urban experience, and it is interesting to see the poetry of youth so based. When Miss

Rukeyser thinks of energy, she thinks of a dynamo rather than a river, an electric spark rather than a trampling hoof—and that is interesting, too.

Perhaps that makes her verse sound like verse of the "Oh, Grandmother Dynamo, what great big wheels you have!" school—and that, most decidedly, it is not. Witness "Song for Dead Children," "Breathing Landscape," and the beautiful and original "Thousands of Days," with its serene and successful assonance. She can write powerfully; she can also write delicately, to a new and light-footed pattern. Her technique is sure, and is developing in original directions. Her long poem, "Theory of Flight," is a rather unusual achievement for a girl in her twenties. It has passages of confusion and journalistic passages, it also has passages that remind one of structural steel. There is a largeness of attempt about it which is one of the surest signs of genuine ability. Her later lyrics, particularly the ones I have mentioned, are more successfully and surely integrated. But only an original mind could have accomplished both.

Miss Rukeyser is twenty-one. She was born and brought up in New York City and has attended Vassar, the Columbia Summer School, and the Roosevelt School of the Air (the latter to gather material for "Theory of Flight"). At present, she is on the staff of "New Theatre." I think we may expect a good deal from her in the future. And it would seem to me that in this first book she displays an accomplishment which ranks her among the most interesting and individual of our younger poets.

Rukeyser addressed the title and themes of TOF in a letter of June 23, 1978, to translator Jan Berg: "The Roosevelt School of Air was the flying school in New York, connected with Roosevelt Field on Long Island. I could not get my parents' permission to study or fly, and I was a minor, so I worked in the school's office . . . in exchange for my tuition at ground school. The first part of the mechanics' course was called *Theory of Flight*, the title of my first book. It was a period of radial engines, cowlings, and the cry of "Contact" when the starter took hold. The hope of young mechanics was that there would be mechanical islands at two or three points in the Atlantic to allow for refueling of heavy cargo planes. This was several years after Lindbergh. To me, the image of flight and return to ground was extremely important, particularly in relation to freedom and heresy and to what I felt to be their ancestors and their rhythms" (LCII).

Poem Out of Childhood

I

Not Angles, angels: According to legend, the young Pope Gregory (590–604), when told that the fair-haired young boys he saw being sold as slaves in Britain were called "Angles," responded, *"Non Angli, sed angeli"* (Not Angles, angels).

while the syphilitic woman turned her mouldered face / intruding upon Brahms: In 1933, the year of his centenary, the work of composer Johannes Brahms (1833–1897) was being celebrated with frequent performances. Brahms became lovers with Clara Schumann, widow of his mentor Richard Schumann, after Schumann's death by syphilis.

Loeb and Leopold: In June 1924, teenagers Richard Loeb and Nathan Leopold were tried and convicted of kidnapping and murdering fourteen-year-old Bobby Franks just to see if they could commit the "perfect crime." Author Kevin Tierney suggests: "Inevitably Leopold and Loeb were regarded as examples of a golden generation gone wrong, symbols of a postwar emancipation that was both envied and feared by their elders" (328).

Not Sappho, Sacco: As an indication of Rukeyser's longstanding interest in Sacco, see Daniel Gabriel's narrative long poem, *Sacco and Vanzetti,* which has a foreword by Muriel Rukeyser. Also see Rukeyser's essay, "The Flown Arrow: The Aftermath of the Sacco-Vanzetti Case."

2

Prinzip: Gavrilo Princip (alternate spelling), the Serbian nationalist who assassinated Archduke Franz Ferdinand and his wife on June 28, 1914. Though Rukeyser was actually born in 1913, having been born in December of that year, she often viewed herself as more connected, by birth, to the following year, as illustrated in the poem, "Born in December" (BW).

playing in sandboxes to escape paralysis: A common belief at the time of Rukeyser's childhood was that plenty of outdoor play would deter the chances of a young child contracting polio.

Allies Advance, we see, / Six Miles South to Soissons: the first newspaper headline that the young poet was able to read on her own (see LP 206). The Allies' advance to Soissons took place in the summer of 1918. Rukeyser would have been younger than five years old at the time.

watching / the music and the shoulders and how the war was over: One of the first public events the young Rukeyser remembered from her childhood was the announcement of the end of World War I on November 7, 1918— eleven days before the actual armistice occurred (LP 190).

In a Dark House

Both of the lines annotated below are engraved on the facade of the New York Public Library, a location Rukeyser describes further in the poem, e.g., "the bird-marked stones" and "shallow-carven letters". In TF and CP, Rukeyser indicated the allusion with an asterisk next to each of these lines, and a footnote that read simply "New York Public Library."

Beauty Old Yet Ever New: from John Greenleaf Whittier's "The Shadow and the Light," stanza 21.

But Of All Things Truth Beareth Away / The Victory: From the Apocrypha, 1 Esdras 3:12.

Notes for a Poem

A close reading of this poem suggests that Rukeyser is beginning her work in these "notes" for her great long poem "The Book of the Dead" (US1). The first line, "Here are the long fields inviolate of thought" echoes in the first line of the later poem, where she expresses a similar desire to geographically locate the poem: "These are roads to take when you think of your country".

Place-Rituals

Tradition of This Acre

Semiramis: Early Assyrian/Babylonian Queen, commonly associated with the beginnings of goddess worship.

Wooden Spring

How horrible late spring is, with the full death of the frozen tight bulbs and **The ghosts swim, lipless, eyeless, upward:** These images recall key attitudes and images in "The Burial of the Dead" section of T. S. Eliot's "The Wasteland"— "April is the cruelest month, breeding / Lilacs out of the dead land" and "the drowned Phoenician Sailor / (Those are pearls that were his eyes. Look!)." Rukeyser seems to be, among other things, parodying Eliot's bleak vision of modernity—see, for example, her lines: "but we must strip nascent earth bare of green mystery. / Trees do not grow high as skyscrapers in my town".

Wedding Presents

2

Where'er you walk, cool gales will fan the glade / . . . trees, where you sit, will crowd into a shade: These lines are taken from Alexander Pope's, "Pastorals," (Summer, 73); they are also sung as part of Handel's opera, "Semele."

The Gyroscope

This poem is an early example of what became Rukeyser's lifelong interest in science and technology and her interest in fusing the exploration of scientific principles and inventions with emotional or psychological explorations (e.g., "All directions are *out*, / all desire turns outward").

The Lynchings of Jesus

2 The Committee-Room

Tom Mooney: (1882–1942) Socialist organizer and union activist who was convicted (and later pardoned) of murder as a result of a bomb explosion at a San Francisco parade in 1916. Mooney's initial death sentence resulted in years of agitation and protest by his political supporters.

Hilliard: According to a report titled *Thirty Years of Lynching in the United States, 1889–1918*, published by the NAACP (New York, 1919), a Henry Hilliard was murdered by lynching in Tyler, Smith County, Texas on October 29, 1895 (96). The details of the lynching represented in this poem seem, in fact, to be from those of a Robert Henson Hilliard, whose lynching in Tyler, Texas in 1897 was described in the same NAACP report. Rukeyser has notes from this report among her papers in LC1, which quotes from a traveling exhibition about Robert Henson Hilliard's lynching advertised in a poster produced by the Breckinridge-Suggs Company. It announces: "We have sixteen large views under powerful magnifying lens now on exhibition. These views are true to life and show the

Negro's attack, the scuffle, the murder, body as found, etc. With eight views of the trial and burning. . . . Don't fail to see this." The report of the crime, written by an eyewitness, is also recorded in the NAACP report. It documents that Hilliard's lower limbs "burned off before he lost consciousness and his body looked to be burned to the hollow. Was it decreed by an avenging God as well as an avenging people that his sufferings should be prolonged beyond the ordinary endurance of mortals?" (12).

3 The Trial

Godfrey's Jerusalem: The crusader Godfrey of Bouillon (1058–1100), regarded by some as the ideal Christian knight, assumed control of Jerusalem after conquering the city in 1099 and killing its Muslim and Jewish citizens.

Calas: (1698–1762) The French merchant whose execution for allegedly hanging his own son in retaliation for his son's conversion to Catholicism inspired the writer Voltaire to fight for religious tolerance within the French legal system.

Herndon: Angelo Herndon, a nineteen-year-old African American Communist, arrested in June 1932 for attempting to incite insurrection against the state of Georgia. He was convicted in 1934.

Nine dark boys: In March 1931, nine African American teenagers (ranging in age from thirteen to nineteen) were arrested in Scottsboro, Alabama, for allegedly raping two white women. In the subsequent trial, eight were convicted and given the death penalty and the ninth was convicted and sentenced to life in prison. What came to be known as the case of the "Scottsboro Boys" sparked international outrage as many believed that a racist social climate prevented any possibility of a fair trial. At the time of writing this poem, Rukeyser had already traveled to Alabama to cover one of the Scottsboro trials for the leftist student newspaper, *Student Review*. See Rukeyser's first-person narrative of attending the court hearings: "From Scottsboro to Decatur."

The Tunnel

2

tiger it may rage abroad: An allusion to "'Queen Mab: A Philosophical Poem. With Notes" by Percy Bysshe Shelley, which includes the lines, "And silent those sweet lips, / Once breathing eloquence / That might have soothed a tiger's rage".

dead and not yet arisen: An allusion to 1 Corinthians 15:15–23.

a bush upon a barren darkening plain: This may be a reference to the closing lines of Matthew Arnold's "Dover Beach" (1867), which read: "Nor certitude, nor peace, nor help for pain; / And we are here as on a darkling plain / Swept with confused alarms of struggle and flight, / Where ignorant armies clash by night."

Shall we losing our ego gain it: An allusion to Matthew 16:24–26.

dihedral: The angle between an airplane's wing and a horizontal line.

3

cowling: Metal cover of an airplane's engine.

The Structure of the Plane

1 The Structure of the Plane

Peter Ronsard: Pierre de Ronsard (1524–1585), celebrated French Renaissance poet who was recognized for adapting the sonnet form to the French language with great skill and beauty. One of his most famous sonnets is called "Roses," thus perhaps Rukeyser's phrase, "Peter Ronsard finger-deep in roses".

3 The Blood Is Justified

This section of TF both participates in and modifies the tradition of the pastoral elegy (e.g., Milton's "Lycidas"). Rukeyser dedicates "For Memory" to Ruth Lehman, a college friend who came from a wealthy family and dedicated herself to helping the poor and disenfranchised.

For Memory

Holy Dying

See "The Rules and Exercises of Holy Dying," by Jeremy Taylor (1613–1667).

Ritual for Death

See Sir James George Frazier's "The Ritual of Death and Resurrection" in *The Golden Bough,* chapter 64, section 7.

City of Monuments

This poem is inspired by the events surrounding the Bonus March of 1932, in which thousands of World War I veterans marched to Washington from all over the United States to demand their benefit pay. Veterans and their families camped out in the mud flats of Anacostia before being forcibly dispersed with sabers and tear gas under the order of President Hoover.

Citation for Horace Gregory

Horace Gregory: (1898–1982) Well-known American poet and critic; husband of poet Marya Zaturenska and friend and mentor of Rukeyser. Coauthor with Zaturenska of the significant critical work, *A History of American Poetry, 1900–1940* (1946). Rukeyser dedicated her second book, *U.S. 1,* to Gregory.

Cats and a Cock

Eleanor Clark: (1913–1996) Widely admired as a travel writer, Eleanor Clarke was also a reviewer, essayist, and novelist. As a young woman, she "became a conspicuous part of [New York] City's intellectual left, writing for *The Partisan Review, The New Republic,* and *The Nation*" (*New York Times* 19 Feb. 1996: B5). Clark and her older sister, Eunice, were good friends of Rukeyser's while they were at Vassar, and Rukeyser and Eleanor coedited a literary magazine called

Housatonic in the summer of 1932. Eleanor shared Rukeyser's political passions and participated with her in labor marches and protests held in Poughkeepsie and New York City.

Rosa Luxemburg: (1871–1919) Political thinker and revolutionary who contributed significantly to the development of Socialist, Marxist, and Communist discourse. She was killed in January 1919 because of her antiwar declarations, and her body was thrown into the Landwehr Canal.

The Blood Is Justified

Augusta Coller: Rukeyser's paternal grandmother who lived in Milwaukee, Wisconsin.

By these roads shall we come upon our country: This line clearly leads into the opening line of "The Book of the Dead" in Rukeyser's next book, *U.S. 1.*

U.S. 1. New York: Covici Friede, 1938.

Rukeyser's original dedication read: "for Horace Gregory."
Rukeyser's original acknowledgments read:

Some of these poems have been printed in *Poetry: A Magazine of Verse, Life and Letters To-Day, Forum, New Caravan, New Masses, Nation, New Republic, New Republic Anthology, Fiction Parade, Common Sense, Partisan Review* (1936), *Signatures, Transition, Best Poems of 1937,* and *New Letters in America.*

1 The Book of the Dead

Rukeyser provided the following endnote regarding "The Book of the Dead" at the end of *U.S. 1.* The note's reference to "a planned work, *U.S. 1.*" seems, on first reading, to be an error, appearing as it does at the back of *U.S. 1.* It is possible, however, that Rukeyser was working at this time toward a larger work that she intended to call, once again, *U.S. 1.* To date, the editors have not found any archival material to resolve this question.

"The Book of the Dead" will eventually be one part of a planned work, *U.S. 1.* This is to be a summary poem of the life of the Atlantic coast of this country, nourished by the communications which run down it. Gauley Bridge is inland, but it was created by theories, systems and workmen from many coastal sections—factors which are, in the end, not regional or national. Local images have one kind of reality. *U.S. 1* will, I hope, have that kind and another too. Poetry can extend the document.

The material in "The Book of the Dead" comes from many sources, the chief of which include:

An Investigation Relating to Health Conditions of Workers Employed in the Construction and Maintenance of Public Utilities. Hearings before a Subcommittee of the Committee of Labor, House of Representatives, Seventy-fourth Congress, Second Session, on H. J. Res. 449, January 16, 17, 20, 21, 22, 27, 28, 29 and February 4, 1936. United States Printing Office. Washington: 1936.

Congressional Record, Seventy-fourth Congress, Second Session, Washington, Wednesday, April 1, 1936.

Other documents, including the Egyptian *Book of the Dead* (in various translations), magazine and newspaper articles on Gauley Bridge, letters, and photographs.

I should like to thank Betty and George Marshall; Glenn Griswold, M.C., Fifth District, Indiana; Nancy Naumburg; Eunice Clark; the work of many investigators and writers, notably Philippa Allen; who made the poem possible.

"The Book of the Dead" focuses on what is now acknowledged to be one of the greatest American industrial tragedies: the building and mining of the Hawk's Nest Tunnel in Gauley Bridge, West Virginia, between March 1930 and December 1931 (see Cherniack, *The Hawk's Nest Incident*). Unsafe drilling conditions resulted in death by silicosis poisoning of many workers, the largest percentage of whom were African American migrant workers from the south. Rukeyser also published a filmscript treatment of this incident in *Films: A Quarterly Discussion and Analysis.*

Additionally, the following "Note to Gauley Bridge" (LCII) indicates that Rukeyser also developed a radio script based on the same events:

This is a documentary radio oratorio, based on materials in the U.S. Senate Hearings on the Gauley Bridge tunnel story, and on material known personally to the writer. It should be played as a Living Newspaper is, with a free, staccato movement, laced with music and sound effects.

In recent years, there has been intense scholarly interest in this poem. See essays by Stephanie Hartman, John Lowney, Leslie Ann Minot, and Shoshana Wechsler in Herzog and Kaufman, *"How Shall We Tell Each Other of the Poet?"* Also see: Dayton, *Muriel Rukeyser's The Book of the Dead;* Kadlec, "X-Ray Testimonials in Muriel Rukeyser"; Kalaidjian, "Muriel Rukeyser and the Poetics of Specific Critique"; Shulman, "Muriel Rukeyser's *The Book of the Dead*"; and Thurston, "Documentary Modernism as Popular Front Poetics."

The Road

the photographer: Rukeyser traveled to West Virginia with her photographer and Vassar College friend, Nancy Naumburg, who was interested in photography and later worked in film.

John Marshall: (1755–1835) Outdoorsman and the fourth chief justice of the United States Supreme Court.

West Virginia

Thomes Batts, Robert Fallam, Thomas Wood, the Indian Perecute: Rukeyser used Arthur Fallam's *A Journey from Virginia to Beyond the Appalachian Mountains* (1671) along with other materials she obtained through historical research to assist her in evoking the particulars of this geographical area. Batts, Fallam, and Wood were early English explorers of West Virginia. (Batts's first name appears to have been mistyped in the poem, appearing elsewhere in multiple published documents as "Thomas.") Fallam listed Penecute (note spelling difference from Rukeyser's usage), an Apomatack Indian, as the exploring party's guide.

Kanawha Falls: Part of the Kanawha or Great Kanawha River, located in west-central West Virginia, formed by the joining of the New and Gauley Rivers at Gauley Bridge.

Point Pleasant: West Virginia site of violent battle between settlers and American Indians in 1774.

Fort Henry: Built by the Confederate Army during the American Civil War, located on the banks of the Tennessee River.

Statement: Philippa Allen

Philippa Allen: Social worker who testified before Congress on January 16–17, 1936, as the first of twelve witnesses to speak on the Gauley Bridge incident (*Hearings on H. J. Res. 449* 2–33). See Rukeyser's note to "The Book of the Dead" (above) for her citation of the Congressional Hearings and recognition of Philippa Allen's investigation.

New Kanawha Power Co.: Union Carbide formed the New Kanawha Power Company in 1927 for oversight of a number of its New River projects dedicated to hydroelectric power generation. See Cherniack, *The Hawk's Nest Incident.*

Vanetta: West Virginian coal mining town in existence until approximately 1925; it was located approximately forty miles from Charleston. The migrant black workers recruited for the Gauley Bridge project lived predominantly in Vanetta.

George Robinson: Blues

The character of George Robinson is based on the real life George Robison (Rukeyser altered the spelling of his name) who testified as one of the miners in the abovementioned Congressional Hearings on January 20, 1936 (*Hearings on H. J. Res. 449* 66–74). Rukeyser intended the poem to be "a free fantasy on the blues form." Asked how her poem is connected to social justice and equality, she stated: "George Robinson was a real man to me. He speaks for a great many things—not only the dust—much more for the men, and the women and children behind them. It seems to me that social justice comes in here as a matter of what is happening to lives—the way in which horizons are opened up, the way in which they are thrown away" (Interview by Dr. Harry T. Moore 130–31).

Juanita Tinsley

Juanita Tinsley: Local Gauley Bridge social worker who was active in the local defense committee (see Nelson 669).

The Cornfield

Heaven's My Destination: Thornton Wilder novel published in 1935, contemporaneous to the Hawk's Nest Tunnel incident.

Arthur Peyton

Arthur Peyton: Silicosis-afflicted engineer who testified in support of the miners on January 20, 1936 (*Hearings on H. J. Res. 449* 53–66).

Power

"Hail, holy light, offspring of Heav'n first-born, . . .": See Milton's *Paradise Lost*, Book III, lines 1–3. This quotation, along with her reference to "Adam unparadiz'd," reinforces Rukeyser's framing of this industrial tragedy in epic terms.

The Disease: After-Effects

Grenz rays: a type of black light, similar to but weaker than ultraviolet light, X rays, and gamma rays. Sometimes referred to as soft X rays.

Tom Mooney: (1882–1942) Socialist organizer and union activist who was convicted (and later pardoned) of murder as a result of a bomb explosion at a San Francisco parade in 1916.

Eel

Rukeyser's title plays off of the term for the "El," the elevated subway. Underground subways were under rapid construction in New York during the period of Rukeyser's adolescence.

Ann Burlak: (1911–2002) A working-class labor organizer, primarily active in the 1930s and 1940s in the textile mills of New England. Newspapers of the time commonly referred to Burlak as the "Red Flame," calling attention to her affiliation with the Communist Party. In her response to a letter from Rukeyser, Burlak narrates key moments in her personal history, stating that she "went to work in a silk mill at the age of 14 in Bethlehem, PA," and that she was a "charter member" of the National Textile Workers' Union, first joining in 1928 (LCI). The letter is dated only June 14, with no year indicated. Rukeyser chose Ann Burlak as a subject for one of her "Lives" poems in TW.

Trophies

"To prevent repetition . . .": This quoted material is taken directly from the report of Major General George H. Thomas, U.S. Army Corps, September 30, 1863, detailing important battles near the Tennessee River at Battle's Creek.

Three Black Women

In her 1978 *CP*, the title of this poem was changed from "Three Negresses" to "Three Black Women."

Night-Music

This poem is dedicated to Marya Zaturenska (1902–1982), poet who won the Pulitzer Prize in 1938 for *Cold Morning Sky* (which she dedicated to Rukeyser). Zaturenska was married to poet Horace Gregory and, with him, coauthored *A History of American Poetry, 1900–1940* (1946).

The Cruise

Rukeyser's experience in Spain where she witnessed the outbreak of the Spanish Civil War had a profound effect on her for the rest of her life. Some of that experience is suggested in this allegorical and sometimes surreal poem, which begins with a portrayal of the carefree activities of a cast of representative characters aboard a luxury-liner cruise (the captain, the barmaid, the poet, the union men, the wealthy financier). The relationships and attitudes of these individuals toward one another and the world are soon observed in a different light when fighting breaks out on shore, and no port for safe landing can be found.

Later in her life, Rukeyser came to believe that the failure of the western countries to come to the aid of the Spanish Republicans was the first in a long line of twentieth-century political betrayals.

Funera plango, fulgura frango, Sabbata pango / excito lentos, dissipo ventos, paco cruentos: Latin dedication often engraved on church bells to indicate their function; an old Catholic monks' hymn, chanted and commonly translated as: "Death's tale I tell, the winds dispel, ill-feeling quell, the slothful shake, the storm-clouds break, the Sabbath awake." Henry Wadsworth Longfellow also uses these words in his poem "Prologue: The Spire of Strasburg Cathedral".

'Free grace and dyin love, . . .': Line from a traditional spiritual. See 2 Corinthians 9.

"Remember the landslide on Chartreuse": Chartreux (alternate spelling) was the monastic home of the Carthusian order, first built by St. Bruno in 1084 and destroyed by avalanche in 1132.

Mediterranean

This poem was previously published first in *New Masses* (1937), and then in booklet form by the Writers and Artists Committee as part of an effort to fund the construction of American hospitals in Spain. This booklet version varies significantly from the version published in *U.S.1*. A copy of the booklet can be seen at the Berg collection, New York Public Library (reference number 79-236). On its back cover, the following appeal for funds is printed under the title "Today in Spain": "Eight American hospitals have been established by the Medical Bureau to aid Spanish Democracy. One hundred and thirteen surgeons, nurses and ambulance drivers, with fifty-two ambulances and tons of medical equipment are saving hundreds of lives daily. What you contribute today, will receive the heartfelt thanks of a heroic people."

See the introduction to LP for Rukeyser's prose description of her experience evacuating from Spain, including this passage: "We were on a small ship, five times past our capacity in refugees, sailing for the first port at peace. On the deck that night, people talked quietly about what they had just seen and what it might mean to the world. . . . Our realization was fresh and young, we had seen the parts of our lives in a new arrangement" (2–3).

I

Otto Boch: German athlete whom Rukeyser met and fell in love with in the summer of 1936 while traveling to the People's Olympiad in Barcelona, an alternative Olympics arranged to protest the rise in fascism. Rukeyser was covering the event as a journalist for the British publication *Life and Letters Today*. Boch stayed in Spain to fight for the International Cause and was killed in battle in 1938. While Boch and Rukeyser only knew each other for roughly six days, Rukeyser's personal correspondence repeatedly references Boch (in both the Library of Congress and the New York Public Library's Berg Collection), and various poems allude to him, attesting to the significance of this relationship in her life. See also the poems "The Book of the Dead" (US1), "Moment of Proof" (TW), "One Soldier" (BV), "Segre Song" (SD), "Voices" (BO), and "Searching/

Not Searching" (BO). See also Rukeyser's "We Came for the Games" and Mariani's "'Barcelona, 1936'—A Moment of Proof for Muriel Rukeyser."

2

Narbo: Caesar marched to Narbo in 52 BCE. It was Rome's first overseas colony.

A Turning Wind. New York: Viking Press, 1939.

Rukeyser's original dedication read:

Elisabeth and George Marshall
  Their Book

Rukeyser's original acknowledgments read:

Some of these poems have already appeared in magazines including *Poetry: A Magazine of Verse, Yale Review, Life and Letters To-Day, Kenyon Review, Twice a Year, Nation, New Republic, New Masses, Atlantic Monthly, Harper's Bazaar, Saturday Review of Literature, Southern Review.*

The first through fifth elegies first appeared together in the first section of *A Turning Wind.*

Otherworld

The Island

Herbert . . . Charles . . . Lancelot Andrewes: Rukeyser traveled to London and Chester in June 1936, prior to her trip to Barcelona. These lines appear to describe the stained glass windows of a cloister in Chester where George Herbert (1593–1633), King Charles I (1600–1649), and Lancelot Andrewes (1555–1626) were depicted together.

Noguchi

Hideyo Noguchi: (1876–1928) Japanese bacteriologist best known for his successful culturing of the agent of syphilis. The reference to "Noguchi's mother with her scalded child" is inspired by an accident suffered by Noguchi at the age of two, when he fell into a hearth fire and severely burned his left hand.

2 Lives

Rukeyser wrote a long prefatory note to *A Turning Wind.* This note is similar to Rukeyser's endnote in "The Book of the Dead," in which she speaks of a projected work called *U.S. 1,* while having already published a book of that title. The note read:

The last section, "Lives," is intended to stand with "The Book of the Dead" as part of a projected work, *U.S. 1.* The five people around whom it is written are Americans—New Englanders—whose value to our generation is very great and partly unacknowledged. The material for "Gibbs" came chiefly from the writings of Pierre Duhem, J. G. Crowther, and Josiah Willard Gibbs (to whose work much of twentieth-century physics and chemical energetics refers, including many of Einstein's researches), and to the conversation of Dr. Theodore Shedlofsky. The material for "Ryder" came chiefly from the writings of F. N.

Price, Paul Rosenfeld, Walter Pach, and Marsden Hartley, on whose conversation, as well as that of William Gropper, I have drawn. The material for "Chapman" came chiefly from the writings of M. A. De Wolfe Howe, William James, Edmund Wilson, John Jay Chapman's own work, and the conversation of Earl Davidson. The material for "Ann Burlak" came chiefly from Ann Burlak herself, Waldo Frank's writings, and the conversation of Rebecca Pitts, to whom and to whose book, a study in art and democracy that is nearing completion, I am deeply indebted for ground-material throughout this book. The material for "Ives" came chiefly from the work of Charles E. Ives, Henry Cowell, and Aaron Copland, and from the conversation of Lehman Engel and Aaron Copland.

When Rukeyser reprinted this series of poems in *Waterlily Fire* (1962), she included a condensed version of the above in an endnote, adding that she conceived of her biographical poems as a group to include: "Gibbs," "Ryder," "Chapman," "Ann Burlak," "Ives," "Timothy Dexter," "Akiba," "Käthe Kollwitz," "Bessie Smith," and "Boas." She also acknowledged: "my debt to Horace Gregory; . . . to Ives's "Essays Before a Sonata"; to the staff of the Portsmouth Public Library, and to Richardson Wright's and John P. Marquand's books about Timothy Dexter; to Louis Finkelstein's biography, and my mother's story that we were descended from Akiba." The poem "Suite for Lord Timothy Dexter" was published later in BW (1958), and "Akiba" and "Käthe Kollwitz" appeared in SD (1968). The first section of "Akiba," called "The Way Out," was published on its own in WF. To the best of our knowledge, however, Rukeyser never published "Lives" poems on Smith and Boas and did not complete her extensively researched biography project on Boas.

Gibbs

J. Willard Gibbs: (1839–1903) An American mathematician and physicist who established the basic theory for physical chemistry, Gibbs is considered the "father of thermodynamics" and "discoverer of the phase rule, what Rukeyser calls 'one of the most celebrated and beautiful laws of theoretical physics'" (Levi 70). See Rukeyser's biography, *Willard Gibbs* (1942).

Ryder

Albert Pinkham Ryder: (1847–1917) An American visionary painter known especially for his landscapes and figure studies. See LP (134–35) for Rukeyser's description of Ryder's particular artistic achievement and the manner in which his paintings became "most memorable" for her.

Ann Burlak

Ann Burlak: A working-class labor organizer, primarily active in the 1930s and 1940s in the textile mills of New England; also mentioned in "The Disease: After-Effects" in US1.

Rosa: Rosa Luxemburg (1871–1919), political thinker and revolutionary who contributed significantly to the development of Socialist, Marxist, and Communist discourse. See also "Cats and a Cock" (TF).

Beast in View. Garden City, NY: Doubleday, 1944.

Rukeyser's original acknowledgments read:

I thank the following, who first published some of the poems of this book: *Decision, Kenyon Review, Poetry, Accent, New Poems 1940, Horizon, Life and Letters To-Day, Twice a Year, The American Scholar, Harper's Bazaar, New Poems 1942, Tomorrow, New Poems 1943, The Manitoban* (of Winnipeg), *Rueca* (of Mexico, D.F.) and Mr. Norman Holmes Pearson; Mr. Louis Untermeyer, editor of Modern American Poetry; Mr. Lee Ault and Mr. Rudolf C. von Ripper.

The sixth through ninth elegies first appeared together as the fourth section of BV, after "The Soul and Body of John Brown." A number of poems in this volume have specific dates recorded at their conclusions. In her final note page for this collection, Rukeyser commented that she had "dated several poems in the first section, and one elegy (the sixth), to indicate with particularity their time of writing during the months just before this country entered the war."

One Soldier

This poem both addresses and refers to Otto Boch, the German athlete whom Rukeyser met in 1936. See the annotation to "The Book of the Dead" (US1).

Ajanta

Rukeyser's endnote in BV reads, "The title 'Ajanta' refers to the caves of that name in India, on whose walls appear the great frescoes, with their religious analogy between space and the space of the body, and their acceptance of reality which may be filled with creation" (98). In SP Rukeyser included a footnote explaining that the frescoes were created by "painter-monks" and that the religious analogy "involves an acceptance of reality which defines art as other than the changing of reality, the *looking-through* the wall of Western painting. The wall is accepted; the air, the space between the walls and the observer, is filled with creation."

Nelson and Kaufman contribute further: "The Ajanta caves in India are a series of twenty-nine Buddhist cave-temples and monasteries cut into cliffs in the north, near Ajanta, Maharashtra. Built over several centuries beginning in the second century BC, they were abandoned in the seventh century and rediscovered in 1819. Most of the cave walls have large-scale tempura murals depicting the lives of the Buddha, while the ceilings are decorated with flowers and animals. The compositions are rhythmic, naturalistic, and generally drawn with soft, curving lines. Rukeyser had not seen the caves themselves, basing her descriptions, as in 'Les Tendresses Bestiales,' on a large portfolio of reproductions. In her sequence the caves are not only a space for collective narrative representation but also a space of the body and of the self." See also LP 153–55, and Nayar, "Trans-formations: Muriel Rukeyser's 'Ajanta'" (1994).

Wreath of Women

Vesalian: Refers to the work of Andreas Vesalius (1514–1564), a key figure in the development of modern anatomy. His *De Humani Corporis Fabrica* (1543) marks the beginning of a more scientific understanding of the human body, based as it was on human cadaver studies.

Walpurga: See also "Mrs. Walpurga" (GW). Name of Benedictine missionary from England (c. 710–779) who served as the abbess for an eighth-century monastery in Heidenheim, Germany. Her name seems to have been conflated with that of the pre-Christian "Waldborg" who was a fertility goddess. The name "Walpurga" (also "Walburga") is also associated with a traditional witches' celebration of German origin on the eve of May 1, Walpurgis Night.

The Minotaur

Rukeyser's endnote in BV dedicates this poem to "Charles Naginski, who shortly before his death wrote the music for a ballet of the same name" (98). Rukeyser was friendly with Naginski (1909–1940) and may have met him at the Yaddo Writer's Colony.

from "To the Unborn Child"

Rukeyser's endnote reads, "The translation from Hans Carossa is a fragment of a long poem. The two lines which begin the last verse are addressed, in the original, to the unborn child. This poem was first printed as a Christmas poem by Norman Holmes Pearson." In BV, the note following the poem read "Written in Germany in 1936, Translation by Elizabeth Mayer and Muriel Rukeyser."

Long Past Moncada

The title of this poem refers to Moncada, Spain, Rukeyser's last train stop on her journey to Barcelona, July 1936, where she went to report on the People's Olympiad. To read Rukeyser's first-person account of the chaotic days during which her train was held over in Moncada due to the outbreak of fighting fifteen miles away in Barcelona, see "Barcelona on the Barricades."

Chapultepec Park—1 and 2

Chapultepec Park: In Mexico City, where Rukeyser spent the latter half of 1939.

Letter to the Front

See Schweik, "The Letter and the Body: Muriel Rukeyser's 'Letter to the Front.'"

7

To be a Jew in the twentieth century: This section was reprinted as a stand-alone poem in BO, immediately following "A Louis Sonnet," with both poems appearing under the heading "Two Sonnets." In BO, Rukeyser included an endnote indicating that this poem "was written during World War II" and had been included in what was then the new Reform Jewish prayer book, *The Service of the Heart* (1967). The poem is currently included in *Gates of Prayer*, the contemporary Reform prayer book. See Kaufman, "'But not the study': Writing as a Jew," and Mort, "The Poetry of Muriel Rukeyser."

8

Malicioso King: Rukeyser's nickname for Generoso Pope Sr. (1891–1950), business partner of her father's in Colonial Sand and Stone. Pope late became a prominent publisher of one of the largest circulation Italian-language newspapers in America, *Il Progresso*, and a strong supporter of fascism.

Wheeler, Nye, Pegler, Hearst, . . . / . . . McCormick: Senator Burton K. Wheeler, Senator Gerald P. Nye, journalist Westwood Pegler, and publisher William Randolph Hearst. Rukeyser was critical of each of these individuals due to each one's noninterventionist stance in response to the growing threat of Nazism.

The Soul and Body of John Brown

On her final note page for BV (98), Rukeyser pointed out that the first version of this poem "appeared as the text (with the old song) of a portfolio of etchings by Rudolf C. von Ripper. The portfolio was published in 1940 by Lee Ault and R. C. von Ripper, and was first shown at the Bignou Galleries, New York City, in January 1941." While copies of this book are rare, interested scholars or readers will be rewarded for their efforts to view it. Ripper's etchings are both extraordinary and disturbing. The setting of Rukeyser's poem alongside of the folk song "John Brown's Body" ("John Brown's body lies a-mould'ring in the grave . . .") is moving and very much in sympathy with Rukeyser's regard for folk music as poetry of the "public domain" (LP 97). Explaining her fascination for John Brown, Rukeyser wrote: "In this country, one man who cut through to the imagination of all was John Brown, that meteor, whose blood was love and rage, in fury until the love was burned away" (LP 36).

According to William L. Rukeyser, the poet's son, Baron Rudolf Carol von Ripper was a painter and lithographer and an early anti-Nazi who served time in a concentration camp. The Austrian prime minister intervened with the German government to have von Ripper expelled rather than executed. Von Ripper served and was wounded while flying with the Spanish (Republican) Air Force during the Spanish Civil War. He then came to the United States where he met Rukeyser and collaborated on the John Brown project.

The Green Wave. Garden City, New York: Doubleday, 1948.

Rukeyser dedicated this book to Marie de L. Welch (Marie West after her marriage), a California poet who was a friend and supporter of Rukeyser's work. She lived in Los Gatos, south of San Jose, and moved in Leftist literary circles.

Rukeyser's original acknowledgments read:

I wish to thank the Guggenheim Foundation for a fellowship which helped with the time of this book, a play, and poems in my book *Beast in View*.

Some of these poems have appeared in *Kenyon Review, Poetry, Twice a Year, Tomorrow,* and the *California Poetry Folios.* The play, *The Middle of the Air,* was produced in Iowa City in 1945 by Hallie Flanagan.

The tenth elegy originally appeared in GW in its own section of the book between "Private Life of the Sphinx" and "Nine Poems for the unborn child."

Song, from "Mr. Amazeen on the River"

Amazeen: Luther Amazeen was a lobsterman who owned a home in New Castle, New Hampshire. He had a small house on the river and rented a room in it to Rukeyser. She liked to go to his home often and was there on at least two occasions with May Sarton in the early 1940s.

"And the sea / Gave up its dead": See Revelation 20:13.

His Head Is Full of Faces

Bernard Perlin: (1918–) New York artist who worked for the Office of War Information Projects Administration during and prior to World War II creating post office mural posters related to the war effort. Rukeyser knew Perlin from her work affiliated with the OWI. Rukeyser had been hired in December 1942 as a "visual information specialist" for the Domestic Branch of the Graphics Division (Design and Services section). Along with many other writers and artists, she was hired to design posters to support the war's anti-Nazi effort. She resigned under pressure in 1943, at which point she had become uncomfortable with a growing tendency to demonize the enemy at OWI.

The following, dated October 27, 1943, was written by Thomas D. Mabry, formerly Assistant Chief, Bureau of Publications, Graphics Division, Office of War Information, to the *Partisan Review* in response to their "rebuke" of Rukeyser:

Miss Rukeyser was invited to join the staff of the Office of War Information, Domestic Branch, in July 1942, where she remained until July 1943. The OWI Publications Bureau asked Miss Rukeyser to act as liaison between poster (graphic) production and writers outside OWI. She also wrote captions for posters and more generally helped develop the entire OWI graphics program. The Publications Bureau employed Miss Rukeyser not only because it respected her talent for incisive imagery and the unambiguous use of words— essential to the joining of words and images together in a popular medium like war posters—but also because of her experience in writing continuity for photographic stories, editing photographic sequences and in writing documentary films. (LC, OWI file)

Mrs. Walpurga

Rukeyser included an endnote for this poem when it was published in WF: "Dr. Rene Dubos saying to me, 'Pasteur said, "La vie, c'est l'oeuf et son devenir." ' " (Editor's translation: Life, it's the egg and its becoming.) Dubos was a French-born, American Pulitzer Prize–winning bacteriologist whose work led to the development of penicillin and other antibiotics. Walpurga is also mentioned in "Wreath of Women" (BV).

When first printed in *Poetry*, February 1947, this poem was presented as a series entitled "Mrs. Walpurga: Five Poems," which were called "Mrs. Walpurga," "Foghorn in Horror," "A Charm for Cantinflas," "A Certain Music," and "Motive." These became separate poems in GW, reordered and sometimes separated by other poems but titled the same way in each case except for "Motive," which became "The Motive of All of It."

A Charm for Cantinflas

Cantinflas: Born in Mexico City as Mario Moreno (1911–1993), the hugely popular Latin American entertainer performed during various points of his life as a musician, acrobat, clown, and other roles. Rukeyser may have seen Cantinflas perform in Mexico while she was there in 1939.

Traditional Tune

Godfrey King: the Crusader Godfrey of Bouillon (1058–1100) assumed control of Jerusalem after conquering the city in 1099 and murdering all of the Muslim and Jewish citizens.

Summer, the Sacramento

Rukeyser lived in California from 1944–1949. This poem refers to the Sacramento River.

Speech of the Mother, from *The Middle of the Air*

The Middle of the Air: Hallie Flanagan was director of the WPA Theatre Project, and Rukeyser first knew her in her capacity as a faculty member at Vassar College. They maintained a lifelong friendship and, as Rukeyser notes in the prefatory pages of GW: "The play, *The Middle of the Air,* was produced in Iowa City in 1945." Rukeyser's play in verse focuses on the corruption of an idealistic young aviator by power. This poem is taken directly from the play, produced and directed by Hallie Flanagan.

Translations: Six Poems by Octavio Paz

Rukeyser met Octavio Paz in California in 1944. She became one of his first English translators and translated his *Selected Poems: 1935–1955* and *Sun Stone,* in addition to numerous other individual poems.

In GW, Rukeyser included the following introductory note to the "Six Poems": "Octavio Paz was born in Mexico in 1914. His collected works (1935–41) appeared in 1942; after a while in this country, he is now with the Mexican Embassy at Paris. These translations are by Octavio Paz and Muriel Rukeyser."

Rari from the Marquesas

In GW, the following note by Rukeyser preceded this poem:

The *rari,* or love-chant—as Samuel Elbert has pointed out—is now a museum-piece revived only on July 14. Until 1935, it was the popular song, the poetry, of the Marquesas; but it was fought relentlessly by the missionaries because of the "erotic symbolism of some of the words."

Rari means tie or bind, love spell. *Rari kou fau* means love spells accompanied by hibiscus batons. The vocabulary of these poems is a picture language, like those of the American Indians. The images are clear, but interchangeable. Samuel Elbert speaks of the use of "mists gathering about a mountain" for a person garlanded with leis; of the following words for "lovers": night-moths, birds, mists, mountain, wreaths; of these male images: root, comet, sun, stick, fruit-pole, trade-winds; and these female images: glittering leaf, garland of red pandanus keys, fruit, bud, flower, sea-shell conch.

The ancient chants were simple and direct: "A god constant as sunlight is her lover . . ."

"The leading poet" of the nineteenth century "was Moa Tetua." He was a blind leper who could neither read nor write; he was so popular as a composer-poet that "natives gathered illegally every night outside the leprosarium to listen" to these songs. He sings of the loves of his son, Piu, he sings stories brought to the wall by lovers and those who mourn.

The first four *rari* are by Moa Tetua. The others are later.

These translations are by Samuel Elbert and Muriel Rukeyser.

These songs are like the songs that Melville heard.

Private Life of the Sphinx

Ella Winter: Longtime Left journalist and activist and the second wife of Lincoln Steffens. Winter and Rukeyser shared a sustaining friendship over many years, beginning in the 1930s.

Nine Poems for the unborn child

Rukeyser wrote this sonnet sequence about her experience of pregnancy. Her only child, William L. Rukeyser, was born on September 25, 1947, in Berkeley, California. See Eisenberg, "'Changing Waters Carry Voices': 'Nine Poems for the Unborn Child.'" In a typed draft for the 1978 CP table of contents, Rukeyser titled the nine sections of this poem according to the first lines of each section and then added a typed margin note: "These subtitles are not to be used in the body of the book. Keep numerals only."

Orpheus. San Francisco: Centaur Press, 1949.

Orpheus was first published in a special edition of five hundred copies, with a frontispiece drawing by Picasso. The poem was reprinted in Rukeyser's SP in 1951 and then in the 1978 CP. In LP Rukeyser describes her process of writing *Orpheus* (182–86); a version of this description was reprinted in Ciardi's *Mid-Century American Poets* under the title "The Genesis of Orpheus." In a letter to Frank Baron dated February 16, 1963, Rukeyser requested—for a possible second printing—that the title she initially gave the essay, "A Way of Writing," be restored: "The editor put on the very pretentious title it now has" (LCII).

Elegies. Norfolk, CT: New Directions, 1949.

When Rukeyser included these elegies in SP, she included a footnote for them: "Ten poems whose development is based on growing connections of images and processes, over a period of ten years." The publication history of these poems is discussed in the Editors' Notes.

Rukeyser included the following endnote for elegies six through nine when they appeared in BV:

The elegies are of the same group as those in *A Turning Wind* (Viking, 1939). They are the sixth, seventh, eighth, and ninth, of ten poems. I have no wish to change the structure of these poems, and so I shall not add the explanatory notes that often mean that something should have been added or taken away from the poem itself. But a reader might be glad to know this of the "Dream-Singing Elegy": that there was a religious revival among the

American Indians as they were defeated, as there is likely to be a revival of faith among the deprived, and that this story is told in a paper by Philleo Nash. And of the "Children's Elegy," that these cries of loss are among us in American children and refugee children here, that they may be seen in newsreels of Spanish and English and Chinese and countless other children, and that some of these stories are told with finality in Anna Freud's book, *Children and War.*

Third Elegy. The Fear of Form

Comtesse de Noailles: Anna-Elisabeth de Brancovan, Comtesse de Noailles (1876–1933), a French poet, of noble Romanian lineage.

Tenth Elegy. Elegy in Joy

I feare, and hope : I burne, and frese like yse . . . and ***I find no peace, and all my warres are done:*** See the sonnet called "I find no peace" in *Tottel's miscellany. Songes and Sonettes by Henry Howard, Earl of Surrey, Sir Thomas Wyatt, the Elder, Nicholas Grimald, and uncertain authors,* which reads: "Description of the contrarious passions in a louer. / I Find no peace, and all my warre is done: / I feare, and hope: I burne, and frese like yse".

Body of Waking. New York: Harper, 1958.

Rukeyser dedicated this book to Frances G. Wickes. Wickes was a leading Jungian analyst in the United States with whom Rukeyser corresponded from 1958–1967, the year of Wickes's death. Rukeyser described her work with Wickes as follows: "The work I did for Frances Wickes was a combination of expert 'evoking' and editing. . . . Mrs. Wickes' writing nor my writing are commercial; this, however, was exacting, concentrated, one-to-one work with professional publication as an end." Rukeyser worked on both the revised edition of Wickes's *The Inner World of Childhood* and *The Inner World of Choice* (LCI). "Voices of Waking" (BW) and "The Blue Flower" (SD) are both dedicated to Wickes.

Rukeyser's original acknowledgements read:

Some of the poems in this volume were first published in: *Poetry, The Saturday Review, The Nation, Tomorrow,* and *Montevallo Review.*

Others were published previously in *One Life,* Simon and Schuster, 1957.

One poem entitled "Night Feeding" was published originally in *Mid-Century American Poets,* 1950, Twayne Publishers, Inc., edited by John Ciardi.

Several of the poems originally appeared in *Discovery, No. 3,* Vance Bourjaily, editor, published by Pocket Books.

Eighteen of the poems in section four of this book first appeared in *One Life* (for more on this 1957 work, what was included, and how selections from that book were made for this one, please see the introduction to this volume). Five of the poems appear to have been previously unpublished, and their placement in this section suggests that Rukeyser saw them as connected to the OL poems: "The sky is as black as it was when you lay down"; "On your journey you will come to a time of waking"; "This is the net of begetting and belief"; "Body of Waking"; and "Then full awake you will recognize the voice".

Phaneron

This endnote appeared with the poem in BW: "Phaneron—anything over the threshold of sense; a perception word first used by Charles S. Pierce."

Ringling

Toni: Antoinette Willson, a San Francisco friend who was a writer and taught English and writing at San Francisco State College (now University).

Night Feeding

In 1947, Rukeyser gave birth to her son, William L. Rukeyser. This poem is among the first American poems on the subject of breastfeeding. While Rukeyser did not comment in prose about nursing, in her 1949 review of Charlotte Marletto's book, *Jewel of Our Longing,* entitled "A Simple Theme," she asserted, "There is no poetry of birth in the literature that reaches us. In our own time, we can count the poems on our fingers; there is a great blank behind us, in our classic and religious literature. There we might expect to find the clues to human process and common experience."

F. O. M.

Rukeyser read and commented on F. O. Matthiesen's writing, and in 1944, Matthiessen defended her after she had been attacked in *Partisan Review* (see Kertesz 175, 180). Matthiesen was himself criticized for his spirit of internationalism and accused of being a naive intellectual. He committed suicide in 1950, leaving the following note, "How much the state of the world has to do with my state of mind, I do not know. But as a Christian and Socialist, believing in international peace, I find myself terribly oppressed by the present tensions" (Kertesz 271).

Exile of Music

Naginski: Charles Naginski, also mentioned in "The Minotaur" (BV), was a classical composer with whom Rukeyser was friendly.

The Watchers

Carson and Reeves: The writer Carson McCullers and her husband, James Reeves McCullers, with whom Rukeyser was friends.

Born in December

Nancy Marshall: The daughter of George and Elizabeth Marshall, lifelong friends of Rukeyser's with whom she went to England in 1936.

Voices of Waking

Frances G. Wickes: A Jungian analyst with whom Rukeyser corresponded. See the opening annotation to BW.

[Untitled] ("In her splendor islanded)"

[Untitled] ("Like ivy the creeper with a thousand hands")

These poems appear untitled both in BW and in Rukeyser's bilingual translation of *Selected Poems of Octavio Paz* (1963); in both books, these poems are titled by their first lines in the table of contents.

from Sun Stone

In BW, the following note appeared at the end of the poem: "'Sun Stone' is a poem whose 585 lines, of eleven syllables, stand for the 585 days of the cycle of Venus to that planet's conjunction with the sun, as the unit was used in the Aztec calendar."

Suite for Lord Timothy Dexter

A contribution to Rukeyser's sequence of "Lives" poems (see the annotation to the "Lives" section of TW). Timothy Dexter (1743–1806) was a rags-to-riches character, an eccentric, prominent citizen of Newburyport, Massachusetts. He was supposedly given the title of "Lord" and adopted it as a proper name—not a title—as he mocked everything ruthlessly, including English snobbery. His booklet about his philosophy of the world, *A Pickle for the Knowing Ones*, was devoid of punctuation and, when criticized for this, he added a page at the end of his second edition consisting only of punctuation, suggesting that he added enough that his readers could "peper and solt [the text] as they please" (see the end of section 5 of this poem). As Louise Kertesz writes, "in Dexter's belief that the world is one creature, Rukeyser met her own profound conviction" (264).

Fields Where We Slept

This poem first appeared in OL. Rukeyser added an endnote when she reprinted it in BO: "'Fields Where We Slept' has its scene in the South, where a manmade lake of the TVA system now lies over some of the land of the Scottsboro Trial actions, the revealing clash of 1933 underwater now. 'Remember they say . . .'"

Waterlily Fire: Poems 1935–1962. New York: Macmillan, 1962.

Rukeyser dedicated the book as follows: "My thanks to Marie de L. Welch and to M. L. Rosenthal—both poets, critics, friends—who helped me select the poems in this book."

Rukeyser's original acknowledgments read:

For permission to publish the poems in the last part of this book, I wish to acknowledge the kindness of the following magazines: *Poetry, The Vassar Review, American Judaism.* These publishers have granted permission to print poems which first appeared in books: New Directions, Harper and Brothers, Simon and Schuster, Inc. This selection was made from the following books: *Theory of Flight, U.S. 1., A Turning Wind, Beast in View, The Green Wave, Elegies, Selected Poems, One Life, Body of Waking.* This volume is published by arrangement with New Directions.

The Speaking Tree

Richard Lannoy writes in *The Speaking Tree: The Speaking Tree: A Study of Indian Culture and Society* (1971):

When Alexander the Great reached 'the furthest forests of India,' the inhabitants led him, in the dead of night, to an oracular tree which could answer questions in the language of any man who addressed it. The trunk was made of snakes, animal heads sprouted from the boughs, and it bore fruit like beautiful women, who sang the praises of the Sun and Moon. According to Pseudo-Callisthenes, the tree warned Alexander of the futility of invading India with intent to obtain dominion over it.

Known as the Waqwaq Tree in Islamic tradition, it was often portrayed on Harappan seals four millennia ago as sprouting heads of a bovine unicorn, encircling a female divinity, or even growing from her body.

Robert Payne: A prolific literary scholar, translator, and chair of the translation committee of P.E.N. when Rukeyser was its president. Rukeyser came to know Payne (1911–1983) after he came to the United States in 1946 and became founding editor of *Montevallo Review*, to which Rukeyser was a contributor. He authored 110 books and his writings included novels, political studies, poetry, literary criticism, translations, operas, philosophy, travel writing, filmscripts, plays, journalism, and critically acclaimed biographies, among which is one about Alexander the Great.

Waterlily Fire

Rukeyser included the following endnote for "Waterlily Fire":

The time of this poem is the period in New York City from April, 1958, when I witnessed the destruction of Monet's *Waterlilies* by fire at the Museum of Modern Art, to the present moment.

The two spans of time assumed are the history of Manhattan Island and my lifetime on the island. I was born in an apartment house that had as another of its tenants the notorious gangster Gyp the Blood. Nearby was Grant's Tomb and the grave of the Amiable Child. This child died very young when this part of New York was open country. The place with its memory of amiability has been protected among all the rest. My father, in the building business, made us part of the building, tearing down, and rebuilding of the city, with all that that implies. Part II is based on that time, when building still meant the throwing of red-hot rivets, and only partly the pouring of concrete of the later episodes.

Part IV deals with an actual television interview with Suzuki, the Zen teacher, in which he answered a question about a most important moment in the teachings of Buddha.

The long body of Part V is an idea from India of one's lifetime body as a ribbon of images, all our changes seen in process.

The "island of people" was the group who stayed out in the open in City Hall Park in April of 1961, while the rest of the city took shelter at the warning sound of the sirens. The protest against this nuclear-war practice drill was, in essence, a protest against war itself and an attempt to ask for some other way to deal with the emotions that make people make war.

Before the Museum of Modern Art was built, I worked for a while in the house that then occupied that place. On the day of the fire, I arrived to see it as a place in the air. I was coming to keep an appointment with my friend the Curator of the Museum's Film Library, Richard Griffith, to whom this poem is dedicated.

For a contemporary and appreciative review of the poem, see Adkins, "The Esthetics of Science: Muriel Rukeyser's 'Waterlily Fire.'"

The Speed of Darkness. New York: Random House, 1968.

Rukeyser's original acknowledgments read:

The author wishes to thank the editors and publishers of the following magazines, in which some of these poems first appeared: *Kenyon Review, The Nation, The Observer* (London), *Atlantic Monthly, Ikon, Liberation, Ladies' Home Journal, Saturday Review, American Judaism, Poetry* (Chicago), *New Directions, Annual, The New Yorker,* Macmillan, Unicorn Press, *Sarah Lawrence Journal, Poets for Peace,* War Resisters Calendar, *Chelsea, Ramparts, Evergreen Review.* The poem "Endless" appeared originally in *The New Yorker.* The poems "The Outer Banks" and "Delta Poems" appeared originally in *Poetry.*

"Delta Poems" was first read at Angry Arts Week; "Käthe Kollwitz" was first read at Syracuse University; "The Speed of Darkness" was first read at M.I.T.

The author wishes to thank the National Council on the Arts for a grant during the time of which many of these poems were written.

The Poem as Mask

Orpheus

The poem's opening—"When I wrote of the women in their dances and wildness. . . ,"—refers to Rukeyser's long poem *Orpheus,* written and published in chapbook form in 1949 (included in this volume as a separate section), and then included in the 1951 SP. As Lorrie Goldensohn argues, this poem became a feminist manifesto and one of its lines, "No more masks!" became the title of an enduring anthology of American women's poetry compiled by Florence Howe and first published in 1973.

the rescued child: Rukeyser's son was born by caesarean section September 25, 1947, after medical personnel determined he was presenting in the breech position. More than one friend had urged Rukeyser to abort the baby or place him for adoption, both unacceptable choices to her. Rukeyser had a long and difficult labor and was asked, more than once, if only one of the two (mother and child) could be saved, which would it be. She answered "the baby."

Junk-Heap at Murano

Joby West: The daughter of Marie de L. Welch West. Joby saw "the glass" on a visit to Venice.

Clues

Indian Baptiste saying: A possible clue to this reference can be found in the third stanza of the manuscript notes (SD, ms file, LCI):

> There is a people of Indians on a river
> on the north Pacific that do this:
> Baptiste Ironstone told me: With the passing

Of the old people, all knowledge of painting
Will disappear. Red signifies "good." It also expresses
Life, existence, blood, heat, fire, day. Some said
It also meant the earth. And self, friendship, success.
Black is opposite to red: evil, death, cold, darkness, night.
Also "person the opposite of self, enemy antagonism, bad luck."
Yellow is also earth, and what comes from it, and . . . dawn.
Green is seldom used; for rainbow. Blue is sky. White is spirit
And the spirit world, ghost, skeleton, dead people, sickness, bones.

Double Dialogue:

Homage to Robert Frost

Frost's son, Carol, committed suicide in October 1940.

The Six Canons

after Binyon: Lawrence Binyon (1869–1943), British poet and Asian art authority who, among many other writings, translated the late fifth-century Taoist painter Hsieh-Ho's "Six Canons of Chinese Painting." Rukeyser's "Six Canons," as expressed in the poem, do not restate the six canons but can be read as a metaphysical expression of the principles of life and art she extrapolated from them.

Cries from Chiapas

Rukeyser traveled in Mexico in 1939 and likely visited Chiapas, where she would have become familiar with the conflict and anticlerical purges there.

Poem

For a discussion of this poem addressing its place within twentieth-century American poetry and, in particular, the nuclear arms buildup, see True's essay "The Authentic Voice" and his book *An Energy Field More Intense Than War*.

The Seeming

Helen Lynd: A friend and colleague from Rukeyser's teaching days at Sarah Lawrence. Lynd was a sociologist best known for the series *Middletown: A Study in American Culture* (1929), which she and Robert Lynd coauthored.

Song from *Puck Fair*

Dating back to 200 BCE, Puck Fair is considered Ireland's oldest festival. In addition to this poem, Rukeyser wrote a novel based on Puck Fair, *The Orgy*.

Segre Song

Otto Boch, the German athlete whom Rukeyser met in 1936, joined the anti-Franco forces in the Spanish Civil War and died in 1938, in a protracted struggle between the Republicans and Fascist forces on the banks of the Segre River. See the annotation to "The Book of the Dead" (US1).

Bunk Johnson Blowing

William Gary "Bunk" Johnson (1879–1949), legendary New Orleans trumpet player, re-"discovered" by musicologist Alan Lomax while conducting folklore research for the WPA in the mid-1930s. Johnson had given up his playing when he lost his teeth, and when Lomax and other now-established jazz musicians encouraged him to come to New York, he said he couldn't play. They raised the money to buy him a set of dentures and brought him north, where he became quite popular, playing with many of the other legendary jazz musicians of his time including Leadbelly and Louis Armstrong.

Cannibal Bratuscha

In 1900, Franz Bratuscha was sentenced to death for murdering and cannibalizing his twelve-year old daughter; his wife, convicted as an accessory, was sentenced to a three-year prison term. The judgments and sentences were based on the Bratuschas' own false confessions, and the convictions were overturned in 1903 after their daughter turned up alive.

The Blue Flower

Frances G. Wickes: a leading Jungian analyst in the United States with whom Rukeyser exchanged analyses. See the opening annotation to BW.

Word of Mouth

The poem first appeared with this note: "The country is the Catalan border of France and Spain. The two times are July, 1936, the beginning of the war, and the time of my return to the border in 1963."

1 The Return

Sardana music: very popular style of Catalonian folk music and dance.

2 Word of Mouth

Amor, pena, desig, somni, dolor: An endnote to this section of the poem read: "The line is from a Catalan poem in *Cantilena* by Joseph Sebastien Pons. *Love, agony, desire, dream, suffering.*"

The Backside of the Academy

The "Academy" is the American Academy of Arts and Letters in New York City.

ART REMAINS THE ONE WAY . . . : from Robert Browning's *The Ring and the Book* (1868), L.842.

WE ARE YOUNG AND WE ARE FRIENDS OF TIME: from Edward Arlington Robinson's poem "Captain Craig" (1902).

CONSCIOUS UTTERANCE OF THOUGHT BY SPEECH . . . : from Ralph Waldo Emerson's "Society and Solitude" (1870).

WITHOUT VISION THE PEO: "Without vision the people perish," from Proverbs 29:18.

IVE BY BREAD ALONE: "Man shall not live by bread alone," from Matthew 4:4.

Mountain : One from Bryant

The poem carried this endnote: "This is a poem of William Cullen Bryant's that is run backward ("What?" said Denise Levertov. "You mean 'Foul Water' instead of 'Waterfowl'?" "Exactly," I said.) The poem is "Monument Mountain," out of which I took key words and phrases and ran the film backward."

Rukeyser was fascinated by the relationship between film and poetry and began writing about it in the 1930s. Discussing film in LP, she wrote: "The selection and ordering are a work of preparation and equilibrium of the breaking of the balance and the further growth. The single image, which arrives with its own speed, takes its place in a sequence which reinforces that image" (143). Rukeyser studied with the famous film editor Helen van Dongen in the 1930s and went on to work herself as a film editor.

The Outer Banks

The poem carried this note:

This country, the Outer Banks of North Carolina, is a strong country of imagination: Raleigh's first settlements, in which Thomas Hariot the scientist served a year in the New World, were here; the Wright Brothers flew from here; Hart Crane's "Hatteras" is set among these sand-bars, these waters. Several journeys here, the last one for the sake of the traces of Thomas Hariot (toward a biography I am writing) led me to this poem. The *Tiger*, in the last part of the poem, is one of the ships sent out by Raleigh. The quotations are from Selma, Alabama, in 1965. The truncated wing is a monument to the Wright Brothers. The spiral lighthouse is Hatteras light.

Rukeyser first published this poem in *Poetry* (Sept. 1965) and then as a chapbook by the Unicorn Press, 1967. She added the footnote when she included the poem in SD. The biography of Thomas Hariot referred to in the note was published in 1971.

5

"Book of Changes": A reference to the ancient Chinese *Book of Changes* or the *I Ching*, assumed to be by the legendary Chinese Emperor Fu Hsi (2953–2838 BCE) and originating from a prehistoric divination technique. An I Ching is "cast" or performed by making a hexagram with six solid or broken lines.

4 *Lives*

This section of the book was first published with this note: "These two 'Lives' are part of a sequence. Akiba is the Jewish shepherd-scholar of the first and second century, identified with the Song of Songs and with the insurrection against Hadrian's Rome, led in A.D. 132 by Bar Cochba (Son of the Star). After this lightning war, Jerusalem captured, the Romans driven out of the south, Rome increased its military machine; by 135, the last defenses fell, Bar Cochba was killed, Akiba was tortured to death at the command of his friend, the Roman Rufus, and a harrow was drawn over the ground where Jerusalem had stood, leaving only a corner of wall. The story in my mother's family is that we are descended from Akiba—unverifiable, but a great gift to a child."

Rukeyser included a second paragraph to her note to "Akiba," indicating that this poem and "Käthe Kollwitz" belong to her "Lives" series and, "To come are Franz Boas and Bessie Smith," indicating that she still envisioned writing additional poems. See also the annotations to the "Lives" section of TW.

Akiba

The Way Out

In the first section of the poem, Rukeyser imposes a detail from the life of Yochanan ben Zakkai, the distinguished rabbi and disciple of the scholar Hillel, onto Akiba. According to tradition, it was not Akiba, but ben Zakkai, a pacifist, who staged his own death during Vespasian's siege of Jerusalem in 68 CE and was carried out of Jerusalem in a coffin rather than surrender. See also the annotations to the "Lives" section of TW.

The Bonds

Rachel: Akiba's wife. According to the Talmudic story, in marrying Akiba, Rachel went from a life of luxury to poverty and, intuiting God's will and grasping Akiba's potential for greatness, she encouraged him to go off and study, which left her alone first for twelve years and then for another twelve years. His achievement and strength of leadership are subtly attributed to her vision and moral power.

For an extended analysis of this poem, see Kaufman, "'But not the study': Writing as a Jew."

Käthe Kollwitz

Käthe Kollwitz: (1867–1945) German printmaker and sculptor whose art was notable for its passionate social conscience as well as its antiwar conviction. Her pacifism was personal as well as philosophical, as her youngest son was killed in World War I and her grandson in World War II.

For a discussion of Rukeyser's representation of Kollwitz's life and the correspondences she found between her life and Kollwitz's, see Porritt, "'Unforgetting Eyes': Rukeyser Portraying Kollwitz's Truth." Also see Kearns's biography, *Käthe Kollwitz: Woman and Artist,* and her essay, "Martha Kearns on Muriel Rukeyser and Käthe Kollwitz."

"Nie wieder Krieg": "Never again war."

The Speed of Darkness

7

In a letter dated September 1, 1976, with a list of addressees including American and international figures such as Betty Ford, Bella Abzug, Martha Graham, Jane Hart, Gloria Steinem, Gerald Ford, Jimmy Carter, "Bucky" Fuller, Robert Jay Lifton, Kurt Vonnegut, Golda Meir, and Simone de Beauvoir, among many others, Rukeyser explained her desire to form an activist group of Americans called "ARNO" to "move against the word and concept of bastardy."

She wrote: "It is beginning to be clear that we can end the concept of illegitimacy as applied to children. This punishment of children can go the way of other punishments and torments that have been dropped in our own time. The word 'bastard' can stay as a pejorative, if people want it, but, like 'villain,' a class-word from the same stock, it can let go of its group meaning.// There are no bastards. There are only children; and parents, responsible or irresponsible . . ." Please sign below, affirming: "'THERE ARE NO BASTARDS. THERE ARE CHILDREN. ARNO.'" Robert Jay Lifton's returned, signed letter is in the ARNO file (LCII).

Breaking Open. *New York: Random House, 1973.*

Rukeyser's original acknowledgments read:

My thanks to the following publications and to their editors. Poems in this book first appeared: "Looking at Each Other" in *New York Quarterly;* "Despisals" in *Antaeus;* "This Morning" in *Mademoiselle;* "Ballad of Orange and Grape" in *New American Review;* "The Writer" in *The World of Translation* (P.E.N.); "Wherever," "Fields Where We Slept" in *29 Poems* by Muriel Rukeyser (Rapp & Whiting/André Deutsch, London); "All the Little Animals;" "After Melville" in *Poetry Review* (London); "To Be a Jew" in the Reform Jewish prayerbook, *Service of the Heart* (London), and *Beast in View* (Doubleday) and *Selected Poems of Muriel Rukeyser* (New Directions); "Fire" and "City of Paradise" in *Mundus Artium;* "The Running of the Grunion" in *Ararat;* "Iris" (part 1) in *The New Yorker,* the entire poem in *29 Poems;* "In the Underworld" in *Transatlantic Review;* "Bringing" in *Green Flag* (City Lights Books); "Next" in *Stony Brook Review;* "Flying to Hanoi" in *American Report;* "Waiting for Icarus" in *Vogue;* "It is There" in *American Review.*

The group of poems, "Searching/Not Searching" in *New York Quarterly.*

From the poem "Breaking Open," parts 19 & 20 in *Poetry Magazine;* parts 8, 11, 12, 13 in *The Nation;* first part of 1, 2, 10, 17 in *Antaeus.*

Waking This Morning

a violent woman in the violent day: In a public reading in 1969, recorded for the "Spoken Arts Treasury: 100 Modern Poets" series, Rukeyser commented humorously, "I think of myself as a violent woman who tries like the members of AA; I try not to be violent one more day."

What Do We See?

In a public reading in New York in 1983, Rukeyser commented: "[This poem] has a cadenza in it, that is, a place for you, a place for the reader or witness or hearer, to move from the last question in any way you yourself move, to the next place in the poem" ("New Letters on the Air"). The idea of the reader being part of the poem was central to Rukeyser's poetics. As early as 1949, in LP, Rukeyser wrote that she would like to use another word for "audience," "reader," or "listener": "I suggest the old word 'witness,' which includes the act of seeing or knowing by personal experience, as well as the act of giving evidence. The overtone of responsibility in this word is not present in the others; and the tension of the law makes a climate here which is that climate of excitement and revelation giving air to the work of art, announcing with the poem that we are about to change, that work is being done on the self. // These three terms of relationship—poet, poem, and witness—are none of them static. We are changing, living beings, experiencing the inner change of poetry. // The relationships are the meanings, and we have very few of the words for them" (175).

Desdichada

Desdichada: A Spanish word that translates as "poor, wretched one," or "unfortunate, unlucky one."

ewig: A German word that translates as "eternal" or "eternally," "everlasting," "perpetual," or "imperishably."

Voices

The endnote to this poem read: "Aug. 26, 1968—by invitation for the Olympics. For Otto Boch, who came to Barcelona July 1936 to run in the Antifascist Olympics." See the annotation to "The Book of the Dead" (US1).

Fire
from City of Paradise

Both of these poems are translations from the work of Vicente Aleixandre (1898–1984), who was born in Seville and spent most of his childhood in Malaga. A contemporary of Jimenez and Lorca, he was publishing, in Spanish, as early as 1932. The first full-book translations of Aleixandre's work into English were done by Lewis Hyde and Robert Bly in 1977, the year Aleixandre also won the Nobel Prize for Literature.

Searching / Not Searching

I

In this first section of the poem, Rukeyser alludes to subjects she writes about in other poems and prose: **the blackened miners** suggest the Gauley Bridge mining disaster, the subject of Rukeyser's poem "The Book of the Dead" (US1); **that Elizabethan man** refers to Thomas Hariot, the scientist and explorer about whom Rukeyser wrote the biography *The Traces of Thomas Hariot;* and **that man forgotten for belief** suggests Otto Boch, who appears in many of Rukeyser's poems in relation to the Spanish Civil War. See the annotation to "The Book of the Dead" (US1).

3 For Dolci

Danilo Dolci, known as "the Sicilian Gandhi" was twice a nominee for the Nobel Peace Prize. An architect, engineer, and writer, Dolci dedicated his life to serving and speaking out on behalf of the poor, the illiterate, the oppressed, and the hopeless. An inventive leader of nonviolent action, he also wrote poetry, published interviews with workers, and authored a number of books, including *To Feed the Hungry.* He was renowned for his work teaching children and, in the 1960s, became somewhat of a cult figure in northern Europe and the United States.

4 Concrete

They are pouring the city . . . / . . . I am pouring my poems: For a discussion of the relationship between Rukeyser's poetics and her father's work in the building industry, see Daniels, "Muriel Rukeyser and Her Literary Critics" (253–54).

6 Reading the *Kieu*

As Rukeyser noted in her original endnote, the *Kieu* is the national epic of Vietnam.

8 H. F. D.

H. F. D. was Hallie Flanagan Davis, director of the WPA's Federal Theatre Project, whom Rukeyser first knew in her capacity as a faculty member at Vassar College. They maintained a lifelong friendship.

9 The Artist as Social Critic

the voice of my son speaking half-world away / coming clear on the radio into my room / out of blazing Belfast: William L. Rukeyser, the poet's son, worked as a reporter and photographer in Belfast from 1971–1972, a period marked by what he has called the "large scale intensification of problems" in Ireland, which included bombings and arson. Muriel Rukeyser would work late into the night with the radio on and would hear him broadcasting from Belfast.

13

after Camus, 1946: Camus was in New York in 1946, the year *The Stranger* was published, as part of a three-month lecture tour of North America.

Boys of These Men Full Speed

Jane Cooper: Poet who taught with Rukeyser at Sarah Lawrence College. Cooper was a longtime friend of Rukeyser's and wrote the foreword, entitled "Meeting-Places," for the reissued edition of LP (1996).

Next

Charles Morice: (1861–1919) French critic and symbolist poet. It is likely that, because Morice's poems were included, at Paul Gauguin's request, in a notebook of sketches and writings that Gauguin published after his return from Tahiti (*Noa Noa,* 1895), Rukeyser would have come across Morice's work when she was completing her translations of the rari poems, published in 1948 (GW). At the bottom of a typescript of "Next," Rukeyser includes a typed note to a Mr. Quasha at the *Stony Brook Review:* "XIX-cent. French, of course, to be found written on the verse of one of Gauguin's Tahitian watercolors; and, in our time in popular form as the Star Baby of *2001.*" She continues: "*Please believe the punctuation.* I have a rubber stamp for that, but it's in storage with my things," and indicates that the poem is forthcoming in BO. Rukeyser did, in fact, have such a rubber stamp made and used it to emphasize to editors the preciseness of her punctuation and spacing decisions in her typescripts.

Two Years

Frances Bucholtz (formerly Sussman), Rukeyser's sister, died of prolonged cancer in New York in 1971. She was seven years younger than Rukeyser. The disease was particularly "bitter" because her physicians failed to catch it early when it would likely have been treatable.

Ballad of Orange and Grape

Rukeyser prefaced a public reading of this poem with the following discussion:

[This poem] has to do with a very hot summer in East Harlem. I was working with young black writers and high school kids, very brilliant black high school kids who were beginning to write. And there was a lot of street fighting that summer in the night. And those kids, there was one who talked to me the most, said all last night he hung onto his bed trying to keep himself from going out into the street. He did keep himself. And I did an exercise with them, which I think of under the name of "A piece of paper." . . . [I] show them a sheet. Say, "Here it is with its properties and its possibilities," and crumple it and throw it down. Then I say, "Here it is now, with its properties and its possibilities." And then I say something like "Write" or "Do something with it." I think I said "Do something with it," because that boy who hung onto his bed struck a match and lit the paper and half of it went up. And I said "Yes, we know that. We really, we know that." I was trying to do something in words. Could he do it in words? And he took another piece of paper, and he wrote little and middle sized and big: Help HELP **HELP**.

And we would leave, the white people who worked, you know, with attache cases, portfolios, would leave about 5:30 everyday and go downtown. And I was waiting for the building to be built where I now live and thinking I should be living here where I work. And I would stop across the street on the next corner, I suppose partly to delay leaving. . . . [There] was a hot dog stand opened to the heat in the corner, with just two tanks. One said orange and one said grape. And [the man behind the counter] was pouring. And he was pouring a dark purple drink in the tank marked orange . . . ("Just Before the Gates").

Don Baty, the Draft Resister

The endnote from BO reads, "Don Baty, a draft resister, took sanctuary in the Washington Square church during the war in Vietnam. Many of us took bread and wine with him and said, 'I am Don Baty.' When the police came for him and asked, 'Who is Don Baty?' everyone said, 'I am Don Baty.'"

Te Hanh : Long-Ago Garden

The note to this poem in BO read: "The Vietnamese poet Te Hanh (1921–) was born in the South, was in the Resistance and in jail. He is now in Hanoi. His 4 books of poems are *Adolescence, South Heart, To North Vietnam, Wave Song*. He is one of the foremost poets of Vietnam."

This poem appears to be a translation. Rukeyser apparently met Te Hanh, president of the Foreign Commission of the Vietnamese Writers' Union, on her 1972 trip to Vietnam with Denise Levertov and Jane Hart. In a letter to potential publishers dated March 13, 1973, Rukeyser explains: "Late in 1972 I went to Vietnam with a letter from P.E.N. (of which Rukeyser was president, 1975–1976) authorizing me to invite Vietnamese writers to set up with American writers a translation exchange program." In a letter to Dr. Spock, dated April 2, 1973, Rukeyser thanks him for hand-delivering a letter to Te Hanh and another poet, Nguyen dinh Thi, along with an authorization note for them to sign to give permission for their work to be published in English (LCII).

Ripe tenth-month fig, and fifth-month dragon-eye: This line originally appeared with the following note: "Dragon's eye, longan, related to the lichee nut, is the fruit of the tree *Euphoria longana*."

Secrets of American Civilization

Staughton Lynd: Labor activist, lawyer, historian, and author of numerous books. The son of Helen and Robert Lynd (see annotation to "The Seeming," SD) and a Yale professor, Lynd was active in the anti–Indochina war effort and made one of the first visits to Hanoi by an American during the war, a controversial decision that resulted in damaging professional consequences.

A Louis Sonnet

Louis Untermeyer: (1885–1977) American poet and anthologist. Well known as an editor of the *Masses*, Untermeyer later became an anthologist and selected many of Rukeyser's poems for publication. His favorable reviews were particularly important early in her career. She thanked Untermeyer in the original acknowledgments to BV.

After Melville

Bett and Walter Bezanson: Friends of Rukeyser's who met her in New Haven in the early 1940s when she was researching the biography of Willard Gibbs. Walter was both a scholar and editor of Melville and taught at Rutgers.

The Writer

Isaac Bashevis Singer: (1904–1991) The 1978 Nobel Laureate in Literature whose writing marked an era of Yiddish and American literature. Polish born, Singer came to the United States in 1935. Rukeyser was an acquaintance of Singer's in the mid-1960s.

Gradus Ad Parnassum

Gradus Ad Parnassum: Latin for "steps to Parnassus." Refers here to a common exercise book for aspiring pianists.

Flying to Hanoi

In 1972, Rukeyser traveled to Hanoi with the poet Denise Levertov and Jane Hart on an unofficial peace mission. See Daniels, "Searching/Not Searching: Writing the Biography of Muriel Rukeyser" and Levertov, "On Muriel Rukeyser."

It Is There

In a letter to the editor accompanying her typescript submission for BO, Rukeyser wrote: "The newest poems are 'It Is There'—which is Hanoi New York and might be marked that . . ."

Sacred Lake

orante: According to the *New Advent Catholic Encyclopedia,* Orante, or Orans, refers to subjects depicted in the art of the Russian catacombs, a female figure with extended arms who prays and is a symbol of the deceased's soul in heaven. See http://www.newadvent.org/cathen/11269a.htm.

3 Northern Poems

Rukeyser's endnote: "The Eskimo poems were translated by Paul Radin and Muriel Rukeyser from texts given by Rasmussen and others. They have been adapted from material in: *The Netsilik Eskimos—Social Life and Spiritual Culture,* by Knud Rasmussen; Gyldendalske Boghandel, Nordisk Forlag, Copenhagen; *Intellectual Culture of the Caribou Eskimos—Iglulik and Caribou Eskimo Texts,* by Knud Rasmussen, same publisher; *The Ammassalik Eskimo II:* Nr. 3, W. Thalbitzer; *Language and Folklore,* C. A. Reitzel, Boghandel, Kobenhaven. The glossary used was *Five Hundred Eskimo Words,* by Kaj Birket-Smith. The last drafts were written in 1973, after the death of Paul Radin, that incomparable man." Rasmussen was a Danish explorer whose books were based on his journeys to the arctic Alaskan coast in the early 1920s. Paul Radin was a well-known anthropologist and former student of Franz Boas, whom Rukeyser interviewed for her research on Boas.

Breaking Open

Westbeth: Since 1967, when the building it occupies was converted from Bell Labs, Westbeth has been an artists' colony/residence in Greenwich Village. Rukeyser, one of the first tenants, moved into Westbeth in 1970 and maintained this residence through the end of her life. In a reading in New York City, Rukeyser talked about Westbeth: "I live in a very curious place in New York. It used to be the lab building of the phone company and has been made over. It's now, for instance, an enormous building, a big city block large, and holds 1100 people, and each member—I can't say the head of each family because I don't think that way—but one person in each family is an artist. It's the first artists' building in this country. And there are writers and painters and musicians, film people and dancers and other people who consider themselves artists, and I commend it to you to look at, to make other buildings like it. It has a certain danger. That is, when you go down to your mail, many people want you to back them for Guggenheims (laughter)" ("New Letters on the Air").

The Gates. *New York: McGraw-Hill, 1976.*

The title *The Gates* refers to the entrance of the South Korean prison in which the poet Kim Chi Ha was held and which Rukeyser visited in the summer

of 1975. Rukeyser's original dedication read: "For Jacob & Kang / & the future."
Jacob is Rukeyser's first grandchild, who had just been born, and Kang is Kim
Chi Ha's baby son, whom Rukeyser met in Korea.

Rukeyser's original acknowledgements read:

Some of the poems in this book have appeared in the following publications: *American
Poetry Review, American Writing, American Scholar, Antaeus, Black Box, Lilith, Ms., Neruda
Reader, Ontario Review, Writers and Teachers Magazine.* To these publications and to their edi-
tors, my thanks.

Dream–Drumming

raga: a South Asian Indian musical scale.

Double Ode

Bill & Alison: In a New York City reading, Rukeyser explained the dedica-
tion to this poem: "My son and his wife, at a time when they were still in exile
and waiting for their first child. In exile in Canada, from which they have been
able to come home without going through the president's amnesty. Through a
crack in the drafting it became possible" ("New Letters on the Air").

4

**But these two figures are not the statues east and west / at my long
window . . . :** "The two figures, the two stone figures, are the corners of the
long set of windows where I live . . . the female and male blackstone figures are
Mexican obsidian figures, and they're on the floor" ("New Letters on the Air").

How We Did It

We knew we would climb the Senate steps: Rukeyser commented at a
poetry reading, "This is based on a document. This is the night in Washington be-
fore we went to the Senate. This was to present the petition to ask the Senate to
stop the war in Vietnam" ("New Letters on the Air"). Rukeyser engaged in an
antiwar act of civil disobedience in June 1972. She was detained overnight at the
Women's Detention Center, and later recorded details of the event:

We were five women in a one-person cell in Washington, on a hot day a month ago, and
the trial for the action for which 111 men and women were arrested will take place on
Thursday (July 27th) in Superior Court, Washington. It was our act of civil disobedience:
we are a group who went to Washington to present a citizens' petition to the Senate to
stop whatever was before them and because of urgent necessity to end the war in Vietnam.
Knowing from long experience that there would be no quick response, we made our ges-
ture.

   We lay down on the floor outside the Senate. We were arrested, and we allowed our-
selves to be arrested peaceably, as we had done the action. This group was part of Redress,
a movement of the Concerned Clergy and Layman which had acted a month before in
the House. But this act in the Senate is considered a misdemeanor, and we are to be tried
with the possibility of a maximum sentence of $500 fine and 6 months in jail. The defense
of some of us will be the Nuremberg obligation.

   The leaders of the group were Robert Jay Lifton, Richard Falk, Grace Paley, and Dr
Spock. (LC)

See also "Parallel Invention" (G).

The doctor: Dr. Spock.

Hypnogogic Figure

This is a translation of a poem by Gunnar Ekelöf. The endnote to this poem in G read: "English by Leif Sjoberg and Muriel Rukeyser."

For Kay Boyle

Kay Boyle: (c. 1902–1992) A novelist, short-story writer, poet, and translator who lived in Europe (primarily Paris) from 1923–1941, when she returned to the United States. She taught at San Francisco University from 1963 onward and was a political activist, anti-Vietnam War figure, and friend of Rukeyser's. Her novel, *Avalanche* (1944), became required reading for the U.S. Army.

Resurrection of the Right Side

Rukeyser prefaced a reading of this poem with the following, "In this kind of illness [stroke], and this kind of recovery, there's a kind of half-life. Half of the body and half of the imagination is quite alive and well, and the other half is somehow dragged along behind the other side. I spoil this story for you by giving you this context and in the hospital, there was a man who said there was a dead man in the bed all night. 'It was beside me, cold and inert.' And they said, 'No, it didn't happen.' And he said, 'It did happen. I felt him there all night long.' And they said, 'Not only did it not happen. It couldn't happen in this place.' And he said, 'It did happen and I'm going to sue the hospital.' And they found out what it was, his repudiated, injured, ailing side. And he had repudiated half of himself. And that is the trap in this. And the recovery comes very slowly, but it does come. And they say to you it doesn't come as recovery. 'You were doing what we called denial.' And you say, 'I'm not. You're talking about the arm and the leg, I'm talking about the whole person, myself'" ("New Letters on the Air").

The Sun-Artist

Bob Miller: In the documentary film featuring Rukeyser, *They Are Their Own Gifts,* the poet discusses Bob Miller as an artist who made sun screens in the San Francisco Exploratorium. She stated: "[The sun screen] is an art in which the viewer, the witness, can be part of the making of the work. I care about it very much, because as the witnesses, the audiences to what I read are part of the making. They don't change the poem, however. This is a matter of changing what is on the screen by intercepting out colors. You can choose out the red and make it quite a different work. And it's the next kind of art, in a way, in which *you* are part of the art. . . . I could play the music experiments there, and I would go back and stand and wave my arms or dance slowly before the screen." Rukeyser herself served as artist-in-residence for the Exploratorium and details her proposals for an eleven-part exhibit of language processes in a memo to the director dated June 1976 (LCII).

Fable

Herbert Kohl: A writer and educator, Kohl was a friend of Rukeyser from the 1960s and 1970s. In 1967, they cofounded Teachers and Writers Collaborative, a nonprofit organization of writers and educators who bring living writers into classrooms to contribute to young writers and the teaching of writing.

Neruda, the Wine

This poem is an elegy to Chilean poet Pablo Neruda, whom Rukeyser met several times. He once told her that his campaign for the Chilean Senate would involve banging a drum. She sent him a drum.

He died in a moment of general dying: Refers to the assassination of Chilean president Salvador Allende, who was killed during an army coup in 1973, also the year of Neruda's death.

Work, for the Day Is Coming

Rukeyser prefaced a reading of this poem: "This name is of course a variation on the hymn ["Work, for the Night Is Coming"], but I don't feel that way about the night. I do a great deal of my life at night, and I do a great deal of my work at night . . ." ("New Letters on the Air").

Parallel Invention

In G, Rukeyser included a note following this poem: "After reading an essay by Robert McC. Adams in *Civilization*—found in the Women's Detention Center, Washington D.C." (See also "How We Did It.") Accompanying this note was bibliographic information for the footnote to *Civilization:* "Edited by Williams et al. 6th edition. Published by Scott Foresman, 1969."

Slow Death of the Dragon

Rukeyser dates this poem "Summer 1936–Winter 1975": 1936 marks the year she traveled to Spain and the outbreak of the Spanish Civil War, and 1975 marks Franco's death.

Mendings

Alfred Marshak: A geneticist and political radical, and a friend of Rukeyser's from when she lived and taught at the California Labor School in the mid-1940s.

The Gates

The following notes come from the Henry W. and Albert A. Berg Collection and parallel, in slightly different form, the prose introduction to "The Gates" that Rukeyser did publish. Both refer to Rukeyser's 1975 trip to Korea.

Clues (being what the librettoes call the Argument)

The woman who is speaking is sent to Asia, where a stinging poet is in prison, in solitary. Through the power of his writing and his life under a galling oppression.

The woman makes the attempt she is sent for: to appeal to the ministers in power for the poet's release. She does this, and the journey turns into a search for the poet, the "house of the poet."

She sees his small son, a strong infant just beginning to run—separated from his father, who is in extreme immediate danger of execution or life imprisonment.

The baby transforms for her into her own son years ago, cut off from his own father for reasons of the imprisoning culture of that time and what it did to men and women.

She goes further in the present-day search—through the poet's poems, through the well-wishers (who cannot now be named), through the courts of government "it's like Kafka," one of her guides says, and finally to the House of the Poet.

It is the huge prison and the prison yard. . . . She remembers. She stands vigil. At the end of the day, which is also the Day of Atonement after the trial of the poet has *not* been held—the gates swing open, surprisingly, for a crowded bus. The thin Chinese-red posts of another gate are visible. The busload of prisoners goes in.

This is the apparatus of the group of poems, The Gates. It is my hope that this note can be removed in later printings. I have been lucky: This has been possible several times before, as the material of my earlier poems became more known to readers—poems dealing with the cave-paintings of Ajanta, the life of the scientist Willard Gibbs, the life of the composer Charles Ives. People used to say, "Ives? You mean Bill Ives? Currier and Ives? (The Gates, folder 3)

For further commentary on this poem, see Michelle Ware's essay, "Opening the Gates: Muriel Rukeyser and the Poetry of Witness."

6 The Church of Galilee

In 1974, Rukeyser traveled to Israel and visited the area of the Galilee, including the Church of the Annunciation.

7 The Dream of Galilee

Akiba at rest over Kinneret: On this trip, Rukeyser also visited Akiba's grave. "Kinneret" is the Hebrew term for the Galilee.

Juvenilia

These poems were written in Rukeyser's early and late adolescence, during her years at the Ethical Culture and Fieldston schools and at Vassar. For more information on these poems, please refer to the introduction to this volume. For comments on the significance of these poems in Rukeyser's personal history as well as some speculation on her decision not to include them in later volumes, see Daniels, "A Note on the Place Poems" (27–28).

A New Poem
An Unborn Poet

This is the only poem we know of that Rukeyser wrote and published between 1978, when her CP came out, and her death in 1980. Rukeyser read this poem publicly at a celebration in her honor at Sarah Lawrence College in 1979, and it was published in *American Poetry Review*, November/December 1979, 8:6. Rukeyser prefaced a reading of this poem by saying: "I have a new poem. I finished it last night. I don't know whether it's a first draft. . . . It's a poem after a long gap of illness and recovery and getting over that big book that holds back a big door [CP] and it's very hard to get past it and write a poem after. And it's a poem for Alice Walker, for whom I've been trying to write for years. It's called 'An Unborn Poet' and that's not Alice Walker, that's me (laughter)" ("New Letters on the Air").

Alice Walker transferred from Spelman College to Sarah Lawrence College in 1964 and graduated from Sarah Lawrence College in January 1966. On Rukeyser's influence, Walker stated: "What I learned from Muriel is that poetry, done well, is always about the truth; that it is subversive; that you can't shut it up and that it stays" (White 109). Walker's relationship with Rukeyser was complicated; interested readers may wish to consult Evelyn White's biography, *Alice Walker: A Life* (2004).

her hurt eye: Here and elsewhere in the poem, when Rukeyser refers to a young female student from the south with an injury to her eye, it is Alice Walker, one of Rukeyser's students at Sarah Lawrence College. See Walker's essay that discusses her injury: "Beauty: When the Other Dancer is the Self" (361–370).

Zora: Zora Neale Hurston (1891–1960) African American novelist and folklorist. Alice Walker is largely credited for recovering and promoting Hurston's many contributions as a writer and intellect. See Walker's essays "Zora Neale Hurston: A Cautionary Tale and a Partisan View" and "Looking for Zora" (83–92, 93–116).

Berenice: Berenice Abbott (1898–1991) A major twentieth-century photographer, known for her New York photographs and portraits of major intellects and artists of her time. Abbott was a longtime friend of Rukeyser and fellow Greenwich Village resident. She took photographs of Rukeyser on more than one occasion, including the ultra closeup of Rukeyser's eye that decorated Rukeyser's biography of Thomas Hariot. Rukeyser wrote the foreword to Abbott's 1970 book of photos.

Grace, Denise: the writers Grace Paley and Denise Levertov, friends of Rukeyser's.

❧ TEXTUAL NOTES

Conventions and Considerations in the Text

1. When sections of long poems are indicated by number, Arabic numbers are used throughout. Rukeyser's first editions varied in their usage of Roman or Arabic numerals for this purpose.

2. Setting Rukeyser's poems is challenging in part because of the way she uses spacing. Her editor for *29 Poems* wrote her about this, and we quote from her letter here because it articulates the challenge quite well:

> On the question of intentional spaces between words we have found that confusion often arises about how much space the poet would like to have left on the printed page, and in order to avoid unnecessary correction at proof I would be most grateful if we could settle this point now. The problem arises in that typewritten character spaces are usually much wider than the printed character, which of course vary anyway depending on what typeface one uses. Would we, therefore, be correct if we instructed the printer to gauge the spaces by aligning them to whichever character they fall below in the typewritten MS? I enclose an example of how "Bringing their life" would be treated to illustrate what I mean. In following this method, we are, of course, assuming that the spacing is intentionally uneven within each poem, and has been typewritten exactly as it should appear in print and hope we are correct in this.

To this, Rukeyser replies in the margin, "yes, thank you very much"; we have thus used this approach as our guide, as did the editor for *29 Poems*. Sometimes different editions of poems have a different look, as in the Elegies series, which appears in part in *A Turning Wind, Beast in View, Green Wave,* and as a whole in *Elegies, Selected Poems* (excerpts), *Waterlily Fire,* and *Collected Poems.* In such cases, we studied all the editions of each poem and approximated as closely as possible what seemed to be Rukeyser's intent for the poems' setting. In some cases, we made compromises between different versions.

3. Enjambment: Rukeyser is known for her long lines. Although we use her first editions as copy texts, wherever possible we have reduced the enjambment that was compulsory in those editions due to margin length. When that is impossible, we have wrapped the line around to the next line and indented it. Where it has been difficult to tell whether or not a given line was intentionally or necessarily enjambed, we have determined this by studying and comparing the line breaks of the poem in question in all editions of the poem.

4. Separate, unnumbered sections of long poems are indicated by an ornamented line space. Rukeyser often used asterisks to separate sections of a poem and, as with the spacing in her poems, was highly attuned to the look of the poem on the page. The editor of *Selected Poems* (1951) wrote to ask her whether the asterisks should be centered according to page width or according to the length of longest line on the page. The editor commented: "I like them best when they are visually centered on each page. You cannot exactly go by the longest line, particularly where there is only one long line on a page. You have to go by the 'feel' of the page, so to speak." Underneath this, Rukeyser wrote "Yes." (SP TS 2465, p. 4). Our design here marks an effort to achieve consistency in the visual appearance of the poems.

5. Rukeyser often wanted more vertical spaces between stanzas, and between titles and first lines of poems, than her publishers would provide. For instance, in "Madboy's Song," she requested four vertical spaces between the penultimate and last lines (SP TS 2464, p. 44). In "The Speed of Darkness," she wanted triple spaces between titles and first lines, and between stanzas (LCII). In this poem, and throughout her books, she wanted poems printed on their own pages whenever possible.

6. After we had completed our research for this project, the Library of Congress reorganized the Rukeyser holdings to categorize and catalogue a significant portion of archival papers that had previously been designated as "unprocessed." The Rukeyser collection is now arranged into two sections, Part I and Part II. We have been advised by the Manuscript Division Literary Specialist at the Library of Congress not to use previous file and box designation numbers in our citations as they may now be obsolete due to the recent work on the Rukeyser holdings. We have been assured that the newly drafted register to the Rukeyser holdings will assist any future researchers in locating the materials they seek.

7. In some cases, Rukeyser has varied spellings within the same poem or section. In these cases, we have standardized spellings and made them contemporary. Thus "Postoffice" in "Gauley Bridge" and "post-office" in "Praise of the Committee" has become "post office"; "blonde" in "The Cruise" has become "blond"; and "travellers" in "Letter to the Front" has become "travelers".

Tracking the Text

Below we have acknowledged and detailed changes made to the copy texts, variances in different published editions of Rukeyser's poems, and mistakes in the 1978 *Collected Poems.*

In identifying the location of each item, we have noted the poem's title and, if applicable, subtitle or number of subsection. Poems divided into unnumbered sections by ornaments are counted by section (the section under the title is 1; a new section begins after each ornament); then stanza number (within the section in a poem with ornaments or else counting from the start of the poem); then line number (within the stanza). When counting lines we have included all lines of text, including runovers of enjambed lines. The locators, then, look like this:

Poem Title
Section Title or Section number (where applicable)
section#: stanza#: line# (for poems with ornaments)
or
stanza#: line# (for poems with no ornaments)

Theory of Flight (1935)
Wedding Presents

I

3:3: By typographical error, CP changes "breath-intake" to "breath-inake".

Three Sides of a Coin

3

2:7: CP adds a stanza break after the line "this is a different story."

The Lynchings of Jesus

2 The Committee-Room

1:5: TF reads "with it" and CP inserts a period.

1:6: TF reads, "into a series of nights" and CP presents a variant printing, "into a series of flights". In TF and CP, the same line continues "rocking sea-like" but in SP, Rukeyser changed this to "a sea rocking". She marked this change in her page proofs for SP (PP 2467).

3 The Trial

1:7:5: CP erroneously adds a period at the end of the phrase "In the Square."

2:1:1: TF reads "Earth, include sky   ;" and CP prints this line with a colon: "Earth, include sky   :"

The Tunnel

1

5:3: TF and CP read "mines graveyards." This edition adds a missing apostrophe to "mines' graveyards."

Night Flight : New York

1:8:2: "Futility stands". Apparently in error, "futility" was not capitalized in the 1978 CP as it was in TF.

For Memory

Life and Works

3:6 and 3:12: TF reads "Remember" and CP prints: "Remembering".

Holy Dying

2:7: TF reads "the young days" and CP changes this to "the younger days".

Child and Mother

3:4: In TF, the end of this line has a semicolon, and the CP changes the punctuation to a colon.

Burlesque

6:3: In TF, stanza six is six lines in length; CP inserted a stanza break after line three of stanza six, creating an additional stanza.

Cats and a Cock

9:1:1–2: Before the quote by Melville, TF inserts a section break and CP does not. We followed TF here, to parallel the section break preceding the quoted passage from Rosa Luxemburg (at 5:1:1–2).

The Blood Is Justified

10:2 (penultimate stanza): TF reads "those other lands" and CP prints: "these other lands".

U.S. 1 (1938)

The Face of the Dam: Vivian Jones

4:4: By typographical error, CP changes "into" to "innto".

George Robinson: Blues

8:1: CP removes the stanza break between the stanza beginning "The water they would bring" and the stanza beginning "Looked like somebody sprinkled".

A Flashing Cliff

4:4: US1 and CP print "catalept!" and SP replaces the exclamation point with a period. Rukeyser marked this correction on SP TS 2464.

Boy with His Hair Cut Short

1:1: US1 reads "on this twentieth" and SP changes this to "on a twentieth". Rukeyser indicated this correction on SP TS 2464

1:2: CP changes the letter "L" to the word "El."

The Cruise

25:22: US1 reads "The voice of life" and CP prints: "That voice of life".

32:5: In the line "'Now,'" wrote the captain, "'boats of madness'", CP corrects the misplaced closed quotation mark in US1 following the word "captain" and moves it to be an open quotation before "boats."

33:6: By typographical error, CP changes "ineffective rancid idle" to "ineffective racid idle".

Mediterranean

Prose introduction: US1 reads "the Americans with Anti-Fascist Olympic Games" and CP corrects this to read "Americans with the Anti-Fascist Olympic Games".

1

3:3: US1 reads "during machinggun battle" and CP changes this to read "during machine gun battle";

2

2:4: CP erroneously adds a period after "and pale".

3:4: reads "Machine-gun marks" and CP changes this to "Machine gun".

3

1:1: US1 reads "Seething, and falling black" and by editorial decision we are following the CP: "Seething, and falling back".

2:4: CP changes "plaster" to "plastic".

4

2:5: US1 reads "France, Cost Brava" and CP corrects this to "France, Costa Brava".

A Turning Wind (1939)

Reading Time : 1 Minute 26 Seconds

TW includes a final line in this poem that does not appear in either the 1951 SP, following Rukeyser's request, or the CP. In TW, the final two lines read: "the yellow joy after the song of the sun, / aftermath proof, extended radiance."

Song, the Brain-Coral

3:1: TW reads "Let the great night" and CP prints: "Let the green night".

Otherworld

Landing at Liverpool

1:1:1: TW reads "dream-journey" and CP, in typographical error, prints: "dream-journal".

1:6:3: TW reads "the great island," and CP prints this without the comma: "the great island".

The Island

1:1:16: TW reads "winding the," and CP prints this without the comma: "winding the".

1:1:22: TW reads "Lancelot Andrewes" and CP erroneously changes the spelling to "Andrews".

2:1:10: TW reads "see the street see the marchers" and CP reads "see the street see the marches".

Correspondences

Correspondences

1:14: In TW, the end of the line reads "the dust-land," and in CP "the dust".

8:3: In TW the end of the line reads "brick," and in CP "bricks,".

Noguchi

1:3: TW reads "turning up" and CP shows a variant printing: "turned up".

4:2: TW reads "did you walk down?" and CP reads: "did you walk," and omits the question mark.

The Shortest Way Home

4:11: TW reads "leaps the rose" and CP prints this with a comma: "leaps the rose,".

Paper Anniversary

1:1: TW reads "the crash" and CP reads "the Crash".

7:1: TW reads "no golf tomorrow" and CP corrects this by capitalizing "No".

M-Day's Child

Title: TW and CP have the title "M-Day's Child is Fair of Face". In SP, the current title appears and MR's TS 2464 confirms that she intended this change.

Gibbs

6:11: In TW, "Years of driving" read "In livery, driving". In a letter to Jan Berg, June 23, 1978, Rukeyser wrote: "I made one howler in the GIBBS poem when I wrote 'in livery, driving'—this is a line spoken to me, and repeated out of ignorance. It is totally out of character, and I have tried to remove it whenever the poem is reprinted. If you are translating GIBBS, I shall be grateful if you will delete the words 'in livery'" (LC).

6:16: In TW, "plotted curves" read "platted curves". CP emended this.

11:4: CP omitted the period at the end of the line after "spiralling through a dream".

Chapman

2:4: CP erroneously added a period from TW's "he writes" to "he writes."

Ives

4:8: TW reads "great to greater" and CP, apparently erroneously, reads: "greater to greater".

Beast in View (1944)
Mortal Girl

2:1: In a variant printing, the CP adds two spaces after "Sang:" and before the word "When".

2:4: BV reads "In whiteness lay" and CP reads "In whiteness I lay".

Darkness Music

Rukeyser cut all but the first and concluding lines of this poem before its reprinting in the CP. The BV version reads:

> The days grow and the stars cross over
> Drawing you nightly
> Along my human love.
> Alone at the vertical wall and wild with tears
> I watch your line of windows.
> Dance of eyes,
> Their constellation steers me from my death,
> Away, persuading me of
> Wavering dawn.
> Breeze of lilac in the sleepless night;
> Here overflown by bells
> Black altitudes,
> And my wild bed turns slowly among the stars.

Chapultepec Park—2

4:3: CP changes end punctuation from a period to a comma.

A Game of Ball

Title: BV reads "A Game of Ball," while CP reads "The Game of Ball."

Evening Plaza, San Miguel

6:3: In BV, the last stanza is six lines; CP emends this by adding a stanza break after the third line to create two tercets.

Letter to the Front

3

4:2: BV reads "Ideas of peace are bargained for." CP prints this line with a comma: "Ideas of peace are bargained for,".

5:4: CP changes "make" to "makes".

4 Sestina

Title: "Sestina" as a title for section 4 was added to the CP.

The Soul and Body of John Brown

6:1: JB reads "O my scene! My mother!" and we have followed this. BV, CP do not capitalize the second "my": "O my scene! my mother!"

The Green Wave (1948)

A Charm for Cantinflas

1:9: GW reads "Slow. Slow. Slow." and CP omits third "Slow."

Then I Saw What the Calling Was

Title: In her manuscript, Rukeyser titled this poem, "The Road Past Los Altos" ("Before 1945" folder, LCII).

Private Life of the Sphinx

4

1:11: CP, apparently erroneously, added a period after "our two faces" and before the em-dash.

Orpheus

I

1:8: O reads "treetrunks" and SP, CP reads "treetops".

2

I

2:2: SP, CP read "unity," and O reads "unity—".

2:5: O has a stanza break following this line and SP has a page break so we cannot determine whether this is also meant to be a stanza break. The CP does not have a stanza break here.

3

1:9: O and SP show a stanza break after this line but CP does not.

6

2:3: SP, CP read "murder," and O reads "murder".

2:5: O, SP read "in circus" and CP corrects this to "in the circus."

3:2: O reads "the shape of plants". We have followed this. SP, CP read "the shapes of plants".

7

2:6: Following this line, O has a stanza break. SP, CP do not.

8

1:9: O reads "tree of air." This was changed to "tree of nerves" in SP and indicated by Rukeyser in her SP galleys (PP 2467).

3

1:18: O reads "they are made mouths" and SP, CP read "they are mouths".

3:5: O reads "All poets and powers" and SP, CP read "All the poets and powers".

10:12: O reads "the young and the unborn" and SP, CP read "the young and unborn".

Elegies (1949)

Third Elegy. The Fear of Form

2:3:10: TW, WF, and CP read "girls by the thousand curve" and E reads "girls by the thousand curl".

2:8:4: TW, WF, and CP read "optic of grandiose delusion" and E reads "optic of grandiose illusion".

Fourth Elegy. The Refugees

2:7: TW, WF, and CP read "before the circle" and E reads "before this circle".

4:2: TW, WF, and CP read "They made a circle" and E reads "They make a circle".

8:1: E, TW, and CP read "Of bells" while WF reads "O bells."

Fifth Elegy. A Turning Wind

1:1:1–2: E, TW, and WF read "the midway travels of migrant" and CP, apparently erroneously, reads "the midway to migrant".

2:11:2: TW, WF, and CP read "stacks" and E reads "stalks".

2:11:3: TW, WF, and CP read "reflection" and E reads "reflections".

2:15:2: TW, WF, and CP read "these" and E reads "those".

Sixth Elegy. River Elegy

This elegy was first published in *Twice a Year* 5–6 (Fall–Winter 1940/Spring–Summer 1941). The first stanza differs significantly from subsequent publications.

1:5: WF incorrectly places a comma instead of a period following "grief".

6:9: WF incorrectly prints "slows" instead of "slow".

Seventh Elegy. Dream-Singing Elegy

2:2:4: BV, WF, and CP read "for a first time" and E reads "for the first time".

2:2:5: BV, WF, and CP read "our blond fields" and E reads "our blond hills".

2:7:8: We followed CP's addition of a second and final section break after "And all the dancers answer 'Yes.'" This break does not occur in BV, WF, or E.

Eighth Elegy. Children's Elegy

1:5:2: BV and WF do not mark the first section break that appears after this line.

2:2:4: CP incorrectly changes "bring" to "brings".

2:3:4: BV, WF, and CP read "if you" and E reads "if they".

2:6:4: BV, WF, and CP read "I wish, I wish for home." and E reads "I wish for home."

Ninth Elegy. The Antagonists

1:1:8: BV, WF, and CP read "smile, and revenge" and E leaves out the comma.

1:3:9: WF incorrectly prints "redeems" instead of "redeem".

2:2:13: BV, WF, and CP read "The doubled phantoms" and E reads "The troubled phantoms".

3:4:4: BV, WF, and CP read "built:" and E reads "built;".

Tenth Elegy. Elegy in Joy

3:2:4: WF reads, "The blessing is the seed." We have followed the E, GW, and CP version, which read "The blessing is in the seed."

Body of Waking (1958)

Phaneron

First appears in OL with the first line as the title.

After Their Quarrel

First appears in very different form in *Discovery, No. 3.*

Tree

4:6: CP erroneously adds a third "s" to the word "process."

The Return

First appears as a shorter poem in *Discovery, No. 3.*

F. O. M.

First appears in very different form in *Discovery, No. 3.*

[Untitled] ("Make and be eaten, the poet says")

In BW, this poem is set without a title; the table of contents lists it under its complete first line. The CP shortens the title and includes it within the body of the text.

Of Money. And the Past

3:5: BW reads "For here there is nothing." CP prints: "From here there is nothing."

[Untitled] ("Long enough. Long enough")

As with "Make and be eaten," in BW this poem is set without a title; the table of contents lists it under its complete first line. The CP shortens the title and inserts it into the body of the text.

2:6: CP, apparently erroneously, changes "May" to "My".

Suite for Lord Timothy Dexter

I

1:8: BW reads "In whitness" and CP reads "In witness".

2:1: BW reads "But that power pours here." CP omits the final period, "But that power pours here".

3 Three Nights I Dreamed

4:3: right margin text: BW reads "sayings, cats" and CP reads "saying, cats".

4

3:12: CP eliminates a section break after line 12, "My gold spread-eagle on the cu-palow."

5 The Pickle, the Temple

THE PICKLE

6:1:7: CP erroneously modernizes the spelling of "plese" to "please" in the line, "And solt it as they plese."

Powerplant

CP removes this title, which was printed in BW. Also, BW inserts a stanza break after "water-black" that is not in OL or CP. CP, apparently erroneously, removes the hyphen from "water-black" in 1:5.

Fields Where We Slept

This poem first appeared in OL and was then included, untitled, in the *One Life* section of BW. Later, Rukeyser also reprinted it with its current title in BO, following "Te Hanh : Long-Ago Garden."

He Had a Quality of Growth

This poem appeared untitled in BW; it was titled in both OL and CP.

The Speed of Darkness (1968)

Rukeyser's typescripts indicate that the title for SD was initially conceived as "Word of Mouth," the title of one of the poems in SD. In a drafted table of contents for this volume, thirty-three poems are listed that never appeared in SD, along with a section of translations entitled "The Birds of Attar," which refers to the twelfth-century Sufi poet Attar and his best-known work, *The Conference of the Birds*.

The Poem as Mask

Orpheus

1:3: CP, in seeming error, changes "god-hunting" to "gold-hunting." Common versions of the Orpheus story maintain that the Thracian maidens who attack and kill Orpheus do so because they are angered by his disinterest and inattention toward them. They are "god-hunting" for Orpheus, not gold-hunting as in the CP.

The Conjugation of the Paramecium

9:1: In the final stanza, CP erroneously changes "This is called" to "This called".

Clues

The manuscript title for this poem was "One Person Said Spots Also Stood for Stars."

Among Roses

In SD, this poem was titled "Among Grass." Rukeyser changed the title to "Among Roses" when she reprinted it in her 1972 volume of selected poems, 29P. According to a letter from Carole Fries of Andre Deutsch, Ltd. (April 21, 1971, LCII), Rukeyser confirmed her decision to change the title in the 29P manuscript.

Niobe Now

1:4: In SD, the fourth line reads "at all". CP corrects this to "as all".

For My Son

1:31 : CP prints, in error, "man play playing" instead of "man playing".

Cannibal Bratuscha

4:1: The "it's" in "it's Thursday" is missing the apostrophe in SD; CP corrects.

The Outer Banks

On the first page of the page proofs for this poem, commenting on the layout of the individual sections, Rukeyser wrote: "These are to be treated as separate poems with much space."

5
1:3: SD reads "female line" and CP offers a variant, "female line."

6
2:1: OB has a stanza break between these lines; SD has a page break between them and thus possibly a stanza break. In the first printing of this poem in *Poetry* 106.6 (Sept 1965: 381–87), there is also a stanza break. The CP omits this break and we have reinstated it.

9
4:4: In OB, this line reads "Body, eye, head . . . ." We have followed the SD and CP version, which, along with the *Poetry* edition, have this word in the plural—"eyes".

Akiba

Akiba Martyr

2:3: In SD, the word "Temple" is not followed by a period. CP corrects this.

The Speed of Darkness

As with "The Outer Banks," Rukeyser wrote in her page proofs for this poem: "These must be treated as separate poems," and indicated that she wanted "more spaces between sections" and more than a standard double space between each stanza and between the section number and first line of each section.

Breaking Open *(1973)*
Waking This Morning

Title: In BO, the title is "This Morning". In an LC TS and the CP, Rukeyser expanded the title to "Waking This Morning".

Despisals

4:2: In BO, the sentence reads, "Not to despise . . ." and in CP it reads, "Nor to despise . . . ."

In Her Burning

1:12: BO reads "off the moon" and CP prints "of the moon".

Searching / Not Searching

5 Brecht's *Galileo*

Title: In BO, the name of the play is not distinguished by typeface, and the CP underlines "Galileo."

8 H. F. D.

3:3: BO reads "the tremor of bone" and CP prints "tremor of bone".

All the Little Animals

First appears in *Poetry Review* 62.3 (Autumn 1971) as only the first three lines.

Iris

First appears in the *New Yorker*, May 16, 1970, as only the first stanza.

Ballad of Orange and Grape

1:3: CP erroneously changes "after you've read" to "after you're read."

In the Underworld

5:1:3: BO does not italicize "are" in "Baby, you *are* in trouble." CP adds the italics.

Flying to Hanoi

Title: In BO, the title is "Flying There : Hanoi" and CP changes this. Rukeyser indicated this change in NP TS (LC).

Breaking Open

8:1:5: BO reads "An old" and CP variantly reads "And old".

Rational Man

1:16: BO reads "with the word of Hanoi" and CP reads "with the world of Hanoi".

The Gates *(1976)*
Resurrection of the Right Side

1:6: CP erroneously added a period after the word "rhythms".

The Sun-Artist

4

1:2: SD reads "yellow of tellows". CP corrects this to "yellow of yellows".

1:9: SD reads "just countered the movement". CP changes this to "counters", a change Rukeyser indicated in a TS.

The Gates

Prose introduction: CP adds concluding sentence to first paragraph, which G does not have: "He is Kim Chi Ha."

10

6:3: CP erroneously changed "loved" to "love".

Juvenilia

Antigone

Dated "1926, probably March," Berg TS, folder 6.

Cities of the Morning

Dated "May 4, 1927," Berg TS, folder 17.

Autumn in the Garden

Librarian's note reads "in school magazine? Ca. 1929," Berg TS, folder 8.

The Ballad of the Missing Lines

Dated "November 1930," Berg TS, folder 9.

November Sketches

Sections 1, 3, and 4 of this poem were published in *The English Leaflet*, XXVII: 239, April 1928, a journal published by the New England Association of Teachers of English in Boston. The poems appeared here after winning second prize in a first annual national contest for high school students. According to William L. Rukeyser, the poet's son, this publication marks the first known instance of Rukeyser and May Sarton being published together (LCII).

To a Lady Turning Middle-Aged

Published in *Inklings* 27 (June 1928): 17. This was a magazine "published five times a year by the students of the Ethical Culture School" (LCII).

1:22: In *Inklings,* this line reads "I have but grown nature". We changed this apparent error so that the line now ends with "mature".

Place-Poems: New York

These nine poems were first printed in the *Vassar Review* (Feb. 1932): 10–12. Three of the poems ("O City," "College Special," and "Empire State Tower") were reprinted the following year in *Poetry* 42 (1933):16–17. Of these, "O City" was slightly revised, and "College Special" was renamed from the original "Grand Central—Vassar Special." We have printed these two as they appeared in *Poetry*, incorporating Rukeyser's revisions. "Place-Poems: New York" also appear in *Poetry East* 16–17 (Spring/Summer 1985): 29–43, a special issue focused on Rukeyser.

For an Aesthete

Published in *The Fieldglass*, the Fieldston School yearbook, c. 1930, p. 66.

Pastorale No. 2

Published in the *Vassar Review* (June 1932): 22–23 (LCII). We have been unable to locate a "Pastorale No. 1."

A New Poem

An Unborn Poet

Published in *American Poetry Review*, November/December 1979, 8:6, and *Poetry East* 16–17 (Spring/Summer 1985): 13–16.

∾ BIBLIOGRAPHY

Abbott, Berenice. *Berenice Abbott Photographs*. Foreword by Muriel Rukeyser. New York: Horizon Press, 1970.

Adkins, Joan F. "The Esthetics of Science: Muriel Rukeyser's 'Waterlily Fire.'" *Contemporary Poetry* 1.2 (1973): 23–27.

Benet, William Rose. "Contemporary Poetry." *Saturday Review* 7 Dec. 1935: 46–47.

Bernikow, Louise, ed. *The World Split Open: Four Centuries of Women Poets in England and America, 1552–1950*. New York: Random House, 1974.

Bourjaily, Vance, ed. *Discovery, No. 3*. Four Poems by Muriel Rukeyser. New York: Pocket Books, 1954.

Brock, James. "The Perils of a 'Poster Girl': Rukeyser, *Partisan Review*, and *Wake Island*." Herzog and Kaufman 254–63.

Cherniack, Martin. *The Hawk's Nest Incident: America's Worst Industrial Disaster*. New Haven: Yale UP, 1986.

Ciardi, John, ed. *Mid-Century American Poets*. 2nd ed. New York: Twayne, 1952.

Daniels, Kate. "Muriel Rukeyser and Her Literary Critics." Dickie and Travisano 247–63.

———. "A Note on the Place Poems." *Poetry East* 16–17 (Spring/Summer 1985): 27–28.

———. "Searching/Not Searching: Writing the Biography of Muriel Rukeyser." *Poetry East* 16–17 (Spring/Summer 1985): 70–93.

Dayton, Tim. *Muriel Rukeyser's* The Book of the Dead. Columbia, MO: U Missouri P, 2003.

Dickie, Margaret, and Thomas Travisano, eds. *Gendered Modernisms*. Philadelphia: U Penn P, 1996.

Eisenberg, Susan. "'Changing Waters Carry Voices': 'Nine Poems for the unborn child.'" Herzog and Kaufman 184–92.

Ekelöf, Gunnar. *Selected Poems*. Trans. Muriel Rukeyser and Leif Sjöberg. New York: Irvington, 1967.

Flynn, Richard. "'The Buried Life and the Body of Waking': Muriel Rukeyser and the Politics of Literary History." Dickie and Travisano 264–79.

Folsom, Merrill. "Sarah Lawrence Again Under Fire." *New York Times* 14 Nov. 1958: 11.

Gabriel, Daniel. *Sacco and Vanzetti*. Foreword by Muriel Rukeyser. Brooklyn, New York: Gull Books, 1983.

Goldensohn, Lorrie. "Our Mother Muriel." Herzog and Kaufman 121–34.

Hartman, Stephanie. "All Systems Go: Muriel Rukeyser's 'The Book of the Dead' and the Reinvention of Modernist Poetics." Herzog and Kaufman 209–23.

Herzog, Anne, and Janet Kaufman, eds. *"How Shall We Tell Each Other of the Poet?": The Life and Writing of Muriel Rukeyser*. New York: St. Martin's Press, 1999.

Howe, Florence, and Ellen Bass, eds. *No More Masks!: An Anthology of Twentieth-Century American Women Poets*. Rev. ed. New York: HarperPerennial, 1993.

Kadlec, David. "X-Ray Testimonials in Muriel Rukeyser," *Modernism/Modernity*, 5.1 (January 1998): 23–47.

Kalaidjian, Walter. "Muriel Rukeyser and the Poetics of Specific Critique: Rereading 'The Book of the Dead,'" *Cultural-Critique* 20 (Winter 1991–1992): 65–88.

Kaufman, Janet E. "'But not the study': Writing as a Jew." Herzog and Kaufman 45–61.

Kearns, Martha. *Käthe Kollwitz: Woman and Artist*. Old Westbury, New York: Feminist Press, 1976.

———. "Martha Kearns on Muriel Rukeyser and Käthe Kollwitz." *Voices of Women: 3 Critics on 3 Poets on 3 Heroines.* Ed. Kearns. New York: Midmarch Associates, 1980.

Kertesz, Louise. *The Poetic Vision of Muriel Rukeyser.* Baton Rouge: Louisiana State UP, 1980.

Lannoy, Richard. *The Speaking Tree: A Study of Indian Culture and Society.* New York: Oxford UP, 1971, xxv.

Levertov, Denise. "On Muriel Rukeyser." *Light Up the Cave.* By Levertov. New York: New Directions, 1981, 189–95. Rpt. in Herzog and Kaufman 289–93.

Levi, Jan Heller, ed. *A Muriel Rukeyser Reader.* New York: W. W. Norton and Co., 1994.

Lowney, John. "Truths of Outrage, Truths of Possibility: Muriel Rukeyser's 'The Book of the Dead.'" Herzog and Kaufman 195–208.

Mariani, Gigliola Sacerdoti. "'Barcelona, 1936'—A Moment of Proof for Muriel Rukeyser," *Revista di Studi Anglo-Americani* 6.8 (1990): 387–96.

McEwen, Christian. "Four Women at the Beginning of Teachers and Writers Collaborative." *Teachers and Writers* 24.4 (Mar.–Apr. 1993): 1–6.

Melville, Herman. "The Conflict of Convictions." *Battle-Pieces and Aspects of the War.* 1866. l.38–39. Rpt. in *Battle-Pieces and Aspects of the War: A Facsimile Reproduction.* Gainesville, FL: Scholars' Facsimiles & Reprints, 1960.

Minot, Leslie Ann. "'Kodak as You Go': The Photographic Metaphor in the Work of Muriel Rukeyser." Herzog and Kaufman 264–76.

Mort, Jo-Ann. "The Poetry of Muriel Rukeyser." *Jewish Quarterly,* 28.4 (Winter 1980–1981): 20–21.

Nayar, Pramod K. "Trans-formations: Muriel Rukeyser's 'Ajanta.'" *Journal of American Studies* 24.1 (Winter 1994): 55–59.

Nelson, Cary, ed. *Anthology of Modern American Poetry.* New York: Oxford, 2000.

Nelson, Cary, and Janet Kaufman. "Muriel Rukeyser." *Heath Anthology of American Literature Instructor's Guide.* 24 Dec. 2003. http://www.georgetown.edu/bassr/heath/syllabuild/iguide/rukeyser.html

Paz, Octavio. *Sun Stone.* Trans. Muriel Rukeyser. New York: New Directions, 1963.

———. *The Early Poems of Octavio Paz, 1935–1955.* Trans. Muriel Rukeyser. Bloomington: Indiana UP, 1963.

Plath, Sylvia. *Ariel.* New York: Harper & Row, 1965.

Porritt, Ruth. "'Unforgetting Eyes': Rukeyser Portraying Kollwitz's Truth." Herzog and Kaufman 163–83.

Rexroth, Kenneth. *American Poetry in the Twentieth Century.* New York: Herder and Herder, 1971.

Rukeyser, Muriel. *Beast in View.* Garden City, New York: Doubleday, 1944.

———. *Body of Waking.* New York: Harper and Brothers, 1958.

———. *Breaking Open.* New York: Random House, 1973.

———. *The Collected Poems of Muriel Rukeyser.* New York: McGraw-Hill, 1978.

———. "Craft Interview." *The Craft of Poetry.* Ed. William Packard. Garden City, New York: Doubleday, 1974, 153–76.

———. "Death in Spain: Barcelona on the Barricades," *New Masses,* 1 Sept. 1936, 9–11.

———. "The Education of a Poet." *A Muriel Rukeyser Reader.* Levi 277–85.

———. *Elegies.* New York: New Directions, 1949.

———. "The Flown Arrow: The Aftermath of the Sacco-Vanzetti Case." *Housatonic.* 1 Aug. 1932. 9–10, 24–26.

———. "From Scottsboro to Decatur." *Student Review* 2.6 (April 1933):12–15.

———. "Gauley Bridge." *Films: A Quarterly Discussion and Analysis* 1.3 (Summer 1940): 51–64. Rukeyser's filmscript treatment of the Hawk's Nest tragedy.

———. *The Gates*. New York: McGraw-Hill, 1976.

———. *The Green Wave*. New York: Doubleday, 1948.

———. *Houdini: A Musical*. Ed. Jan Freeman. Ashfield, MA: Paris Press, 2002.

———. *Houdini:* A Play by Muriel Rukeyser. Ed. Richard Jones and Kate Daniels. *Poetry East* 16–17 (Spring/Summer 1985): 96–220.

———. Interview by Dr. Harry T. Moore. *Talks with Authors*. Ed. Charles F. Madden. Carbondale, IL: Southern Illinois UP, 1968, 125–50.

———. Introduction. *An American Portrait 1776–1976*. Ed. Alex J. Rosenberg. New York: Transworld Art Corporation, 1975.

———. *Just Before the Gates*. Poems read by the author. Audiocasette. Watershed Recording, #c-105. Recorded at the Textile Museum, Washington DC, Jan. 1975.

———. *The Life of Poetry*. 1949. Ashfield, MA: Paris Press, 1996.

———. *Mediterranean*. New York: Writers and Artists Committee, Medical Bureau to Aid Spanish Democracy, 1938.

———. "The Music of Translation." *The World of Translation*. New York: P.E.N. American Center, 1970, 187–93.

———. "New Letters on the Air." Introduced and produced by Dennis Bernstein. Kansas City, MO. 7 Jan. 1983. Selections from Muriel Rukeyser reading at the 92nd Street YM/YWHA, recorded by Jeffrey Norton Publisher.

———. "Notes for a Preface." Library of Congress, Manuscript Division, Rukeyser archives, Part II.

———. *One Life*. New York: Simon and Schuster, 1970.

———. *The Orgy*. 1965. Ashfield, MA: Paris Press, 1997.

———. *Orpheus*. With drawing by Picasso. San Francisco: Centaur Press, 1949.

———. *The Outer Banks* (chapbook). Greensboro, NC: Unicorn Press Inc., 1965.

———. *Out of Silence: Selected Poems*. Ed. Kate Daniels. Evanston, IL: TriQuarterly, 1992.

———. *Selected Poems*. New York: New Directions, 1951.

———. *Selected Poems*. Ed. Adrienne Rich. Library of America, 2004.

———. "A Simple Theme." Review of Charlotte Marletto's *Jewel of Our Longing*. *Poetry* 74 (1949): 236–39.

———. "Sixth Elegy." *Twice a Year* 5.6 (Fall–Winter 1940/Spring–Summer 1941). New York: Kraus Reprint Corporation, 1967, 323–26.

———. *The Soul and Body of John Brown*. With etchings by Rudolf C. von Ripper. New York: Lee Ault and R. C. von Ripper, 1940.

———. *The Speed of Darkness*. New York: Random House, 1968

———. *Theory of Flight*. New Haven: Yale UP, 1935.

———. "To Be a Jew in the Twentieth Century." *Gates of Prayer*. New York: Central Conference of American Rabbis, 1975, 706. Rpt. in *The Service of the Heart*. London: Union of Liberal and Progressive Synagogues, 1967.

———. *The Traces of Thomas Hariot*. New York: Random House, 1971.

———. *A Turning Wind*. New York: Viking Press, 1939.

———. *29 Poems*. Great Britain: Rapp & Whiting/André Deutsch, 1972.

———. *U.S. 1*. New York: Covici Friede, 1938.

———. *Wake Island*. Garden City, New York: Doubleday, 1942.

———. *Waterlily Fire: Poems 1935–1962*. New York: Macmillan, 1962.

———. *Willard Gibbs*. Woodbridge, CT: Oxbow Press, 1988.

Schweik, Susan. "The Letter and the Body: Muriel Rukeyser's 'Letter to the Front.'" *A Gulf So Deeply Cut: American Women Poets and the Second World War*. Madison: U of Wisconsin P, 1991, 140–70.

Shulman, Robert. *The Power of Political Art: The 1930's Literary Left Reconsidered*. Chapel Hill: U North Carolina P, 2000.

Spoken Arts Treasury: 100 Modern Poets. Audiocassette. Vol. 11. Rukeyser reads her own poems. Rec. 1969. New Rochelle, New York: Spoken Arts, 1985.

They Are Their Own Gifts. Film. Dir. Lucille Rhodes and Margaret Murphy. Distr. Women Make Movies, 1978.

Thurston, Michael. "Documentary Modernism as Popular Front Poetics: Muriel Rukeyser's 'Book of the Dead.'" *Modern Language Quarterly: A Journal of Literary History* 60.1 (March 1999): 59–83.

———. *Making Something Happen: American Political Poetry Between the World Wars*. Chapel Hill: U North Carolina P, 2001.

Tierney, Kevin. *Darrow: A Biography*. New York: Crowell, 1979.

True, Michael. "The Authentic Voice." Herzog and Kaufman 91–99.

———. *An Energy Field More Intense Than War: The Nonviolent Tradition and American Literature*. Syracuse, New York: Syracuse UP, 1995.

"Under Forty: A Symposium on American Literature and the Younger Generation of American Jews." *Contemporary Jewish Record* (February 1944): 4–9.

Walker, Alice. *In Search of Our Mother's Gardens*. Orlando, FL: Harcourt Brace Jovanovich, 1983.

Ware, Michelle S. "Opening 'The Gates': Muriel Rukeyser and the Poetry of Witness." *Women's Studies* 22 (1993): 297–308.

"We Came for the Games," *Esquire* 82 (Oct. 1974): 192–94, 368–70.

Wechsler, Shoshana. "A Ma(t)ter of Fact and Vision: The Objectivity Question and 'The Book of the Dead.'" Herzog and Kaufman 226–40.

White, Evelyn. *Alice Walker: A Life*. New York, W. W. Norton and Co., 2004.

∾INDEX OF TITLES

Subtitles appear in italics and are listed twice; once alphabetically as main entries and once indented under the main title in sequence. First lines (in quotation marks) appear when a poem or subtitle is unnnamed. Alphabetical order disregards initial articles in titles and subtitles.

Absalom, 83
Adventures, Midnight, 126
After Melville, 500
After Their Quarrel, 338
Afterwards, 507
Air, 423
"Air fills with fear and the kinds of fear", 565
Ajanta, 207
    The Journey, 207
    The Cave, 208
    Les Tendresses Bestiales, 209
    Black Blood, 210
    The Broken World, 210
Akiba, 454
    The Way Out, 454
    for *The Song of Songs, 455*
    The Bonds, 457
    Akiba Martyr, 458
    The Witness, 459
Akiba Martyr, 458
"All day the rain", 568
All Souls, 236
All the Little Animals, 489
Alloy, 95
Along History, 488
"Among all the waste there are the intense stories", 244
Among Roses, 420
"Among the days", 563
Anemone, 428
Ann Burlak, 191
Antigone, 573
Are You Born?—I, 379
Are You Born?—II, 399
Arthur Peyton, 94
Artifact, 540
The Artist as Social Critic, 484
Asleep and Awake, 349
Asylum Song, 174
"At daybreak go looking for your newborn name", 360
Autumn in the Garden, 574
The Baby on the Mountain—Stroking Song, 519
Back Tooth, 555
The Backside of the Academy, 445
Ballad of Orange and Grape, 492
The Ballad of the Missing Lines, 575
A Ballad Theme, 348
Beast in View, 238
Before Danger, 551

Being Born, 520
Believing in Those Inexorable Laws, 421
The Bill, 104
The Bird, 268
A Birth, 334
The Birth of Venus, 356
The Birthday, 131
Black Blood, 210
The Black Ones, the Great Ones, 516
The Blood Is Justified, 68
The Blue Flower, 440
Blue Spruce, 539
Body of Waking, 390
The Bonds, 457
The Book of the Dead, 106
Born in December, 354
Boy with His Hair Cut Short, 119
Boys in the Branches, 541
Boys of These Men Full Speed, 488
Breaking Open, 521
    Columbus, 523
    Burning the Dreams, 526
    Death and the Dancer, 526
    Rational Man, 526
    The Hostages, 528
Breathing Landscape, 19
Brecht's Galileo, 482
Bringing, 498
The Broken World, 210
Bubble of Air, 231
Bunk Johnson Blowing, 434
Burlesque, 59
The Burning, 405
Burning Bush, 112
Burning the Dreams, 526
Burnishing, Oakland, 557
"The Cabinet minister speaks of liberation", 563
Canal, 544
Cannibal Bratuscha, 435
Careful of the Day, 273
Cats and a Cock, 63
The Cave, 208
A Certain Music, 259
Chapman, 188
Chapultepec Park—1, 233
Chapultepec Park—2, 234
A Charm for Cantinflas, 263
Child and Mother, 53
The Child Asleep, 124
Child in the Great Wood, 212
Children, the Sandbar, That Summer, 353

The Children's Orchard, 261
Christmas Eve, 261
The Church of Galilee, 564
Citation for Horace Gregory, 62
Cities of the Morning, 573
City of Monuments, 51
Clouds, Airs, Carried Me Away, 255
Clues, 416
College Special, 581
Columbus, 523
The Committee-Room, 26
Concrete, 482
The Conjugation of the Paramecium, 414
The Cornfield, 92
Correspondences, 164
    Democritus Laughed, 164
    Tree of Days, 164
    1/26/39, 165
    Correspondences, 166
Correspondences, 166
Course, 120
Crayon House, 262
Cries from Chiapas, 424
"Crucified child—is he crucified? he is tortured",
   567
The Cruise, 133
The Dam, 99
Darkness Music, 215
Day, 361
"Dear place, sweet home", 583
Death and the Dancer, 526
Delta Poems, 426
Democritus Laughed, 164
Desdichada, 474
Despisals, 471
Destruction of Grief, 555
The Disease, 86
The Disease: After-Effects, 102
Divining Water, 358
The Doctors, 89
Don Baty, the Draft Resister, 495
Double Dialogue:
    Homage To Robert Frost, 417
Double Ode, 534
Dream-Drumming, 534
The Dream of Galilee, 564
Driveway, 128
The Drowning Young Man, 119
Drunken Girl, 222
Easter Eve 1945, 276
Eccentric Motion, 55
Eel, 113
Effort at Speech between Two People, 9
Eighth Elegy. Children's Elegy, 321
Empire State Tower, 582
Endless, 445
"Even during war, moments of delicate peace", 239

"Evening, bringing me out of the government
   building", 243
Evening Plaza, San Miguel, 237
Exile of Music, 344
Eyes of Night-Time, 253
Fable [*Body of Waking*], 360
Fable [*The Gates*], 549
The Face of the Dam: Vivian Jones, 78
Facing Sentencing, 497
Fields Where We Slept, 384
Fifth Elegy. A Turning Wind, 310
Fighting for Roses, 428
Fire, 475
First Elegy. Rotten Lake, 299
A Flashing Cliff, 111
The Floor of Ocean, 483
The Flying Red Horse, 447
Flying to Hanoi, 508
Foghorn in Horror, 265
F. O. M., 343
For a Mexican Painter, 404
For an Aesthete, 583
For Dolci, 481
For Fun, 162
For Kay Boyle, 545
For Memory, 48
    Life and Works, 48
    Holy Dying, 49
    Ritual for Death, 50
For My Son, 429
"For that I cannot name the names", 567
for *the Song of Songs, 455*
Forerunners, 418
Forgetting and Remembering, 441
Formosa, 122
Four in a Family, 19
Fourteenth Street, 579
Fourth Elegy. The Refugees, 307
Fragile, 409
From a Play : Publisher's Song, 503
from City of Paradise, 477
from Sun Stone, 366
From the Duck-Pond to the Carousel, 174
from "To the Unborn Child", 229
A Game of Ball, 235
The Gates, 561
Gauley Bridge, 77
    "Waiting to leave all day I hear the words",
    561
    "Walking the world to find the poet of these
    cries", 562
    New Friends, 562
    "The Cabinet minister speaks of liberation",
    563
    "Among the days", 563
    The Church of Galilee, 564
    The Dream of Galilee, 564

Mother as Pitchfork, 565
"You grief woman   you gave me a scarlet
    coverlet", 565
"Air fills with fear and the kinds of fear",
    565
"Long ago, soon after my son's birth", 567
"For that I cannot name the names", 567
"Crucified child—is he crucified?   he is
    tortured", 567
"So I became very dark very large", 568
"All day the rain", 569
George Robinson: Blues, 87
Gibbs, 182
Gift, 424
Gift-Poem [Beast in View], 224
Gift-Poem [U.S. 1], 130
Girl at the Play, 111
A Girl for a Boy—Stroking Song, 518
Gold Leaf, 236
Gradus Ad Parnassum, 502
Green Limits, 260
Guessing Time, 377
The Gyroscope, 24
The Handclap, 115
"The hand of day opens", 359
Haying before Storm, 333
He Had a Quality of Growth, 398
"Held among wars, watching", 462
"Held between wars", 460
Hero Speech, 346
H. F. D., 483
His Head Is Full of Faces, 257
Holy Dying, 49
Holy Family, 228
Homage to Literature, 115
Homage To Robert Frost, 417
"Home thoughts from home; we read you every
    day", 242
The Hostages, 528
How Lovely It Is, 517
How to Impress Massachusetts, 367
How We Did It, 538
Hypnogogic Figure, 542
I Recognize This Song, 515
I'm Here Again, 513
In a Dark House, 6
In Hades, Orpheus, 118
In Her Burning, 478
"In her splendor islanded", 362
In Our Time, 417
"In the last hour of night, a zebra racing
    dawn", 384
In the Night the Sound Woke Us, 503
In the Underworld, 503
"In your time, there have been those who
    spoke clearly", 397
Inland, Away, 512

Iris, 490
The Iris-Eaters, 558
The Island [Otherworld], 158
The Island [Waterlily Fire], 406
Islands, 538
It Is There, 508
Ives, 195
The Journey, 207
Journey Changes, 408
Juanita Tinsley, 88
Judith, 179
Junk-Heap at Murano, 415
Käthe Kollwitz, 460
    "Held between wars", 460
    "Woman as gates, saying", 461
    "Held among wars, watching", 462
    Song : The Calling-Up, 463
    Self-Portrait, 463
The Key, 214
The Kind of Woman, 376
Kings and Contemporaries, 370
King's Mountain, 335
Landing at Liverpool, 157
Landscape with Wave Approaching, 433
Leg in a Plaster Cast, 230
Les Tendresses Bestiales, 209
"Let poems and bodies love and be given to air",
    252
Letter to the Front, 239
    "Women and poets see the truth arrive", 239
    "Even during war, moments of delicate
        peace", 239
    "They called us to a change of heart", 240
    Sestina, 241
    "Much later, I lie in a white seaport night",
        242
    "Home thoughts from home; we read you
        every day", 242
    "To be a Jew in the twentieth century", 243
    "Evening, bringing me out of the government
        building", 243
    "Among all the waste there are the intense
        stories", 244
    "Surely it is time for the true grace of
        women", 246
Letter, Unposted, 14
Life and Works, 48
Life of the Poet, 363
"Like ivy the creeper with a thousand hands",
    363
A Little Stone in the Middle of the Road, in
    Florida, 440
The Loan, 352
"Long ago, soon after my son's birth", 567
The Long Body, 409
"Long enough. Long enough", 351
Long Past Moncada, 232

Looking, 494
Looking at Each Other, 473
The Lost Romans, 543
A Louis Sonnet, 499
Love and Its Doors and Windows, 222
The Lover, 42
Lover as Fox, 129
Lovers, 270
The Lynchings of Jesus, 25
    Passage to Godhead, 25
    The Committee-Room, 26
    The Trial, 29
Madboy's Song, 221
"Make and be eaten, the poet says", 345
Martin Luther King, Malcolm X, 494
M-Day's Child, 177
Mearl Blankenship, 82
Mediterranean, 144
The Meeting, 213
Mendings, 560
Metaphor to Action, 61
The Minotaur, 223
Miriam : The Red Sea, 481
More Clues, 479
More of a Corpse than a Woman, 121
Mortal Girl, 211
Mother as Pitchfork, 565
Mother Garden's Round, 336
The Motive of All of It, 259
Mountain : One from Bryant, 447
Movie, 60
Mrs. Walpurga, 257
Ms. Lot, 540
"Much later, I lie in a white seaport night", 242
"Murmurs from the earth of this land, from
   the caves and craters", 380
My Breath, 514
Myth, 480
Neruda, the Wine, 550
Nevertheless the Moon, 354
The New Bridge, 581
New Friends, 562
The New School for Social Research, 580
Next, 490
Night Feeding, 340
Night Flight : New York, 44
Night-Music, 123
    Time Exposures, 123
    The Child Asleep, 124
    Adventures, Midnight, 126
    Night-Music, 127
Night-Music, 127
Nine Poems for the unborn child, 280
Ninth Elegy. The Antagonists, 325
Niobe Now, 422
Noguchi, 168
Not before I Fall Asleep, 275

Not Much Good, 514
Not Searching, 485
Not to Be Printed, Not to Be Said, Not to Be
   Thought, 554
Not Yet, 432
Notes for a Poem, 11
November Sketches, 576
Nuns in the Wind, 161
O City, 579
Of Money. And the Past, 350
The Old Days, 512
On the Death of Her Mother, 344
"On your journey you will come to a time of
   waking", 389
One Month, 438
One Soldier, 207
1/26/39, 165
Orgy, 419
Orpheus, 287
Orpheus, 413
Otherworld, 157
    Landing at Liverpool, 157
    The Island, 158
    Otherworld, 159
Otherworld, 159
The Outer Banks, 448
Outpost, 132
The Overthrow of One O'Clock at Night,
   420
Painters, 537
Palos Verdes Cliffs, 171
Panacea, 117
Paper Anniversary, 172
Parallel Invention, 553
Park Avenue, 581
Passage to Godhead, 25
Pastorale No. 2, 584
Phaneron, 333
The Pickle, the Temple, 372
The Place at Alert Bay, 357
Place-Poems: New York, 579
    O City, 579
    Fourteenth Street, 579
    The New School for Social Research, 580
    Sheridan Square Conversation, 580
    The New Bridge, 581
    Park Avenue, 581
    College Special, 582
    Empire State Tower, 582
    "Dear place, sweet home", 583
Place-Rituals, 12
    Tradition of This Acre, 12
    Ritual of Blessing, 12
Poem [The Gates], 554
Poem [Speed of Darkness], 430
The Poem as Mask, 413
    Orpheus, 413

Poem out of Childhood, 3
Poem   White Page   White Page   Poem,
   549
Poet's Epitaph, 268
Portrait of a Man, with a Background of
   Holdings, 385
Pouring Milk Away, 353
Power, 96
"Power never dominion", 387
The Power of Suicide, 430
"The power of war leads to a plan of lives",
   381
Powerplant, 383
Praise of the Committee, 79
Preamble, 21
The President and the Laser Bomb, 484
The Prisoner, 364
Private Life of the Sphinx, 277
Proverbs, 362
The Question, 477
The Question, 485
Rari, 274
Rari for Hepuheku, 273
Rari for O'Otua, 272
Rari for Tahia and Piu, 271
Rari, to Be Bothered by Mosquitos, 274
Rari to Encourage Youth, 274
Rational Man, 526
Reading the Kieu, *482*
Reading Time : 1 Minute 26 Seconds, 155
Recovering, 552
"A red bridge fastening this city to the
   forest", 386
Resurrection of the Right Side, 545
The Return, 341
The Return, 442
Ringling, 338
"The risen image shines, its force escapes,
   we are all named", 181
Rite, 337
Ritual for Death, 50
Ritual of Blessing, 12
The Road, 73
Rock Flow, River Mix, 493
Rondel, 479
Rune, 537
The Running of the Grunion, 509
Ryder, 185
Sacred Lake, 511
Salamander, 256
Sand-Quarry with Moving Figures, 15
"The sea has opened, the limit of his dream",
   382
Sea Mercy, 232
Searching / Not Searching, 480
   *"What kind of woman goes searching and
      searching?", 480*

Miriam : The Red Sea, 481
For Dolci, 481
Concrete, 482
Brecht's Galileo, *482*
Reading the Kieu, *482*
The Floor of Ocean, 483
H. F. D., 483
The Artist as Social Critic, 484
The President and the Laser Bomb, 484
Not Searching, 485
The Question, 485
   *"Searching/not searching.   To make
      closeness", 486*
      "What did I see? What did I not see?", 486
*"Searching/not searching.   To make closeness",
   486*
Second Elegy. Age of Magicians, 302
Secrets of American Civilization, 497
The Seeming, 431
Segre Song, 434
Self-Portrait, 463
Sestina, 241
Seventh Avenue, 169
Seventh Elegy. Dream-Singing Elegy, 318
Sheridan Square Conversation, 580
Shooting Gallery, 216
Shooting Star, 520
The Shortest Way Home, 170
Silence of Volcanoes, 439
A Simple Experiment, 487
The Six Canons, 418
Sixth Elegy. River Elegy, 314
The Sixth Night: Waking, 354
"The sky is as black as it was when you lay
   down", 388
Slow Death of the Dragon, 558
"So I became very dark very large", 568
Song [*Beast in View*], 215
Song [*Waterlily Fire*], 405
Song for Dead Children, 5
Song, from "Mr. Amazeen On The River",
   255
Song from *Puck Fair,* 432
Song : Love in Whose Rich Honor, 422
Song : Lying in Daylight, 542
A Song of Another Tribe, 404
Song : Remembering Movies, 551
Song, the Brain-Coral, 155
Song : The Calling-Up, 463
Song : The Star in the Nets of Heaven, 423
Songs of the Barren Grounds, 512
   The Old Days, 512
   Inland, Away, 512
   I'm Here Again, 513
   Not Much Good, 514
   My Breath, 514
Sonnet, 13

The Soul and Body of John Brown, 247
"Sounds of night in the country of the opposites", 395
Spark, 269
The Speaking Tree, 403
Speech for the Assistant, from *Houdini*, 178
Speech of the Mother, from *The Middle of the Air*, 266
The Speed of Darkness, 465
Speed, We Say, 355
Spirals and Fugues, 427
St. Roach, 533
Statement: Phillippa Allen, 75
The Street, 269
The Strike, 31
Stroking Songs, 518
    A Girl for a Boy—Stroking Song, 518
    The Baby on the Mountain—Stroking Song, 519
    The Wiping Moss from the Ruins, 519
Stroking Songs, Childhood Songs, 520
    Being Born, 520
    Shooting Star, 520
The Structure of the Plane, 38
    The Structure of the Plane, 38
    The Strike, 41
    The Lover, 42
The Structure of the Plane, 38
Study in a Late Subway, 53
Suicide Blues, 216
Suite for Lord Timothy Dexter, 367
    "They face us in sea-noon sun, just as he saw them waiting", 367
    How to Impress Massachusetts, 367
    Three Nights I Dreamed, 369
    Kings and Contemporaries, 370
    The Pickle, the Temple, 372
    The Kind of Woman, 376
    Guessing Time, 377
Summer, the Sacramento, 265
The Sun-Artist, 547
Sundays, They Sleep Late, 56
"Surely it is time for the true grace of women", 246
The Surrounded, 58
Target Practice, 156
Te Hanh : Long-Ago Garden, 496
Tenth Elegy. Elegy In Joy, 328
Then, 561
"Then full awake you will recognize the voice", 396
Then I Saw What the Calling Was, 267
Theory of Flight, 47
"They called us to a change of heart", 240
"They face us in sea-noon sun, just as he saw them waiting", 367
Third Elegy. The Fear of Form, 304
This House, This Country, 20

"This is the net of begetting and belief", 389
This Place in the Ways, 254
Thousands of Days, 57
Three Black Women, 122
Three Nights I Dreamed, 369
Three Sides of a Coin, 16
Time Exposures, 123
To a Lady Turning Middle-Aged, 578
"To be a Jew in the twentieth century", 243
To Enter That Rhythm Where the Self Is Lost, 403
Tradition of This Acre, 12
Traditional Tune, 264
The Transgress, 414
Tree, 339
Tree of Days, 164
"A tree of rivers flowing through our lives", 382
"The tree of rivers seen and forgotten, 380
The Trial, 29
Trinity Churchyard, 556
Trophies, 116
Trout Fishing, 517
A True Confession, 272
The Tunnel, 31
Two Bodies, 269
The Two Illuminations, 342
Two Years, 490
An Unborn Poet, 591
Unborn Song, 342
The Victims, a Play for the Home, 175
Voices, 475
Voices of Waking, 357
Waiting for Icarus, 476
"Waiting to leave all day I hear the words", 561
Wake Island, 201
Waking This Morning, 471
"Walking the world to find the poet of these cries", 562
The War Comes into My Room, 425
The Wards, 546
The Watchers, 347
Water Night, 253
Waterlily Fire, 405
    The Burning, 405
    The Island, 406
    Journey Changes, 408
    Fragile, 409
    The Long Body, 409
The Way Out, 454
Wedding Presents, 15
Welcome from War, 496
West Virginia, 74
"What did I see? What did I not see?", 486
What Do I Give You?, 413
What Do We See?, 472

What Have You Brought Home from the
    Wars?, 437
What I See, 421
*"What kind of woman goes searching and
    searching?"*, 480
What They Said, 439
Wherever, 498
Who in One Lifetime, 228
Willkie in *The Gulliver,* 396
The Wiping Moss from the Ruins, 519
The Witness, 459
Woman and Bird, 131
Woman and Emblems, 131
    Woman and Bird, 131
    The Birthday, 131
    Woman and Music, 132
Woman and Music, 132

"Woman as gates, saying", 461
Woman as Market, 441
    Forgetting and Remembering, 441
"Women and poets see the truth arrive", 239
Wooden Spring, 13
Word of Mouth, 442
    The Return, 442
    Word of Mouth, 443
Word of Mouth, 443
The Word-Fisher, 518
Work, for the Day Is Coming, 551
Wreath of Women, 217
The Writer, 502
"You grief woman   you gave me a scarlet covelet",
    565
The Young Girl of the Mississippi Valley, 334

ᴖINDEX OF FIRST LINES

First lines of poems appear in roman; first lines of subsections appear in italics. Alphabetical order disregards initial articles in titles and subtitles.

Across the country, iron hands push up chimneys, 49

Act I, Sc. 4. She is lit, standing high, with the lit line of Anne's, 266

After I am dead, darling, 439

After the black ones!, 516

After the last cold mountain, 132

After the last freeze, in easy air, 428

After the lifting of the mist, 465

After the lights and after the rumba and after the bourbon, 263

After the quarrel in the house I walked the grasses of the field, 338

After the revolution came the Fuehrer, 264

After this crisis, 485

After you finish your work, 492

Air fills with fear and the kinds of fear, 565

All day the rain, 568

All of the people of the play were there, 433

All of the people of the play were there, 434

All power is saved, having no end. Rises, 99

All the voices of the wood called "Muriel!", 267

All this time, 438

Along history, forever, 488

Always I travelled farther, 20

Am I in your light?, 16

Among all the waste there are the intense stories, 244

Among leaf-green, 426

Among the days, 563

And for the man with one nightmare, the student of clouds, the bitter, 178

And if the cliffs themselves produced the major illusion, 171

And if the curtain lifts, it is a window-shade, 175

And the child sitting alone planning her hope, 307

And turn and arise and give these wounds their song, 292

Angel of declaring, you opened before us walls, 481

Another day. I stand before the screen, 548

Another day. No sun. The fog is down, 548

Answer with me these certainties, 42

Antaeus was once strong, when his feet, locked in earth, 586

As I came out of the New York Public Library, 161

As I went down the road to the water, the river to the sea, 174

As I went down to Rotten Lake I remembered, 299

As we climb to the church of Galilee, 564

Asleep and awake, I wake, 349

At daybreak go looking for your newborn name, 360

At one shock, speechlessness, 452

At the end of July, exile. We watched the gangplank go, 144

A baroque night advances in its clouds, 302

Battles whose names I do not know, 494

Be bold, friend ; all your nymphs have disappeared, 16

Be proud you people of these graves, 51

Beat out continuance in the choking veins, 68

Believing in those inexorable laws, 421

Between between, 466

Between the illuminations of great mornings, 431

Big-boned man young and of my dream, 467

A bird flew out of a cloud, 131

Black parental mysteries, 536

Bleeding of the mountains, 494

Blue in the green trees, what are they climbing?, 541

The body cannot lie, but its betrayals, 115

Born of this river and this rock island, I relate, 406

Boys of these men, 488

Break of light! Sun in his colors, 548

Breathe-in experience, breathe-out poetry, 3

Brecht saying : Galileo talking astronomy, 482

Bringing their life these young, 498

The brown, dead leaves, 576

The bubbles in the blood sprang free, 231

But that was years ago. My child is grown, 536

But these two figures are not the statues east and west, 535

But this is our desire, and of its worth, 24

By day white moths, the nightlong meteors, 433

The cabinet minister speaks of liberation, 563

Call himself unbegun, for the sea made him; assemblages of waters, 185

The calling and the melody all night long, 233

Came in my full youth to the midnight cave, 207

Came to Ajanta cave, the painted space of the breast, 210

Camera at the crossing sees the city, 77

Care for love tenderly, it is deep in me, 273

Carlos, your art is embryos, 404

The cattle-trains edge along the river, bringing morning on a white vibration, 35

A child is in the dark room where the dim lights
    swim, 585
A child riding the stormy mane of noon, 399
the child, the poems, the child, the poems, the
    journeys, 424
Child who within me gives me dreams and sleep,
    282
The childless years alone without a home, 280
Children remembering sadness grieve, they
    grieve, 497
The choice proposed : ascends, the nervy
    conductor, 116
City, 579
The city of the heart, 234
The city of the past. The past as a city, 434
Climbing the air, prophet beyond prophet, 483
Clouds, airs, carried me away, 255
The clouds are dark, 275
Colors move on a screen. The doors open again,
    548
Come back to us, little grey sister, 576
Come : you are the one chosen, by them,
    to serve them, 490
Coming among the living, 159
Coming to Spain on the first day of the fighting,
    241
The concert-hall was crowded the night of
    the crash, 172
Configurations of time and singing, 238
Consumed. Eaten away. And love across the
    street, 94
Crucified child — is he crucified? he is tortured,
    567
Darkness, giving us dream's black unity, 318
Dashing in glass we race, 55
A day is lost, 361
The day of life and death offers its flowers,
    236
The days are incestuous, each with its yester-
    day, 56
The days grow and the stars cross over, 215
Dear place, sweet home, 583
Death flowing down past me, past me, death, 474
Death is here, death is guarded by swords, 491
Death's threat!   Today I have known laughter,
    282
December steel done, flowers open color, 130
Deeper than sleep but not so deep as death,
    340
The deepest blue, green, not the streams of the sea,
    547
Democritus laughed when he, 164
Depth of petals, May iris, 491
Do you know the name of the average
    animal?, 222
Dream of the world, 552

The dream-image fades, with its red pandanu
    keys, 271
Driven, at midnight, to growth, the city's
    wistful turnings, 129
The drowning young man lifted his face from
    the river, 119
Early, before the huge explosions, 592
Early, before the reservoir, 591
Earth, bind us close, and time   ;   nor, sky,
    deride, 21
Eating sleep, eating sunlight, eating meat, 281
Emerge, city, from your evening   :   allay me,
    sleep, 33
Ends of the earth join tonight, 466
Error, disease, snow, sudden weather, 92
Eve walked in the Garden of a Sunday
    morning, 575
Even after the letters, there is work, 88
Even during war, moments of delicate peace, 239
Evening, bringing me out of the government build-
    ing, 243
Faced with furnace demands during its
    education, 112
Faithful ever to thy brother, 573
The far lands melt to orange and to grey, 582
Father and I drove to the sand-quarry across
    the ruined marshlands, 15
The father and mother sat, and the sister
    beside her, 19
The fear of poetry is the, 155
A feat of laughter and a coastwise dance, 377
The fertile season ending in a glitter, 434
Fields where we slept, 384
The fire entire, 475
Fire-thread in the valley. Bird-voice in
    darkness, 390
Five brick panels, three small windows, six
    lions' heads, 445
Flickering, 493
Flood over ocean, 449
Flower of time, and a plague of white trilling in
    sunlight, 434
Flowers of air, 423
Fly down, Death: Call me, 221
For that I cannot name the names, 567
For that I never knew you, I only learned to
    dread you, 533
For that you never acknowledged me, I
    acknowledge, 474
Forerunners of images, 418
Frail it is and can be intercepted, 579
From you I learned the dark potential, 483
Frontier of Europe, the tideless sea, a field of power,
    145
Gauley Bridge is a good town for Negroes,
    they let us stand, 87

Ghostly in my house, 376

The girl being chosen stood in her naked room, 211

Girl grown woman   fire   mother of fire, 405

Give a dime to a beggar for I have seen a sight, 126

Give them my regards when you go to the school reunion, 121

"Goodbye!" called the stockholders as the ship pulled out, 133

Great Alexander sailing was from his true course turned, 403

Green going through the jungle of those years, 554

Griefs, 15

Guilt   said the bony man, 404

A habit leading to murder, smoky laughter, 210

A hall at the National Pawnshop crowded with unsold bureaus, 439

The hand of day opens, 359

Have you heard about Mr. Bratuscha?, 435

Having come to this place, 254

He said he would be back and we'd drink wine together, 476

He sang until his death, 268

He speaks in a big voice through all the air, 484

He stood against the stove, 82

He turned the lights on and walked to the window, 18

He walks toward me.   A black man in the sun, 450

Held among wars, watching, 462

Held between wars, 460

Here, again. A smell of dying in the milk-pale carton, 353

Here are the long fields inviolate of thought, 11

Here is a long and silent street, 269

Here's the story, my darling, of the dancing flower, 274

High above shores and times, 481

High wind, and spring restless in the ground, 584

His life is in the body of the living, 247

His tears fell from his veins, 502

History melts my houses, 222

Home thoughts from home; we read you every day, 242

Horizon of islands shifting, 448

How can I speak to them today? What can I know, 370

How horrible late spring is, with the full death of the frozen tight bulbs, 13

How lovely it is to, 517

How will you catch these clues at the moment of waking, 416

However the voices rise, 455

Hunger, 424

Hurricane, skullface, the sky's size, 452

I answer!   I fly reborn from deep escape!, 278

I braced the drum to my arm, a flat drum, and began to play, 534

I come into the room   The room stands waiting, 521

I first discovered what was killing these men, 83

I go a road, 503

I hold a key in my hand, 214

I know that behind these walls is the city, over these rooftops is the sun, 265

I know what I want in my words, 518

I lie in the bath and I contemplate the toilet-paper, 503

I lived in the first century of world wars, 430

I look across at the real, 466

I Muriel stood at the altar-table, 495

I recognize this little song, 515

I stand in the strong sun before a bank of prisms, 547

I think of the image brought into my room, 409

I thought I was going to the poets, but I am, 508

I told myself coming after a long time to my poem, 592

I want to speak in my voice!, 216

I was born in winter when, 164

I wear a garland and take my beloved's hand, 274

I will say what I mean here; in a book, 372

I'd rather be Muriel, 554

An Idea ran about the world, 341

Idols of luxury, 581

If I could write   :   Summer waits your coming, 14

I'm here again, 513

I'm not much good at any of this, 514

In adolescence I knew travellers, 4

In agony saying : "The last night of his life," 417

In all the cities of this year, 335

In burning summer I saw a season of betrayal, 314

In her splendor islanded, 362

In our period, they say there is free speech, 417

In the cave with a long-ago flare, 537

In the full sun.   In the fruitfall season, 261

In the human cities, never again to, 471

In the last bus last night that dead musician, 344

In the last hour of night, a zebra racing dawn, 384

In the night the sound woke us, 503

In the water-cave, 491

In the wine country, poverty, they drink no wine,
457

In wet green midspring, midnight and the
wind, 257

In woods you know stands the wonder-
working madonna, 542

In your time, there have been those who
spoke clearly, 397

Inland, away, 512

Inner greet.   Greenberg said it, 523

Invading nightmare, spinning up through
sleep, 122

Inverted torrents, fountains with strong trunks of
water, 585

is my concern.   That's this moment, 420

It is all much worse than I dreamed, 212

It is the poem, yes, 551

It seemed at the time like a slow road and late
afternoon, 339

It was like everything else, like everything, 558

It was long before the national performance,
162

It was much later in his life he rose, 182

It was much stronger than they said. Noisier,
343

It's still my little big "big brother," isn't it?, 518

Jefferson spoke of freedom but he held slaves,
497

The jokes, the feuds, the puns, the punish-
ments, 499

Kitty Hawk is a Caesar among monuments,
38

Knowing again, 425

Knowing the shape of the country. Knowing
the midway travels of, 310

Knowing the voices of the country, gathering,
195

Land; and only to stand on the ground, stand on
the brick, 158

Last night she died, 50

Lately having escaped three-kinded death, 334

Lattice of his back grows, the dolphin-
arching, till, 338

Launching themselves, 509

Let her be seen, a voice on a platform, heard,
191

Let poems and bodies love and be given to air, 252

Let the wounds change.   Let them not cry aloud,
292

Let us be introduced to our superiors, the voting
men, 26

Lie still, be still, love, be thou not shaken, 155

Lie there, in sweat and dream, I do, and
"there", 421

Life the announcer, 466

The light tumbles in cubes, boxes of light through
my window, 586

Like ivy the creeper with a thousand hands,
363

Long after you beat down the powerful hand,
111

Long afterward, Oedipus, old and blinded,
walked the, 480

Long ago, soon after my son's birth, 567

The long-ago garden is green deepened on
green, 496

"Long enough. Long enough", 351

A long road and a village, 228

"Look!" he said, "all green!" but she, 118

"Look," the city child said, "they have built over
the river", 581

Love, 422

Lucid at dusk the city lies revealed, 44

Lying, 467

Lying here among grass, am I dead am I
sleeping, 420

Lying in daylight, in the strong, 542

Lying in the grass, 270

Lying in the moment, she climbs white
snows, 546

Lying in the sun, 19

Make and be eaten, the poet says, 345

Make me well, I said. — And the delighted
touch, 117

A man is walking toward me across the water, 450

A man riding on the meaning of rivers, 379

A man who is bones is close to me, 451

Many of us   Each in his own life waiting, 408

The marker at Auschwitz, 526

M-Day's child is fair of face, 177

Microscopically, the ground moves. Dark creases in
the soil, 586

Middle of May, when the iris blows, 490

The moon revolves outside; possibly, black air,
53

The moon is not a crescent, 577

More lovely this, 574

Morning cried by the bed, 57

Mother and listener she is, but she does not
listen, 477

Mother, because you never spoke to me, 479

The motive of all of it was loneliness, 259

The mountains and the shadows move away,
439

The mountains rear, and are deathly terrifying, 584

The mountaintop stands in silence a minute
after the murder, 287

Mouth looking directly at you, 463

Mr. T. S. Eliot knows the potency of music, 580

Much later, I lie in a white seaport night, 242

Murmurs from the earth of this land, from the
caves and craters, 380

My body is set against disorder.   Risen among
enigmas, 278

My eyes are closing, my eyes are opening, 428
My father groaned; my mother wept, 337
My large back tooth, without a mate for years, 555
My limits crowd around me, 260
My night awake, 467
My son as child saying, 440
My thoughts through yours refracted into speech, 13
A name's a name but, 367
Near Mexico, near April, in the morning, 156
Near the end now, morning. Sleepers cover the decks, 148
Near the waterfront, 557
Never to hear, I know in myself complete, 259
Nevertheless the moon, 354
The new friend comes into my hotel room, 562
The night is covered with signs. The body and face of man, 454
Night. What do you know about the light?, 548
Niobe, 422
No longer speaking, 465
No one ever walking this our only earth, various, very clouded, 398
No one will ever understand that evening, 237
No pagan gods are dancing in these fields, 577
NO WORK is master of the mine today, 31
Nothing was less than it seemed, my darling, 232
Now green, now burning, I make a way for peace, 328
Now he has become one who upon that coast, 257
Now that I am fifty-six, 479
Now the ideas all change to animals, 281
now the world stands visible through your body, 366
O for God's sake, 538
O my singing lover, 273
Of all green trees, I love a nevergreen, 539
Oh I know, 502
On a ground beaten gold by running and, 235
on a spring morning of young wood, green wood, 526
On all the streetcorners the children are standing, 447
On the hour he shuts the door and walks out of town, 78
On the roads at night I saw the glitter of eyes, 253
On your journey you will come to a time of waking, 389
One cornstalk is all cornfields, 362
One o'clock in the letter-box, 213
Only there is a wound that cries all night, 291
Open war with its images of love and death, 278

Open with care the journal of those years, 48
The opening of the doors.   Dark, 547
Oranges smell of the south. Chestnuts are warm. The paint, 579
Organize the full results of that rich past, 5
Over the water, where I lie alive, 255
Passage to godhead, fitfully glared upon, 25
Past the darkness a lashing of color, 547
Peddler, drowned pier, birdcage—images, 591
Pieces of animals, pieces of all my friends, 325
Playing a phonograph record of a windy morning, 174
Plush lines the metal train, making the steel, 582
Poem   white page   white page   poem, 549
The potflower on the windowsill says to me, 430
Power never dominion, 387
The power of war leads to a plan of lives, 381
A procession of caresses alters the ancient sky, 209
PROOF OF AMERICA! A fire on the sea, 201
The Proud colors and brittle cloths, the supple smoke rising, 12
The quick sun brings, exciting mountains warm, 96
Rabbits breed, flies breed, said the virgin lady, 342
Raging from every quarter, 217
The randy old, 478
A red bridge fastening this city to the forest, 386
Red leaf.   And beside it, a red leaf alive, 256
remembering movies   love, 551
Returns to punishment as we all return, in agonized initiation proving America, 188
Revolution shall be a toy of peace to you, 53
Rider of dream, the body as an image, 283
The risen image shines, its force escapes, we are all named, 181
Risen in a, 356
The river flows past the city, 467
Rumor, stir of ripeness, 463
Running from death, 526
Running to me, 519
Sand nailed down, 510
Sands have washed, sea has flown over us, 449
The sand's still blue with receding water, sky topples, 122
The sea dances its morning, 232
The sea has opened, the limit of his dream, 382
The sea produced that town : Sète, which the boat turns to, 150
A seacoast late at night and a wheel of wind, 344

The sea-coast looks at the sea, and the cities pour, 500

Searching/not searching.　　To make closeness, 486

Sea-shouldering Ithaca, 544

Seawave, 510

The secret child walks down the street, 261

Seething, and falling black, a sea of stars, 147

Seize structure, 418

A shadowy arch calling the clouds of the sun, 236

Sharp clouds and a sea-moon sang to me, 369

She said to me, He lay there sleeping, 347

She tells, 348

She was unloaded and delivered to us, glory be!, 520

Shifting of islands on this horizon, 449

The sickness poured through the roads, 558

Silence of the air, of the light, of sky, 268

Silver, 511

Simply because of a question, my life is implicated, 277

Since very soon it is required of you, 168

The sky behind the farthest shore, 253

The sky is as black as it was when you lay down, 388

So I became very dark very large, 568

some flushed-earth-color pueblo, 511

Something is over and under this deep blue, 490

A song I sing, strong I sing, 514

Song-calling, 512

A sound lying on the fantastic air, 131

Sounds of night in the country of the opposites, 395

The South is green with coming spring　;　re-vival, 29

Space to the mind, the painted cave of dream, 208

Sparks of fishes, 269

Speak to it, says the light, 450

Speak to me.　　Take my hand.　　What are you now?, 9

Speed, we say of our time: racing my writing word, 355

Speeding back from the border, 443

Speeding from city, feeling day, 128

Spinning on his heel, the traveller, 111

Spirals and fugues, the power most like music, 427

Spotlight her face　　her face has no light in it, 60

St. Thomas' House: "And now I will believe", 580

Stallions go leap, and rimfire knows, 334

Standing against the gorge, he sees the slides of light, 385

Standing high on the shoulders of all things, all things, 357

The star in the nets of heaven blazed past your breastbone, 423

The state of fire and the state of air, 360

Stillness during war, the lake, 465

Storm and disorder and the giant emotions, 342

Stroke by stroke, in the country of the fragile, 440

A structure is rising.　It takes on shape, it takes on meaning, 383

The subcommittee submits, 104

The sun climbs, hot and burning overhead, 272

Sunday shuts down on this twentieth-century evening, 119

Sunlight the tall women may never have seen, 353

Surely it is time for the true grace of women, 246

Tell the jury your name, 89

That first green night of their dreaming, asleep beneath the Tree, 354

That night, a flute, 564

That summer midnight under her aurora, 414

Then full awake you will recognize the voice, 396

There is a place.　　There is a miracle, 280

There was always a murder within another murder, 482

There was frost on my window, 576

There was I led by a maternal hand, 477

There was no place on that plain for a city, 170

There were poems all over Broadway that morning, 551

There were three of them that night, 419

These are our brave, these with their hands in on the work, 62

These are roads to take when you think of your country, 73

These are the lines on which a committee is formed, 79

These coins and calendars stood for the moon, strong boys, 350

These creatures, 510

These images will parade until the morning, 216

These roads will take you into your own country, 106

These things are the heart of Autumn, 577

They are pouring the city, 482

They began to breathe and glitter.　Morning, 534

They called us to a change of heart, 240

They came to me and said, "There is a child", 280

They come into our lives, Melville and Whitman who, 500

They escape before, but their shadows walk behind, 58

They face us in sea-noon sun, just as he saw them waiting, 367

They found him in the fields and called him back to music, 434

They have asked me to speak in public, 484

They saw rivers flow west and hoped again, 74

They think I answer and strangle.   They are wrong, 279

The thin, black fingers of the ash-tree, 576

This has nothing, 414

This is a dark woman at a telephone, 179

This is a lung disease. Silicate dust makes it, 86

This is a tall woman walking through a square, 132

This is the cripples' hour on Seventh Avenue, 169

This is the dream-journey, knowing the earth slips under, 157

This is the life of a Congressman, 102

This is the most audacious landscape. The gangster's, 95

This is the music of the cities of the morning, 573

This is the net of begetting and belief, 389

This is the word our lips caress, our teeth bite, 12

This journey is exploring us. Where the child stood, 409

This sky is unmistakable. Not lurid, not low, not black, 333

Time comes into it, 467

A time of destruction. Of the most rigid powers in ascendance, 432

To be a Jew in the twentieth century, 243

To the poem. Alice, you left a sheet, 593

To enter that rhythm where the self is lost, 403

To keep and conceal may be, in times of crisis, 229

To this bridge the pale river and flickers away in images of blue, 265

Today I asked Aileen, 555

Tonight I will try again for the music of truth, 535

Torrent that rushes down, 432

Touch me!   Love me!   Speak to me!, 292

Trapped, blinded, led; and in the end betrayed, 223

A tree of rivers flowing through our lives, 382

The tree of rivers seen and forgotten, 380

A true confession!, 272

Two bodies face to face, 269

Two on the stairs in a house where they had loved, 6

Two or three lines across;   the black ones, down, 262

Two years ago, 578

Two years of my sister's bitter illness, 490

Tyranny of method! the outrageous smile, 304

Under the tall black sky you look out of your body, 445

Up against the mountain-side, 519

Up in the second balcony, 59

A voice flew out of the river as morning flew, 405

Voices of all our voices, running past an imagined race, 475

Waiting.   A good deal like real life, 548

Waiting to leave all day I hear the words, 561

Waking this morning, 471

Walking the world to find the poet of these cries, 562

Wars between wars, laughter behind the lines, 166

Wary of time O it seizes the soul tonight, 276

Wave of the sea, 449

We all had a good time, 17

We all traveled into that big room, 538

We are the antlers of that white animal, 507

We are the seas through whom the great fish passed, 550

We in our season like progress and inventions, 553

We look through our lives at each other, 591

"Well," he said, "George, I never thought you were with us", 41

Well, if he treats me like a young girl still, 540

Well, I'm back again, 517

We set great wreaths of brightness on the graves of the passionate, 5

We started to walk but it was wading-slow, 113

We stood around the raw new-planted garden, 358

Westward from Sète, 442

What did I miss as I went searching?, 485

What did I see? What did I not see?, 486

What do I give you?   This memory, 413

What have you brought, 437

What hill can ever hold us?, 63

What is the skill of this waking?   Heard the singing, 545

What kind of woman goes searching and searching?, 480

What was it? What was it?, 441

Whatever roams the air is traveling, 333

What's over England? A cloud. What's over France? A   flame, 124

The wheel in the water, green, behind my head, 149

When a magnet is, 487

When a man's body is young, 274

When after the screens of the evening of defeat, 396

When at last he was well enough to take the sun, 230

When Barcelona fell, the darkened glass, 165

When his death confronted him, it had the face of his friend, 458

When I am dead, even then, 561

When I stand with these three, 528

When I think of him, midnight, 207

When I wrote of the women in their dances and wildness, 413

When the exposed spirit, busy in daytime, 123

When the half-body dies its frightful death, 545

When the hero of the threshold enters our lives and our houses, 346

When they're decent about women, they're frightful about, 472

When this hand is gone to earth, 540

When those who can never again forgive them selves, 127

When you imagine trumpet-faced musicians, 115

Whenever you wake, you will find journeying, 357

Where are they, not those young men, not those, 543

Wherever, 498

Wherever I walked I went green among young growing, 556

Whether it is a speaker, taut on a platform, 61

While this my day and my people are a country not yet born, 474

Who in one lifetime sees all causes lost, 228

Who is the witness? What voice moves across time, 459

Who will speak to the wounds?   Who will have grace, 290

Whoever despises the clitoris despises the penis, 465

Wildflowers withering with the same death, 447

The wind is an insolent braggart, 577

Wine and oil gleaming within their heads, 534

Woman as gates, saying, 461

A woman has been begging for ninety-seven years, 439

A woman looks at the sea, 501

Woman seen as a slender instrument, 565

The woman to the man, 496

Women and poets see the truth arrive, 239

The word in the bread feeds me, 537

Words? Yes, made of air, 363

Working with these students. This, 592

The world is full of loss; bring, wind, my love, 215

The wounds   :   Love me!, 290

The wounds   :   Speak to me!, 290

The wounds   :   Touch me!   Love me!   Speak to me!, 289

The wounds   :   Touch me!   Speak to me!   Love me!, 289

The wreck of the Tiger, the early pirate, the blood-clam's, 453

The year in its cold beginning, 224

The year was river-throated, with the stare of legend, 336

Years before action when the wish alone, 120

Yes, I have seen their eyes.   In peaceful gardens, 321

Yes, it is there, the city full of music, 508

Yes it was the prince's kiss, 549

Yes, we were looking at each other, 473

You are like me born at the end of the year, 354

"You are not pregnant," said the man, 489

You come from poets, kings, bankrupts, preachers, 429

You dynamiting the structure of our loves, 47

You grief woman   you gave me a scarlet coverlet, 565

You have made an art in which the sun is standing, 548

You have not disappeared, 364

You like the State of West Virginia very much, do you not?, 75

You made healing as you wanted us to make bread and poems, 560

You star up there, 520

You told me resurrection in images of roots, 352

You told me : they all went in and saw the glass, 415

You will enter the world where death by fear and explosion, 282

You would have loveliness in a cup and spoon, 583

A young woman stands at the door of my small room, 591

Your song where you lie long dead on the shore of a Spanish river, 434